EXECUTION OF LOUNT AND MATTHEWS [date and artist unknown].
Public Archives of Canada, C–1242.

THE REBELLION OF 1837
IN UPPER CANADA

THE
REBELLION OF
1837
IN UPPER
CANADA

A Collection of Documents

Edited with an Introduction by

Colin Read and
Ronald J. Stagg

CARLETON UNIVERSITY PRESS

OTTAWA, CANADA

1988

ISBN 0-88629-026-0 (paperback)

Printed in Canada

Second printing September 1988

Major funding towards this publication was provided by the Ontario Heritage Foundation, Ontario Ministry of Citizenship and Culture.

Carleton University Press gratefully acknowledges the support extended to its publishing programme by the Canada Council and the Ontario Arts Council.

Canadian Cataloguing in Publication Data

Main entry under title:
    The Rebellion of 1837 in Upper Canada

(Carleton Library Series ; 134)
ISBN 0-88629-032-5 (bound for members of the
Champlain Society). — ISBN 0-88629-026-0 (pbk.)

1. Canada—History—Rebellion, 1837–1838.
I. Read, Colin Frederick, 1943–   II. Stagg,
Ronald John, 1942–   III. Series: The
Carleton Library ; no. 134.

FC454.R42 1985   971.03′8   C85-090050-6
F1032.R42 1985

Distributed by: Oxford University Press Canada,
                70 Wynford Drive,
                Don Mills, Ontario, Canada, M3C 1J9

(416)441-2941

FOREWORD

THE Rebellion of 1837 is one of the central events of Ontario's history, as those with even the slightest familiarity with our past will know. Among its characters, William Lyon Mackenzie is undoubtedly the most famous, and he occupies a central role in these documents. The failure of his rebellion decisively repudiated the armed uprising as a means to effect change in Upper Canada; soon afterwards, reactionary ultra-tory extremism was equally undermined and discredited. Thus, the rebellion was at once the most marked break in the evolutionary pattern that has so largely characterized the province's political development over its two-hundred-year history and a confirmation of that more moderate, gradualist tradition.

It was the belief of the Honourable Leslie Frost, through whose initiative the Ontario Series of the Champlain Society was founded and long sustained, that a documentary approach to the province's history offered the best way to avoid the bias of narrow partisanship. For the Rebellion, which will remain a controversial episode in our past, and one more likely than most to be subject to mythology, this is particularly valuable. All the major documents and an extensive selection of other relevant material can be assembled in a single volume, through which those who rebelled, and those who resisted, can speak directly to us.

Ideas, communications, information, and misinformation play an important part in the story revealed in these documents. Would there have been a rebellion at all if the British government had better understood events in distant Upper Canada and sent someone other than Sir Francis Bond Head as lieutenant-governor? Would there have been a rebellion in Upper Canada if the actual outcome of events in Lower Canada had been known? Would those who followed Mackenzie at Toronto have done so if he had not himself been their main source of information about the mood of the city? And would Charles Duncombe and his followers have risen in the west if they had had accurate news of what was happening in Toronto? It would be wrong to suggest that the tragic (and sometimes comic) events of 1837–8 were simply a result of that all-purpose modern diagnosis, a "failure of communications" (for clearly they were not), but how the actual events happened can be properly understood only by going beyond the brief summaries found in most textbooks. Hindsight is easy and invites simplistic judgments; these documents restore our sense of the confused and complex reality of 1837 Upper Canada.

The Ontario Series is produced through the cooperation of the Government of Ontario and the Champlain Society, which has been publishing historical documentary studies for more than seventy-five years. The Society selects and guides the editors for each volume, while the costs of preparation and publication are defrayed by the Government of Ontario and the Ontario Heritage Foundation. The volume editors' task is to assemble a selection of documents that will illuminate their subject as fully as possible and to write an introduction that will enable the reader to appreciate the significance of the documents.

This volume is the twelfth in the series and continues its recent emphasis on thematic as well as regional studies. Indeed, in its attention to all of the province's regions in 1837, it nicely combines regional and thematic approaches. The next volume to appear in the series will have as its focus one of the most important and least understood of Upper Canada's institutions, the Bank of Upper Canada.

Queen's Park,   WILLIAM G. DAVIS
Toronto   *Premier of Ontario*
11 July 1984

PREFACE

THE Upper Canadian rebellions of 1837 have assumed a central place in Canadian historiography. In the nineteenth-century liberal view the rebellions were integral to the development of Canadian freedoms, and although in the twentieth century this predominant idea was attacked by a number of authorities, the ensuing controversy added to, rather than detracted from, interest in the revolts. This book of documents is designed to help satisfy the continuing interest in the risings and to shed new light on areas which, though often much discussed, have not always been closely examined.

Perhaps surprisingly there is a large amount of documentation extant on the rebellions, much of which has not been considered. The editors have attempted to produce in whole, or in part, all the important documents of the period from 1836 to the end of the rebellions' immediate aftermath, even those reproduced elsewhere. We have also tried to survey all of the province and, consequently, have canvassed a wide spectrum of material. Faced with an abundance of documentation, we have typically opted for contemporary material over reminiscences and the like, which are often coloured by time and self-interest. Inevitably, we have omitted many documents which we could have included, but we feel that this collection presents those which best represent the range of available materials and which canvass the issues of the day most clearly and comprehensively.

We have adopted a number of conventions in the text. We have standardized the names of the writers and recipients of letters. Those who signed their correspondence in several ways – "John Askin," "John B. Askin," for example – have been assigned just one signature in the document headings. Similarly, we have standardized the places from which letters were written and the dates of their writing: "London, 30 March 1838." We have included salutations and complimentary closes in correspondence only on those few occasions when they are important to the meaning or tenor of particular documents. We have not attempted, for reasons of space and economy, to reproduce all the varied spacing and type faces of newspaper articles, government proclamations, and the like. We have used ellipses to indicate the omission of material from the documents but not for the omission of salutations and complimentary closes in correspondence. We have chosen to regard diary entries for individual days and the testimony of individual witnesses in trials as constituting separate documents in their own right. We have used *sic* sparingly, for mistakes in the originals that are not obvious ones, or for ones that if not so designated might be thought ours; and we have taken the liberty of removing from previously edited documents that we have republished those *sics*, as well as other editorial additions, that are not consistent with the usages and conventions we have adopted. We have allowed original punctuation to stand and provided additional punctuation only when the meaning of passages would have been obscured without it. In such cases the punctuation inserted appears in square brackets and is consistent with the punctuation used in the rest of the document. Where documents have ended without punctuation we have included the appropriate concluding punctuation in square brackets. We have added material in square brackets elsewhere. Those, such as "th[at]," "complete mutilated words or passages or provide missing letters for words that could not be readily understood without them. Others, such as "dep [deponent]," explain potentially confusing abbreviations. We have also added material in square brackets to supply words or phrases necessary to an understanding of the text.

We have attempted to reproduce faithfully the wording and punctuation of the documents. Here, our attempts have been plagued by the all-too-frequent necessity of consulting microfilm rather than the original documents, and by the consequent difficulties of distinguishing between dust specks and periods, flecks in the paper and commas, scratches in the film and dashes – problems all exacerbated by the fact that microfilming makes faint handwriting even fainter! Hence we particularly regret the fact that we were denied permission to examine the originals of the documents in the Upper Canada Sundries collection, many of which we have published here. Further, the failure of many writers to distinguish clearly between their upper and lower case letters has often made it exceedingly difficult for us to determine with certainty precisely which words they have capitalized and which they have not.

Inevitably, the documents chosen abound with the names of individuals and places. We have identified as many of the former as we could in our footnotes and placed as many of the latter as possible on our maps. We believe those maps to be reasonably accurate, though the exact routes of pioneer roads are not always certain, nor indeed are the precise limits of a few counties and districts. As for the counties and districts, we have chosen to indicate their boundaries as they actually operated, not as they were intended to operate. In the preparation of the maps we have benefited from the information provided us by Professor Charles Whebell of the University of Western Ontario, Professor John C. Weaver of McMaster University, and Bernadine Dodge, archivist of Trent University. To them we are much indebted, as we are to Professor Grant Head and Ms. Pam Schaus of Wilfrid Laurier University, who prepared the maps for publication.

We also wish to thank the archivists at the Archives of Ontario, the Baldwin Room at the Metropolitan Toronto Library, and the Public Archives of Canada, particularly Dr. Jean L'Espérance, who helped us gather the prints and photographs we have reproduced here. Many of the portraits and several of the scenes selected date from the post-rebellion era. Unfortunately, contemporary illustrations of the events of the risings are relatively rare. None the less, all the depictions we have selected for inclusion have value. Those of more recent vintage, those of the battle of Montgomery's for example, help show how the events of the rebellion passed into folklore, becoming mythologized in the process.

As the acknowledgements cited above suggest, the difficulties we have encountered in producing this volume have been outweighed many times over by the courtesies and kindnesses extended us. We have many other debts to acknowledge. We wish to thank those who generously granted permission to publish documents: the Archives of Ontario; the Douglas Library, Queen's University; Hamilton Public Library; London Public Libraries; the Metropolitan Toronto Library; the Toronto Public Library; the Norfolk Historical Society; the Provincial Archives of Manitoba; the Public Archives of Canada; the Regional History Collection, University of Western Ontario; the Sarnia Public Library and Art Gallery; the Trent University Archives; the United Church Archives; and Professor Robin S. Harris of the University of Toronto. We have made every reasonable effort to secure permission to publish the documents included here, but we would appreciate being informed of any oversights we may have committed on this score.

The archivists, librarians, and technicians of the various institutions cited above have been most helpful, as have those at the Archives of the Anglican Church of Canada. We owe particular gratitude to the staffs of the Archives of Ontario and of Government Publications and of the Regional History Collection of the University of Ontario's Weldon Library, who helped us with much of our later work and who answered many of our vexing questions.

The biographical footnotes in this volume, which are italicized in the index, are reasonably extensive. We did not work on them unaided. The staff of the *Dictionary of Canadian Biography* opened up their biographical files to us, as did Professors Keith Johnson of Carleton University and Frederick H. Armstrong of the University of Western Ontario. Such largesse is hard to repay. Mrs. B.D. Boyce and Mr. Gerald Boyce of Belleville, Mr. Dan Brock and Mr. Raymond Crinklaw of London, the Reverend David George Bowyer of Lambeth, Mrs. Alice M. Hughes of Merrickville and other members of the Merrickville and District Historical Society, Mrs. Ethel Poth of the Huron County Historical Society, Mr. William Yeager, Curator of the Eva Brook Donly Museum in Simcoe, and Professors Donald B. Smith of the University of Calgary and Douglas Leighton of Huron College all offered useful biographical information to us, for which we are deeply grateful.

We wish to thank the editors of the Champlain Society: Dr. William Ormsby, Archivist of Ontario, who was in charge of the Ontario Series when this volume was assigned to us, and Douglas McCalla of Trent University, who became the editor prior to our submitting material. Professor McCalla has been an extremely conscientious editor, subjecting successive drafts of our work to thorough, thoughtful criticism. Throughout, he has provided the greatest intellectual and moral support, despite his own crowded schedule. Equally, Diane Mew of Carleton University Press has been a tower of strength.

Ryerson Polytechnical Institute and Huron College, University of Western Ontario generously provided funds for the typing of the final drafts of the manuscript.

For their encouragement and sound advice over the years we express our thanks to Professors J.M.S. Careless and G.M. Craig of the University of Toronto and to Professor Fred Armstrong of the University of Western Ontario. We are grateful to our families – Geoffrey, Jackie, and Sydney – for accepting the neglect caused by our scholarly commitments. We would like to thank Sydney for her help in typing parts of the preliminary manuscript and Jackie for typing the final copy.

Colin Read's debts, intellectual and otherwise, to the late Professor Donald F. Forster, President of the University of Guelph, are immense, and he wishes to dedicate his efforts in producing this volume to him.

COLIN READ
RONALD J. STAGG

CONTENTS

ILLUSTRATIONS AND MAPS

Frontispiece   The Execution of Lount and Matthews

The section of illustrations will be found between pages 188 and 189.

Maps

THE REBELLION OF 1837
IN UPPER CANADA

INTRODUCTION

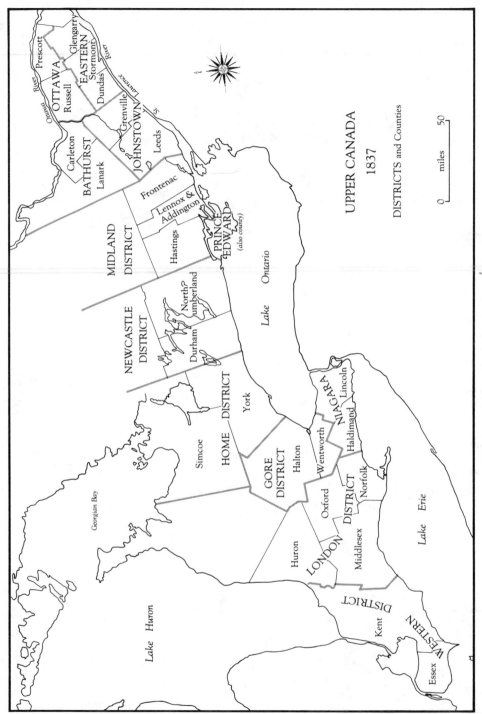

UPPER CANADA
1837

DISTRICTS and Counties

0   miles   50

1: Districts and Counties in Upper Canada, 1837

A.   THE CAUSES OF THE REBELLION

ANGRY MEN in homespun clothing debating at public meetings;
neighbour fighting neighbour over their right to disagree; tired
farmers slogging down a muddy December road, a wagon load of
assorted rifles, fowling pieces, pikes, axes, and pitchforks
accompanying their dogged march; a lone steamboat sailing a
frigid winter lake bearing a motley cargo of gentlemen,
storekeepers, and more farmers, all determined to stop the
advance of the group that came by road; the thump of a trapdoor
pitching two men to their deaths at the end of a rope; men fleeing
by land and water, cold, tired, and frightened. These are just a
few impressions of the uprisings of 1837 in the colony of Upper
Canada, uprisings of which much has been written but much
remains unknown.

The Upper Canadian rebellions have left behind a curious
legacy. The uprising in the London District, often called the
Duncombe Rebellion after its chief character, has been largely
ignored in accounts of the troubles of 1837. A very few books,
such as John Charles Dent's *The Story of the Upper Canadian
Rebellion . . .* (1885), have attempted to describe the events of
the outbreak. Most works on the period contain little more than a
mention that an uprising was contemplated by Duncombe but
was suppressed before it was fully organized. Even in the case of
Dent's book, which displays considerable research on the
Toronto area rising, the section dealing with the western rising is
based on a much less substantial knowledge of the subject. A few
works, such as Fred Landon's "The Duncombe Uprising and
Some of Its Consequences," published in 1931, have gone
beyond the usual well-worn phrases about the western revolt, but
not until 1982 and the appearance of Colin Read's *The Rising in
Western Upper Canada, 1837–8: The Duncombe Revolt and
After* did that rebellion receive any extended treatment.

The Home District outbreak, variously called the Mackenzie
Rebellion, the Yonge Street Rebellion or, rather grandly, the
Upper Canadian Rebellion, has not been well served by
historians either. Here, self-justification, prejudice, and political
motivation have combined to obscure matters. Although on the
surface well known, the events and significance of the rising
have in reality been almost as shrouded as those of the

Duncombe rising. The major published studies of the rebellion include Dent's work cited above, Charles Lindsey's *The Life and Times of William Lyon Mackenzie, With an Account of the Canadian Rebellion of 1837, and the Subsequent Frontier Disturbances, Chiefly from Unpublished Documents* (1862), and Sir Francis Bond Head's two works, *A Narrative* (1839) and *The Emigrant* (1846). These works, the most recent of which is one hundred years old, form the major sources of information on the uprising, yet each has significant failings.

Dent's two-volume study is characterized by an intense dislike of William Lyon Mackenzie and an exceptionally generous view of the conduct of Dr. John Rolph, a man of whom most other writers on Upper Canada/Canada West have been considerably more critical. Dent's obvious prejudice has led those who looked with favour on Mackenzie's conduct, not an insubstantial number, to disregard much of Dent's otherwise well-researched work and to turn elsewhere, particularly to Lindsey. The latter's two-volume work is basically an uncritical presentation, by Mackenzie's son-in-law, of material from Mackenzie's private papers, in a pre-digested form. Both Francis Bond Head and William Lyon Mackenzie tended to alter events in describing them in order to throw the best possible light on themselves. Since all later major works on the uprising, such as D.B. Read's *The Canadian Rebellion of 1837* (1896) and W. Kilbourn's *The Firebrand: William Lyon Mackenzie and the Rebellion of Upper Canada* (1956), depend heavily on these earlier histories, none gives an entirely accurate picture of events.

In the twentieth century another interpretation has been grafted on descriptions of the risings. Using what is essentially a Lindsey version of events, authors such as Stanley B. Ryerson in *1837: The Birth of Canadian Democracy* (1937) and in *Unequal Union* . . . (1968), and Greg Keilty in *1837: Revolution in the Canadas* (1974) have developed an essentially Marxist interpretation. In their version the labourers identified on the official list of those arrested in 1837 become largely industrial workers and the rebel forces are seen to be composed of farmers and workers. The underlying reason for the rebellion's failure is said to be the "immature level of industrial capitalism."[1] Since the labourers referred to were in reality mainly farm labourers, this analysis does not stand up to close scrutiny.

We have each examined in detail one of the rebellions in a

[1]Stanley B. Ryerson, *Unequal Union* . . . (Toronto, 1968), p. 132.

doctoral thesis – C.F. Read in "The Rising in Western Upper Canada, 1837–38 . . ." (University of Toronto, 1974) and R.J. Stagg in "The Yonge Street Rebellion of 1837: An Examination of the Social Background and a Reassessment of the Events" (University of Toronto, 1976), but neither deals with events in south-central or eastern Upper Canada, an omission common to all material on the uprisings. This volume is designed with the limitations of available work in mind. It presents a broad documentary coverage of the rebellions and material on areas of Upper Canada not directly threatened by them. It reproduces all the major documents of the day and a representative sampling of those canvassing the main themes. A judicious reading of all this should provide a sound knowledge of the risings, though, inevitably, it will not acquaint the reader with every detail of the period. Only a much larger, and possibly less useful, volume would do that. Further, this collection does not cover the "patriot" raids of 1837–8 launched by Canadian refugees and American sympathizers, the assumption being that this volume should concentrate on the restoration of public order within the province during the immediate aftermath of the revolts.

A complete understanding of the rebellions requires that they be seen in context. Since the period of rising discontent in Upper Canada following the War of 1812 is covered more than adequately elsewhere – for example, in Aileen Dunham, *Political Unrest in Upper Canada, 1815–1836* (1927) and G.M. Craig, *Upper Canada: The Formative Years, 1784–1841* (1963), the documents in this volume deal only with the situation immediately prior to the uprisings, the years 1836–7. In order that the documents do not stand in isolation, a brief examination of this broader setting is presented here, but the reader is encouraged to look elsewhere for a complete discussion of the issues involved.

The grievances which underlay the rebellions were of long duration, their roots entangled in the provisions of the Constitutional Act of 1791 which had created Upper Canada's political framework. The provisions of the act had been governed by the British desire to prevent a second revolt against imperial rule in North America. The lesson of the American Revolution learned by Secretary of State William Grenville and others was that they must retard in their fledgling colony "the growth of a republican or independent spirit."[2] This was to be done by

[2]Gerald M. Craig, *Upper Canada: The Formative Years, 1784–1841* (Toronto, 1963), p. 15.

checking closely the influence in the colony's government of those inhabitants of little education and wealth, who, it was thought, could easily be led astray by men of liberal ideas. The voice of the common man might be heard in the Assembly but it was to have limited strength.[3] As a curb on the power of the people an appointed upper house, the Legislative Council, and a lieutenant-governor, appointed by and responsible to the British government, had also to approve legislation. As well, an Executive Council, technically only an advisory body to the lieutenant-governor but in actuality a body which heavily influenced executive policy, could impede the popular will as expressed by the Assembly.

Since members of the Executive Council tended also to be appointed to the Legislative Council and the lieutenant-governor had a remarkably similar philosophical outlook to that of many of the executive councillors, the upper strata of the colonial government more often than not acted as a unit. Local officials throughout the colony – sheriffs, district clerks and treasurers, justices of the peace and so on – were appointed by the executive from the more affluent conservative segment of colonial society, and in many if not most cases men with outlooks similar to those of the executive councillors and lieutenant-governors were chosen. With real power at the local level residing in these men, especially with the justices of the peace, instead of with locally elected officials, the voice of the common man was muted indeed. The small group of men who wielded so much power at the provincial capital became known as the Family Compact, but small family compacts emerged across the colony occupying most of the official positions in the local areas, often having social and economic ties to the central elite.

In the very early life of the colony its oligarchic form of government worked reasonably well, for the province's settlers were less concerned with politics than they were with wresting a living from their new land. Then as population swelled political strife developed. Before the War of 1812 such strife was limited, revolving as it did about a few prominent personalities who were dissatisfied with their positions in the colony. After the war political tensions heightened as colonial officials, convinced that American aggression was a symptom of mob rule or democracy and doubly frightened by the apparent extent of disloyal conduct

---

[3]The existence of a property franchise for the Assembly helped limit somewhat the influence of the common man there.

among Upper Canadians during the war, determined to control the menace by denying American immigrants land and the right to hold political office.

The Alien Question, as it became known, caused consternation among a large proportion of the population. The British government's interpretation of the executive's actions, if carried to its logical conclusion, would have deprived many long-established settlers of their rights as British citizens. By the time the Colonial Office imposed a compromise solution in 1826, alliances had formed in opposition to the executive's policies which, though often shifting or ephemeral, provided organizational precedents for future action. In the mid-1820s a whole series of issues, most of which involved questions of education, religion, land development, and internal improvements, arose and brought men together in a more cohesive group, the Reform Movement, which disagreed with the Family Compact's attempts to impose its values and priorities on the society.

Striving as they were to create a conservative British society with as many safeguards against popular democracy as possible, the oligarchy offended not only those who felt the people could be trusted to make political decisions but also those who objected to the Compact's interpretation of Britishness and loyalty. Religious questions offer an example. Until 1831, when the Assembly finally altered the policy, only magistrates and ministers of the established faiths, those denominations which were state churches in other countries, the Church of England, Church of Scotland, and Roman Catholic Church, were allowed to perform marriages. The other denominations were deemed too dominated by their American parent churches to be trustworthy. Attacks on the loyalty of what was probably the largest religious sect in Upper Canada, the Methodists, by the Compact's religious leader and one of its chief spokesmen, John Strachan, only exacerbated the situation.

Religious tensions were compounded by the Compact's reserves policy. The Constitutional Act and a later proclamation had established clergy and crown reserves totalling two-sevenths of the surveyed lands of the province. Spread out as they were across the colony, these reserves angered many, because few people would rent or later buy the lots while land was available very cheaply in much of the province. Without settlement the reserve lands were not developed and thus local communications in many areas were made difficult. But, beyond this, the clergy reserves gave the Church of England a privileged position. Interpreting the ambiguous wording of the Constitutional Act to mean that the Church of England was the established church in the province, and believing that an established church was needed to assist in providing stability by checking the base nature of the common man, the Compact insisted that all revenues from the reserves belonged to this denomination alone.

Though the British government admitted in 1820 the possibility of the Church of Scotland's sharing in the reserve revenues, the Kirk continued to be excluded from them, as were other non-Anglican denominations. Unlike the Kirk, however, most of the latter were voluntarist, believing that no church should receive state aid. Instead the money from the reserves should be used for education and internal improvements.

By the late 1820s the Family Compact was accused of sins as diverse as trying to force education into a mould created by the Church of England and failing to develop roads within the colony. It was seen as too closely allied with major business concerns such as the Bank of Upper Canada, the Welland Canal Company, and the Canada Company, the last of which had taken over the sale of crown reserves and of considerable undistributed crown lands in 1826, in return for an annual payment to the executive. Numerous other contentious issues, major and minor, caused hostility against the Compact among certain segments of the population and, together, all the issues suggested to them the necessity of change. In 1828 the province's electorate returned a majority of reformers to the Assembly.

Winning one election did not guarantee reform victory. In 1830 the tories turned the reformers out in the election and gained control of the House. In many ways they represented as diverse a collection of individuals and views as did the reformers. A minority were outright Family Compact supporters, while others advocated many of the same practical reforms as their opponents. They did not, however, call for constitutional reforms to break the power of the Compact, as increasingly the reform movement did; and, whatever may have divided them internally, they shared a common loyalty to the British crown. To the men in the Legislative and Executive Councils this was the key. Though the members of the Compact might be frustrated at times by the tory Assembly's actions, at least that Assembly could be counted on not to try to alter the British system of colonial government.

To Compact members, certain segments of the reform group appeared to be courting disaster. The Baldwins, Robert and his father William Warren, might advocate responsible government and the handing over of power to the Assembly, but other reformers, with William Lyon Mackenzie in the lead, openly flirted with American-style democracy as the answer to Upper Canada's problems. The political liability of this latter position was that both those who advocated it and the reform movement as a whole could be branded as disloyal to the monarch and to the mother country. The Compact and many other tories were not above doing this, even though the Baldwin solution was well within the sphere of British political discussion.

Though in the 1830s the reform movement often appeared united because of its policy of not criticizing its own members even when there were disagreements of principle, it was in fact composed of diverse factions and led by many men, of whom Robert Baldwin, John Rolph, Marshall Spring Bidwell, and William Lyon Mackenzie were the most notable. On the other hand, the tories, or "constitutionalists" as they preferred being called, though divided on questions of change, were united in their opposition to disloyalty. They had considerable public appeal and in the 1830s were able to compete on reasonably equal terms with the reformers at the polls. They took the election of 1830, but then the electorate, obviously dissatisfied with their glacial approach to reform and angered over the continued expulsion of William Lyon Mackenzie from the Assembly, which he continually criticized, returned the reformers in 1834. Mackenzie, hoping to strike a mortal blow at the Compact and its supporter the lieutenant-governor, set up a committee of the Assembly to investigate grievances and abuses of power. Its report, largely Mackenzie's own work, was a compendium of reform grievances, but its intemperate tone and emphasis on concerns not shared by all reform members embarrassed many of his colleagues. Nevertheless it had important results, helping persuade the British government to remove Sir John Colborne, the lieutenant-governor, and to appoint someone it believed more acceptable.

In January of 1836, the year in which the documents in this book commence, Upper Canada received its new governor, a rather improbable one, in the person of Sir Francis Bond Head. A sometime adventurer and more recently senior poor law commissioner in Kent, he had no political experience or finesse and soon collided violently with the reform majority in the Assembly. At first Head tried conciliation, in the hopes of heading off demands for constitutional reform. In February he admitted Robert Baldwin and John Rolph to his Executive Council, the very body that Baldwin wanted to make responsible to the people, through the Assembly. The accommodation was short-lived. Baldwin, who had been reluctant to enter the Council, soon tired of the position in which he found himself: while the Council might tender the governor advice, the latter could ignore it, as Head was wont to do. He persuaded the five remaining councillors to present Head with a document, dated 4 March, insisting that they be given greater influence in the affairs of state (A 2). Head refused publicly (A 3) and insisted that the six join in withdrawing the document. When all did not, he installed six new councillors, all tories. Battle was then joined in earnest.

The reform-dominated Assembly established a select committee to investigate the affair. The committee reported in April that responsible government had already been incorporated into Upper Canada's constitution! To secure Head's recognition of this, it advised the House to stop the supplies. The Assembly agreed. Head retaliated by refusing to grant contingency funds and by withholding assent from money bills already passed. In May he informed the electors of Toronto that he was not the instigator of "the stoppage of . . . Supplies [that] has caused a general stagnation of business, which will probably end in the ruin of many of the inhabitants of this city"(A 5). He then dissolved the Assembly, denounced his opponents as disloyal in terms which made many Compact statements seem mild, and accused them of conspiring with external enemies, obviously Americans. He challenged those enemies. *"Let them come if they dare!"* (A 6). In the ensuing election he was not above making public denunciations of the "republican" reformers. All this was extraordinary but highly effective conduct.

Head having made the issue of the election one of loyalty to the crown, tories of every stripe mustered behind him. Some re-established the defunct British Constitutional Society, originally founded in York in 1832 to preserve the British tie (A 8). Particularly in western Upper Canada this body busily solicited support for "constitutional candidates." Clerics of the Church of England, Church of Scotland, and Roman Catholic Church also actively joined the cause of loyalty. The Catholic bishop, Alexander Macdonell, actually enjoined his priests to secure results favourable to the lieutenant-governor.[4]

More damning for the reform cause was the attitude of the largest Methodist faction, the Canadian Wesleyan Methodist Church, which was the product of an 1833 merger of the major Canadian body with the smaller British Wesleyan Methodist one. To this union, the British Methodists brought with them a small government grant for Indian missions. Many reform votes had traditionally come from Methodists, but William Lyon Mackenzie had alienated large numbers by attacking the leadership of the denomination for accepting government money in defiance of their voluntarist principles and for their generally conservative political and social views. In fact, his campaign degenerated to a large degree into a personal vendetta against that youthful but formidable figure, the Reverend Egerton Ryerson. Not surprisingly, many "Ryersonian" Methodists turned to the "constitutional" cause (A 16).

Also working for Head was that host of government functionaries who could, in quiet ways, do so much to influence the course of an election. Land patents, which conferred the right to vote, were made available to sympathetic voters in several areas. For example, officials of the Crown Lands Office agreed to a request from the tory candidate in the town of London, Mahlon Burwell, that they give several applicants from London their land patents, to qualify them as voters (A 10). To oblige Burwell, those involved had to date at least one patent improperly, but this helped influence an election where but thirty-eight votes were cast, thirty-one of them for Burwell.[5] Other official intervention saw returning officers discounting the votes of reformers by insisting on proof of citizenship from men well known to them and local officials arranging for sympathetic voters to be treated to free liquor. Just how widespread these practices were is impossible to assess, but reformers were convinced they were widespread indeed, far more so than in any previous election. This electoral fraud and the unprecedented intervention of the lieutenant-governor largely explained, they felt, the defeat they had suffered.

[4]John Alexander Macdonell, *A Sketch of the Life of the Honourable and Right Reverend Alexander Macdonell* . . . (Alexandria, 1890), pp. 38–9.
[5]Public Record Office (PRO), microfilm in Public Archives of Ontario (PAO), CO 42, v. 440, p. 97, "Extracts from the Poll-Books. . . ."

From the reform standpoint the election was a catastrophe. More than twice as many tories as reformers were elected. Many prominent reformers, Bidwell, Robert Baldwin, and Mackenzie among them, were defeated. Mackenzie gathered evidence of corruption to present to the assembly but illness prevented him from submitting the material within the time limit for contesting election results. An unsympathetic Assembly refused to extend the deadline.[6] Dr. Charles Duncombe, a successful reform candidate in Oxford County, did Mackenzie one better. He took his convictions and his charges to England in a petition to the House of Commons. Duncombe claimed that he had "been deputed by the Reformers" of the province to apprise the Commons of widespread electoral fraud, when he had been sent, in actual fact, by just some of the Toronto reformers. If his backing was small, his charges were many. The instances of corruption cited in the petition, "encouraged by the Lieutenant Governor and public functionaries in every part of the Province," had, he claimed, "overwhelmed" "the real Electors" (A 17).

While the petition did reach the House of Commons, Duncombe was unsuccessful in his bid to present it to the colonial secretary, Lord Glenelg. The latter, importuned by Head,[7] refused to see the infuriated reformer (A 18). A co-traveller with Duncombe, Robert Baldwin, also had cause to be displeased, for he discovered while in Britain that a vengeful Upper Canadian government was seeking out its enemies and had dismissed a variety of reformers from their posts. Among these was his father, who lost his District and Surrogate Court judgeships (A 19).

For the reformers, grievance seemed to pile upon grievance, and little remedy appeared available to them within the existing system. This was underlined in January of 1837 when an Assembly committee, controlled and directed by tories, reported that it had investigated Duncombe's petition and its majority had concluded that all of the doctor's charges were without foundation. While a reading of the report and of Duncombe's petition shows that some charges were laid to rest, others not dealt with convincingly, and still others not addressed at all, this mattered little to the crushed reformers. Clearly the whole report was a tory device to hide tory sins.

[6]Charles Lindsey, *The Life and Times of William Lyon Mackenzie* . . ., i (Toronto, 1862), p. 382.
[7]Sir Francis Bond Head, *A Narrative, with Notes by William Lyon Mackenzie*, edited by S.F. Wise (Toronto, 1969), pp. 61–2.

From the reform perspective the end of 1836 and the early months of 1837 brought forth a whole catalogue of Family Compact and tory iniquities. Some of them were old and some were new but all emphasized the forces ranged against social and political change. The report, largely Mackenzie's work, of a committee appointed by the old Assembly to inquire into the Welland Canal Company affair charged that the officers of this government-subsidized body had committed serious defalcations of funds and had abused their power of granting contracts (A 21). It was learned that Sir John Colborne, just before leaving office, had endowed fifty-seven rectories of the Church of England (A 23). Increasingly, establishment churches and the Wesleyan Methodists were seen as being in the pockets of government (A 26, A 27). The anti-Catholic, pro-monarchy Orange Order was also denounced as a government tool because of its support of constitutional candidates in the election, although it had never previously taken a public anti-reform stand (A 29, A 30, A 31, A 32). The Canada Company, the Bank of Upper Canada, and all the old enemies were still active, while a deepening economic crisis gripped the province.

In 1836 much of the western world had been afflicted by a tightening of credit following hard on the heels of a long period of economic expansion in both Great Britain and the United States. By early 1837, with the international economy in confusion, money was in short supply in Upper Canada. The provincial banks responded by asking the provincial government for the right to suspend specie payments, as had been done elsewhere in British North America, in order to prevent a run on their reserves by citizens fearing for the security of their deposits and by those who distrusted the value of paper currency. Before the Bank of Upper Canada received such permission, it was reduced to having its friends and supporters clog the bank all day to make withdrawals, which were quietly returned to the vaults by night.[8] This shortage of cash was felt in all aspects of the province's affairs, not just by men like Mackenzie who believed banks conspired against the public good (A 33, A 34, A 35, A 37).

Agricultural problems also took their toll. The crop yields had been at best uneven.[9] Consequently, in 1837 foodstuffs were in

---

[8]Lindsey, *The Life and Times of William Lyon Mackenzie*, II, p. 34.
[9]*United Secession Magazine*, VI (April 1838), p. 211, extract of a letter from Rev. Wm. Proudfoot, London, 1 Jan. 1838.

short supply and prices rose all through the spring and summer. With the populace eagerly awaiting the new crop, that also proved deficient. Well-established farmers with crops to sell probably suffered little economic hardship from the short-falls in the harvests, benefiting as they did from higher prices. But those who had to buy those crops – townsfolk, newer farmers, and those in areas particularly hard hit by crop failures – suffered. Food shortages provided another economic concern; to many reformers, deficient crops, the bank crisis, and rising interest rates were all interconnected, flowing inevitably from Compact policies.

For Mackenzie, if not for all reformers, the final straw seems to have been Lord John Russell's "Ten Resolutions" of March 1837, which allowed government by executive decree in Lower Canada. If the British government could treat one province this way, reasoned Mackenzie, then it was certain to treat Upper Canada similarly. It was no longer possible to hope, as reformers previously had, for aid from the mother country.[10] After their defeat at the hands of the lieutenant-governor and after seeing the actions the new Assembly took in 1837 to prolong its life beyond the expected death of the king, leading reformers such as Robert Baldwin and Marshall Spring Bidwell had withdrawn from politics. A vacuum existed in the reform leadership which radicals such as Mackenzie, eager to try new solutions, could fill.

These radicals decided that the British government would have to be pressured to make changes through extra-parliamentary action. In October of 1836 a group of reformers, seeking to organize such action and desiring to revitalize the reform movement, had created the City of Toronto Political Union. Upper Canada was no stranger to political unions, the device having been used following the example set in Britain at the time of the great Reform Bill in the early 1830s. It was an excellent way to express frustrations that could no longer be vented through the assembly. More than this, it was a way of demonstrating what the radicals felt were the legitimate desires of the people for reform.

In the summer of 1837, Mackenzie, who had recently begun to discuss the possibility of rebellion in his newspaper the

[10]R.J. Stagg, "The Yonge Street Rebellion of 1837: An Examination of the Social Background and a Reassessment of the Events" (PH.D. thesis, University of Toronto, 1976), pp. 31-2.

Constitution and had pointed out the similarities between the grievances of Upper Canada and those that led to the American Declaration of Independence, suggested that the province's reformers create a pyramidal structure of political unions. These could, he observed, "be easily transferred . . . to military purposes," but would not be (A 48). At the end of July he was instrumental in having the Toronto Political Union publish an address calling for an end to political corruption and unrepresentative government, the creation of a network of political unions, a boycott of imported goods, the formation of a close working relationship with reformers from Lower Canada, and the establishment of a joint convention of the two provinces to discuss their common afflictions (A 50).

The Toronto declaration brought swift results. Reform newspapers across the province reprinted it, and reformers in many locales followed the example of those in the capital. Unions sprang up in the Home District, then elsewhere. Beginning in August, Mackenzie, as agent and corresponding secretary of the "Committee of Vigilance" created by the Toronto meeting, scheduled fifteen meetings to organize unions throughout the Home District.[11] Of these, two were broken up by gangs of Orangemen, although one was later held in a private home, and two, to be held in Peel County, centre of Orange strength in the District, were never convened. At three more, the reformers found themselves outvoted by tory supporters and were forced to meet separately to pass their resolutions.

It is hard to argue that the meetings which were held were intended as the prelude to rebellion. Only three of the Home District meetings passed resolutions which could be interpreted as calls to use force to achieve change, and the meeting which issued the most blatant statement, that at Whitby, was not attended by any of those later associated with the leadership of the Toronto rising.[12] On the other hand, the Lloydtown meeting, held in the centre of one of the most disaffected areas and attended by Mackenzie and others who drafted beforehand many of the resolutions passed at those meetings, resolved that "the resistance we contemplate is not that of physical force, much may be done without blood."[13] Essentially, those at the meetings

[11]*Constitution* (Toronto), 2 Aug. 1837, 13 Sept. 1837.
[12]*Patriot* (Toronto), 11 Oct. 1837.
[13]*Constitution*, 9 Aug. 1837.

were trying to demonstrate their resolution to have reform, not their resolution to seize it by force of arms.

In the months to come reformers in other centres – Brockville, Belleville, and Hamilton, for example – established political unions. Among the most ardent supporters of the movement were the reformers in the London District. Its three southern counties, Norfolk, Oxford, and Middlesex, had in 1836 bucked the provincial trend by returning only reformers to the Assembly. Also, the district had the leading reform journal west of Hamilton, the St. Thomas *Liberal*. In 1837 this was edited by thirty-nine-year-old John Talbot, son of a prominent London Township pioneer and a distant relative of that irascible and unregenerate tory, Colonel Thomas Talbot. The latter, who had been involved in organizing the settling of no less than twenty-seven townships,[14] thought himself entitled to exercise paternal authority over the settlers. Despite his best efforts, the reformers in the west, or Liberals as they styled themselves, had grown from strength to strength. Many, among them John Talbot (A 51), welcomed the call to unionize.

The meetings in the London District went very much as had those in the Home. Some, such as those at Sodom in Norwich Township[15] and at Sparta in Yarmouth,[16] endorsed the principles of the Toronto reformers. Others, such as the Richmond meeting, in Bayham, resulted in a set-to with tory forces (A 62). The outcome of the riot was disputed by the two sides, but it was clear that the Liberals were a force to be reckoned with in the District. This was proved beyond a doubt by the Westminster meeting of 6 October, when over one thousand reformers swarmed onto the field,[17] pushing out local tories who had met to condemn those who spread sedition in Upper and Lower Canada (A 64, A 65).

The tories became very alarmed at this display of strength and at a public meeting on 21 October requested government assistance (A 68). Head replied with assurances that the laws of the province would be upheld by "the vigilance of the Magistracy & the loyalty of" the people (A 70). In fact, he had already demonstrated such confidence in the citizens of the

[14]*Appendix to the Journals of the House of Assembly of Upper Canada*, Second Session, Twelfth Parliament, 1836, v. 1, no. 22, p. 24.

[15]*Constitution*, 13 Sept. 1837.

[16]See *Liberal*, ibid., 27 Sept. 1837.

[17]*Gazette* (London), ibid., 18 Oct. 1837.

colony by readily complying with the request of Sir John Colborne, now stationed in Lower Canada as lieutenant-general commanding the forces, to send as many men as possible from the British regiment in the province, the 24th, to aid the Lower Canadian authorities.[18] By early November the province was denuded of troops.

Although the move to organize unions was winding up in the Home District by early fall, it continued in the London District and was spreading to other districts. In early November, Charles Duncombe began to take part in this work. Since his return from England he had maintained a low profile, perhaps because of the shock and subsequent grief at finding that his teenage son, Charles, had died during his absence. Now he was ready for action. He spoke with "eloquence and spirit."[19] To a correspondent he explained, "it is high time for the reformers to be up and doing" for "the time has come when we are to decide whether we will be bondsmen or slaves" (A 66).

The meetings spread into the farthest corners of the district, one being held in the Huron Tract on 10 November. In November also, the organizational activity spread to the Gore District, with meetings at Hamilton (A 80) and Guelph. To the south, in the Niagara District, the reformers of the Short Hills, back of St. Catharines, held their meeting in early December.[20] Scattered about the province were other unions. In total, however, the number organized probably did not exceed two score.

Writers such as William Lyon Mackenzie have given an inflated idea of the extent of the political union movement. Building on this, Charles Lindsey and those who have followed his line of thought have suggested that a great many political unions were created, with the intention of organizing the members for rebellion. As proof of this, the military "trainings" held in the Home District at the time of the formation of the unions are cited as being the next step in the organization. But Mackenzie reported only one training prior to October, in the Home District, and none at all were held in the London District. Although some Hamilton men decided to purchase rifles (A 77),

[18]Public Archives of Canada (PAC), RG7 G16A, Lieutenant-Governor's Internal Letter Books, v. 2, p. 2, Head to Colborne, 17 Oct. 1837.
[19]*Constitution*, 15 Nov. 1837.
[20]PAC, RG 9 I B1, Adjutant General's Office, Correspondence (AGOC), v. 29, Lincoln file, Deposition of Solomon Camp, 26 Feb. 1838.

and others at Wellington Square determined to form a rifle company,[21] the Gore District saw such actions only a short time before the outbreak, and these seemed to be no part of a coherent and widespread plan.

Everywhere, the union meetings were merely attempts to show the strong resolve of the people to have reform. As Mackenzie put it in the *Constitution* of 13 September, the unions' purpose was "Agitation! agitation! agitation!" to convince the government that it did not have the support of the people, thereby bringing about change. The culmination of all of this activity was to be the great convention of citizens which the Toronto reformers had suggested in their declaration of July. This would prove even to the imperial authorities the necessity of reform.

Why is it widely believed that the organization of political unions was the first link in a chain leading to rebellion? Certainly Lindsey's work had a great deal to do with creating this belief, as does the human desire to see neat linear progressions. When no positive evidence exists to support such a progression, it must be substantiated by circumstantial means. Thus Mackenzie's publication of a draft constitution for Upper Canada on 16 November (A 78) has been held to show that a revolutionary plot was well under way. Such historical assumptions, based on no concrete evidence, can create serious distortions. It is highly unlikely that Mackenzie's constitution was part of a longstanding and widespread plot. All of the men who acted as leaders in the Toronto rising who later commented on it insisted that they knew nothing of a rising until shortly before the rebellion took place.[22] Far from being a widespread conspiracy, the uprising at Toronto was uniquely the creation of a frustrated William Lyon Mackenzie.

Only one piece of evidence exists to suggest an organized effort at rebellion, the correspondence of John G. Parker, a wealthy American-born Hamilton merchant and radical reformer. He and a handful of cohorts in and about Hamilton diligently worked for rebellion. In his letters to acquaintances in the province and in Lower Canada he was eager to spur on the faint-hearted, to give the impression that all was ready for rebellion. He informed one correspondent, "Upper Canada is at this time in a great excitement and should Lower Canada

[21]Ibid., RG5 A1, Upper Canada Sundries (UCS), v. 185, p. 103594, Deposition of John S. McCollom, 29 Dec. 1837.
[22]Stagg, "The Yonge Street Rebellion of 1837," p. 53 n. 32.

revolutionize, Upper Canada would follow at once and join the States. . . . The country is already well organized by the formation of Political Unions."[23] Parker was arrested in early December and his correspondence seized. Authorities reading it then and those perusing it since have found it easy to believe that the course of rebellion had long been charted. Yet Parker was not plotting with any of those who later organized the uprisings. No other seized correspondence or other correspondence that has survived from the period suggests there was any organization. To use this isolated evidence as proof of a general movement is to make a general case from an exceptional one.

The lack of planning by those who rebelled explains a noteworthy feature of the pre-rebellion documents of this volume. In October of 1837 Mackenzie swore he had not written "a line in politics to any person" in the London District "for months past."[24] Neither did he correspond frequently with reformers elsewhere; nor did his colleagues. They had no deeply laid plans for rebellion, and hence were not in constant contact with each other. This fact is reflected in the documents chosen here. Relatively few are drawn from private correspondence; most come from newspapers, official documents and the like – the usual instruments of political dialogue in the province, and those in most use in the days before the outbreak of rebellion.

What existed then in Upper Canada in the summer and early fall of 1837 was a movement of extra-parliamentary protest by the more radical elements of the reform movement. Even the military trainings that were held appear to have been just more emphatic demonstrations of determination than the political unions were. No attempt was made to arm the trainees, and the men who later led the Toronto rising claimed afterwards that they did not know while the trainings were going on that there was to be a rising. No doubt there were many frustrated individuals, but only in November and December would an attempt be made to direct this frustration to armed action against the government.

[23]PRO, CO 42, v. 467, p. 13, John G. Parker to J. Williams, Hamilton, 1 Dec. 1837.
[24]*Constitution*, 18 Oct. 1837.

B. THE MACKENZIE RISING

ON OCCASION IN 1837 the radicals in and about Toronto had couched their rhetoric in revolutionary phraseology, but few had spoken of rebellion. None the less, radicals from the Home District did join in arms against the government in December of that year. The available evidence points to the conclusion that, in doing so, they were not carrying out some deeply laid plot, but were acting more or less on the spur of the moment, having been aroused to do so largely by one man, William Lyon Mackenzie.

The precise date of Mackenzie's decision to incite revolt cannot be established. Here, approximations must suffice. It is noteworthy that it was not until the fall of 1837 that Mackenzie's newspaper, the *Constitution,* began to grow strident, often intemperate, in discussing how to end "oppression" in Upper Canada. Thus it is likely that Mackenzie decided on rebellion only in the autumn of 1837, or, at the earliest, in the late summer of that year. This conclusion is reinforced by the fact that he is not known to have broached the question of revolt with others until late October,[1] at a meeting at the home of a prominent Toronto brewer, John Doel. That meeting saw Mackenzie begin his campaign to persuade fellow radicals to join him in rebellion.

Mackenzie suggested to the approximately ten radical reformers assembled at Doel's that, with the soldiers withdrawn from the province, now was the time to strike and eliminate the oppressive regime in power at Toronto. It would be possible to organize the farmers, "who were quite prepared for resistance" but it would be better to use "Dutcher's foundry-men and Armstrong's axe-makers" (that is, the radical employees of two radical reformers) to seize the lieutenant-governor, several thousand muskets stored in the city hall, and the garrison, for all of which the only protection was two constables. Then the

---

[1]*Trial of Dr. Morrison, M.P.P., for High Treason, at Toronto, on Wednesday, April 24, 1838* (Toronto, 1838), pp. 2-3, testimony of John Elliott and Robert McKay. There is disagreement about the date of this meeting, but most evidence suggests the end of October. For a complete discussion of the date, see Stagg, "The Yonge Street Rebellion,"pp. 40-2. Those known to have been at the meeting are W.L. Mackenzie, Dr. T.D. Morrison, John Elliott, John Doel, John McIntosh, Robert McKay, John Armstrong, Timothy Parsons, Thomas Armstrong, and John Mills.

successful rebels would only have to wait for their friends and supporters among the farmers to arrive in the city. At this point Dr. T.D. Morrison jumped up, denounced the idea as treason, and stormed out, breaking up the meeting.[2]

Mackenzie did not in the least abandon his idea of overthrowing the government. The next day he went to speak to Dr. John Rolph, one leading reformer who kept himself aloof from the various factions within the movement. Mackenzie proved himself a good judge of character, for when he suggested the possibility of overthrowing the government, Rolph was guardedly interested. What Mackenzie said was not recorded, but it seems likely that he argued, as he was to do later, that those who signed the political union lists had actually been expressing their willingness to act against the government. He must have indicated that Lower Canada was also ready to rise.[3]

Rolph and Mackenzie soon thereafter went to see Dr. Morrison. A cautious man and a follower rather than a leader, Morrison fell in line with Rolph, whom he admired, and agreed to consider supporting action against the government if more concrete information could be obtained of the people's intentions. The three agreed to despatch Jesse Lloyd, founder of Lloydtown in King Township and a strong supporter of Mackenzie, to ask the leaders of the radicals in Lower Canada for specific information of their plans.[4] When Lloyd arrived in Montreal in the second week in November, he did more than ask for this information. He also informed his contacts that the Upper Canadians were going to attack Toronto.[5]

It seems likely that by this point Mackenzie had been joined by Silas Fletcher,[6] another of his supporters from north of Toronto, as well as by Jesse Lloyd, in his conviction that a rebellion was the only possible way to end oppression. Mackenzie's suggestion of a quick surprise attack by a few men having been rejected at the meeting at Doel's, he, Lloyd, and probably Fletcher, attempted a much more elaborate scheme to draw into rebellion not only Rolph and Morrison but also a large portion of those people in and around Toronto who supported radical reform. The first step involved a letter from Thomas Storrow Brown which

[2]Lindsey, *The Life and Times of William Lyon Mackenzie*, II, pp. 53-6.
[3]J.C. Dent, *The Story of the Upper Canadian Rebellion . . .*, I, pp. 380-1.
[4]Ibid., I, p. 383, and II, p. 21n.
[5]T.S. Brown, *1837 – My Connection with It* (Quebec, 1898), pp. 21-2.
[6]See J. Barnett, "Silas Fletcher, Instigator of the Upper Canadian Rebellion," *Ontario History*, XLI (1949), pp. 11-13, for a discussion of Fletcher's role.

Lloyd brought back from Lower Canada. It appeared to be an innocuous business letter, but Mackenzie purported to read between the lines for the two doctors, explaining that Lower Canada was about to rebel but wished Upper Canada to do so first, in order to confuse the British forces. Brown himself could not have written such a message since, as he later wrote, he knew of no plans for rebellion in Lower Canada. When this evidence failed to convince Rolph and Morrison, Mackenzie agreed to ride north of Toronto and secure positive assurances of large-scale support.[7] When he went north, probably about the middle of November, instead of looking for proof of support, which had never in fact been given, Mackenzie set about convincing key men that a rising was both possible and necessary. While he had claimed great popular backing for rebellion to tempt Rolph and Morrison, he now told others that the two doctors were prepared to lead the rebellion.[8]

Mackenzie first approached Samuel Lount, farmer and blacksmith, probably the most popular reformer north of Toronto and a man whose generosity to new settlers and to the Indians of the region was remembered long after he was dead.[9] Once he had convinced Lount, Mackenzie called a meeting of influential radicals from about Toronto, in the third week of November. Present were Lount, Lloyd, and Fletcher, James Bolton from Albion, the founder of Boltontown (Bolton), Nelson Gorham, a young, well-educated inhabitant of Newmarket, where his father ran one of Upper Canada's few cloth mills, and possibly Peter Matthews, a prominent farmer from Pickering. His elaborate arguments and the prearranged support of three of the men ensured Mackenzie of little trouble in convincing the meeting. The date of the rising was set for 7 December and the details were essentially those that Rolph, Morrison, and Mackenzie had tentatively agreed to in Toronto.[10] A surprise descent on Toronto would lead to the seizure of the arms, the lieutenant-governor, and other prominent officials. Rolph was to become head of a provisional government.[11]

[7]Brown, *1837*, pp. 21-3; Dent, *The Story*, I, pp. 382-4 and statement by Dr. Morrison; ibid., II, pp. 20-2n.

[8]Ibid., I, pp. 9-10, Dr. Morrison's statement, p. 22n; PAC, MG24 B24, Dr. John Rolph Papers, v. 3, W.T. Aikin to John Rolph, Toronto, 11 Nov. 1852.

[9]For a modest assessment of Lount's efforts, see PAO, Mackenzie–Lindsey Papers, Mackenzie Correspondence, Elizabeth Lount to W.L. Mackenzie, Pontiac, Michigan, 12 April 1850.

[10]Dent, *The Story*, II, p. 9; PAO, David Gibson Papers, D. Gibson to John Rolph, Grovsend, 1 Dec. 1852 and D. Gibson to John Rolph, York Mills, 20 May 1854.

[11]Dent, *The Story*, I, pp. 382-4 and II, pp. 20-2n.

Mackenzie rode back to Toronto, to face the wrath of Rolph and Morrison, who had heard of Mackenzie's misuse of their names.[12] Mackenzie, giving quick and firm assurances of the support of four or five thousand men, bolstered by his lists of union members, assuaged their anger. Probably somewhat reluctantly, Rolph and Morrison gave their support.[13] They insisted, however, that the rebels secure a competent military leader. Mackenzie willingly agreed, suggesting Colonel Anthony Van Egmond, who had served with the Dutch, French, and Prussian forces during the Napoleonic wars. Although an employee of the Canada Company, Van Egmond was a strong critic of this concern and its supporters, the members of the Family Compact (A 20).[14]

Mackenzie's ability to win over intelligent and cautious men demonstrated one of his strengths. The next weeks were to demonstrate one of his great weaknesses – his inability to plan and execute large scale ventures. Aside from a speech Lount gave to the men of the settlement of Hope (Sharon) (B 5), there appears to have been no attempt to organize the men who were expected to march on Toronto, until the weekend of 2-3 December.

Even then Mackenzie did little. Having returned to the north shortly after his discussions with Rolph and Morrison, on Friday, 1 December, he dashed off, over breakfast, an appeal to Upper Canadians to rise in arms (B 3), suggesting neither time nor plan. He sent it south to his brother-in-law who lived at the site of the future Willowdale, who ran it off on a small press for distribution outside Toronto.[15] Mackenzie also called a meeting at Stoverville (Stouffville) for Saturday. If he really hoped to secure several thousand men for the descent on Toronto, his organizational efforts should have been more far-reaching. Even if, as he

[12]Ibid., II, pp. 9, 11-12; PAO, Gibson Papers, D. Gibson to John Rolph, Grovsend, 1 Dec. 1852 and D. Gibson to John Rolph, York Mills, 20 May 1854.

[13]A certain amount can be assumed about this conversation. Mackenzie insisted for the rest of his life that thousands would have joined the rising. See *Mackenzie's Gazette* (New York), 15 Dec. 1838 and his account in the Watertown, New York, *Jeffersonian*, reprinted in *Mackenzie's Gazette*, 12 May 1838.

Many individuals suggested that Mackenzie misrepresented the nature of the union lists. See UCS, v. 193, pp. 107510-23, Petition of Joseph Gould, 4 May 1838 and v. 180, pp. 99487-8, Examination of Bartholemew Plank, 19 Dec. 1837.

[14]See Robina and Kathleen Lizars, *In the Days of the Canada Company* . . . (Toronto 1896), pp. 111-12; and PAO, Scrapbook, "The Canada Company and Anthony Van Egmond – The Story of 1837 in Huron County,"for Van Egmond's earlier career.

[15]PAO, Mackenzie–Lindsey Papers, Mackenzie Clippings, no. 6017, rough notes in Mackenzie's handwriting.

told several people, not more than six hundred were required,[16] his contention that most of these would be informed, and thus secured, by word of mouth demonstrated a singular lack of practicality on his part.

At Stoverville Mackenzie employed the arguments he had used to win over Lount and other prominent radicals. He was in his element in haranguing a crowd. Few people could hold the attention of an audience as he could. And his message at Stoverville was a dramatic one. Of course he went over all the old grievances, linking the economic depression and agricultural shortages of 1837 to Family Compact policies, but he went far beyond this. The people of Lower Canada, Mackenzie explained, had risen in rebellion and carried all before them. The government of Upper Canada, in order to prevent a similar occurrence, was about to declare martial law. Thousands of arms stored in the Toronto city hall were to be given out to Indians, blacks, and Orangemen, all loyal government supporters, who would be allowed to murder and pillage at will. Now was the time to resist, while the St. Lawrence was closed to reinforcements by the Lower Canadians. In fact, a general rising had been organized across the province through the political union movement. The people north of Toronto were to march into the capital and seize control of the government before it could act. This would not be difficult because prominent reformers like John Rolph were for the movement, as were members of the Family Compact who were disgusted with Bond Head's arbitrary actions.

As proof of this latter dramatic statement, Mackenzie pointed out that Peter Robinson, G.H. Markland, and J.H. Dunn had all resigned from the Executive Council in protest at Head's actions. Moreover, John Beverley Robinson had told his fellow executive councillors not to prosecute Mackenzie for sedition. While this was true, the audience had no way of knowing that Robinson had acted because he felt Mackenzie had the sympathy of too many people for the government to secure an impartial jury for his trial, not because he approved of Mackenzie's conduct. The only problem, Mackenzie said, might arise if a few die-hard tories resisted, but this could be prevented if the people carried weapons on their march to Toronto. This would actually avert bloodshed, and officials like John Beverley Robinson would feel

[16]See, for example, UCS, v. 180, pp. 99351-2, Examination of Nathaniel Pearson, 16 Dec. 1837.

justified in turning the government over to the people. Those who participated in the movement would be rewarded with free land from the crown and clergy reserves seized from the government. Those who resisted might be punished by losing their lands, as had the tories of the American Revolution (B 4, B 7, B 8, B 9, B 12).[17]

To understand why Mackenzie's audience deemed this argument credible, it is necessary to remember that most people of the day took their news from only one source. Thus those who had obtained their information only from Mackenzie's *Constitution* or the recently defunct *Correspondent and Advocate* could easily believe Mackenzie's version of events. Additionally, most Upper Canadians knew that armed demonstrations had been a feature of the agitation which had preceded the great Reform Bill in Britain. Such a demonstration in Upper Canada might be seen as providing a similarly tolerable, though not strictly constitutional, action, as Mackenzie might have known.

Mackenzie spent the night at Stoverville, secure in the belief that his message would be carried far and wide and that, while the initial response might involve only a few hundred, ultimately thousands would march on Toronto. On Sunday he rode towards the capital to inform Rolph that the rebellion was now organized (B 14). In the evening he arrived at the home of David Gibson, a prominent York Township radical. Although Gibson had been very active in the meetings and trainings of the summer and fall, Mackenzie had not informed him of the projected rebellion when stopping at the Gibson farm just a week before on the way to organize the rising. Gibson first learned what was afoot early on the Sunday morning when a message came for Mackenzie from Rolph. Rolph had heard rumours that the government was about to call out the militia and arrest ringleaders in order to forestall rebellion. He therefore urged a Monday assault on the city with whatever forces could be gathered. Gibson, not knowing Mackenzie's whereabouts, had sent the message on to Samuel Lount.[18]

Upon hearing Gibson's story, Mackenzie sent word to stop the

[17]Dent, *The Story*, I, p. 376 and II, p. 16; PAC, Rolph Papers, v. 3, D. Gibson to John Rolph, 1 Dec. 1852; UCS, v. 188, pp. 104986–5013, Petition of Charles Low, 16 March 1838; ibid., v. 204, pp. 113202-37, Documents re Hugh D. Willson, including Petition of Hugh D. Willson, 14 March 1838; ibid., v. 180, pp. 99441-2, Confession of William Bunce, 18 Dec. 1838; ibid., v. 180, pp. 99487-8, Examination of Bartholemew Plank, 19 Dec. 1837; ibid., Petition of William Doan, v. 188, pp. 105073-94; ibid., v. 193, pp. 107638-46, Petition of Peter Rogers, 5 May 1838.

[18]PAC, Rolph Papers, v. 3, Notes by David Gibson on the rising and D. Gibson to

early rising because he believed, correctly, that Rolph was wrong. In fact, on Monday the government only sent orders to the commanders of the various militia regiments in the province to be ready to call out their men if requested (B 18). On the rebel side, meanwhile, word had spread in the area south of Lake Simcoe to turn out on Monday morning. By the time Mackenzie's message to stop arrived, too many people knew of the plan. For better or worse, the rising was about to begin.[19]

Early Monday morning, men began to march from Holland Landing, Sharon, Lloydtown, and other centres (B 5). Some carried weapons but many had none. Mackenzie had let it be known that weapons and food would be available at the inn of John Montgomery, a fellow radical, north of the city, so the shortage of weapons was not considered a problem.[20] As they marched, enough men carried weapons to alarm supporters of the government along the route, and by the time the first men reached Montgomery's, men behind them were already preparing to warn Toronto.[21] A few men had arrived at Montgomery's by seven o'clock but the first large group did not arrive until about ten. There they found that Montgomery had, within the last few days, rented his inn to a tory, John Linfoot, who was to act in the days ahead as a somewhat unwilling host to the rebels. Exhausted, and finding little food and no weapons, his erstwhile guests were confused as to what to do next. Mackenzie decided to take three men and reconnoitre in order to determine if Toronto had been warned.[22]

John Rolph, Grovsend, 1 Dec. 1852; PAO, Gibson Papers, nos. 233 and 239; ibid., Mackenzie–Lindsey Papers, Mackenzie Correspondence, Memorandum of W.L. Mackenzie of a conversation with Mrs. Lount re 4 Dec. 1837; *The Caroline Almanack and American Freeman's Chronicle for 1840* (Rochester, 1839), p. 98.

[19]*The Caroline Almanack*, pp. 98, 100; PAO, Mackenzie–Lindsey Papers, Mackenzie Clippings, no. 6017, rough notes in Mackenzie's handwriting; ibid., Mackenzie Correspondence, Memorandum of W.L. Mackenzie of a conversation with Mrs. Lount re 4 Dec. 1837; PAC, Rolph Papers, v. 1, Flag of Truce, Statement of John Hawke re 3–5 Dec. 1837.

[20]PAC, Rolph Papers, v. 1, Flag of Truce, Statement of John Hawke re 3–5 Dec. 1837; PAO, Mackenzie–Lindsey Papers, Mackenzie Clippings, no. 6017, "Recollections."

[21]"Resident Here in 1810 – Settler Tells Life Story," *Era & Express* (Newmarket), 20 Dec. 1946; *Records of the Lives of Ellen Free Pickton and Featherstone Lake Osler* (London, 1915), Second Journal of Featherstone Osler, pp. 170-7.

[22]UCS, v. 180, pp. 99085-6, Statement of John Montgomery, 11 Dec. 1837; PAO, Mackenzie–Lindsey Papers, Mackenzie Correspondence, Affidavits re the refusal of John Montgomery's rebellion losses claim, 19 Aug. 1852, Affidavit of William Hill; PAC, Rolph Papers, v. 1, Flag of Truce, Statement of John Hawke re 3–5 Dec. 1837; Dent, *The Story*, II, pp. 38, 43-4.

Although by Monday night very specific rumours of an uprising had been circulating, most people, the lieutenant-governor among them, paid little heed. The one man who had been convinced for some weeks that trouble was imminent, James FitzGibbon, a minor hero of the War of 1812, was dismissed by most as a crank and his efforts to organize local defence forces had been discouraged. He and several others rode up Yonge Street that night to find out if there was any truth to the rumours. Some, including FitzGibbon, turned back. Others went on and were captured (B 19).[23] Two of these, alderman John Powell and wharfinger Archibald MacDonell (McDonald) were taken by Mackenzie and his three-man party. Two of the party were detailed to escort the prisoners to Montgomery's. On the way there, the group was surprised by a fast-galloping man who recognized Powell's voice and shouted that Colonel Moodie had been shot. The man continued towards the city. Fearing for his life, Powell drew one of two pistols he had concealed under his coat and shot one of his captors, Anthony Anderson. Anderson, the only man with any military experience among the rebel force, died instantly. Powell and MacDonell then broke away and rode hard for the city. MacDonell was captured by Mackenzie, but, after some difficulty, Powell reached the city with the first reliable news of the revolt (B 20, B 21).

While Mackenzie was away, a party of seven men, loyalists who lived on or near Yonge Street north of Montgomery's, attempted to get by, to warn Toronto. Three broke through the lines of guards at the inn, one turned back, and the rest were captured. One of them, Colonel Robert Moodie, fired a pistol in the air to intimidate his captors. He was shot from his horse and died a few hours later, in great pain (B 27). The men who broke through did not reach the city until after Powell.

In Toronto all was confusion. Defence of the city would, in the normal course of events, be undertaken by the soldiers of the garrison. With these in Lower Canada, the militia of the district could be called out to meet an emergency, but this was a slow and not always satisfactory process. In theory, all the male citizens aged sixteen to sixty were obliged to serve when called upon, but in practice some regiments had too few or poorly qualified officers who neglected their duties and the regiments

[23]M.A. FitzGibbon, *A Veteran of 1812* (Toronto, 1894), pp. 188-96; James FitzGibbon, *An Appeal to the People of the Late Province of Upper Canada* (Montreal, 1847), pp. 10-13.

existed only on paper. Even where regiments did exist, training consisted of one day a year. A traveller, David Wilkie, commented on those in training at Hamilton in 1834:

they presented a most laughter-stirring spectacle. . . . As far as we could discern, not one garment was kin to another . . . the weapons that dangled from the fists of the doughty heroes would have been still more difficult to classify. Guns, whips, bludgeons, hoes, umbrellas, canes, sticks, &c.[24]

Since militia weapons had to be drawn from the British army commissariat in time of war, the militia was under normal circumstances very poorly armed, rifles and muskets not being in plentiful supply among the populace. Wartime duties were, in fact, usually delegated to specially incorporated and trained militia units, rather than the nominal ones of the various counties. Thus little attention had been paid to the unprepared state of the sedentary militia. The newly appointed adjutant general at Toronto, Richard Bullock, concluded in January 1838 that it had suffered from years of "total neglect."[25]

Since FitzGibbon had been discouraged from organizing to meet any attack on the city, there was little that could be done at the last minute. It would take days to organize the militia of the province, where it could be organized, and in the reform areas the loyalty of the men would be very much in question. In Toronto the bells of the city were rung to summon the population to defend the government but many did not hear them while others ignored them, thinking they were a call to fight a fire in some other part of the city.[26]

The lieutenant-governor, somewhat flustered, helped to escort the ladies of his household to the solicitor general's home, which was a less obvious target than Government House (B 23, B 24). He then went to the city hall, which with the market building beneath was to become his fortified headquarters. Muskets were handed out to volunteers and messages requesting aid were sent east to Kingston and west to Hamilton and the Niagara peninsula. Throughout the night volunteers came in, but by morning only

[24]K. David Wilkie, *Sketches of a Summer Trip to New York and the Canadas* (Edinburgh, 1837), pp. 158-9.
[25]PAC, RG9 I B1, Adjutant General's Office, Upper Canada, Letter Books, v. 68, p. 20, Richard Bullock to P.B. de Blaquiere, Toronto, 5 Jan. 1838. In 1838 a new militia law was passed, designed to tighten up things.
[26]Egerton Ryerson, *"The Story of My Life,"* J.G. Hodgins, ed. (Toronto, 1883), p. 177, William Ryerson to Egerton Ryerson, 5 Dec. 1837; PAC, Rolph Papers, v. 3, Account of John G. Howard.

two hundred to two hundred and fifty had arrived to defend the government (B 39).[27]

All was confusion at Montgomery's as well. There was to have been no bloodshed, but Anderson and Moodie were dead. The promised food and arms were not there. Perhaps worst of all, the city now knew of the attack. It was decided that nothing could be done until morning. Morning in fact brought the rebels good news in the shape of a large body of their fellows. Their forces now numbered between three and five hundred.[28] Beyond the city and Montgomery's, loyalists and rebels were organizing everywhere in the Home District, the former either to go to the aid of Toronto or simply to defend themselves, the latter to reinforce the group at Montgomery's. Many reformers responded to Mackenzie's call, relayed by word of mouth, to join the demonstration at Toronto, but others came to Montgomery's for different reasons. In some cases men were told just that there was an important meeting they should attend at Montgomery's. In at least one instance a determined recruiter threated to shoot someone who would not go there.[29]

Tuesday was Mackenzie's day. He had superior forces and the psychological advantage as well. In the city it was believed that there were several thousand rebels at Montgomery's. Unfortunately for Mackenzie, he chose to lead his forces into Toronto himself. Under normal circumstances he was not a great leader of men, but under the stress of leading a rebellion, he became very erratic (B 39), wasting the rebel advantage. Early in the morning, he mustered the men. Taking Toronto would be so easy, he said, that, if they had no weapons, they "should take pipes in their mouths as they could take the City with pipes as well as with fire arms" (B 30). The men were then formed in ranks as they had been taught to do at the various trainings and marched towards Toronto. Many wore white tape on their left arms. Mackenzie rode at their head, wearing several overcoats, all buttoned to his chin, to protect him from bullets.[30]

[27]The estimate given here is Mackenzie's. Head set loyalist numbers at about 300 (B 22), but the body of evidence suggests that Mackenzie's estimate was the more reliable.

[28]PAO, Gibson Papers, Diary O, 5 Dec. 1837.

[29]PAC, RG5 C1, Correspondence of the Provincial Secretary's Office (CPSO), v. 9, file 1209, Depositions and extracts from depositions affecting Samuel Lount on a charge of High Treason, extract from the Statement of Joshua B. Woodward, n.d.; UCS, v. 191, pp. 106639-42, Petition of Titus Root.

[30]Samuel Thompson, *Reminiscences of a Canadian Pioneer* . . . (Toronto, 1968,

Before long things began to go wrong; while making their way slowly towards the city the party arrived at Gallows Hill (the present site of St. Clair Avenue), only to catch sight of what appeared to be a cannon coming up the road towards them. The rebels immediately panicked and ran from the road.[31] When it was discovered that the cannon was really a wagon, Mackenzie did not attempt to get the column moving again. David Gibson and a small party then took all the prisoners who had been brought from Montgomery's west to the home of Augustus Baldwin, a Family Compact associate, in search of food. Samuel Lount kept the main body training on Gallows Hill, and Mackenzie took about fifty men and rode to the nearby house of J.S. Howard, postmaster of Toronto, where he demanded food for all fifty from Mrs. Howard.[32] Meanwhile, the road to the city was wide open. Francis Bond Head was so insecure in his position that he had pulled all his forces back to the market area, including a guard which had been placed at the first toll gate on Yonge Street against his wishes.[33] A resident who lived south of Gallows Hill, Dr. Horne, found while riding into the city on Tuesday morning that few people were enthusiastic to defend it (B 35). Mackenzie could have had his forces in the city by early afternoon.

So weak did Head feel his position to be that he decided to send negotiators, under a flag of truce, to find out what the rebels wanted. He hoped either to dissuade the rebels or at least to buy some time.[34] After he had negotiated with several prominent reformers, Robert Baldwin and John Rolph accepted the commission, the latter reluctantly.[35] What followed was the most controversial incident of the rebellion period.

The agreed upon facts are these. Rolph, Baldwin, and Hugh Carmichael, another reformer, who carried the flag, rode out to Gallows Hill, where they spoke with Lount. Shortly after, Mackenzie arrived and took over negotiations. After some discussion it was agreed that Rolph and Baldwin would go back

reprint), pp. 130-1; PRO, CO 42, v. 447, p. 205, Trial of Gilbert Fields Morden, Testimony of Morden.

[31]PAO, Mackenzie–Lindsey Papers, Mackenzie Clippings, no. 4687, Captain Stewart's narrative and A. MacDonell to *Herald* [Toronto ?], 21 July 1843.

[32]Ibid.; Thompson, *Reminiscences*, pp. 130-1.

[33]FitzGibbon, *A Veteran of 1812*, pp. 214-15.

[34]Dent, *The Story*, II, pp. 62-3.

[35]Ibid., II, p. 64; James H. Price in the Assembly quoted in *Mackenzie's Weekly Message* (Toronto), 7 April 1854.

and get the lieutenant-governor's offer of an amnesty in writing. Meanwhile the rebels would not move beyond the toll gate south of Gallows Hill (B 31).[36] As Rolph left, he saw Isaac Robinson, a tailor of tory leanings, standing nearby. Rolph ordered him to stay where he was and the rebels came down and seized him.[37] When the negotiators reached Toronto, the lieutenant-governor, evidently having learned something of the true strength of the rebels, ordered negotiations terminated (B 31).[38] Rolph and Baldwin rode out again and passed on the news. Rolph then had a brief conversation with Mackenzie while Baldwin and Carmichael waited a bit further down the road.[39] By this time Mackenzie had moved about one hundred and fifty of his men to the head of College (now University) Avenue, ready to march (B 31).[40]

The controversy arose because Lount later claimed that after the first arrival of Head's emissaries, Rolph told Lount to ignore the message and continue the march into the city (B 33). If Rolph did so, of course, he violated his position as a neutral emissary. In later years he and Mackenzie collected statements from numerous individuals to prove either that he had not or had spoken to Lount. Mackenzie rewrote his accounts of the rebellion and played up the role of an unnamed executive, obviously Rolph, who had been responsible for the failure of the rising.[41] Rolph always maintained that he had not spoken to Lount until after the second trip, when the mission for the lieutenant-governor had been completed. The whole debate appears pointless. Even had Rolph spoken only when his mission was

[36]UCS, v. 192, pp. 107033-8, Petition of Samuel Lount, 10 March 1838; PAC, Rolph Papers, v. 3, John Hawke to John Rolph, Hawksville, 1 June 1854 and v. 3, Nelson Gorham to T.T. Rolph, 7 June 1884; PAO, Mackenzie–Lindsey Papers, Mackenzie Correspondence, "Remarks on Sir Francis Head's Speech of December 28, 1837," filed under 4 Dec. 1837; PAO, C.H. Graham Papers, Thomas I. Patterson to C.H. Graham, Wellington, 15 Dec. 1837; PAO, Gibson Papers, no. 233.

[37]PAO, Rebellion Papers, 1837-8, no. 15, Information of Hugh Carmichael, 21 Dec. 1837 and no. 16, Information of Isaac Robinson, 21 Dec. 1837.

[38]PAO, C.H. Graham Papers, Thomas I. Patterson to C.H. Graham, Wellington, 15 Dec. 1837.

[39]PAC, Rolph Papers, v. 1, Statement of T. Parsons, 30 Oct. 1838 and v. 3, Statement of William Ware, 20 Dec. 1837 and v. 3, Statement of Robert Baldwin, 13 Dec. 1837.

[40]*Mackenzie's Gazette* (New York), 8 Sept. 1838; PAC, Rolph Papers, v. 3, Statement of William Ware, 20 Dec. 1837; PAO, John Beverley Robinson Casebook, Trial of Robert Stibbert, 9 April 1838, Testimony of Joseph Lusty and Titus Valentine.

[41]See *Mackenzie's Gazette*, 12 May 1838; *The Caroline Almanack*, pp. 41, 98, 102; *Mackenzie's Weekly Message*, 31 March 1854.

technically over, he had clearly violated the trust Head had placed in him. Nor would his defence likely have stood up in a court of law. As well, on the first trip he apparently told a young reformer, William Ketchum, to spread stories in the city of the great strength of the rebels (B 36).

Whatever the case, Rolph fully expected Mackenzie to follow him into the city as soon as possible. The doctor and Carmichael parted with Baldwin inside the city limits and Rolph rode to Elliot's Tavern, the reform establishment at Lot (Queen) Street and Yonge. There he told a large crowd of perhaps one hundred to two hundred men gathered in the street that Mackenzie was on his way in and that they should arm themselves and meet him, Rolph, at Doel's brewery. When no sign was seen of Mackenzie's advance, Rolph sent one of his students, H.H. Wright, to find out why, then went to Doel's (B 43, B 44).[42] About one hundred men were there. The doctor urged them to get any weapons they could, by seizing them from the tories if necessary, and then either wait for Mackenzie or go to his aid. Many of those present appear to have followed his advice. Rolph then went to a back room of Elliot's Tavern, where he waited news of the rebels' arrival.[43]

Wright, in his search for Mackenzie, had to go a long way. After the flag of truce had returned to the city about 3 P.M., Mackenzie, instead of ordering the advance, went over to the nearby house of Dr. Horne, who was a public critic of Mackenzie and assistant cashier of the Bank of Upper Canada. Despite pleas from Lount and disagreement from some of the rebel force, Mackenzie and a few others set it on fire.[44] Mackenzie then rode purposefully towards Rosedale, the home of Sheriff W.B. Jarvis. At this point David Gibson, who was returning to Montgomery's with the prisoners, and Lount interceded forcefully and prevented further arson.[45] Their leader did not, however, return to the march on Toronto. He went back to postmaster Howard's house where, finding that Mrs. Howard had not produced the food for his men, he dragged her to the window and threatened to

[42]PAC, Rolph Papers, v. 3, Statement of H.H. Wright, 7 July 1838 and Statement of George Coulthard, 7 Sept. 1839 and Statement of Robert Baldwin, 13 Dec. 1837.

[43]Ibid.; Metropolitan Toronto Public Library, Reminiscences of Dr. James H. Richardson, 1905, no. 3 (typescript) p. 3; PAO, Mackenzie–Lindsey Papers, Mackenzie Clippings, no. 227, rough notes re Dr. Rolph.

[44]PAC, Rolph Papers, v. 3, Nelson Gorham to T.T. Rolph, 7 June 1884; UCS, v. 192, pp. 107033-8, Petition of Samuel Lount, 10 March 1838; PAO, Rebellion Papers, 1837–8, no. 13, Statement of Charles Doan, 15 Dec. 1837.

[45]UCS, v. 192, pp. 107033-8, Petition of Samuel Lount, 10 March 1838; PAO, Gibson Papers, no. 233.

do the same to her house as he had done to Horne's, which was burning below. At this moment Lount felt obliged to step in and assure Mrs. Howard all would be well.[46] Lount explained that Mackenzie was not his usual self. Several men commented on the "lunatic" behaviour of their leader on this day.[47]

Mackenzie next returned to Montgomery's, where Wright found him and convinced him that the way to the city was clear, that numerous reformers were armed and ready to assist them, and that the loyalist forces were relatively small and confined to the market area. Mackenzie then decided to renew his attack (B 44). But by now many who would have gone earlier were discouraged, while others did not want to advance in the fast-approaching December darkness. Journeying back down Yonge Street, Mackenzie persuaded as many as he could to turn around and head for the city.[48] Although he had from five to seven hundred men in his force, only part of this number now advanced.

Many who went with Mackenzie were from Lloydtown, and these men were among the best trained of the rebels. But when they did meet trouble, in the form of a picket guard under Sheriff Jarvis, which, against Head's orders, the indefatigable James FitzGibbon had placed at the side of the road south of the present College Street (B 37), this training proved a hindrance. Seeing the advancing rebel column, the picket opened fire and then, as they numbered only about twenty, turned and ran. The front rank of the rebel force also fired, then dropped to the ground, as they had been trained to do, so that the next rank could fire while they reloaded. It was now evening. In the poor light some men in the rebel force thought that those who had dropped to the ground had been shot. They turned and ran, causing panic among their fellows (B 38, B 40). Mackenzie, for once, acted strongly and tried to stop the retreat, but could not (B 38).[49] It did not stop until Montgomery's, and in some cases, not even then, as many rebels decided to go home. Although men continued to arrive over the next two days, the rebel force was never larger than on Tuesday. As fast as new arrivals added to rebel numbers, others

[46]Thompson, *Reminiscences*, p. 132.

[47]See Dent, *The Story*, II, p. 93n, p. 94n.

[48]PAO, Rebellion Papers, 1837–8, no. 13, Statement of Charles Doan, 15 Dec. 1837.

[49]PAO, Mackenzie–Lindsey Papers, Mackenzie Correspondence, notes filed under 4 Dec. 1837; PAO, Rebellion Papers, 1837–8, no. 20, Statement of Charles Doan, 15 Dec. 1837.

left, either discouraged by the failure to get into Toronto or
annoyed because they had been misled as to the nature of the
advance on Toronto or as to the purpose of the gathering at
Montgomery's.

The initiative now passed to the loyalist side. The first large
party of reinforcements from outside the city arrived between
nine and ten o'clock Tuesday night. Some sixty or seventy "men
of Gore" arrived by steamer from Hamilton, under command of
Colonel Allan MacNab, Speaker of the House of Assembly.[50]
Later about twenty men, the vanguard of a force from
Scarborough Township to the east, arrived under Colonel Allan
Maclean (B 45). While earlier that evening Head had been so
concerned that Toronto might fall that he had put the families of
government officials on a steamer in the harbour, ready to sail for
the United States, he now felt confident enough to disperse some
of his troops by placing guards on other buildings around the city
(B 41, B 42).

With the increased loyalist activity, Rolph felt it unwise to
continue the attack on Toronto. He sent two messengers to
Mackenzie explaining the state of the city and suggesting
dispersing the rebel force.[51] Mackenzie and his fellow leaders
decided instead to hold off the attack until Thursday, the day
originally planned for the rebellion, when more men and their
military commander, Van Egmond, would have arrived.[52] This
decision they sent back to Rolph with a request for more
information on the state of Toronto.[53] About 11 P.M. Rolph and
the others waiting at Elliot's gave up and left: Rolph went home
to pack. Shortly after he left the tavern the government put a
guard on it.[54]

On Wednesday Mackenzie seems hardly to have known what
to do while waiting for Thursday. While other men took it upon

[50]Head gave the day incorrectly in *A Narrative* (London, 1839), p. 332, Head to
Lord Glenelg, Toronto, 19 Dec. 1837. He corrected the date in *The Emigrant*
(London, 1846), p. 174.

[51]PAO, Gibson Papers, nos. 233, 239, 284; Mackenzie–Lindsey Papers, Mackenzie Correspondence, rough notes re John Rolph, 4 Dec. 1837.

[52]PAO, Mackenzie–Lindsey Papers, Mackenzie Correspondence, rough notes, 4
Dec. 1837; PAC, Rolph Papers, v. 3, Nelson Gorham to T.T. Rolph, 7 June 1884;
Dent, *The Story*, II, p. 105.

[53]PAO, Mackenzie–Lindsey Papers, Mackenzie Correspondence, notes in Mackenzie's handwriting filed under Dec. 1837, and Mackenzie Clippings, no. 6017, rough
notes on the rebellion; PAC, Rolph Papers, v. 3, Nelson Gorham to T.T. Rolph, 7
June 1884.

[54]PAC, Rolph Papers, v. 3, Statement of George Coulthard, 7 Sept. 1839.

themselves to do necessary tasks such as searching for food,[55] he wandered about the rebel camp until midday, when he decided that it would be wise to intercept the western mail, in order to find out what was going on in Toronto (B 48).[56] The only constructive action he had previously taken that day was the sending of three men to inform Dr. Charles Duncombe, the most influential radical leader in the west, of the rising. For whatever reason, they did not reach Duncombe, but they evidently did reach the United States, for they appear to have formed the party which arrived there, requesting aid.[57]

Along with Lount and forty or fifty men, Mackenzie rode out the Davenport Lane (Davenport Road) to intercept the stage at the Peacock Tavern on Dundas Street (near the present Keele Street).[58] While he was gone, little happened at Montgomery's, and security became so lax that several prisoners escaped, carrying information about rebel strength to the city, information corroborated by a young girl, Cornelia De Grassi, aged about thirteen, who rode out from the city and under pretext of visiting a local shop, examined the rebel camp. Soon after, she reported what she had seen to the lieutenant-governor.[59]

At the Peacock Tavern, Mackenzie robbed the patrons and a servant girl, or at least according to them he did – Mackenzie always denied it.[60] When the stage arrived, he ordered the passengers, save one, an American, and the guard off and searched all the baggage except that of a young Hamilton lawyer, Charles Durand. Durand was a radical, known to Mackenzie, who had visited the rebel camp on Tuesday but refused to join the rising. The two men had a talk about the state of Toronto; Durand said the defence was weak and Mackenzie asserted that the rebels

[55]PRO, CO 42, v. 447, p. 202, Trial of John Montgomery, Statement of Philip Wideman; PAO, Rebellion Papers, 1837–8, no. 6, Information of William Gymer, 11 Dec. 1837; W.H. Higgins, *The Life and Times of Joseph Gould* (Belleville, 1972, reprint), p. 107.

[56]*Mackenzie's Gazette*, 12 May 1838.

[57]Dent, *The Story*, II, pp. 106, 177.

[58]PAO, Rebellion Papers, 1837–8, no. 3, Information of Ephriam Livers, 8 Dec. 1837, and no. 4, Information of James Partridge, 8 Dec. 1837.

[59]For the ease of the prisoners' escape, see PAO, Rebellion Papers, 1837–8, no. 2, Information of John Peverin, 8 Dec. 1837, and no. 3, Information of Ephriam Livers, 8 Dec. 1837. The De Grassi information is found in University of Toronto, Fisher Library, De Grassi Papers, Reminiscences and clipping from *Albion* (New York), 13 Oct. 1838.

[60]*Christian Guardian* (Toronto), supplement, 17 Feb. 1838, Statement of Thomas Cooper; PRO, CO 42, v. 447, p. 214, Trial of Charles Durand, Testimony of Mary Ann Seely.

were strong and would be victorious.[61] Durand and the other passengers were then allowed to walk westward. As he travelled, Durand told others of the rebellion at Toronto and its success. One of the men he informed, Martin Switzer, travelled to the London District where he alerted radicals in the Yarmouth area, south of London, to the rising and its reputed success.[62] Mackenzie's party took the stage, driver, and one passenger, together with other prisoners they had captured, back to Montgomery's, where Mackenzie read the letters in the mail long into the night. Some later claimed Mackenzie had told them that he had also seized money from the mail, but again Mackenzie always denied this charge. Curiously perhaps, he had considerable money with him for the next few days, even though he was usually very short of cash.[63]

More men came to Montgomery's during the day to augment the depleted rebel ranks. The biggest party to arrive was probably that headed by Peter Matthews, consisting of about sixty men (B 50). While the men at Montgomery's stayed idle, however, far more were to reinforce the city. They came by water from as far away as Niagara and Ancaster and by road from distant townships such as Chinguacousy in Peel County.[64] Other men were organizing behind the rebels to go to the aid of Toronto (B 64, B 65). Potentially even more reinforcements were available as word of the revolt reached loyalists as far away as Kingston. By Wednesday night Toronto's besiegers were losing the war of numbers. With five to six hundred rebels they were then facing up to fifteen hundred defenders, with many more on the way.[65] The lieutenant-governor felt confident enough during

[61]PRO, CO 42, v. 447, pp. 211-23, Trial of Charles Durand; PAO, Gibson Papers, no. 116; PAO, Mackenzie–Lindsey Papers, Mackenzie Correspondence, Charles Durand to W.L. Mackenzie, Buffalo, 10 Oct. 1838; Thompson, *Reminiscences*, p. 214.

[62]UCS, v. 204, pp. 113188-93, Petition of Martin Switzer, 5 Sept. 1838.

[63]PRO, CO 42, v. 447, p. 213, Trial of Charles Durand, Testimony of James Partridge; PAO, Rebellion Papers, 1837–8, no. 2, Information of John Peverin, 8 Dec. 1837, and no. 3, Information of Ephriam Livers, 8 Dec. 1837, and no. 9, Information of George D. Reed, 13 Dec. 1837.

[64]Thompson, *Reminiscences*, p. 124; *Upper Canada Herald* (Toronto), 12 Dec. 1837; T.A. Reed, "Extracts from the Diary of a Loyalist of 1837," *York Pioneer and Historical Association Report* (1948), p. 15; *Commercial Herald* (Toronto), 11 and 20 Dec. 1837; W.P. Bull, *From Brock to Currie* . . . (Toronto, 1935), p. 150.

[65]UCS, v. 193, pp. 99487-8, Petition of Joseph Gould, 4 May 1838; *Christian Guardian*, 12 Dec. 1837; C.R. Sanderson, ed., *The Arthur Papers* . . . (Toronto, 1957), I, p. 171, R.B. Sullivan's Report on the State of the Province, 16 July 1838; Thompson, *Reminiscences*, p. 124.

the day to move his headquarters to the less secure parliament buildings and to begin arresting suspected rebels,[66] but he was reluctant to attack the rebel camp. Like Mackenzie, he hoped time would bring more reinforcements. Dr. Rolph, feeling the cause was lost, did not wait to be arrested, but slipped out of the city and headed for the United States.[67]

By evening, word of the city's growing strength reached the rebel camp, producing more defections there.[68] Mackenzie pinned his hopes on the arrival of large scale reinforcements for his cause once the original day set for rebellion, 7 December, arrived. He was up all night (B 48)[69] and in the morning welcomed a bleary Anthony Van Egmond. The old soldier took one look at the situation and recommended either a retreat to the United States or disbanding. Mackenzie would have none of this and pointed a pistol at his military commander's head. The rebellion, he said, must go on.[70]

Mackenzie decided that a diversion must be created by sending Matthews and a party of good marksmen to burn the bridge over the Don River, which provided access to the city from the east. While loyalist forces were dealing with this, the main rebel body would attack Toronto. All the other leading rebels disagreed with this but, unable to suggest an alternate plan, gave in to Mackenzie.[71] Matthews and sixty of the best men were sent off (B 50) and the leading rebels continued their discussions. A short time later one of the advance guards brought word that the loyalist forces were in sight.[72]

On Wednesday afternoon Head had finally conceded that an attack should be made on Thursday, after many leading government figures and James FitzGibbon had urged him to authorize an assault. Initially he gave the command to Allan MacNab,[73] but after much complaint from FitzGibbon, who felt he deserved the command because of experience and because of

[66]Thompson, *Reminiscences*, p. 124; *Upper Canada Herald*, 12 Dec. 1837; *Commercial Herald*, 11 and 20 Dec. 1837.

[67]Dent, *The Story*, II, pp. 112-14.

[68]PAO, Gibson Papers, no. 233.

[69]PAO, Mackenzie–Lindsey Papers, Mackenzie Clippings, no. 4687, Captain Stewart's narrative.

[70]PAO, Gibson Papers, no. 233.

[71]Ibid.; *Examiner* (Toronto), 27 March 1850, Statement of John Stewart Jr., 12 Dec. 1849.

[72]PAO, Mackenzie–Lindsey Papers, Mackenzie Clippings, no. 4687, Captain Stewart's narrative; *The Caroline Almanack*, p. 102; Dent, *The Story*, II, p. 123.

[73]FitzGibbon, *A Veteran of 1812*, pp. 218-21; FitzGibbon, *An Appeal*, pp. 25-6.

his role in forecasting the rebellion, Head gave it to the old soldier. After only a few hours sleep, FitzGibbon rose early on Thursday and began the monumental task of organizing a force out of the untrained and unorganized volunteers. Whether by skill or by luck, all was arranged before 11 A.M.[74] Three columns totalling between one thousand and fifteen hundred men were ready to march, the largest up Yonge Street and the smaller ones to the east and west (B 60).[75] By all accounts the central column was impressive, its members marching to the martial music provided by two bands, their bayonets glistening in the sun. Many residents along the route waved small flags from windows, while other citizens, including several ministers, followed the column until the firing started.[76]

The ensuing battle, wrongly called that of Gallows Hill since the fighting took place beyond the hill, was rather anti-climactic. The loyalist forces expected to confront a formidable enemy of over one thousand men (B 60).[77] Instead only about four hundred remained at Montgomery's and only about half took part in the fight.[78] The rest, unarmed, took shelter in the tavern until cannon fire drove them out, or helped David Gibson escort the prisoners out of the battle zone.[79] The actual battle took only a few minutes. What the loyalists lacked in training, they made up in fire-power. With two cannon and over a thousand muskets they easily put the rebels to flight, though killing or wounding only a few.

Bond Head, who had accompanied the troops waving a miniature flag, ordered Montgomery's burned and sent a troop several miles north to burn David Gibson's house. When the officer assigned to the latter task expressed fear for his life, FitzGibbon, who disapproved of the action, carried it out.

[74]FitzGibbon, *A Veteran of 1812*, pp. 222-4; FitzGibbon, *An Appeal*, pp. 25-6; James FitzGibbon, *Narrative of Occurrences in Toronto Upper Canada, 1837*, quoted in Dent, *The Story*, II, p. 117.
    [75]*Upper Canada Herald*, 12 Dec. 1837; *Commercial Herald*, 11 and 20 Dec. 1837; *Christian Guardian*, 27 Dec. 1837; Dent, *The Story*, II, p. 118; Ryerson, *"The Story of My Life,"* pp. 177-8.
    [76]Head, *The Emigrant*, p. 177; PAO, J.W. Hunt, "The Stirring Times of Fifty Years Ago"; Dent, *The Story*, II, p. 119.
    [77]*Commercial Herald*, 11 and 20 Dec. 1837.
    [78]Dent, *The Story*, II, p. 124; PAC, MG24 I26, Alexander Hamilton Papers, Order Book, 7 Dec. 1837; Higgins, *Joseph Gould*, p. 107.
    [79]PAO, Gibson Papers, no. 23; PAO, Mackenzie–Lindsey Papers, Mackenzie Clippings, no. 4687, A. MacDonell to *Herald*, Toronto, 21 July 1843 and Captain Stewart's narrative; Thompson, *Reminiscences*, pp. 125-6.

Coming on top of the trials and tensions of the past weeks, this so sickened him that the next day he resigned the post of adjutant-general of militia, the post he had been given in order to organize the defence of Toronto.[80] Some of the more enthusiastic mounted loyalists set off in pursuit of the rebel leaders but all escaped, at least for the time.

A group of men, some of them probably not rebels, was collected from the field of battle and from nearby homes by the loyalist forces and brought before Head. The lieutenant-governor, who liked grandiloquent gestures, lectured the men on loyalty and granted them their freedom.[81] This same spirit was to influence the proclamation Head later issued offering rewards for the leading rebels but offering the possibility of clemency to less important rebels who returned to their allegiance (B 67). While the men were being collected and lectured, loyalist volunteers were streaming by, loaded with the spoils of war, including food and farm animals, removed from houses as far north as Gibson's.[82] Perhaps the plundering of food was a good idea. Since the rebellion had cut off normal supplies to Toronto, there was by Thursday a real shortage in the city.[83]

To the east of Toronto, Matthews' attack also failed. A large force had been left in the city to protect it and the fire companies had been standing by their machines for two days because of rumours that the rebels intended to fire the city to cover their attack. The Don bridge and the houses around it were set alight but almost immediately loyalist forces and a fire engine arrived and the rebels were driven off (B 52, B 53).[84] Matthews' party was soon fleeing Toronto and the rebellion there was over.

No evidence exists that large numbers of rebel supporters were on their way to Montgomery's on Thursday. There is ample evidence, however, that thousands of loyalists were on their way to Toronto, so many that they would soon pose a problem, due to the lack of food and lodgings in the city. Some, like the Indians of the Orillia area, were turned back when word arrived of the

[80]FitzGibbon, *A Veteran of 1812*, pp. 228-9.

[81]PAO, Mackenzie–Lindsey Papers, Mackenzie Clippings, no. 6017, *Mackenzie's Gazette*, J.M. to W.L. Mackenzie, Chapinville, 16 July 1838; Dent, *The Story*, II, p. 132n; Head, *The Emigrant*, p. 181.

[82]PAO, Mackenzie–Lindsey Papers, Mackenzie Clippings, no. 6017, *Mackenzie's Gazette*, J.M. to W.L. Mackenzie, Chapinville, 16 July 1838; Thompson, *Reminiscences*, p. 127.

[83]FitzGibbon, *A Veteran of 1812*, pp. 218-21; FitzGibbon, *An Appeal*, pp. 25-6.

[84]*Mackenzie's Gazette*, 12 May 1838; Dent, *The Story*, II, pp. 144-5 and notes.

rebel defeat (B 68), but many more were to reach Toronto before they could be halted. It seems clear that Van Egmond's assessment of Thursday morning was quite correct. Once the rebels had lost the advantage of surprise and numbers on Monday and Tuesday, they lacked the mass support needed to recover that advantage.

The government's perception of the seriousness of the situation was a different matter. A thousand or more men came to Montgomery's during the four days of the rising and people in Toronto thought there were more. A thousand represented 10 per cent of the total population of the Toronto area or over 5 per cent of the adult male population of the Home District. It is easy to see why a government with no army to defend it and with a local population which did not rush to its aid in the early stages of the rising was extremely worried. This concern was to be reflected in the manner in which the government dealt with the population in the vicinity of the capital after the rising.

As for the rebels who were either attempting to flee the country after the rebellion or were trying to hide in the anonymity of their everyday occupations, their background and motivations became a subject of enduring interest, both to the loyalists of the day and to historians. Although at the time and later the rebels were thought to be largely of American origins and therefore easily disloyal, or to be ignorant farm lads, easily duped,[85] neither assumption was true. While the rebel ranks did not contain anyone who was extremely wealthy and the loyalists perhaps were supported by a higher percentage of the poor, in most other respects the loyalists and rebels were very similar. The Home District rebels represented a cross-section of society from the poor to the quite well off. A large majority were married, with an average age of thirty-two. While slightly over half the rebels were of American ancestry, only about one-quarter had been born in the United States, about one-third had been born in Canada, and about one-third in Great Britain.

In two respects there was a significant difference between the two groups. The loyalist cause was supported by blacks, Indians, and Orangemen, the three groups Mackenzie had claimed would attack the reform population of Upper Canada if it did not act. The first two defended a government which they felt had always looked after them; the blacks were very conscious of the

[85]For a contemporary assessment, see Sanderson, ed., *The Arthur Papers*, I, p. 170, R.B. Sullivan's Report on the State of the Province, 16 July 1838.

treatment of their race in the United States, and the Indians stood by their traditional alliance with the crown. Orangemen had always held loyalty to the monarch as one of their guiding principles. Rebels and loyalists differed also in religion. Those who turned out against the government tended to follow no religion or to belong to a dissenting sect which did not preach loyalty to the established order. Reformers who belonged to dissenting bodies like the Wesleyan Methodists, which opposed the Family Compact but also stressed acceptance of the legal order of society as part of their teachings, tended to be neutral in the rising. These facts suggest that it was to a large extent reformers who had nothing to balance their antagonism to government policies and attitudes who accepted Mackenzie's idea of an armed demonstration leading to a change in government. While arguably not illegal, if executed as Mackenzie said it would be, such a course of action was not strictly legal either. Thus anyone who was concerned with preserving the legal forms which gave balance and order to life was much less likely to become involved. This is not to say that there was a complete absence of such people in the rebel ranks, but they were the exception rather than the rule.[86]

Undoubtedly the popularity of local leaders such as Samuel Lount, Jesse Lloyd, and Peter Matthews encouraged men to join the rising. Since, however, many men from the home townships of these prominent individuals did not turn out, while men from other townships which had no local leader did join, this was not a major fact. It must be remembered as well that Mackenzie attracted men like Lount who brought others with them. Rumours or false reports obviously brought some men to Montgomery's. The issues that underlay the rebellion were not in themselves sufficient to cause the turnout or else many more reformers would have joined. Thus the role of Mackenzie and the susceptibility of those of his audience who joined him must be credited with the major role in creating rebels out of average citizens desirous of reform.

[86]For a complete discussion of the background of the rebels, see Stagg, "The Yonge Street Rebellion," chapters 6, 8, and 9.

C. THE DUNCOMBE RISING

NEWS OF MACKENZIE'S REBELLION spread quickly from Toronto but, graphically indicating the state of the communications of the day, the first report generally received throughout the province was that the capital had fallen to the rebels. Many about the colony based their actions on that rumour. In no part of the province was Mackenzie's reported success to have more telling consequences than in the section of the southwest between Brantford and St. Thomas. Young George Washington Case of Hamilton brought the news of Mackenzie's success to the village of Scotland in Oakland Township south of Brantford on 6 or 7 December. He brought, too, the report that "the Sheriffs" were about to arrest two prominent local reformers – Charles Duncombe and Eliakim Malcolm (C 1), a report made more plausible by the arrest of John G. Parker in Hamilton on the fifth.

Two local radicals, Malcolm and schoolteacher William McGuire, immediately began organizing revolt in the Scotland area, to protect themselves from the threat presumed posed by the local authorities and to take advantage of the supposed opportunity of overthrowing the tories. They spread word of that opportunity among the area's radicals, claiming wrongly that they were cooperating with Mackenzie (C 41). Within a few days they had about them over one hundred recruits, who had evidently been told that the Grand River Indians intended attacking them and that the rebellion had been "approved by their Sovereign and her Ministers at home."[1] The rebels drilled, investigated suspected tories (C 2), collected arms and ammunition, and planned to intercept the Long Point mail and attack Brantford.

Charles Duncombe, who lived in Burford, close to Oakland and his reform associate Malcolm, was also actively spreading rebellion – doubtless having agreed to concert his activities with those organizing the Oakland area. Responding to the rumour of Mackenzie's success, Duncombe drafted letters intended to incite rebellion and sent them to various area reformers. On 6 December he led a small group into nearby Norwich, informing

[1]UCS, v. 193, p. 107829, Deposition of Lyman Chapin, 4 March 1838.

the residents there that warrants were out for "six or eight" township reformers who "were to be tried by martial law and forthwith executed"(C 4). Duncombe was embellishing what he believed to be true; he certainly thought there was a warrant out for his arrest. When informed by his son-in-law on 11 December that this was not so, he replied he could not "risk" his safety on that assurance (C 12).

Duncombe organized two meetings at Norwich, presenting at each an inaccurate version of events, expanding the rumours he had heard. At the first, on the seventh, he helped create a small group to defend the Quaker township.[2] At the second, on the eighth or ninth, he and others enrolled some eighty men,[3] and established a small vigilance committee to collect arms (C 15) and cow local tories (see, for example, C 14). On 12 December the Norwich men mustered, ready to move to Oakland to join those raised there. John Treffry, a recent British immigrant, recorded that a banner inscribed "British constitution and the rights of the people" flew over the rebels but that Duncombe told them that, as they might later have to call on the United States for aid, they had best take it down. Down it came, replaced by a liberty flag (C 16).

Aside from his activities in Norwich, Duncombe, prevailing on the services of local followers, sent recruiting letters to various people in the area; one led to a meeting at the home of miller Elisha Hall of Oxford (Ingersoll) and helped decide those attending to join Duncombe's force (C 19). A second meeting in West Oxford produced another score or so for Duncombe's growing army.[4] Another of Duncombe's letters led his fellow Oxford MLA Robert Alway to meet with various Dereham reformers. After reviewing the facts as he had them, Alway reportedly advised rebellion (C 17), helping persuade a few Dereham men to enlist with Duncombe's force.

Members of the numerous Malcolm clan were also sending out letters. On 7 December, Eliakim Malcolm's brother James of Oakland wrote to nephew Finlay, who lived in Bayham, a township along the Erie shore, informing him that Mackenzie had taken Toronto and urging him to bring men to Oakland, where a force was gathering before marching on Hamilton to free

[2]Ibid., v. 203, pp. 112555-6, Petition of John Tidey, London Gaol, 9 March 1838.
[3]PAC, RG5 B36, Records of the London District Magistrates (RLDM), v. II, Deposition of Joseph J. Lancaster, 18 Dec. 1837.
[4]Ibid., v. I, p. 35, Examination of Charles Travers, 29 Dec. 1837.

innocent men jailed there.[5] Finlay responded, on 10 December addressing some thirty people at nearby Dereham Forge in Dereham.[6] His eloquence spurred them on to Oakland, the party including some "seven or eight hands" from George Tillson's foundry.[7] Finlay might have played a role, too, in persuading a second, smaller group to leave Bayham for Oakland.[8]

Finlay also conferred with Ebenezer Wilcox, an American-born farmer living in Malahide, the township west of Bayham. Wilcox helped organize a meeting in Malahide on 11 December. Reportedly, he advised the sixty or so attending to arm themselves. At a second gathering later in the week he urged the signing of a union paper, in which the signatories "agreed . . . to defend one another and their property" (C 24). Wilcox and others evidently feared attack from the tories (C 25). In any case, if Finlay had expected Wilcox to secure rebel recruits, he must have been disappointed, for the Malahide meetings produced none. Finlay and others, however, enjoyed greater success in adjacent Yarmouth.

The residents of the south of Yarmouth, many of them Quakers, had long had a reputation for radicalism. Consequently, Finlay Malcolm came to urge them to revolt,[9] evidently bringing uncle James' letter with him (C 26). Also, Dr. Duncombe sent an emissary, Elias Snider of Norwich, with an open letter "To our Reform friends in Middlesex," apprising them of the rebels' activities. The alleged signatures of MLAS Robert Alway and Thomas Parke and of owner Bela Shaw and editor John Talbot of the *Liberal* graced a pledge of support to the rebel cause. These, however, "were written in" Duncombe's "hand" (C 27). Finally Martin Switzer, a long-time resident of Streetsville and a friend of William Lyon Mackenzie, showed up in Yarmouth. While he almost certainly did not appear at Mackenzie's behest, some made the logical assumption he had.[10] If so, he represented Mackenzie's sole recruiting activity in the London District. Switzer himself later indicated he had gone to

[5]Ibid., v. I, p. 11, Examination of Finlay Malcolm, 25 Jan. 1838, and v. II, Examination of Finlay Malcolm, 23 Dec. 1837.

[6]PRO, CO 42, v. 447, pp. 261-2, *The Queen* vs. *Ebenezer Wilcox and Enoch Moore*, Testimony of Wm. A. Anderson; UCS, v. 181, p. 99979, Deposition of Stevens Newell, 21 Dec. 1837.

[7]UCS, v. 199, p. 110454, John Burn to "Dear Sirs," Dereham, 19 July 1838.

[8]See ibid., v. 193, p. 107362, *The Queen* vs. *Robert Cook*, Testimony of Robert Cook.

[9]RLDM, v. I, p. 73, Examination of Isaac Moore, 12 Jan. 1838.

[10]UCS, v. 184, p. 102968, John Burwell to R.S. Jameson, Port Burwell, 8 Jan. 1838.

Yarmouth to see an old acquaintance, MLA Elias Moore.[11] Whatever the case, once in the township, he did his best to persuade its residents to rebel. He attended meetings at Sparta on 9 and 11 December, helping to attract some fifty men into the rebel ranks. He then accompanied the Yarmouth rebels, the western-most ones to join Duncombe, and their leader, David Anderson, part way on their march to Oakland (C 31).

To the north of Oakland approximately twenty people held a meeting on the Blenheim-Dumfries town line on 12 December. Some decided to cast their lots with the rebels (C 34) and formed a company to scour the neighbourhood for arms and ammunition (see C 35). To the south, in Townsend on 12 December, Eliakim and James Malcolm led an armed party to a meeting in the village of Waterford. Eliakim did not claim that Toronto had fallen to Mackenzie, though he allowed that it was about to fall (C 37). He and others passed a recruiting circular round the meeting,[12] then he and James led their followers back to Oakland, taking with them the weapons they had requisitioned (C 41).

By the thirteenth, Duncombe had approximately five hundred men with him. Only a few had serviceable arms, though Duncombe expected to acquire more. In fact, he had brought eleven empty baggage wagons with him from Norwich, vowing "to fill them at Brantford" (C 40). In the meantime, a local blacksmith, Peter Coon, worked to help fill the void, turning out pikes (C 41). Still, certain rebels, noting that "some had arms, & some had none" (C 42), were unimpressed with arrangements, particularly in view of the great discrepancy between the actual number gathered at Oakland and the several thousand or so they had been told they would find there. They would have been even more disconsolate had they known of the mustering of the loyalists.

Once the rebellion had broken out at Toronto, the authorities there, mindful of the agitation of the fall, expected a similar rising in the west. Allan MacNab, after assisting in dispersing Mackenzie's rebels, was ordered on "special service to the London district" with "about 500 volunteers" (C 39). Loyalists in the west itself were stirring. Militiamen about Brantford had already been ordered out (see C 44), while those about Simcoe turned out on the eleventh (C 45).

[11]Ibid., v. 204, p. 113190-2, Account of Switzer's actions enclosed in Petition of Martin Switzer, 5 Sept. 1838.

[12]Ibid., v. 181, p. 99805, Examination of Baldwin Walker, 2[8?] Dec. 1837.

On the twelfth, Francis Evans, the Anglican rector of Woodhouse, left Simcoe with eight other men for Brantford. His party hoped to concert the activities of the loyalists north and south of the insurgents. After reaching Brantford and completing his mission, Evans went off to Oakland to plead with the rebels to take advantage of the lieutenant-governor's proclamation of 7 December promising amnesty to those returning to their homes and their allegiance (C 47). He was detained.[13] Doubtless some insurgents were discomfitted by Evans' confirmation of rumours already about that Mackenzie's rising had failed.[14] That night the leaders were doubly disturbed when a rider from Brantford brought the startling news that MacNab had arrived there with his force (C 56).

Other loyalists were closing in on the rebels, for the movement of the Yarmouth band to Oakland had incited two groups of loyalists to action. The first, and numerically the less significant, consisted of some thirty Bayham men who tried to intercept Anderson's band in their township. Unsuccessful, they pushed on to Simcoe (C 52). The second group was led by John Askin. On 12 December he had left London for St. Thomas to arrest John Talbot, only to find that he had fled, that Duncombe had raised revolt, and that Anderson was leading a party to bolster Duncombe's army. Askin "instantly beat up for Volunteers and in less than three hours was on the march for Scotland"(C 53). Before long he had about one hundred and fifty men (C 55). Anderson and company, apprised of their pursuit, eluded them.

By the evening of the thirteenth, the rebel leaders knew that Mackenzie had been defeated, that MacNab was in Brantford, that the loyalists in Simcoe were on the alert, and that Askin was rushing in upon them from the west. Faced with all this, they dithered. First, they mustered their men, told them they were going to intercept a force from Simcoe and marched them for a distance, only to return them to camp before dismissing them (C 57). Anderson then urged his brother officers (Duncombe was the general) to launch an attack on Brantford or Simcoe (C 59). His advice fell on deaf ears. The officers reassembled their men, telling them they were off to Simcoe, but they were not. On the march Duncombe and others revealed to some of the rank and file that they were, in fact, retreating to Sodom, in Norwich (C 57). Confusion set in. Eliakim Malcolm ordered his men

[13]Ibid., v. 204, pp. 112709-12, Francis Evans to Sir George Arthur, 14 April 1838.
[14]For those rumours, see C 38.

home (C 59), others deserted (C 58). Early on the fourteenth the bedraggled and reduced army struggled into Sodom. Some found sleeping places, others slipped away. By daybreak most had gone. Duncombe, who was still about, "much frightened, said that if he was taken he should be executed" (C 59). From Evans he knew of Head's proclamation of 7 December. He advised those few he met, while preparing to flee to Michigan, "to lay down their Arms, go home and submit to the laws of the Country" (C 60).

In the meantime, MacNab had acted, hoping to capture the rebel force by a master stroke. Learning of the approach of Askin's volunteers, he had sent an *"express"* to them "via *Simco . . .* with instructions to march as expeditiously as possible & get as near the Rebels as possible" (C 55). By his own reckoning he had well over five hundred men – three hundred from Hamilton, one hundred and fifty from Brantford, and one hundred from the Six Nations Reserve. All these he led out of Brantford at one o'clock on the morning of the fourteenth, intending to catch the rebels in Oakland by surprise (C 62).

As the force approached Scotland from three directions, the cavalry spurred ahead and swept into the village. A few isolated shots rang out from sentries left behind, but these did little damage. The sentries fled (C 63). "The *Indians* were let slip in pursuit & three of the unfortunate men were shot down & scalped" (C 63).[15] MacNab's men occupied Scotland. By that afternoon they were joined by "not less than one thousand volunteers,"who poured in on all sides. The troops scoured the village and environs, taking Duncombe's and Malcolm's papers. Despite initial hopes (C 62), these proved to be of little consequence.

On the fourteenth MacNab busied himself laying plans for invading Norwich (C 62), finding time, though, to deal with deputations from contrite rebels (C 67). On the fifteenth he and his men moved into Norwich, impressing weapons and supplies as they thought necessary and frightening many residents in the process. That same day, loyalists from the Woodstock area, after scouring East and West Oxford, moved into the rear of Norwich (C 66). They intended, in concert with MacNab's men, to scoop

---

[15]Considerable doubt exists whether the Indians did, in fact, kill anyone at Scotland. None of the reports of such deaths came from eyewitnesses. Also, after the rebellion, petitions from rebels and their families and friends poured in upon the government. These documents frequently rehearsed individual grievances, and it is odd that none referred to such killings.

up all the insurgents then hiding in the township. In this they enjoyed some success.

Ensconced at Sodom, MacNab received a petition from 103 former rebels herded before him by his troops. The petitioners had, they swore, been "led away by Charles Duncombe, Eliakim Malcolm, and other wicked and designing leaders, who have induced us by promise of large grants of land and great pay for our services" to rebel (E 8). MacNab reminded the petitioners of the enormity of their crimes, detained their leaders, and allowed the rest to return home on the understanding they would surrender themselves if the lieutenant-governor failed to grant them clemency (C 69). Head, in fact, did consent to MacNab's "liberating such of them as are not known to have committed acts of violence against . . . persons or property" after binding them over "to answer any complaint that may be brought against them" (E 9). In total, by 18 December MacNab and his men had taken almost five hundred real or suspected rebels (C 69). Most they released but those they deemed leaders they despatched to either the London or Hamilton gaol, though, in fact, they captured no leaders of the first rank.

After subduing Norwich, MacNab's force left on 19 December, heading for Ingersoll and, ultimately, London. MacNab intended to organize volunteer companies in these centres, as well as in Simcoe and Brantford, and intended, too, to allow most of the loyalists with him to return home (C 72). The work of pacification, he obviously felt, was nearing its end. Yet MacNab was not the only one detaining and arresting suspected rebels. In various parts of the disaffected townships local magistrates and militia officers were also doing so. Most notably, the returning Yarmouth volunteers, who had left Norwich on the eighteenth, took prisoners on their way west. They made a particular point of visiting the Sparta area, and reached St. Thomas on the twentieth with thirty-eight suspects in tow, much to the disgust of one of the volunteers, Adam Hope, a political moderate and a friend of John Talbot, who felt that the "mistaken & misguided" men should not have been taken at all.

Hope was a thoughtful man, but he could not understand why those taken prisoner and their former comrades had rebelled. He searched for some explanation in the characters of those involved, but this proved unsatisfactory, for, while "the leaders of the Rebels . . . were perhaps a sett [sic] of as consumate [sic] ruffians as ever disgraced humanity," an amazing "number of

people of *property* & respectability" were "implicated" in the
Toronto and Oakland risings (C 79).

Research indicates that Hope was right in thinking that many
such people were involved in the rebellions. Generally, the
Duncombe rebels, like the Mackenzie ones, came from a
comparatively productive farming area and formed a fairly
stable, reasonably prosperous sector of Upper Canadian society.
Data, regrettably less complete than might be desired, can be
found regarding almost two hundred western rebels. They show
that the insurgents could be divided into three broad occupational
categories: farmers, labourers, and innkeepers, craftsmen,
professionals, merchants and the like. The average age of those
in the rebel sample was 30.2 years, and most were married.[16]
Such evidence strongly suggests that Duncombe's men were well
settled and not economically disadvantaged in comparison with
other members of their own rural society.

Of considerable concern to contemporaries was the national
complexion of the insurgents, for national tensions and troubles
had long bedevilled the province. The townships from which the
rebels came had been first settled primarily by Americans. Given
this, it is not surprising to find that most in the rebel sample
discussed above were North American-born,[17] which helps
explain the increased tempo of anti-Americanism in the west
after the revolt. Somewhat surprising, in light of the limited
British immigration to the disaffected townships, is the fact that
one-fifth of the sample whose nationalities are known were
Irishmen and Englishmen, though none were Scots. No British
rebels came from homogeneous European settlements, leaving
room for the twin notions that the rebelling Europeans had been
prevailed upon by their North American neighbours to shoulder
arms, or had lived among those neighbours long enough to have
accepted their norms of behaviour. On balance, it seems that the
Duncombe rising was somewhat more American in personnel
and inspiration than was the Mackenzie one, though such
differences were in degree, not kind. It is notable, for example,
that in the west, as around Toronto, blacks, Indians, and
Orangemen were all enthusiastic supporters of the government,
suggesting powerful similarities in the character of the loyalists
in both regions.

[16]Colin Read, *The Rising in Western Upper Canada, 1837–8: The Duncombe Revolt
and After* (Toronto, 1982), pp. 172-4, 178.
[17]Ibid., p. 179.

Another area of broad similarity involves religion. The Duncombe rebels, like the Mackenzie ones, tended to be drawn from dissenting sects. Unlike the loyalists, few had ties to that rock of British and colonial society, the Church of England.[18] That church had not had the opportunity of preaching loyalty, due subordination, and the British way to the western rebels. In this sense, religion played a role in determining who mustered for and against the rising.

The immediate cause of the Duncombe rising seems straightforward enough – the rumours attendant upon Mackenzie's revolt – but the underlying causes are not as clear-cut. Certainly political grievances played a part, as did short-term economic distress which, in the form of tight money, high interest rates, and failed harvests – the latter offset to some extent by high prices – adversely affected the western peninsula. Too, the North American character of the rebel townships may have helped dispose some inhabitants to shoulder arms against a colonial government which could be seen as the child of a distant and foreign power. Family connections and personal loyalties doubtless influenced others. The rebels' communities were rural and relatively long-settled ones with developing political cultures in which kinship connections and personal affinities were important. When a James Malcolm called for help, a Finlay Malcolm responded. When some decided to take up arms to prevent outrages and right wrongs, relatives and friends followed. On balance, then, no single explanation – a solitary significant political grievance, a depressed economy, a general hunger for land or food – suffices to explain why men shouldered arms.

[18]Ibid., pp. 184-97, 201, 203.

D. REBELLION DAYS AROUND THE PROVINCE

WHILE THE TORONTO AND BRANTFORD areas were most affected by the events of the rebellions, other parts of the province also felt the effects to varying degrees. In large measure, the extent to which any given area was caught up in the turmoil of the period depended upon how close it was to one of the risings, how near it was to the American border, whence came raids by escaped rebels and their American sympathizers, and how much reform activity there had been in the area prior to the outbreaks. Occasionally, special local circumstances also had some influence.

The easternmost portion of Upper Canada, the Eastern, Ottawa, and Bathurst districts, was caught up as much or more in the events in the lower province as it was in those of the upper. This was particularly true of the Eastern District, which included the counties of Glengarry, Stormont, and Dundas. The disaffected areas of Lower Canada, south and north of Montreal, were quite close, and the rebellion there began with the opening shots at Longueuil, on 16 November. Thus attention was drawn eastwards fully half a month before the Upper Canadian troubles. In addition, the crisis in Lower Canada had religious overtones, being seen by some as setting Catholics against Protestants. As a result, groundless fears existed in the Eastern District that the Catholic Highlanders of Glengarry might decide to cooperate in rebellion with their co-religionists in the lower province (D 1, D 2).

Sir John Colborne did not share these fears, and on several occasions in November fruitlessly asked Bond Head for permission to use the Glengarry militia in suppressing the rebellion in the lower province. Finally, on 8 December, Colborne wrote directly to the Glengarry colonels, instructing them to prepare, should Head approve, to muster their men and march them to the Lake of Two Mountains area, northwest of Montreal. Two thousand Highlanders answered the call. By the time Bond Head felt secure enough to allow their use outside Upper Canada, the Glengarry men were no longer needed.[1]

[1]Elinor Senior, "The Glengarry Highlanders and the Suppression of the Rebellions in Lower Canada, 1837–38," *Journal of the Society for Army Historical Research*, LVI

When news arrived of the uprising at Toronto, the Glengarry regiments volunteered to serve in either province, although they still expected that they would be used in the closer conflict, around Montreal (see D 4), and indeed, during 1838 they did serve several times in Lower Canada. Both the Glengarry and the Stormont militia, which also expected to serve in the lower province, suffered from a shortage of weapons in December 1837 (D 3). Some of the militiamen were mustered, however, and were used to garrison the area.[2] Others, in concert with the Glengarry men, secured the approaches to the lower province, along the St. Lawrence (D 7).

The Ottawa District (Prescott and Russell counties) lay above the Eastern, along the Ottawa River. Residents here were completely caught up in events in Lower Canada and gave only a minimum of attention to events at Toronto. The greatest concern in the district was the possibility of attack from across the river (D 3). In the contiguous Bathurst District, composed of Carleton and Lanark counties, there was, however, a greater concern about events at Toronto. Prominent residents volunteered the services of the militia in November,[3] to serve in Lower Canada if needed, and again in December, for possible use at Toronto or elsewhere in Upper Canada. When, in answer to a call from Head, that feudal anachronism, the Laird of MacNab, tried to raise his Highland settlers, he provided the only evidence of possible disloyalty in the district, as he found the men very reluctant to come forward.[4] This tardiness probably had more to do with his unpopularity among the settlers, whom he tried to keep in a form of vassalage to himself, than with any political principles. It is true that some magistrates about Perth doubted the loyalty of that area's Catholics, but a Catholic justice of the peace, Anthony Leslie, collected the signatures of local Catholics on a petition to the lieutenant-governor protesting their loyalty (D 13, D 14).

South of Bathurst, stretching down to the St. Lawrence, was the Johnstown District, which took in Grenville and Leeds

---

(1978), pp. 143-59. Dr. Senior points out that, though some sources indicate that the Glengarry men served in Lower Canada in December 1837, there are good reasons for thinking that they did not.

[2] J.F. Pringle, *Lunenburgh, or, the Old Eastern District, Its Settlement and Early Progress* . . . (Cornwall, 1890), p. 260.

[3] UCS, v. 179, p. 98674, Loyal address of sundry inhabitants of Bytown and vicinity, 7 Nov. 1837.

[4] Ibid., v. 180, pp. 99231-2, Loyal address from Fitz Roy Harbour, 15 Dec. 1837.

counties. Here official concern about the disloyalty of some citizens went much further. Towards the rear of the district, not far from Bathurst, magistrates along the Rideau were sufficiently unsure of some inhabitants that they held formal inquiries, trials in fact, examining those residents' loyalties and their actions in November and December. On learning of the outbreak at Toronto, the justices decided to investigate those belonging to the alleged "secret society," the political union, formed in Wolford Township. Here a pattern observable elsewhere appeared; that is, after the rebellion at Toronto, magistrates around the province decided to investigate the local political unions and their members, suspecting that, since Mackenzie had been the prime mover of both the unions and the rebellion, the two must be inextricably linked.

The six Wolford trials did little to substantiate this conclusion. The most spectacular revelation was that a local tailor, John Graff, during militia training in November, had said while "inebriated" that "he was a full Blooded *Papanau* [*sic*] man" (D 21). None the less, the examining magistrates saw cause to take alarm and bound three of the accused, Graff among them, over to the next assizes.[5] A further indication of the agitated state of the magistrates was the fact that they reported one of their own number to Head, because he had held private discussions with the father of one of the accused (D 24). Despite the justices' fears concerning the populace, no one was jailed for an extended period. Only one local resident, from the neighbouring township of Kitley, was deemed guilty enough of disloyal conduct to be incarcerated. William H. Sherman, a shoemaker, was judged to have used such "seditious language"[6] that he was to spend several months in gaol before being released.[7]

Further south in the district, along the St. Lawrence, magistrates and loyalists generally had more cause for alarm than those in Wolford and Kitley, for here they faced the possibility that, if there were disaffected in the area, the latter could concert their activities with sympathetic Americans, just across the river. Such a rumour did circulate in the Prescott area, in the eastern part of the district, early in December (D 3). Nothing came of it, however. West of Prescott, the loyalists of Brockville were also afraid. In part this was because Brockville had a political union,

[5]See D 20. Evidently nothing further came of this.
[6]*Recorder* (Brockville), *Journal* (St. Catharines), 1 Feb. 1838.
[7]Prisoner list in Lindsey, *The Life and Times of William Lyon Mackenzie*, II, p. 374.

and once again the union and rebel activities were associated in the minds of the authorities. Consequently, after news of the Mackenzie rising reached Brockville on 8 December (D 15), they arrested suspected traitors in and about the town. They took up at least nine people and issued warrants for three others, including Samuel Chollett Frey, member of the local union and one of the founders of the Wolford one, and William Benjamin Wells, Grenville MLA, an associate of Mackenzie, and a well-known radical (D 17, D 18). Both managed to escape. The authorities seized Wells's papers and allegedly found a "plan for burning . . . Brockville – releasing the Prisoners from the Court House & seizing the Arms" (D 19).

So tense was the atmosphere in the town at this point that William Buell, ex-MLA, who published the leading reform journal, the *Recorder*, felt impelled to print a statement on 14 December that, while he had criticized the Upper Canadian government in the past, he had never encouraged rebellion.[8] The immediate fears concerning local activity of a rebellious nature quickly subsided, and those arrested were soon out of gaol, their punishments relatively light, although tensions were to increase again in 1838 with the Patriot raids by Canadian refugees and American sympathizers. In retrospect, there seems to have been little danger of treasonous activity on any substantial scale in this area, or in the whole of the eastern section of the colony.

The Midland District, consisting of the counties of Lennox and Addington, Frontenac, and Hastings, was the most easterly to be directly caught up in the Toronto rising. This involvement stemmed in large part from Kingston's role as the military centre of the colony. From the beginning, Kingston was overwhelmingly loyal. As early as 2 November, citizens, alarmed by the deteriorating situation in Lower Canada, had called for the establishment of a volunteer corps in their city.[9] When news of Mackenzie's outbreak reached Kingston, in a despatch from Head which arrived 6 December (D 26), Kingstonians responded quickly to the emergency, hurrying to replace the regular troops withdrawn to Lower Canada. That night cavalry patrols took to the streets and the following day flank companies of militia were summoned to occupy the fort and strong points in the town (D 28).

[8]*Recorder*, 14 Dec. 1837.
[9]UCS, v. 179, p. 98589, Loyal Address from Kingston, 2 Nov. 1837.

The remaining officers in the fort despatched the steamer *Traveller* to Toronto on 8 December, with arms, ammunition, and ordinance to aid the loyalists in the capital (D 29). They also decided to send arms west to Belleville, in case the authorities in this rather radical area might need them. After a trip during which Colonel Anthony Manahan, the militia officer in charge of the conveyance of the arms from Culbertson's Wharf (Deseronto) onward, often felt threatened by the supposed disloyalty of the inhabitants on the route, the weapons arrived safely in Belleville (D 31). There local magistrates had already been attempting to organize a defence. In fact, as early as 7 December they had made arrangements to summon the militia.[10]

Evidence of disloyalty existed in the Belleville area. Many of the militia were unwilling to take the oath of allegiance; political unions were very active in and around Belleville; and the magistrates discovered that "rifles guns & Powder have been purchased here under fictitious pretenses – and 7 Guns & rifles have been found in a vacant house in Town" (D 32). When one thousand men of the 1st and 2nd Hastings Regiments had assembled in Belleville, on 11 December, the magistrates chose two hundred and forty of the most loyal to aid them in their duties,[11] which involved hunting down and jailing the disloyal of the neighbourhood. Arrests began immediately and continued through the month. In Belleville two men were charged with high treason, supposedly because of revelations found in Duncombe's captured papers.[12] Merchant Peter Robertson of Belleville was intercepted in Brockville, and taken up for having joined the Belleville political union.[13] Four settlers in the northeast corner of Camden were imprisoned, accused of sedition. Indeed, the Anglican priest at Bath, A.F. Atkinson, who believed his village awash with rebels, thought Camden equally inundated.[14]

In total, those arrested from Belleville and nearby townships in December 1837 numbered between seventeen and twenty-nine.

[10]AGOC, v. 22, Hastings file, Thomas Coleman to Captain McNabb, Belleville, 8 Dec. 1837.

[11]Ibid., v. 22, Hastings file, Thomas Coleman to Colonel FitzGibbon, Belleville Park, 14 Dec. 1837; Coleman to FitzGibbon, Belleville, 16 Dec. 1837.

[12]PAO, Wallbridge Papers, L. Wallbridge to Mrs. M. Howard, Belleville, 26 Dec. 1837. Wallbridge had it that the earlier arrests had occurred because of findings in the Mackenzie papers.

[13]UCS, v. 180, pp. 99448-9, Copy of Affidavit of Paul Glasford, Brockville, 18 Dec. 1837.

[14]CPSO, v. 9, file 1220, A.F. Atkinson to J. Joseph, Bath, 27 Dec. 1837, *Private*.

Doubtless most were arrested on suspicion, not on firm proof, that they had intended or committed treason. Typical of those arrested were two former MLAS, Joseph Lockwood and Reuben White. They were sent off to the Kingston gaol along with six others, Lockwood for signing a "republican" constitution and White for attending "seditious" meetings. The other six were sent to Kingston for similar indiscretions (D 35). Perhaps also some of those arrested in the Belleville area were, like prisoners in other areas, taken up on totally spurious grounds.

Most of the Belleville and area prisoners were soon released. In fact only two, Anson Day of Camden and merchant Nelson Reynolds, showed up on the province-wide list of prisoners, compiled the following November, as having spent prolonged periods in gaol;[15] and in Reynolds's case, that return does not show that he was bailed[16] and subsequently re-arrested on other charges. Clearly there was no proof of widespread disloyalty. None the less the magistrates at Belleville felt there had been treason in the area, and were confirmed in this belief when they discovered, in February of 1838, what they were convinced had been a plot to burn Belleville, back in December.[17] Belleville continued to have the reputation of being disloyal.

To the south of Belleville lay the Prince Edward District, consisting of the single county which gave the district its name. Here, December was essentially quiet, for the population was largely loyal. After word of the rebellion reached the district, some militiamen refused to turn out when ordered to do so,[18] and some others mustered but would not take the oath of allegiance.[19] The vast majority though threw their support behind the government, and by 14 December some one thousand men paraded at Picton in a display of loyalty (D 42). Like militiamen elsewhere in the province, those of Prince Edward County were kept on duty throughout December, guarding roads and garrisoning their locality.

The district west of Midland was Newcastle, comprising the counties of Northumberland and Durham. As far as Henry Ruttan

[15]See the prisoner list in Lindsey, *The Life and Times of William Lyon Mackenzie*, II, p. 374.

[16]UCS, v. 180, pp. 99495-6, Paul Glasford to ——, Brockville, 19 Dec. 1837.

[17]AGOC, v. 28, Hastings file, Bella Flint to ——, enclosed in Bella Flint to Colonel Bullock, Belleville, 27 March 1838.

[18]Ibid., v. 22, Prince Edward file, Cornelius Vanalstine to Richard Bullock, Hallowell, 23 Dec. 1837.

[19]Ibid., James Cotter to James FitzGibbon, Picton, 19 Dec. 1837.

of Cobourg, MLA, district sheriff and colonel of the 3rd Northumberland Regiment, was concerned, the whole district was loyal. His regiment turned out with enthusiasm and was stationed at key points in Northumberland to intercept fleeing "traitors," and to provide security for the country (D 44). Ruttan despised the "refractory spirits" across the district line, in the Belleville area, and would no doubt have enjoyed an excuse to move his men into the region (D 45, D 47). Yet not everyone felt that the district was as overwhelmingly loyal as he claimed. The magistrates arrested eight men of the district in December and held them for some time.[20] In November a Methodist preacher, Anson Green, had confided his strong suspicions about the loyalty of the populace in the Cobourg–Port Hope area to Egerton Ryerson;[21] and Ryerson, who happened to pass through Cobourg on 6 December, also questioned the loyalty of the inhabitants, although he admitted that about seven hundred men had left the area that day to march to the defence of Toronto (D 53). In addition, Cobourg was to be the site of the "Cobourg conspiracy" in 1839, when Canadian exiles and some local citizens concocted a plot to capture the town.[22]

Further back in the Newcastle District, at Peterborough in the rear of Northumberland County, the lieutenant-governor's summons to arms had arrived, along with first reports of the outbreak at Toronto, on 6 December (D 49). The magistrates in the area began to investigate the loyalty of the local citizenry while the militia was being organized. Most appear to have been loyal although, as in Cobourg and other centres, certain individuals in the area fell under suspicion. Dr. John Gilchrist of the village of Keene, who had been an MLA from 1834 to 1836, was one of those whose reform background and alleged close connection with Mackenzie caused him to be questioned. As in many similar cases throughout the province, no evidence beyond his background could be found against him and he was released.[23] Reportedly, nearly a dozen others were examined,[24]

[20]Prisoner list in Lindsey, *The Life and Times of William Lyon Mackenzie*, II, p. 376.

[21]United Church Archives, Ryerson Papers, Anson Green to Egerton Ryerson, Cobourg, 16 Nov. 1837.

[22]For one account of the conspiracy, see E.C. Guillet, *The Lives and Times of the Patriots* . . . (Toronto, 1938), pp. 167-73. Support for the conspiracy seemed limited to only a few individuals. Perhaps there were other disaffected citizens too fearful to take part in such disloyal activity.

[23]CPSO, v. 9, file 1224, John Gilchrist to John Joseph, Otonabee, 15 Dec. 1837.

[24]*History of the County of Peterborough, Ontario* (Toronto, 1884), pp. 319-20.

and Catharine Parr Traill recorded that two spies were captured in Peterborough and despatched to the district gaol at Amherst (Cobourg) (D 50). How much of such reports was hearsay and how much was fact is difficult to determine since records for the period are so scanty.

Several hundred men from the Peterborough area mustered over the next few days and set off for Port Hope on the lakefront, the staging area for those district loyalists prepared to march to Toronto (D 50). A total of about one thousand volunteers moved into Port Hope (D 51), although not all arrived in time to march to the capital. Several hundred left on 6 December, and to the west were joined by another five hundred or so who had mustered in Bowmanville (D 56). In fact, perhaps as many as two thousand men from the various parts of the Newcastle District eventually reached Toronto, though too late to assist in the suppression of the rising there.[25] Some of those who arrived at Port Hope after the volunteers had left for Toronto were employed elsewhere. For example, some of the Peterborough area volunteers came to Port Hope only after word had arrived there of Mackenzie's defeat. They were then instructed to march to Ops and Mariposa townships in the northwestern section of the district "to bring some radicals to their senses."[26] Towards the end of December the militiamen stationed in these two townships returned home, their tour of duty an uneventful one (D 50).

Just as the Newcastle District, on the Home's eastern boundary, was heavily caught up in the rising at Toronto, so too was the Gore District, on the western boundary, but in the Gore there was considerable evidence of sympathy for, and even attempted participation in, the rising. The district consisted of two counties, Halton and Wentworth, and in parts of Halton close to Toronto, men actually did muster for Mackenzie's rebel army. A few left Nelson Township, at the head of Lake Ontario, for Toronto, but found Mackenzie already defeated when they arrived. They turned back, only to be arrested on the return journey (D 58). In Nassagaweya, inland from Nelson, some individuals made concerted efforts to attract support for the

[25]*Star* (Cobourg), Letter of Lieutenant-Colonel George Ham, Darlington, 8 Dec. 1837; Reed, "Extracts from the Diary of a Loyalist of 1837,"p. 15; E.M. Morphy, *A York Pioneer Looking Back* . . . (Toronto, 1890), pp. 21-2; *Commercial Herald* (Toronto), 20 Dec. 1837.

[26]Public Archives of Manitoba, photostats in Trent University Archives, B75 O11, Kirkpatrick Letters, Stafford Kirkpatrick to Alexander Kirkpatrick, Peterboro, 10 Jan. 1838.

rebels from the township's predominantly Scots population. When news of the Toronto rising first arrived there on 6 or 7 December, those individuals organized a meeting of twenty-five or thirty people and held it in Gaelic. Most decided to support Mackenzie and scattered in search of arms, but then heard that the first reports that had Mackenzie triumphant were wrong.[27] Before long, several of the leading spirits in Nassagaweya were fleeing the province,[28] leaving some of their unfortunate comrades to be questioned by the local justices.

In Nassagaweya's northern neighbour, Eramosa, events took a similar turn. Here, on 7 or 8 December between sixty and one hundred people[29] came to a meeting, after hearing the rumour that the rebels had taken Toronto. Their first object was to acquire reliable information, and, to that end, they decided to send an emissary to see if the capital had indeed fallen (D 62). Clearly, several of the meeting's speakers favoured the rebels' cause (see D 60 and D 61), while at least some of the audience inclined to the government. The latter, deeming the proceedings "highly Treasonable,"informed the magistrates of nearby Guelph of what had occurred (D 60). The justices then organized a force of some thirty men and swept into Eramosa on the night of the thirteenth. They immediately rounded up those they considered the local ringleaders. In the next few weeks, they continued to detain and question Eramosa inhabitants, binding over twenty-three people and sending three off to the district gaol at Hamilton.[30] The Guelph justices also found some work to do at home. Here, they arrested Robert Armstrong, identified in the captured correspondence of John G. Parker as a moving spirit behind the political unions, on a charge of purchasing ammunition in Preston "for the use of the Rebels in this Province" (D 63). Parker's arrest on 5 December had helped spark the Duncombe rising. In Hamilton itself it also had repercussions. Like another prominent Hamiltonian implicated in

[27]UCS, v. 180, pp. 99239-41, Deposition of Duncan McPhederain, 13 Dec. 1837. See also D 54.

[28]PRO, CO 42, v. 447, p. 296, "Copy of the Solicitor General's Report Respecting the Prisoners, in the District of Gore, who have petitioned,"16 May 1838, W.H. Draper.

[29]PAO, Mackenzie–Lindsey Papers, Mackenzie Clippings, no. 453, extract from the Hamilton *Express*, n.d., entitled "Trials for High Treason, Thurs, Mar 27/38," Testimony of William Campbell and Walter King.

[30]Colin Frederick Read, "The Rising in Western Upper Canada, 1837–38: The Duncombe Revolt and After" (PH.D. thesis, University of Toronto, 1974), p. 308.

the rebellion, Charles Durand, Parker was a parishioner of the local Niagara Presbyterian Church; and, on his arrest, the minister of that church, James Marr, fled the town, fearing widespread violence. Marr fully expected some fifteen hundred men to fall upon Hamilton, rescue Parker, and burn "the public buildings" (D 66). Though his fears, or hopes, were wildly overdrawn, the people of Hamilton, buffeted by the events of both Mackenzie's and Duncombe's risings, were thrown into some turmoil.

Hamilton, which provided men for the suppression of both rebellions in the province, was not without its own coterie of radicals. And, as the experience of Parker suggests, once the local officials learned of the outbreak of rebellion to the east, they began inquiring closely into the loyalty of certain area residents. They discovered that gunsmith Michael Marcellus Mills was supposed to have made a bargain with Parker to supply him with one hundred rifles[31] and that Mills had accumulated ammunition and buried it in his orchard (D 64). This was the most spectacular revelation unearthed by the authorities, who in the course of their investigations, questioned some of the members of the Hamilton political union and local residents suspected of helping fleeing Mackenzie rebels to escape (see D 73). The Hamilton *Gazette*, magisterially surveying these activities and the score or more of arrests made, decided that, on balance, few of the latter were of "any consequence" (D 67). Clearly, the tory *Gazette* approved of the officials' energy and of the reaction of Hamilton's populace, as well as that of the people of nearby Ancaster, to the crisis. It approved far less of the response of the inhabitants of that "pestilent swamp,"Dundas. These had disgraced themselves in the *Gazette*'s eyes by rallying not at all to the Queen's colours (D 69). Indeed, the Gore District's sheriff, Allan Macdonell, took a similar attitude. Alarmed by a meeting of "several suspected" individuals held in Dundas on 11 December, he rode off to that centre and seized the papers and ammunition of those involved (D 70).

Macdonell and other civil officials, such as the magistrates, represented one branch of the local authorities active in Hamilton in December. The members of the militia establishment comprised the other, and the two branches did not always get along well. For instance, Robert Land, lieutenant-colonel of the

[31]UCS, v. 180, p. 99046, Colin C. Ferrie to the Attorney General, Hamilton, 8 Dec. 1837.

3rd Gore Regiment, who commanded at Hamilton, complained
that the civil authorities failed to keep him in touch with their
activities and released dangerous characters handed over to them
by the militia (D 72). The civil and military authorities in
Hamilton continued to fuss and feud throughout December. Such
confusion and conflict were perhaps inevitable in the community's unprecedented situation between the twin revolts in the
province and close to the point at which, soon after, invasion
from the United States was most threatened. These circumstances called for the mobilization of large numbers of
militiamen and involved the confinement of many suspected
traitors in the district gaol.

  To the south of Hamilton and the Gore District lay the counties
of Lincoln and Haldimand, which comprised the Niagara
District. Though the western sections of Haldimand were directly
affected by the Duncombe rising, the Niagara District was
touched far less by that revolt than by the one at Toronto. Indeed,
some of the peninsular loyalists about the Ontario shore helped
subdue Mackenzie's rebellion. That rebellion in turn led
indirectly to increased fears about the loyalty of certain Niagara
District inhabitants. In the district several locales were considered radical, most notably the Short Hills, back of St.
Catharines. In November some residents of the Short Hills
formed a political union. After news of the Home District rising
reached the area in early December, the chairman of that union,
Moses Brady, came to St. Catharines to assure the authorities
there that its members merely sought peaceable reform. His
assurance did little to assuage the fears of local officials, who
formed a troop at St. Catharines and sent it back through the
Short Hills to look for escaped rebels. In the meantime,
Mackenzie, with the aid of a local resident, Samuel Chandler,
slipped through the Short Hills on his way to the United States.[32]
The troop brought back "2 suspicious characters" for questioning, but the justices freed both (D 74). Another resident was later
taken to St. Catharines for examination and then released. He
told his neighbours he had escaped. In the opinion of one worried
magistrate, Henry Mittleburger, this helped "create an alarming
excitement among the disaffected" (D 75). Mittleburger, the
chairman of the district's quarter sessions, asked the lieutenant-
governor what he could do about those who "have urged Militia

[32]Colin Read, "Samuel Chandler," *Dictionary of Canadian Biography*, IX
(Toronto, 1976), p. 124.

men not to turn out" or who organized reform meetings or societies (D 75). Head, however, gave no comfort. He merely instructed the magistrate to watch suspicious citizens closely (D 76).

Events along the Niagara frontier heightened the fears of local loyalists. Mackenzie, having escaped the province, addressed curious crowds at Buffalo. To them he announced his intention of invading Upper Canada with an army of liberation and, on 14 December, he and a few Canadian and American sympathizers seized British-owned Navy Island in the Niagara River above the falls. Mackenzie's escapades redoubled the anxieties of district loyalists about the local disaffected, and authorities feared a local rising if an invasion or uprising occurred elsewhere (see D 77). Just how great was the actual disaffection in the area is difficult to determine. Certainly the Short Hills raid of June 1838 was to provide some proof to the loyal of their suspicions, but the very limited support that the raid received suggests either that the disloyal were fearful of reprisals or that there was not much support for rebellious activity in the area.[33]

To the west of the Niagara District lay the London District, one of the province's largest. It consisted of four counties – Norfolk, Oxford, Middlesex, and Huron. Many residents of the first three were intimately affected, as we have seen, by the Duncombe revolt. The settlers of parts of Middlesex, and all of Huron, however, were only indirectly touched by that rising, and it is to these latter areas that we now turn. Like many reformers elsewhere in the province, those in the town of London were caught by surprise by the news of the Mackenzie rebellion. On 8 December a score or more (D 80) met in the barroom of Flannagan's Tavern to decide what to do. Fearing that the local tories would attack them in retaliation for the Toronto outrage, they formed a defensive association. They decided to "assemble in the neighbourhood of the Scotch [United Secession Presbyterian] Church on a signal being given, which signal was to be the firing of two Guns and the blowing of a Bugle" (D 78).

On the eleventh, John B. Askin, the district clerk, and sheriff James Hamilton received a garbled account of these proceedings, which had it that the reformers were to fall upon London that night after firing their two guns and blowing their bugle. Askin then raised "all the inhabitants that could be relied upon." These,

[33]See Colin Read, "The Short Hills Raid of June, 1838, and Its Aftermath," *Ontario History*, LXVIII (1976), pp. 93-115.

to the number of two hundred, readied the court house for defence. That night nothing happened, leaving Askin convinced "that the Zeal displayed by the Loyalist[s] . . . frustrated such plans as might have been in progress . . . by the Rebels" (D 79). The next day, Hamilton stayed in London, while Askin, on the instructions of the attorney general, left for St. Thomas to arrest John Talbot of the *Liberal*. There, of course, he found Talbot flown and the town buzzing with the news of the Duncombe rising. He then helped organize the force which he accompanied to the east, off to Oakland (D 79).

The news of Duncombe's activities reached London soon after St. Thomas, and galvanized Hamilton and other officials into further action. On 14 December they summoned London's militiamen and sent them to St. Thomas. Their place in London was meanwhile taken by two hundred militiamen who arrived that evening from Goderich (D 80). Other local militiamen were called out and told to search for the "arms, and ammunition . . . of such as have not come forward to serve" (D 81). London was soon in the grip of a "military mania," heavily guarded and prepared for the worst (D 83, D 84). The attempts by officialdom to round up arms produced resistance. In Nissouri Township, to the east of London, Robert Davis, author of *The Canadian Farmer's Travels* . . ., and others armed themselves to fend off "the Tories who They Heard were coming out to Seize arms for the Queens service." Reportedly, Davis commanded one hundred and thirty armed men (D 82). He, however, quickly realized that resistance was futile and fled to the United States, where he enlisted in the Patriot service; this was to cost him his life.

Mackenzie's revolt, Duncombe's rising, the mustering of the local loyalists, and all of the various rumours attendant upon each produced such a state of confusion about London that some reformers in the area met to consider the several reports and decide what action to take. Liberals from Dorchester, to the southwest of London, held such a meeting on 12 December. Two days later seventy-five residents of Dorchester and adjacent townships "unanimously resolved to form a *mutual safety association*."[34] Such associations were common in areas of the province where residents did not want to take a stand for the rebels or loyalists or were fearful of attack by either side.

The Dorchester area men were among the many Upper

[34]RLDM, v. II, Petition of Nathaniel Deo, n.d.

Canadian reformers fearful that the tories were about to fall upon them, employing local Indians in the process.[35] Indeed, in December, authorities did call on Indian forces in several places – near Belleville, at Rice Lake back of Port Hope, in the Orillia area, and at Oakland. At no place in the west was fear of the Indian stronger than in Delaware Township, immediately west of London, where there was a reserve of Munceys, Chippawas, and Delawares. In early December the local Liberals had formed a political union. On the fifteenth news of Duncombe's defeat finally reached them.[36] At once, like the reformers of Dorchester, they organized a mutual protection society. It turned out that they had nothing to fear; although J.B. Clench, the local Indian Superintendent, wished the authorities to use his warriors (D 86), they were not needed and were not called out. If, as seems unlikely, the reformers of Delaware ever contemplated any treasonous activity, the ever-present threat of Indian attack must have dissuaded them. The local Church of England priest, Richard Flood, summed up the attitude of most white residents when he commented that, had the Indians been used, they "would probably have resorted to all those horrid barbarities of scalping and burning."[37]

Some twenty miles beyond Delaware, on the District's western boundary, in Adelaide and Mosa townships, the rebellions also had repercussions. Here, the local militiamen were summoned in mid-month. In Adelaide some thirty from the Irish settlement of Katesville refused to respond.[38] In Mosa, to the south, on the fifteenth, Alexander Roberts, a local farmer, showed up at a militia mustering with men he had already gathered. He urged the militiamen to quit their ranks and join his volunteers on their way to St. Thomas[39] to aid Duncombe. Seventeen men heeded his call,[40] swelling the numbers of his band to fifty or more. Roberts was not yet prepared to move his force eastward, and he promised its members to get them arms from Detroit. It is clear from the fact that Roberts's men then

[35]Ibid.

[36]UCS, v. 204, pp. 112765-7, Petition of Alvaro Ladd, 2 June 1838.

[37]W.J.D. Waddilove, *The Stewart Missions: A Series of Letters and Journals Calculated to Exhibit to British Christians the Spiritual Destitution of the Emigrants Settled in the Remote Parts of Upper Canada* (London, 1838), p. 182, extract of a letter from Richard Flood to Rev. W.J.D. Waddilove, Caradoc, 27 Dec. 1837.

[38]UCS, v. 185, p. 103305, Robert Johnston to the Adjutant General of Militia, near Katesville, London District, 21 Jan. 1838.

[39]RLDM, v. II, Deposition of Richard Neale, 22 Dec. 1837.

[40]Ibid., Information of Adam Hatelie, 22 Dec. 1837.

agreed to try to get Mackenzie's draft constitution for Upper
Canada introduced (D 89) that they did not yet know of the
defeat of either Mackenzie or Duncombe. Soon, though, they
had that news,[41] and Roberts, instead of leading a victorious
column eastward, was fleeing westward to safety in Detroit,
where he enrolled in the Patriot cause.

The events in Mosa helped convince the Middlesex loyalists
that disaffection was widespread in the county. To some, the
actions of the Liberals of London, Dorchester, Delaware, and
Nissouri were of a piece with those of Roberts and his cohorts in
Mosa, indeed of a piece with those of arch-traitors Duncombe
and Mackenzie. Consequently, various Middlesex inhabitants
would find themselves obliged to give accounts of their actions
once the rebellion was over, the province secured, and formal,
systematic investigations into the loyalty of individuals begun.

Middlesex's northwestern neighbour, Huron County, was less
troubled by the events of December. Though one of Mackenzie's
leading lieutenants, Anthony Van Egmond, journeyed from the
Huron Tract to Toronto to support the rebel cause, he had "made
few converts" in the Tract itself, "and these of the most
unimportant classes" (D 94). Significantly, when an attempt to
dissuade the militiamen about Goderich from mustering and
marching to London occurred on 11 December it was made by a
Middlesex resident, Joseph Alway, and his effort was unsuccessful (D 93). The Tract was relatively remote from the rest of
the province, but its residents were not entirely unaffected by the
revolt's repercussions. For one thing, they heard alarming
reports of Indian activities, causing them to conjure up visions of
atrocities and depredations (see D 92). For another, just as the
Huron militiamen were called on to serve in the London area, so
too would they later be summoned to the Detroit frontier to help
turn back the Patriots. In fact, the men of the Huron Tract
probably were more involved in the events of 1837–8 than many
who were closer to the actual scenes of the December uprisings.

Like the Huron Tract, the Western District, composed of Kent
and Essex counties, harboured few rebellious spirits in December
1837. No arrests of local residents occurred, though some
doubted very much the loyalty of the many French Canadians
living along the Detroit frontier.[42] As along the Niagara border,

[41] Ibid., Deposition of William Gardiner, 23 Dec. 1837.
[42] See, for example, Metropolitan Toronto Public Library, James Hamilton Papers,
Lt. Col. John Prince to Col. Hamilton, The Park Farm, 28 Dec. 1837.

the threat to peace here came not from local inhabitants but from the Patriots. In mid-month, after the failure of the Mackenzie and Duncombe risings, magistrate and MLA John Prince of Windsor found it necessary to cross over to Detroit to apprise the people and officials there of the true state of affairs in Upper Canada. Though he felt his efforts would be rewarded (D 90), he was wrong, as the patriots were to grow from strength to strength. The militia of the Western District was "in a comparatively unorganized state,"[43] and by the end of the month the authorities were making frantic efforts to prepare it to resist the looming Patriot menace (see D 91). In the year ahead, the Patriot invasions were to throw the western frontier, and the province at large, into turmoil.

In summary, then, it can be said that the eastern portion of Upper Canada was overwhelmingly loyal and largely oriented towards the troubles in the lower province. Further west, the vast majority of citizens were loyal, with many actively supporting the government, though there were pockets of anti-government activity, most notably at Belleville, Cobourg, and perhaps Port Hope. Immediately west of the Home District, in the Gore District, was the greatest concentration of rebel sympathy and rebel activity outside of the two rebel areas of the province. South of this there existed pockets of disloyalty, but nothing on the scale found in the Gore District. In those areas of the London District not directly involved in the Duncombe rising the reformers seemed divided between those who wished only to protect themselves from the tories and Indians and those who wished to join the rebellion. The Western District was largely uninvolved in the rebellions of 1837 and, like the eastern part of the province, seemed more concerned with events outside the colony than those inside. Had the risings in the London and Home districts been even briefly successful, it is possible that more evidence of disaffection would have emerged in the province. Events undoubtedly influenced how certain segments of the population reacted. It seems, however, that the desire to rebel affected only a small portion of the population and, no matter what happened, the vast majority of the population would have remained neutral or else have rallied to the defence of the government.

[43]CPSO, v. 10, file 1370, John Prince *et al.* to Sir George Arthur, Toronto, 1 April 1838.

E. AFTERMATH

FOLLOWING THE FLIGHT of the rebels from Montgomery's Tavern and the despatch of forces to put down the rebellion in the London District, the lieutenant-governor and Executive Council took action to insure that no further armed anti-government activity took place in the Home District. Hampered by lack of accurate information as to the size of the rebel force and to the extent of support for the rebellion in the countryside, the disconcerted authorities made policy on an ad hoc basis, being governed by their current perceptions of conditions in the province. When in mid-December the rebels in the London District fled before MacNab's advance, the executive's measures were carried out in that district as well.

Although initially disposed to be generous and to allow those rebels who would return to their allegiance their freedom, provided they had been involved in no serious crime, Head and his advisers soon decided that all those taken up by loyalist forces must be held for questioning (E 1). Because so many men had been brought in by the magistrates, militia officers, and loyalist enthusiasts, a further order was issued within a few days, advising that arrests must now be left to the magistrates and to legal procedures, except where "notorious offenders" were involved (E 6). By this time officials had been appointed in both the Home and London districts to examine those suspected or accused of treasonable practices (E 5, E 10).

These appointments were absolutely essential in that the gaol facilities were becoming severely overcrowded. Even the Gore District gaol was flooded with prisoners (E 15), although the district had been only marginally involved in the actual fighting. At Toronto not only the gaol but also the market buildings and a section of the Parliament Buildings were pressed into service to hold the prisoners. Even with this extra space in use, one man later complained of the accommodation that he shared with "28 or 29," two small rooms sixteen or seventeen feet square.[1] Many were pressed into such facilities. A list of prisoners in the gaol and Parliament Buildings, made on 13 December, lists three

[1]PAO, Miscellaneous, 1896, Rev. J. Doel, *Some Recollections of the "Rebellion" so called in 1837 & 1838*, pp. 6-7.

hundred and twenty men. One for the market lists ninety-two.[2]

The cause of this overcrowding was the enthusiasm with which loyalist volunteers, organized to go to the aid of the capital, rounded up suspected rebels and rebel sympathizers, combined with the continued activities of legal and extra-legal forces after the rebellion was crushed. It is quite apparent that in the Home District, at least, and in areas adjacent to it, many excesses were perpetrated: people were brought in only because of their known reform sympathies, blank warrants were issued for the arrest of suspects, and individuals were taken up because of personal dislike on the part of a loyalist or loyalists (E 16, E 17, E 18, E 21, E 22). In some cases these professed loyalists appear to have been little more than bandits, looting and smashing as they searched for evidence of rebel activity or sympathy (E 17, E 27, E 28).

While the majority of the leaders of the rebellions were making their way by various means out of the country, a widespread paranoia about reform took hold. With everything reform being suspected of being rebel, even those not taken into custody were persecuted. Once again this activity was greatest in the Home District, where protection of the seat of government gave some justification for excessive zeal. The most famous incident associated with this persecution of reform was the virtual expulsion from the colony of Marshall Spring Bidwell (E 26), but other incidents of note took place as well. The Bank of the People, formed by reformers to provide an alternative to the Compact-linked Bank of Upper Canada, was accused of aiding the rebels (E 30), and men were quartered in the premises of prominent reformers (E 85) or set to monitor the activities of influential reformers.[3] In the general anti-reform climate which prevailed, the Brockville *Recorder* was moved to publish an editorial explaining why a desire for reform was not a desire for rebellion, and pledging loyalty to the government (E 40). With the mixture of fear and anger pervading the tory camp and affecting many of the supporters of constitutional government, even the most innocent of statements could bring arrest, or cause near panic, if taken the wrong way. A Roman Catholic official, returning from the United States in late December, "gave serious alarm" to some people in Kingston when he announced that the number of Lower Canadian Patriots on the American side

[2]UCS, v. 180, pp. 99146-60, List of prisoners, 13 Dec. 1837.

[3]See, for example, W.R. Wood, *Past Years in Pickering: Sketches of the History of the Community* (Toronto, 1911), p. 29.

"should not be underrated." Such a simple statement caused sufficient apprehension and doubt about his loyalty that he was moved to write a letter to the *Chronicle & Gazette* explaining that his words had been taken to mean far more than he intended (E 29).

Uncertainty as to what was reform and what was rebellion in the province was fuelled by the situation on the American frontier. Many of the leaders and a substantial number of participants in the rebellion in Upper and Lower Canada had reached the American side and were stirring up the border states with tales of Canadian oppression. One result of this agitation was Mackenzie's takeover of Navy Island, where a republic of Upper Canada was proclaimed and an armed force, at one time amounting to several hundred, established. Soon fears of a rebellion within the colony were intensified by concern over a coordinated invasion. Rumours of such joint threats circulated in the colony in December.[4]

The many volunteers who had flooded Toronto in the days after the rebellion had by mid-December been sent home, with the exception of the Bank Guards, enrolled during the rebellion. To meet the threat of invasion and further internal troubles, City Guards were created on 23 December to maintain law and order in Toronto, and similar bodies were soon created in other urban centres. Judging from reports of the day, these volunteers were a mixed blessing. Sometimes overzealous, sometimes less than effective, they none the less provided a basic defence force in the months to come (E 31, E 32, E 33).

The Navy Island invasion force withdrew on 14 January, after Canadian volunteers burned its American supply boat, the *Caroline*, causing an international incident in the process; but three abortive attempts to invade Upper Canada occurred on the western frontier in January and February. The justices of the Midland District became aware in February of a complicated plot in which raiders from the United States, in concert with radicals about Belleville had laid plans to attack Kingston (E 54). A preventative arrest of suspects was at once carried out.[5] Whether the patriots' intentions were as desperate as the magistrates felt is far from certain, for the justices' actions helped prevent the conspirators from translating their plans into action.

---

[4]C.P. Stacey, ed., "The Crisis of 1837 in a Back Township, Being the Diary of Joseph Richard Thompson," *Canadian Historical Review*, xi (1930), p. 231.

[5]All those tried for involvement in this episode were acquitted.

A major raid did, however, take place in February, at Pelee Island in Lake Erie. A large force of Americans occupied the island, only to be driven from it in early March by a force of British regulars and militiamen, after a bloody battle. The Patriots had to struggle back over uncertain ice to the American shore.[6] Almost as bad as the raids themselves were the constant rumours of invasions (E 34, E 35). Instead of gradually subsiding, the fear and anger of those who had chosen to support the government in December was kept at a fever pitch throughout early 1838.

To meet these real or perceived threats the authorities in Toronto felt it necessary from time to time to increase the strength of forces within the colony. On 25 January, for instance, it was announced that the lieutenant-governor had accepted the services of two volunteer companies to serve with the City Guards in Toronto. The authority of the latter was extended over the whole province on 15 February. While some of the militia that had been incorporated, or enrolled, in mid-December to serve until 1 July 1838 were withdrawn from the Niagara frontier, where the threat of large-scale imminent invasion had subsided, militiamen were kept on for a time in the capital.[7]

Despite, or perhaps because of, the continuing insecurity, Francis Bond Head decided to declare a day of thanksgiving for deliverance from the uprising in early February. Those who spoke against or ignored the occasion he threatened with God's wrath and earthly punishment (E 36). This did not prevent some ministers of dissenting sects from declining to honour the day. In Toronto the Congregationalist minister John Roaf refused not only to take part in the observances, but also to pay the subsequent fine or to allow the quartering of soldiers in his house (E 38). In London, the Reverend William Proudfoot of the United Secession Church refused to mark the day, as did the members of his congregation (E 37). In each case the refusal was at least partly based on the belief that the lieutenant-governor did not have the right to tell worshippers when and about what they should pray.

Not surprisingly, such recusancy brought accusations of disloyalty. In the months after the rebellion there was much

[6]Guillet, The Lives and Times, pp. 99-103.
[7]Upper Canada Gazette (Toronto), 25 Jan., 15 Feb., 10 April, 26 July 1838; Patriot (Toronto), 12 Jan. 1838. Incorporated or enrolled militiamen were given pay, clothing, and some training, unlike the sedentary militiamen who received an allowance during time of service but no clothing.

comment from loyalists concerning the seditious, even treasonous attitude of various dissenting sects. The Reverend Thomas
Green, an itinerant Church of England missionary in the London
District, for instance, informed the readers of *The Stewart
Missions* . . ., published in England, that he was convinced that
"a large body of the disaffected are Universalists . . . . nearly
two-thirds of the prisoners at present confined in the jail here are
connected with this most unscriptural body." Similarly, many
"*professed* Baptists" as well as Norwich Quakers had been
implicated in the Duncombe rising. On the other hand he knew of
no Anglican "being detected in aiding or abetting the unnatural
and unwarrantable outbreak" (E 39).

Against this calumny and continued suspicion of all associated
with the reform cause, a few voices were raised in public protest.
In Toronto the *Mirror* spoke against attempts to proscribe reform
(E 41) and the Niagara *Reporter* cautioned, "If the magnates of
the land are permitted to suppose, for a moment, that the
Loyalists of Upper Canada rose to secure to them the possession
of that power which too many of them abuse, our rights will be
trampled upon, and there is danger of another and a worse
rebellion" (E 42). One response to expressions of concern such
as these was an act of the provincial parliament, passed on 6
March which granted all those who had taken action to suppress
the rebellion immunity from prosecution, whether their conduct
had been legal or illegal. Anyone choosing to take one of the
loyalists to court, would have to pay the defendant "double
costs" (E 52).

A second bill passed on 6 March was designed to prevent men
from assembling "clandestinely and unlawfully" to train in arms.
The authorities were instructed to disperse and arrest those
drilling and to seize the weapons of those suspected of being
disloyal (E 53). This act clearly demonstrates the depth of
loyalist fears in the months after the risings, as the climate of
rumour and insecurity in the colony continued unabated.

In the midst of this hostile environment the trials for treason of
those arrested for their activities in December took place. Some
sections of the community pressed for the death penalty (see, for
example, E 43), and initial indications were that the government
intended to deal harshly with the prisoners. A statute passed in
January severely abridged their rights of habeas corpus and
declared that only those named by the lieutenant-governor could
be bailed (E 44). This act had considerable force at Hamilton,

Toronto, and elsewhere, but its effects were limited at London by the fact that the magistrates there had freed many on bail before its passage. Even after the act was passed, they admitted at least one man "to bail for the limits of the town" (E 45).

Shortly before the trials began, the government took a further step which, although it might seem in some ways to be a measure of clemency, was in fact an attempt to reduce the number of cases to be tried, while still allowing strong punishment to be administered. On 6 March a law, 1 Victoria, c. 10, was passed making it possible for those charged with treason to petition the lieutenant-governor for pardon. "Pardon," the act declared, "shall have the same effect as an attainder of the person therein named for the crime of High Treason, so far as regards the forfeiture of his Estate and property real and personal." Recipients might also face transportation to a penal colony or banishment from the province (E 46). In spite of the possible consequences of petitioning under the act, 43 of 81 prisoners indicted at London, 14 of the 47 at Hamilton,[8] and 124 of 134 indicted at Toronto petitioned under it.[9] Of all those who petitioned, only three were refused: Isaac Moore, accused of aiding the Yarmouth rebels, in the London District, and Samuel Lount and Peter Matthews, who were considered principal figures in the Home District. Moore fared better than many who petitioned, being tried and acquitted (see E 47, E 48, E 49). Lount and Matthews paid the ultimate penalty.

The prisoners who stood trial for their parts in the rebellion were all charged with various forms of treason, charges far too serious to be handled by the justices of the peace. All had been indicted by grand juries of the districts where their trials were held. Those not indicted were freed. All trials were held under the normal legal procedures of the colony, in the Courts of Oyer and Terminer and General Gaol Delivery, presided over by a judge of the Court of King's Bench. Appeals from these courts went to the lieutenant-governor and Executive Council and from there to the Queen-in-Council.

Of the twelve men who stood trial in Toronto, six were

[8]Read, *The Rising*, pp. 125, 129. The statistics given here and in E 65 do not quite agree; the latter are in error.

[9]There are three or four more men who may have been indicted at Toronto. The courts evidently ignored some indictments. One of these men escaped from the hospital before he could be tried. See *Return to an Address of the Honourable The House of Commons, dated 8 May 1838; for Return of the Names and Quality or Station of the Several Persons Arrested in Upper Canada . . .* (Toronto, 1839).

acquitted and six convicted. Of those acquitted, five had had
little or no part in the rising and had obviously chosen to stand
trial because of this. Donald Cameron of Thorah, for instance,
had gathered men to go to the aid of Toronto, not Mackenzie,
witnesses claimed at his trial.[10] The only case of note among
those acquitted was that of Dr. Thomas D. Morrison. Morrison
had, of course, been forward in supporting the rising from the
beginning, but evidence at his trial was contradictory and did not
clearly show that he had taken an active role.[11] Shortly after his
acquittal, Morrison, hearing that additional charges were being
prepared against him, fled the country.

The six who were convicted were a mixture of minor and
major figures. One, John Montgomery, had apparently taken no
direct part in the rising, although a minority of witnesses said he
had. His main crime, it seems, was that he had remained at his
inn, the rebel headquarters, during the rising instead of leaving
and taking news of rebel activity to Toronto.[12] Another, Charles
Durand, was the rather muddled young lawyer from Hamilton
who had spread news of rebel success at Toronto as he travelled
westwards, suggesting all the while that perhaps it was time to be
"up and doing."[13] The two defendants who attracted most
attention were Samuel Lount and Peter Matthews, each accused
of having led a section of the rebel forces. As the highest-ranking
rebels captured after the Toronto rising, they were used as
examples to those who still harboured rebellious ideas.

Both Lount and Matthews pleaded guilty, as they had done in
their petitions seeking executive clemency, and thus deprived
themselves of public defences. In pronouncing the death
sentence on the two, Chief Justice John Beverley Robinson gave
them a long lecture on their duties to the government and to God,
duties which he felt they had ignored because of "envy and
hatred towards your rulers" and not because they had grievances
or were oppressed (E 59). The Executive Council, which

[10]PAO, Special Commission for Trial of Treason and Misprision of Treason
committed in any Districts of the Province, John Beverley Robinson Casebook. It
would appear that Ewen Cameron, listed as discharged by the commission, was tried
along with Donald Cameron and also acquitted. This Donald Cameron is probably the
same one who appears in two places on the official prisoner list cited in footnote 9,
since he was brought in twice for examination.
[11]*Trial of Dr. Morrison, M.P.P. for High Treason, at Toronto, on Wednesday,
April 24, 1838* (Toronto, 1838).
[12]PRO, CO 42, v. 447, pp. 181-204, Trial of John Montgomery.
[13]Ibid., v. 447, pp. 211-23, Trial of Charles Durand.

included the chief justice, and the prosecutor at their trial, met twice within a few days of this sentencing. Despite instructions from Lord Glenelg, the colonial secretary, conveyed to them by the new lieutenant-governor, Sir George Arthur, on 31 March[14] to avoid executing anyone unless absolutely necessary, the councillors decided that the two men must die as examples to others and to satisfy the loyalist element in the population (E 60, E 61, E 62). A frantic campaign was begun to collect signatures in favour of clemency for the two men and many thousands were gathered,[15] but neither these nor Mrs. Lount's personal plea to Sir George Arthur made on bended knee, could change the council's mind.[16] Within two weeks of their sentencing, Lount and Matthews walked to their deaths in the gaol-yard at Toronto. The rebel cause now had two more martyrs to join Anthony Van Egmond, who had died on 30 December 1837 from the cold, damp conditions in his basement cell.

The Hamilton trials began on 26 March. Ultimately, cases proceeded against twenty-six men. Seven of them were charged for their parts in the Eramosa meeting of December; all were acquitted.[17] Eighteen others faced charges stemming directly from the Duncombe rising. Of these, ten were judged guilty of treason. The twenty-sixth prisoner, Willard Sherman, accused of hoarding weapons about Hamilton in preparation for the revolt, was found not guilty.[18]

By the time the London trials opened on 30 April, the Executive Council, having made an example of Lount and Matthews, felt secure enough to follow a generally lenient policy with regard to most of the other accused, in keeping with the spirit of Glenelg's despatch. The council recommended that in all but serious cases, those on bail should not be brought to trial (see E 70). This change in attitude helps to explain why only fifteen people were tried for treason at London.

Three men tried for their part in Flannagan's meeting in London on 8 December were acquitted, as were three of the

[14]PAC, RG1 E3, Upper Canada State Papers, v. 50, pp. 3-11, Minute read before the Executive Council, 31 March 1838.

[15]The exact number of signatures is unknown. The government minimized the number, while reformers insisted it was very high indeed. The evidence suggests between 12,000 and 20,000 signed petitions for Lount and/or Matthews. See PAC, Upper Canada State Papers, v. 46, no. 27, pp. 131-79 and no. 35, pp. 239-64.

[16]PAO, Mackenzie–Lindsey Papers, Mackenzie Clippings, Box 11, no. 831, Mrs. Lount to W.L. Mackenzie, Utica, Michigan, 8 Dec. 1838 (printed).

[17]*Journal* (St. Catharines), 5 April 1838.

[18]Read, *The Rising*, pp. 126-7.

four charged with involvement in the "Delaware conspiracy." The fourth, Alvaro Ladd, was found guilty, but his case was then reserved by the judge, Henry Sherwood, who doubted that enough evidence had been mustered against him to support a conviction. Five of the eight prisoners accused of involvement in the Duncombe rising were found guilty of treason.[19] Fortunately for them, although several feared they would be hanged (see, for example, E 72), Lount's and Matthews' executions and Glenelg's announced hostility to widespread use of the death penalty helped secure remission of their sentences. The Upper Canadian government now had to decide among banishment, transportation to the penal colonies, prison terms, and release for the remainder of the confessed or convicted prisoners.

Since the Executive Council had to deal with day-to-day executive affairs, the cases of many prisoners, the defence of the colony, and the complaints of many individuals suffering because of the difficult times, it did not always handle matters with despatch. For many who were incarcerated, official action was slow in coming, with consequent hardships on the prisoners. On 5 June, for example, nine of those who had petitioned for pardon from the London gaol reminded the government that their petitions had not been answered in some three months, while they had recently been moved to considerably more crowded and uncomfortable quarters. Their sense of grievance was compounded by the fact that they felt their crimes to be far less heinous than those of many "Toronto characters" already released (E 76). Over fifty petitioners had been released from the Toronto gaol in May, and the authorities were now in the midst of considering the cases of fifty-six of the London and Gore District prisoners who had petitioned under 1 Victoria, c. 10. Later that month it ordered thirty-five of them freed.[20] At Toronto there were still many cases to consider. One man, Jesse Cleaver, complained that after being held almost five months he had not yet been examined and had no idea of the charges against him (E 77). He was later banished. At Kingston, seventeen prisoners sent there either for imprisonment or transportation to a penal colony were treated like Cleaver. No one had bothered to inform them of their sentences! The warden had to write twice asking permission to tell them what these were (E 78).

The long wait for action in some prisoners' cases, the lack of

[19]Ibid., pp. 130-1.
[20]Ibid., pp. 148-9.

information on the fate of certain men, the seeming severity of some of the sentences, and the continued harassment by those professing to be loyalists, were problems that the families of those remaining in gaol had to suffer. Through the spring and summer a stready stream of petitions came from family members and prisoners asking for clemency on the grounds that families were suffering from the absence of fathers, husbands, and sons. Of all the petitions surviving from the rebellion period, these are perhaps the most despairing and pathetic. Many families were shocked by the prospect that male members would be gone for years, perhaps forever. Some faced great economic difficulties. Appealing to the newly arrived governor general, Lord Durham, Phoebe Willson, wife of Hugh D., one of those sentenced to transportation for life, summarized the despair many felt when she wrote, "you are the last I can look to under heaven for a remady" (E 83; see also E 81, E 82, E 84).

Prisoners and their families were not the only ones suffering. The disorganization and panic consequent upon the rebellion and the distrust of those who were reformers or who had remained neutral in December 1837 led to injustices and to other petitions. The most notable cases here were those of Toronto's postmaster, James S. Howard, and the Lesslie brothers.

Howard was removed from his important position because his loyalty was in question. Although of conservative temperment, he had been friendly with both tories and reformers prior to the rebellion. When the rising occurred, government officials felt they could learn of rebel activities by opening the mails. They thus discovered that John and Joseph Lesslie of Dundas had sent letters care of Howard to their brothers James and William, both prominent radicals and close associates of Mackenzie. This cost John Lesslie his job as postmaster at Dundas and, when combined with Howard's failure to take up arms during the revolt, damned him in official eyes and led to his dismissal too. Howard appealed for an investigation, but the council felt that none was needed since he was charged with no crime (E 87). His case clearly suggests that the lieutenant-governor and his councillors could be ruthless when dealing with government employees, feeling that their loyalty, above all, should be unimpeachable.

As the case of James and William Lesslie indicates, the executive also took a direct, albeit a small, role in persecuting neutral reformers. Incarcerated for two weeks at the conclusion of the Toronto rising and their premises occupied by soldiers in their absence, the Lesslies were never charged with any crime. Released, William travelled to Kingston to get married, but, recognized on the way, was arrested once again. Hearing this, James approached Bond Head, first for an order for William's release, then for a pass allowing him to go to his brother's aid. Refused on both counts, James could only wait until William in due course was examined and freed.[21] The Lesslies appealed this conduct, which they considered both arbitrary and unlawful, but the councillors informed them that people such as they had to expect such treatment in such times. Spreading "seditious and dangerous sentiments" ending "in rebellion" had yielded them, the councillors thought, a just, if bitter, reward (E 86).

While Howard and the Lesslies suffered because of their positions, one as a government employee in a suddenly highly sensitive post, the others as prominent members of a political faction from which the rebels had been drawn, other perhaps less notable people were injured by the circumstances of the moment. For example, James Lockhart, a merchant from Niagara, was unlucky enough to have had a case of fowling pieces in Toronto at the time of the rebellion. The guns, seized by Alderman Alexander Dixon for use in defending the city, subsequently disappeared. Lockhart applied to the courts for redress, but was told that the law passed in March to prevent actions against those who had been active in defence of the government barred compensation. In fact, he was forced to pay all court costs. He then petitioned the executive for compensation (E 90) but was told that the council knew "of no fund from which" he could "be indemnified" (E 91).

In the Upper Canada of 1838 where some innocents suffered along with the guilty and where citizens of reform persuasion saw the Family Compact secured in its place of power by the rebellion, those leaving for the United States increased greatly in number. Just how many fled will never be known. Judging from population statistics and immigration records for 1836 to 1839, a massive shift of population did not occur, but enough left to sustain the contemporary impression of a large-scale movement. In April a Toronto Township settler recorded that "a great many are daily leaving the Province for the United States, some through dread of punishment, others disgusted with the

[21]PAC, Rolph Papers, v. 3, J. Lesslie to Charles Dent, Eglinton, 16 March 1885.

administration of government" (E 93). Elija Duncombe, brother to Charles, claimed that "Nearly 1/3 of the Inhabitants have left and are leaving – for the United States and all the Leading Reformers are gone and a great many Moderate Tories" (E 95). George Arthur, the lieutenant-governor, was moved to comment: "The number of persons who have left the Province and gone to the States is astonishing. I do not believe that all are disloyal but many have emigrated from fear."[22]

Political motivation probably drove many to the States, as did "the overthrow of commercial business" (E 99), the economic recession which continued to grip the western world in 1838 and which was made worse in Upper Canada by the unsettled times. It is probable, however, that the lack of money and the low value of land kept as many people in the colony as they drove out. The persecution of, or at least hostility to, various reform denominations probably also contributed to the exodus. The Reverend William Proudfoot noted in a letter of 14 August the persecution of his congregation by the tories and the consequent desire to emigrate, but, he also observed, the economic state of the province made such emigration difficult (E 100).

So strong was the desire of some segments of the population to leave that the Mississippi Emigration Society was founded in Toronto by prominent reformers such as James Lesslie and MLA Peter Perry, as well as by lesser known reformers such as Francis Hincks, cashier of the Bank of the People. The intention of this society was to found a colony on the Mississippi in the Iowa Territory.[23] The colony proved largely abortive, though some emigrated to Iowa under the society's auspices. There they found disease and hardship, so the British Colonist reported on 20 September 1838, adding that those who could had already returned to the province.

A seeming contradiction exists in the fact that, while the lines of division between tories and reformers hardened, as evidenced by the flight of some of the latter from the province, the executive began in late summer to deal more leniently with the sentenced traitors. The Patriot raids, particularly the Short Hills one and its repercussions and results, help explain this apparent contradiction.

[22]Sanderson, ed., The Arthur Papers, v. I, p. 430, Arthur to Colborne, Toronto, 8 Dec. 1838.
[23]Metropolitan Toronto Public Library, James Lesslie, Resume of events and people in Toronto 1822-38."

Rumours about projected raids had been in constant circulation all through the winter and spring of 1837–8. They began assuming a semblance of reality when at the end of May a group of sympathizing brigands attacked and burnt the Upper Canadian-owned steamboat *Sir Robert Peel* in the Thousand Islands. Then in June about thirty men, though the loyalists later thought the force much larger, crossed the Niagara River, moved into the Short Hills, and attacked a small troop of cavalry stationed in the village of St. Johns. The militia in various parts of the province were ordered out in anticipation of a large-scale invasion. In the Short Hills, loyalists soon hunted down most of the raiders, though some, including Dr. Duncan Wilson of Yarmouth, escaped. He was then captured at Norwich, but, when two bailiffs attempted to convey him to London, was freed by an armed band. Once more he fled, this time to Yarmouth, where he was recaptured.[24]

Although the militia generally was disbanded as the threat diminished, not so in Norwich. Following Wilson's release, militia forces descended on that township where they became convinced that plans for an invasion and simultaneous uprising were maturing. They arrested several Norwich settlers and stationed themselves around the township, congratulating themselves when no revolt occurred (E 103, E 104). At the end of June, London authorities had a similar scare when a report was received that one thousand or more Patriots were about to attack. The expected assault failed to materialize, and twenty-six settlers from about Chatham, said to be in league with the Patriots, soon found themselves in gaol (E 106).

While there were no raids in July and August, the continuing sense of threat divided the public over how the state prisoners should be treated (see, for example, E 106, E 107). The Executive Council and the lieutenant-governor had to consider these opinions, as well as the wishes of the British authorities, whose desire for clemency was by now further emphasized by the presence in North America of Lord Durham.

The opportunity to punish convicted Short Hills raiders severely to demonstrate to potential rebels the harsh realities of attempted treason[25] helped decide the executive councillors that they could now treat the state prisoners from December 1837

[24]Read, *The Rising*, pp. 137-9.
[25]PAC, Upper Canada State Papers, v. 64, pp. 90-2, Minute of the Executive Council, 30 Aug. 1838.

with greater leniency. Accordingly, between July and October they freed almost fifty petitioners from the Toronto, Hamilton, and London gaols, and reduced the sentences of a number more, including seventeen whom they banished. In fact, a further ten who had been sentenced to three years imprisonment, followed by banishment, seem only to have suffered the latter punishment. As for the rest of the Hamilton and London prisoners, three settled matters themselves, two by escaping, one by dying. The councillors sent a fourth to the penitentiary. Deeming the last two western prisoners held from the December troubles, Finlay Malcolm of Bayham and Paul Bedford of Norwich, among the most guilty, they ordered them transported,[26] as they did approximately eighteen from the Toronto gaol. All those to be transported were taken to Fort Henry in transit for England from where they were to be shipped to one of the Australian penal colonies. With the assistance of a friendly employee at the fort, fifteen of the prisoners escaped and twelve reached the United States, three being retaken.[27] Of those who did not escape, one was kept at Fort Henry and the remaining prisoners were sent to England. As it turned out, this was the worst punishment they were to suffer for their crimes. Whether by design or neglect, the conditions they experienced on the voyage were extremely unpleasant (E 79, E 80). When they finally reached England, a series of legal manoeuvres secured their release.[28]

The executive took one last measure of leniency on 25 October 1838. A proclamation ordered sixty-one men who had been indicted for treason but had fled the province to surrender by 1 February 1839, or suffer the penalties of those convicted of treason. All others not yet charged with treason, misprision of treason, or treasonable practices were free to return home (E 110). While some, like the editor of the Toronto *Mirror*, were quick to point out that, as an amnesty, the proclamation excluded many,[29] it was one more step towards winding up the rebellion cases. The government also showed some generosity in not moving to confiscate the property of those exempted from the amnesty, although in the coming months the Executive Council was to advise such action (E 111).

While the authorities were tidying up these loose ends of

[26]Read, *The Rising*, pp. 150-3, 161.
[27]Guillet, *The Lives and Times*, pp. 115-18.
[28]Lindsey, *The Life and Times of William Lyon Mackenzie*, II, pp. 233-4.
[29]*Mirror* (Toronto), 26 Oct. 1838.

December 1837, military activity increased on the frontier, as did fears of rebel activity in the colony. From both the Lake Erie shore and from the area north of Toronto loyalists reported in October and November the disaffected segment of the population ready to act in concert with any invasion (E 112, E 113). Featherstone Osler, the Church of England minister at Bond Head north of Toronto, made the following entry in his diary in mid-October: "Rumours were again afloat this week of another projected rebellion, on a more extensive scale than the last, and that the Americans were preparing to aid the rebels with both men and money."[30] On 5 November, he wrote a friend in England and told him that 40,000 were expected from the United States. As a Church of England minister, he expected to be killed.[31]

So strong were these rumours that the government created some sixteen battalions of incorporated militia, four to serve eighteen months and twelve or so to serve six months. These were stationed in sensitive areas, especially where the loyalty of the population was suspect. In addition, portions of the sedentary local militia were called up and the 93rd Regiment was moved from Lower Canada. Blockhouses were built at all the approaches to Toronto. When the Patriot forces were defeated at Prescott in mid-November and at Windsor in early December, the government felt secure enough to disband most of the militia, although troops remained stationed in disaffected areas well into 1839.[32]

These raids renewed fears of invasion and coordinated rebellion and unleashed another wave of repressive activity against reform sympathizers, usually perpetrated by the incorporated militia. Two of the most serious incidents occurred east of Toronto, where a prominent reform lawyer, James E. Small, who had defended a number of those charged with rebel activities, was stopped on the road and beaten quite severely (E 115). Further east, Thomas Conant, patriarch of a prominent reform family whose ships had ferried a number of escaped rebels to the United States, was foolish enough to accuse a

[30]*Records of the Lives of Ellen Free Pickton and Featherstone Lake Osler* (London, 1915), Second Journal of Featherstone Osler, week of 14 Oct. 1838, pp. 216-17.
[31]PAO, Osler Family Papers, Letterbook 2, F. Osler to F. Proctor, Tecumseh, 5 Nov. 1838.
[32]*Mackenzie's Gazette* (Rochester), 30 March 1839; *Upper Canada Gazette* (Toronto), 25 Oct., 8 Nov., 15 Nov., 22 Nov., 29 Nov., 13 Dec. 1838.

despatch rider of drinking on duty. The rider drew his sword and cleaved Conant's skull (E 114). Tried for murder, the rider was acquitted because the only witness could not positively identify him.[33]

While the Patriot raids ceased after the bloody defeats at Windsor and Prescott, loyalists and tories remained suspicious of reformers. Most would not resort to the kinds of actions taken against Conant and Small. None the less, so ready were they to associate reform with rebellion that others found it difficult to espouse the cause of reform in the years after the uprising for fear of being accused of engaging in seditious activity. When reformers wished in 1839 to express their support for Lord Durham's report, they founded Durham clubs, rather than putting themselves forward as part of the reform movement. Even these clubs were persecuted by tories anxious to root out rebellious feelings. As to the ex-rebels who had been allowed to return to their day-to-day lives, John B. Askin wrote, "true it is, they regret; – not the Participation they had with the Rebels; but, that they failed in their attempt, which is only permitted to slumber for a time only to revive with more Energy" (E 117). On the other side of the coin, many reformers and many who had borne arms in December 1837 with Mackenzie and Duncombe had little reason to love the tories. One radical schoolteacher, for example, went to the extreme of instructing his charges to copy "over and over again, . . . – 'Death to the Tories.' –"[34]

Obviously the Upper Canadian rebellions had results: the jailing of many rebels, the flight of others from the colony, the unleashing of the Patriot raids, the deepening of the commercial depression, albeit alleviated in some measure by British garrison expenditures,[35] the creation of an atmosphere of suspicion and recrimination, and so on. Unfortunately, these were all undesirable. Hence, by almost any measure the revolts had been abject failures. Hastily organized, they were easily crushed, thereby helping vault the ultra-tories into the ascendancy at least for a time. In so doing, they did nothing in the short term to

[33]See *Mackenzie's Gazette* (New York), 15 Dec. 1838; Thomas Conant, *Upper Canada Sketches* (Toronto, 1898), p. 78.

[34]The Rev. John P.K. Hanshaw, *The Late Bishop of Quebec's Upper Canadian Travelling Mission Fund – Reminiscences of the Late Hon. and Rt. Rev. C.H. James Stewart, Lord Bishop of Quebec* (Hexam, England, [1840 ?]), p. 91, K. Green to W.J.D. Waddilove, Wellington Square, 29 Dec. 1839.

[35]Douglas McCalla, *The Upper Canada Trade 1834–1872: A Study of the Buchanans' Business* (Toronto, 1979), p. 31.

further meaningful political reform. And it is by no means clear that they did so in the long run either. Traditionally, the argument has been that they hastened the advent of responsible government by persuading the British government to send out Lord Durham, whose celebrated report led to the granting of responsible government to the Canadas. This argument, however, ignores the fact that the Colonial Office was moving to a policy of conciliation before the rebellions and that, had Gosford in Lower and Head in Upper Canada been unable to produce political harmony, British officialdom would likely have implemented significant reforms, possibly responsible government among them. Nor does the argument recognize that the Upper Canadian risings were not necessary to generate Durham's mission, as the Lower Canadian rebellion ensured his despatch. Once here, Durham had remarkably little interest in the upper province, spending most of his time in Lower Canada. And while he did recommend the establishment of responsible government in the Canadas, the recommendation was ignored by a British government loathe to grant that concession to colonies which had recently witnessed rebellions. Hence it is difficult to see how the Upper Canadian risings directly advanced the cause of responsible government, especially since responsible government was not formally achieved in the Canadas until 1848, two months after its implementation in Nova Scotia, which, Joseph Howe liked to point out,[36] had not suffered rebellion.

Possibly, however, the Upper Canadian revolts and their repercussions did lead indirectly and circuitously to responsible government by discrediting the extremists on either side, thus paving the way for the rise to power of moderate leaders who had been largely neutral in the rebellion[37] and who spearheaded the successful drive for responsible government. But the generalization that the extremists were discredited and the neutrals triumphant needs further study, for the careers of Allan MacNab, John Beverley Robinson, and W.H. Draper, who were extraordinarily active for the tories in 1837–8, suggest that not all tories were in decline in the post-rebellion period. As for their old

[36]See, for example, J. Murray Beck, *Joseph Howe: Voice of Nova Scotia* (Toronto, 1964), p. 4.

[37]The most recent expression of this argument has been advanced by Michael Cross in the "Afterword" to *The Wait Letters*, introduced by Mary Brown and written by Benjamin Wait (Erin, Ont., 1976), p. 157. Cross's piece has been reprinted in Michael S. Cross and Gregory S. Kealey, eds. *Readings in Canadian Social History*, 2: *Pre-Industrial Canada, 1760–1849* (Toronto, 1982), pp. 139-58.

opponents, the rebels, some like William Lyon Mackenzie rose to fight again, if only figuratively. Too, the net effect of the rebellion era on the moderate reformers is far from clear. Some, like Marshall Spring Bidwell, fled or quit the colony forever, while others like Robert Baldwin and Francis Hincks emerged in the 1840s with a considerable following, their political positions aided considerably by the union of the two Canadas and the alliance forged with the French Canadian reformers. Had they been obliged, however, to work within a purely Upper Canadian political system and to rely upon a purely Upper Canadian constituency, their influence would have been greatly diminished. In any case, those who wish to argue that the risings in Upper Canada helped achieve responsible government might maintain that they did so by helping, in whatever degree, to produce the Durham mission, which led to the union of the Canadas, which in turn saw the alliance of the Upper and Lower Canadian reformers, who eventually formed the first responsible government in the Canadas, though not in British North America. Such logic, however, is rather finely spun.

Obviously the long-term significance of the rebellions is a matter of considerable debate. Indeed, before 1838 drew to a close, heated controversies about the significance, and causes and events, of the risings had begun to develop. These have lasted to the present day. The documents that follow will not resolve all issues or settle all points of difference, but they should help clarify matters by presenting the events of the rebellion era clearly, thus providing a solid basis for the formation of sound judgments about the causes, courses, and consequences of Upper Canada's twin revolts.

THE REBELLION OF 1837
IN UPPER CANADA

DOCUMENTS

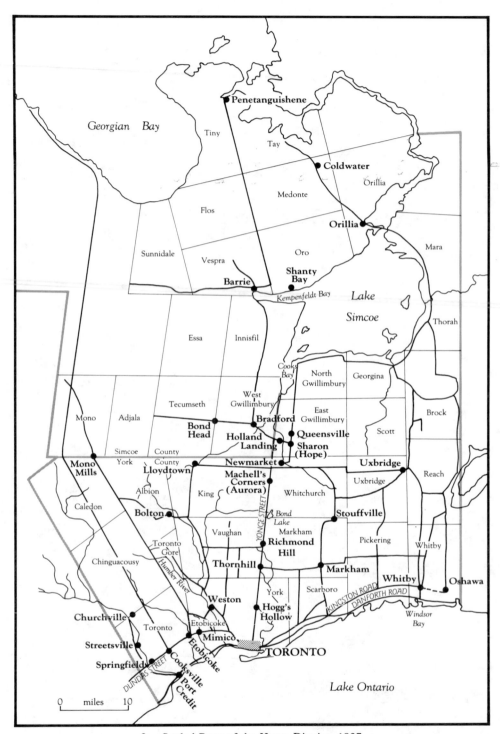

2:   Settled Parts of the Home District, 1837

A. THE CAUSES OF THE REBELLION

A 1 "A LOYAL REFORMER" TO THE *Liberal*
6 February 1836
[Liberal, *St. Thomas, 18 Feb. 1836*]

"What do the Radicals want?" is a question which the Tories ask continually, without waiting for a reply, with which the most illiterate Reformer could furnish them. . . . I will tell you what the Reformers want. (The Reformers are not Radicals in the Tory acceptation of the term; they are Radicals in the liberal sense of the word, so far, that they wish to root out of our Government, every person and thing radically bad – to eradicate every abuse, and to lay the axe at the root of all oppression and misrule.) They want our Parliament to be a fair representation of public sentiment – the dissolution of the unholy union of Church and State. They want their Representatives to have the control of the Public Revenues; the full benefit of the munificent bequest of George the Third for the education of the people; they want a cheap Government. The present ruinous mode of disposing of the public lands superseded by a system which will turn the tide of emigration from a foreign land to our own forest home. They want a commercial intercourse betwixt this country and the United States, on a system of perfect reciprocity. These are the wants of the people, and who dare say that they are extravagant in their demands. . . .

A 2 EXECUTIVE COUNCIL TO SIR F.B. HEAD[1]
4 March 1836
[Correspondent and Advocate, *Toronto, 17 March 1836*]

. . . The Executive Council recognize the truth of the opinion expressed by LORD GLENELG,[2] that "the present is an era of more

[1]Sir Francis Bond Head (1793–1875) was born in England and trained as an engineer at the Royal Military Academy, Woolwich. He served at various locations in the Mediterranean area and Europe before retiring on half pay in 1825. His writings concerning his subsequent short career as manager of the Rio Plata Mining Association in Argentina brought him to public notice and in 1834 he became senior assistant poor law commissioner in Kent. In 1835 he was offered the position of lieutenant-governor of Upper Canada. In return for accepting, he received a baronetcy in 1836. In September of 1837 he resigned over a policy dispute with the Colonial Office and returned to England, where he occupied the remainder of his life with writing.

[2]Charles Grant, Baron Glenelg (1778–1866) was a Whig politician. He had a long career during which he advocated such things as conciliation for Ireland and abolition of slavery. He was colonial secretary from April of 1835 to February of 1839. His attempts to please Canadians by conciliatory measures were not enough to satisfy the colonials and caused substantial criticisms at home. This criticism increased with the rebellions and Glenelg resigned in 1839.

difficulty and importance than any which has hitherto occurred in the history of this part of His Majesty's dominions." This unhappy condition they ascribe, in a very great degree, to the hitherto unconstitutional abridgment of the duties of the Executive Council. It appears from the proceedings of the House of Assembly, and from the reiteration of established opinion in the Country, that neither will public expectation be satisfied, nor contentment be restored, until the system of Local Government is altered and conducted according to the true spirit and meaning of the constitutional Act. . . .

The Council meeting once a week upon Land matters, while the affairs of the Country are withheld from their consideration and advice, is as imperfect a fulfilment of the Constitutional Act, as if the Provincial Parliament were summoned once a year, to meet the letter of the Law, and immediately prorgued [sic] upon answering the Speech from the Throne. In both cases the true meaning and spirit of the Constitutional Act require, that the Parliament should have a general and practicable opportunity to Legislate, and the Executive Council to advise, upon the affairs of the Country. In the former case, the Representative of the King can withhold the Royal Assent from bills, and in the latter, reject the advice offered; but their respective proceedings can not be constitutionally [sic] circumscribed or denied because they need the expression of the Royal pleasure thereon for their consummation. . . .

(Signed,) PETER ROBINSON,[3]
GEO. H. MARKLAND,[4]
JOSEPH WELLS,[5]
JOHN H. DUNN,[6]
ROBERT BALDWIN,[7]
JOHN ROLPH.[8]

[3]Peter Robinson (1785–1838) was the eldest son of loyalist parents. He served in the War of 1812 and in 1824–5 was the Upper Canadian agent for the British government in an assisted immigration scheme, whereby Irish settlers were located near the site of Peterborough, named after Robinson. From the late 1820s until 1836 he served on the Executive and Legislative councils. His other positions included that of commissioner of crown lands, 1827–36, and member of the Legislative Assembly, 1816–24. Robinson was brother to William B. and John Beverley.

[4]George Herchmer Markland (ca. 1790–1862) was born at Kingston. A student of John Strachan, he was considered a clever man by fellow members of the Family Compact. He was given various positions involving the clergy reserves and school matters. In addition, he was appointed to the Legislative Council in 1820 and the Executive Council in 1827. In 1833 he became inspector general of public accounts. Markland resigned all his positions in 1838, after being accused of homosexual activities.

[5]Joseph Wells (1773?–1853) entered the British army in 1798 and served in the Napoleonic Wars before coming to Canada as inspecting officer in 1815 with the rank of lieutenant-colonel. He retired on half-pay that year, at York, Upper Canada, and served as a legislative councillor, 1820–41, and executive councillor, 1830–36. In addition, he was bursar of King's College from 1827 to 1839, when he defalcated on college funds, having made unauthorized loans.

A 3　SIR F.B. HEAD'S REPLY TO AN ADDRESS OF TORONTO CITIZENS
[Correspondent and Advocate Extra, *Toronto, 28 March 1836*]

. . . Now, as regards the House of Assembly, you must know that being your representatives, they are of course answerable to you for their conduct, and as regards the Lieutenant Governor, I publicly declare to you that I am liable to be dismissed in case I should neglect your interest.

But, contrary to the practice which has existed in this or any other British colony – to Colonel Simcoe's[9] practice, or to the practice of any other Lieutenant Governor who has ever been stationed in this Province, it has suddenly been demanded of me, that the Executive Council are to be responsible for my acts, and because, I have refused, at a moment's warning, to surrender that responsibility which I owe to the people whose real interest I will never abandon, I find that every possible political effort is now making [*sic*] to blind the public mind, and to irritate its most violent passions. . . .

[6]John Henry Dunn (1794–1854) was born on the island of St. Helena and spent his early working years in the East India Company service. Coming to Upper Canada in 1820 as receiver general, he had a long career as a public servant without strong political affiliation. From 1822 to 1841 he sat on the Legislative Council and on the Executive Council in 1836. After the union of 1841 he continued to serve as receiver general and sat, for a time, as a member of the Assembly from Toronto. In 1843 he resigned his positions and later returned to England.

[7]Robert Baldwin (1804–1858) was born at York, Upper Canada. He became clerk in his father, W.W. Baldwin's, office in 1820. In the late 1820s he became active in reform politics and was recognized as a leading figure of the movement. He became the chief spokesman for the idea of responsible government in the colony. He disagreed with the ideas of the radicals and dropped out of politics after the 1836 election. Active again after the rebellion, he became joint leader, with Louis H. LaFontaine, of the reform party of Canada East and Canada West, and in 1848 headed, with LaFontaine, the first responsible government in the Canadas. He resigned in 1851.

[8]John Rolph (1793–1870) was born in Thornbury, England. He emigrated to Upper Canada in 1812 and served in the militia during the War of 1812. From 1818 to 1821 he studied law, medicine, and divinity in England. After his return he was elected to the Assembly for Middlesex in 1824. Very early in his political career he took a position for reform and became highly respected by all political factions. He refused to be identified with either moderate or radical elements in the reform movement. By 1832 he had stopped practising law and had moved to York. He was briefly a city councillor in 1834 until he resigned, and was one of the few reformers elected to the Assembly in 1836. Implicated in the rebellion, he fled to the United States where he resided until 1843. After his return, he set up a medical school in Toronto and was active in the new Clear Grit movement. In 1851–4 he was in the cabinet as a Grit minister. During the period after 1843 controversy and hostility surrounded his actions almost constantly.

[9]John Graves Simcoe (1752–1806) was prominent in the American Revolutionary War as commander of the Queen's Rangers. He became the first lieutenant-governor of Upper Canada (1791–9). During his stay in the province, which ended in 1796, he attempted to make the colonial constitution the "image and transcript" of that of Britain. In later years reformers and tories argued over the exact meaning of what Simcoe had attempted.

How can gentlemen who are sworn to be dumb be responsible to the yeomanry & people of this rising Province? How could they possibly undertake to administer this Government with mouths sealed by an oath which forbids them to disclose to any one, the valuable advice they may conscientiously impart to me? The answer to these questions is very short.

The political party which demands responsibility for my Counsel, know perfectly well, that the power and patronage of the Crown are attached to it, and it is too evident, that if they could but obtain this marrow, the empty bone of contention, namely, responsibility to the people, they would soon be too happy to throw away, and from that fatal moment would all those who nobly appreciate Liberty, who have property to lose, and who have children to think of, deeply lament that they had listened to sophistry, had been frightened by clamour, and had deserted the Representative of their Gracious Sovereign, to seek British Justice from his mute but confidential advisers.

This supposition, however, I will not permit to be realized, for never will I surrender the serious responsibility I owe to the people of this Province, and I have that reliance in their honesty. . . . I well know, the more I am assailed by a Faction, the stronger will be their loyal support —. . . .

With respect to my late council, I regret as much as you can do their resignation, but before they took the oath of secrecy (which appears to my judgment to be an oath of non-responsibility to the people) I addressed to them a note, which clearly forewarned them as follows: "I shall rely on your giving me your unbiassed opinion on all subjects respecting which I may feel it advisable to require it." Three weeks after they had joined the council they altogether in a body disputed this arrangement and accordingly we parted on a matter of dry law.

No one can deny that my view of the subject agrees with the practice of Col. Simcoe and of all the succeeding Governors of this Province down to the day of Sir J. Colborne's[10] departure – . . .

A 4   "To the Constituency of Upper Canada"
[Correspondent and Advocate, *Toronto, 27 April 1836*]

. . . Having, therefore, pointed out some of our grievances, as the fruits of the past mismanagement of our affairs, our Representatives

[10]Sir John Colborne (1778–1863) was born in Lyndhurst, England. Between his birth and death in England, he was a career soldier, rising from ensign in 1794 to field marshal. After the Napoleonic Wars he served in administrative posts in Guernsey, 1821–8, and then in Upper Canada, 1828–36. Recalled in 1836 mainly because of local criticism of his work as lieutenant-governor, Colborne was sent to Lower Canada as commander of the forces in Canada. As such he suppressed the Lower Canadian rebellions. He left Canada at the end of 1839 and was made Lord Seaton. He later served the British government in the Ionian Islands and in Ireland.

have repeatedly begged not merely for their redress, but for such an indispensible improvement of that *bad management*, as would prevent the like evils being again produced to our injury, or entailed upon our children.

Under a deep sense of the duty and responsibility they owe to the people, they, the Session before last, in a specific address to His Majesty, besides the Grievance Report, prayed in substance, that the Executive Council, appointed under the Constitutional Act to advise the Governor upon the affairs of the Province, should hereafter, consist of persons alike possessing the confidence of the King and the people. For it was then, and still is, the prevailing opinion, that a stranger arriving from England in the character of Governor, ignorant of the country, and of the wants and wishes of its inhabitants, must seek advice from some person, and from none could he procure it more properly, than from such a Council, expressly provided for that purpose, by the Constitution, and selected by the King for their talents, integrity, and public acceptability. . . .

Sir F. B. Head, in answer to these complaints, has come out, as he says, to carry into effect "remedial measures." But we ask how has he done it?

Upon his arrival here, it is true, he so far complied with the reiterated prayer of the representative body, as to introduce into the Executive Council Messrs. Dunn, Baldwin, and Rolph, in addition to the old Members – Messrs. Robinson, Markland and Wells. The people were satisfied and thankful. So were their representatives. We all felt, that, with such Councillors, Sir Francis would, though a stranger, pursue good government, which could not yield the grievances of past corruption.

We thought these appointments to the Executive Council were made in honor and good faith. But we were bitterly, cruelly and disgracefully deceived. For having sworn the Council to secrecy, as he alleges, he kept them *mute* and *dumb* from giving any advice, while in breach of all good faith, both towards them and the country, he pursued his own unadvised and arbitrary pleasure, now confirmed to be *after the fashion of his predecessors*. During three weeks, this deceitful and fraudulent system was, secretly carried, on, while it was supposed Sir Francis was in faithful and useful intercourse with the Executive Council, upon the most important affairs of the Province. . . . After three weeks, however, it was brought to light, by the honest and honorable conduct of the late Executive Council; for when they found themselves duped by Sir Francis Head, by his swearing them to secrecy, and as an act of unparralleled [sic] duplicity, never, during that period, consuling [sic] them on public affairs, according to the public expectation he had himself excited, they addressed to him a secret & confidential representation, in which they unanimously prayed, that they might according to the oath they had taken, advise

His Excellency, upon our public affairs, previously to his final and discretionary action on these affairs; and if he could not allow them to fulfil the duties so expected from them by the people and their representatives, that they might be allowed to disabuse the public mind respecting the nature and extent of the duties confided to them.

This manly and noble conduct against political fraud and deception in the secret mismanagement of our affairs, forced Sir Francis to an alternative, namely; – either to fulfil his implied pledges to the country by allowing the Executive Council to do their lawful duties, or to unveil to the public the idleness of their office, that they might not be a party to the wicked deception of the people, or be blamed for measures upon which they were never allowed to give advice.

What was the answer of Sir F. Head? – He gets into a passion with his Council and endeavours to bully them into obedience to his arbitrary Government, by telling them in plain English *to retire from their principles or leave the Council!* No doubt, in putting this alternative, he had mistaken his men; for to his surprise they adhered to their principles, and rather than dishonorably abandon them they tendered rheir [*sic*] resignations, . . .

Having thus got rid of the Council, he looks about for men to form another after his own heart; . . . voluntarily to act the part of mutes and dummies to Sir F. Head !!!

Is this the sort of government for which the people's representatives ought, out of their hard earnings, to grant supplies? . . .

A 5   SIR F.B. HEAD'S REPLY TO AN ADDRESS OF TORONTO ELECTORS
[Patriot, *Toronto, 20 May 1836*]

HIS EXCELLENCY'S REPLY.

GENTLEMEN, – No one can be more sensible that I am, that the stoppage of the Supplies has caused a general stagnation of business, which will probably end in the ruin of many of the inhabitants of this city; and in proportion as the Metropolis of the Province is impoverished, the farmers' market must be lowered, for, how can he possibly receive money when those who should consume his produce are seen flying in all directions from a land from which industry has been publicly repelled?

But I am guiltless of the distress which Upper Canada must shortly most bitterly endure; for, in my Legislative capacity I have never lost an opportunity of entreating that I might be assisted in attracting into this Province, by tranquillity, the wealth and population of the Mother Country. In this simple, peaceful doctrine I have, however, been opposed by a fatal declaration, which emanated, I regret to say, from the Metropolitan County, that "THE CONSTITUTION WAS IN DANGER!!! – and that *"the grand object was to* STOP THE SUPPLIES!"

Well, Gentlemen, this "grand object" has been gained for you, and what, I ask, has been the result?

The clerks and messengers of the Government Offices, who during a long Session have laboured unremittingly for the public service, are now surrounded by their families, perhaps penniless. Money, which would not only have improved your roads, but would have given profit and employment to thousands of deserving people, is now stagnant; – the sufferers in the late war have lost the remuneration, which was absolutely almost in their hands; – Emigration has been arrested; and instead of the English yeoman's arriving with his capital in this free British country, its mechanics in groups are seen escaping from it in every direction, as if it were a land of pestilence and famine; – all just claim for assistance from the Mother Country has vanished; every expectation of relief from internal industry is hourly diminishing. . . .

With feelings of deep melancholy I acknowledge myself to have been apparently defeated.

The object of my mission – my exertions – my opinions – my earnest recommendations, have been received by language to which I have no desire to allude, and the *grand object* of "stopping the Supplies" is now termed by its promoters the 'Victory of Reform.'

Gentlemen – I have no hesitation in saying, that another such victory would ruin this country.

But this opinion is hourly gaining ground; the good sense of the country has been aroused; the yeoman has caught a glimpse of his real enemy; the farmer begins to see who is his best friend; – in short, people of all denominations, of all religions and of different politics, rallying round the *British Flag*, are now loudly calling upon me to grant them constitutional redress.

When the verdict of the country shall have been sufficiently declared, I will promptly communicate my decision.

A 6   Sir F.B. Head's Reply to an Address of Home District Electors
[Upper Canada Gazette, *Toronto, quoted* Correspondent and Advocate, *Toronto, 8 June 1836*]

Gentlemen, – The addresses I have received, requesting me to dissolve the present House of Assembly are so numerous – the signatures are so respectable, and the firm, manly language conveyed to me from all parts of the Province, is so strongly corroborative of a feeling of general disapprobation of the harsh measures that has been resorted to by stopping the Supplies, that I shall no longer hesitate to exercise my prerogative, by dissolving the assembly.

With respect to a certain letter which you state, was "laid on the table of the House of Assembly a few hours before the prorogation of the Legislature, purporting to come from the Speaker of the House of

Assembly of Lower Canada,[11] . . ." he was not authorized to tack to his official communication his own private sentiments, nor was he in any way justified in proclaiming them in the first person plural, as follows: – ". . . If misrule went on unchecked in any of those neighboring Colonies without exciting our sympathy, your ills would soon become our ills, and ours would reach you in return." "If you have to complain of evils similar to ours, or of any other evils, all Constitutional means in the power of the people of this Province, would readily be resorted to, to aid you in their removal. . . ."

The people of Upper Canada detest democracy, they revere their Constitutional Charter, and are consequently staunch in allegiance to their King.

They are perfectly aware that there exist in the Lower Province one or two individuals who inculcate the idea, that this Province is about to be disturbed by the interference of foreigners, whose power and whose numbers will prove invincible.

In the name of every Regiment of Militia in Upper Canada, I publicly promulgate – *Let them come if they dare!*

A 7   REFORMERS OF TORONTO TO SIR F.B. HEAD, 1 JUNE 1836
[Correspondent and Advocate, *Toronto, 8 June 1836*]

A REFUTATION
OF SIR FRANCIS BOND HEAD'S
SLANDERS AND MISTATEMENTS. [*sic*]

To His Excellency Sir F. Bond Head.

Having observed that a portion of our fellow citizens have addressed your Excellency upon the subject of the stoppage of the supplies and that the said address purports to be from the "*Electors* of the City of Toronto,"we deem it a duty we owe to our representatives, our fellow subjects throughout the Province, and to ourselves, to address Your Excellency and disabuse the public mind upon the subject which now agitates the Province, and to assign some of the causes which have brought us into our present unhappy condition. – But before we enter

[11]The letter referred to was sent by Louis-Joseph Papineau (1786–1871). A native of Quebec, he was called to the bar in 1811 and elected a member of the Assembly of Lower Canada in 1814, after serving in the War of 1812. In 1815 he was made Speaker, a position he held almost continually until the rebellion. One of the most popular politicians in Lower Canada, he was radical in his policies. Implicated in the rebellion, he fled the country once its fortunes took a downward turn. He lived in the United States, then France until 1844. From 1848 to 1851 and from 1852 to 1854 he served in the Assembly of the united Canadas.

The letter in question here contained some personal political reflections, though it was supposed to be an official communication.

further upon the subject we desire, in answer to the repeated slanders freely circulated by those who profess admiration of your Excellency's administration, (although limited to the brief period of four months) and would have your Excellency believe that all those who disagree with them in politics, are desirous of separating this colony from the mother country; most unequivocally and solemnly, in the face of the country to declare our warm attachment to our revered Sovereign and the Constitution, and our earnest desire that by a continuation of the subsisting connection between the mother country and this colony our posterity for ages yet to come may glory in the name of Britons. – Yet as we never can, we trust they never will, submit to tyranny and oppression; . . .

In following up the objects we have in view, we will not stop to remark upon the address headed, "we the inhabitant electors of the City of Toronto," and signed only by three or four hundred persons, many of whom do not reside even within the township of York! but shall proceed freely to canvass your Excellency's reply thereto; . . . we can assure your Excellency that as the representative of our most gracious Sovereign you command the highest considerations of our respect; but we regret to say, our personal respect for you as an individual is impaired when we perceive you say *"No one can be more sensible than I am that the stoppage of the supplies has caused a general stagnation of business which will probably end in the ruin of many of the Inhabitants of the city."* What! your Excellency *sensible* that the nonpayment of about *four thousand pounds next July*, and the like sum in *January next* has *already causnd* [*sic*] *a general stagnation of business*! Is it possible! that the evil Councillors by whom your Excellency is surrounded have not explained to your Excellency that stopping the supplies by the House of Assembly was nothing more than saying, "The amount of about £8000 which you require to pay the Clerks of the public offices their half yearly salary in July and January next, we will not grant to you in advance, you have refused to listen to our opinions as the representatives of the people, in the appointment of your Executive Council, we have no confidence in the men you have chosen, and therefore to grant you the money of our constituents in advance would be falsiifying [*sic*] our declared opinions;" . . . We feel as British subjects, as men possessing independent minds, & moral honesty! that weare [*sic*] bound to contradict the assertion, that the stoppage of these paltry payments in July and January next is the cause of the general "stagnation of business," or even of a depression in trade; and you know, or ought to know by your advisers [*sic*] information this stagnation commenced before your arrival in this colony, arising from daily pressure on our industry by the accumulating evils of bad government, while now you yourself are actually capping the deformed pyramid the sooner to tumble to the ground, preparatory to this ruin. Other auxilary [*sic*] circumstances have occurred to increase the depression you speak of, as the failure of the wheat crops last year, which being generally grown was not marketable, another was a difference in the relative value of gold and silver between the United States and this Province which afforded the Americans the means of draining our Banks during the last winter of upwards of fifty thousand pounds in specie, and which necessarily obliged our Banks to lessen their discounts.

But there is another and more immediate cause. Your Excellency in another part of your answer is made to say "But I am guiltless of the distress which Upper Canada must shortly most bitterly endure." We wish, sincerely wish, we could endorse this assertion of Your Excellency, but it is impossible. Who we would ask was it kept the clerks and messengers of the Legislature . . . out of their hard earnings; *but Your Excellency*? Who we would ask has been the cause of "money remaining stagnant which would not only have improved our roads, but would have given profit and employment to thousands of deserving people," *but Your Excellency*? . . . Who has withheld the means of Education from the children of the several districts in the Province, *but Your Excellency*? . . . Who has prevented the improvement of various Bridges that are going to decay in the several districts of the Province, *but Your Excellency*? . . . Did not Your Excellency refuse to authorize in the usual way the contingencies of the Legislature to be paid, thereby depriving the clerks and servants of the two Houses of their wages justly due, . . . and did the stoppage of the supplies by the House *necessarily* oblige Your Excellency to do this wrong, any more than it did Earl Gosford,[12] who had no supplies granted, yet nevertheless paid the contingencies? Did stopping the supplies necessarily compel Your Excellency to withhold the assent of our Gracious Sovereign to all the bills providing for the expenditure of money upon the various public improvements and for other purposes herein before recited to the amount of *one hundred and fifty thousand pounds*, any more than it did *Earl Gosford*, who had no *supplies granted*, yet gave the royal assent to all the money bills that were passed for the various improvements proposed in Lower Canada.

If the Colonial Minister has furnished one set of instructions for the Lower Province and another for the Upper Province, we pray Your Excellency to make public those upon which you acted . . . and we shall then most readily acquit Your Excellency of any intention to inflict punishment upon the people of this Province, . . . but should Your Excellency not condescend, or be unable to do so, we cannot but believe that the advice upon which Your Excellency acted was given

---

[12] Archibald Acheson, second Earl of Gosford (1776–1849) was an Irish earl and a Whig. He was lord lieutenant of Ireland, 1832–5, and then governor-in-chief of British North America, 1835–7. He also headed a royal commission to inquire into the state of affairs in Lower Canada. Gosford resigned just days before the rebellion there, when it was clear his neutral position on local affairs pleased no one.

by interested individuals, devoid of principle and honor, whose only aim was to embroil Your Excellency with our representatives, in the hope that you might be induced to dissolve the Parliament and afford them an opportunity of again obtaining power by imposing upon the credulity of the people.

We deeply regret to perceive that your Excellency has been induced to liken the country of our birth and adoption, to a *"land of pestilence and famine."* For although we have before remarked there was to a certain extent a failure in some of the crops last year, yet we have no reason to believe that the supreme Being, has visited any portion of this naturally highly favored Province with the heavy dispensations expressed by your Excellency; and with the exception of that dreadful malady the Cholera, with which we were afflicted in the years 1832 and 1834, we know of no pestilence existing besides that of your Excellency being surrounded by parasites and sycophants who will sacrifice the best interests of the Province to secure their own aggrandizement. . . .

For us again to request your Excellency to dismiss such men from your Council would, we are convinced, prove useless; but we confidently await the views and pleasure of his Majesty's Government on the subject, satisfied that the Constitntional [*sic*] Sovereign of the British Empire will ever uphold the constitutional rights of his loyal Canadian subjects, and will require that his representative so exercise the prerogative of the Crown, as to ensure the peace, welfare and prosperity of the People.

A 8   DECLARATION OF THE BRITISH CONSTITUTIONAL SOCIETY
Toronto, 10 May 1836
[*Public Archives of Canada (PAC), Alpheus Jones Papers, v. 1, pamphlet*]

. . . The fundamental principle and object of the Society is to PERPETUATE THE CONNEXION BETWEEN UPPER CANADA AND THE UNITED KINGDOM OF GREAT BRITAIN AND IRELAND. This is the END – all other objects of the Society are but means for securing that end . . . satisfied that the Constitution conferred on us by the Mother Country is well adapted to secure our peace, welfare, and good government, we desire to uphold that Constitution in its integrity, and are determined to resist all innovation upon it, whether proceeding from open enemies, or from the more insidious attacks of pretended friends.

A calm and dispassionate review of the events that have occurred for some time past has led us to the conclusion, that a crisis has arrived which renders it the bounden duty of every true lover of his country to stand forth and join heart and hand with his fellow-subjects in sustaining the Constitution, and resisting the attempts at its subversion which have lately assumed a more tangible shape, and which *must be put down*, unless we are disposed to submit tamely to be revolutionized without even a shew of resistance. . . .

In this uncalled for proceeding [the assembly's stopping of the money bills], more than in any other, the revolutionary views of the party are disclosed. Let the honest, intelligent, and loyal Farmer, or other inhabitant of this Province, ask himself this plain question – Whether he at any time desires to see the Courts of Justice impeded in their progress – the prisoners confined in the gaols of the Province left untried – the Offices of the Surveyor General – the Register – the Receiver General – in short, all those Offices in which their own business, and that of their fellow-subjects is transacted closed, and access to them completely denied? – Would they not pronounce those who would wantonly produce such a state of things, as enemies to the peace, welfare, and good government of the Province, and wholly undeserving of their confidence. . . . these men under the name of Reform seek *Revolution*, . . .

Under these circumstances the British Constitutional Society is re-organized. Not for any party purpose – not for any local or minor consideration, but because we think the facts above detailed prove, that there is danger at hand – danger to our peace – danger to our established rights – danger to our Constitution. We, therefore, call on all loyal men to join us. *The rallying word is the maintenance of the Union with the Mother Country – if need arise, it shall be the battle cry* – . . .

W.B. JARVIS,[13]
PRESIDENT,
British Constitutional Society.

GEORGE GURNETT,[14] }
JOHN KENT,[15]   }   *Joint Secretaries.*

[13]William Botsford Jarvis (1799–1864) was born in Fredericton, New Brunswick, and moved at an early age to Upper Canada, becoming a student of John Strachan at York. In 1827 he was appointed sheriff of the Home District, a position he held until 1849. In 1830, a government supporter, he was elected MLA for the town of York, though he lost the election of 1834. During the rebellion he commanded a regiment of militia.

[14]George Gurnett (*ca.* 1792–1861) was born in Sussex, England, emigrating to North America while quite young. Some time before 1826 he settled in Ancaster, publishing the *Gore Gazette* there. In 1829 he began publication of the *Courier of Upper Canada* in York and continued to do so until 1837. That year he became both mayor of Toronto and clerk of the Home District, a position he held until 1861. In the rebellion year, 1837, he was also a justice of the peace and a major in the militia. In later years he continued to be active in city affairs.

[15]John Kent (*fl.* 1807–1888) was born in England in 1807 and came to Upper Canada in 1833 as headmaster of Upper Canada College's preparatory school. He left the college in 1838, serving for a time as Lieutenant-Governor Arthur's secretary. Earlier the editor of the ephemeral *Canadian Literary Magazine*, he edited the

A 9   Rev. Alexander Ross[16] to John Joseph[17]
St. Thomas, 22 June 1836
[*PAC, Upper Canada Sundries, v. 167, pp. 91476-9*]

. . . In my letter of the 13th May I had expressed my belief that radicalism in this part of the country might be greatly reduced if some wise and firm efforts were made for the purpose. It occurred to me that the most promising mode of accomplishing the object in view would be to form all the loyal inhabitants of Dunwich, Aldborough, Orford. & Howard into a constitutional society. For this purpose two meetings were held, one at Orford on the 14th, & one at Dunwich on the 15th – The meeting at Orford was numerous, and the business of the day proceeded with the greatest regularity, and, altogether to my satisfaction. At Dunwich matters were also managed sufficiently well, but the meeting was not numerous. This was owing, I think, to a defect in the notice previously given for the purpose of calling the people together – This however is a matter of slight moment, as the Society has been fully constituted, and the members of the committee are now active in obtaining subscribers. I took care that in the resolutions framing the constitution of the Society nothing of a disputable nature should be inserted, while they are sufficiently implicit in excluding every shade of radicalism. In a very short time I hope to be able to transmit to you a list of the members of the Society, with an address to His Excellency, and a copy of the resolutions . . . . I had expected that a St. Thomas constitutional society should have been formed ere now. Had this been done, It would I believe have been better – They had however a meeting for the purpose of securing as many votes as possible at the ensuing election for constitutional candidates – and this in existing circumstances may answer the same end. The candidates are Cols. Bostwick[18] and Clench.[19] perhaps we cannot calculate with

---

Anglican newspaper, the *Church*, 1841–3. He later moved to England, then to Madeira and the Azores.

[16]Alexander Ross, who settled in Upper Canada about 1830, was the Church of Scotland minister in Aldborough Township. Evidently he did not win much favour among his parishioners, the editor of the *Christian Examiner and Presbyterian Review* recording in 1838 that he was "a dull, lifeless person – naturally *dazed* – and perhaps of late somewhat avaricious," and a drunkard into the bargain. In 1839 he was removed from his post.

[17]John Joseph (1801?–1851), a Jewish English civil servant, accompanied Francis Bond Head to Upper Canada in 1836 as his civil secretary. He was reappointed by Sir George Arthur in 1838 but, soon considered inadequate by Arthur for the appointment, he was moved to the clerkship of the Legislative Council. From 1847 to.1851 he served as clerk of the Executive Council. He may have died by his own hand.

[18]John Bostwick (1780–1849) was born in Massachusetts, the son of a Church of England priest. Arriving in Upper Canada prior to 1804, he fought for the British in the War of 1812. He settled at Port Stanley in 1817, where he established a warehouse. Sheriff of the London District, 1805–17, he also became a colonel in the militia, postmaster, a magistrate, and a collector of customs. In 1836 he was an unsuccessful tory candidate in Middlesex. Suffering financial misfortunes, he died almost penniless.

[19]Joseph Brant Clench (*ca.* 1790–1857), a veteran of the War of 1812, was an

certainty on their return, as the county of Middlesex has been for some
years back extremely fertile in producing the weeds of radicalism.
With this I transmit you a copy of what our precious agitators call the
British constitution. This vile stuff is a specimen of the jargon with
which the party endeavour to wile our simple minded yeomanry into
the gulph of treason & destruction. It is quite well understood here that
the party is led by one Bela Shaw[20] a storeKeeper from the states. He is
also /unluckily/ postmaster of the village. It may truly be said that he
carries on his work under ground. The visible instruments are Kent[21]
and Talbot,[22] editors of the liberal newspaper – Kent is a scotch,
Talbot an Irish adventurer. The title *liberal* given to the said paper
furnishes a fair example of the singular application of words in which
the party delight so much. They have certainly made no small progress
in the act of perverting language. We may however now rest satisfied
that they cannot proceed much farther. Even in Middlesex I have good
hopes that they shall be beat. The Rev. Dond. McKenzie[23] of Zorra
who lately visited this part of the country for the purpose of assisting
me in certain pastoral duties, is now here. He intends to visit London,
Lobo, and Williams if it be in his power. His influence with our
countrymen is undoubtedly considerable, and he is quite disposed to
exert it to the utmost – We separate to day, and hope to meet again at

Indian storekeeper at Fort George from 1813 to 1826. From 1821 to about 1828 he
served as clerk of the Niagara District Court. In 1829 he was a clerk in the Indian
Office at York, and the next year was appointed superintendent of the Bay of Quinté
and Rice Lake Indians. He later moved to Middlesex, running unsuccessfully as a
candidate there in the 1836 elections. In 1837 he became the superintendent of the
Chippewas and Munceys of the Thames. In 1854 charges of mismanagement led to his
removal from that post.

[20]Bela Shaw, an American who had entered Upper Canada about 1823, became the
owner of a thriving general store in St. Thomas. A prominent local politician and
owner of the St. Thomas *Liberal*, he was elected clerk of Yarmouth Township in 1836
and 1837 and president of the St. Thomas political union in 1837. His political
activities led to his dismissal as postmaster in 1836 and to his being questioned over
possible involvement in the rebellion in 1837.

[21]John Kent, who was evidently a Scot, came into the St. Thomas area from New
York State in 1828. From 1834 to 1836 he edited the *Liberal*, publishing briefly the
Enquirer after the demise of the *Liberal* in 1837.

[22]John Talbot (1797–1874) was the son of Richard Talbot who brought his family
and a group of Irish Anglican immigrants into London Township in 1818. A former
schoolteacher, John Talbot became an editor of the *Liberal* in 1836, carrying on the
paper after John Kent left it. Though not a rebel, he fled the province on the outbreak
of rebellion, fearing tory reprisals. He settled in the United States, dying in Illinois.

[23]Donald McKenzie (1798–1884) was born in Inverness, Scotland, and came to
Canada with Alexander Ross about 1830. McKenzie was ordained a Church of
Scotland minister in 1834. That year he came to Zorra Township, largely settled by
Highlanders, assuming direction of the church there in 1835. Conducting his services
in Gaelic for a time at least, he exercised considerable control over his parishioners and
did so until his retirement in 1872. Over the years he preached temperance as well as
the Gospel.

the London election, and afterwards Mr. McKenzie will proceed with all expedition to the Oxford election. Upon the whole our horizon is not cloudy. As to the final result of matters in the province we cannot for a moment doubt. I think that I can see distinctly radicalism writhing in the throes of death; and I cannot but believe that the name of Sir Francis Bond Head will long, long, be remembered for having transfixed the monster –

A 10   MAHLON BURWELL[24] TO JOHN JOSEPH
Port Talbot, 11 June 1836
[*PAC, Upper Canada Sundries, v. 167, pp. 91306-8*]

Confidential

Sir,

I believe you have heard through Mr. Askin[25] the Clerk of the Peace for the London District that I am a candidate for the representation of the Town of London. A majority of the Freeholders have promised to give me their suffrages, but there is no security for mens actions in these trying times. The persons whose names follow have performed their Settlement duties in the Town of London and obtained Colonel Talbot's[26] certificates to that effect – namely – Christopher Williams,

[24]Mahlon Burwell (1783–1846) was born in New Jersey. His family emigrated to Upper Canada after the American Revolution, and his father James became a registered United Empire Loyalist. Mahlon settled in Southwold in 1802. A surveyor, he laid out many townships in the western part of the province, acquiring large properties for himself and founding the village of Port Burwell. In 1809 he was appointed registrar of Middlesex County. He served in the War of 1812 and was captured by the Americans. Thereafter he was active in the militia, becoming colonel of the 2nd Regiment of Middlesex in 1822. A close associate of Thomas Talbot, he was elected to the Assembly in 1812, 1816, 1820, 1830, and 1836, where he gained a reputation as a vigorous tory. Though raised a Quaker, he had become an Anglican and he strongly championed the interests of his church in the Assembly. He also took a strong interest in educational matters there. Like many men of influence, he acquired a host of offices, serving as a magistrate, a postmaster, and a collector of customs among other things. This helped make him particularly obnoxious to local reformers.

[25]John Baptist Askin (1788–1869) was born at Detroit into a prominent fur-trading family. Having served in the War of 1812, he held a post in the army commissariat until 1819, when he moved to Vittoria in the London District. That year he became the district clerk and the next year the clerk of the District Court. In 1832 after London had become the district capital he and his wife moved there, where he built up large properties. A strident tory, he was active in many aspects of public life, holding a commission as a major in the militia in 1837.

[26]Thomas Talbot (1771–1853) was born at Malahide in County Dublin, Ireland. He served in the British army, rising to the rank of colonel and serving in Upper Canada as John Graves Simcoe's aide-de-camp. In 1801 he secured 5,000 acres of land on the north shore of Lake Erie and began his settlement activities there in 1803. Over time he helped settled twenty-seven townships, acquiring almost 50,000 acres for himself. Something of a despot by inclination, he became a controversial figure, revered by

Peter Rogers,[27] Michael Burk, William Snell, John O'Brien, Robert Fennel, & Isaac Carling[28] – their Petitions will be forwarded to an agent at Toronto (I believe a Mr. James Henderson[29]) by the same mail which takes this letter, and if they are acted upon immediately,[30] and the Patents enveloped by mail to "John B. Askin, Esquire, Clerk of the Peace – London" in a few days they may be in time for the Town Election, and then, there will be no question of my return. I left London immediately after getting through with my street canvass, and am exerting myself with many others of the friends to the Kings Government to secure the Election of Messrs. Bostwick & Clench for the County of Middlesex instead of Parke[31] and Moore.[32] By the bye, the Petitions I have mentioned may have left London by this evening's mail, and referred to the Executive Council before this letter will arrive – In that event a memorandum of the names of the Petitioners might be given to Mr. Beikie[33] to prevent any of them being forgotten.

---

some, despised by others. Reformers objected to his high-handedness and his tory sympathies, while many in the provincial administration disliked his virtual independence of their authority. In 1838 the British and provincial governments removed the Talbot Settlement from his control.

[27]This may have been the Peter Rogers who accompanied Richard Talbot's settlers into London Township in 1818. He came as a servant or an apprentice.

[28]Isaac Carling was the Upper Canadian-born son of Thomas Carling who established the Carling Brewing and Malting Company in London ca. 1840. In 1848 Isaac and his brother John formed a partnership to operate a tannery in Exeter.

[29]This may have referred to James Henderson of Toronto (1800–1874), a Scot who had come to Upper Canada in 1832.

[30]The various names mentioned in the document as seeking patents all have check marks beside them. All got their patents in good time.

[31]Thomas Parke (d. 1864) was born in County Wicklow, Ireland, and settled in Upper Canada in 1820. A London builder and architect, he represented Middlesex in the Assembly from 1834 to 1844. After the rebellion he did all he could to maintain the reform cause in the Assembly, but upon joining the Sydenham ministry in 1841 was held by many to have deserted reform ranks. From 1841 until 1845 he was the surveyor general of the united Canadas.

[32]Elias Moore (b. ca. 1776) was a native of New Jersey. His Quaker father fled the Revolution, settling his family first in Nova Scotia, then in 1811 in Upper Canada, where Elias and several of his brothers became prosperous farmers near the Erie shore. A temperance advocate and a philanthropist, he was popular in his locale, holding several township offices in Yarmouth and being elected as a reformer to the Assembly in 1834 and 1836 from Middlesex. In 1837 he became a member of the St. Thomas political union. He was accused of complicity in the revolt and, indeed, a son of his did go to Oakland. After the rebellion he was jailed at London for several months but was never tried. This seems not to have ended his public influence, for in 1842 he was made a magistrate.

[33]John Beikie (1766–1839), born in Gibraltar, was living in Cornwall, Upper Canada, in the 1790s. He moved to York about 1800, becoming sheriff of the Home District from 1810 to 1815. He was Stormont and Russell's representative in the Assembly, 1812–16, serving later as the clerk of the Executive Council. An Anglican, he was deputy provincial grand master of the Masons from 1825 to 1839.

P.*S*. – Two other persons, by name, – John Douglas,[34] & Edmund Raymond,[35] have sent their Petitions – they will vote for me – Please to refer their Petitions to the Executive Council as soon as presented.

A 11   STAFFORD KIRKPATRICK[36] TO ALEXANDER KIRKPATRICK[37]
Peterborough, 18 July 1836
[*Public Archives of Manitoba, Stafford Kirkpatrick Letters, photostats at Trent University Archives*]

I am quite ashamed of my long silence but the fact is that our new general election has but just terminated and in common with all good & loyal subjects I have been as busy as possible – The revolutionists have been defeated as there have been returned 43 Constitutionalists & 19 only [revolutionists ?]. I dont think the supplies will be stopped again in a hurry. . . .

A 12   "THE LATE UPPER CANADA ELECTIONS"
[Liberal, *St. Thomas*, *quoted* Correspondent and Advocate, *Toronto, 3 Aug. 1836*]

We have now the Election returns from all parts of the Province, and we are enabled to state, that the same means were made use of in every Town and County, that so disgracefully signalized the Middlesex Election. the [*sic*] same unholy exertions of the State-paid Priests – the same exhibition of ruffianism, club-law and intimidation; and above all, heaps of new Deeds, *the ink scarcely dry on them*, were sent in all directions, not only the week proceeding [*sic*], but absolutely the very week of the Elections. . . .

A 13   NELSON GORHAM[38] ON THE NORTH RIDING OF YORK
ELECTION
[*Gorham to* Constitution, *Toronto, 4 July 1836*]

. . . After a few votes had been polled, to the surprise and

[34]John Douglas, Upper Canadian-born, moved from Fort Erie to the town of London about 1834, where he became active in the militia, holding the rank of captain in 1837. He was a prominent figure locally, being appointed an associate justice in 1839 and running unsuccessfully as a conservative in the Assembly elections of 1841. Shortly thereafter financial disaster struck. His firm went bankrupt and he fled to the United States, possibly to Alabama.

[35]This was probably Edmund Raymond the hatter and furrier (1809–1888), born in Buffalo, who had moved to Fort Erie before locating in London in 1831.

[36]Stafford Kirkpatrick (1809–1858) was an Irish Protestant who emigrated to Upper Canada in 1829 to escape a paternity suit. He settled in Toronto, where, under his brother Thomas, he completed his training for the bar. He became Peterborough's first lawyer, then moved for a time to Kingston before finally establishing himself and his family in Peterborough in 1837.

[37]Alexander Kirkpatrick, who lived near Dublin, Ireland, was Stafford's father.

[38]Nelson Gorham (b. *ca.* 1812) was an Upper Canadian. He was the son of Eli

astonishment of every body but those with whom the vile plot had originated, an objection was raised against receiving the votes of those electors who had once resided in the United States, unless the voter produced a written certificate of his having taken the oath of allegiance before some person duly authorized to administer the same; by this Tory stroke of policy about 100 were deprived of their elective franchise, and of all voice in the representation of their country. In vain was it that Mr. M'Intosh[39] protested against this most unjust, partial and tyrannical decision. In vain was it for him to argue the question; argument and justness were of no avail. In vain was it to desire the Returning Officer to qualify the electors to their subjectship, and to refer him to the form of the oath Captain M'Auly[40] had handed to him, and by which he had sworn several. In vain was it that he was told there was nothing between the lids of the Provincial Statutes requiring any such certificate. In vain was he told that many of those voters had volunteered their services, and fought and bled during the last war (the names of such will be given if required.) In vain was he told that the most of those voters were men who had been in the country for twenty, thirty, thirty-five, and forty years – men who were the first to penetrate the forests of Canada, and encounter every obstacle and disadvantage incident to a new and wilderness country – that they were the men whose exertions had subdued and cultivated all the fine country north of the ridge, and brought it to its present state of improvement – men, too, who have long believed themselves the dupes and objects of oppression, by an irresponsible Government; and though goaded, galled, and vexed into a state of feeling almost beyond forbearance, yet were never heard to talk of "casting about in their minds' eye for some new state of political existence,"or to begin to openly form themselves

---

Gorham who came from Connecticut in 1808 and who opened the first woollen mill in the province. Nelson had completed his education at a college in Aurora, New York, by 1831. He then worked in mills in Upper Canada. He was a nephew by marriage to Samuel Lount.

[39]John McIntosh (1796–1853) was born in Scotland. His family emigrated in 1801, settling in York in 1803. John served in the War of 1812 and afterwards he and his two brothers operated a schooner. About 1825 he built the Sun Tavern which his brother-in-law Thomas Elliot took over about 1830. With extensive real estate interests, McIntosh dropped out of most other business ventures in the 1830s. He represented the north riding of York in the Assembly, 1834–41, and was related to William Lyon Mackenzie by marriage.

[40]John Simcoe Macaulay (McAuly) (1791–1855) was the son of an army surgeon who accompanied John Graves Simcoe to Upper Canada. He became an officer of the Royal Engineers, hence his popular name "Captain Macaulay," and became, too, a professor of fortifications at the Royal Military Academy at Woolwich. In 1838, a colonel, he commanded the militia forces in Toronto and helped plan fortifications at Port Colborne. A wealthy man, he sat on the Legislative Council, 1839–41, and served as a government commissioner of the Welland Canal. In the 1841 elections to the Assembly he ran unsuccessfully in the third riding of York as a government supporter. In 1843 he retired to England.

into rifle corps. . . . A Mr. Abram Lepard[41] came forward to vote, who had been in the country thirty-five years, had drawn land from the Crown in the Township of Whitchurch, but had sold that land, and bought another lot in the same Township, for which he had held a transfer deed in fee simple for twenty years past; he was refused his vote, for want of a certificate of having taken the oath of allegiance; he returned home, and procured the Crown deed of the first-mentioned lot, and offered it as a sufficient certificate, but was refused, because the deed, though in his name, yet was not for the identical land for which he intended voting. A third time he pressed his vote and was refused and had eventually to go and take the oath of allegiance again, and get a certificate, though he had taken it before three times. Men, too, there were who when they came forward to vote, though personally known to the Returning-Officer to be worth from $20,000 to $30,000, and mostly in freehold property, yet were required to swear to their freehold, as if to insult and trample upon their feelings by such vindictive proceedings. . . .

A 14   ELECTION CORRUPTION
[Correspondent and Advocate, *Toronto, 6 July 1836*]

. . . Previous to and even during the election a vast number of deeds under Sir F.B. Head's name and seal of office were issued by the Government, under unusual and extraordinary circumstances, and were distributed at the very hustings by Government Agents to poor men, whose integrity was not sufficient to bear up against such disgraceful corruption. This was notoriously the case in the County of Simcoe. Men only for a short time residing in the country were thus brought up to the hustings to exercise the elective franchise in favor of Sir Francis Bond Head, their mistaken benefactor, whilst the votes of many old inhabitants of thirty or forty years standing, who fought and bled in defence of the Province during the last war; men of considerable property and influence, whose right to the franchise was never before questioned, were ignominiously rejected, ostensibly because they could not immediately produce their certificate of sworn allegiance to His Majesty which, being never before required, they neglected to bring with them, but in reality because they were known to be favorable to Reform, and hostile to the policy of the Executive. . . .

Even government deeds for quarter acre lots near the mouth of the Credit were executed during the very week of the election, and voted on immediately after, in order to prevent the return of Mr.

---

[41] Abram Lepard was an early settler in Whitchurch Township and was probably one of the Pennsylvania Germans who migrated to the province about the turn of the nineteenth century.

MACKENZIE.[42] The reader may form some idea of the means employed to defeat that gentleman, from the fact, that he polled fifty votes more this election, than he did in the election of 1834, and was yet beaten by a majority of 95, shewing in one small riding an increase in the constituent body of 145, notwithstanding the announcement lately made that the industrious classes were flying from a country, from which *industry had been publicly repelled, as if it were a land of pestilence and famine.* . . .

That similar sinister influences were also used in other parts of the Province there can be little, if any, doubt. For instance in the County of Halton several voted on Government Deeds, executed between the 25th and 29th of last month. . . .

A 15   HARMANNUS SMITH'S[43] REPLY TO THE REFORMERS OF BRANTFORD
Barton, 17 August 1836
[Archives of Ontario (PAO), Mackenzie–Lindsey Clippings, No. 2464]

Gentlemen – I thank you for the expression of approbation and confidence in my capacity of representative of this county, and agree with you that it was not public opinion that put me down, but was accomplished by many bad votes – votes on freeholds within the corporation of the town of Hamilton, that is represented by its own member – the foreign auxiliaries – the votes of married women, whose husbands voted at the some [*sic*] poll, which is a species of votes I never heard of being received by any returning officer in Canada before[44] – and lastly, and most corruptly of all, by votes on patent deeds issued from the Government office for the express purpose, and some of them dated after the election commenced. A pretty effectual way this to get a verdict of the country. . . .

[42]William Lyon Mackenzie (1795–1861) was born near Dundee, Scotland. He had a rather erratic education and little success in various business ventures. In 1820 he went out to Canada under the sponsorship of the Lesslie family. He worked as a partner with the Lesslies as a merchant at Dundas until 1823, when the partnership was dissolved because of personal differences. In 1824 he founded the *Colonial Advocate* newspaper at Queenston, but soon moved it to the capital, York, where he quickly became a strong critic of the Family Compact. First elected to the Assembly in 1828, he survived repeated expulsions by tory elements to emerge as a radical leader of the reform movement; he was very popular in his riding north of Toronto. Frustration with the lack of progress turned him to rebellion in 1837. After a long exile in the United States, he returned to Canada West in 1850 and resumed both his journalistic career and his political activity. Though relatively prominent in the 1850s, he did not have the influence he had had in the 1830s.

[43]Harmannus Smith (1790–1872) was born in the Gore District. He trained as both a lawyer and a doctor but devoted himself to medicine. He enjoyed a long political career. Elected as a reformer in Wentworth in 1834, he was also a successful candidate for the Assembly of the united Canadas in 1841, 1844, and 1848. In 1856 he became a legislative councillor but was defeated in the council elections of 1860.

[44]Widows who owned patented property could vote in elections.

A 16   REV. JOHN RYERSON[45] TO REV. EGERTON RYERSON[46]
Toronto, 25 September 1836
[*United Church Archives, Ryerson Papers*]

. . . there is nothing *new* in this *new* part of the world. The late ellections agitated the Societies very Much in some places, but they are now very generally, I believe, settling down in "quietness & assureance," . . .

The Political State of the Province is, I think better than what it has been for Many years. The present house of Parliment, is decidedly superior – in respectability & talent to any we have ever had in this province & I Doubt not will prove so in point [of] honour & usefulness. The Radicals Met with a Most tremendous overthrow & they come Down so suddenly & so swiftly from their lofty ellivation. that they felt it & still feel it most sensiblely. They were just about to Cease [seize] the prey & behold it was instantly & forever hid, if not from their wicked eyes – yet from the reach of their [rotten?] grasp. Not one Radical was returned from the bounds of the Bay of Quinty District, The Preache[r]s & I laboured to the utmost extent of our ability to keep every scamp of them out, & we succeeded. & had the Preachers of Done their Duty in every place; not a *ninny* of them would have been returned to this parlement. But as it is there is just enough "escaped" to tell the fate of the rest. & to Moan over the Dissolotions of their Miserably wicked & ruinous crafts. . . . The Governor is a talented man; but very little Magisterial Dignity about him[.] He is also a frolicking little Cur as you ever saw[47] & he takes good care to let every one know that *he* esteams every Day alike, traveling on sabbaths the *same* as other *Days*: indeed he seams to have no idea of Relegion atall, but is purely a Man of plasure. . . .

[45]John Ryerson (1800–1878) was born in Charlotteville, Upper Canada, into a United Empire Loyalist and Anglican family. He served in the War of 1812, and, like some of his family, converted to Methodism in the postwar period. He began preaching in 1820 and in 1825 was made an elder. He was extremely prominent in church affairs, helping create the independent Canadian church and negotiate its union with the British Wesleyans. He largely designed the policy pursued in the 1830s of avoiding any church association with political radicalism. In 1843 he became president of the Wesleyan Methodists and continued to be active within the church until his death.
[46]Adolphus Egerton Ryerson (1803–1882) was born at Charlotteville, Upper Canada. He was educated at the district grammar school and entered the Methodist ministry in 1825, quickly becoming one of the church's most prominent clerics. In 1829 he became the editor of the influential *Christian Guardian*. He was editor until 1831, and served as such 1833–7 and 1838–40, wielding considerable political power in the process and coming into conflict with the radical reformers. As the province's chief superintendent of education, 1844–76, he made an enduring contribution to the province.
[47]The passage from "cur" to "saw" has been struck with pencil and "Man" substituted.

A 17   CHARLES DUNCOMBE'S[48] PETITION TO THE HOUSE OF
COMMONS
*[Public Record Office (PRO), CO 42, v. 437, p. 32, microfilm in
PAO]*

HUMBLEY SHEWETH,

That your Petitioner has been deputed by the Reformers of that
Province [Upper Canada] to lay before His Majesty's Government
and your Honourable House the dangerous crisis at which the affairs of
that Province have unhappily arrived, through the unconstitutional
violence and outrage practised and sanctioned by Sir F. Head, the
present Lieutenant Governor, and those under his immediate influence
and control, at the late elections, for the purpose of obtaining a
majority in the House of Assembly.

That in the County of Oxford, where your Petitioner was a
successful candidate, John B. Askin, Esq. Returning Officer, in the
early part of his election, while the contest was doubtful, refused to
take the votes of many Reformers, long resident in the Province,
though they had voted at former elections, and offered to take the oaths
required by the Statute, some of whom had taken the Oath of
Allegiance before James Ferguson,[49] Esq., Returning Officer at the
last election, and now the opposing Candidate and Registrar for the
County of Oxford, upon the ground that they had not the certificate
with them of their having taken the Oath which had not formerly been
required at any of your Petitioner's previous elections. They declared

---

[48]Charles Duncombe (1792–1867) was born in Connecticut, acquiring a medical
education in New York City. In 1819 he moved to Upper Canada, settling first in
Delaware Township in the London District, then in St. Thomas, where he established a
large practice. In 1828 he moved his family to Bishopsgate, near Brantford,
developing large property holdings in that area. He was well known and widely
respected, becoming the regimental surgeon of the 2nd Middlesex militia in 1825 and a
member of the provincial Board of Health in 1832. He took an interest in politics,
holding moderate views, and was elected to the Assembly for Oxford in 1830 and
1834. Public and private grievances led to his becoming a radical reformer in the
1834–6 House. In December 1837 he led the rebellion in the Brantford area.
Unsuccessful, he fled the province to become active with the Patriots. He eventually
settled in California, where he was elected to the state legislature as a Republican.

[49]The document reproduced is a printed version of Duncombe's petition. An error
was obviously made in transcription, for Duncombe must have referred here, not to
James Ferguson, but to James Ingersoll (1801–1886), the registrar of Oxford and
defeated tory candidate in the election of 1836.

Ingersoll was the son of Thomas Ingersoll, the founder of Oxford Village
(Ingersoll), and the brother of Laura Secord. A general merchant, he became a person
of considerable local influence, being appointed a magistrate in 1833 and registrar of
Oxford the next year, holding the latter post until his death. A militia officer, he was
gazetted a major on 8 February 1838. When the county's registry office was moved to
Woodstock in 1847, he followed, continuing, however, through a nephew, to run his
Ingersoll store.

It is a notable coincidence that a James Ferguson (1810–1884) became in 1858 the
registrar for east and north Middlesex.

their willingness to take the Oath of Allegiance at the hustings, where it had frequently been administered at former elections, but which was utterly refused on this occasion by Mr. Askin, the Returning Officer.

That after the election closed in Oxford, your Petitioner, who is a freeholder of Middlesex, proceeded on the last day of the election to the polling for that County; on arriving within a mile and a half of the village of London, where the election was held, he met Mr. Moore, one of the successful Reform Candidates, escaping from the Orangemen, whom he said had threatened his life, and that he should not be returned, and who were driving with clubs the Reformers from the hustings, and beating them wherever they found them. – That your Petitioner believes such would have been less likely to occur, had the election for this County been held at the village of St. Thomas, where it had formerly been held, and where it was firstly appointed by Sir Francis Head to have been held, as it was not the residence of the Officers of the Government, who at London, with Mr. Cronyn,[50] a Clergyman of the Church of England, who had been recently inducted into the Rectory of that place, were constantly hurraing and cheering on the Orangemen, who were seen running through the streets intoxicated, with clubs, threatening the Reformers with instant death if they shouted reform: and Mr. Moore said, that when the rioting commenced in the early part of the election, Edward Allan Talbot[51] and John Scatchard,[52] Esquires, Magistrates of that place, swore in some twenty special constables to keep the peace.

[50]Benjamin Cronyn (1802–1871), born in Kilkenny, Ireland, and educated at Trinity College, Dublin, was ordained a priest of the Church of Ireland in 1827. In 1832 he brought his family to Upper Canada, where he was to minister to the needs of the settlers of Adelaide Township west of London. He preferred London to Adelaide, however, and located himself there, where he received government favour in the form of two rectories – one in London Township, the other in London town. He was a well-known Anglican evangelical, and when the Diocese of Huron was created in 1857, he became its first bishop.

[51]Edward Allen (Allan) Talbot (ca. 1801–1838) was born in Tipperary, Ireland, a son of Richard Talbot, who brought out settlers from Ireland to London Township in 1818. Edward was an eccentric; plagued by ill health and interested in inventing a perpetual motion machine, he also had an urge to write, producing in 1824 Five Years' Residence in the Canadas . . ., a fanciful account of life in Upper Canada. Later he published a newspaper in London. His family was evidently accustomed to penury. Initially inclined to the government side of politics, he was appointed a magistrate in 1829 and kept his post until 1836. By the latter year, however, he was in the reform camp and was dismissed as a magistrate after the elections to the Assembly. When rebellion broke out, he was suspected of treason and jailed for a short time. He then left the province, dying shortly thereafter in New York State.

[52]John Scatcherd (Scatchard) (fl. 1821–1858) emigrated from Yorkshire, England, to Upper Canada in 1821, settling in Nissouri Township in 1822, marrying and raising twelve children there. He became a farmer and merchant and then a magistrate, losing his appointment after the 1836 election, which had seen him run unsuccessfully for the legislature as a reformer in the town of London. In 1854 and 1858 he was elected, however, for Middlesex to the Assembly of the united Canadas.

That Mr. Wilson,[53] the Returning Officer, forbade the Magistrates from interfering with the rioters during the election, and when Mr. Talbot insisted on his right as a Magistrate to keep the peace, at any place, not immediately about the hustings, the Returning Officer threatened to commit him to prison.

That of the many complaints the people of Upper Canada have to prefer, the following deserve the immediate attention of your Honorable House.

That the Lieutenant Governor, the Attorney General,[54] and Solicitor Generals,[55] and in general every public functionary, made common cause with the Tories and Orangemen against the Reformers, using every means in their power to overcome the Reformers, and influence the Election in favour of the Tory Candidates.

That the Returning Officers were appointed by the Lieutenant Governor of such persons as were known most likely to forward his views.

That the elections were fixed by the Lieutenant Governor at places to favor the Tory Candidates, and, as in Middlesex, where the place first appointed and where former elections had been held, were changed, because that place first fixed was considered favorable to the Reformers.

That by the general law of Upper Canada, no Elector can vote upon a freehold, the transfer title of which has been less than three months in his possession, and registered as such.

[53]John Wilson (1807–1869) was a Scot, born at Paisley, whose family moved to Nova Scotia, then to Perth, Upper Canada, about 1823. As a young law student at Perth, Wilson in 1833 killed a fellow student in a celebrated duel. Acquitted of murder, he pursued his career, practising law for a time in the 1830s in Niagara before settling in London, where he became a notable public figure; his wife was the daughter of a St. Thomas judge. After the rebellion he defended a number of those accused of treason, but this did not blight his career, as he was elected to the Assembly of the united Canadas in 1847 and 1848 as a conservative. As a judge, he later became involved in the Fenian trials.

[54]This was Robert Sympson Jameson (d. 1854), a native of England who had pursued a legal career. After serving as a judge in Dominica, he came to Upper Canada in 1833 to be attorney general. In 1837 he was named vice-chancellor of the newly created Court of Chancery, a post he held for the rest of his working life. He was briefly a member of the Assembly in 1834–5 and served on the Legislative Council under the union, being Speaker until 1843 when he resigned as a result of the move of the capital from Kingston to Montreal.

[55]Christopher Alexander Hagerman (1792–1847) was born in Adolphustown, into a United Empire Loyalist family. In 1812 he was chosen an aide-de-camp to the governor general. In 1815 he was called to the bar of Upper Canada and appointed to the province's Executive Council. A power in Kingston, he represented that town in the Assembly, 1820–4 and 1830–41. Appointed a District Court judge for Johnstown, 1826–8, he acquired ever more influence, and became solicitor general in 1829, though he was removed for a time from that post on the representations of W.L. Mackenzie to the Colonial Office. In 1837 he was made attorney general, serving as such until 1840 when he was appointed a puisne judge of the Court of Queen's Bench.

That Sir Francis Head, in order to overwhelm these legally registered Electors, issued large numbers of patents or grants of lands, under the Great Seal, in many cases for only a quarter of an acre of wild uncultivated land, on which no buildings were erected, such grants being generally dated subsequent to the dissolution of Parliament, and in some cases even after the opening of the poll, at which the holders of such grants actually voted.

That the holders of such grants, as in the case of the Rev. Dr. Phillips,[56] one of the new Rectors of the Established Church of England, were called upon at the hustings to swear to the value of such grants being forty shillings: he declined to do so, and could not vote.

That the number of such patents to be prepared was so great as to require an additional number of clerks to get them ready, and your Petitioner believes, he would be able to prove thousands of such grants of land were issued and voted upon at the election.

That such grants were distributed openly at the places of election, to persons who had not applied at that time for such patents, and who received them to enable them to vote, without paying the usual fees. At Simcoe, one of the many instances, Mr. Ritchie, the Government Emigration Agent, thus issued hundreds of these grants to persons who voted immediately on them.

That heretofore the uniform practice has been not to issue the patents until the purchase money and fees have been paid, and all the conditions of the order in Council been complied with.

That bands of Orangemen, supposed to have been organized by their lodges, committed acts of outrage and violence at many of the elections, and the Returning Officers, as at London, refused to allow the Magistrates to interfere to prevent such breaches of the peace.

That at Leeds, these bands generally armed with clubs or knives, drove the Reformers and their candidates from the hustings – and at Leeds, procured the return of the Grand Master Ogle R. Gowan,[57] as Member for that County.

---

[56]Thomas Phillips (1781–1849), an Englishman, was from 1825 to 1829 the headmaster of the district grammar school at York, and later the assistant principal of Upper Canada College. A doctor of divinity, he left the college in 1834 for Etobicoke, where he became the rector of St. Philip's.

[57]Ogle R. Gowan (1796–1876) was born in County Wexford, Ireland. He was a journalist in Dublin from 1822 to 1829 before coming to Upper Canada in the latter year. In Upper Canada he edited a succession of newspapers until 1855 and served as member of the Assembly for Leeds, 1836–41, 1844–47, and 1858–61. A committed Orangeman, he founded the Orange Association of British North America in 1830 to organize and expand the movement in Canada. He was grand master until 1853. His political views are difficult to describe. On many issues he was in agreement with reform ideas, but in the 1830s was believed by many to be a government supporter because his views on the value of the Orange Order and on loyalty were close to those of the Compact. A lieutenant-colonel in the militia, in November 1838 he raised his regiment in Brockville against the Patriots.

That the rioters then proceeded to Grenville, where the Reform Candidates were at the head of the poll – pulled down the hustings, and destroyed the poll booths [books].

That by these, and many other unconstitutional acts, encouraged by the Lieutenant Governor and public functionaries in every part of the Province, the real Electors have been overwhelmed, and their franchise rendered of no avail.

Your Petitioner therefore humbly begs, that your Honorable House will institute such enquiry into these grievances, and adopt such measures as shall do justice to the people of Upper Canada.

A 18   CHARLES DUNCOMBE TO ROBERT BALDWIN
Charing Cross, England, 15 September 1836
[*Metropolitan Toronto Public Library (MTPL), Robert Baldwin Papers, Section I*]

Since you left I have been engaged in calling upon Reformers, discussing Canadian politics, and corresponding with the Colonial Office; I went to Worthing to see Mr. Hume[58] where he resides constantly; Lord Glenelg has refused to see me upon my private business, . . . I hate a snake in the grass, I hate a Tory in a reformers coat – I have seen many of the subs here and they say reformers are for independance only they dare not openly avow it, I wish the people of Upper Canada could see exactly how these whigs manage matters, they would soon see that if ever they have good government in Canada they must look among themselves for the means of producing it, for they care very little for the people of Canada other than as a source of patronage or revenue to the Colonial Office[;] That must be changed . . . .

A 19   ROBERT BALDWIN TO W.W. BALDWIN[59]
Cork, Ireland, 24 September 1836
[*MTPL, W.W. Baldwin Papers, v. B105, pp. 151-4*]

. . . The conduct of the Executive Government cannot indeed be too strongly condemned – They are hastening the crisis which I would

---

[58]Joseph Hume (1777–1855) was a surgeon and served as such with the East India Company in Persia. He returned to England a wealthy man, and was elected to Parliament as a tory in 1812. In 1818 he was elected again as a liberal, and led the parliamentary radicals, except for 1841 when he was out of Parliament, until his death. An ally of colonial reformers, he attacked the Orange Order in 1835–6.

[59]William Warren Baldwin (1775–1844) emigrated from Ireland with his father to Upper Canada in the latter 1790s, settling in York in 1802. Trained as a doctor and lawyer, he worked mainly in the latter profession, but along with Drs. T.D. Morrison and J.E. Tims ran the York Dispensary, 1832–3, and was head of the Board of Health. A wealthy man after his wife inherited money, he gave the reform cause a great deal of respectability. He was a member of the Assembly, 1820–4 and 1828–30, and sat for

earnestly wish to see avoided – I suppose they do not see it – . . . I told
Ridout[60] before I left Toronto that he would be removed and indeed
had I thought of your Surrogateship I should have been equally certain
of your removal[61] – but in fact it was a matter of such insignificance
that I never once thought of it at all – The unconstitutional outrage
however is not the less because the place was to you of no consequence
– . . . I dare say the principle regret was that you *could not* be made
feel the lash – . . .

With respect to the methodists – Their Clergy have I dare say done
much mischeif – That is the consequence of their being the pentioners
of the Government – . . .

A 20   "THE CURSE OF THE CANADA COMPANY" – A. VAN EGMOND[62]
[Constitution, *Toronto, 4 Oct. 1836*]

. . . The question naturally arises here – What has Goderich, with this
whole tract, both begun to settle in 1828, nearly three times as old as
Chicago, and by water at least 500 miles nearer to New York,
Montreal, Quebec, or any other seaport than Chicago, to shew, bearing

---

Norfolk in the Assembly of the united Canadas. In 1843 he was made a legislative
councillor. He may have been the first to propose the idea of responsible government
for Upper Canada, an idea which his son Robert did much to carry into effect.

[60]George Ridout (1791–1871) was born in Quebec. His family became prominent
citizens of York, and sent him to John Strachan's school at Cornwall. He fought in the
War of 1812 and was later active in the militia. In 1813 he was admitted to the bar and
in 1828 was appointed judge of the Niagara District Court. In politics he was a
moderate, running several times unsuccessfully for public office. He was active in the
municipal affairs of York (Toronto), and helped found the Bank of Upper Canada.

[61]W.W. Baldwin and Ridout lost their positions because their names appeared on a
list of those who had supported an address of the Constitutional Society. After their
dismissals in July 1836, both insisted they had nothing to do with the address, though
Baldwin said he agreed with it. Baldwin lost his judgeship of the Surrogate Court of
the Home District, while Ridout was removed as a judge of the District Court of
Niagara, a magistrate, and colonel of the 2nd Regiment, East York militia. Glenelg,
reacting to a petition from Ridout, ordered his reinstatement. Head resigned, rather
than comply with this and with instructions to appoint M.S. Bidwell a judge.

[62]Anthony G.W.G. Van Egmond (1771–1837) was a native of Holland. He was
reputed to be of noble birth with extensive military experience in the Dutch and French
armies during the Napoleonic Wars and with the allies at its conclusion. He claimed to
have served from about 1780 to 1815 and to have risen to the rank of
lieutenant-colonel. In 1819 he emigrated to Pennsylvania, where he became a
storekeeper and in 1827 came to Waterloo County, Upper Canada. In 1828 he began to
do work for the Canada Company, assisting particularly in opening the Huron Road
along which he had an inn, store, and mill in time. After a few years he owned 13,000
acres in the Huron Tract, the large parcel of land stretching from Guelph to Goderich
which was sold to the Canada Company. He lent some of his wealth to settlers and to
the company and was quite popular. In the mid-1830s he had a falling out with the
company and became a strong critic of it. He participated in the rebellion and died
because of prison conditions.

any resemblance of improvements? Nothing but unparalelled [*sic*] poverty, distress, and discontent, with a consequent daily loss and desertion of inhabitants and settlers.

What is the cause of that difference – so great success there, and such non-success here? Because the lands for the town and country *there* belonged to just and humane men, knowing their business and their own interest, and because their settlers and inhabitants feel, and do, by their manly acts, shew that they feel, their intrinsic worth *as white and free-born men*; while the lands *here* belonged to hard-hearted, arrogant, oppressing, and tyrannical [*sic*] disposed men, ignorant of the requisites for the settling of large tracts of wild lands, besides looking down upon the farmers – styled "peasantry," clowns, rustics, &c. by them, and upon mechanics – styled *the lowest order*, as if they both belonged to the brute creation. And which feelings they but too plainly express, as they have frequently done to myself – saying, "Bah! the peasants to be allowed to appear at public meetings and to have a vote – no! they should be allowed to clear off and till their lands and nothing more;" . . .

A 21   THIRD REPORT FROM THE SELECT COMMITTEE ON THE WELLAND CANAL
[Appendix to the Journals of the Assembly, *Second Session, Twelfth Parliament, 1836, v. 2, No. 90, pp. 5-9*]

. . . Upon the investigation of the 20th charge, your committee find that there are important estimates, and other documents amounting to large sums of money, belonging to the Company missing, and of which the officers can give no satisfactory account. . . .

upon an investigation of Mr. [W.B.] Robinson's[63] accounts, who was the Commissioner entrusted by his brother commissioners to expend £7,500, there appears a deficiency (after allowing sums claimed without vouchers; as also vouchers for sums paid, executed with a cross without a witness) of about £300 – . . . your Committee cannot acquit Mr. Robinson as a Commissioner, entrusted with the expenditure of public money, of a very great dereliction of duty, in not having been prepared long before the commencement of the present session with a detailed statement of his expenditures, corroborated by such vouchers as would defy a suspicion, . . .

Your committee having thus remarked upon all the charges brought before them, would state, in conclusion, that, after the investigation they have been able to make, they are fully satisfied, that for some

---

[63]William B. Robinson (1797–1873) was born in Kingston, a younger brother to Peter and John B. He was a member of Parliament for Simcoe, 1830–41 and 1844–57, a commissioner of the Welland Canal Company, and a large landowner in the Newmarket area.

years past the affairs of the Company have been conducted in a very loose and unsatisfactory manner, which may have, and no doubt has, originated in their being frequently much cramped for means to carry on the necessary repairs required to keep the canal open; and when your committee take into consideration the magnitude of the undertaking, and the many unforeseen disadvantages the Directors have had to struggle against, they feel inclined to put the most favorable construction upon their general conduct, and to acquit them of any *intentional* abuse of the powers vested in them – although it is difficult for your committee to account for or excuse their conduct in the sale of the Hydraulic Works, or in the relinquishment of the £7,500 to Oliver Phelps,[64] who appears to have received advantages withheld from other contractors, in the opinion of your committee much more deserving. Their conduct also in the purchase of £1,340 worth of timber for a tunnel, which was abandoned, is also highly reprehensible, as it appears that a portion of this timber was allowed to be stolen and lost to the Company, without one shilling's worth ever being accounted for; another portion appears to have been purchased by Gilbert M'Micking, Esq., M.P.P.,[65] and others, without any authority from the Directors, or the Company deriving any advantages from such sales; and large quantities of it made use of by Oliver Phelps in the Locks, for which he does not appear to have been charged. . . .

A 22   FAMILY COMPACT CORRUPTION
[Constitution, *Toronto, 3 May 1837*]

Mr. Robinson's Default. – It appears that Mr. Hamilton Merritt's[66] Welland Canal career has ended in ousting him from the concern, now when the two millions are wasted and nothing to be made. The defalcations, the rascality, the tricks of the canal, are recorded in a large folio volume, and altho' there were many facts which could not be got at, and altho' one valuable chapter of evidence was, thro' undue influence, suppressed by the committee, yet there is enough on record

---

[64]Oliver Phelps came from the United States to work on the Welland Canal, and eventually became a contractor on the project.

[65]Gilbert McMicking (*fl.* 1819–1841) was a large-scale merchant in the Chippawa-Queenston area. He owned a mill, was the local agent for an American steamboat in 1831, and was a magistrate. From 1834 to 1841, he represented the fourth riding of Lincoln in the Assembly.

[66]William Hamilton Merritt (1793–1862) was born in Bedford, New York. His father had served under Simcoe and received land which William later farmed. The younger Merritt opened a store and later became a miller and distiller. In 1818 he developed the idea of the Welland Canal. Starting with a private company in 1824, he was very soon accepting large amounts of government aid. He sat in the Assembly for Haldimand from 1832 until the union and identified himself with the Family Compact. After the union he sat in Parliament for Lincoln for most of the forties and fifties and served briefly on the Executive Council at the end of the 1840s.

for ever to disgrace the whole tribe. But Mr. Peter Robinson's default[67] – nearer to £20,000 than £15,000; a default which has upheld the orange mobs, and fed their leaders – that default, tho' well known throughout the country, is not mentioned by one other press in Upper Canada, the *Liberal* excepted. So much for the attention of the press to financial matters. . . .

A 23   JOHN ROLPH ON THE CLERGY RESERVES[68]
14 December 1836
[Constitution, *Toronto, 28 Dec. 1836*]

. . . I envy not the casuist or the divine, who, neither from the motions of the heart, nor the principles of reason, can perceive or understand the palpable selfishness and injustice of admitting one church to monopolize wealth and power, to the exclusion of every other. . . . Are the other churches, in any respect, less deserving? – Are they less useful members of the general community? – Are they less industrious in their respective avocations? – Do they less display the domestic and social virtues? – Are they less loyal to the King or patriotic to their country, – Are they, in any respect whatever, inferior subjects either in peace or war? . . . It is wrong, then, to make artificial distinctions, when there is no real christian difference. All indeed, may not think alike, and the systematic theologian may draw lines of demarcation. But they are branches of the same vine, . . . The claim by any one Church to a continuation of the existing monopoly, affords proof of the Church being already corrupted by it. "It is easier for a camel to pass through the eye of a needle than for a rich man to enter the kingdom of Heaven." . . .

if such Executive favours are to be given to any christian churches in our community, they should be given to all; but as such a lucrative alliance with the State is inexpedient, anti-christian and unsafe, it should neither be countenanced in any, nor arbitrarily confined to one. – . . .

Fifty-seven rectories have in open defiance of universal sentiment, been erected within our borders, richly endowed, and armed with

[67]William Lyon Mackenzie, as a radical reformer, was quick to point out corruption and overspending among government officials. In the case of Mackenzie, of William John O'Grady of the *Correspondent and Advocate*, and of other radical editors, this did not just reflect their dislike of waste through incompetence or intent but also their desire to show what government officials who did not answer to the public would do. The default referred to here was a shortfall in the accounts of the commissioner of crown lands, Peter Robinson. Within a few months in 1836 Mackenzie had linked two of the three Robinson brothers, pillars of the Family Compact, to bad financial management or corrupt practices.

[68]This speech, delivered in the Assembly, was considered by the reformers to be a tour de force of oratory.

exclusive ecclesiastical and spiritual rights and privileges;[69] while with similar defiance, clergy reserves are sold under an English act of parliament passed without our knowledge and consent, to the amount of £70,000, and that amount abstracted from our impoverished land, and paid into the military chest. This is despotism as undeserved by Canada as it is unworthy the parent state. We have not the physical strength, if we had the moral courage of the Scotch, to resist the evil; and therefore necessity may doom us to bow to wrongs, which, because of our weakness, it was ungenerous to inflict. How keenly are we at this hour feeling the scourge which has thus been visited upon us by the ascendancy of the Church which in England maintains its adulterous union with the State. Perhaps providence may have in reserve for us some unseen way of escape from the impending corruption of religion and wound of the dearest privileges of an outraged dependency. . . .

A 24   ROBERT DAVIS[70] ON CHURCH ESTABLISHMENT
[*Robert Davis*, The Canadian Farmer's Travels . . . *(Buffalo, 1837), pp. 70-1*]

. . . For though Canadians boasted, till very lately, that there was no church establishment in Canada, yet they are now made to understand that fifty-seven rectories are given to them as an earnest of more: for it is not unlikely that ere long the fifty-seven will be increased to five hundred and seventy, or perhaps a greater number.

Now, no man of common sense believes that any civil government establishes a church for the sake of spreading the gospel; but merely because it is impossible to keep together a despotic government without a state priesthood. A free government requires no established church, and in very deed, *they cannot exist together. A free*

[69]One of the major irritants to the reform movement in the 1830s was the creation of fifty-seven Church of England rectories by Sir John Colborne just before he left the province in 1836. Since these rectories were to be supported by money from the clergy reserves, the reform movement, which objected to state aid to religious denominations, was strongly opposed to them. News of the creation of the rectories did not reach the reformers until Colborne was out of the province, leaving them unable to protest directly to their architect.

[70]Robert Davis (*ca.* 1799–1838) was born in County Cavan, Ireland. He came with his family to Upper Canada about 1810 and settled in Nissouri Township in 1818 or 1819. A farmer, he was also a Methodist exhorter who felt keenly the religious discriminations practised by the government in Upper Canada. Inevitably, he was attracted to the reform cause. His book, *The Canadian Farmer's Travels in the United States of America* . . ., was a reform tract. Contrasting the freedom and prosperity of the United States with the despotism and poverty of Upper Canada, it was excerpted in the *Constitution*. Active in the reform agitation of the fall of 1837, Davis tried to raise the settlers against the mustering of the militia in December. Unsuccessful, he fled to the United States, and joined the Patriots in a raid near Fort Malden in January 1838. He later died from wounds suffered in the escapade, leaving a wife and young family.

government, and a pure christian church, can no more be united than heaven and hell: for said Christ, "my kingdom is not of this world." And farther, *a free government, and an impure church cannot be united*: for the church will destroy the *freedom* of the state!!! Any evidence required on the above facts will be found in that luminous speech delivered in our house of assembly on the 14th Dec. 1836, by Doctor John Rolph, which speech contains a flood of light on church establishments, sufficient to convince any man, except those whose eyes are blind by *established* gold or silver dust, that to unite church and state is an attempt to unite God and mammon. These religious ministers who receive government bounty, are considered *State servants*, and as such must please their patrons. But St. Paul says. "If we strive to please men, we are not the servants of Christ." Consequently, such will have to reckon with the master whom they have served. I have been long of the opinion, that the continued degraded state of the heathen world is chargeable to established churches; and that the devil is more successful by getting state churches established, than by all other ways put together. The rapidity of the gospel before Constantine professed the christian faith, and the slowness of its progress since, is one strong proof. Established church ministers, are generally too idle and worldly to become missionaries, and their luxuries need all the money they can get, without sending it abroad. Dissenters have shoved a few into the field, but only a few; it takes too much to shove them and convert them. . . .

A 25   W. L. MACKENZIE ON THE WESLEYAN METHODISTS
[Constitution, *Toronto, 22 March 1837*]

. . . When a religious body lay down principles for the guidance of the public, and then desert those principles for a little money and the hope of more, they deserve to be shunned and held up to public scorn by every man and woman of true piety. That such has been the conduct of the *Guardian* and its preachers no candid reader will deny. They got up a College or Academy subscription paper, and . . . although they now come forward and ask $16,400 of the funds of the province wherewith to endow an incorporated school, exclusively under the guidance of their own preachers, they collected the money of the Reformers to build a very different institution, by declaring that to give the public money to sectarian colleges would be no bad excuse for a glorious revolution. . . .

Before the gilden pill was presented to Egerton Ryerson's imagination, he detested the whole race of British Wesleyans, as a vile nest of tory humbugs, and his brother George[71] did not hesitate to say as much of them. Egerton in his reply to Colborne's burst of

---

[71]George Ryerson (1791–1882) was born in Sunbury County, New Brunswick, into a United Empire Loyalist family which moved to Upper Canada near the turn of the

indignation against the Methodists declared very plainly he wanted no
Wesleyans. . . .

Think of the time when we expressed a fear that a Judas would be
found among your black coats, and blush, if the evidence of shame has
not long since left your face, when you think of the political crusade
your abandoned and lost fraternity carried on against the best and
boldest of the faithful and true reformers at the last election. Like
wasps from an evil hive your Conference turned out to humble and
disgrace Lennox and Addington, by inducing these whose votes ye
could command to prefer John Solomon Cartwright,[72] the high church
tory and Bank President, to Mr. Speaker Bidwell,[73] the ornament and
pride of the Canadian Senate, and who will again grace the people's
house, when your base and polluted priesthood will be without a
congregation in the counties which witnessed your deep disgrace. . . .

A 26   ON RELIGIOUS CORRUPTION
[Correspondent and Advocate, *Toronto, 23 Nov. 1836*]

*Extract of a letter sent by a person in this city to his brother in the West
of England:*

*   *   *   *   *   *   *

Religion is in a very low state in Upper Canada, the Government
having corrupted the Clergy of the four denominations, which have
descended to prostitution, v[i]z – the Church of England, Scotland,

---

century. George served in the War of 1812, and after it studied as an Anglican priest,
though he was unable to secure a position within the church in Upper Canada. He
migrated slowly to the Methodist church of his brothers, and in 1828 presented a
petition to the House of Commons on behalf of the non-Anglicans of the province.
That same year he became a Methodist preacher, but in 1831, when in England,
converted to the Catholic Apostolic Church of William Irvine. He returned to Toronto
in 1836, and in 1837 was placed in charge of a congregation there, remaining active
with the Irvingites until his death.

[72]John Solomon Cartwright (1804–1845) was the son of the Honourable Richard
Cartwright of Kingston. John Solomon studied law in England and returned to Upper
Canada in 1830. He was the first president of the Commercial Bank of the Midland
District in 1831 and sat in the Assembly for Lennox and Addington from 1836 as a
Family Compact supporter. In December 1837, as its lieutenant-colonel, he mustered
the 2nd Regiment of Lennox militia for duty.

[73]Marshall Spring Bidwell (1792–1872) was born in Massachusetts and came to
Canada in 1810 with his father Barnabas. In 1821 he was called to the bar and was
elected to the Assembly for Lennox and Addington. He was prevented from holding
the seat until 1825, when the law concerning the rights of aliens was settled. From
1825 to 1836 he sat as a moderate reformer and was a leading spokesman for reform.
He was speaker, 1828–30 and 1834–6. Defeated in 1836, he took a small role in the
protests of 1836–7 against the way the colony was governed. In 1837 he was unfairly
accused of being associated with the rebels by Francis Bond Head and moved to the
United States, becoming an eminent lawyer in New York City, and in 1858 receiving a
doctor of laws from Yale.

Roman Catholic, and Wesleyan Methodist, in consequence of which the societies of each of the above denominations throughout Upper Canada, are torn in pieces. Never did I see or read of such intrigue and deception as I have seen used by the leading Methodist Preachers. . . . You know that I have been a Member in the Methodist connexion for many years and that nothing short of a deviation from the truths of the Gospel of Christ, by the leading members of that body, would induce me to withdraw from their communion: But I and hundreds of others have done so, since the last Canada Conference, . . .

A 27   ROBERT DAVIS ON HALF-PAY OFFICERS AND THE "POLITICAL PRIESTHOOD".
[*Robert Davis*, The Canadian Farmer's Travels . . . *(Buffalo, 1837), pp. 9-10]*

. . . No man who has seen Canada and the United States can long be at a loss as to what causes the contrast between the two countries. The curse of Canada is an *unprincipled* aristocracy, whose pretensions to superiority above other settlers, would disgust a dog. Many of these *would-be* aristocrats came out from the old country under the title of *half-pay officers*, but who, in fact, had commuted their pensions before they left home, to help to convey them across the Atlantic; and then getting posssession [*sic*] of a few hundred acres of wild land, thought themselves Lords of Canada. – Many of these have been Ensigns in the old country, but when they arrived in Canada they called themselves *Captains*. For instance, in the township of Adelaide there are hosts of Captains, while the fact is, there is only *one* captain among them all. I mean Captain Johnston.[74] These pretended captains get put into every office of trust and profit. They are slaves and sycophants to the Governor, and at elections are the captains of Orange mobs. But there is another way in which these men become a nuisance to the independent settlers of Canada: nearly the whole of them become magistrates, and it is in vain for reformers to expect justice from such tory sycophants. They also form the grand jury at the district courts, and commissioners of the courts of requests. Such being the state of things, how can an independent settler of reform principles be comfortable and prosper? Bad as the above is, there is another curse, if possible still worse, I mean the *political priesthood*. The government has been sufficiently crafty, and the priests sufficiently wicked, to amalgamate in order to put down reform principles. The government has hired that portion of the priesthood, who appear to have the greatest influence. For these political priests think they can serve God and Mammon at the same time. . . .

[74]This was likely Captain William W. Johnston of Adelaide, who may have been the William Johnston of Adelaide who in 1835 was treasurer and secretary of the Acting Committee of the Emigrant Society of the London District.

A 28   STATE SUPPORT FOR CHURCHES
[Constitution, *Toronto, 11 Oct. 1837*]

PAPISTS AND PROTESTANTS.

The Government of Sir F. Head and Lord Glenelg pay £200 a year to the Church of England parsons for damning the Roman Catholics, and £600 to the Papist Bishop at Kingston, and £1000 more to the Papist Bishop of Quebec for sending to Hell the Protestant heretics of the unbelieving Churches of England and Scotland – these payments are out of the taxes, while £6 a year of starvation money is allowed to the poor schoolmaster. . . .

A 29   W.L. MACKENZIE ON THE ORANGE ORDER
[Constitution, *Toronto, 19 July 1836*]

ORANGE LODGES. – It is our intention, in an early number of this Journal, to place before our readers the interesting debate in the British House of Commons, on the 23rd of February last, which terminated in an address to the Crown for the suppression of these pernicious and unlawful combinations, the Orange Lodges of the United Kingdom. Orange Lodges in this Colony are a dangerous nuisance, of the most strictly exclusive kind, from which Catholics are always kept, and their main object is to oppose and oppress the Catholics. . . . The Judges have solemnly denounced Orangeism from the Bench, the King has called upon its factious bands to disperse, the people's representatives have denounced it in the House of Commons, the public authorities have, by royal order, intimated that any civil officer of the government connected with an Orange Society shall be instantly cashiered, and the Commander in Chief has announced his Majesty's directions, at the head of every regiment in the service, that any soldier who shall dare to enter an Orange Lodge, will do so on pain of a Court Martial. How, then, comes it that the heads of the government here, trifling with the powers entrusted to them, are cherishing this public pest? Why are the *paid* ministers of religion in open connexion with men, who, on pretence of superior loyalty, are displaying the standard of rebellion to their lawful Sovereign? Is Orange loyalty to the government here, and defiance of the imperial government by the sworn officers of the state to be tolerated? Are our elections to be at the mercy of illegal desperadoes, and is the arm of the law to become powerless for the protection of the peaceable subjects of the King in the exercise of their elective franchise? Look at Leeds, at Middlesex, at Grenville and other places? [*sic*] . . .

A 30   C.J. BALDWIN[75] TO THE *Constitution*
[Constitution, *Toronto, 1 March 1837*]

It is with much satisfaction I hasten to correct an error in my letter of the 8th instant. . . . The person who headed th[a]t party holds some Rank amongst the Orangemen, and, as I am informed, exerted himself to prevent that procession, and accompanied it chiefly for the purpose of preventing party and offensive tunes being played, in both which attempts he failed.

Can any stronger argument be used, to shew the mischievous tendency of that system, than that the orange body cannot be controlled by their leaders, when they wish to prevent insult or outrages, . . .? I again say, that unless the legislature interfere to put down orangeism, there cannot exist any security to the rest of the population of this Province, for freedom of action, or property, or for life.

I would now ask what is the real object of orangeism here, what is meant by their recruiting and orgies and oaths? Is it loyalty? Certainly not. . . . Theirs is a calculating conditional loyalty. They will support their King whilst he supports their ascendancy and countenances their outrages. . . . I therefore again repeat that the question with the Province, is not – the baneful domination of the mother country, or of Downing–street, or of the tories, or of an irresponsible executive, – but, Shall we submit to orange domination and dictation? . . .

A 31   ANONYMOUS TO THE *Constitution*
[Constitution, *Toronto, 30 Aug. 1837*]

. . . I do not think you do us justice as a body. It was an orangman who sat 30 hours in the new-plaistered jury room of the assize court here, to announce as foreman of the special jury that they gave you $2500 for the loss of your types: . . . at least a hundred orangemen voted for you to be Mayor, or for the Reformers in that struggle; in your election for the county in '30, and at other times, orangemen were not so much your enemies as you assert, and if they have since become so, your own remarks and copying Mr. Hume's speech and Colonel Baldwin's letters are the causes. You *had* friends among us, that I know, and it would be as well for you not to take so much pains to change them. . . .

---

[75]Connell James Baldwin (1777–1861) was born in County Cork, Ireland. He pursued a military career after his education, until 1826 when he retired on half-pay as brigade-major. After two years of raising troops for the emperor of Brazil, he settled in Upper Canada, west of Toronto, among men he had commanded in the Peninsular War and again in Brazil. William John O'Grady was one of these. A moderate reformer and a Catholic, Baldwin was linked to William Lyon Mackenzie through his dislike of the Orange Order. Baldwin raised a troop in the rebellion of 1837 at his expense to oppose his ex-ally Mackenzie. In the letter quoted, he referred to an Orange parade which had recently taken place in his area.

A 32   "THE ORANGEMEN AND THE REFORMERS" – A LETTER BY
"T.P."
[Constitution, *Toronto, 1 Nov. 1837*]

I like to read your paper, but if it contained fewer remarks derogatory to the character of those of your protestant neighbours who are members of the orange society, I think its influence would be greater in this township. You will never win the orangemen by abusing them – drop that, and you will find many good reformers in our lodges. Hundreds of orangemen have voted for you at elections who now oppose you, although in their hearts they want to bring about the same changes that you are evidently striving to effect. You had yourself to blame last election for the opposition you met with. . . . There are changes – we have not been well used, and some of us see it – Sir Francis Head is far from being popular here – he promised much – we have given him a trial, and he has deceived us. The country never was in such a state as now, and he is not the man to relieve it with his Bubbles. If you had witnessed, or if I durst tell you what passed at a late meeting here, you would have proof that orangemen are neither blind fools to their own interest nor yet enemies of reform – but we will never consent to catholic ascendancy – . . . But we would join, at least one half of us would join the reformers, and so there would be no need of war, which is seldom to the farmer's profit – what would be good for one would be good for all, only dont abuse us in the paper. . . . Sir Francis Head, His Excellency, was polite and friendly to us before the late election, and told us fine stories, and promised great things, but now that he can make no use of us we are cast off like a dog that has lost his teeth. He has a House of Assembly which is to do us no good, but its members have taken care of themselves – two have been made judges at £1000 a year, one made attorney general [Christopher Hagerman], one made solicitor general,[76] and other offices given them – if you leave the orangemen alone they will join the reformers. . . .

[76]The solicitor general was William Henry Draper (1801–1877). Born in England, he ran away to sea at age 15 and then emigrated to Upper Canada in 1820. Soon after, he took up the study of law and was called to the bar in 1828, his legal and personal connections being with the Family Compact. Elected to the Assembly in 1836, he was appointed to the Executive Council that same year, becoming solicitor general in 1837. In this latter position he was responsible for the prosecutions which followed the rebellions and the border raids. With the union of 1840–1 Draper, who had become attorney general, worked to create a modern conservative party. In 1842 he resigned from the Executive Council to make way for Governor Bagot's compromise with Baldwin and LaFontaine. In 1843, however, he returned to the council to assist the new governor, Sir Charles Metcalfe, and until 1847 he was leader of the government forces. In this latter year, having a weak ministry and a new governor more sympathetic to the reformers, he resigned, spending the rest of his public career on the bench.

A 33   W.L. MACKENZIE ON THE FINANCIAL CRISIS
[Constitution, *Toronto, 7 June 1837*]

Get Gold and Silver for your Bank Promises before Head's Parliament meet, and oblige you to take paper money, ten dollars of which you will perhaps be soon able to buy with five dollars of silver.

I told you, courteous reader, a short time ago, that although the Chartered Banks were protected from making honest payments to the public by means of the British Sixpenny and Shilling law of 1836,[77] they would, unless supplied with the specie kept for paying the forces, be driven to bankruptcy, or, as they call it, to suspension.[78] – Am I mistaken? Look at the proclamation of Governor Head, to do what Canada has not seen done before for many a long year, call the Legislature together, to sit and frame laws to protect rotten banks from the consequences of prosecutions by their creditors. To sow the seeds of anarchy and confusion among us by obliging the farmer who gave his wheat for bank paper, to accept rags never perhaps to be redeemed,
. . .

A 34   W.L. MACKENZIE ON TAXES
[Constitution, *Toronto, 12 July 1837*]

Canadians! Brother Colonists! Your Mock Parliament has done its duty. For four long weeks has its members been marched and counter-marched, by our Kentish drill-sargeant, aided by Corporals McNab[79] and Robinson.[80] Bills and badgerings have followed each

[77]This law was an Upper Canadian one. It overvalued the British shilling, thus making it the colony's dominant coin.

[78]At the outset of 1837 there were four banks in Upper Canada which were not chartered banks but joint stock companies: the Agricultural Bank, the Farmers' Bank, the Bank of the People, and the Niagara Suspension Bridge Bank. The Agricultural Bank failed during the crisis of 1837; thereafter no new private banks were allowed. In 1837 there were three chartered banks in the colony: the Commercial Bank of the Midland District, the Gore Bank, and the Bank of Upper Canada. A special session of the legislature, called for 19 June 1837, passed legislation allowing the chartered banks to suspend specie payments. All three subsequently did so, the Commercial Bank in September 1837 and the other two in March 1838.

[79]Allan Napier MacNab (McNab) (1798–1862) was born in Newark, Upper Canada. Son of one of Simcoe's Queen's Rangers, he had a rather indifferent early career. Called to the bar in 1826, he moved from York to Hamilton. Through hard work and connections with prominent tories, he prospered. He entered the Assembly in 1830 and identified himself with many of the ideals of the Family Compact but not with the Compact itself, with which he was often in conflict over business dealings. He was a land speculator on a grand scale and had other extensive business interests. In December 1837 he led a small band of volunteers to aid Toronto. For this and his role in the leadership of the force which displaced the rebels from the Toronto area, MacNab was given command of the force sent to deal with the Duncombe rising and then command of the forces defending the Niagara frontier in early 1838. After the union of 1841, he became identified with the old-line tories in the provincial parliament. He served as premier, 1854–6. Much of his time in the 1840s and 1850s was spent in railway speculation.

[80]This was William B. Robinson.

other in quick succession – and the end of the farce is that the Banks and the province have been handed over by a sham legislative enactment to Sir Francis, . . . to be made the most of, for the use of its foreign owners and creditors, or like a farm held for a term of years at a rack rent to be improverished in every possible shape by the holder before it be given up.

Ye False Canadians! Tories! Pensioners! Placemen! Profligates! Orangmen! Churchmen! Spies! Informers! Brokers! Gamblers! Parasites, and knaves of every cast and description, allow me to congratulate you! Never was a vagabond race more prosperous. Never did successful villainy rejoice in brighter visions of the future than ye may indulge. Ye may plunder and rob with impunity – your feet is on the people's necks, they are transformed into tame, crouching slaves, ready to be trampled on. . . .

The four pound loaf is at a Halifax shilling, the barrel of flour brings twelve dollars, woe and wailing, and pauperism and crime meet us at every corner of the streets. The settlers and their families on the Ottawa, in Simcoe, in the rear of the London District, and many new settlements seldom taste a morsel of bread, and are glad to gnaw the bark off the trees, or sell their improvements for a morsel to keep away starvation.

The settlers are leaving the country in thousands, for lands less favored by nature, but blessed with free institutions and just government.

The merchants are going to ruin, one after another – even sycophancy and degrading servility have failed to save them this time. . . .

But why are Want and Misery come among us? Ah, ye rebels to christianity, ye detest the truth, ye shut your ears against that which is right.

Your country is taxed, priest ridden, sold to strangers, and ruined. What then? Ye share the plunder! . . .

Have you taken 1 farthing off the £80000 of salaries and incomes of which the rich placemen rob the poor labourer? No! you have added to the yoke.

Have you reduced the many thousands of pounds squandered at home and abroad on pensions to the vile and the worthless? No! on the contrary you have, as it were with acclamation, during your short session, taxed the country twelve hundred dollars a year, for the term of his life, to bestow another PENSION on Colonel Coffin,[81] who has been a pensioner as an Ensign for half a hundred years, and has had besides £365 a year, with the sinecure of Adjutant General of Militia,

---

[81]Colonel Nathaniel Coffin (d. 1846) entered the British army in 1783 and became provincial aide-de-camp in 1812 while his brother-in-law, Sir Roger Sheaffe, was military administrator of Upper Canada. In 1815 he became adjutant general of the provincial militia and remained such until the outbreak of the rebellion in 1837.

and £200 more from the poor people to pay a Deputy to do the work for him. . . .

Have ye lessened our taxes? – No! – within the last twelve months I have paid in direct taxation to the task-master, in this colony, Ten hundred dollars and more. Indirectly and directly I have paid more than $1,200. – £10,000 of the sales of our Public Lands are annually collected from the farmers and shipped to England. No wonder they had to sell grain in the fall cheap, and buy it in the spring dear! – £25,000 a year do we pay for taxes to the Rag Barons, and now it is to be doubled. The law preventing Americans from holding or selling land is a loss to us of at least £20,000 a year. The Canada Company of foreign adventurers swindle, (mind the word Mr. T.M. Jones)[82] swindle our poor people, small farmers and settlers out of £25,000 a year to be shipped to Europe. Our letter and newspaper postage are doubled to create a revenue of £10,000 a year surplus to be shipped to England and augment salaries at Quebec, without our will, and you, ye poor slaves, dare not complain. No, ye share the plunder. – Our foreign governor and his minions fill the offices, and after getting too odious to be longer borne, march off to England with the plunder of our poor bleeding country. . . .

O, but say some "We are not taxed heavily." Yes, most cruelly. Taxes on the clothes ye wear, on the food ye eat – on the goods sold at auction – on the pedlar's pack – on the cow and horse and house and hearth and cultivated land and wild land – and under which a few speculators have grasped a million of acres of choice lands sold by the Sheriffs. Taxes! Why the province pays a million of dollars nearly every year in Law taxes, and the parliament have added to the scourge "a Court of Chancery" – a serpent basking in corruption's rays, till it gather strength to suck your very heart's blood. Taxes! Your shops are taxed – your tea is prohibited from the cheapest market and you are forced into the dearest. If you want a cheap book, the custom house officer asks the invoice and demands £30 per £100 in taxes. If you buy oil in the States where it is cheap, the broad arrow of seizure is fixed upon the barrel, and a third of the spoil goes to F.B. Head! Taxes! You pay £3,000 a year for M.P.P.'s to scourge and rob you by wholesale enactments. Ye pay the penalty of prohibition from free trade with all the world, through the Hudson, because your foreign task-masters exact heavy duties on American goods and exclude their grain and provisions. Taxes! What else are the 57 rectories, with

[82]Thomas Mercer Jones (1795–1868) was born in England. He was apprenticed to Ellice, Kinnear and Company in 1815. Ellice became deputy-governor of the Canada Company, and in 1829 arranged for Jones to replace John Galt in running the Upper Canadian operations of the company. Jones was given the management of the Huron Tract, as the former crown reserves were put under separate management. He moved from Toronto to the Tract in the late 1830s and spent a long but controversial period developing the area. In 1852 he was dismissed after losing touch with the philosophy of the management in England.

spiritual and temporal powers to harrass you to death. Taxes! What else is the refusal of the government to permit the primogeniture law to be repealed? Taxes! What is the land selling and granting system but a robbery of the country! Taxes! Are not your farms mortgaged to British creditors for £600,000? Is not the money scattered to the four winds of heaven? – What is the £250,000 pretended to be expended on the St. Lawrence, where all work is stopt? What is the £400,000 alledged to be thrown into the Welland? In what condition are your roads, your bridges, your light houses, your rail roads? . . .

A 35 CURRENCY SCARCE AROUND LONDON
[University of Western Ontario (UWO), Proudfoot Family Papers, Proudfoot[83] Diary 27]

Friday. July 7. [1837]

. . . The mercantile world has undergone a great revolution – Poverty has come upon thousands, and many a tale of heart rending distress I have heard, . . .

Monday. July 10th

Went into the village to discount a bill of £15[.] The bank would give no more than 5 pCent which I would not take – And there was no storekeeper who had as much cash as was sufficient. – The tree is indeed girdled!!! . . .

Wednesday. July 12. –1837.

. . . The country is looking fine – There is a prospect of plenty, May God grant that it may all be safely got home. – What distress do I every day hear of.

Wednesday July 26. 1837–

. . . The state of the country is becoming critical more & more every day. – The Liberal party is becoming more confident and the Tories more quiet than they have been for some time back. – . . .

A 36 POST OFFICE NOTICE
Quebec, 15 July 1837
[Constitution, Toronto, 2 Aug. 1837]

. . . The Deputy Post Master General[84] begs to inform the public that

---

[83]William Proudfoot (1788–1851) was born in Scotland, and attended the University of Edinburgh. A United Secession Church minister, he was ordained in 1813. In 1832 he moved his family to Upper Canada, settling just outside London and ministering to several charges in the area. He became involved in political controversy, writing several articles for the *Liberal* in 1836 on the church question. His reform bias and the fact that a nephew, James Aitchison, was captured in the Patriot raid on Windsor in December 1838, damaged his ministry for a time as he lost parishioners.

[84]This was Thomas Allen Stayner (1788–1868) who had served in the British army

he is under the necessity of requiring from this time forth the payment of *all postages* in SPECIE. The Deputy Post Master General has refrained from resorting to this measure, which he is aware must add to the inconvenience experienced by all classes from the scarcity of hard money, until he finds that he cannot otherwise conduct the duties of his Department.

A 37   JOHN GRUBB[85] TO MR. WILSON
Etobicoke, 7 October 1837
[*Queen's University Archives, typescript, History of the Grubb[e]
Family, Letterbook, pp. 84-5*]

. . . We are greatly convulsed in political matters and as for the banks and their promises to pay, beggars description. All these incorporated bodies have refused payment but the Upper Canada Bank who protects itself by only issuing Lower Canada Bank notes, that is not payable in specie. This is trick upon trick and trick upon travellers too; Yet as of old we live upon faith and worthless paper. A sovereign is worth and is exchanged readily for $5.50 and even $6. of the paper currency. These are the times for the emigrants whose pockets are stored with gold. . . .

A 38   ADAM HOPE[86] TO ROBERT HOPE[87]
Hamilton, 26 February 1837
[*Hamilton Public Library, (HPL), Adam Hope Letters, typescripts*]

. . . The Wheat crop throughout the whole county of Oxford was more deficient than perhaps any other part of the Province. This is a great privation to the new settlers, as Wheat can't be got under the rate it fetches in Hamilton 12/- to 14/- or 7/6d to 8/9d cy pr bush.[88] & the most of them have all their provisions to buy. In the Township of Zorra where a great many Highland Scotch are settled, and but recently

from about 1808 to 1823. In 1824 he became postmaster at Quebec and in 1827 succeeded his father-in-law as postmaster general for Upper and Lower Canada. He received much of the blame for the poor service in the colonies, which was largely due to the general policies of the British post office. He survived the criticism and became wealthy on the proceeds from the rates he set on newspapers, but gradually had his powers reduced until, in 1851, the Assembly of the Canadas gained control and he retired.

[85]John Grubb (1783–1850) was an immigrant from Scotland. He bought land in Etobicoke and farmed there for the remainder of his life.

[86]Adam Hope (1813–1882) was born in East Lothian, Scotland, and emigrated on his own to Upper Canada in 1834. In Hamilton he worked for the firm of Young, Weir and Company, leaving them in 1837 to begin his own business in St. Thomas. He eventually extended his own business concerns to London, Hamilton, and beyond, becoming a partner in the well-known firm of the Buchanans. In 1877 he was appointed to the Canadian Senate.

[87]Robert Hope was Adam Hope's father.

[88]In the early 1830s wheat prices were generally about one-half of those quoted.

settled the scarcity of provisions, especially bread stuffs is very great. . . .

A 39   FOOD SHORTAGES
[*UWO, William Wood*[89] *Diary, typescript, pp. 16, 19*]

MONDAY JUNE 26 [1837]
Digging in the garden this morning and part of the evening [,] hoeing my potatoes for the remainder of the day. Cloudy[.] Setting our cabbages fater [after] tea – great distress prevails in every part of the country from scarcity of provisions particularly flour .

TUESDAY AUGUST 15
Logging with Mr. Pugsley[90] all day[–] he drank tea with me and agreed to take the mare up to Dover and get us some flour. I furnished him with a dollar for us and another for himself on account of Mr. Grey's[91] not returning our flour[–] we are nearly starved[,] no bread whatever.

WEDNESDAY AUGUST 16
Mr Pugsley went up to Dover to procure us some flour if possible which he returned with this evening [–] 17 lbs very very dear at the rate of £12 4s per barrel[–] hard hard times [–] however we are glad of [*sic*] it at any rate[,] having tasted little besides potatoes a long time: underbrushing part of the day.

THURSDAY AUGUST 17
Carrying out manure this morning and being rainy in the evening[,] the weather clearing off – logging with Mr. Pugsley[,] Thank God we have bread once more and good it is to a hungry soul filled with nothing more for the last ten days but potatoes and cucumbers with a little milk as a treat.

A 40   FLOUR PRICES
[*PAO, Diary of John Thomson*[92]]

Sat. 24 [June 1837]. . . . Alexr. retd. last evening with a Barl [barrel] of Flour $9. the highest price I ever gave by $2. – . . .

---

[89]William Wood was an Englishman who emigrated to the Lake Erie shore near Port Dover some time before 1830. He farmed and raised his family there. In December 1837 he went with the Walpole militia on their march to the Niagara District to oppose Mackenzie at Navy Island. Later, he quit farming and studied for the Anglican ministry. He was ordained a deacon in 1858 and a priest in 1859, becoming the incumbent at St. John's Church at Port Rowan.

[90]Puglsey farmed near Port Dover. He seems to have done contract work from time to time for William Wood on Wood's farm. In December 1837 he went with the Walpole militia to the Niagara District to oppose Mackenzie at Navy Island.

[91]Grey lived near Port Dover. In December 1837 he set off with the Walpole militia, marching to the Niagara District to oppose Mackenzie at Navy Island.

[92]John Thomson (b. 1787) had a career of twenty-eight years as a seaman before

Tuesd. 18. [July]. . . . I was at the Village [Orillia] & bought a Barl. of flour at $12. – . . .

Mond. 7 [August]. . . . I went to the Village & got a Cask of Flour $11. –

Wed. 13. [September]. . . . Pat ploughing[,] sent to Village for a few pounds of Flour[.] it is not to be got but with difficulty. – . . .

Tuesd. 10 [October] . . . went to Village about Flour[.] got a Barl. $8. – . . .

A 41   JOHN MACAULAY[93] TO ANN MACAULAY[94]
Toronto, 7 July 1837
[*PAO, Macaulay Papers*]

. . . Flour has risen to 11 dollars a barrel here & in many places there is great distress, & absolute famine. If the weather should now become warm & dry, we shall have abundant [harvests?] this year & they are much wanted[.]

A 42   ANN MACAULAY TO JOHN MACAULAY
Kingston, 7 December 1837
[*PAO, Macaulay Papers*]

. . . I am afraid provisions will be dear this winter[:] within these 2 weeks flour has risen from 5 to 9 and ten dollars. I bought 2 Barrels to day for 19 dollars and it is expected to rise still more. . . .

A 43   C.P. TRAILL[95] ON FLOUR AND GRAIN PRICES
[*C.P. Traill*, The Backwoods of Canada . . . *(Toronto, 1929), p. 323*]

[Writing in December 1837]
. . . The price of grain has been very high during the last years, which has been a great thing for those who had it to sell. It appears likely to be a high price this winter also. During the latter part of the summer, just before the harvest commenced, flour rose to twelve dollars a

---

retiring in 1832 and settling in South Orillia Township, Upper Canada, where he farmed.

[93]John Macaulay (1792–1857) was born in Kingston, Upper Canada. He attended John Strachan's school in Kingston and in 1813 became postmaster of that place. With good connections to the Family Compact, he became a legislative councillor, 1836–42, and surveyor general, 1836–8. He also served as civil secretary to the lieutenant-governor, 1838–9, inspector general, 1839–42, and collector of customs at Kingston, 1845–6. He was one of the two founders of the Kingston *Chronicle*.

[94]Ann Macaulay was the mother of John.

[95]Catharine Parr Traill (1802–1899) was born in London, England. She married in 1832 and came to Upper Canada, settling near Peterborough. She was the sister of Samuel Strickland and Susanna Moodie. All three of them later wrote of their pioneering experiences.

barrel, and in some cases even higher than that, and pork was eighteen dollars a barrel. Owing to the extreme wetness and lateness of the harvest, many of the small growers were without flour, . . . Owing to the warm, moist weather and heavy rains after the wheat was cut, a great deal of the grain sprouted in the sheaf, and even in the ear, uncut. . . .

A 44   REV. WILLIAM PROUDFOOT ON SHORT HARVESTS AND
FINANCIAL DISTRESS
London, 1 January 1838
[United Secession Magazine, *VI (April 1838), pp. 211-12*]

The crop of 1836 was so deficient, that many of the people had to buy their bread for from two to eight months. Wheat used to be the only article for which they got cash of late years, – that they have had to buy at from twelve to fourteen dollars per barrel. The severity of the winter that followed was such, that very few had sufficient fodder to bring the cattle through; in consequence, very many of them died. These unfavourable circumstances left the farmers in great straits. The crop of 1837 was better than the preceding; but it will do no more than support the farmers' families, at least in this district. There will be very little to pay their debts in the stores. Then came on the embarrassments produced by the heavy failures in the States, – that has led to a scarcity of specie, and also of good paper. The Montreal merchants, pressed for money, drew in their credit with the storekeepers all over the country. The storekeepers sued for payment in every direction, and the farmers have had to part with any thing that could be sold, for any thing they could get; and thus, from so many untoward causes, a state of great embarrassment and distress has been produced. . . .

A 45   "THE LATE ELECTIONS – TORONTO POLITICAL UNIONS"
[Constitution, *Toronto, 12 Oct. 1836*]

At a numerous meeting of influential Reformers, hald [*sic*] at Mr. T. Elliot's[96] Hotel, in the City of Toronto, on the evening of Monday, the 10th October, 1836: WILLIAM W. BALDWIN, Esquire, was called to the chair, and Mr. JOHN ELLIOTT[97] requested to act as Secretary.

[96]Thomas Elliot was a Scot who emigrated to Upper Canada before 1830. He took over the Sun Tavern, at the southeast corner of Yonge and Lot (Queen), from John Montgomery. He was the brother of John Elliot of Vaughan Township, another active reformer.

[97]John Elliot (Elliott), a native of England, was a Toronto Lawyer who had offices at 55 Lot Street.

Mr. Price,[98] seconded by Mr. Sheldon Ward,[99] moves, that it be

Resolved 1st – That this meeting feel deeply impressed with the necessity of considering the measures necessary to be taken, with a view to obviate, as far as possible, the evil effects of the unconstitutional proceedings pursued at the late general elections in the Province – *proceedings*, which, if not promptly checked, must irretrievably lead to the extinction of Civil and Religious Liberty. – Carried, unanimously.

Dr. O'Grady,[100] seconded by F. Hincks,[101] Esquire, moves, that it be

Resolved 2nd – That this meeting rejoice in the FIRMNESS AND DIGNITY OF CONDUCT manifested by the House of Assembly in LOWER CANADA, in defence of their just rights, and that, weighing the deplorable reluctance of the Colonial Office in London to listen to the repeated remonstrances from this Province, it has, at last, become our immutable opinion, that we can, in no way, preserve our constitutional rights but by following the noble example set by the *Assembly of our sister Province*. – Carried, nem. con.

---

[98]James Hervey Price (1797–1882) was born in Cumberland, England. He emigrated to Upper Canada in 1828 and was called to the bar in 1833. He was Toronto city clerk, 1834–5, and in 1836 was elected councillor for St. David's Ward. An active reformer, he helped to found the Bank of the People, a reform effort to break the monopoly of the government chartered banks. In 1838, when many reformers felt it best to leave the country because of hostility over the rebellion, Price was a founder and director of the Mississippi Emigration Society. He was a member of Parliament, 1841–51, and commissioner of crown lands in the Baldwin–LaFontaine government, 1848–51. He later returned to England.

[99]Sheldon Ward was a bricklayer and mason on Berkeley Street, Toronto.

[100]Rev. Dr. William John O'Grady (d. 1840) was born in Ireland and ordained in the diocese of Cork. He was one of the men who served under Connell James Baldwin in Brazil in 1828. He came to Upper Canada with Baldwin and others of Baldwin's troop that year and settled in York. At first he did well in the Catholic Church, becoming a vicar general in 1830. O'Grady had a disagreement with his congregation, however, and refused Bishop Macdonell's attempt to transfer him, resulting in his suspension. He then set up the *Canadian Correspondent* (the *Correspondent and Advocate* after 1834) and became associated with the reform movement. He unsuccessfully contested the Kingston riding in the 1834 provincial election. In 1837 he retired and sold his business to Charles Fothergill.

[101]Francis Hincks (1807–1885) was born in Cork, Ireland. In 1832 he and his wife emigrated to York. At first he opened a wholesale dry goods and liquor business but soon accepted the position of cashier (manager) of the Farmers' Bank. When the reformers involved with this venture left it and formed the Bank of the People, he became cashier there. He joined the Mississippi Emigration Society in 1838 and went to Washington as an agent for it, to inquire about the availability of land in the American west. Also in 1838, he founded the *Examiner* at Toronto, the first new reform paper to appear after the rebellion. Active in politics after the union, he became a close associate of Robert Baldwin, and succeeded him as joint premier in 1851. In 1854, after a premiership marked by English-French conflict within the political groupings of the Canadas and charges of corruption and mismanagement, he resigned.

Mr. Richard Harper,[102] seconded by Mr. James Beaty,[103] moves, that it be

Resolved 3rd – That a committee be appointed to draft resolutions conformable to the objects of this meeting, and to report the same forthwith, and that such committee do consist of Dr. O'Grady, Messrs. Price and Hincks. – Carried nem. con.

The committee then retired, and shortly after submitted a series of resolutions, containing a plan for the organization of POLITICAL UNIONS throughout the Province – which resolutions were adopted unanimously.

Mr. Alderman Harper, seconded by Mr. Doel,[104] moves, that a committee of the present meeting be now appointed to communicate to the friends of Reform throughout the Province, the views and sentiments of this meeting, as respects the present public *emergency*, and that his worship the Mayor,[105] W.W. Baldwin, Esquire, Dr. O'Grady, Mr. Price, Mr. Hincks, and Mr. J. Elliot be such committee.

Dr. Baldwin having left the chair, the Mayor took his place – when it was moved by John McIntosh, Esquire, M.P.P. – that this meeting do now resolve itself into a Society, to be called *The City of Toronto Political Union*. . . .

A 46   THE TORONTO POLITICAL UNION
[Constitution, *Toronto, 14 Dec. 1836*]

. . . The following pledge has been taken and subscribed by all the members of the Union.

We who have signed our names in this Book as Members of the "CITY OF TORONTO POLITICAL UNION," do hereby PLEDGE ourselves to co-operate in all legal and constitutional ways and means, in our power, to aid the cause of Political Reform in this Province, especially in these important points, viz: –

1. The protection of the Elective Franchise from the baneful effects

---

[102]Richard Harper was a carpenter with a large lumberyard on Hospital Street, Toronto. He served as an alderman for the town in 1836.

[103]James Beaty was a shoemaker. The firm of Beaty and Armstrong Boot and Shoemakers was located at 55 and 57 King Street.

[104]John Doel (1790–1871) was born in Somerset, England. He arrived in York in 1818, where he opened a brewery at Bay and Adelaide streets. He was an active radical reformer and meetings were often held in his business premises. From 1834 to 1836 he was on city council.

[105]This was Dr. Thomas David Morrison (1796?–1856) who had been born in Lower Canada and who had moved to York in 1816. At first the chief clerk in the surveyor general's office, he was fired. He became a doctor in 1824, was a reform member of the Assembly from 1834 to 1838, and mayor of Toronto in 1836. He was tried in 1838 for his alleged part in the rebellion and, although acquitted, fled to the United States after hearing rumours of further charges. He returned to Upper Canada in 1843.

of corruption and all undue influence, whether by bribery, intimidation, misrepresentation, or other unlawful or unconstitutional devices.

2. The establishment of an EXECUTIVE COUNCIL, responsible in this Province, agreeably to the spirit of our constitutional Act, and that of the English principles of government.

3. The control of the PUBLIC REVENUE of the Province of every kind, agreeably to the spirit of the said constitutional Act, and the principles of English government.

4. the amendment of the Constitutional Act of the 31st Geo. III, in so far, as to render the LEGISLATIVE COUNCIL "ELECTIVE."

5. The non-interference of the Imperial Legislature or the Colonial Minister, in our local affairs, except in so far as the 31st Geo. III, explicitly reserves to his Majesty and the British Parliament the powers of interference in matters therein expressed. . . .

A 47   RESOLUTIONS OF THE TORONTO POLITICAL UNION
27 March 1837
[Constitution, *Toronto, 12 April 1837*]

. . . J.E. Small,[106] V.P. in the Chair.

1st. Mr. Thos. Elliot, seconded by Mr. James Bolton,[107] moves that it be resolved, that in the opinion of this Union, the conduct of Sir Francis B. Head, as Lieut. Governor of this Province, has been arbitrary, tyrannical and unconstitutional. That he has in endeavouring to justify his conduct upon several occasions, perverted the truth to the great discredit of the Sovereign whom he unworthily represents, and has consequently forfeited the confidence of all good men. That his being longer retained in the Government of this Province will tend to bring Royalty itself into contempt, to alienate the affections of His Majesty's faithful and loyal subjects from His Majesty's person and government, and that it is therefore the imperative duty of all

[106]James E. Small (1798–1869) was born at York, Upper Canada, his father having been in John Graves Simcoe's entourage. After service in the War of 1812, he studied law and was called to the bar in 1821. He sat as the member of the Assembly for Toronto, 1834–6, and replaced T.D. Morrison as the representative for the third riding of York in 1839, holding the seat until 1849. From 1840 to 1843 he was also solicitor general for Canada West. After leaving Parliament in 1849, he became a county judge in Middlesex and served as such for the rest of his life. A moderate reformer, he acted for William Lyon Mackenzie against those Family Compact members who had destroyed Mackenzie's press and type in 1826. In 1836 Head removed him as a commissioner of the Court of Requests for his election activities. After the rebellion, he acted for a number of those accused of being rebels.

[107]This was probably James Bolton (d. 1838) who came from Norfolk, England, about 1819 with his family. A carpenter, he built a number of mills in the Home District before settling at the future sight of Bolton in Albion Township and, with his nephew George, building Bolton's Mills. He died in September 1838 in the western United States, having fled after the rebellion. Although a participant in the rising, he seems to have had a very minor role in it.

constitutional Reformers to unite in making such representations to His Majesty and the Imperial Parliament, as will enlighten them *upon the true state of affairs in this Province*. – Carried.

2nd. Mr. Doel, seconded by Mr. James Armstrong,[108] moved that it be resolved, That the conduct of the House of Assembly during the last session, has incontrovertibly proved that that body does not represent the free and independent electors of this Province, but that the majority are the mere servile instruments of Sir F.B. Head, bound by their interests to obey his mandate, inasmuch as they were elected if not by his immediate direction, yet with his knowledge and concurrence, by means of an illegal and unconstitutional issue of a large number of patent deeds to individuals who had not performed the duties required of them upon location, before any patent should issue, and in many cases dispensing with the payment of large sums of money to the government, which were originally stipulated to be paid before such grants should have been made; as well as by other corrupt and unconstitutional influences. – Carried.

3rd. Mr. R. McIntosh[109] seconded by Mr. Joseph Elliot,[110] moves, That it be resolved, that after the unconstitutional reference to, and adjudication by the House of Assembly on the serious charges contained in the petition of Dr. C. Duncombe to the British House of Commons upon which the Assembly studiously avoided making such inquiry as would have led to a confirmation of many of the charges therein contained, this Union feel assured that the Province can never derive any beneficial results from their deliberations, but on the contrary that should they be allowed to finish their terms of four years, the Province will not only be involved in debt beyond the possibility of redemption, but will be driven to seek protection in the last resource of an oppressed people. – Carried.

4th. Mr. Hunter[111] seconded by Mr. Reed,[112] moves that it be

[108]This was probably James Rogers Armstrong (1787–1873), born at Dorchester, Quebec. He became a merchant in Kingston and in 1828 moved to York, where he opened a wholesale and retail dry goods store. Possibly because he retained business connections in the eastern portion of the province, he sat as the member of the Assembly for Prince Edward County, 1836–40. In the 1840s he set up the City Foundry which operated for many years. The James Armstrong cited, however, may have been the saddler, who resided at 31 Yonge Street.

[109]Robert McIntosh was one of two brothers of John. All three had houses side by side on Yonge Street. John was by far the most active in politics. Robert had continued to captain lake ships after John had retired from that occupation, and was known as Captain Robert.

[110]Joseph Elliot may have been a labourer, a recent arrival in Toronto, or a visitor from outside the city.

[111]James Hunter was a tailor at Hunter's Place, George Street, Toronto.

[112]This could have been any of several Reeds or Reids in Toronto but was quite possibly James Reid, a young reformer of Scottish birth who worked as a clerk in one of the banks, probably the Bank of the People. He was a son of one of Mackenzie's classmates in Scotland.

resolved, . . . that the lives and liberties of the people of this Province in the exercise of their dearest rights, are insecure, and that the arbitrary powers assumed by Sir Francis B. Head, and so unequivocally justified by Lord Glenelg, in His Majesty's name, in defiance of every principle of honor and justice, convince us that without an unqualified authority to regulate all our internal affairs by a constitution recognizing the people as the source of power we can never enjoy good government in this Province. – Carried.

5th. Dr. O'Grady, seconded by Mr. Shannon,[113] moves that it be resolved, That in the opinion of this Union, there remain no hopes of an amelioration of our present condition or a redress of grievance, unless the friends of civil and religious freedom throughout the Province unite heart and hand in a respectful but firm representation to the Commons of Great Britain and Ireland – and that as we have reason to believe great political changes are contemplated by His Majesty's Ministers in the constitution of this Province, the time has now arrived when the Reformers of Upper Canada should express their opinion with freedom and determination, and that with a view to act with unanimity upon all subjects affecting our liberties and privileges, *A Convention of Delegates* should be held at some place to be agreed upon among themselves with as little delay as possible, said Delegates to be elected by the inhabitants of the several towns and counties in the Province, now entitled to send Representatives to Parliament – *Carried*.

6th. Dr. Tims,[114] seconded by Mr. Laurie,[115] moves that Messrs. Small, Morrison, Gibson,[116] John McIntosh, Lesslie,[117] Price and

[113]James Shannon was a shoemaker at 113 King Street, Toronto.

[114]Dr. John Edward Tims (d. 1839) came from Ireland to York in 1828 and established a medical practice at 219 King Street. A reformer in politics, he was an alderman in 1834.

[115]Archibald Laurie had a wholesale and retail dry goods store at 195 King Street, Toronto.

[116]David Gibson (1804–1864) was born in Forfarshire, Scotland. He apprenticed as a surveyor and in 1825 came to Canada to try his luck at getting a job. Referred to the lieutenant-governor of Upper Canada, Gibson secured government work when it became available in 1828, as well as private employment. He became involved in politics on the reform side and associated with radicals such as his countryman William Lyon Mackenzie, but he did not acquire the radical reputation of his associates. He represented the first riding of York from 1836 to 1838 but then fled the country because of his involvement in the rising. Avoiding the border troubles, Gibson secured employment as a surveyor and did very well, choosing not to return to Upper Canada under the general pardon of 1843. In 1848 he lost his job and returned to Canada, where he became a government employee under the Baldwin–LaFontaine ministry and worked as a surveyor till his death.

[117]James Lesslie (1802–1885) was born in Dundee, Scotland, and emigrated to Upper Canada with most of his family in 1822. He opened a store at Kingston, while his father, brothers, and William Lyon Mackenzie, whom they had sponsored, opened stores at York and Dundas. Lesslie took over the York store in 1826. An active radical

O'Grady, do compose a committee to prepare and report at a future meeting of the Society, an appeal to the Reformers of the Province at large, impressing upon them the urgent necessity at this peculiar crisis of our affairs, to meet in convention, pursuant to the last resolution. – *Carried nem*[.] *con.*

7th. Dr. O'Grady, seconded by Mr. Doel, moves that it be resolved, That an humble address be presented to his Majesty, on the present deplorable state of the Province, and the reckless legislation of the present unconstitutional House of Assembly, which is daily alienating the affections of His Majesty's loyal subjects from the Parent State, and that Messrs. Price and James Lesslie, be a committee to prepare the same. – Carried. . . .

A 48   W.L. MACKENZIE'S POLITICAL UNION SCHEME
[Constitution, *Toronto, 19 July 1837*]

. . . *The Leading Features of a Project for Uniting and Organizing the Reformers of Upper Canada, as a Political Union, for the establishment of the Constitution on the broad basis of civil and religious liberty and equal rights.*

THE POLITICAL UNION.

1. In order to avoid the mixture of persons unknown to each other, no society is to consist of more than twelve persons, and these to be resident as nearly as possible in the same neighbourhood, street, or village. . . .

9. A Union like the above would be perfectly legal, and therefore it appears to me that all oaths should be dispensed with, . . .

10. It will have been observed that successive layers of delegated authority are provided, each exercising a superintendence over that immediately below it, by means of which the whole body of the reformers of this province may be most efficiently organized, for the common good of the whole. . . .

11. It is true that a plan such as I have suggested, could be easily transferred without change of its structure to military purposes. . . . But such is not my object. The organization I suggest is purely civil, for although I am honestly of the opinion that the young men of any one of our most populous townships possess more physical strength than the government and its genuine supporters, yet I do not conceive

---

reformer all his life, he worked tirelessly for the disadvantaged. A founder of the Mechanics' Institute in 1831 and a founder of the Bank of the People in 1835, he also served as a delegate from the Mississippi Emigration Society to the American government in 1838–9 and as a city alderman in 1834. He did not participate in the rebellion but was harassed after the rising because of his radical views. In the 1850s he was active in the Clear Grits. Lesslie was one of the few people who remained a friend of William Lyon Mackenzie over many years, despite his fellow Scot's ingratitude.

that among an educated and armed yeomanry like us Upper Canadians, any such bill as that of Mr. Gowan and the government for the militia, or any such military structure as the above will be wanted. Sir F. Head may cry "Come if ye dare!" and Don Quixotte may engage Wind Mills in due form of battle, but our object is of a purely civil nature, and confined to the embodying and expression of public opinion, in the 1st instance.

I have only given the outline of the system I would recommend. Minor regulations would be easily added. . . .

I think it is time the trial were made whether the people can form one efficient society or union to go a step further than reformers have hitherto moved, on behalf of the injured interests of the many. If union, and an enthusiastic feeling in favor of Justice to Canada, do not work miracles before long, I shall consider myself a bad calculator.

A 49   RESOLUTIONS OF THE TORONTO UNION
28 July 1837
[Constitution, *Toronto, 2 Aug. 1837*]
MEETING
OF
FRIENDS OF REFORM.

At a Meeting of Friends of Reform, held on the premises of Mr. John Doel, Brewer, in the City of Toronto, on the evening of Friday, the 28th of July, 1837, Mr. John Mills[118] was called to the Chair, and Mr. John Elliot, appointed to act as Secretary.

[The Chairman and Secretary were of opinion that this was perhaps the largest assemblage of the Reformers of the City which ever met in Toronto.][119] . . .

Resolved, 2. That the Reformers of Upper Canada are called upon by every tie of feeling, interest, and duty, to make common cause with their fellow citizens of Lower Canada, whose successful coercion would doubtless be in time visited upon us. . . .

Resolved, 3. That a Convention of Delegates be appointed by the Inhabitants of the several Townships, Towns, Counties and Ridings in this Province, to assemble at Toronto, at as early a period as possible to take into consideration the State of the Province, the causes of the present pecuniary and other difficulties, and the means whereby they may be effectually removed. . . .

Resolved, 4. That it be an instruction to the said Convention to appoint seven persons of approved judgment, discretion and patriotism, to proceed to Lower Canada, there to meet the Delegates of

[118]John Mills, a native of Scotland, was a hatter at 191 King Street, Toronto. He was active in the reform movement and in the rebellion. After the failure of the rising, he fled to Adrian, Michigan.
[119]The square brackets occur in the original.

any Congress of these provinces which may be appointed to sit and deliberate on matters of mutual interest to the Colonies during the present year. . . .

Proposed by Mr. Mackenzie, . . .

Resolved, 6, That it is expedient to adopt the following project for uniting, organizing and registering the Reformers of Upper Canada as a political Union, for the establishment of the Constitution on the broad basis of freedom, peace, and justice. – Carried.

1. In order to avoid the mixture of persons unknown to each other, no society is to consist of less than 12 or more than 40 persons, and those to be resident as nearly as possible in the same neighbourhood.

2. Each of these Societies shall choose one of their number to be their secretary.

3. The Secretaries of five of these Societies shall form a Committee, to be called the Township Committee.

4. Ten of these Township Committees, of Citizens residing in places the most convenient to each other, shall each select one of their number, and the persons so chosen shall form the County Committee.

5. The District Committee shall consist of one member to be chosen from each County Committee within the limits of such district.

6. Upper Canada shall be divided into four grand divisions. . . .

7. Within each of these divisions there shall be a Committee of Division to be composed of 2 or 3 members elected from each of the District Committees within the same.

8. The Executive shall consist of three persons, to be chosen from among the members of the several Committees of Division, and be invested with the necessary powers to promote the objects for which the Union is to be constituted.

Mr. Thomas Elliott, seconded by Mr. Kennedy,[120] moves that when this meeting adjourns it do stand adjourned to the same place on Monday evening at a quarter to seven, to receive and decide upon the report of the special committee. – Carried. . . .

A 50   THE TORONTO UNION TO THE REFORMERS OF UPPER CANADA
31 July 1837
[Constitution, *Toronto, 2 Aug. 1837*]
City Reform Meeting.
LAST MONDAY.

The Reformers met, pursuant to adjournment, at seven in the evening, in the large room at Mr. Doel's Brewery – the meeting was called to

---

[120]This was probably William T. Kennedy, who was clerk to William Lyon Mackenzie. Imprisoned for three weeks after the rebellion and without a job, he crossed to the United States, where prospects seemed brighter.

order by Mr. Armstrong – after which John Mackintosh, Esq., M.P.P., was called to the Chair, Mr. Mills being absent.

Dr. Morrison, M.P.P., Chairman of the Special Committee appointed to report a Declaration of the Reformers of this City to their friends throughout the colony, reported the following draft, which was read, and called forth from the meeting the most unequivocal marks of approbation:

THE

DECLARATION

OF THE

REFORMERS

OF THE

CITY OF TORONTO

TO THEIR

FELLOW-REFORMERS

IN

UPPER CANADA

The time has arrived, after nearly half a century's forbearance under increasing and aggravated misrule, when the duty we owe our country and posterity requires from us the assertion of our rights and the redress of our wrongs.

Government is founded on the authority and is instituted for the benefit of a people; when, therefore, any government long and systematically ceases to answer the great ends of its foundation, the people have a natural right given them by their Creator to seek after and establish such institutions as will yield the greatest quantity of happiness to the greatest number.

Our forbearance heretofore has only been rewarded with an aggravation of our grievances; and our past inattention to our rights has been ungenerously and unjustly urged as evidence of the surrender of them. We have now to choose on the one hand between submission to the same blighting policy as has desolated Ireland, and on the other hand, the patriotic achievement of cheap, honest, and responsible government.

The right was conceded to the present United States at the close of a successful revolution, to form a constitution for themselves; and the loyalists with their descendants and others, now peopling this portion of America, are entitled to the same liberty without the shedding of blood – more they do not ask; less they ought not to have. – But, while the revolution of the former has been rewarded with a consecutive prosperity, unexampled in the history of the world, the loyal valor of the latter alone remains amidst the blight of misgovernment to tell them what they might have been as the not less valiant sons of American Independence. Sir Francis Head has too truly portrayed our country "as standing in the flourishing continent of North America like a girdled tree with its drooping branches." But the laws of nature do not, and those of man ought not longer to doom this remnant of the new world to exhibit this invidious and humiliating comparison.

The affairs of this country have been ever against the spirit of the Constitutional Act, subjected in the most injurious manner to the interferences and interdictions of a succession of Colonial Ministers in England who have never visited the country, and can never possibly become acquainted with the state of parties, or the conduct of public functionaries, except through official channels in the province, which are illy calculated to convey the information necessary to disclose official delinquencies and correct public abuses. – A painful experience has proved how impracticable it is for such a succession of strangers beneficially to direct and control the affairs of the people four thousand miles off; and being an impracticable system, felt to be intolerable by those for whose good it was professedly intended, it ought to be abolished, and the domestic institutions of the province so improved and administered by the local authorities as to render the people happy and contented. – This system of baneful domination has been uniformly furthered by a Lieutenant Governor sent amongst us as an uninformed, unsympathising stranger, who, like Sir Francis, has not a single feeling in common with the people, and whose hopes and responsibilities begin and end in Downing Street. And this baneful domination is further cherished by a Legislative Council not elected and therefore responsible to people for whom they legislate, but appointed by the ever changing Colonial Minister for life, from pensioners on the bounty of the Crown, official dependents and needy expectants.

Under this mockery of human Government we have been insulted, injured and reduced to the brink of ruin. The due influence and purity of all our institutions have been utterly destroyed. Our Governors are the mere instruments for effecting domination from Downing Street; Legislative Councillors have been intimidated into executive compliance, as in the case of the late Chief Justice Powell,[121] Mr. Baby,[122] and others; the Executive Council has been stript of every shadow of responsibility, and of every shade of duty; the freedom and purity of elections have lately received, under Sir Francis Head, a final and irretrievable blow; our revenue has been and still is decreasing to such

[121]William Dummer Powell (1755–1834) was born in Boston. Educated in law in Britain, he came to Montreal in 1779. He was, successively, one of the first judges in Upper Canada in 1789, judge of the Court of King's Bench in 1794, and chief justice, 1816–25. In addition he was on the Legislative Council from 1816 to his death and on the Executive Council from 1808 to his death.

[122]James or Jacques Baby (1763–1833) was a member of a prominent Quebec family who moved to Detroit. A prosperous fur trader, he was appointed to the Legislative and Executive councils in 1792. In 1815 he became inspector general of accounts. These positions he held until his death. When he became inspector general he moved to York.

an extent as to render heavy additional taxation indispensable for the payment of the interest of our public debt incurred by a system of improvident and profligate expenditure; our public lands, although a chief source of wealth to a new country, have been sold at a low valuation to speculating companies in London, and resold to the settlers at very advanced rates, the excess being remitted to England to the serious impoverishment of the country; the ministers of religion have been corrupted by the prostitution of the casual and territorial revenue to salary and influence them; our clergy reserves, instead of being devoted to the purpose of general education, though so much needed and loudly demanded, have been in part sold to the amount of upwards of 300,000 dollars, paid into the military chest and sent to England; numerous rectories have been established, against the almost unanimous wishes of the people, with certain exclusive, ecclesiastical and spiritual rights and privileges, according to the Established Church of England, to the destruction of equal religious rights; public salaries, pensions and sinecures, have been augmented in number and amount, notwithstanding the impoverishment of our revenue and country; and this parliament have, under the name of arrearages, paid the retrenchments made in past years by reform parliaments; our Judges have, in spite of our condition, been doubled, and wholly selected from the most violent political partizans against our equal, civil and religious liberties, and a court of chancery suddenly adopted by a subservient parliament, against the long cherished expectations of the people against it, and its operation fearfully extended into the past so as to jeopardize every title and transaction from the beginning of the Province to the present time. A law has been passed enabling Magistrates, appointed during pleasure, at the representation of a Grand Jury selected by a Sheriff holding office during pleasure, to tax the people at pleasure, without their previous knowledge or consent, upon all their rateable property to build and support work-houses for the refuge of the paupers invited by Sir Francis from the parishes in Great Britain; thus unjustly and wickedly laying the foundation of a system which must result in taxation, pestilence and famine. Public loans have been authorized by improvident legislation to nearly 8 millions of dollars, the surest way to make the people both poor and dependent; the parliament, subservient to Sir Francis Head's blighting administration, has, by an unconstitutional act sanctioned by him, prolonged their duration after the demise of the crown, thereby evading their present responsibility to the people, depriving them of the exercise of their elective franchise on the present occasion, and extending the period of their unjust, unconstitutional and ruinous legislation with Sir Francis Head; our best and most worthy citizens have been dismissed from the bench of Justice, from the militia, and other stations of honour and usefulness, for exercising their rights as freemen in attending public meetings for the regeneration of our condition, as instanced in the case of Dr. Baldwin, Messrs. Scatchard, Johnson, Small, Ridout,[123] and others; those of our fellow subjects who go to England to represent our deplorable condition are denied a hearing, by a partial, unjust and oppressive government, while the authors and promoters of our wrongs are cordially and graciously received, and enlisted in the cause of our further wrongs and misgovernment; our public revenues are plundered and misapplied without redress, and unavailable securities make up the late defalcation of Mr. P. Robinson the Commissioner of Public Lands to the amount of 80,000 dollars. Interdicts are continually sent by the colonial minister to the Governor, and by the Governor to the Provincial Parliament, to restrain and render futile their legislation, which ought to be free and unshackled; these instructions, if favourable to the views and policy of the enemies of our country, are rigidly observed; if favourable to public liberty they are, as in the case of Earl Ripon's[124] despatch, utterly contemned, even to the passing of the ever to be remembered and detestable everlasting Salary Bill; Lord Glenelg has sanctioned, in the King's name, all the violations of truth and of the constitution by Sir Francis Head, and both thanked and titled him for conduct, which, under any civilized government, would be the ground of impeachment.

The British Government, by themselves and through the Legislative Council of their appointment, have refused their assent to laws the most wholesome and necessary for the public good, among which we may enumerate the Intestate Estate equal distribution Bill; the Bill to sell the Clergy Reserves for educational purposes; the Bill to remove the corrupt influence of the executive in the choosing of juries, and to secure a fair and free trial by jury; the several bills to encourage emigration from foreign parts; the bills to secure the independency of the Assembly; the bill to amend the law of libel; the bills to appoint commissioners to meet others appointed by Lower Canada, to treat on matters of trade and other matters of deep interest; the bills to extend the blessings of Education to the humbler classes in every township, and to appropriate annually a sum of money for that purpose; the bill to dispose of the school lands in aid of education; several bills for the improvement of the highways; the bill to secure independence to voters by establishing the vote by ballot; the bill for the better regulation of

[123]All those mentioned lost public offices and positions for their parts in the election of 1836.

[124]Frederick John Robinson, Viscount Goderich, afterwards Earl of Ripon (1782–1859), was elected to Parliament in 1806 and held that position until elevated to the peerage. A Whig, he served in various senior government positions, particularly in the Admiralty and the Board of Trade. In 1827 and again from 1830 to 1833 he was secretary of state for war and the colonies. The issue referred to in this section of the address involved the salaries of government officials. The "Everlasting Salary Bill" of 1831 created a permanent civil list so that the officials would be paid without the administration's consulting the provincial assembly.

elections of members of the Assembly, and to provide that they be held at places convenient for the people; the bills for the relief of Quakers, Menonists and Tunkers; the bill to amend the present obnoxious courts of requests laws, by allowing the people to choose the commissioners, and to have a trial by jury if desired; with other bills to improve the administration of justice and diminish unnecessary costs; the bills to amend the Charter of King's College University so as to remove its partial and arbitrary system of government and education; and the bill to allow free competition in Banking.

The King of England has forbidden his governors to pass laws of immediate and pressing importance, unless suspended in their operation till his assent should be obtained; and when so suspended, he has utterly neglected to attend to them. He has interfered with the freedom of elections, and appointed elections to be held at places dangerous, unconvenient and unsafe for the people to assemble at, for the purpose of fatiguing them into his measures, through the agency of pretended representatives; and has through his legislative council, prevented provision from being made for quiet and peaceable elections, as in the case of the late returns at Beverley.

He has dissolved the late House of Assembly for opposing with manly firmness Sir Francis Head's invasion of the right of the people to a wholesome control over the revenue, and for insisting that the persons conducting the government should be responsible for their official conduct to the country through its representatives.

He has endeavoured to prevent the peopling of this province and its advancement in wealth; for that purpose obstructing the laws for the naturalization of foreigners, refusing to pass others to encourage their migration hither, and raising the conditions of new appropriations of the public lands, large tracts of which he has bestowed upon unworthy persons his favorites, while deserving settlers from Germany and other countries have been used cruelly.

He has rendered the administration of Justice liable to suspicion and distrust, by obstructing laws for establishing a fair trial by Jury, by refusing to exclude the chief criminal judge from interfering in political business, and by selecting as the judiciary violent and notorious partizans of his arbitrary power.

He has sent a standing army into the sister province to coerce them to his unlawful and unconstitutional measures, in open violation of their rights and liberties, and has received with marks of high approbation military officers who interfered with the citizens of Montreal, in the midst of an election of their representatives, and brought the troops to coerce them, who shot several persons dead wantonly in the public streets.

Considering the great number of lucrative appointments held by strangers to the country, whose chief merit appears to be their subservience to any and every administration, we may say with our brother colonists of old – "He has sent hither swarms of new officers to harass our people and eat out their substance."

The English Parliament have interfered with our internal affairs and regulations, by the passage of grievous and tyrannical enactments, for taxing us heavily without our consent, for prohibiting us to purchase many articles of the first importance at the cheapest European or American markets, and compelling us to buy such goods and merchandize at an exorbitant price in markets of which England has a monopoly.

They have passed resolutions for our coercion,[125] of a character so cruel and arbitrary, that Lord Chancellor Brougham[126] has recorded on the Journals of the House of Peers, that "they set all considerations of sound policy, of generosity, and of justice at defiance," are wholly subversive of "the fundamental principle of the British Constitution, that no part of the taxes levied on the people shall be applied to any purpose whatever, without the consent of the representatives in parliament," and that the Canadian "precedent of 1837, will ever after be cited in the support of such oppressive proceedings, as often as the Commons of any Colony may withhold supplies, how justifiable soever their refusal may be;" and (adds his lordship) "those proceedings, so closely resembling the fatal measures that severed the United States from Great Britain, have their origin in principles, and derive their support from reasonings, which form a prodigious contrast to the whole grounds, and the only defence, of the policy during latter years, and so justly and so wisely sanctioned by the Imperial Parliament, in administering the affairs of the mother country. Nor is it easy to imagine that the inhabitants of either the American or the European branches of the empire should contemplate so strange a contrast, without drawing inferences therefrom discreditable to the character of the legislature, and injurious to the future safety of the state, when they mark with what different measures we mete to six hundred thousand inhabitants of a remote province, unrepresented in Parliament, and to six millions of our fellow citizens nearer home, and making themselves heard by their representatives. The reflection will assuredly arise in Canada, and may possibly find its way into Ireland, that the sacred rules of justice, the most worthy feelings of national generosity, and the soundest principles of enlightened policy, may be appealed to in vain, if the demands of the suitor be not also supported by personal interests, and party views, and political fears, among those

[125]These were Lord John Russell's Ten Resolutions of 2 March 1837 allowing the crown to acquire public monies without the Lower Canadian Assembly's approval. Among other things, the resolutions declared against an elected Legislative Council and a responsible executive one.

[126]Henry Peter Brougham, Baron Brougham and Vaux (1778–1868), was one of the more liberal Whigs. He championed an end to slavery, an extension of the franchise, and law reform. He was lord chancellor from 1831 to 1834.

whose aid he seeks; while all men perceiving that many persons have found themselves at liberty to hold a course towards an important but remote province, which their constituents never would suffer to be pursued towards the most inconsiderable burgh of the United Kingdom, an impression will inevitably be propagated most dangerous to the maintenance of colonial dominion, that the people can never safely intrust the powers of government to any supreme authority not residing among themselves."

In every stage of these proceedings we have petitioned for redress in the most humble terms; our repeated petitions have been answered only by repeated injuries.

Nor have we been wanting in attention to our British brethren. We have warned them from time to time of attempts by their legislature to extend an unwarrantable jurisdiction over us. We have reminded them of the circumstances of our emigration and settlement here, we have appealed to their native justice and magnanimity, and we have conjured them by the ties of our common kindred to disavow these usurpations which would inevitably interrupt our connection and correspondence. They too have been deaf to the voice of justice and consanguinity.

We, therefore, the Reformers of the City of Toronto, sympathizing with our fellow citizens here and throughout the North American Colonies, who desire to obtain cheap, honest, and responsible government, the want of which has been the source of all their past grievances, as its continuance would lead to their utter ruin and desolation, are of opinion, 1. That the warmest thanks and admiration are due from the Reformers of Upper Canada to the Honorable Louis Joseph Papineau, Esq., Speaker of the House of Assembly of Lower Canada, and his compatriots in and out of the Legislature, for their past uniform, manly, and noble independence, in favour of civil and religious liberty; and for their present devoted, honorable and patriotic opposition to the attempt of the British Government to violate their constitution without their consent, subvert the powers and privileges of their local parliament, and overawe them by coercive measures into a disgraceful abandonment of their just and reasonable wishes.

2. And that the Reformers of Upper Canada are called upon by every tie of feeling, interest, and duty, to make common cause with their fellow citizens of Lower Canada, whose successful coercion would doubtless be in time visited upon us, and the redress of whose grievances would be the best guarantee for the redress of our own.

To render this co-operation the more effectual, we earnestly recommend to our fellow citizens that they exert themselves to organize political associations; that public meetings be held throughout the province; and that a convention of delegates be elected, and assembled at Toronto, to take into consideration the political condition of Upper Canada, with authority to its members to appoint commissioners to meet others to be named on behalf of Lower Canada and any of the other colonies, armed with suitable powers as a Congress, to seek an effectual remedy for the grievances of the colonists.

T.D. MORRISON, *Chairman of Com.*   JOHN ELLIOT, *Secretary.*

COMMITTEE.

DAVID GIBSON,	JAMES H. PRICE,
JOHN MACINTOSH,	JOHN DOEL,
WM. J. O'GRADY,	M. REYNOLDS,[131]
EDWARD WRIGHT,[127]	JAMES ARMSTRONG,
ROBERT McKAY,[128]	JAMES HUNTER,
THOMAS ELLIOTT,	JOHN ARMSTRONG,[132]
E.B GILBERT,[129]	WILLIAM KETCHUM,[133]
JOHN MONTGOMERY,[130]	WM. L. MACKENZIE.
JOHN EDWARD TIMS,	

Dr. Morrison addressed the meeting at great length, and was enthusiastically cheered. He then moved, seconded by Mr. E.B. Gilbert, that the report of the special committee, just read as above, be

[127]Edward Wright was a tailor who lived in the north end of Toronto.

[128]Robert McKay was a Scot who opened a wholesale and retail grocery business in York in 1832. His business was at 48 King Street at the time of the rebellion. A radical reformer, he was at the October meeting when Mackenzie proposed a quick seizure of the government, and was active inside the city during the subsequent rising until arrested on 7 December. He left Toronto some time after his release, and in July of 1839 opened a grocery store in Rochester, where many Upper Canadian exiles lived. His brother Alexander had a business at 46 King Street.

[129]Elisha Benjamin Gilbert was a cabinet-maker on Bay Street in Toronto.

[130]John Montgomery (1788–1879) was born in Gagetown, New Brunswick. He came to Upper Canada in time to serve in the War of 1812. He then opened a tavern on Yonge Street in York. In the mid-1830s he opened a new tavern on Yonge Street north of the present Eglinton Avenue. Although he had just rented the tavern when the rebellion broke out, he remained there during the rising and was caught, tried, and sentenced to transportation. In 1838 he escaped from Fort Henry in company with several other convicted rebels and reached the United States, where he remained until the general amnesty of 1843. Upon his return, he resumed innkeeping.

[131]Michael Reynolds was a printer who lived on York Street in Toronto. He may have worked for William Lyon Mackenzie.

[132]John Armstrong took over an existing axe-making firm in the mid-1830s. An active radical, he served on city council in 1835, and was at the October 1837 meeting at which W.L. Mackenzie proposed using "Armstrong's axe men and Dutcher's foundry men" to seize the government. He appears to have left the city after the rebellion.

[133]William Ketchum (b. *ca.* 1807) was born north of Toronto, son of the tanner and social reformer, Jesse Ketchum. William became a tanner himself. His property in the village of Markham was used for a political union meeting in September 1837. After the rebellion he fled to the United States because he feared he would be tried as a rebel, although his only crime appears to have been to withhold information of the strength of the rebels and on the conduct of John Rolph during the flag of truce incident of 6 December.

adopted as the sense of this meeting, and that the declaration of the Reformers of this city be countersigned by the Secretary on behalf of this meeting.

Which was agreed to, by acclamation, none dissenting.

Edward Wright, Esq., seconded by Mr. James Armstrong, moves that it be

Resolved, That reposing the greatest confidence in our fellow citizens,

> JOHN ROLPH, M.P.P.,
> MARSHAL S. BIDWELL,
> T.D. MORRISON, M.P.P.,
> JAMES LESSLIE,
> JAMES H. PRICE,
> JOHN EDWARD TIMS, and
> ROBERT McKAY, ESQUIRES,

we do hereby nominate and appoint them members of the Provincial Convention for the City of Toronto. – Carried unanimously and by acclamation.

Moved by John Edw. Tims, Esq., seconded by Mr. Robert McKay.

Resolved, That the members of the Committee who have reported the draft of a declaration of the Reformers of Toronto, be a permanent Committee of Vigilance, for this city and liberties, and to carry into immediate and practical effect the resolutions of this meeting for the effectual organization of the Reformers of Upper Canada – that Mr. John Elliot be requested to continue to officiate as the secretary in ordinary – that W.L. Mackenzie, Esq., be invited to perform the important duties of Agent and Corresponding Secretary – and that when this meeting adjourns it stand adjourned to the call of the said committee through its chairman. – Carried unanimously.

Mr. John Doel, seconded by Mr. M. Reynolds, moves that it be

Resolved, that we will, in the pursuit of the objects of this meeting as far as possible rigidly abstain, so long as our duty to our country requires it, from the consumption of articles coming from beyond [the] sea, or paying duties, in order that no revenues raised from the people shall be made instrumental in the continuance of their bad government, which will assuredly be perpetuated as long as our folly supplies the means. – Carried – ten to one.

Mr. Mackenzie, seconded by Mr. James Hunter, moves –

Resolved, That the right of obtaining articles of luxury, or necessity, in the cheapest market, is inherent in the people, who only consent to the imposition of duties for the creation of revenues with the express understanding that the revenues so raised from them shall be devoted to the necessary expenses of government, and apportioned by the people's Representatives; and therefore when the contract is broken by an Executive or any foreign authority, the people are released from their engagement, and are no longer under any moral obligation to contribute to, or aid in the collection of, such revenues. Mr. M., briefly addressed the meeting in favour of the resolution, which was put and carried without opposition. . . .

A 51   THE *Liberal* ON THE DECLARATION OF THE TORONTO UNION
[Liberal, *St. Thomas, quoted* Constitution, *Toronto, 30 Aug. 1837*]

THE DECLARATION, &c. – Need we call attention to "the *Declaration* of the reformers of Toronto?["] They have bearded the lion in his den, and like the insulted colonies of old, they fling their Declaration in the teeth of despotism. It is a noble document – the production of men of muscle – every one of them a CHOPPER! It will stimulate the friends of equal rights to vigorous action, as it already begins to make the enemies of good government tremble. It will be read with pleasure and every sentence treasured up by a brave people struggling to be free. Times are changing – read the accounts of the reform meetings in the County of York, and if ever you allowed yourself to doubt the principles or spirit of the Canadian people, dismiss your doubts for ever. "Now is the time and now is the hour," your co-operation is required. This is not the winter of our political existence, in which we might read and sleep, wrapt round and round in conscious security, while the winds whistled through the woods and the torrents tumbled from the hills; this is the spring time of reform for the Canadas; and it becomes the paramount duty of every man to put his hand to the plough, or lay his axe at the root of the tree of abuse. Bear a part in the labor now, that you may hereafter share in the honor and blessings of the political regeneration of your country.

We earnestly recommend every township to form political unions; to hold meetings and to express boldly and above board their determination to rise or fall with their brethren in Lower Canada. This is not enough – they must at the same time, let the world know, that they are determined to shake the locust from their own "girdled tree" – from this land of *bubble*-Governors, *pestilence*-Parliaments and *famine*-officials. These are grievances which can never be removed by "humble petitions,"neither the Lord Glenelg nor the Imperial Parliament will listen to your complaints; nor can your cries ever be permitted to disturb the frills or the frolics of that young damsel that sits as Queen, and flirts her fan over the empire.

A 52   W.L. MACKENZIE ON THE STATE OF THE PROVINCE
[Constitution, *Toronto, 16 Aug. 1837*]

DREADFUL AFFRAY.

What a terrible situation this country is in! An Editor offends a few of the servants of government, and his types are sent to the bottom of

Lake Ontario! A Scottish gentleman expresses political opinions, and eight months in a dungeon, are followed by banishment, because he would not go away! . . . A Judge, from England, interprets the law, that one Judge is not three, and for his honesty is dragged from the bench of justice! – Another (Thorpe) expresses a wish for the prosperity of our country, and poverty, banishment and disgrace await him![134] . . . The English nation and legislature denounce orangeism, the King desires his inferior magistrates to put down the abomination, and Sir Francis Head declares he neither has put it down, nor has he any such intention! Magistrates, Commissioners of Requests, and officers of government boast of their connexion with the order, and receive at court more favour! Processions, with party tunes, drums, guns, pistols, dirks, cutlasses and swords, figure in our streets and churches, and the *established* church bestows its blessing! An Assembly, for a wonder, is honest to the country, and dissolution is their reward! Patents and corruption yield a more subservient parliament, and year after year is added to their duration! What wonder is it then, that when the reformers have called peaceful meetings to state and express public opinion as to the causes of the agricultural and commercial distress, orange mobs, with rifles, clubs, and other such arguments, should fall upon them like demons and shed innocent blood. The government, the orangemen, and the magistracy understand each other perfectly. . . .

A 53   THE ALBION UNION MEETING
Boltontown, 7 August 1837
[Constitution, *Toronto, 16 Aug. 1837*]

ALBION MEETING.

Agreeable to the notification, a Reform Meeting was this day held in this place. – About half past twelve, JAMES COATS[135] was appointed Chairman, and JAMES BOLTON, Secretary.

The meeting was scarcely organized before great clamour and interruption took place and continued for the space of an hour. In the mean time, a blue flag was hoisted containing the words – "The Constitution""Albion For Ever." "No Surrender," in large yellow letters. The Declaration of the city Reformers of Monday last was,

---

[134]The reform movement in criticizing the Compact often referred to past incidents to illustrate the vindictive and unyielding nature of the government. Mackenzie referred here to the dumping of his type in the lake in 1826 and then mentioned three of the most quoted examples of the way the Compact acted: the harassment of Robert Gourlay, 1818–19, the removal of Judge John Walpole Willis from the Court of King's Bench in 1828 for insisting that the court could not sit unless all three judges were present, and the removal of Puisne Judge Robert Thorpe in 1807 for stirring up opposition to government policies.

[135]James Coats lived on lot 23, concession 8, Albion.

however, passed, without any apparent opposition at the time; but *all* after that was confusion and uproar. James Johnson,[136] Esq., Commissioner of Requests, kindly used much exertion to restore order among his countrymen and fellow protestants, but to no effect. The Reformers, although we believe this class far the most respectable as to appearance and numbers, soon after the Declaration passed, and for the sake of the King's peace, and the cause of humanity, concluded to adjourn the remainder of their business to Mr. Charles Boltons,[137] which was accordingly done.

(Signed) JAMES COATS Chairman,
(Signed) JAMES BOLTON Sec'y. . . .

A 54 "THE BATTLE OF ALBION
[Constitution, *Toronto, 16 Aug. 1837*]

Mr. Mackenzie left Lloydtown accompanied only by a couple of friends. . . . News in the meantime had reached Lloydtown that the Orangemen were to try to raise a riot in Albion, and about 50 stout young farmers on horseback resolved to escort Mr. Mackenzie to the village, and see fair play. They overtook him 3 miles to the north of it, and it was soon made evident that their presence would be of service. After Mr. Coats, brother to the worthy magistrate for Albion, had taken the chair, the orangemen boldly avowed they had come to put down the meeting, by force if necessary. – They were few in number compared to the reformers, but although they heard Mr. Mackenzie with great patience, they thrice interrupted the reading of the Toronto declaration; and grew more and more enraged and vociferous when its adoption by the township could not be prevented. . . . They told the Lloydtown reformers to leave the ground in 5 minutes, hoisted a flag with "the Constitution" and "no surrender" on it, and gave out that they had fire arms loaded and ready in one of the houses. Their threats and warnings were disregarded, the remainder of the business was done at Mr. Bolton's, and some hours after when many reformers had gone away, the young gentlemen from King mounted their horses, and twenty six of them were leaving together, fine stout athletic fellows, when as the last of them was crossing the river, a leader of the tories from whom I would have expected better things, seized hold of him by the thigh, thinking to throw both man and horse over the bridge into the Humber. Two others were attacked at the same time. But they had mistaken their men. The whole of them were off their horses in an instant, and in a minute the bridge was cleared, and a more terrible infliction was never given to men than these unfortunate tories there

[136]James Johnson lived on lot 14, concession 6, Albion.
[137]Charles Bolton, not "Boltons," was the son of James Bolton. He was born in England in 1804.

received. With rails, sticks, and their heavy fists, they made the blood
flow very freely – and a number of the men whose insults we had borne
with patience, lay groaning with pain, and some of them admitted that
they had deserved all they got. . . .

A 55   "ERIN GO BRAGH" TO THE *Patriot*
Albion, 8 August 1837
[Patriot, *Toronto, 15 Aug. 1837*]

. . . Mr. Mackenzie entered this loyal township, according to his
appointment, on Monday last at about 10 o'clock in the morning,
accompanied by a cavalcade of 40 persons to proclaim King Papineau,
O'Connell[138] and himself, with the Eagle and Stars for their rallying
point. The loyal boys of Albion, however, shewed no disposition to
swear allegiance to such a government, but on the contrary, disgusted
and enraged beyond all endurance at the impudence of those who had
"*dared to invade the borders of their realm*" to preach sedition against
our gracious Queen and glorious Constitution, adopted a very
summary mode of ridding themselves of the whole gang. No sooner
had little Mackenzie mounted the *fatal* cart, with his chairman and
secretary, than in the twinkling of a bed-post, with the well known
shout of "*Faugh a Ballagh*," (anglice "*clear the way!*") the whole
concern was shoved into the Humber, and the rebel army was made to
feel the power of an Irish Shillelagh. It was impossible to restrain the
fury of our people, and the consequence was that many of their
enemies were left weltering in their blood. Poor Mackenzie begged his
life – Lloyd[139] of Lloydstown lost his *eye* tooth, and *Squire* Lount[140]
his hat, and a little of his Yankee blood. We picked up, as the spoils of

[138]Daniel O'Connell (1775–1847) was an Irish lawyer and moderate reformer. He
worked for Catholic emancipation and for better conditions for Irish Catholics. He won
a seat in the British Parliament in 1828 and proved himself conservative on issues such
as an extended franchise and trade unionism. He was a hero to Irish Catholics because
of his work on their behalf.

[139]Jesse Lloyd (1786–1838) came from Pennsylvania in 1812 and began to build
mills on the Holland River. In the mid-1820s he acquired land in King Township,
subdividing part of it to form the village of Lloydtown, which was flourishing by the
early 1830s, as was Lloyd. Born a Quaker, he was expelled from the local meeting in
1831 because of his reform activities. A vigorous supporter of the rebellion from the
beginning, he fled to the United States on its failure and died of fever in the Indiana
Territory.

[140]Samuel Lount (1791–1838) was born in Pennsylvania. He came to Whitchurch
Township in Upper Canada with his father and family in 1811 but returned to the
United States during the War of 1812, coming back to Upper Canada to stay in 1815.
He worked variously as a blacksmith, surveyor, tavernkeeper, storekeeper, and farmer
in Whitchurch and West Gwillimbury townships. As a result of his surveying and
exploring for the government, he became a good friend of immigrants and the Indians,
a man of great popularity. He also accumulated valuable properties and helped build
the first steamer on Lake Simcoe. After resisting pressure to run for the Assembly for
some years, he stood for election in 1834 and was successful. In 1837 he served as

war, *thirty-two hats* after the action was over, and I take it for granted that the heads that wore them may have required a little plastering to fit them for new ones if they can be obtained. The cavalry cleared off without sound of trumpet, or waiting to put the bridles in the mouths of their chargers, and you may rest assured, Sir, that Jack Lawless,[141] the aid-de-camp of O'Connell, never met a *warmer* reception in Ballybay, than did W.L. Mackenzie in Albion, on Monday last. . . .

A 56   JAMES GOWAN[142] TO OGLE GOWAN, [DRAFT]
Albion, 24 August 1837
[*PAO, James R. and Ogle Gowan Papers*]

. . . I remained in the Country till the 4th Inst. but not long enough to witness the McKenzie meeting at Boultons Mill but the acct he gives in his paper of it is strictly incorrect [–] The truth was as Mr. [Steven?] who witnessed the whole [transaction?] tells me he brought [some ?] 40 yunge men from the neighburing Township who we[re] equipped in complete row stile short jackets cap; and clubs & well ins[t]ructed to awe the Albion [loyaales?] tho the truth ends there for after out voting them the Torys drove from the villiage McK's support[er]s who were oblidged to flee with the utmost precipitation to save themselves [–] the tale of the castigation given by his men and the Viva's for Panieu [Papineau] &c is without foundation, . . .

A 57   "ANTI-COERCION MEETING IN VAUGHAN"
19 August 1837
[Constitution, *Toronto, 23 Aug. 1837*]

The people of the Township of Vaughan, ever true to the principle of Reform, met on Saturday the 19th of August, 1837, to form political associations, express public sympathy with Lower Canada, and elect delegates to the U.C. Convention – . . .

Mackenzie's chief lieutenant during the rebellion. Captured in an open boat on Lake Erie after the rebels' defeat, he was imprisoned. Tried, he was found guilty of treason and was executed in April 1838 with Peter Matthews.

[141]John Lawless (1773–1837) was an Irish reformer who was trained in law but not allowed to practise because he was considered too radical. He preferred public meetings and agitation to parliamentary reform, and opposed the more moderate Daniel O'Connell on several major issues.

[142]James Robert Gowan (1815–1909) was a cousin of Ogle Gowan. James emigrated to Albion, Upper Canada, in 1832. He articled as a lawyer with James E. Small in 1833 and in 1838 became his partner. He fought against the rebels of 1837 but helped Small defend some of them afterwards. This experience gave him a lasting interest in reform. He was appointed judge of the new District of Simcoe in 1843. In the succeeding years he was very active in organizing and consolidating the laws of Canada West, Ontario, and of Canada. He retired in 1883 and was appointed to the Senate, where he spoke for imperial unity.

Resolved, 1. That Government is founded on the authority, and is instituted for the benefit [*sic*] of a a people [*sic*], or community, and not for the benefit, honour, or profit of any man, or any class of men, who are only a part of that community; that the doctrine of non-resistance to arbitrary power is slavish, absurd and discreditable to a people who can appreciate their privileges; and that it is therefore their inherent right as well as incumbent duty, to meet and discuss whatever relates to them in a public capacity. . . .

Resolved, 2. That though in a first settlement of a colony, or during the first possession of a ceded country, the people by admitting the authority of a foreign Legislature, may for a time forego the exercise of their natural privileges, yet as they possess the indefeasable right of altering, reforming, or changing that Government, whenever their safety, happiness or prosperity require it, or when public liberty is endangered, they may resume their rights, and act upon their own energies, whenever their efforts to obtain redress elsewhere have proved ineffectual. . . .

Resolved, 3. That at no time in the history of our country was union among the people more necessary for its salvation from much difficulty. Corruption reigns in the Legislature – the violent partizan fills the seat of Justice – the governing power has now no check on this side of the ocean, except it were the apprehension of popular indignation suddenly expressed – and the friends of reform have as yet been baffled in their honest efforts to bring about a better state of things. We acknowledge the existence of the manifold abuses pointed out in the declaration of reformers of Toronto City, dated 31 July last, and approve of their proceedings, especially in the formation of primary societies of between 12 and 40 members, for maintaining political rights, and producing union and strength among the reformers; and we accord our meed of praise to the gallant conduct of the people and assembly of Lower Canada; who, with their able leader, Mr. Speaker Papineau, are taking the stand we would have gladly taken here. . . . And we solemnly pledge ourselves to abstain, as far as possible, from the purchase or use of British goods which have paid taxes to a government which openly declares its bad faith, by resolving to rob the exchequer of the sister colony, and keep her people without education, and by continuing from year to year to plunder us of many thousands of pounds annually, for the worst of purposes. . . .

Resolved, 4. That we adopt the principles laid down in an address to His Majesty King Wm. 4th, by the 11th House of Assembly, . . . wherein they ask for self government; solemnly protesting against any interference in their internal affairs, on the part of Great Britain, . . . since (as they say) "His Majesty's Ministers at a distance of more than 4000 miles; not at all accountable to" the people of Upper Canada; and "possessing necessarily a slight and imperfect knowledge of their country, the wants and habits and feelings of its inhabitants, and the mode of transacting business;" are "beyond the reach and operation of the public opinion of the Province." . . .

Resolved, 5. That Ireland, from which many of the people of this country or their parents emigrated, has suffered severely, by absentee proprietors of lands, by an established church of a few and proscribed or persecuted sects comprising the many, by an executive government which public opinion has seldom reached, by the want of free trade, by native legislatures at one period and a foreign one at another which only used their power to rivet the fetters on the country, by domestic factions and parties caring only for ascendency [*sic*], by a corrupt administration of the laws, and sometimes by the suspension of law – but above all, by fomenting discord, jealousy, animosity, and bitter enmity between the protestant and catholic population, and encouraging rival associations founded on religious differences. . . . Upper Canada, from like causes, has been compared to a "girdled tree with its drooping branches" standing in the middle of the North American Continent, overshadowed by "the tree of abuse," which latter our lieutenant governors daily water, and our rectory established clergy regard its growth with more than parental anxiety. . . .

Resolved, 7. That the £20,000 defalcation by Mr. Peter Robinson, the £300,000 expended on the Welland Canal, the £50,000 given to political parsons, chiefly of the Church of England, the £60,000 sent to London . . . of post office taxation, the £80,000 sent to the same place from the Clergy Reserves Sales, the £150,000 paid to War loss claimants from monies borrowed, the £5,000 and upwards given as a reward for political services to one sort of Methodists, the many thousand [*sic*] of pounds paid for sham parliamentary sessions which could result in no positive good; these, and the enormous pension monies profligately thrown away, . . . and the vast profits so unjustly bestowed on the Canada Company, with the proceeds of land sales paid to Europe on account of persons who have had splendid free grants in a country they never resided in, and of the princely incomes of Governors and their assistants, who came from and returned to Europe, have involved us £40,000 a year in debt, mortgaged our revenue, injured our trade, withdrawn the means by which the merchant and banker might do business to advantage, and put a stop to much that would be useful as public improvements. . . .

Resolved, 8. That we agree with Lord Stanley[143] in the opinion he expresses in a letter to W.W. Baldwin, Esq. that "the Legislative Council is at the root of all the evils complained of in both provinces;"and that the Lower Canada Assembly, when all other

---

[143]Edward George Geoffrey Smith Stanley, fourteenth Earl of Derby (1852) and Lord Stanley (1834) (1799–1869), was a Whig who entered Parliament in 1822. He served as chief secretary for Ireland, 1830–3, and as colonial secretary, 1833–4. He was reappointed to the latter post in 1841.

means of remedying this radical evil had failed, did right to adopt his lordship's suggestion to stop the supplies. . . .

Resolved, 9. That a Committee of public safety and good correspondence be established in the township, . . .

A 58   THE VAUGHAN MEETING
[Constitution, *Toronto, 23 Aug. 1837*]

GLORIOUS EFFECT OF ARMED ASSOCIATIONS,
VAUGHAN MEETING.
THE ORANGE RUFFIANS SCARED.

Couriers carried the tidings of Friday to Vaughan (the next township) in good time to enable the yeomanry to attend the meeting on lot 4 in 11 concession, next morning each man with a solid oak or hickory stick; and by eleven, one hundred and fifty farmers were assembled on the green near the German [Lutheran] Church, who increased their number to four hundred, including a good number of well dressed ladies, between 2 and 3 in the afternoon. Colonel Moody,[144] and Squires Parsons,[145] Bridgeford,[146] Boyd[147] & Barwick,[148] came with their orangemen, but the formidable and unexpected array of oak and hickory troubled them sore, and for fear of their skins they sent a deputation to Mr. Gibson, but would not venture upon Mr. Mussulmen's[149] grounds although that gentleman repeatedly invited

[144]Colonel Robert Moodie (Moody) (d. 1837) was a native of Fifeshire, Scotland. He entered the army in 1796 and served in the Peninsular War and in the War of 1812. In 1814 he was put on half-pay as lieutenant-colonel. In 1835 he emigrated with his family to Upper Canada, settling on lot 49, concession 1 of Markham Township, just north of Richmond Hill. He was killed attempting to warn Toronto of the rebellion on 4 December 1837.

[145]William Parsons (d. 1866) emigrated from Dorset, England, in 1817 with his brother-in-law Benjamin Thorne. They settled in what became Thornhill, on Yonge Street. Parsons kept a store and was the first postmaster of the village, a position he kept until 1860.

[146]David Bridgeford (b. *ca.* 1792) came to Canada from New York at age seven, with his mother and stepfather. He served in the War of 1812 and was subsequently appointed colonel of the sedentary militia. Known as Captain Bridgeford, he bought lot 47 and part of lot 45, concession 1 in Vaughan Township in 1818.

[147]Francis Boyd arrived in Upper Canada in 1835 or 1836 and bought lot 53, concession 1 of Vaughan Township. He is likely the same Francis Boyd who, an English farmer, was recommended to be elevated to the Legislative Council in 1838 but whose appointment was never made, and who also served as a director of the Bank of Upper Canada from 1842 to 1859.

[148]John Barwick (1806–1881) was born in St. Petersburg, Russia. He served in the British army, reaching the rank of lieutenant-colonel. In 1832 he emigrated to Upper Canada, and settled on lot 34, concession 1 of Vaughan, which formed part of the village of Thornhill. He had a sawmill as of 1834 cr 1835, and in 1843 took over the Red Mills at Holland Landing from Benjamin Thorne. He then moved to the latter place. In 1837–8 he raised a troop at his own expense to fight the rebels.

[149]"Mussulmen" may have been Abraham Musselman who farmed on lot 11, concession 4 of Vaughan, a lot owned by his brother Peter, a Lutheran minister.

all who knew how to behave themselves quietly. They expostulated about the clubs and Mr. Gibson frankly told them that their unmanly conduct on the Friday was properly resented by the farmers, and that hereafter at public meetings they (the farmers) would teach them and such as them how to keep the peace. Guilt is fearful, and their worships and their desperadoes shewed it, for they sneaked off without beat of drum, leaving their boast of scattering the d_____d radicals to be fulfilled when, as in Churchville, the people may not be prepared with weapons of self defence. . . .

A 59 "THE POLITICAL UNIONS"
[Constitution, *Toronto, 13 Sept. 1837*]

. . . The cry hath hitherto been – "Get a good House of Assembly." It is a false cry. You may vote in fifty reform parliaments as you please, but until the great body of the people have considered and decided, in their Unions and town meetings, what measures ought to be carried to insure the promotion of the general welfare, and until they have determined that these measures shall be carried, what can a House of Assembly do, even if it be a reform one? – . . .

Agitation! agitation! agitation! then, ought to be your watchword; and when the great questions on which the prosperity of the country rests are temporately discussed and fully understood out of doors, there will be no difficulty in making any Governor or any Assembly respect the public will truly and solemnly expressed. – . . .

A 60 THE WHITBY MEETING
14 September 1837
[Patriot, *Toronto, 19 Sept. 1837*]

. . . More interest attached to this meeting in the minds of many from the unusual circumstances of the people, who were invited to attend, being *recommended to come armed*. At the hour appointed, one o'clock, a considerable number of persons, amongst whom were many of the first respectability in the neighbourhood, and others from the adjoining townships, assembled at the Baptist Meeting House – the place named in the advertisement. But here there was very *properly no admission*. An adjournment to the stores of Mr. Peter Perry[150] was then proposed and agreed to, and a numerous body of people was soon congregated in front of Mr. Perry's dwelling. But no Mackenzie made his appearance! A full hour was given him and his adherents to

---

[150]Peter Perry (1793–1851) was born near Kingston into a United Empire Loyalist family. He was joint member of the Assembly for Lennox and Addington with M.S. Bidwell from 1824 to 1836 when he was defeated in the general rout of reformers. By then he was recognized as a leader of the radicals. He then moved to Perry's Corners (Whitby), where he kept a store. In 1849 he was one of the founders of the Clear Grits.

organize their meeting. Two o'clock came, but still no Mackenzie!! At half past two, seeing no probability of his arrival, or any open advocacy of his cause, the Conservatives adjourned to the long room in Bennett's Tavern, from the middle window of which the union flag of Old England was displayed . . ., as a rallying point, and the room was speedily filled. . . .

Mr. *Fothergill*[151] rose, and introduced a series of resolutions applicable to the occasion, in a speech of considerable length, in which he inveighed in strong terms on the conduct of those who in any degree aided and abetted the unprincipled disturbers of the peace; and he particularly warned those who were inclined to think lightly of such pranks as bearing arms *of any sort* in support of the Revolutionists or their opinions, or their meetings – even though such arms *should* be no other than "*hiccory staves*," for there were magistrates, notwithstanding the aspersions which had been thrown upon them, who *would do their duty*. Mr. Fothergill pointed out how easily well intentioned but half-informed people might be drawn into seditious practices by designing malcontents; expatiated on the happy circumstances of the Provinces, and our brightening prospects – congratulated his fellow subjects on the near prospect of better times, . . .

"1. Resolved, – That as a public meeting of the inhabitants of Whitby, and the adjacent townships, has been called at this very busy and inconvenient season (being in the midst of harvest), for political purposes of the vilest nature, the majority of this meeting avail themselves of the opportunity thus afforded them, to express their abhorrence and indignation at this additional attempt to disturb the peace of this otherwise tranquil, rich, and flourishing section of our noble Province." . . .

"2. Resolved, – That it is a matter of surprise to all our well-disposed inhabitants, that such men as Mackenzie, and his associates and adherents, whether open or secret, are *permitted* so long and so often to annoy by their pernicious fooleries and rank sedition, an enlightened and loyal people, who are unalienably attached to the principles of their government, and to their long cherished and highly venerated institutions, which they are determined to support and defend, if necessary, with their lives and property." . . .

"4. Resolved, – That whilst we feel ourselves called upon thus to express our detestation of the cause which has this day called us together, we rely with implicit confidence on the patriotism and

---

[151]Charles Fothergill (1782–1840) came to Upper Canada from Yorkshire in 1816 and settled at Port Hope in 1817, where he had a general store and post office. From 1824 to 1830 he was a member of the Assembly for Durham, and from 1822 to 1826 was King's Printer and editor of the *Upper Canada Gazette*. He sometimes spoke against the administration and in 1826 was dismissed as King's Printer and postmaster. In 1837 he bought the equipment of the retiring William J. O'Grady and from 1837–40 he and his son published the *Palladium of British America*. Fothergill was well known for his naturalist interests and collection.

firmness of his Excellency the Lieutenant Governor under the enlightened and benevolent policy of the Mother Country to carry into execution every measure calculated to develope the manifold resources, and promote the welfare of this extensive and fruitful province." . . .

A 61   THE BAYHAM MEETING
23 September 1837
[Patriot, *Toronto, 6 Oct. 1837*]

. . . Glorious result of a Public Meeting at the Township of Bayham, on Saturday the 23rd instant, convened by the enemies of the Queen and Constitution, for the purpose of subverting the lawful authority of the Government, as appeared in the notice thereof in the rebel newspaper published at St. Thomas [the *Liberal*].

The people having heard of the proceedings held two weeks before at a small Yankee village called Sparta, determined upon rallying round the standard of the Queen, to frustrate their knavish tricks, met the enemy at the appointed hour, when lo, the rebels finding themselves outnumbered, refused to organize their meeting, but with clubs, pikes, guns, hatchets, dirks, knives, brandished about with the most awful imprecations against the Queen's people, and in true Robespierrean style hurraing for Papineau and Liberty – ('being of course Reformers upon British principles only,') – but the good people, nothing dismayed, took ground where this meeting was advertised, and on hoisting the national flag of England, proceeded in due form to organize the meeting, when Philip Hodgkinson,[152] Esq., was called to the Chair, and Doyle McKenny,[153] Esq., appointed Secretary. The chairman explained the object for which they had met, being to defeat the designs of the enemies of their peace, when John Burwell,[154] Esq., after reading the Queen's Proclamation, addressed the meeting at considerable length, during which he was several times cheered by the people; after which the following Resolutions were severally put, and unanimously adopted. –

[152]Philip Hodgkinson, the son of a United Empire Loyalist, moved into the Malahide Township area from Grantham. On occasion he helped his brothers George and Thomas edit St. Thomas' first newspaper, the *Journal*, which was established in 1831 and in other editorial hands by 1833. Philip was appointed a magistrate in either 1833 or 1836 and postmaster of Aylmer in 1837. He held the latter post until 1875.
[153]Doyle McKenny (b. *ca.* 1797) was a Canadian-born Malahide farmer and Canada Company agent who acquired extensive land holdings by purchasing UEL rights. A veteran of the War of 1812 and appointed a magistrate in 1835, he was active in suppressing the Duncombe rising in his area. He became an ensign of the militia in December 1837 and a captain in July 1838. Shortly after the rebellion he drowned crossing the Niagara River.
[154]John Burwell (1794–1864) was born in Upper Canada into a family which claimed a United Empire Loyalist heritage. He lived in Port Burwell, a village

1st. Resolved, That this meeting fully and affectionately acknowledge the Government of our Sovereign Lady the Queen, as by the Grace of God permitted and sanctioned.

2d. Resolved, That the people of these Townships, fully appreciating the advantages attendant on the blessings of honest industry, do not desire any invasions of their comforts by a constant agitation of the public mind – only to subserve the hopes and views of the idle and vicious for selfish gain from the credulity of the unwary.

3d. Resolved, – That this Meeting solemnly pledge themselves to stand by and defend the Government of their lawful Sovereign against the insidious attempts of the seditious and disaffected to promote a rebellion in this happy land.

4th. Resolved, – That without Law, honestly obeyed, there is no liberty.

5th. Resolved, – That the flag of England is the only lawful flag to be exhibited in this Province, and that all others are forgeries upon our rights and liberties.[155]

6th. Resolved, – That this Meeting repudiates the attempts that have been made in some parts of this District to promote the cause of rebellion in our sister Province of Lower Canada.

7th. Resolved, – That this Meeting regards the arrival of Sir Francis Head in this province as a measure under the Providence of God, of checking the seeds of rebellion, then rapidly growing up.

8th. Resolved, – That this meeting retains grateful recollection of the protection of the British Government, and do not desire any change in its organization in this Province, to promote confusion, strife and uncertainty.

9th. Resolved, – That this meeting return their warm and grateful thanks to the Hon. Colonel Talbot, for his fatherly protection of this settlement.

10th. Resolved, – That this meeting do now disperse, and the people return to their respective homes, loyally holding themselves in readiness to obey the commands of their Sovereign and laws, whenever required.

The thanks of the meeting were then severally given to the Chairman and Secretary, for their steady conduct, and also to John Burwell,

---

established by his elder brother Mahlon. There he was the central figure of a little tory clique, the "Bayham Club," and was a commissioner of the Court of Requests, a magistrate, the collector of customs, postmaster, and coroner. A veteran of the War of 1812, he was active in suppressing the rebellion and was commissioned a lieutenant-colonel in the militia in January 1838, but he was such a violent tory partisan in the post-rebellion period that he was stripped of his magistracy in 1839. None the less, he retained sufficient popularity to be elected to the district council in 1842.

[155]This resolution presented a protest against the flying of liberty flags at some reform meetings.

Esq., for his address to the people, and for the resolutions he had prepared.

PHILIP HODGKINSON, *Chairman*.
DOYLE M'KENNY, *Secretary*.

Thus ended, and in the most peaceful manner, the PUBLIC MEETING called by the rebels for quite a different purpose, who seeing themselves so completely out numbered, *ran away* to a log heap, at some distance – and some boys, whose curiosity induced them to follow them, informed us that nothing could be understood among them but *huzzas* for "Papineau and Liberty," as not one among the motley crew could audibly read the resolutions which Mackenzie had transmitted for their adoption – and certainly a more unintellectual, ignorant and murderous-looking set of vagrants could not be gleaned from the most worthless of this District – the loyalists then went to Cook's Inn, and partook of refreshment, and then returned home; when the rebels, most of whom being from the south part of Yarmouth, found it convenient to *"clear out"* without waiting to get anything to eat.

A friend of ours says, that the Bayham meeting was a scene past description; and that the conduct of the club and pike men, from the south of Yarmouth, was so brutish, that had there not been a sufficient number of good and loyal men to wrest from them their war clubs and allay their fury, the consequences would have been awful. But let the *impartial* give an account of their barbarous actions, and then say who displayed the better feeling. Let the liberal talk no more of blood and butchery, but go home and wipe the stains from his own skirts, and ask forgiveness in sackcloth and ashes.

A 62   THE RICHMOND RIOT
23 September 1837
[Constitution, *Toronto, 4 Oct. 1837*]

MEETING OF BAYHAM AND MALAHIDE.

[From the Correspondent of the St. Thomas Liberal][156]
The meeting was organized at Richmond. *   *   *   *   *   *.
It had been reported that the Radicals would be hunted off the ground – and they accordingly provided themselves with sticks. The aforesaid Tisdal struck a Reformer & then boasted he could *whip* any one of them. His challenge was instantly accepted by a Mr. Cook,[157] who

---

[156]The square brackets occur in the original.
[157]Robert Cook (b. *ca.* 1798) was born into a United Empire Loyalist family in the Niagara District. He settled in Bayham, where he and his wife had by 1837 acquired 150 patented acres which they farmed. In December Robert was a lieutenant in the

thrashed him to his heart's content in less than two minutes. Another reformer was struck at the same time with a brick and a club, then the battle became general and the Tories fell in all directions[.] When the ruffians had thus succeeded in raising a tremendous riot, Doyle M'Kenney went up stairs, put his head out of a window and *commencing reading the riot act*, in the name of *"our Sovereign* LORD *the Queen!"* as he styled Her Majesty. Squire M'K. was not long at his riot-act reading vocation, when himself and his aid-de-camp, one Metcalf,[158] were taken by the necks and waistbands and thrown, head foremost, down stairs, with as little ceremony as you would throw a pair of blind pups into a frog pond, or shake a couple of dead rats out of a trap.[159] The Tories then brought out *scores of clubs*, which they had in a great measure concealed until now – and commenced the battle anew. But before you could say Arnold Ryerson[160] they were discomfited. Some were seen flying like Indian dogs before a white man's whip, while others were seen sprawling like wounded snakes, and cursing their *worships* that brought them in such a scrape.

The Reformers by this time had mounted their horses, and got into their waggons, and were proceeding homeward, when the Tories who had re-assembled at Cook's Tavern, commenced throwing brick-bats, stones and heavy clubs at them as they passed. The Reformers promptly turned back – gave all who stood their ground another severe thrashing – marched up and down with their flag flying, and then left the village in triumph, – Burwell as usual, though the instigator of all the mischief – kept himself in safety, and Doyle M'Kenney ran home, with the remnant of the *riot* act and his torn breeches dangling at his tail. It would make you laugh to see M'Kenney when he found himself all in a heap at the foot of the stairs – the big tear stood trembling in his eye – he looked as pale as death's horse in the Revelations – in fact, Sir, he was such a sight as is seldom seen – and barren must be the imagination which could not trace a resemblance between him and the Devil when he was thrown down from heaven for his *riot acts*.

Bayham party of rebels who marched to Oakland. Jailed in London, he was tried there in the spring, found guilty of treason, and released on bail in September. Unattached to any church, he was described by one government official at the time as "very dissipated. & Drunken & a person of no importance."

[158]This was Henry Medcalf (*ca.* 1778–1849) who had been born in Dublin, Ireland, and who had emigrated to British North America about 1806. He was a quarter-master in the War of 1812, and thereafter was active in the militia. He helped raise the loyalists against the Duncombe rebels and was commissioned a major in 1838. A clothier, he owned a mill in Bayham in the 1830s.

[159]This incident led to charges of assault being laid against Robert Cook and two other reformers. That fall true bills were found against them and they were released on bail. Their cases seem to have been forgotten in the turmoil attendant upon the rebellion.

[160]This seems to have been a comment upon Egerton Ryerson's supposed treachery to the reform cause, combining as it does his name with that of Benedict Arnold.

A 63   JOHN GEORGE BRIDGES[161] TO JOHN JOSEPH
London, 4 September 1837
[PAC, Correspondence of the Provincial Secretary's Office, v. 7, file 899]

John B Askin Esqr being from home, I am at a loss with whom to advise, and conceiving it of importance at this eventual crisis, that the Government should be made acquainted with all matters current, having an inimical tendency to its interests – I at once determined to write you Sir, in order that his Excellency may be through you informed thereof – In this last past week Dr. Chas Duncombe made a sojourn in our town of London, of some days, during which time it was apparent, from the incessant agitation of some of the principal adherents of the radical faction in this part, and from their nightly meetings that something was concocting, and though not positively ascertained when, there is no doubt but it is their intention to hold a meeting shortly, and that London is to be the scene of their grand [rush ?], of this I am well advised and also that they have their companies scouting the Country, passing from place to place telegraphing their intentions – If they carry their intentions into effect, and, as they threaten "Come prepared with fire arms." the result will be no doubt, serious and attended with loss of life, for, the loyal subjects are determined at all hazards to oppose their nefarious designs

I thought it my duty Sir, to apprize the Executive of what we have just cause to apprehend.

A 64   THE WESTMINSTER TORY MEETING
6 October 1837
[Gazette, London, quoted Patriot, Toronto, 13 Oct. 1837]

Glorious Defeat of the Westminster Radicals in their own Strong Hold.

Pursuant to public notice as given in the St. Thomas rebel newspaper [the *Liberal*], and also in various hand bills, calling a meeting of the revolutionists of the County of Middlesex, the constitutionalists assembled in the market square [of London] early yesterday morning, and having organized their body, marched out to meet the rebels on their own ground and at their own time and place. A more resolute,

[161]Dr. John George Bridges (*ca.* 1802–1845) was an ardent tory. Before and after the rebellion he bombarded the government with tales of treason and found some favour, being raised in March 1838 from an ensign of the 1st Oxford Regiment to its surgeon. He moved to Norwich in order to be able to watch the people of that township for treason more closely. Not surprisingly, he was unpopular there and fled it in May 1839, but, oddly, was appointed a magistrate for Norwich in 1840. In 1839 he published a pamphlet on the British constitution to educate the radicals to its glories, and continued writing through 1839–40 as editor of the Caledonia Springs *Mercury*. He later moved to Ottawa, becoming the owner of the Ottawa *Advocate*, which he edited until his death.

determined and devotedly loyal body of men we never saw. The rebels had vauntingly boasted of their spears & rifles, which in the language of the revolutionary editor would make the clubs of the tories and vile Irish "as harmless as boiled parsnips," yet not a weapon was found in the hands of a single constitutionalist. On they marched with firmness and spirit, and by the time they reached Griffin's Inn,[162] the place chosen by the rebels, their numbers amounted to near 400.

When within a few rods of the stage, they gave three tremendous cheers for Victoria our Queen, and then dashing forward at a quick pace, what a scampering was seen in the rebel ranks!! Some fled to the woods – others got concealed in garrets and hay lofts, and the few who screwed their courage up to sticking point to stand their ground, seemed palsied and ghastly as Egyptian mummies. Not a word did they attempt to utter; in fact they seemed so conscience stricken that they could hardly breathe through fear.

The friends of the Queen's Government immediately proceeded to organize the meeting by calling Lawrence Lawrason,[163] Esquire, to the Chair, and appointing Hamilton R. O'Reily,[164] Esq. to act as Secretary, when the following resolutions were unanimously carried amid the most deafening cheers. On the reading of each resolution the rebels were asked if they had any thing to say against it, or any objection to make, but not a word did they utter. Their whole demeanor was like that of criminals on their way to execution.

1. *Resolved*, That all the noisy and senseless clamour raised in this happy province, under the able administration of our present liberal and enlightened Lieutenant Governor, has been made by a gang of unprincipled and selfish demagogues, who, to subserve their own base purposes, and entrap the ignorant and unwary, promulgate the grossest

[162]"Griffin's" Inn was owned by Nathan Griffiths (*ca.* 1790–1862) of Westminster Township. He had emigrated from the United States to Upper Canada about 1812 and fought for his newly adopted country in the conflict that broke out that year. He was a popular man in Westminster and came to hold various township offices. In 1837 he was the town clerk. Besides his tavern, he also owned a brickyard, and was an early advocate of what came to be the Great Western Railroad.

[163]Laurence (Lawrence) Laurason (Lawrason) (1803–1882) was born in Ancaster into a loyalist family. In 1822 he bought over 500 acres in London Township, establishing a general store, an ashery, and a distillery there. In 1832 he moved his family into the village of London, opening a dry goods business and a general store in association with J.G. Goodhue. As a merchant he was interested in improving the navigation of the Thames and in securing London a railroad. A militia officer and a tory, he was appointed a magistrate in 1835, and was very active in examining those imprisoned at London in the wake of the rebellion. In 1844 he was elected to the Assembly of the united Canadas.

[164]Hamilton R. O'Reilly (O'Reily), a lawyer and a brother of Miles O'Reilly, the District Court judge of Gore, 1837–49, had lived in Hamilton before coming to London. In December 1837 he was with Captain Drew in cutting out the *Caroline*. He returned to Hamilton in 1838, transferring his militia commission as a lieutenant to the 3rd Gore. He married a daughter of Abel Land, a prominent Hamiltonian, in 1839. He later became a judge.

falsehoods and inflame the minds of the multitude with their seditious publications; until they have at length arrived at the conclusion, that both their moral and physical strength is such, that they can throw off their allegiance to the Queen, and must accordingly rebel.

2. *Resolved*, That this meeting is composed of True Reformers, but not of Revolutionists – they wish to reform every grievance which they can discover to exist, while they are determined to resist, with all their powers, every effort at rebellion against the Government of Her Majesty the Queen, and every attempt which may be made in violation of our happy and free Constitution.

3. *Resolved*, That this loyal and constitutional meeting views with more regret than anger many well-meaning though ignorant men of this fine country, who, under the specious pretext of reform, have been drawn by this rebellious cabal almost to the very vortex of self immolation.

4. *Resolved*, That as far as in us lies, we will use our best endeavors to cure all the description of persons mentioned in the above resolution; and that should the incurables incur our vengeance, their day of mercy we must consider past.

5. *Resolved*, That should any have the audacity to insult and outrage British feeling by raising any republican flag in any part of this District, we solemnly and firmly pledge ourselves, if within our reach or knowledge, to tear it to pieces and punish the miscreants who dared to hoist it.

6. *Resolved*, – That so far from the Papineau faction in Lower Canada deserving our sympathy or condolence, they are entitled to our deepest execration from the whole tenor of their conduct, for a series of years past, by their illiberal attempts to ruin [the] trade, commerce, and agricultural prosperity of Upper and Lower Canada through no other motives than the most black and diabolical hatred to those of British origin, to clog the whole of the administration and hurl odium and contempt upon our rulers.

7. *Resolved*, That, from the anti commercial and anti-agricultural disposition that has been uniformly displayed by the malcontents of Lower Canada up to the present period, the commercial and agricultural spirit of this province has been greatly checked and restrained in the development of its internal resources, and in the completing of various works of public improvement, within the limits of this province.

8[.] *Resolved*, That while Upper Canada, from its limited means, has appropriated large sums of money for completing immense improvements on the noble river St. Lawrence, and making it navigable for large steamers and schooners as far as the lower limits of this province extend – has constructed the Welland Canal – is improving the navigation of the Ottawa and the Trent – is engaged in the construction of railroads and various other improvements; the inhabitants of Lower Canada, with a much larger population and revenue, content themselves, so far as public improvements are concerned, with a trifling (Lachine) canal, of small extent, fit only for the accomodation of small bateaux: thus by their apathy and inactivity excluding us from free access to the ocean, in which we, as subjects of the same government, have an equal right with themselves.

9. *Resolved*, That while the paltry improvements they have made act only as an obstacle to our enterprise, they have passed laws in that province by which they tax our rafts of lumber, and the boats which take our produce to market, they also levy a polltax on emigrants from the mother country, while they admit free of impost the inhabitants of all foreign countries, which tends greatly to retard the rapid settlement of this province, by the only people who, besides the Colonies respectively, have a positive right to settle within its limits.

10. *Resolved*, That although this meeting was called by those styling themselves Reformers for the purpose of expressing their sympathies for the dominant faction in Lower Canada, this meeting can discover no cause for sympathy; on the contrary, they hold the rebellious conduct of the faction in that province in utter abhorrence.

11. *Resolved*. That this meeting view with astonishment and regret the conduct of the Executive of this province in suffering William Lyon Mackenzie to exercise all manner of treason and sedition without noticing them – and that it is the desire of this meeting that the Executive should institute prosecutions for the suppression of such treason and sedition.

John S. Cummins,[165] Esq. being called to the chair, the thanks of the meeting were voted to Mr. Lawrason for his dignified conduct as chairman of the most respectable and constitutional meeting ever held in the County of Middlesex, and also to the Secretary for his able and impartial conduct.

The meeting having given three cheers for our young Queen, three for Sir Francis Bond Head, and three loud and long ones, for that truly constitutional personage Bishop McDonell,[166] broke up but remained on the ground till twenty minutes after one o'clock, lest the *skulking* rebels might return and report that they had fled. Just before taking

[165]John Swete Cummins (*fl.* 1837–48) arrived in Delaware Township in the mid-1830s from Ireland, though he may have been English-born. Though youthful, he was to look after the lands of a British nobleman in the colony. In 1838 he was appointed a captain in the Middlesex militia and a magistrate for both Lobo Township and Amherst Island. A journalist and author, he produced a number of works. He died in the pre-Confederation era.

[166]Alexander Macdonell (McDonell) (1762–1840) was a Scottish Catholic cleric who organized the Glengarry Fencibles, a Catholic Highland regiment which served in the Irish rebellion of 1798. In 1804 he brought out several hundred Highland settlers to eastern Ontario. Ever loyal to the crown, he served in the War of 1812 as a military chaplain. He became the Bishop of Regiopolis in 1826 and was appointed to the Legislative Council in 1831. He was particularly active in the election of 1836, rallying the Catholics of the province behind Head.

their departure, a few rebels came up, who appearing to walk rather stiffly, notwithstanding the ample dimensions of their Yankee trousers, were seized and disarmed of five rifles and double barrelled guns, which had been stuck below their nether garments. These firelocks are now in possession of one of our most respectable magistrates of this town, and clearly indicate the bloody intention of the party had they not been checked by the friends of good order. Thus have treason and Radicalism for ever found their grave in the township of Westminster, once supposed to be the hotbed of rebellion. – *Requiescant in pace*.

A 65   THE WESTMINSTER REFORM MEETING
6 October 1837
[*Constitution, Toronto, 25 Oct. 1837*]

RESOLUTIONS
OF THE
Great Middlesex Meeting
of 1,000 Men.

The following Resolutions were put, and passed by acclamation, not a solitary hand was raised against them.

Moved by Wm. O'Dell,[167] seconded by Ewd. Beatie.

Resolved 1. That when the Interests and Prosperity of a country are brought into a state of derangement and ruin, by the misconduct of those to whom its government and affairs are entrusted; it becomes an imperative duty which the people owe to themselves and their offspring, to meet in their respective Townships, to discuss the cause of their country's distress, and adopt and suggest such measures as may be thought expedient for its relief.

Moved by Albert S. O'Dell,[168] seconded by Wm. Norton.[169]

Resolved 2. That inhabiting a soil of the richest and most fertile description, which was at the commencement of our settlement placed in the hands of the government free and unencumbered – and to which has been added the continued labor of an industrious and energetic

[167]The O'Dell family had moved into Westminster Township in 1810–11. A William O'Dell was a tax collector in Westminster in 1837. He was likely the William O'Dell cited here and a member of that branch of the O'Dells who were early settlers. A William O'Dell, however, born in New York State, did move into Westminster from Lower Canada in 1837.

[168]Albert S. O'Dell settled in Westminster in 1810, holding over the years various township offices. In 1834 he was a supporter of the projected London and Gore Railroad.

[169]William Norton (b. *ca.* 1793) emigrated to Upper Canada from Lower Canada, his birthplace, in 1811 and settled in Westminster, where he and his wife had acquired by 1837 over 250 patented acres and ran an inn. In 1823 and 1828 he was elected a pathmaster for the township. In December 1837 he helped two Duncombe rebels, Walter Chase and David Anderson, escape. For this he was jailed at London on 17 December 1837 and freed on bail 26 January 1838.

people, together with the vast sums of money brought into the country by emigration, as well as the thousands derived from the sale of public lands, and the large amounts borrowed, for the interest of which our revenue from every source (though insufficient) is pledged, Upper Canada with even a moderate share of good management, possesses every requisite to make a most prosperous country.

Moved by Cyrus W. Sumner,[170] seconded by James Elliot.[171]

Resolved 3. That notwithstanding these numerous advantages and blessings, we view with alarm and dread the deplorable state of ruin and misery to which our country is fast verging; and we hold, that it could only be to mismanagement of the most blasting description, and intentions and objects the most base and foul on the part of those entrusted with the public weal, that could bring our country to its present depressed condition.

Moved by Hiram Crawford,[172] seconded by Captain O'Dell.[173]

Resolved 4. That all powers of Government should be derived from, – accountable to, and controlled by the people, – and that we view as the primary cause of all our difficulties an irresponsible system of Government, having not the prosperity of the country, but selfish interests to advance, and to the furthering of which, the best interests of Upper Canada have been continually sacrificed; it would therefore be the height of insanity any longer to expect the country to flourish while under such unjust management.

Moved by Nathan Griffiths, seconded by Robert Frank.[174]

Resolved 5. That the present House of Assembly of this Province having been elected to serve for a limited period that is to say. [*sic*] until the demise of the king – any other way of prolonging their existence, than by the suffrages of the people, is a usurpation – and the sanction given by the Governor and Legislative Council to a Bill passed by the House of Assembly, to elect themselves as representatives without the consent of their constituents, was an act of combined treason against the people of Upper Canada, and any law they may

---

[170]Cyrus W. Sumner (1803–1880) was born in Upper Canada's Blenheim Township. A mason, he held in 1837 150 patented acres in Westminster.

[171]This may have been the James Elliott (1811–1863) who was born in Roxboroughshire, Scotland, and emigrated with his family to New Brunswick in 1811, where he learned the building trade. Living for a time in the United States, Elliott then came to the village of London in 1834, where he opened a building business in 1844.

[172]Hiram Crawford, a Westminster landowner, sat on the London District Council for that township in 1842.

[173]Joseph O'Dell, who settled in Westminster in 1811, fought for Upper Canada in the War of 1812. Ironically, he lost his captaincy in the militia for participating in the reform agitation of 1837.

[174]Robert Frank of Westminster was a Westminster town warden in 1817 and 1826. He appears to be the same Robert Frank who supplied the authorities in January 1838 with information against the suspected traitor John Grieve.

pass during the continuance of such usurpation, should be as strongly resisted as the usurpation and treason are base and perfidious.[175]

Moved by Charles Reeves,[176] seconded by William Munro.

Resolved 6. That at the time Great Britain conceded to Canada a *Constitution*! she reserved to herself ample powers for the exercise of the most arbitrary and degrading system of Colonial vassalage, – among which may be mentioned, the power of regulating our trade and commerce, which she has ever done to the enriching of herself, and the impoverishing of us; – the appointing the Executive, which has uniformly sacrificed the dearest interest of the many to promote the rapacious objects of the few; – the creating, from a kind of pauper and ignorant Aristocracy, a kind of mock peerage, called a Legislative Council which has seconded the schemes of the Executive and opposed every measure beneficial to the country and desired by the people; – the uncontrolled management of the largest portion of the Canadian revenue; which added to the undue interference of the Executive at elections, and the appointment to office of the Members of Assembly afterwards – have at last placed all Legislative as well as Executive power in the hands of one man.

Moved by Calvin Burch,[177] seconded by John O'Dell.[178]

Resolved 7. That we deem the Resolutions lately passed by the Parliament of the United Kingdom[179] a subversion of the Chartered rights of these Provinces; and we therefore applaud the patriotic stand taken against their baneful operation by our brethren in the Lower Province; we approve of their determination, respecting the disuse of tax-paying articles, and we recommend their example as worthy of imitation in this Province, until the obnoxious Resolutions be annulled, and until both Provinces obtain such an amelioration in the

---

[175]This resolution indicates the increasing radicalization of some reformers, urging as it did outright opposition to the laws of the Assembly.

[176]Charles Reeves (b. *ca.* 1801) was an American who emigrated to Upper Canada about 1821. By 1837 he had acquired 50 patented acres in Westminster on lot 76, on the west side of the north branch of the Talbot Road. There he farmed and ran a tavern. In the 1830s he served several times as an overseer of highways for Westminster. On 17 December 1837 he was jailed at London for using seditious language and granted bail on 2 January 1838.

[177]Calvin Burtch (Burch) (1798–1863 or 1865) was born in New York State into a family which claimed loyalist connections. In 1802 he was re-united with family members already resident in Upper Canada. He fought for the colony in the War of 1812, thereafter teaching school for a time before turning to farming. In 1837 he owned 150 patented acres of lot 75 on the east side of the north branch of the Talbot Road in Westminster. Suspected of having urged the militia not to turn out to quell rebellion, he was examined in London in January 1838 and released on bail.

[178]In 1811 John O'Dell settled in Westminster. He became an overseer of highways for that township in 1831.

[179]These were Russell's Ten Resolutions.

Constitution as will enable our respective Legislatures to redress the grievances which have long pressed heavily on the people, and which have checked the prosperity of the Province, and engendered such discontents as have at last destroyed the credit of the Province abroad, and plunged it into bankruptcy at home.

Moved by C.W. Taylor, seconded by William Dyer.

Resolved 10. That we find no language in which we can adequately express our indignation at the conduct of those Magistrates of the Home District, who having collected a mob of ignorant and misguided men, so disgracefully disturbed by the most brutal outrages the Reformers of that district, when convened for the purpose of peaceably and Constitutionally deliberating upon measures for the public good. That these riotous and illegal acts of the Magistrates, whose peculiar province it is to keep the peace[,] maintain good order, and execute justice, connived at as they have been by the Governor and Executive and by that portion of the press retained by the present Administration as their official organ: we look upon as almost tantamount on the part of the Government to a declaration of civil war, and that we are determined to frustrate as far as in us lies, the anarchical endeavors of those officers, who have been converting the civil sword into a weapon of assassination, instead of wearing it as the instrument of justice.

Moved by Ira M. Sumner, seconded by Nathan Griffith.

Resolved 11. That time after time, both in this Province and in Great Britain, most loyally, nay, most servilely have we petitioned for a redress of the long and frightful catalogue of the wrongs of Canada. – Our prayers have been spurned, and our feelings have been deeply wounded by the insults that have accompanied the contemptuous disregard of our most humble supplications for justice – that we have too longed [*sic*] hawked our wrongs, as the beggar doth his sores, at the fastidious threshold of haughty oppression, when derided and mocked we have been sent empty away; that since our iron-hearted rulers have turned a deaf ear to the voice of our complaints, we confiding in the goodness of our cause resting as it wholly does on reason, truth, and equity for its support, will call upon the God of Justice to aid us in our holy struggle for our rights as Britons and as men.

Moved by Albert S. O'Dell, seconded by Wm. Munro.

Resolved 13. That we heartily concur in the Address by the Reformers of Toronto; that we highly approve of the measures being taken throughout the Province to provide a Convention of Delegates to deliberate on the causes that have sunk our country into ruin and distress, to devise and suggest some measures for her restoration and to preserve, if possible, her few remaining advantages; and that in pursuance of the recommendations contained in that address, we do hereby appoint the following Members to attend on our behalf, viz. –

HUGH CARMICHAEL,[180] }
JOSEPH ALWAY,[181]   }   *Lobo*

CALVIN BURCH,   }
JOHN GREEVE,[182]   }   *Westminster*

Moved by Captain O'Dell, seconded by Calvin Burch.
Resolved 14. That the thanks of this Meeting are eminently due to
Mr. John Talbot for his patriotic conduct on all occasions, and
particularly for his attendance here this day, and also that the thanks of
this Meeting be given to Dr. Rolph and Dr. Duncombe, and the rest of
the minority of the House of Assembly.

GIDEON TIFFANY,[183] *Chairman*,

JOSEPH S. O'DELL,   }   *Secretaries*
CHARLES LATIMER.[184] }   *Westminster, Oct.* 6, 1836. [*sic*]

When the business was concluded, the friends of Canada in the
British Parliament were loudly cheered; Papineau & the Patriots of
Lower Canada were loudly cheered; and the whole concluded by three
hearty cheers for the Queen, and three groans for the *Hanoverians*.

[180]Hugh Carmichael (1796–1872) of Argyleshire, Scotland, came to Upper Canada
about 1820, settling in Lobo Township, where he and his family farmed 200 patented
acres in 1837. In 1831 and 1837 he was elected town clerk of Lobo. In December 1837
he was examined and then granted bail by London magistrates suspicious of his reform
activity in the fall.

[181]Joseph Alway (b. *ca*. 1800) of Lobo, an Englishman, was the brother of the
prominent reform MLA for Oxford, Robert Alway. Joseph came with his family to
Upper Canada in 1810, acquiring by 1837 over 300 acres of property. He lived on lot
10, concession 2 of Lobo.

[182]John Grieve (Greeve) (1808–1838), who was born in Roxboroughshire,
Scotland, came to Upper Canada about 1817. A Westminster farmer who owned 200
patented acres in 1837, he was a parishioner of William Proudfoot and active in local
affairs, having held a number of township offices. Jailed on suspicion of treason in
December 1837, he was not indicted and was freed on 10 April 1838. He died from
"jail fever" on 1 June 1838, leaving a wife and two daughters.

[183]Gideon Tiffany (1774–1854) was born in New Hampshire and came to Upper
Canada about 1797, editing Upper Canada's first newspaper, the *Upper Canada
Gazette or American Chronicle*, at Newark that year. In 1801 or 1802 he founded the
village of Delaware, near London, where he raised his family. He became a
well-known figure locally, holding a lieutenancy in the militia, being elected a
township commissioner in 1836, and acquiring extensive properties, worth in 1837, he
claimed, over $10,000. Suspected of treason in December because of his reform
activity in the fall, he was jailed at London, tried in the spring, and acquitted.

[184]Charles Latimer (d. 1844) of Oxford, England, was in 1837 a lawyer unable to
practise in Upper Canada because he had not yet met the stringent residence
requirements of the legal profession in the colony. About 1835 he and a partner had
opened a general store in London. An able man, he was particularly active in the
reform agitation of the fall of 1837 and was jailed in London in December as a
consequence. Tried in the spring for treason, he was acquitted and, a bachelor, headed
off for the United States, where he joined the Patriot cause, working on a scheme to
encourage Canadian emigration. In 1839 he was admitted to the Illinois bar. He was
later killed in a duel in Wisconsin Territory.

The meeting adjourned in the utmost good order, not an angry word was spoken, all were well armed, and before they left the ground they fired a *fue de joie*. There could not be less than five hundred guns and pistols discharged.

A 66   CHARLES DUNCOMBE TO ROBERT DAVIS
Burford, 24 October 1837
[*PAC, Upper Canada Sundries, v. 178, pp. 98408-11*]

Your favor of the 17th instant has this moment come to hand, in which you say that the time has come when reformers ought to be on the alert in forming political unions and in organising for our common safety;

I heartily concur with you that it is high time for the reformers to be up and doing, When Sir Francis Head declares that the British Government never intended any such absurdity as giving us the British Constitution, (of course we are to continue to be governed by the Oligarchy of Toronto,) And when the doors of the Colonial Office are closed against reformers (or republicans as Sir Francis Head tauntingly styles us;) because we are guilty of the crime of appealing to His Majestys Government with our complaints, And when we see this Province under the dynasty of a foreign Governor and an Orange Oligarchy, retrograding in one year as much as it had advanced in five, the only interest our oppressors have in the Province being the plunder they can amass and carry away with them; I think any one not wilfully blind, not interested in the continuance of the abuses, must see, that while this baneful domination continues we have not the slightest chance for prosperity and that if we will be well governed we must govern ourselves; Our oppressors have shown us more clearly than ever before, that their great object is to make the rich richer and the poor poorer, for if the people should become wealthy they would become inteligent and unwilling slaves; my maxim has always been educate the people, this can be now done only upon a few matters upon politics[;] we may do much by "the assembling our selves together" and hearing political lectures, by the forming political unions, publishing periodicals and encouraging the circulation of reform news-papers – this can best be done by union and by our devoting the few pence we save from our grog bills to the purchase of correct information upon the subject of our own affairs – and the time formerly spent in drinking to reading and reflection; I shall be most happy to meet with you at any time after next week (as I have heard that there is to be a reform meeting in Oakland one day next week but have not heard what day) – and I must (God willing) be there;

I have just received a note from our trusty friend Hall[185] upon the

---

[185]Elisha Hall (1800–1868), Upper Canadian-born, in 1837 owned a sawmill in Ingersoll and 245 patented acres thereabouts, some, at least, of which he farmed. He was well known locally, having been a district constable in 1835 and an agent for the

same subject & he mentions Capt. Curtisses[186] as a proper place for the meeting but does not mention the time. I hope when you appoint the time you will let me know as the time has come when we are to decide whether we will be bondsmen or slaves – The reformers of Westminster have done nobly; your name I see among the immortal patriots who feel the oppressors iron rod; thank God we are strong in the justice of our cause, and although we may suffer for a time, we shall assuredly in the end prevail; "A nation never can rebel" those only are rebels who resist the will of the people; from them (the people) eminates all legitimate, constitutional government;

I highly approve the plan both you and Mr. Hall propose and shall be much obliged by your leting me know when the meeting is to be and I shall endeavor to be with you – God prosper the right and every m[an] come prepared to defend himself.

A 67   ARM YOURSELVES!
[Gazette, *Hamilton, 31 Oct. 1837*]

The Editor of the Liberal in addressing the heroes – the gun men of the Sparta. – Bayham and Westminster Meetings – *very Loyally* says, "Let your motto be Liberty and down with the baneful domination of Bond Head. The laws afford you no protection – protect yourselves, do as you did at the Westminster Meetings – and your enemies and the enemies of *peace* and good order, will, as they did from Westminster fly at your approach. The time mentioned in holy writ seems to have arrived – when he who has no sword should sell his coat and buy one!!![''']

A 68   A TORY MEETING AT LONDON
21 October 1837
[Liberal, *St. Thomas, 2 Nov. 1837*]

. . . We are indebted to that pink of papers, the London Gazette "extraordinary" for the following account of the Meeting held by the Tories of Middlesex, in London, on the 21st of October last. . . .

Liberal in 1837. He helped muster the rebels of his locale in December 1837 but was hurt in a fall from his horse before he could join Duncombe. Captured by loyalist forces, he escaped, fleeing to the United States. He returned to the province in 1840, though charges still pended against him. He was finally pardoned in 1843. In 1863 he was made an Ingersoll magistrate.

[186]This was David Curtis's tavern in West Oxford. Curtis (*ca.* 1776–1862) had settled in West Oxford from the United States in 1794, where he held a number of township offices over the years. He fought in the War of 1812 and after it held a captaincy in the militia. A mason and an Open Communion Baptist, he was both an innkeeper and a farmer and acquired 350 acres, 150 of it patented. Suspected of being a Duncombe rebel, he was jailed at London on 20 December 1837. After being freed on bail on 12 February 1838 because of ill health, he returned to his wife and family.

"The following resolutions were severally put and carried without a dissenting voice. . . .

"3d. Moved by Lawrence Lawrason, Esq. seconded by Captain Thomas H. Ball.[187]

"That this meeting have learned with deep concern, that on several occasions a number of persons from the Township of Yarmouth and its neighborhood, have lately attended public meetings, unlawfully armed with loaded fire arms and other dangerous weapons, for the avowed purpose of carrying their measures at such meetings by force, and preventing a free expression of public opinion.

"4th. Moved by Captain John Cummins and seconded by Nicholas Gaffney, sen.[188] Esq.

"That it is the opinion of this meeting, that if this organized and armed body who follow the satellites of Mackenzie from meeting to meeting be not suppressed by Her Majesty's Government, either the people of this District and the Province generally, must submit to the arrogant and insolent assumption *of its name*, by a mob for purposes held in scorn and execration by the vast majority, *or bloodshed must ensue*.

"5th. Moved by William Robertson,[189] Esq. and seconded by Mr. Edward Fitzgerald.[190]

"That the firmness, decision, and wisdom evinced by Sir Francis Bond Head, during his administration, commencing as it did, at one of the most critical periods, which our annals exhibit, entitle His Excellency to our fullest confidence, and we entertain no doubt that His Excellency will adopt such measures, as will best ensure the public tranquillity *at this juncture*. . . .

A 69   CHARLES LATIMER TO JOHN TALBOT
London, 22 October 1837
[PAC, Records of the London District Magistrates, v. II]

. . . I suppose you want some news – well – Squires Hall[191] & McKenzie[192] were heard at a Camp Meeting the other day talking

---

[187]Thomas H. Ball was appointed both a magistrate and lieutenant-colonel of the 4th Regiment of Middlesex militia in 1838. In December 1838 he served with his regiment on the western frontier.

[188]Nicholas Gaffney (Gaffny) was evidently of Irish origin. He was an early backer of the proposed London and Gore Railroad.

[189]William Robertson, a London Township Scot, was appointed a magistrate in 1829. In 1831 he was elected a road commissioner for the town of London, where he was the local agent of the Bank of Upper Canada.

[190]This seems to have been the Edward Fitzgerald (1759–1841) who left Ireland and settled in London Township in 1819, becoming a farmer there. His wife was related to Irish nobility.

[191]Cyrenius Hall (*ca.* 1788–1860) was born in New Hampshire, emigrating in 1810 to the Fort Erie area of Upper Canada before settling in Westminster Township, where he raised a family and seems to have operated a tannery for a time at Byron. He was appointed a magistrate in 1836.

[192]Duncan McKenzie (1787–1875) was born in Scotland. In 1808 he joined the 5th

about *taking up* the Subscribers to the Liberal *under the summary punishment act* –

The Tory & orange Meeting yesterday was a signal failure – 65 or 70 are the most that were counted – & several of these were persons who seeing a waggon in the middle of the Square or Market place with some persons round it might have supposed that some Sheriff's Sale or auction was going on – I am told that the signers of the requisition expected this to be the largest meeting there had ever been in the District – they calculated on the assemblage of at least 3 or 400 – (three or four thousand) souls – 6 or 700 hundred wd: have been a failure – then what must we say of 60 or 70 being all that cd: be mustered from the whole Cty. of Middlesex to sanction their unjust, illegal, & unconstitutional proceedings – When the show of hands was calld for not half of those assembled displayed any token of their being interested in the proceedings – . . . it is supposed that had the Meeting taken place on any other than Market Day that 60 or 70 wd: have been reduced to 6 or 7 – The resolutions are not yet out – nor can any one give any acct– of what was said as they cd: not even gather the substance of it – The orators did not speak out – The whole proceedings lasted about half an hour – or so – The Gazette it is said is at a loss what to say about the numbers – but its ingenuity has at length decided on giving it that the numbers were so great that the Court House wd not contain them & they were obliged to adjourn to the Square – . . . There were some Tories who went there with the view of putting down armed meetings – but the resolutions proposed were of so irritating & harassing a character that they came away without taking any part in the business – The Tories here are evidently splitting – they denounce the violence of some of their party & strongly condemn their attempt at interrupting the people at their last reform meeting – if these men wd: join the constitutional Reformers in obtaining those organic changes which alone can give satisfaction & diffuse amongst us the blessings of peace, happiness & prosperity – they might yet save this country from evils which it is more easy for a thinking man to predict with certainty than depict with truth – . . .

A 70   JOHN JOSEPH TO JOHN B. ASKIN
Government House, 1 November 1837
*[PAC, Governor-General's Office, Letter Books, Upper Canada,
1793–1841, v. 42, pp. 245-6]*

Having laid before his Excy. the Lieut: Governor your letter of the 23rd Ulto. transmitting for His Excellency's information the Resolu-

---

Battalion of Royal Artillery and fought at the battle of Waterloo. In 1817 he and his family emigrated to New Brunswick, moving to Upper Canada and a farm site in London Township the next year. He was elected the township's clerk throughout the 1820s and in 1829 was appointed a magistrate. In 1823 he was made a militia captain and commanded a battery at Chippawa, 1837–8.

tions adopted at a Public Meeting of the Inhabitants of the County of Middlesex held on the 21st of October last, I have the honor to convey through you His Excellency's thanks for the loyal & patriotic sentiments, which those Resolutions contain.

His Excellency at the same time directs me to remark, that however unworthy of notice as an object of apprehension the body of mis-guided men may be, who libel the loyal Inhabitants of this Province by assuming the name of the people, and who under that name disturb the public peace, His Excellency fully agrees with the Meeting, that the Laws of the Province ought not to be permitted to be impugned with impunity, –

His Excellency is well assured that for the suppression of sedition & insubordination, He will not call in vain upon the vigilance of the Magistracy & the loyalty of of [sic] the people, and His Excy. desires me to assure you, that he is perfectly ready to afford every assistance and protection to those, whose duty it is to enforce the Laws, and that he will not be wanting in firmly maintaining unimpaired the blessings, which Her Majesty's subjects in this Province enjoy under our most happy constitution.

A 71   PREPAREDNESS AGAINST REBELLION
[Patriot, *Toronto, 24 Oct. 1837*]

The prompt determination of His Excellency the Lieutenant Governor to confide the defence of the Province to the Constitutional force, its gallant Militia, will, we are convinced, be hailed with joy by every loyal and true hearted subject of our gracious Queen. Confidence of this kind can never be misplaced; and sure we are that, if need should arise, thousands are ready to turn out, as in days long since past, but not forgotten, to defend, to the death, the honor of that flag which proudly flutters to the breeze on the residence of Her Majesty's honored representative. . . . That there is any special necessity for an assembly of the Militia forces we do not believe; but, in the event of the whole of the regular troops being sent below, it might be advisable, as has been suggested by a highly respectable individual, to call out some of the flank companies and officer them with the old soldiers of the late war accustomed to military service. Such a force would be highly efficient for garrison duty, and being formed of the *elite* of our Provincial battalions, would serve as an admirable body guard to the Executive, as well as a most effective corps to keep in check any hostile movement which our restless demagogues may be so abundantly foolish as to attempt against the peace and harmony of society. We repeat that we give them credit for more method in their madness, more wit in their anger, than to leave their safe and profitable trade of agitation, the war of *words*, for one of a more terrific character, since they must know, though their wretched and ignorant

dupes may not, that the sword of law and justice, like that of
Damocles, is suspended over their heads by a single hair, and the first
step taken in overt acts of treason to the State, will cause it to descend
with fearful effect upon them. Meantime let the loyal and peaceful be
assured that the Executive neither slumbers nor sleeps, but is wide
awake, nay correctly informed of the most minute and secret intentions
of the Revolutionary party. Precautionary measures of the most
effective kind have been taken to protect the Government and
inhabitants of the country generally, from all danger; and the gallant
Sir John Colborne, our late esteemed Governor, is quite prepared, and
disposed, with Sir Francis Head, to say –
"Let them come if they dare!"

A 72   JOHN JOSEPH TO THE MAYOR OF TORONTO[193]
Government House, 29 October 1837
[Patriot, *Toronto, 3 Nov. 1837*]

I am commanded by the Lieut. Governor to inform you, that in
consequence of the disturbed state of the Lower Province, His
Excellency has cheerfully consented to the immediate withdrawal of
Her Majesty's Troops from Toronto, and that His Excellency has
moreover offered to Sir John Colborne the assistance of the Military
stationed at Kingston.

As the 24th Regiment quits the Barracks at this Port to-morrow,
about six thousand stand of Arms and accoutrements complete will
require to be protected, and the Lieutenant Governor desires me to
express to you, that he has very great pleasure in offering to commit
this highly important trust to the loyalty and fidelity of the Mayor,
Aldermen, and Commonalty of the City of Toronto.

A 73   COL. JAMES FITZGIBBON[194] TO JOHN JOSEPH
Government House, 31 October 1837
[Patriot, *Toronto, 3 Nov. 1837*]

Seeing that Her Majesty's Royal Troops have all left the seat of the
Government, and having had a Volunteer Company of young
militia-men of this City placed under my command, in the month of

[193]The mayor of Toronto was George Gurnett.

[194]James FitzGibbon (1780–1863) was born in Glin, Ireland. He came to Canada
with the 49th Regiment in 1801. As a lieutenant he arranged for the surrender of the
American forces at Beaver Dams in 1813. In 1827 he was appointed clerk of the
Assembly. FitzGibbon was convinced that trouble was coming in 1837 and tried very
hard to persuade the lieutenant-governor and members of the Executive Council to
prepare. He was unsuccessful. When the rising came, FitzGibbon, who commanded a
volunteer company of militia, was made acting adjutant general, since the incumbent,
Colonel Coffin, was infirm, and he organized the forces which defeated the rebels on 7
December. In 1846 he went to live in England, where he was made a military Knight
of Windsor in 1850.

May 1835, by the late Lieut. Governor, for the purpose of being drilled, I beg leave in their behalf to offer their services to His Excellency the Lieut. Governor, to be employed in furnishing the usual guard for the Government House, or any other duty which His Excellency may be pleased to order.

A 74   JOHN JOSEPH TO COL. JAMES FITZGIBBON
Government House, 31 October 1837
[Patriot, *Toronto, 3 Nov. 1837*]

I have had the honor to lay before His Excellency the Lieut. Governor your letter of this day's date, and in reply am commanded by His Excellency to request that you will convey to the Volunteer Company of young militia-men of this City, placed under your command in the month of May 1835, by the late Lieut Governor, for the purpose of being drilled, His Excellency's thanks for their prompt offer to furnish a guard for the Government House, or to perform any other duty which His Excellency may be pleased to order.

I am further commanded by His Excellency to state, that in case the lives or property of Her Majesty's subjects in this Province should require defence, His Excellency will instantly avail himself of the services which have so zealously been offered to him; but placing implicit reliance on the loyalty of the inhabitants of Upper Canada, the Lieut. Governor must decline to accept any other personal protection than that which the Laws afford to every inhabitant of this noble Province.

A 75   JOHN MACAULAY TO ANN MACAULAY
Toronto, 30 October 1837
[*PAO, Macaulay Papers*]

. . . In the rear of this Town the disaffected meet in squads with arms. and are drilling & I have no doubt they are in correspondence with the Lower Canadian Malcontents – The time may not be far distant when our muskets may again [bear ?] requisition – not in foreign, but civil war – The Papineau and Mackenzie factions seem almost infuriated & I do not see how matters can end but in a resort to arms [–] Feelings such as now exist are seldom appeased in any other way – and it unfortunately happens that when persons are long allowed to talk sedition, they learn to act treason – . . .

A 76   JOHN MACAULAY TO ANN MACAULAY
Toronto, 6 November 1837
[*PAO, Macaulay Papers*]

. . . Sir Francis has paid our Militia the compliment of relying entirely on them for the protection of his Government against the disaffected and in this he has acted with as much judgment as gallantry. . . .

A 77   CHARLES DURAND[195] TO W.L. MACKENZIE
Hamilton, 16 November 1837
[Patriot, *Toronto, 15 May 1838*]

I send you herewith a list of persons living in Guelph who have been so spirited as to subscribe some money towards paying the costs of your trial at Niagara,[196] although the sum is small, still it is a token of their good will towards you which you will no doubt fully appreciate . . . . since writing my letter of the 13th, a person in this town named Mr. Mills,[197] Gunsmith, Hamilton, desires to take your paper till forbid. You will please to send him one. He is a rifle-maker – says he will make 100 good ones for $1000. . . .

We are raising two or three Unions here in Hamilton, and will do so I think.

Armstrong[198] will raise one in Guelph. . . .

N.B. – . . . I would advise you by all means not to go out at night unless you are well armed and with some friends. . . . Great sympathy is felt for you here.

A 78   W. L. MACKENZIE'S CONSTITUTION
[Constitution, *Toronto, 15 Nov. 1837*]

To the Convention of Farmers, Mechanics, Labourers, and other Inhabitants of Toronto, met at the Royal Oak Hotel, to consider of and take measures for effectually maintaining in this colony, a free constitution and democratic form of government.

The Committee appointed to report a popular Constitution, with guards

[195]Charles Morrison Durand (1811–1905) was born in Barton Township, Upper Canada, and studied law in Hamilton. In 1834 he became the town's clerk and assessor and in 1835 its treasurer, collector, and assessor. A Methodist, then a member of the Niagara Presbyterian Church, he was an ardent temperance advocate. His brother James was an MLA for Halton, 1834–6. Charles adopted his brother's reform principles, contributing articles to the reform Hamilton *Free Press*. He became connected to the prominent reform and mercantile family, the Parkers, through marriage. During the Toronto rising he met Mackenzie, then spread the word of what he believed to be the successful rising. Arrested early in December, he was tried the following spring for treason. Found guilty, he was eventually banished from the province, locating in Buffalo in 1838 and Chicago in 1839. Pardoned in 1844, he returned to the colony. In 1897 he published his remarkably chaotic *Reminiscences*. The *Patriot* published his letter to Mackenzie in its report on Durand's trial.

[196]Mackenzie was being tried in November at Niagara for libel over charges he had made concerning the Welland Canal's operation.

[197]Michael Marcellus Mills (1804–1847) was an active reformer, being a member of the Gore Constitutional Reform Society formed in 1836 and attending a radical meeting in Trafalgar in August 1837. He and a brother made guns, and, after the revolt, being suspected on rather good evidence of having plotted to deliver rifles to the rebels, he was indicted for treason. He had already fled, however, and had joined Mackenzie at Navy Island. Attainted a traitor in 1838, he was pardoned in 1844 but seems not to have returned to the colony, dying in Indiana.

[198]Robert Armstrong was a Scottish wagon-maker and blacksmith who opened a

suitable for this Province, in case the British system of government shall be positively denied us, respectfully submit the following draft:

WHEREAS the solemn covenant made with the people of Upper and Lower Canada, and recorded in the Statute Book of the United Kingdom of Great Britain and Ireland as the 31st Chapter of the Acts passed in the 31st year of the reign of King George III., hath been continually violated by the British Government, and our rights usurped; *And Whereas* our humble petitions, addresses, protests and remonstrances against this injurious interference have been made in vain – WE, the people of the State of Upper Canada, acknowledging with gratitude the grace and beneficence of GOD, in permitting us to make choice of our form of Government, and in order to establish justice, ensure domestic tranquillity, provide for the common defence, promote the general welfare, and secure the blessings of civil and religious liberty to ourselves and our posterity, do establish this Constitution:

1. . . . the legislature shall make no law respecting the establishment of religion, or for the encouragement or the prohibition of any religious denomination.

2. It is ordained and declared that the free exercise and enjoyment of religious profession and worship, without discrimination or preference, shall forever hereafter be allowed within this State to all mankind.

3. The whole of the public lands within the limits of this State, including the lands attempted, by a pretended sale, to be vested in certain adventurers called the Canada Company (except so much of them as may have been disposed of to actual settlers now resident in the State,) and all the lands called crown reserves, clergy reserves and rectories, and also the school lands, and the lands pretended to be appropriated to the uses of the University of King's College, are declared to be the property of the State, and at the disposal of the Legislature, for the public service thereof. The proceeds of one million of acres of the most valuable public lands shall be specially appropriated to the support of Common or Township Schools.

4. No Minister of the Gospel, clergyman, ecclesiastic, bishop or priest of any religious denomination whatsoever, shall, at any time hereafter, under any pretence or description whatever, be eligible to, or capable of holding a seat in the senate or house of assembly, or any civil or military office within this state.

5. In all laws made, or to be made, every person shall be bound alike – neither shall any tenure, estate, charter, degree, birth, or place, confer any exemption from the ordinary course of legal proceedings and responsibilities whereunto others are subjected.

---

wagon-making business in Guelph in 1834. Accused of treason for plotting rebellion, he was jailed at Hamilton on 12 December 1837 and granted bail on 5 January 1838.

6. No hereditary emoluments, privileges, or honours, shall ever be granted by the people of this State.

7. There shall neither be slavery nor involuntary servitude in this State, otherwise than for the punishment of crimes whereof the party shall have been duly convicted. People of Colour, who have come into this State, with the design of becoming permanent inhabitants thereof, *and are now resident therein*, shall be entitled to all the rights of native Canadians, upon taking an oath or affirmation to support the constitution.

8. The people have a right to bear arms for the defence of themselves and the State,

9. No man shall be impressed or forcibly constrained to serve in time of war; because money, the sinews of war, being always at the disposal of the Legislature, they can never want numbers of men apt enough to engage in any just cause.

10. The military shall be kept under strict subordination to the civil power. No soldier shall, in time of peace, be quartered in any house without the consent of the owner, nor in time of war, but in a manner to be prescribed by law.

11. The Governor, with the advice and consent of the Senate, shall choose all militia officers above the rank of Captain. The people shall elect their own officers of the rank of Captain, and under it.

12. The people have a right to assemble together in a peaceable manner, to consult for their common good, to instruct their representatives in the legislature, and to apply to the legislature for redress of grievances.

13. The printing presses shall be open and free to those who may wish to examine the proceedings of any branch of the government, or the conduct of any public officer; and no law shall ever restrain the right thereof.

14. The trial by Jury shall remain for ever inviolate.

15. Treason against this State shall consist only in levying war against it, or adhering to its enemies, giving them aid and comfort. No person shall be convicted of Treason unless on the testimony of two witnesses to the same overt act, or on confession in open court.

15a. No ex-post-facto law, nor any law impairing the validity of legal compacts, grants or contracts, shall ever be made; and no conviction shall work corruption of blood or forfeiture of estate.

16. The real estate of persons dying without making a will shall not descend to the eldest son to the exclusion of his brethren, but be equally divided among the children, male and female.

17. The laws of Entail shall be forever abrogated.

17a. There shall be no lotteries in this State. Lottery tickets shall not be sold therein, whether foreign or domestic.

18. No power of suspending the operation of the laws shall be exercised except by the authority of the Legislature.

19. The people shall be secure in their persons, papers and possessions, from all unwarrantable searches and seizures; general warrants, whereby an officer may be commanded to search suspected places, without probable evidence of the fact committed, or to seize any person or persons not named, whose offences are not particularly described, and without oath or affirmation, are dangerous to liberty, and shall not be granted.

20. Private property ought, and will ever be held inviolate, but always subservient to the public welfare, provided a compensation in money be first made to the owner. Such compensation shall never be less in amount than the actual value of the property.

21. *And Whereas* frauds have been often practised towards the Indians within the limits of this State, it is hereby ordained, that no purchases or contracts for the sale of lands made since the   day of   in the year   , or which may hereafter be made with the Indians within the limits of this State, shall be binding on the Indians and valid, unless made under the authority of the legislature.

22. The legislative authority of this State shall be vested in a General Assembly, which shall consist of a Senate and House of Assembly, both to be elected by the People.

23. . . . the legislature shall every year assemble on the Second Tuesday in January, unless a different day be appointed by law.

24. The Senate shall consist of twenty-four members. The Senators shall be Freeholders and be chosen for four years. The House of Assembly shall consist of seventy-two members, who shall be elected for two years.

25. The State shall be divided into six senate districts, each of which shall choose four senators. . . .

26. An enumeration of the inhabitants of the State shall be taken under the direction of the Legislature, within one year after the first meeting of the General Assembly, and at the end of every four years thereafter; and the senate districts shall be so altered by the legislature after the return of every convention, that each senate district shall contain, as nearly as may be, an equal number of inhabitants, and at all times consist of contiguous territory; and no county shall be divided in the formation of a senate district.

27. The members of the House of Assembly shall be chosen by Counties, and be apportioned among the several counties of the State, as nearly as may be, according to the numbers of their respective inhabitants. . . .

29. All Elections shall be held at those places which may be considered by the electors to be the most central and convenient for them to assemble at. No county, district, or township election shall continue for a longer period than two days.

30. In order to promote the freedom, peace, and quiet of elections, and to secure, in the most ample manner possible, the independence of

the poorer classes of the electors, it is declared that all elections by the People, which shall take place after the first session of the legislature of this State, shall be by ballot, except for such town officers as may by law be directed to be otherwise chosen.

31. Electors shall, in all cases, except treason, felony, or breach of the peace, be privileged from arrest during their attendance at elections, and in going to and returning from them. . . .

34. And as soon as the Senate shall meet, after the first election to be held in pursuance of this Constitution, they shall cause the senators to be divided by lot, into four classes, of six in each, so that every district shall have one senator of each class: the classes to be numbered 1,2,3, and 4. And the seats of the first class shall be vacated at the end of the first year; of the second class, at the end of the second year; of the third class, at the end of the third year; of the fourth class, at the end of the fourth year; in order that one senator may be annually elected in each senate district.

35. A majority of each House shall constitute a quorum to do business, but a smaller number may adjourn from day to day and compel the attendance of absent members. Neither House shall, without the consent of the other, adjourn for more than two days.

36. Each House shall choose its Speaker, Clerk and other Officers.

37. In each House the votes shall, in all cases when taken, be taken openly, and not by ballot, so that the electors may be enabled to judge of the conduct of their representatives.

38. Each House shall keep a Journal of its proceedings, and publish the same except such parts as may require secrecy.

39. Each House may determine the rules of its own proceedings, judge of the qualifications of its members, punish its members for disorderly behaviour, and with the concurrence of two-thirds expel a member, but not a second time for the same cause.

40. Any bill may originate in either House of the Legislature; and all bills passed by one House may be amended or rejected by the other.

41. Every bill shall be read on three different days in each House – unless, in case of urgency, three-fourths of the whole members of the House where such bill is so depending shall deem it expedient to dispense with this rule; in which case the names of the majority or [sic] members present and consenting to dispense with this rule shall be entered on the Journals.

42. Every bill which shall have passed the Senate and Assembly, shall, before it becomes a law, be presented to the Governor. If he approve, he shall sign it; but if not, he should return it with his objections to that House in which it shall have originated, which shall enter the objections on its journal, and proceed to reconsider it. If after such reconsideration, two-thirds of the members present shall agree to pass the bill, it shall be sent, together with the objections, to the other House, by which it shall likewise be reconsidered; and if approved by

two-thirds of the members present it shall become a law. In all such cases, the votes of both Houses shall be determined by yeas and nays, and the names of the persons voting for and against the bill shall be entered on the Journals of each House respectively. If any bill shall not be returned by the Governor within ten days (Sundays excepted) after it shall have been presented to him, the same shall be a law, in like manner as if he had signed it, unless the legislature shall, by its adjournment, prevent its return, in which case it shall not be a law.

43. No member of the legislature, who has taken his seat as such, shall receive any civil appointment from the governor and senate, or from the legislature, during the term for which he shall have been elected.

44. The assent of the Governor, and of three fourths of the members elected to each branch of the legislature, shall be requisite to authorize the passage of every bill appropriating the public monies or property for local or private purposes, or for creating, continuing, altering, or renewing any body politic or corporate; and the yeas and nays shall be entered on the Journals at the time of taking the vote on the final passage of any such bill.

45. The members of the legislature shall receive for their services a compensation to be ascertained by law and paid out of the public treasury.

46. Members of the General Assembly shall, in all cases, except treason, felony, and breach of the peace, be privileged from arrest during their continuance as such members; and for any speech or debate in either House, they shall not be questioned in any other place. . . .

47. No Judge of any Court of law or equity, Secretary of State, Attorney General, Register of Deeds, Clerk of any Court of Record, Collector of Customs or Excise Revenue, Postmaster or Sheriff, shall be eligible as a candidate for, or have a seat in, the General Assembly. . . .

49. All officers holding their offices during good behaviour, or for a term of years, may be removed by joint resolution of the two Houses of the Legislature, if two-thirds of all the members elected to the Assembly, and a majority of all the members elected to the Senate, concur therein.

50. The House of Assembly shall have the sole power of impeaching, but a majority of all its members must concur in an impeachment.

51. All impeachments shall be tried by the Senate, and when sitting for that purpose, its members shall be on oath or affirmation to do justice according to law or evidence; no person shall be convicted without the concurrence of two-thirds of all the Senators.

51. [sic] The Legislature shall have power to pass laws for the peace, welfare, and good government of this State, not inconsistent

with the spirit of this Constitution – To coin money, regulate the value thereof, and provide for the punishment of those who may counterfeit the securities and coin of the State.

    i. To fix the standard of Weights and Measures.

    ii. To establish an uniform rule of naturalization.

    iii. To establish uniform laws on the subject of Bankruptcies.

    iiii. To regulate commerce.

    v. To lay and collect taxes.

    vi. To borrow money on the credit of the State, not, however, without providing at the same time the means, by additional taxation or otherwise of paying the interest, and of liquidating the principal within twenty years.

    vii. To establish Post Offices and Post Roads.

52. Gold and Silver shall be the only lawful tender in payment of debts. . . .

54. There shall be no sinecure offices. – Pensions shall be granted only by authority of the Legislature.

55. The whole public revenue of this State, that is, all money received from the public, shall be paid into the Treasury, without any deduction whatever, and be accounted for without deduction to the Legislature, whose authority shall be necessary for the appropriation of the whole. A regular statement and account of the receipt and expenditures of all public money shall be published once a year or oftener. No fees of office shall be received in any department which are not sanctioned by legislative authority.

56. There shall never be created within this State any incorporated trading companies, or incorporated companies with banking powers. Labour is the only means of creating wealth.

57. Bank Notes of a lesser nominal value than   shall not be allowed to circulate as money, or in lieu thereof.[199]

58. The Executive power shall be vested in a Governor. He shall hold his office for three years. No person shall be eligible to that office who shall not have attained the age of thirty years.

59. The Governor shall be elected by the People at the times and places of choosing members of the legislature. . . .

60. The Governor shall have power to convene the legislature, or the senate only, on extraordinary occasions. He shall communicate by message to the legislature at every session, the condition of the State, and recommend such matters to them as he shall judge expedient. He shall transact all necessary business with the officers of government; expedite all such measures as may be resolved upon by the legislature; and take care that the laws are faithfully executed. . . .

[199]Mackenzie's hard money views suggest that he intended to make paper money as scarce as possible by banning small denominations of it. None the less, his views here seem somewhat confused, for clause fifty-two seemed to interdict paper money entirely.

61. The Governor shall have power to grant reprieves and pardon, after conviction, for all offences, except in cases of impeachment. . . .

62. The Governor shall nominate by message, in writing, and, with the consent of the Senate, shall appoint the Secretary of State, Comptroller, Receiver General, Auditor General, Attorney General, Surveyor General, Postmaster General, and also all judicial officers, except Justices of the Peace and Commissioners of the Courts of Request, or Local Courts. . . .

65. The Judicial power of the State, both as to matters of law and equity, shall be vested in a Supreme Court, the members of which shall hold office during good behaviour, in District or County Courts, in Justices of the Peace, in Courts of Request, and in such other Courts as the Legislature may from time to time establish.

66. A competent number of Justices of the Peace and Commissioners of the Courts of Request shall be elected by the people, for a period of three years, within their respective cities and townships. . . .

69. All persons shall be bailable by sufficient sureties, unless for capital offences, where the proof is evident or the presumption great; and the privilege of the writ of Habeas Corpus shall not be suspended by any act of the Legislature, unless, when in cases of actual rebellion or invasion, the public safety may require it. . . .

74. Sheriffs, Coroners, Clerks of the Peace, and Registers of Counties or Districts, shall be chosen by the electors of the respective Counties or Districts, once in four years, and as often as vacancies happen. Sheriffs shall hold no other office, and be ineligible for the office of Sheriff for the next two years after the termination of their offices.

75. The Governor and all other Civil Officers under this State, shall be liable to impeachment for any misdemeanor in office; . . .

76. After this Constitution shall have gone into effect, no person shall be questioned for any thing said or done in reference to the public differences which have prevailed for some time past, it being for the public welfare and the happiness and peace of families and individuals that no door should be left open for a continued visitation of the effects of past years of misgovernment after the causes shall have passed away.

76a For the encouragement of immigration, the legislature may enable aliens to hold and convey real estate, under such regulations as may be found advantageous to the people of this State. . . .

78. All powers not delegated by this constitution remain with the people. . . .

80. . . . no religious test shall ever be required as a qualification to any office or public trust under this State. . . .

Several clauses for the carrying a constitution like the above into practice are omitted, the whole being only given in illustration of, and for the benefit of a comparison in detail, with other systems.

We have not entered upon the questions, whether any, and if so, what restrictions ought to be laid upon the right of voting, or as to residence in the State, taxation, performance of militia duty, &c. These matters, however, might be advantageously discussed by the public press. . . .

A 79   JOHN G. PARKER[200] TO THOMAS STORROW BROWN[201]
Hamilton, 22 November 1837
[PRO, CO 42, v. 467, p. 12, microfilm in PAO]

Private*

. . . I wish you could write me from official Accounts from the seat of war – The Radicals in Upper Canada are afraid that the C.' [Canadiens] have no spunk, and all will end in talk & smoke. – The Upper Canadians are ready for almost any thing. I have been informed that political Unions are formed all through the Country based on the declaration of the Reformers of Toronto on 31 July last. – We have a rifle Establishment in this Town, and it is said that a great many of the farmers are getting Rifles, in fact every thing here looks squally. There is a nest of Scotch Radicals of the worst sort back of Toronto and I was told by a man from that Quarter that they were getting well *marshalled*, and only waiting for good news from L. Canada, when they will enter the City, and salute the Governor and Nobility in – demonstrations of great joy carrying flags of divers colors. I look for great things this winter, and early in the winter – It is said by some one travelling from

*not for publicity

[200]John Goldsbury Parker (*ca.* 1796–1879) was born in New Hampshire and came to Upper Canada from Rochester about 1817. He settled first in Kingston, then in 1834 in Hamilton. There he and his brother Reuben became successful merchants and steamship owners, though by 1837 their fortunes were on a downward slide. A member of the reform-oriented Niagara Presbyterian Church, Parker was an enthusiastic dispenser of religious tracts and reform principles. In the fall of 1837 he wrote several people suggesting that he was at the centre of a vast revolutionary conspiracy. One correspondent, a Kingston resident, showed his letter to the authorities. This seems to have prompted Parker's arrest on 5 December, but not before his wife had destroyed various papers of his. Parker petitioned under 1 Victoria, c. 10 and was ordered transported for life. In August he and others escaped from the Kingston penitentiary, but he was recaptured and transported to England. There he and eleven other Upper Canadian state prisoners were freed after lengthy court cases revealed that the British government did not have the right to send them on to Van Diemen's Land (Tasmania). He then rejoined his family, settling in Rochester, New York, where he became a grocer.
[201]Thomas Storrow Brown (1803–1888) was born at St. Andrews, New Brunswick. Early in life he moved to Montreal, where he helped found the radical newspaper the *Vindicator*, which tried to make a particular appeal to discontented Irish immigrants. A rebel in 1837, he commanded the Canadiens at the battle of St. Charles, fleeing thereafter to the United States. In 1844 he returned to Montreal, living there until his death.

Lower Canada that the month of December would make known the fate of the Canadas, I hope they will make money plenty so that poor folks may pay their debts. The Banks may yet become very useful – I suppose you have seen the "Home Made constitution" in a late constitution, it takes well here. It may yet be adopted. The London and Western District[s] are said to be boiling over, ready for Reform – The Tories begin to cow in many places, a great many are determined to take no part whatever. – there is I am told 3 or 4 Unions formed in this City in a still quiet way, of determined spirit. The Tories begin to *calculate* that their real Estate will be worth double what it is when the troublesome times are over, and frequently are heard to say "whatever change is to take place let it be done at once" – I do not believe we have any fear of consequences in U.C. – a great many people are anxiously awaiting for the News from below – the Country is excited all over – One of Head's officials/I think Hagerman/ was heard to say "The Canadas are lost" – I wish you could write me – It is said Mr. Papineau has gone to the States for help! – I suppose not. – Do the Americans feel favorable and will they render any assistance? Are the – Canadians united? – There is a report they are divided – No wonder – no organization – no means, no arms, no courage – These things are said by certain friends. –

A 80   RESOLUTION OF THE HAMILTON POLITICAL UNION
24 November 1837
[Express, *Hamilton, quoted* Constitution, *Toronto, 6 Dec. 1837*]

. . . At a meeting of a number of the members of the Political Union, No. 1, for the Town of Hamilton, and its friends, held on Friday evening, the 24th November, 1837 – . . .

The following Resolutions were passed – . . .

8th Resolved – That we repudiate with disdain the stigma that some attempt to throw upon the Gore District, by setting us down as all Tories. On the contrary, we are fully persuaded, and firmly believe, that a large majority of this District agree in sentiment with the Reformers of the Home District, and with the nobly struggling patriots of Lower Canada against British usurpation, and that in case of any urgent conjuncture, there would not be found wanting hundreds who would be willing to aid in the cause of Reform in this Province or in Lower Canada, of this we are convinced from personal knowledge and past experience. The great bulk of the inhabitants of this District, containing upwards of forty thousands are Agriculturalists and Labourers, who of whatever country, in the aggregate, deeply sympathize with Lower Canada in its present struggle. And we wish the inhabitants of this Province to know, that we are willing at any fit conjuncture, in support of our dearest rights, if necessary, to lay down our lives – to expend our property and our time, in the manner of our English forefathers at Runnymede, or of our neighbors the Americans – believing, that to live as slaves is worse than to die. . . .

A 81   THE REFORMERS ARM
[Gazette, *Hamilton, 28 Nov. 1837*]

Mr. Mackenzie, in his last *Advocate & Correspondent*,[202] says –
   "A large quantity of Fire arms have been sent up to the Gore District, part deposited at Hamilton, some sent to Guelph, and some sent to the London District. I am not informed whether any have been sent to the Western District yet."
   And thus *innocently* concludes:
   "*The People* will be informed where to call for the guns when they are needed!!!" . . .
   We are credibly informed that Charles Durand, *Esq..* [*sic*] is canvassing for names, to form a Rifle *Corpse*, to aid and assist the Lower Canadians, if deemed necessary! . . . Well done Charley. . . . thou Prince of Simpletons!

A 82   W.L. MACKENZIE ON RESISTANCE TO OPPRESSION
[Constitution, *Toronto, 22 Nov. 1837*]

Look and deeply consider!!!
PEOPLE OF UPPER CANADA, . . .
   I again say, whatever may have been the grievances complained of hitherto by the Lower Canadians, or how unjust or unfounded soever they may have been, is not now to be considered by us. The question is – Are the British Government right or are the Lower Canadians – the one in taking the taxes of the People against their will, and the last in opposing like freemen this gross aggression by a tyrannizing Executive? Behold the oppressors!! in order to enslave a free People encamp soldiers all over their country!! O! Englishmen in Canada and Upper Canadians, have you no brotherly sympathy for the Lower Canadians? Will you calmly and coldly see them put down by military force? No methinks not. I tell you if they are put down by soldiers you will be so too! If the British Kingdom can tax the People of Lower Canada against their will, they will do so with you when you dare to be free. I tell you, your lot will be like theirs – their fate will be yours!! . . .
   Oh, men of Upper Canada, would you murder a free people! Head has sent down his troops, next he will try and send you down to put

---

[202]After William O'Grady ceased publishing the *Correspondent and Advocate* in August 1837, Mackenzie incorporated it in his *Constitution*, publishing about half the newspaper under the latter title and about half under the former.

down your countrymen. Before you do so pause, and consider the world has its eyes on you – history will mark your conduct – beware lest they condemn. Oh who would not have it said of him that, as an Upper Canadian, he died in the cause of freedom! To die fighting for freedom is truly glorious. Who would live and die a slave?

A FRIEND TO DEMOCRACY

A 83   W.L. MACKENZIE THREATENS TORIES
[Constitution, *Toronto, 22 Nov. 1837*]

WHO WILL LOSE THEIR PROPERTY? –

This is a question people begin to ask each other, and none with more anxious earnestness than the vindictive tories. In the old American war, the lands of those tories who took an active part against their country's independence were very properly sold to pay the expences of the war, and their claims and other valuables confiscated. Those who lay quiet were not disturbed. Why should they? They were peaceable, and men ought not to be punished for entertaining abstract opinions. In the last war, the lands of those who supported the Americans were confiscated. In the next, Sir F.B. Head is to do great things. "Come if you dare! Here goes!"

B. THE MACKENZIE RISING

B 1   "AN ACCOUNT OF THE REBELLION NEAR TORONTO" BY W.L.
MACKENZIE
[Jeffersonian, *Watertown, reprinted in* Mackenzie's Gazette, *New
York City, 12 May 1838*]

For other extracts from this document see B 14, B 25, B 31, B 38, B 48, B 61.

DEAR SIR – I received yesterday three or four of your latest papers, with
a couple of the *U.C. Heralds* of last month, . . . In one of these
Heralds, I find a very incorrect narrative of the insurrection at Toronto;
and as your journal probably circulates in the same section of country,
and there is no likelihood that the Kingston editor would permit me to
correct his errors, I request that you will publish this statement, at your
leisure, in the Jeffersonian. I also send for your perusal the Rochester
Democrat of last Tuesday, with a long article over my signature,
entitled *"Reasons for a Revolution in Canada,"* the perusal of which
might perhaps be acceptable to the olds [*sic*] friends and neighbors of
your cruelly persecuted fellow citizen, John G. Parker.

Ψ

NARRATIVE, &c.

On the 31st of July last, the Reformers of Toronto responded to the
request of their fellow sufferers in Lower Canada, by the appointment
of ward committees of vigilance, the passage of resolutions of
sympathy and co-operation, and the adoption of a declaration of rights
and grievances, which only differed from your great Declaration of
1776, in that it did not at once proclaim the Province independent, nor
enumerate, in all cases, the same complaints.

The Reformers had taken great pains to inform the British
Government of the true state of affairs in Upper Canada, and many
believed that Sir Francis Bond Head would do what he could to remove
the chief causes of discontent, until the proceedings of the executive
previous to and at the last general election of a House of Assembly,
convinced them that nothing but a revolution would relieve the
country. This opinion I was confirmed in, by observing that when the
Assembly of Lower Canada deferred granting supplies until their
wrongs would be redressed, the House of Commons of England, by a
vote of about 10 to 1, and the Lords unanimously, (Lord Brougham

alone dissenting,) resolved, that the proceeds of the revenue raised in that colony, both by provincial and British statutes, should be expended without the consent of the representatives of the people, or the form of law, in keeping up a costly foreign government in which the governed had no share.

In the declaration of grievances of the 31st of July, the British Government were distinctly given to understand that revolt might be the consequence of its base duplicity. And that declaration was read, considered and approved at 200 public meetings in the country; 150 branch associations, agreeing to its principles, were speedily organized, and Sir F.B. Head was informed thro' the press, that the officers of these societies *might* be used as captains and lieutenants of companies, for resistance by force, in case a change of his measures did not soon take place.

The many scenes of violence and outrage which occurred at our public meetings between July and December I need not recount. Let it suffice to say, that we kept up a good understanding with the reformers of Lower Canada; and concluding that arbitrary imprisonments and a declaration of military execution would follow the anticipated outbreak at Montreal, we resolved to second the Lower Canada movements by others equally prompt and decisive.

Some of the members of our branch societies were kept in ignorance of the intended revolt. – Others were fully aware of it. Some whose names were attached to no association were leaders in the revolution – other very active republicans took no part. The presses under my control sent forth nearly 3000 copies of a periodical filled with reasons for revolt, and about the third week in November it was determined that on Thursday the 7th of December, our forces should secretly assemble at Montgomery's Hotel, 3 miles back of Toronto, between 6 and 10 at night, and proceed from thence to the city, join our friends there, seize 4000 stands [sic] of arms, which had been placed by Sir Francis in the city hall, take him into custody with his chief advisers, place the garrison in the hands of the liberals, declare the province free, call a convention together, to frame a suitable constitution, and meantime appoint our friend Dr. Rolph, provincial administrator of the government. WE expected to do all this without shedding blood, well knowing that the vice regal government was too unpopular to have many *real* adherents.

Only in one instance did we forward a notice of the intended movement beyond the limits of the county of York and to Whitby and some other towns in it no circulars were sent. We never doubted the feeling of the province. Sir F. admits, in "his speech from the throne," that we would have cheerfully submitted the whole matter to a convention of the people.

Twelve leading reformers in the city and county agreed one day in November, that on thursday the 7th of December last, between the hours of six and ten in the evening, the friends of freedom in the several townships, led by their captains, would meet at Montgomery's, march to Toronto, seize the arms we so much wanted, dismiss Sir Francis, and proclaim a Republic. The details were left entirely to my management; and an executive in the city was named to correspond with Mr. Papineau and our other friends below, afford intelligence, aid our efforts, and finally, to join the army at Montgomery's. It was also stipulated that no attempt should be made by that executive to alter the time on which we were to revolt, without consulting with me in the first instance. . . .

B 2   STATEMENT OF JAMES LATIMER[1]
21 December 1837
[PAO, Rebellion Papers, 1837–8, no. 18]

For other extracts from this document see B 39, B 51.

. . . For some weeks before the breaking out of the rebellion I observed a great change in the conduct of Mr. MacKenzie: he became much more violent & capricious in his temper; took to swearing a good deal, & became much addicted to drink. My opinion was that he was pushed for the payment of heavy debts due by him at New York – which he was unable to meet – and that this, together with the loss of his trial at Niagara had rendered him desperate. For a week or two before the breaking out of the insurrection he was a good deal in the country – On the Wednesday – I think it was – the 29th Nov. a small press was taken down, and was sent into the country together with a small assortment of type & a bundle of paper, under the charge of Peter Baxter,[2] – Mr. MacKenzies brother in law – I did not know then where the Press & types were sent to, but I afterward learned they were at Montgomery's Tavern. I heard a number of flying reports – but *knew* nothing of what was going on until Monday the 4th Dec. when we heard of the rebels having assembled at Montgomery's. . . .

[1]James Latimer was an apprentice of William Lyon Mackenzie, 1830–4. From 1834 to 1836 he worked for various printers, then after a period of illness returned to work as a journeyman in Mackenzie's Toronto shop in 1837.
[2]Peter Baxter (*fl.* 1800–1853) was the brother-in-law of William Lyon Mackenzie. In the early 1830s he came to York to work as a printer for Mackenzie and in the days before the rebellion he printed, on a portable press, the circular calling the people to arms. This was printed and circulated north of Toronto. He appears to have fled to the United States after the rising but later returned to Toronto.

B 3   W.L. MACKENZIE'S APPEAL TO ARMS[3]
[*Charles Lindsey*, The Life and Times of William Lyon Mackenzie
    . . . *II (Toronto, 1862), pp. 358-62*]

INDEPENDENCE!

*There have been Nineteen Strikes for Independence from European
Tyranny, on the Continent of America. They were all successful! The
Tories, therefore, by helping us will help themselves.*

> The nations are fallen, and thou still art young,
> The sun is but rising when others have set;
> And though Slavery's cloud o'er thy morning hath hung,
> The full tide of Freedom shall beam round thee yet.

BRAVE CANADIANS! God has put into the bold and honest hearts of our
brethren in Lower Canada to revolt – not against "lawful" but against
"unlawful authority." The law says we shall not be taxed without our
consent by the voices of the men of our choice; but a wicked and
tyrannical government has trampled upon that law, robbed the
exchequer, divided the plunder, and declared, that, regardless of
justice, they will continue to roll their splendid carriages, and riot in
their palaces, at our expense; that we are poor, spiritless, ignorant
peasants, who were born to toil for our betters. But the peasants are
beginning to open their eyes and to feel their strength; too long have
they been hoodwinked by Baal's priests – by hired and tampered-with
preachers, wolves in sheep's clothing, who take the wages of sin, and
do the work of iniquity, "each one looking to his gain in his quarter."
    CANADIANS! Do you love freedom? I know you do. Do you hate
oppression? Who dare deny it? Do you wish perpetual peace, and a
government founded upon the eternal heaven-born principle of the
Lord Jesus Christ – a government bound to enforce the law to do to
each other as you wish to be done by? Then buckle on your armor, and
put down the villains who oppress and enslave our country – put them
down in the name of that God who goes forth with the armies of his
people, and whose Bible shows that it is by the same human means
whereby you put to death thieves and murderers, and imprison and
banish wicked individuals, that you must put down, in the strength of
the Almighty, those governments which, like these bad individuals,
trample on the law, and destroy its usefulness. You give a bounty for
wolves' scalps. Why? Because wolves harass you. The bounty you
must pay for freedom (blessed word!) is to give the strength of your
arms to put down tyranny at Toronto. One short hour will deliver our
country from the oppressor; and freedom in religion, peace, and

---

[3]This handbill was printed on Friday, December 1, and circulated outside of Toronto
(see p. xxxix). It was not, as Head later claimed, published in the *Constitution*.

tranquillity, equal laws, and an improved country will be the prize. We contend, that in all laws made, or to be made, every person shall be bound alike – neither should any tenure, estate, charter, degree, birth, or place, confer any exemption from the ordinary course of legal proceedings and responsibilities whereunto others are subjected.

CANADIANS! God has shown that he is with our brethren, for he has given them the encouragement of success. Captains, Colonels, Volunteers, Artillerymen, Privates, the base, the vile hirelings of our unlawful oppressors, have already bit the dust in hundreds in Lower Canada; and although the Roman Catholic and Episcopal Bishops and Archdeacons are bribed by large sums of money to instruct their flocks that they should be obedient to a government which defies the law, and is therefore unlawful, and ought to be put down; yet God has opened the eyes of the people to the wickedness of these reverend sinners, so that they hold them in derision, just as God's prophet Elijah did the priests of Baal of old and their sacrifices. Is there any one afraid to go to fight for freedom, let him remember, that

> God sees with equal eye, as Lord of all,
> A hero perish, or a sparrow fall:

That the power that protected ourselves and our forefathers in the deserts of Canada – that preserved from the cholera those whom he would – that brought us safely to this continent through the dangers of the Atlantic waves – aye, and who has watched over us from infancy to manhood, will be in the midst of us in the day of our struggle for our liberties, and for governors of our free choice, who would not dare to trample on the laws they had sworn to maintain. In the present struggle, we may be sure, that if we do not rise and put down Head and his lawless myrmidons, they will gather all the rogues and villains in the country together – arm them – and then deliver our farms, our families, and our country to their brutality. To that it has come, we must put them down, or they will utterly destroy this country. If we move now, as one man, to crush the tyrant's power, to establish free institutions founded on God's law, we will prosper, for He who commands the winds and waves will be with us; but if we are cowardly and mean-spirited, a woeful and a dark day is surely before us.

CANADIANS! The struggle will be of short duration in Lower Canada, for the people are united as one man. Out of Montreal and Quebec, they are as one hundred to one – here we Reformers are as ten to one; and if we rise with one consent to overthrow despotism, we will make quick work of it.

Mark all those who join our enemies, act as spies for them, fight for them, or aid them; these men's properties shall pay the expense of the struggle; they are traitors to Canadian freedom, and as such we will deal with them.

CANADIANS! It is the design of the friends of liberty to give several hundred acres to every volunteer – to root up the unlawful Canada Company, and give *free deeds* to all settlers who live on their lands; to give free gifts of the Clergy Reserve lots, to good citizens who have settled on them; and the like to settlers on Church of England Glebe lots, so that the yeomanry may feel independent, and be able to improve the country, instead of sending the fruit of their labor to foreign lands. The fifty-seven Rectories will be at once given to the people, and all public lands used for education, internal improvements, and the public good. £100,000, drawn from us in payment of the salaries of bad men in office, will be reduced to one quarter, or much less, and the remainder will go to improve bad roads and to "make crooked paths straight;" law will be ten times more cheap and easy – the bickerings of priests will cease with the funds that keep them up – and men of wealth and property from other lands will soon raise our farms to four times their present value. We have given Head and his employers a trial of forty-five years – five years longer than the Israelites were detained in the wilderness. The promised land is now before us – up then and take it – but set not the torch to one house in Toronto, unless we are fired at from the houses, in which case self-preservation will teach us to put down those who would murder us when up in the defence of the laws. There are some rich men now, as there were in Christ's time, who would go with us in prosperity, but who will skulk in the rear, because of their large possessions – mark them! They are those who in after years will seek to corrupt our people, and change free institutions into an aristocracy of wealth, to grind the poor, and make laws to fetter their energies.

MARK MY WORDS, CANADIANS! The struggle is begun – it might end in freedom; but timidity, cowardice, or tampering on our part, will only delay its close. We cannot be reconciled to Britain – we have humbled ourselves to the Pharaoh of England, to the Ministers and great people, and they will neither rule us justly nor let us go; we are determined never to rest until independence is ours – the prize is a splendid one. A country larger than France or England, natural resources equal to our most boundless wishes; a government of equal laws; religion pure and undefiled; perpetual peace; education to all; millions of acres of lands for revenue; freedom from British tribute; free trade with all the world – but stop – I never could enumerate all the blessings attendant on independence!

Up then, brave Canadians! Get ready your rifles, and make short work of it; a connection with England would involve us in all her wars, undertaken for her own advantage, never for ours; with governors from England, we will have bribery at elections, corruption, villainy, and perpetual discord in every township, but independence would give us the means of enjoying many blessings. Our enemies in Toronto are in terror and dismay; they know their wickedness and dread our vengeance. . . . Is there to be an end of these things? Aye, and now's the day and the hour! Woe be to those who oppose us, for "In God is our trust."

B 4   PETITION OF SAMUEL LOUNT TO SIR F.B. HEAD
10 March 1838
[PAC, Upper Canada Sundries, v. 192, pp. 107033-8]

For another extract from this document see B 34.

. . . during the whole of the Summer of 1837 your petitioner had been employed in the pursuit of agriculture (about two Miles and a half back from Yonge Street in the woods) in Such a place as entirely to exclude him from intercourse with society – Consequently was not aware of any plot existing against the Government until about two weeks before the late insurrection, when he was visited by W.L. McKenzie – who held forth to him the ease with which the people of the Country might possess themselves of the Arms in the City Hall, and by the shew of power have all their political wants accomplished, and that there would be no necessity of taking the life of any individual, and that his defaming the Governor was only a sham to mislead their opponents, to back which assertion he referred your petitioner to sundry articles published in his paper, any one of which he said was sufficient to Condemn him, and that lately a request had been made to the Governor and Council for a Warrant to apprehend him (McKenzie) upon sedition published in his paper but that the Chief Justice[4] winked at his conduct and advised the Governor and Council that if he was apprehended and brought to trial it would only be giving him a Chance of making a long speech, and that they (the Government) would be able to do nothing with him, and that the Chief Justice, the Honorable John Henry Dunn, Christopher Alexander Hagerman Esquire, the Honorable Peter Robinson, Doctor John Rolph and others were as anxious of affecting a Change in the Government as he possibly Could be, but dare not come forward, for fear of a few persons in the City of Toronto, in view of

[4]The Chief Justice was John Beverley Robinson (1791–1863) who had been born at Berthier, Lower Canada, to United Empire Loyalist parents. His family had moved to Kingston in 1792, and a few years later to York. John was educated by John Strachan, who exercised a formative influence on him. Robinson then studied law and served as an officer in the War of 1812. His abilities and connections were signified by his being appointed acting attorney general of the province in 1812, a post he held until 1814. In 1815 he became the province's solicitor general and in 1818 its attorney general. In 1820 he was elected to the Assembly for York, where he served as the leading government spokesman until 1829 when he resigned his seat to become chief justice of the province and Speaker of the Legislative Council and president of the Executive Council. During Colborne's tenure as lieutenant-governor his influence waned, though it waxed again under Head and Arthur. He became a voluble critic of Durham's report and the ensuing union of the Canadas. The 1840s saw the power of the Family Compact decline and with it, Robinson's political influence. Increasingly, he concerned himself with his judicial duties and the fostering of the Church of England.

which all the Troops had been sent from the province, and that there was nothing required but for the people to arm themselves and turn out to the number of two or three hundred (which he said he had already arranged) and then the Governor and those in authority could with propriety grant all that was required, and if done in that way the Government of Great Britain would consent to a friendly seperation without the loss of a single life – With the above arguments and many others of the same tendency such as "see the sedition constantly published in my paper &c.&c.["] meaning thereby to say "you must be sure that many in authority must be my friends or I should be taken up.["] I was led to place implicit confidence in his representations and consequently agreed to acceed to his wishes and as I thought the wishes of the majority in power in the Province, And on Sunday the third day of December last a message was received that all those on the north side of the ridges must be in Toronto on the night of Monday the fourth of December (although the time previously fixed upon was the Seventh) and that the reason of Our being Called upon before the time appointed, was, because such posative information had been made to the Governor and others that they (notwithstanding their friendly disposition to our cause) had been obliged to issue warrants for the apprehension of McKenzie, Rolph, and others. and that unless we Came forward, our intentions and the desires of those in the City friendly to us, would be entirely frustrated – . . .

B 5   STATEMENT OF CHARLES DOAN[5]
15 December 1837
[*PAO, Rebellion Papers, 1837–8, no. 13*]

. . . I live in the town of Hope and belong to the Children of Peace[.] on Monday the 27th Novr. Samuel Lount came into our settlement and called a meeting of the young men at the orphan House Chamber[.] about twenty Per[sons] assembled when Lount addressed them and said there was war in Lower Canada and there was reason to believe that Martial Law would be proclaimed in this Province. in order to prevent which it would be necessary to proceed to take the City, that a number of Influential persons would meet them at Montgomery's amongst them he mentioned the Receiver General Peter Robinson and the Chief Justice with Two hundred men, that four hundred were assembled there. from below the ridges and one hundred from Lloyd

[5]Charles Doan (1808–1895) was the son of one of the founders in Hope (Sharon), East Gwillimbury, of the Children of Peace or Davidites, a schismatic Quaker group. By the time he was 18 Charles had already been a farmer and a shoemaker; he later became a partner in a mercantile business. In 1837 he struck out on his own and in later life enjoyed considerable business success. Like many other members of the Children of Peace, he was active in the rebellion. Arrested on 18 December 1837, he was held until May 1838. After petitioning the lieutenant-governor, he was pardoned upon giving security for three years' good behaviour.

town, and they would come in by hundreds and fifties from other different townships. he said he thought the City would be taken without firing a Gun, that he did not know the exact day the attack was to be made but he would let them know. the young men present said that if there was to be a general turn out they though[t] they would join. Lount recommended us to take such guns as we had with us. On Sunday the third of Decr. he came again to the settlement and rode round to the different houses of people who he thought would go. and told them to be ready to start down at 9 oClock in the morning of Monday[.] he told us to put the arms in the waggon of John D Wilson[6] my brother in law. we accordingly started at the time appointed, about 12 or 13 started at this time and J.D. Wilson started with the waggon containing the arms[.] Mr. Lount went with us and ordered us to stop at Gibsons place. we did so. we went on to Montgomerys that evening and arrived there about 11 oClock. there were about 80 persons when we got there. . . .

B 6   REBELS MUSTER
[PRO, CO 42, v. 447, pp. 205-11, Trial of Gilbert Fields Morden,[7]
microfilm in PAO]

James Severs – knows prisoner, has known him for 7 or 8 months – On 4th December, Monday, met him about 2 or 3 O'Clock, P.M. in the Township of Vaughan, in the road between the 3rd and 4th Concessions – he was armed, had a long fowling peice – coming in towards Yonge Street – About 70 men were with him, armed – Witness had met 20 or more just before – most of them had pikes or rifles – Jesse Lloyd rode in the rear of the party with prisoner, armed with a rifle, Witness spoke to prisoner, he said they had left Lloyd-town about 8 O'Clock that morning – Witness remarked they had travelled fast; prisoner said they could not be too quick in a good cause. He said "We are going to Toronto." . . . This was about 14 or 15 miles from Montgomery's – Witness was going out from Toronto on business as a Sheriff's bailiff –

---

[6]John D. Willson (Wilson) (1797 or 1798–1887) came to Canada as a young boy with his father David, who became the leader of the Children of Peace in Hope, East Gwillimbury. John D. became a leading member of the group. Along with many others from the community, he was involved in the rebellion. Arrested 14 December 1837, he was released in May of the next year, having petitioned for pardon. The condition of pardon was that he give security for three years' good behaviour.

[7]Gilbert Fields Morden (b. *ca.* 1800) worked as a shoemaker in Lloydtown, King Township, *ca.* 1835-7. He took an active part in the rebellion and was sentenced to death at his trial. After this sentence was reduced to transportation, he escaped from Fort Henry while being transferred to England. He crossed to the United States, where he was active in the Patriot movement. Caleb Morden, also a shoemaker from Lloydtown, joined the loyalist side in the rebellion. He may well have been related. Caleb was Canadian-born of United Empire Loyalist parents.

Arthur Armstrong[8] – Is a Captain in the Militia, lives near Lloyd-town in the Township of King – has known prisoner nearly two years – On Monday 4th. December, very early in the morning, prisoner with eight or ten other persons made prisoner of witness in the Township of King – They were armed with pikes and guns – . . . – witness resisted; they threatened him – this prisoner had a long firelock; they desired witness to take Arms and go with them; Witness refused – One Anderson[9] said they would take him at any rate – At last they said they would make him take an Oath that he could not inform – they sent and got a bible, and made Witness swear that he would give no information, which witness agreed to, in order to get away from them, being desirous to raise the Country, and alarm the loyal inhabitants in their rear – Witness did so and armed many persons who came in afterwards under Colonel Dewson[10] – has never seen prisoner since, until today – About 60 or 70 persons had assembled (of the rebels) before witness got away from them – they were chiefly armed – witness Knew prisoner well [–]

B 7   PETITION OF JOSEPH GOULD[11] TO SIR GEORGE ARTHUR[12]
4 May 1838
[PAC, Upper Canada Sundries, v. 193, pp. 107514-18]

. . . I am an inhabitant of the Township of Uxbridge where I was born and have lived all my life it being Principly a wilderness nearly 50 miles from this city, there I lived and knew nothing of the affairs of the

[8]Arthur Armstrong (b. 1812?) came from his native Ireland about 1835 and settled on a farm in King Township on lot 24, concession 9. A captain of militia in 1837, he raised the loyalists in the area near Lloydtown to oppose the rebellion. In 1838 he was appointed a magistrate and in 1838–9 raised a troop which garrisoned the still disloyal Lloydtown for about a year. Armstrong was a member of the Church of England and a devoted Orangeman.
[9]This was Anthony Anderson (d. 1837), a friend and neighbour of Jesse Lloyd of King Township. Having served as a trooper in the War of 1812, he was considered by the radicals to be of great value in the trainings which preceded the rebellion.
[10]Jeremiah Wilkes Dewson (b. 1794) served in his native Staffordshire militia for four years and then spent twenty-five years in the 35th and 15th regiments, rising to the rank of major. He settled in West Gwillimbury Township in the mid-1830s, where he was appointed commissioner of the Court of Requests. He commanded a large party of volunteers from his area who marched to the aid of Toronto in 1837. Afterwards he was allowed to raise a regiment of militia from the same area but almost immediately the command was taken from him and given to W.B. Robinson. In 1838–9 he commanded a volunteer company stationed at Bond Head to prevent further rebellion. Dewson was a member of the Church of England.
[11]Joseph Gould (1806–1886), born in sparsely settled Uxbridge Township, went on to become a very successful local businessman and public figure. A reform supporter for most of his adult life, he was persuaded by his neighbours to take part in the rising of 1837. Captured while fleeing the defeat at Montgomery's, he was sentenced to transportation, but this sentence was reduced to nine months' imprisonment. In October 1838 he was released under the general amnesty then proclaimed.
[12]Sir George Arthur (1784–1854), born at Plymouth, England, entered the army in 1804, serving in various European campaigns. In 1814 he became lieutenant-governor

Provence till within the last year, one of my neighbours presented me with two news papers which he Said he would let me have evry week if I would Send for and return them, which I did, those papers were the Corespondant and Advocate and McKinzie's Constitution paper[,] these two papers were the first and only political prints I ever read and to them I alledge my being placed in the Situation I am at present. I need not set forth any of the principles held forth in those papers for your Honorable Council can I believe inform you better what was their drift than I am able to do. Although I read those papers which in part placed my mind in a Situation to be wrought upon yet I did not attend political meetings nor places of Political discusing until Friday night the first Day of December last[.] William H Doyle[13] came to my house Sometime towards midnight and told me there was to be a meeting at Stouffille on the morrow and requested me to go to it, I refused to go and asked the meaning of the meeting[,] he said McKinzie was to be there and would make known the meaning of the meeting[,] he said that he had been up into Brock and they mosly all were going from them parts[,] he said some of my neighbours were going and that I must go to, which I refused So Strong that he left me[.] In the morning Mr Doyle came to my place with about twenty men with him and said he would go no further till I consented to go with them which I would not consent to do but after being persuaded some time by Mr Doyle and Seeing so many men going I at last consented and went

When we got there we were met by a number of men from the adjoining Township to me but appearently of Some Standing. Soon after McKenzie came in and began to harang us on the affairs of the Provence[,] he told us all things were in readiness now that all the plans were laid[,] that this was the last meeting he had to hold and that we had but two choices which was either to Submit to Governed by the lower Canadians or rise up and Govern ourselves, for that Lower Canada had revolted and the french were driveing all before them[,] he said they had taken Montreal and driven Sir Johns troops to the four winds of heaven with many more such like Statements, he Said he had been all through the country and hel[d] council with the people and they all were dissatisfied with the present state of things and had

<hr>

of Honduras and in 1823 of Van Diemen's Land. From 1838 to 1841 he was lieutenant-governor of Upper Canada at a time when penalties had to be decided for the rebels of 1837. Some considered his actions harsh while others felt him properly firm. After his time in Upper Canada, he was rewarded with a baronetcy for handling a difficult situation well. He served with the government in Bombay until 1846, when he returned to England.

[13]William H. Doyle of Whitchurch Township was a member of a family which was among the first of those settled in Brock Township in the 1820s. The postmaster at Stoverville (now Stouffville), he was active in the political union movement prior to the rebellion and led a company of men from his township and surrounding ones down to Montgomery's Tavern.

unanimously agreed to Join and take this city which he Said could be done without the loss of one life, as all the troops were gone below and there were fifteen hundred men in toronto all ready to Join[,] he said he was nothing but a mear tool in the hands of his council which he Said was Some of the first men in the Provence and mentioned Something about Rolph being intended for the Presadent but would tell no more, nor would he tell the time of action but Said W H Doyle would acquaint all in them parts[,] here McKenzie and Doyle insisted on my Joining the expedition and I seeing none object consented, they then Presented me with a political union paper which had been circulated through our neighbourhood but I had not signed it not knowing its meaning[,] [it] they Said was to unite the people in cases of elections and Such like Political movements and urged me to sign it which I did, the meeting ended and I returnd home and heard no more of the affair until the Tuesday following when word came from Markham that the men from Simcoe Newmarket Lloydtown and all along youngstreet had turned out and marched direct to the city and without adoubt the city was taken by that time, he Said his orders was to warn evry man to turn out for fear of a reaction, a fear I had not before heard expressed by any party; So in the evening there come to my house about ten or twelve men and boys[.] Some were neighbours and Some from other parts, and I Joined with them, we traveled all night[,] in the morning we overtook a company from Brock[,] we came with them the rest of the way down, We plundered no mans house[,] we forced no provisions but paid for all we wanted where they would take pay. We arived at Montgomery's on Wednsday evening about five oclock. . . .

B 8   PETITION OF RANDAL WIXON[14]
10 April 1838
[PAC, Upper Canada Sundries, v. 198, pp. 109984-9]

. . . The petition of the Undersigned Randal Wixson now in the Home District Gaol on a charge of High Treason.

Humbly Sheweth: . . .

That your petitioner's Loyalty stood both unimpeached and unimpeachable up to the evening of the 30th November last, when William H. Doyle of Stouffville came to your Petitioner's residence in the Township of Brock, inquiring for the residences of certain

---

[14]Randal Wixon came with his parents from Steuben County, New York, about 1801, the family being among the first settlers in the north of Pickering Township. Randal was an active Baptist, serving as an elder of the church for many years. He was a school teacher and an active reformer, both in Pickering and in Brock Township, after he moved there in the 1820s. While William Lyon Mackenzie was in England in 1832, Wixon edited the *Colonial Advocate*, and at the time of the rising he encouraged his neighbours to join it, although his participation was limited because he had only one leg. Arrested and sentenced to transportation for fourteen years, Wixon was released by the courts while in England, awaiting shipment to Van Diemen's Land.

individuals in said Township; – whereupon your petitioner asked Mr. Doyle, Why he was in such earnest to see them? To which he replied that there was to be a meeting in Stouffville on the following Saturday, Dec. 2d and that Mr. MacKenzie was particularly desirous that the persons named should be present at the meeting, as there was something of importance to be discussed. Your petitioner then asked Mr. Doyle whether the meeting was to be a private one? To which he replied that he did not consider it so. Your petitioner, thinking by Mr. Doyle's manner, that there must be something more than common [in] the matter, asked what was going on? To which he replied that the Lower Canadians were fighting like the Devil and carrying all before them.

Your petitioner felt very much struck, and, being an Upper Canadian by birth and warmly attached to the interests of his Country, – after a few moments reflection, concluded to attend the meeting at Stouffville and hear for himself what was going on, – which he did in company with several of his neighbors.

On his arrival there, your Petitioner found a large company assembled and assembling apparently without knowing the objects of the meeting further than that Mr. Doyle had warned them to attend. When a number of persons, say from 50 to 100, had gotten together, Mr. Mackenzie made his appearance, and proceeded immediately to explain the objects of the meeting in substance, (as nearly as memory serves,) as follows, viz. That the Lower Canadians were in an actual state of open revolt, – That they were defeating the Queens troops in every engagement, – That he knew from unquestionable authority that the Queens army were literally cut all to pieces, – That Montreal was unquestionably in the hands of Papineau, – That there was little or no room to doubt but that Quebec had followed in the same track as the troops had been withdrawn towards Montreal to such an extent as to leave the citizens of Quebec (who were almost to a man in favor of the insurgents) by far stronger than the soldiery, – That in fact, (although he had not received positive information of it,) he had no more doubt of Quebec's being in the hands of the Canadians, than he had of his own existence.

That under these trying circumstances the people of Upper Canada were imperatively called upon to consider what was to be done, which they had promptly done, – That consultations similar to the present had already been held in various parts of the province, and that more than nine tenths of the people of Upper Canada had agreed to a change of constitution as a matter of expediency, – That people holding a diversity of political opinions on former occasions, were assuming a unanimity on this occasion, naming (as proofs of this unanimity) several distinguished individuals, amongst which were the Hon. Peter Robinson, The Hon. The Chief Justice Robinson, Dr. John Rolph, M.S. Bidwell, Esq. and many others holding, on former occasions a wide difference in political opinions, – explaining the various means by which he had learned the sentiments of the various persons whom he named.

That the reason for the asserted unanimity was very obvious, – That with Lower Canada existing as an independent republic, we could not exist as a British Colony as we would be without a seaport and consequently shut out from, and deprived of, all commercial advantages, – That there was still another consideration of more importance, – That the Lower Canadians would most undoubtedly turn their victorious arms against Upper Canada which was too weak to resist them, assisted as they were, by thousands of riflemen from Vermont and Maine enlisted into the Canadian Service, as volunteers. That under these painful circumstances it was clearly our only alternative to change our constitution and join the American union, or see our Country deluged in blood and covered with devastation.

That the proposed change was not to affect private rights, that person and property were to remain equally protected and equally secure under the new constitution as under the old one, and that commercial transactions were not expected to be impeded for a single week. That the proposed change could not be made, or consistently admitted by those in office without some appearance of military parade; – that it was necessary that there should be a sort of turnout to carry it into effect; but that there would not be a gun fired, or at least, that he had no expectation that there would be.

Your petitioner believes he should be fully able to prove nearly or quite all the material points in the above outline of Mr. Mackenzie's statement. The meeting was not formally organized by the appointment of a chairman and secretary, neither was there any door keeper, but people went out and in as they pleased.

Suffice it to say, that after Mr. Mackenzie had publicly made the foregoing statements and had given the most solemn assurances of their truth when further interogated in private, all doubts having thus been removed from the mind of your Petitioner as to the truth of them, – your Petitioner returned home and mentioned, he thinks, to about a dozen of his acquaintances in Brock, the situation of the public affairs, as he then understood them, some four or five of whom he thinks may have turned out in consequence of what he told them.

That your petitioner by particular request attended a meeting in Brock which was afterwards convened for the purpose of choosing officers. That it was distinctly understood at that meeting that the proposed change was to be carried into effect by the general consent of the leading men of all political parties, or more properly speaking, of the country; – That the choosing of officers was considered a mere matter of form, and that the most moderate and temperate men were chosen to office instead of warriors. . . .

B 9   EXAMINATION OF NATHANIEL PEARSON[15]
16 December 1837
[PAC, Upper Canada Sundries, v. 180, pp. 99351-2]

Nathaniel Pearson, am come here [Newmarket] to give myself up to the authorities, am guilty, had not any arms, I saw Samuel Lount a week or two before I went down who told me there was going to be a change in the government, Dr. Rolph & Dunn were leaders, Peter Robinson and the Chief Justice were favourable but would not act, and that the country were dissatisfied with the Government on account of the bank, and they were going to unite to overturn the Government and would have one of their own choosing – It would be known only a very short time before it took place[,] the first I knew of it was from Gabl. Hawke,[16] it was mentioned by many on the Sunday, Hawke and others were sworn – McKensie came to see me at a tavern, between Whitchurch and Markham, the plan would not be known, the people were to be in readiness[,] the officers only were to know the times[,] they were to get their orders a very short time before, and then use all expedition, if only a few come, there may be some fighting, if 500 or 600 come there would be no opposition, no mention of bank or property, I went with a waggon and provisions intended for myself, but as the people had nothing to eat I gave it. Thos. Holmes[17] went with me, had a rifle, my brother Peter[18] was with me[,] I expected it to be a general strike from Quebec all over the province[,] McKensie had deceived us, got to Montgomery's on Tuesday morning – . . . on Tuesday there were 220 guns, 67 Pikes & 150 unarmed[,] I counted them[,] there were many went in afterwards.

B 10   PETITION OF WILLIAM DOAN[19] TO SIR GEORGE ARTHUR
17 March 1838
[PAC, Upper Canada Sundries, v. 188, pp. 105089-92]

. . . Some short time previous to the fourth of December being in the

[15]Nathaniel Pearson (1803–1880) was a member of a Quaker family which came from Pennsylvania to Whitchurch Township in 1800 or earlier. Quite prosperous by 1837, Pearson supported the rising until he discovered Mackenzie had lied about the populace's overwhelming desire for change. After the rising, he surrendered himself but was only questioned and released. His brother Peter was also involved with the rebels.

[16]Gabriel Hawke was a member of a family which came early in the century to Tecumseth Township from the United States. Three of the sons, Gabriel, Perciphen, and John, were involved in the revolt but Gabriel was not arrested, although his two brothers were.

[17]Thomas Holmes was an inhabitant of Whitchurch. In 1850 he bought lot 15, concession 4.

[18]Peter Pearson of Whitchurch Township was the brother of Nathaniel. Born a Quaker, he nevertheless took part in the political union movement prior to the rebellion. Although taken into Toronto for questioning after the rising, in which he had a minor part, he was not arrested.

[19]William Doan (1807–1892) was brought to Canada from Pennsylvania in 1808.

company of Samuel Lount and William Lyon McKenzie they informed me of their intention to effect a revolution, I opposed the project and objected to participating with them in it, When McKenzie informed me that if I, (as well as others,) did not turn out, it was likely I should lose my property, he further stated that the whole country was ready for a general turnout, and that more than half the inhabitants of the Town were ready to receive the people from the Country – On the fourth of December finding that a large proportion of my neighbours were going down to assemble at Montgomeries Inn, I was induced to accompany them, more out of curiosity than any thing else – Upon my arrival there I soon discovered that the people had been duped by McKenzie, and determined in my own mind to leave them the same night, I communicated my intentions to some of my neighbours in the hope of inducing them to go with me – . . .

B 11   PETITION OF TITUS ROOT[20] TO SIR GEORGE ARTHUR
filed under 20 April 1838
[PAC, Upper Canada Sundries, v. 191, pp. 106639-42]

. . . The Petition of Titus Root – late of the Township of East Gwillimbury in the Home District Yeoman

Humbly Sheweth. . . .

That your petitioner has a wife and *twelve* – children.

That he was warned by Daniel Fletcher[21] who is Sergeant in the Company of Militia to which he belonged on the Morning, early, of the 4th Decmr to attend a general parrade on Monday the fourth of December in the Village of Hope[,] that previous to this time your petitioner had heard nothing of a rising in opposition to the cons[t]ituted authorities and had never attended or taken part in any political meetings[,] that in obedience to what he conceived was a legal notice he attended on the day above mentioned At Hope and was then informed that the training was to take place near the City[,] that in consequence your petitioner proceeded toward Town[,] met with a party at Bonds lake who compelled him to proceed with them to

---

He became a blacksmith in Whitchurch while his father and brothers remained in East Gwillimbury, where they were active members of the Children of Peace. William, as well as his brother Charles, was active in the political union movement in the summer and fall of 1837 and these two, with their brother Jesse, were arrested after participating in the rising. William was pardoned after pleading guilty.

[20]Titus Root was a naturalized citizen of Upper Canada who had bought 100 acres of lot 23, concession 5 of East Gwillimbury Township in 1835. Arrested in March 1838, he was pardoned in May because he had played only a minor role in the uprising.

[21]Daniel Fletcher was the son or nephew of Silas Fletcher, one of Mackenzie's chief organizers in the area north of Toronto. Forward in the political union movement of 1837, Daniel, of East Gwillimbury, also took an active part in encouraging men to join the rebellion. He was indicted for his part but could not be found. In 1839 he was pardoned.

Montgomery's when he for the first time discovered what was the real object, that he immediately attempted to make his escape but was prevented by the different guards that were placed about the premises –
. . .

B 12   PETITION OF CHARLES DOAN TO SIR F.B. HEAD
12 March 1838
[PAC, Upper Canada Sundries, v. 188, pp. 104880-4]

. . . The Petition of Charles Doan – late of the Township of East Gwillimbury in the Home District yeoman
Humbly Sheweth. . . .

That your petitioner in common with many others of those who took part in the late Rebellion was alarmed and deluded by various representations and among others by the following – That the Province of Lower Canada was about to revolt, that then victory was certain, that it was the intention of the Government of upper Canada to place the Country under Martial Law, that in such case the Reformers would not have the liberty of Slaves if they were Suffered to live at all – That in case of Martial Law every one would be subject to be arrested and tried by Court Martial and hung or shot at discretion – –

That there was a great number of Fire Arms in the City, which would be put into the Hands of – Indians, Negroes, and Orange Men, in order to Murder plunder, Burn and destroy the peaceable Inhabitants; and that the present was the only opportunity that the people had to Secure themselves and posterity from a long and barbarous reign of despotism –

That the Government had put it in the power of the people to releive themselves from such a Calamity, which would be very easily accomplished under existing circumstances. – –

That the Garrisons were all destitute of Troops and the Militia had not been called to do duty and were not prepared for defence – That there was an understanding between the principal Men in Government and the Reformers to effect the Change of the administration, without firing a Gun – –

That nevertheless the people should go prepaired if any rise should take place which was likely to occur, a few days after that of Lower Canada – – That there was an understanding with the leaders of the Lower Canadians, and that the matter was duly organized and the Province was all to rise at one time –

That though the time might be postponed, every man should keep it Secret at his peril, for that Independance would certainly prevail and every one should be accountable to the prevailing power – That all who distinguished themselves in the deliverance of their country from the present administration would be well paid in the end and their names honoured in the land –

That your petitioner deluded and alarmed by the representations, was in an unguarded moment unhappily induced to act the part he did in the late criminal Insurrection –

That after your petitioner had arrived at Montgomerys and ascertained the true state of Affairs your petitioner tried to escape but was arrested and detained by McKenzie until the final route of his deluded followers when your petitioner escaped and went home, . . .

B 13   EXTRACT FROM R.B. SULLIVAN'S[22] REPORT TO SIR GEORGE
ARTHUR
Toronto, 16 July 1838
[C.R. Sanderson, ed., The Arthur Papers . . . I (Toronto, 1957),
pp. 132-187, extract p. 170]

. . . In a country accustomed to peace and tranquillity in which there was no police and no military force. two or three hundred young ignorant men were suddenly called together on the 4th. December. under the most false and unfounded pretences. they were told that there would be no resistance, that Lower Canada was in the hands of the Patriots – that the principal functionaries of the Government in this Province had joined the same cause. that all they had to do was to step forward and seize the country[:] that he who was foremost would be promoted and he who remained behind treated as an enemy. . . .[23]

B 14   W.L. MACKENZIE'S ACCOUNT OF THE REBELLION'S
MIS-TIMING
[Jeffersonian, Watertown, reprinted in Mackenzie's Gazette, New
York City, 12 May 1838]

For other extracts from this document see B 1, B 25, B 31, B 38, B 48, B 61.

. . . The country was ripe for a change, and I employed a fortnight previous to Sunday the 3d Dec., in attending secret meetings, assisting in organizing towns and places, and otherwise preparing for the revolution. On that day, I rode from Stouffville, (where I had held two private meetings on the Saturday,) to Yonge Street; and arrived at Mr. Gibson's in the evening. To my astonishment and dismay, I was

[22]Robert Baldwin Sullivan (1802–1853), born at Bendon, Ireland, was a cousin to W.W. Baldwin. He emigrated with his parents to Upper Canada in 1819 and in 1828 was admitted to the bar. In 1835 he was elected mayor of Toronto and the next year appointed an executive councillor. In 1839 he became a legislative councillor. In the 1840s he was considered allied with the reformers. In 1848 he became a judge of the Court of Queen's Bench and in 1850 a judge of the Court of Common Pleas.

[23]This account of Robert Baldwin Sullivan, a Family Compact stalwart, indicates that it was generally accepted that the majority of Mackenzie's followers had been misled, as they claimed. They were not, however, all young and ignorant, as he claimed.

informed by him, that although I had given the captains of townships sealed orders for the Thursday following, the executive, through him, by a mere verbal message, had ordered out the men beyond the ridges to attend at Montgomery's with their arms next day, Monday, and it was probable they were already on the march.

I instantly sent one of Mr. Gibson's servants to the north, countermanded the Monday movement, and begged of Col. Lount not to come down nor in any way to disturb the previous regular arrangement, because neither of the other towns, nor the citizens of Toronto, were in any way prepared for an alteration which if persisted in would surely ruin us. The servant returned on Monday, with a message from Mr. Lount, that it was now too late to stop, that the men were warned, and moving with their guns and pikes, on the march down Yonge street, (a distance of 30 to 40 miles on the worst roads in the world,) and that the object of their rising could therefore be no longer concealed.

I was grieved and so was Mr. Gibson, but we had to make the best of it; accordingly I mounted my horse in the afternoon, rode in towards the city, took five trusty men with me, arrested several men on suspicion that they were going to Sir Francis with information, placed a guard on Yonge street, the main northern avenue to Toronto, at Montgomery's, and another guard on a parallel road, and told them to allow none to pass to the city. I then waited some time, expecting the executive to arrive, but waited in vain – no one came, not even a message – I was therefore left in entire ignorance of the condition of the capital; and instead of entering Toronto on Thursday, with 4000 or 5000 men, was apparently expected to take it on Monday with 200, wearied after a march of 30 or 40 miles through the mud, and in the worst possible humor at finding they had been called from the very extremity of the county, and no one else warned at all. . . .

B 15   Sir F.B. Head to Lord Glenelg
Toronto, 19 December 1837
[F.B. Head, A Narrative (London, 1839), pp. 326-41]

For other extracts from this document see B 22, B 58.

I have the honour to inform your Lordship that on Monday, 4th inst., this city was, in a moment of profound peace, suddenly invaded by a band of armed rebels, amounting, according to report, to 3000 men (but in actual fact to about 500), and commanded by Mr. M'Kenzie, the editor of a republican newspaper; Mr. Van Egmond, an officer who had served under Napoleon; Mr. Gibson, a land-surveyor; Mr. Lount, a blacksmith; Mr. Loydd [sic], and some other notorious characters.

Having, as I informed your Lordship in my despatch, No. 119, dated 3rd ultimo, purposely effected the withdrawal of her Majesty's troops from this province, and having delivered over to the civil authorities the whole of the arms and accoutrements I possessed, I of course found myself without any defence whatever, excepting that which the loyalty and fidelity of the province might think proper to afford me. The crisis, important as it was, was one I had long earnestly anticipated. . . .

As the foregoing statement is an unqualified admission on my part that I was completely surprised by the rebels, I think it proper to remind, rather than to explain, to your Lordship, the course of policy I have been pursuing.

In my despatch, No. 124, dated 18th ult., I respectfully stated to your Lordship, as my opinion, that a civil war must henceforward everywhere be a moral one, and that, in this hemisphere in particular, victory must eventually declare itself in favour of moral, and not of physical preponderance.

Entertaining these sentiments, I observed with satisfaction that Mr. M'Kenzie was pursuing a lawless course of conduct which I felt it would be impolitic for me to arrest.

For a long time he had endeavoured to force me to buoy him up by a Government prosecution, but he sunk in proportion as I neglected him, until becoming desperate, he was eventually driven to reckless behaviour, which I felt confident would very soon create its own punishment.

The traitorous arrangements he made were of that minute nature that it would have been difficult, even if I had desired it, to have suppressed them; for instance, he began by establishing union lists (in number not exceeding forty) of persons desirous of political reform; and who, by an appointed secretary, were recommended to communicate regularly with himself, for the purpose of establishing a meeting of delegates.

As soon as, by most wicked misrepresentations, he had succeeded in seducing a number of well-meaning people to join these squads, his next step was to prevail upon a few of them to attend their meetings armed, for the alleged purpose of firing at a mark.

While these meetings were in continuance, Mr. M'Kenzie, by means of his newspaper, and by constant personal attendance, succeeded in inducing his adherents to believe that he was everywhere strongly supported, and that his means, as well as his forces, would prove invincible.

I was not ignorant of these proceedings; and in proportion as Mr. M'Kenzie's paper became more and more seditious, and in proportion as these armed meetings excited more and more alarm, I was strongly and repeatedly called upon by the peaceable portion of the commuuity [sic] forcibly to suppress both the one and the other. I considered it better, however, under all circumstances, to await the outbreak, which I was confident would be impotent, inversely as it was previously opposed; in short, I considered that, if an attack by the rebels was inevitable, the more I encouraged them to consider me defenceless the better.

Mr. M'Kenzie, under these favourable circumstances, having been freely permitted by me to make every preparation in his power, a concentration of his deluded adherents, and an attack upon the city of Toronto, was secretly settled to take place on the night of the 19th instant. . . .

B 16   COL. JAMES FITZGIBBON ROUSES THE GOVERNMENT
[*James FitzGibbon*, An Appeal to the People of the Late Province of Upper Canada *(Montreal, 1847), pp. 13-15*]

For other extracts from this document see B 19, B 37.

. . . On the morning of Saturday, the 2nd of December, I was in my office taking down the information of a man from the Township of Markham, previous to my swearing him to it, I being then a Justice of the Peace. Before I had gone through with the case, a gentleman from another, and more distant part of the country, north of Toronto,[24] came in, and desired to speak with me alone. I took him into the Speaker's Room, and hearing his statement, which I considered as most important, I determined to take him with me at once to the Government House; but he positively refused to accompany me. He said the rebels knew that he had urgent business to transact in town, and they believed that for that only had he come in; but that if they suspected he came to give information, he had no doubt they would assassinate him. I still urged him, but in vain. He said he could not depend for secrecy upon any one else in town, and he would not.* On going from the Parliament House, I said to him that His Excellency would no doubt desire to hear his statement from his own lips, and again urged him to let me know where in Town I could send for him, should His Excellency insist upon seeing him; and at last he consented, and did tell me.

On arriving at the Government House, and sending in my name, I was shown in to His Excellency's presence, and found assembled with him the Members of his Council, some of the Judges, the Attorney General, and the Speaker of the Assembly. I communicated the information I had just received, and stated the objection made by my informant to his appearing personally before any other person. After some conversation it was decided that I should summon him before His Excellency, and I did so. Before he came, much discussion took place

*To account for this confidence in me, especially, I must state that I had been, for some years before, Deputy Provincial Grand Master of the Free Masons in Upper Canada.

---

[24] This was William Laughton, who lived three lots away from Samuel Lount.

on the state of the Province, in which I was invited or permitted to take a part. No one present appeared to have any apprehension of approaching danger. I expressed mine very strongly, and from time to time urged upon His Excellency the necessity of arming in our defence. Upon one occasion, Judge Jones,[25] who sat next to me on my right hand, turned towards me and said, "You do not mean to say that these people are going to rebel?"To which I answered "Most distinctly I do, sir." Whereupon he turned from me towards His Excellency, and exclaimed, most contemptuously, "Pugh! Pugh!" I instantly threw out my hand, and looked around the circle until I saw all silent, and then said, "Which of you, gentlemen, would have prophesied one month ago that the Lower Canadians would now be in open rebellion as they are? – and have not these people been repeatedly drilled and practised with ball cartridge in the neighbourhood of this City, and will they not go further?" And on my pausing, Mr. Jones said "There is some truth in that." I then thought I had made a convert of him. But no; for on Monday night, only two days after, when I galloped from house to house, calling upon one man to go and call his neighbour, that I might multiply the means of arousing the people from their beds, I sent a gentleman to call Judge Jones, whose residence was opposite; and when the Judge came forth into the street, he roughly asked, "What is all this noise about? who desired you to call me?" he was answered "Colonel Fitz Gibbon," when he exclaimed. "Oh, the over-zeal of that man is giving us a great deal of trouble." And yet had it not been for this over-zeal it is possible that he would have been one of the victims who would in all human probability have been sacrificed by the Rebels, on that night, had they proved successful.

But to return to the meeting of Saturday: On the arrival of the gentleman who had been sent for, His Excellency and the Attorney General examined him in an adjacent room; and on their return the Attorney General said "The statement made to us by Mr. ——, does not make half the impression upon one's mind as was made by Col. Fitz Gibbon's statement: the information he brings is at third or fourth hand." Upon which I said, "The information he brings is at second and third hand, not at fourth hand; – but what impression does it make on the man's own mind? Has he not seen, in a blacksmith's forge, bags filled with what he has no doubt are pike heads? Has he not seen the handles already made, and the timber prepared for more, which he was

---

[25]Jonas Jones (1791–1848) was born in Elizabethtown, Upper Canada, and educated by John Strachan in his school at Cornwall. Jones fought in the War of 1812, and in 1815 became a lawyer, practising in Brockville. He was that town's mayor in 1833. He served as an MLA for Grenville, 1816–28, and for Leeds in 1836–7, surrendering his place in the Assembly when appointed the registrar of Dundas County. In 1837, too, regarded as a leading member of the Family Compact, he was made a judge of the Court of Queen's Bench. A colonel in the militia, he acted as an aide-de-camp to Head.

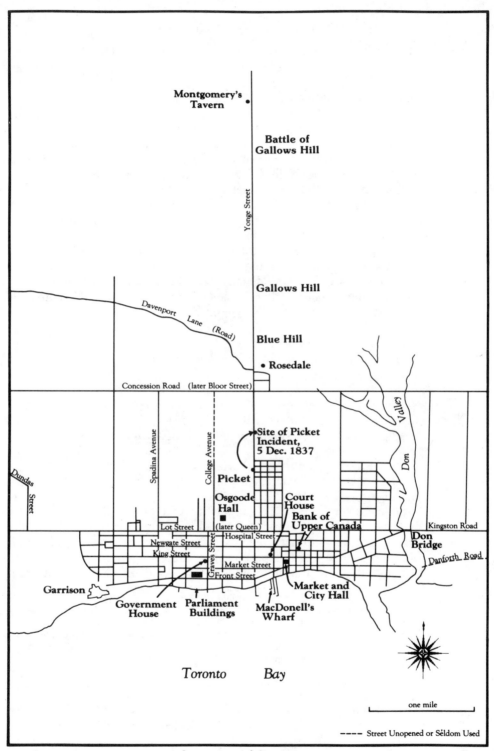

Montgomery's Tavern

Battle of Gallows Hill

Yonge Street

Gallows Hill

Davenport Lane (Road)

Blue Hill

• Rosedale

Concession Road (later Bloor Street)

Don Valley

Don

Spadina Avenue

College Avenue

Site of Picket Incident, 5 Dec. 1837

Picket

Osgoode Hall

Court House

Bank of Upper Canada

(later Queen)

Dundas Street

Lot Street

Kingston Road

Newgate Street

Graves Street

Hospital Street

Don Bridge

King Street

Market Street

Danforth Road

Garrison

Front Street

Market and City Hall

Government House

Parliament Buildings

MacDonell's Wharf

Toronto   Bay

one mile

---- Street Unopened or Seldom Used

3:   Toronto and Environs, 1837

told were intended for hay-rakes or pitch-forks? And has he any doubt at all of the object of the preparations which he, from day to day, has seen making in his neighbourhood?"Whereupon the Hon. William Allan[26] said, "What would you have gentlemen? Do you expect the Rebels will come and give information at first hand? How can you expect such information but at second, third or fourth hand? I am as long in this country as most of you, gentlemen; I know the people of this country as well as most of you, and I agree in every word spoken here to-day by Colonel Fitz Gibbon, and think that an hour should not be lost without preparing ourselves for defence."

Up to this period not a word was spoken by any one present in my support; and these expressions greatly relieved and encouraged me. After Mr. Allan had done speaking, I turned towards His Excellency and said, "In short, Sir, when I came here this morning, I expected that Your Excellency would give me leave to go into the streets and take up every half-pay officer and discharged soldier I could find in the City, and place them this very day, in the Garrison to defend it." To this, His Excellency answered, "What would the people of England say were we thus to arm? And, besides, were you to pass the Militia by, they would feel themselves insulted."To which I replied, "Pardon me, Your Excellency, they would rejoice to see me organise the Military to be a nucleus for them to rally round."

This meeting, or Council, sat for five or six hours, and when I withdrew from it and reflected upon all that had passed, of which I here state but a few particulars, I did fear that I should be looked upon by those present as a presumptuous and arrogant man: for I spoke with great earnestness and fervor.

On Monday morning, between eight and nine o'clock, His Excellency sent his Secretary for me, and on coming into his presence, he had in his hand a Militia General Order, appointing me to act as Adjutant General of Militia; and having read it to me, he told me I may sign the General Orders and other documents issuing from the Department, as Adjutant General. After a moment's pause I observed that if I did so, it would expose me to a charge of assuming to be what I was not: that the law allowed but one Adjutant General, and that

[26]William Allan (1770–1853) emigrated from Scotland to Montreal in 1787. A few years later he moved to York, where he became a successful merchant. He soon acquired government appointments including the posts of collector of customs, inspector of stills and taverns, and postmaster, all for York, and treasurer of the Home District. In the War of 1812 he rose to the rank of colonel in the 3rd Regiment, York militia. Following the war, now a Family Compact intimate, he held a series of important financial posts. He was the first president of the Bank of Upper Canada, 1822–35, and was appointed the first governor of the British America Assurance Company in 1834, as well as a commissioner of the Canada Company in 1829. From 1835 to 1841 he sat in the Legislative Council and from 1836 to 1841 in the Executive Council. As well as becoming a pillar of the Compact, he amassed considerable wealth.

Colonel Coffin still held the office. I therefore ventured to suggest that I should add to my signature "Acting Adjutant General,"to which His Excellency assented. I state this fact here, because it will corroborate other facts which I shall have to state hereafter, and which will show how easily His Excellency departed from a due regard to veracity when his interests or his feelings prompted him to do so.

On this day, Monday, His Excellency prepared a Militia General Order, appealing to the Officers commanding Regiments and Corps in the Province, and conveying instructions for their guidance under the circumstances mentioned therein. A copy of this I took to the Queen's Printer, but it could not be circulated before the out-break, which occurred the night of the same day. . . .

B 17 LADY HEAD[27] TO FRANK HEAD[28]
Toronto, 13 December 1837
[*Bodleian Library, University of Oxford, Letters of Sir Francis and Lady Head to Frank Head, microfilm in PAO*]

For other extracts from this document see B 24, B 41, B 59.

. . . For some time past it has been well known that secret meetings have been held, and drilling has been secretly carried on, but in a country where every man is allowed to carry a gun, it is not easy to arrest those who pretend they are merely going into the woods in search of game – The Law Officers had been long on the Watch for a sufficient plea to arrest him [Mackenzie] for high treason, and on Sunday the 3d a correspondence was intercepted from a Mr. Parker [John G. Parker] which determined your father instantly to issue the General Militia Order which you will see, and on Monday morning it was printed and issued about 4 o'clock; private information however was obtained of this by Dr. Rolph who gave Mackenzie the intelligence that morning, and this determined him to make the attack that night before the militia could arrive.

Your father had been prepared so far, that he had sworn in a number of special constables, and patroles were guarding the streets and the arms, which were deposited in the town hall, and we had plenty of loaded guns and pistols in our bed-rooms – no apprehension of an immediate attack was felt however, . . .

---

[27]Lady Head was the former Julia Valenga Somerville. In 1816 she had married Francis Bond Head, her cousin. The couple, who were devoted to each other, raised four children. She, along with two of her children and other members of the household, joined Head in Upper Canada in March 1837.

[28]Frank Head (b. 1817) was the eldest of the Heads' four children. He was trained at the East India Company's college at Haileybury and posted to India in 1835.

B 18   JOHN BEVERLEY ROBINSON'S COMMENTS ON PREPARATIONS IN
TORONTO

[PAO, John Beverley Robinson Papers, notes made 7 Dec. 1837]

. . . For some weeks past reports were brought to Toronto from the settlements about Newmarket and along Yonge Street that there were people training by hundreds under certain leaders who have been long Known as disaffected, & seditious persons, but who were not supposed to be quite so desperate and daring as to rise in open rebellion against their Sovereign –

The loyal inhabitants in the neighbourhood of these armed meetings were much alarmed, & so many accounts arrived of an intended attack upon Toronto that serious alarm was felt by many of the inhabitants of the City as well as of the Country –

The Lieutenant Governor looked upon these meetings of the rebels as a mere effort to deter him from sending away the troops, to the assistance of our fellow subjects in Lower Canada, where thousands of French Canadians are in arms against the British population; and it was long before he could bring himself to think that any thing more was intended than to put on a threatening appearance and to make it be believed abroad that the people of Upper Canada were ready for revolt against their Sovereign – He did not therefore at first take decisive measures for putting down the seditious movements of Mr. McKenzie and his base followers – but on Sunday last, such particular reports were received of an intended attack, & so much alarm was felt in several parts of the Country that the Lieutenant Governor addressed an order to the different Militia Regiments calling for them to hold themselves ready for duty upon any emergency arising here, or in Lower Canada –

This order was actually ready for distribution on Monday – and the Mayor and Citizens of Toronto aided by the zealous cautions of Cols. Fitzgibbon & Stanton[29] had made some arrangements for guarding the Bank & the City Hall – & such points as were likely to be assailed – but a very inadequate & hurried preparation had been made, . . .

[29]Robert Stanton (1794–1866) was born in Lower Canada and moved with his father to York in 1805. He served in several minor government positions prior to the War of 1812, in which he served as a lieutenant. After the war he moved to Kingston and engaged in business as a merchant while again occupying several minor government positions. In 1826 he was appointed king's printer and moved back to Toronto. There he operated a stationery and book-binding business and for three years published a tory newspaper, as well as the official *Upper Canada Gazette*. He clearly identified himself with the Compact and with toryism. In 1835 he was appointed colonel of the 1st West York Regiment of militia and he helped defend Toronto in 1837. After the union of the Canadas, he lost his job but succeeded in obtaining other positions which provided an income until his death.

B 19   COL. JAMES FITZGIBBON'S ACCOUNT OF EVENTS IN TORONTO
4 DECEMBER

[James FitzGibbon, An Appeal to the People of the Late Province of
Upper Canada (Montreal, 1847), pp. 15-18]

For other extracts from this document see B 16, B 37.

. . . As that night [of 4 Dec.] approached I became more and more
apprehensive of approaching danger. I determined not to sleep again in
my own house, which, being some distance from any other house,
might be readily surrounded, and my capture or destruction easily
accomplished; and McKenzie had recently in his newspaper made
especial mention of me, by name, as the Teacher of the young men of
the Volunteer Corps. I had no doubt, therefore, of being a marked
man. I consequently determined to sleep in my office in the Parliament
House, until I should consider all danger over. Late in the day I invited
several gentlemen to come to the Parliament House and watch with me
during the night, and many came in consequence.

About ten o'clock, because of some occurrence which I now forget,
I went over to the Government House, where I found Mrs.
Dalrymple,[30] His Excellency's sister, and his daughter, Miss Head,[31]
at work with their needles. I told Mrs. Dalrymple that I desired to see
His Excellency. She said he was in bed. "Nevertheless, Madam, I
desire to see him." "He retired early, being fatigued, and it is hard that
he should be disturbed." "Still, Madam, I think it most important that I
should see him; but if he will not come down, I must go [*sic*] his
bedside." He was sent for, and came in his dressing gown. I told him
that I appredended [*sic*] some outbreak would take place that very
night, which fear I deemed it my duty to commuuicate [*sic*] to him,
leaving His Excellency to give it what attention he pleased: That if he
retired again, I would take care that he should not be surprised. He did
retire and I withdrew. Before another hour elapsed I was informed that
a body of the Rebels was approaching the city from the north.
Whereupon I instantly sent Mr. Cameron,[32] then a student at law, and

[30]Mary Dalrymple (b. *ca.* 1783), F.B. Head's widowed sister, had come with the
rest of the Head family to Upper Canada early in 1837.

[31]Julia Head (b. 1820), F.B. Head's daughter, like others in his household, had
joined him in Upper Canada in 1837.

[32]John Hillyard Cameron (1817–1876) was born at Blendecques, France, of military
parents. He had moved to Kingston, Upper Canada, in 1825 and to York in 1831 when
his father had been transferred to those two posts. At York he studied law, and, while a
student, served with the government forces during the rebellion of 1837 and the
subsequent border troubles. After this service, he began a long and successful legal
career. He was less successful at politics. Although he served as an alderman in
Toronto, 1846–7, 1851–2, 1854, and 1855, and was elected to the Assembly,
1846–51, 1854–7, and 1861 till his death, he never achieved the position of power he
seems to have wanted. The closest he came to his goal was to serve as solicitor general
for Upper Canada, 1846–8. In the 1850s and 1860s his power base was the Orange

now the Solicitor General for Canada West, to ring the College bell, which he immediately did. At the same time I mounted a horse belonging to the House Messenger, and in a stable at hand, and galloped from house to house in the west end of the town, calling the people out of their beds, and directing them to run to the Parliament House with their loaded arms, for that the Rebels were approaching the city. I called Mr. Stanton, and made him call Judge McLean,[33] whose house was next to his. I called another gentleman and bade him call Judge Jones; and this I did in order to multiply the means of arousing the people. When Mr. Jones came into the street he asked, angrily, "What is all this noise about? who desired you to call me?" and was answered "Colonel FitzGibbon," when he exclaimed, "Oh! the over zeal of that man is giving us a great deal of trouble." This fact I have already stated, to elucidate more clerly [sic] the force of what I then mentioned, as in connexion with it, and to remove all doubt of the incredulity of the principal Members of the Government, down to the very last moment, with the single exception of the Honorable Wm. Allan.

As I went from house to house, I listened for the ringing of the City bells, but several minutes having elapsed and no bell rung, I galloped to St. James [Anglican] Church, which I found yet shut. I called aloud for some one to run for the keys, and after waiting for some considerable time, I called aloud for axes to break the door open, when at length the keys were brought and the door was opened. In accomplishing this, I lost nearly half an hour of my most valuable time. I then gave directions in the City Hall to break open the cases in which the arms were deposited and to issue them rapidly to the men as they came in.

Everything being now in motion I desired to ascertain what probable time would elapse before the Rebels would enter the City, and I therefore rode out Yonge Street, accompanied by two young students at law, Messrs. Brock[34] and Bellingham,[35] who were then near me,

Order, of which he was the grand master, 1859–70. A successful businessman for a time, the financial crisis of 1857 left him with huge debts he was never able to repay.

[33] Archibald McLean (1791–1865) was born at St. Andrews, Luneburg District, Quebec. He attended John Strachan's school at Cornwall and studied law at York but did not complete his studies until after the War of 1812, in which he distinguished himself. As well as practising law at Cornwall, he represented Stormont in the Assembly, 1820–34, Cornwall, 1834–6, and Stormont, 1836–7. There he acted as a spokesman for Church of Scotland interests. In 1837 he was appointed to the Legislative Council and began the long judicial career that lasted almost until his death. During the rebellion of 1837 he became a colonel in the militia.

[34] Brock was the son of Major Brock of Colchester, England, who had been in the 49th Regiment with FitzGibbon in the War of 1812 and who had entrusted his son to FitzGibbon's care. Young Brock was a law student in 1837 and was probably also a member of the rifle corps FitzGibbon had created prior to the rebellion.

[35] Bellingham was, like Brock, a law student and was likely also a member of FitzGibbon's rifle corps.

and also mounted. We proceeded as far as the bridge and causeway, lately made over the ravine, in front of Rosedale, the Sheriff's residence, about two miles from the market place, and meeting no one and everything being perfectly quiet along the road, I began to think the alarm I gave was premature, and that I was exposing myself to ridicule by my extraordinary proceedings. But seeing that I had now time to return and form a strong piquet and place it on Yonge Street, to meet the Rebels, I determined to gallop back for that purpose. But still desiring to learn where the Rebels were, if indeed at all approaching, I expressed my regret that I had not with me a few more mounted men and with arms, for we were without any, that they might ride as far as Montgomery's, then two miles from us, to reconnoitre. The young men instantly and eagerly offered to do so, but I would not consent, partly because they were unarmed, and partly that Mr. Brock had been sent to Canada, and recommended to my care by his father, Major Brock, of Colchester, who had formerly served in the 49th Regiment with me, and who had, some short time before, generously lent me £1,500 sterling. I shrunk from thus exposing his son to such danger. But the young men pressed me so importunately that I consented. Now, at this moment, the Rebels were within two hundred yards of us, silently marching towards town, and in two minutes after the young men left me, they met them in the dark and were made prisoners. I was then returning rapidly towards town and soon met Mr. Alderman Powell,[36] and Mr. McDonald,[37] the Wharfinger, riding outwards; and on asking them their object in going out, Mr. Powell said he was desirous of ascertaining if the Rebels were, in fact, at Montgomery's, as he had just been told. I expressed my great satisfaction and told him that Messrs. Brock and Bellingham were already proceeding before him for the same purpose, and begged of him to ride on quickly and overtake them, and we parted. In a few minutes after they also met the Rebels, who called upon them to surrender. Mr. Powell, however, being armed, drew a pistol and shot their leader [Anthony Anderson] dead as he approached him, and then turning his horse, he galloped back towards town. On arriving at the Toll-Gate he found it shut, and no one answering his call, and supposing he was pursued, he quitted his horse and ran through the woods and fields to the Government House, and went at once to His Excellency's bedside and acquainted him with what was passing. On my arriving in town, but yet ignorant

[36]John Powell (1809–1881) was born at Niagara, the grandson of William Dummer Powell. John had a rather undistinguished career, broken only by the period 1837–41. Elected a Toronto alderman in 1837, it was he who brought the first convincing evidence of the rebellion's outbreak to Toronto. As a result of this he was elected mayor, 1838–40. In 1841 he was elected alderman but resigned a short time after. He died at St. Catharines.

[37]Archibald MacDonell (McDonald) was a wharfinger (wharf owner) who lived at 36 Front Street. Captured on Monday night, he was held until the rebels fled Montgomery's Tavern on Thursday.

of what had just occurred behind me, I also went to the Governor's House to let His Excellency know all that I had done, where I met Mr. Powell coming down from His Excellency's bed-room, and he told me what had just occurred to him. I passed up to His Excellency and advised him to dress quickly and come with me to the City Hall, and that while he was dressing I would ride down to the end of Yonge Street, and ascertain whether or not the Rebels had yet come so far, as if they had, we must gain the Court House by one of the front streets, not liable, just then, to be traversed by them; and I did so. But on approaching the end of that street I saw some seven or eight men grouped together, and I called aloud, desiring one of them to approach and let me know who they were; but they all quickly ran behind the two corners of that and King Street. Being unarmed and not doubting but that many concealed Rebels were ready in town to join those coming in, I did not venture to approach them, but galloped rapidly back towards the Government House, from which I saw His Excellency issue with two or three of his servants, all armed, and I led him by a front street to the City Hall.

On proceeding to form a piquet I learned that Judge Jones had already formed one and had marched it to the Toll-Gate on Yonge Street, whither I immediately rode, and soon learned that the Rebels had returned to Montgomery's. I afterwards learned that they did so because their leader was killed, and because they heard the bells ringing in the City.

Sentries were now carefully posted, and soon two men on horseback, riding cautiously inwards, were secured by them. These men pretended that they were coming to town on business. They had no arms. They admitted that they passed through the Rebels who did not molest them; and they gave the first information of the shooting of Colonel Moodie, who they saw lying on a bed, dying. I sent them to the City Hall and placed them in custody. The remainder of the night was spent in arming and organizing the citizens. . . .

B 20   JOHN POWELL'S ACCOUNT OF EVENTS
Toronto, 14 February 1838
[Christian Guardian, *Supplement, Toronto, 17 Feb. 1838*]

. . . On Monday Evening, December 4th, about 9 o'clock, when engaged at the City Hall in swearing in special constables and distributing arms, I found, from the number of magistrates present, I could be of more service in taking charge of several volunteers, who had assembled to patrole on horseback the approaches to the city during the night, for the purpose of reconnoitering the body of rebels said to be assembling, and more particularly those who were reported to be in arms on Yonge Street. Mr. A. McDonell offered to accompany me, as I had determined to take the Yonge Street road myself. Just as I had made my arrangements, Captain Fitzgibbon, Mr. Brock, and Mr. Bellingham, rode up to the Hall. Captain Fitzgibbon told me of his intention to go out, and I said we would accompany him; Mr. McDonell went home for his horse, intending to meet me on Yonge Street, and I rode with Captain Fitzgibbon to the foot of Yonge Street, where I left him to go to my own house for arms. When I loaded my gun, I found I had no caps; so abandoned the idea of taking it, and proceeded to overtake the party, having only two small pistols lent me by the high bailiff,[38] as I left the Hall. I went alone as far as the Sheriff's hill (about a mile from the city,) where I met Captain Fitzgibbon returning alone; he said Brock and Bellingham have gone on. I came back with him as far as the toll gate, where we met McDonell coming to join us. Captain Fitzgibbon then said all was quiet up the street, and he would return to town. Mr. McDonell and myself agreed we would proceed up the street to overtake Brock and Bellingham. We were going leisurely along, when, at the rise of the Blue Hill four persons on horseback met us; we thought they were our friends; but as we approached, Mackenzie himself advanced and ordered us to halt; the others immediately surrounded us. Mackenzie was armed with a large horse pistol, the rest had rifles. Mackenzie then told us that we were his prisoners; I demanded by what authority? he replied, he would let us know his authority soon! Anderson (one of them) said, their authority was their rifles! Mackenzie asked us many questions as to the force in town? what guard at the Governor's? and whether we expected an attack that night? To all these questions I returned for answer, He might go to town and find out. This appeared to enrage him very much, and he ordered Anderson and Sheppard[39] to march us to the rear and *"Hurry on the men."* Anderson took charge of me; Sheppard of McDonell. I went first; McDonell was about ten yards in the rear. Anderson was very abusive towards the Governor, and said he would let "Bond Head know something before long." I asked him of what he had to complain, and reasoned with him on the impropriety of their conduct; he replied, "they had borne tyranny and oppression too long, and were now determined to have a government of their own." From all I could gather from him, I found the rebels were on

[38]This was William Higgins (1794–1871), who had come with his family from northern Ireland after the War of 1812. In 1826 he was appointed high constable of the Home District and inspector of police. When Toronto was created in 1834, he became, as well as high constable, high bailiff of Toronto and city inspector. In 1835, while Higgins was in gaol accused of killing a man in a street demonstration, he was replaced as high bailiff. However, the case was dropped, and he remained city inspector and high constable. From 1860 to 1862 he was a councillor in Toronto.

[39]Joseph Shepard (Sheppard) owned half of a 200-acre lot on Yonge Street and came from a very prosperous United Empire Loyalist family. His father had been a prominent farmer, a member of the Church of England, and a reformer in York Township. Joseph and his three brothers Thomas, Michael, and Jacob participated in the uprising. Joseph was arrested at the end of the rebellion and pardoned in May 1838.

their march to town, for the purpose of surprising it, and that they (the four persons who took us prisoners) were the "advanced guard." Opposite Mr. Howard's[40] gate a person on horseback met us; Anderson ordered him to halt, and asked him who he was? he replied, "Thomson"[41] I immediately said, "Mr. Thomson, I claim your protection; I am a prisoner." The person recognized my voice, and said, "Powell, the rebels have shot poor Colonel Moodie, and are coming on to town." He then put spurs to his horse and succeeded in passing them; they turned round to fire, but were prevented by our both being between them and Brooke, who was the person we met. Upon this intelligence, I made up my mind, and determined to make my escape at any hazard, as I felt confident the salvation of the town depended upon correct information being given at once. I made several attempts to fall back; but Anderson, who had me, threatened if I attempted to escape, he would "drive a ball through me." I went on as far as Mr. Heath's Gate, when I suddenly drew my pistol and fired, not being more than two feet from him; he fell and I instantly set off full speed down the street; McDonell did so likewise; Sheppard followed, and fired; the ball passed between us. McDonell was far in the advance; I shouted to him to ride hard and give the alarm as my horse would not keep up. At the Sheriff's Hill we were again met by McKenzie and the other persons. Mackenzie rode after me and presenting his pistol at my head, ordered me to stop. I turned on my horse and snapped my remaining pistol in his face; the pistol must have touched him, I was so near; his horse either took fright, or he could not stop him, and he got some little distance in front of me. I drew up suddenly at Dr. Baldwin's road, galloped up about twenty yards, and then jumped off my horse and ran through the woods. I heard them pursue me, lay down behind a log, for a few minutes, (a person on horseback was within ten yards of the place where I lay,) I then ran down through the College fields and avenue, keeping near the fence. I went immediately to Government House, and after some little difficulty saw the Governor in bed. I related to him in a few words what had passed; he seemed to doubt whether I could be certain as to

[40]James Scott Howard (1798–1866), left his native County Cork, Ireland, in 1819 and settled in York, Upper Canada, in 1820. He had been assistant to William Allan in the Post Office until succeeding to the position of postmaster of York in 1828, an office which he discharged with great skill. Because he knew prominent radicals and had not taken up arms for the government in 1837, Francis Bond Head had him removed from office, and all successive attempts by Howard and others who respected his capabilities failed to win back his position. In 1842 he was appointed treasurer of the Home District and he subsequently discharged the duties of several offices, including that of treasurer of York and Peel counties, very ably.

[41]"Thomson" was Thomas Richard Brooke, a half-pay captain who had bought 76 acres of lot 8, concession 1 of East York Township in 1823. Brooke was an avid Orangeman, and became master of Lodge 207 in 1840 and a member of the grand committee. He was one of those men who accompanied Moodie in his attempt to warn Toronto on 4 December.

Mackenzie, but at last appeared to take the alarm. From Government House I proceeded to the City Hall.

McDonell was re-captured at the Toll Gate, and neither Brooke nor any other person arrived in town until the bells were ringing.

Lount has told several persons that the death of Anderson alone prevented their coming in that night.

B 21   INFORMATION OF ARCHIBALD MACDONELL
20 December 1837
[PAC, Upper Canada Sundries, v. 180, pp. 99588-91]

For another extract from this document see B 63.

The City of Toronto to wit – The Information upon Oath of Archibald Macdonell of the City of Toronto Wharfinger who saith

That about Midnight of Monday the 4th Instant I was riding up Yonge Street on horseback with Mr. John Powell and we had got near Gallows Hill when we were met by Mackenzie and four Riflemen one of whom was Joseph Shephard but I do not know the others except that I was informed afterwards one was Anthony Anderson since dead – Mackenzie ordered us to halt and asked us who we were when we told him – he said you are my prisoners – we disputed his right to take us – he said "might is right – we will settle that another day" – we were put in charge of the said Shephard and Anderson & were sent on towards Montgomery's – when we got about half a Mile a shot was fired I think by Mr Powel – I wheeled my horse around and made my escape – Mr Powell did the same – I proceeded towards Toronto at full speed but was stopped at the Gate by its being closed – I was throwing myself off my horse to escape when Mackenzie and another Rifleman came up to me – Mackenzie presented a pistol at my head – after he ascertained from me that I had escaped he said he would take good care I should not do so again – I was taken back to Montgomery's and on my way saw Anderson dead on the road – Mackenzie accompanied me – In going up he said "Powell snapped his pistol at me but I have done his business for I shot him" – . . .

B 22   SIR F.B. HEAD TO LORD GLENELG
Toronto, 19 December 1837
[F.B. Head, A Narrative (London, 1839), pp. 326-41]

For other extracts from this document see B 15, B 58.

. . . As soon as they had attained this position [at Montgomery's Tavern], Mr. M'Kenzie and a few others, with pistols in their hands, arrested every person on the road, in order to prevent information reaching the town. Colonel Moody, a distinguished veteran officer, accompanied by three gentlemen on horseback, on passing Montgomery's Tavern, was fired at by the rebels, and I deeply regret to say that the Colonel, wounded in two places, was taken prisoner into the tavern, where in three hours he died, leaving a widow and family unprovided for.

As soon as this gallant, meritorious officer, who had honourably fought in this province, fell, I am informed that Mr. M'Kenzie exultingly observed to his followers, *"That, as blood had now been spilled, they were in for it, and had nothing left but to advance."* Accordingly, at about ten o'clock at night they did advance; and I was in bed and asleep when Mr. Alderman Powell awakened me to state that, in riding out of the city towards Montgomery's Tavern, he had been arrested by Mr. M'Kenzie and another principal leader; that the former had snapped a pistol at his breast; that his (Mr. Powell's) pistol also snapped, but that he fired a second, which, causing the death of Mr. M'Kenzie's companion, had enabled him to escape.

As soon as Mr. Powell reached Toronto, the alarm-bell was rung, and, as Mr. M'Kenzie found we might be prepared for him, he forbore to proceed with his attack.

On arriving at the City Hall I appointed Mr. Justice Jones, Mr. Henry Sherwood,[42] Captain Strachan,[43] and Mr. John Robinson,[44] my aid-de-camps [*sic*]. I then ordered the arms to be unpacked, and, manning all the windows of the building, as well as those of opposite houses which flanked it, we awaited the rebels, who, as I have stated,

[42]Henry Sherwood (1807–1855), the son of judge Levius Peters Sherwood, was born in Leeds County, Upper Canada. He studied law and practised first in Prescott and then at Toronto. Keenly interested in politics, he sat on the Toronto city council as alderman, 1842–9, and was mayor, 1842–4. From 1843–54 he sat for Toronto in the Assembly of the United Canadas, where he became a prominent spokesman for ultra-tory interests. Brought in as solicitor general for Canada West to strengthen Bagot's executive, he was forced out when Baldwin and LaFontaine joined the ministry in 1842. When Metcalfe wished to strengthen his conservative-oriented executive, Sherwood again became solicitor general, only to be forced out in 1846 because of his tory stance. In 1847, with Draper's conservative government failing, he took over as leader and attorney general. The government was defeated in the election of that year and replaced by the Baldwin-LaFontaine ministry.

[43]James McGill Strachan (1808–1870) was the eldest son of John Strachan. He purchased an army commission in 1826, staying in the army until 1836 when he returned to York to study law. During the rebellion of 1837 he served as military secretary to F.B. Head. In 1838 he was called to the bar and thereafter became a successful lawyer. He was a partner of John Hillyard Cameron until 1847 and practised on his own thereafter. He was also an unsuccessful speculator and a politician who enjoyed but modest success. He won the Huron County seat in the election of 1841 but lost it on a recount. He sat as a Toronto alderman in 1842 and 1852.

[44]John Beverley Robinson Jr. (1821–1896) was born at York. He attended Upper Canada College and served as an aide-de-camp to F.B. Head in December 1837. In 1844 he was called to the bar. Much of his time was spent in political pursuits. A Toronto alderman in 1851, and 1853–7, he was mayor, 1856–7. From 1858–72 he represented Toronto in the Assembly and the House of Commons. From 1872–4 he sat for Algoma and from 1878–80 for West Toronto. From 1880–7 he was lieutenant-governor of Ontario.

did not consider it advisable to advance. Besides these arrangements, I despatched a message to the Speaker of the House of Assembly, Colonel the Honourable Allan M'Nab, of the Gore District, and to the Colonels of the militia regiments in the Midland and Newcastle Districts: an advanced picquet of thirty volunteers, commanded by my aid-de-camp, Mr. Justice Jones, was placed within a short distance of the rebels.

By the following morning (Tuesday) we mustered about 300 men, . . .

B 23   F.L. BRIDGMAN[45] TO FANNY WEST[46]
Government House, 15 December 1837
[*PAO, Miscellaneous, 1837, typescript*]

For other extracts from this document see B 42, B 66.

. . . Monday night, the 4th, . . . about 12 o'clock a Mr. Powell came breathless to Government House and told Sir Francis that the rebels were in great force within 3 miles of Toronto, and intended to attack us that night. . . . We were very much frightened, I had been in bed some time; we all got up directly and dressed ourselves. Sir Francis with a guard of 12 armed men took Lady Head and all the females of the family to the Solicitor-general's house, as being a place of greater safety than Gt. House, as that was the first place the rebels intended to attack. Mrs. Draper[47] received us with great kindness, and there we passed a miserable night, as you may imagine, apprehending all sorts of horrors. On leaving us, Sir Francis went down to the Town Hall, where he was joined by all the principal people, and there made every arrangement to receive the rebels – they however did not come that night. It seems that under Providence the death of Anderson, who was the most determined and blood-thirsty of their leaders, was the cause of their stopping. McKenzie wanted them to proceed, but they were divided and afraid we should be too well prepared for them. . . . There has been only one person killed on our side, his death is very melancholy and has cast a gloom on our otherwise bloodless victory – Coll. Moody a gallant, courageous man, who lived about 15 miles up Yonge Street, had on Monday received certain intelligence of the intentions of the rebels, he wrote a despatch to his Excellency informing him of this and sent it by a servant; fearing however that he might be stopped, which was the case, he determined to go to Toronto himself and set out for that place accompanied by 4 other gentlemen. They soon came up with a party of the enemy, through whom Coll

[45]F.L. Bridgman was the governess of F.B. Head's daughter Julia. She was about 29 when she and other members of the Head household arrived in Upper Canada in early 1837.
[46]Fanny West lived in Kent, England.
[47]Mrs. Draper was the former Mary White. She and William had married in 1827.

Moody and another pushed their way, but meeting another party, amongst whom was McKenzie, they were again stopped. Coll Moody fired his pistol; he was immediately pulled off his horse and it is said that while on the ground one of the wretches shot him through the body; he was taken to Montgomery's Tavern where he died after lingering 3 hours. . . .

B 24   LADY HEAD TO FRANK HEAD
Toronto, 13 December 1837

[Bodleian Library, University of Oxford, Letters of Sir Francis and
Lady Head to Frank Head, microfilm in PAO]

For other extracts from this document see B 17, B 41, B 59.

. . . Mr. Powell about 12 at night . . . arrived quite breathless to inform us of the intended attack of the rebels. Your father who had gone to bed early with an excruciating sick head-ache now got up and advised us all to leave the house which would probably be one of their points of attack, and under a guard of 80 or 90 men he took us through the garden[,] the alarm bell tolling as we went to the house of the Solicitor General Mr. Draper, which was in a row of brick houses, and not in a marked situation. He then returned home and leaving Orris[48] in charge of Govt. House with a guard of armed men, he proceeded to the Town-Hall, and under the constant expectation of an attack spent the night in fortifying it and the market place, over which it was built. He had so many difficulties to contend with that night, owing to the undisciplined state of his men, the badness of some of the muskets, and the uncertainty as to which of the towns-people were friends or foes, that had Mackenzie prevailed on his men to advance and set fire to the town, it would have been all over with us – providentially, the man whom Mr. Powell shot was a savage fellow who had been urging them on to the attack, and they were discouraged at losing him, and even the alarm bell frightened many of them as they found they could not take the town by surprise – The public events are all detailed in the newspapers, so I shall confine myself to the *family* details which I know will interest you –

Your father sent George[49] to me guarded by a Militia man, as he could do no good poor little fellow, & he thought things in a desperate state the first night – he was armed with his rifle & would have made a

[48]Daniel Orris had been the Heads' footman in England. In Upper Canada he served as Head's butler. After Head left Upper Canada in 1838, he stayed on in the colony, marrying a servant of Head's sister Mary. He worked as a government messenger.

[49]George Head (b. 1822) was the youngest of the Head children. A small, taciturn youth, he travelled out to Upper Canada in 1837 with his mother. He stayed on in Upper Canada for a few months after his parents left in 1838, trying to learn farming with Andrew Drew at Woodstock, but, tiring of that, he returned to England. He eventually became an Anglican cleric in Gloucestershire.

stout resistance had he been allowed to face the danger – we spent Monday night in great suspense, one of us being on the look-out from the upper windows to see if any fire was in the town – all remained quiet, & during the night I received a few lines from your father saying he believed there would be no attack that night, and that by the morning they should be quite prepared for them – . . .

B 25   W.L. MACKENZIE'S DESCRIPTION OF JOHN POWELL'S ESCAPE,
ANTHONY ANDERSON'S DEATH
[Jeffersonian, *Watertown, reprinted in* Mackenzie's Gazette, *New York City, 12 May 1838*]

For other extracts from this document see B 1, B 14, B 31, B 38, B 48, B 61.

. . . About 8 or 9 o'clock, I accompanied Capt. Anderson of Lloydtown, Mr. Sheppard, and two others, on horseback, down Yonge street, intending if no one came with tidings from the city to go there and ascertain how far an attack and seizure of the muskets and bayonets we so much needed, was practicable. There were warrants out for my apprehension, but I did not mind them much.

We had not proceeded far when we met Alderman John Powell, (now the Mayor,) and Mr. Archibald McDonald, late of Kingston, on horseback, acting as a sort of patrol. I rode up to them, presented a double barreled pistol, informed them that the democrats had risen in arms, that we wished to prevent information of that fact from reaching the city, and that they would have to go back to Montgomery's as prisoners, where they would be well treated, fed and lodged, and in no way injured in person or purse – but they must surrender to me their arms. They both assured me they had none, and when I seemed to doubt, repeated the assurance; on which I said, "Well gentlemen, as you are my townsmen, and men of honor, I would be ashamed to show that I question your words by ordering you to be searched;" and turning to Messrs. Sheppard and Anderson, I bade them place the gentlemen in the guard room, and see that they were comfortable, after which I proceeded again towards the city.

Not many minutes afterwards I was overtaken by Alderman Powell, riding in great haste. I asked what it meant, and told him he must not proceed, except at his peril. He kept on, I followed and fired over my horse's head but missed him. He slackened his pace till his horse was beside mine, and while I was expostulating with him, *he suddenly clapt a pistol quite close to my right breast*, but the priming flashed in the pan, and thus I was saved from instant death. At this moment McDonald rode back seemingly in great affright, and Powell escaped from me by the side bar, and by a circuitous route reached Toronto. McDonald appeared unable to explain, I therefore sent him back the second time, and being now alone judged it most prudent to return to

Montgomery's on my way to which I encountered the murdered remains of the brave and generous Capt Anthony Anderson, the victim of Powell's baseness. His body lay stretched in the road but life was extinct. The manner of his death was as follows: Sheppard and Anderson were accompanying Powell and McDonald on their way to the guard room at Montgomery's when Powell was observed to slacken his horse's pace a little – by this means he got behind Anderson, and taking a pistol from his pocket, shot him through the back of his neck, so that he fell and died instantly. Sheppard's horse stumbled at the moment, Powell rode off and McDonald followed. Whether Powell is or is not a murderer let the candid reader say. I give the facts. On arriving at Montgomery's, I was told by the guard that Colonel Moodie of the army had attempted to pass the barrier, that they had told him what guard they were, that he had persisted and fired a pistol at them, on which one of the men levelled his rifle and shot him. He died in an hour or two after. I find it stated in many papers that I killed Colonel Moodie, altho' at the time of his death I was several miles distant, as those then present well know. But I fully approved of the conduct of those who shot him. . . .

B 26   CAPT. HUGH STEWART'S[50] ACCOUNT OF COL. MOODIE'S DEATH
[PAO, Mackenzie–Lindsey Clippings, No. 1851]

. . . On Monday the fourth of December, while I was standing at the front door of Crew's[51] Tavern, Yonge Street, about 4 P.M., a great many men to the number of about 75, passed me, going towards Richmond-Hill; it immediately occurred to me that these men belonged to the Rebels, and were on their way to Toronto. I sent Mr. Crew to inform Mr. Boyd, and others, to meet at Col. Moodie's house. On looking after the men on the road, I observed them perch themselves, in number about 60, opposite Colonel Moodie's house. Fearing their intentions, I walked up inside of the fence amongst them, and endeavored to bring them into conversation, but without effect. By this time their numbers had increased to about 125. I crossed the fence in the midst of them, and crossed the road to Colonel Moodie's house, where I found him and his family, without any knowledge of what was passing. I pointed to the men on the fence, when he directly ordered his arms and loaded them, and stated that if they came inside of his gate he would shoot the first man; and I said I would assist, and took arms for

[50]Hugh Stewart was a retired naval officer who lived on Yonge Street, lot 51, in Markham Township near Richmond Hill.

[51]The tavern was owned by William Babcock Crew (d. 1859), an auctioneer and a one-time commissary agent who kept tavern on lot 49 of Yonge Street in Vaughan Township near Richmond Hill. He is reputed to have been a somewhat unstable individual who tried to hang one of the rebels on 7 December and who made it very difficult for reformers in his area after the rebellion. He took his own life.

that purpose. About half-past four o'clock, they began again to move on from the fence. At this time Mr. Boyd had arrived, and after a brief consultation, it was determined to send a despatch to His Excellency the Lieutenant-Governor, relative to the movements then before us, when Mr. Crew came to the house and volunteered his services, to mount a swift horse and go immediately into Toronto; Colonel Moodie had written this despatch the night before, but adding the additional information, and recommending Mr. Crew to the notice of His Excellency. About a quarter past five Mr. Crew went away alone, and we separated. By this time many men were on the road, some walking, and some on horseback, with a waggon here and there, which we supposed contained arms, there being none in the hands of the men on the road. About six o'clock we received a message at Mr. Crew's tavern, that he had been stopped at Richmond Hill and taken prisoner. From this having taken place so soon after he left Colonel Moodie's, I am induced to believe that he was watched by a man named Aaron Munshaw,[52] whom I saw at Crew's tavern, and who I understood left it for the Hill the moment that Mr. Crew's horse was seen at Colonel Moodie's door. Mr. Crew stated afterwards that they were prepared when he got to them: with rifles and pistols. On learning Mr. Crew's capture, I again proceeded to Colonel Moodie's house, and told him the fate of the despatches. Mr. Bridgeford was with him at the time, when he replied he would go himself, as he could not think of allowing the Governor and people of Toronto to be murdered in their beds, without an effort to save, and do all he could to pass the rebels on the road. I agreed to accompany him, as also did Mr. Bridgeford. We prepared, by loading our pistols, &c. and about 7 o'clock we started, and pushed on, as fast as the state of the roads would permit. . . .

B 27   STATEMENT OF CAPT. HUGH STEWART
n.d.
[PAC, Correspondence of the Provincial Secretary's Office, v. 8, file 1209]

On Monday Night the 4th Decr last in endeavouring to pass Montgomery's Tavern in Company with Coll. Moodie and four others namely – David Bridgford Prime Laurence[53] – George Reed[54] and

[52]Aaron Munshaw was a farmer who owned lot 51 on Yonge Street in Vaughan Township. At least one of his relatives had arrived in Upper Canada at about the time John Graves Simcoe had. An illiterate man with no previous involvement in politics, Munshaw was persuaded while drunk to join the men going to Montgomery's Tavern on Monday, 4 December. After the battle of Thursday he hid out and then fled to the United States. A few months later he returned to Upper Canada. In 1839 he surrendered, confessed, and petitioned for pardon, which was granted.

[53]John Prime Lawrence (Laurence) probably lived near Richmond Hill.

[54]George Decimus Reed kept a store in Markham Township. Walton's Directory lists him as living on lot 26, concession 3, but he did not own it. He was an active Orangeman and in 1840 was master of Lodge 210.

another whose name I do not know. We found a guard placed across the road. We make a dash at them and passed them – on turning round I saw that only two, namely Coll. Moodie and myself had passed. he and I consulted together and determined to pass the second guard. in passing the door at Montgomery's house I heard an order given, either "prepare to fire" or "fire" – I heard the word fire distinctly. I did not know the voice in which the order was given. We put our horses to full speed for the purpose of passing the second guard which was drawn up about fifty yards below Montgomerys. We failed in getting through the second guard. they got hold of the bridles of our horses, they called upon us to stop and surrender. Coll. Moodie said who are you that dare to stop me upon the Queens high way. they replied you will find out that by and bye[,] at that instant Coll. Moodie fired his pistol and immediately three shots were fired by the rebel guard two from the right and one from the left. Coll. Moodie fell upon my horse's neck and said I'm shot, I'm a dead man. I assisted him to regain his saddle, asked him if he thought he could sit for a little while? to which he replied yes. We were then taken prisoners and separated by force. I was taken towards Montgomerys door. I was dragged off my horse and used me in a most barbarous manner, as many as could get round me struck and kicked me. this they continued to do until they got me inside the porch at Montgomery's House, when a Scotchman one of the rebels named Nelson[55] interfered and rescued me from their brutal treatment and led me up to the place appropriated by the rebels as a prison: in the Second Story at Montgomery's Tavern, I had been there but a short time when the prisoner now present Saml. Lount came to me and asked me if I was armed[.] I said I was armed with a pair of pistols, he demanded them from me – and took them away. I asked the Sentinel to send for the prisoner Saml. Lount a second time for the purpose of asking his permission to see Coll. Moodie. he came to me, and for some cause I was not permitted to go then but shortly afterwards he (the prisoner) came to me and permitted me to go and see Coll. Moodie, who I found lying on the floor in a small room bleeding and writhing in agony[,] there was one man holding his head up. I saw no one abuse him or ask him any questions. I asked the prisoner Saml. Lount If I might be permitted to send for a Medical man. he took the note and said he would give it to Mr. McKenzie. I left Coll. Moodie and went back to my prison – Coll. Moodie was then dying. I soon afterwards learned that he was dead. I then sent for Mr. Lount who was

---

[55] William Nelson (1794–1851) came from Fettercairn Parish, Scotland, probably as an indentured worker. In 1835 he bought 50 acres of lot 19, concession 2, East Gwillimbury, on which he farmed. Active in reform politics and in the political union movement prior to the rebellion, he also took a prominent part in the activities at Montgomery's Tavern. Men kept prisoner there later praised him for his efforts to protect them and to see that they were well treated. Captured after the battle of 7 December, he petitioned for pardon and was sentenced to seven years' transportation but in July 1838 he was pardoned.

good enough to come and see what was wanted and requested him to procure an order for a team to take away the body of Coll. Moodie. I asked him for paper & pen & ink which was granted me by Mr. Lount[.] I asked him to get me a pass for the team with the body which he procured for me signed by William Lyon McKenzie. I wrote a note and enclosed the note to Captn. Boyd. . . .

B 28   EVIDENCE OF WILLIAM BABCOCK CREW
[PRO, CO 42, v. 447, pp. 205-211, Trial of Gilbert Fields Morden, microfilm in PAO]

William Babcock Crew, sworn – was taken prisoner on the 4th December last by Samuel Lount and others on Yonge Street – about ten miles from Toronto – taken first to one Shephard's, then to Montgomery's, the party who took him were armed with rifles, muskets, swords, pistols and some of them with long Knives, about a hundred of them – Witness asked why they stopped him on the road, they said they were afraid he was going to town to give information of their coming in; they were then coming in – Witness asked what they were arming for – they said to overturn the Government. Nelson Gorham and others said this. They used witness roughly, and said they knew he was opposed to them – At Shephard's they stopped, and were casting bullets and preparing pikes – There were waggons with them with arms – At Shephards arms and ammunition were dealt out – about 200 pikes were served out there he thinks – Witness was then taken prisoner by them to Montgomery's – this was on Monday night 4th December. About night or very early on Tuesday morning, they got to Montgomery's and halted there – found many armed men there – witness knew many of them; the house was full: he was asked whether he would not like to see his neighbour, Coll. Moodie, & was taken to him in a room in Montgomery's inn; he was lying dead – had two bullet-wounds in the left side – Several of the men said that their guard had shot him, that he imprudently fired at them and the guard shot him – . . .

B 29   INFORMATION OF GEORGE REED
13 December 1837
[PAO, Rebellion Papers, 1837-8, no. 9]

For other extracts from this document see B 32, B 49.

. . . On Monday the 4th. Instant I was taken prisoner at Hoggs hollow[56] by a party of rebels:. . . I was taken to the home of the late

[56]Hogg's Hollow took its name from James Hogg (d. 1839) who came from Lancashire, England, in 1824 and who in 1832 purchased 40 acres of lot 10, concession 1 of York Township, "the hollow," where he operated a mill. In 1831 and

Joseph Sheppard:[57] where I saw David Gibson and a Sadler who lives near Finches Tavern – who was very active among the rebels: there were an immense number – I should think two or three hundred – of the rebels assembled at Sheppards: Old Mrs. Sheppard[58] was particularly active in getting White tape, & White rag, to tye them round the mens arms: & there were several other women who were equally active in furnishing this emblem to the insurgents – . . .

B 30   INFORMATION OF JOHN LINFOOT[59]
14 December 1837
[PAO, Rebellion Papers, 1837–8, no. 12]

For other extracts from this document see B 50, B 62.

. . . The next morning [5 Dec.] they [the rebels at Montgomery's Tavern] spoke amongst themselves of going to Toronto. Mackenzie addressed those present and [said] amongst other things that "those who had not arms should take Pipes in their mouths as they could take the City with Pipes as well as with fire arms" from which I understood him to mean that there would be no opposition. the whole party then left for Toronto and I saw no more of them till dusk. Mackenzie came into the bar room and turned me out telling the men that he would pay for all. some person whose name I did not know told Mackenzie that they might have been in Toronto if they had not got so bad a General[.] Mackenzie told him to take his gun and go home. The person replied that a great many were preparing to do so. . . .

B 31   W.L. MACKENZIE'S ACCOUNT OF THE FLAG OF TRUCE INCIDENT, 5 DECEMBER
[Jeffersonian, *Watertown, reprinted in* Mackenzie's Gazette, *New York City, 12 May 1838*]

For other extracts from this document see B 1, B 14, B 25, B 38, B 48, B 61.

. . . Sir Francis Head admits that he was entirely ignorant of our

---

1835 he bought considerably more land. He was also involved in other business ventures and was a founder of York Mills Presbyterian Church. Previously a reformer, the rebellion made him a loyalist and in the post-rebellion period he denounced a number of his friends and neighbours as rebels.

[57] Joseph Sheppard (Shepard) (1767–1837) came with his family to Upper Canada from New England in 1774 and settled in the Bay of Quinte area. In 1793 or 1794 he moved to York, after working as a fur trader for some years. He became a very prosperous farmer, owning several farms and saw and grist mills. An ardent supporter of the Church of England, he gave land to build a church at York Mills. He was also an ardent supporter of reform. Though he died before the rebellion, his four sons participated keenly in it with the rebels.

[58] Catharine Sheppard was Joseph's wife.

[59] John Linfoot was a tory who had leased Montgomery's Tavern on 1 December 1837. After the rebellion he was able to provide information against several insurgents.

intended movement until awakened out of his bed that night [4 December]. His informant, I believe to have been Cap. Bridgeford. He had the bells set a ringing, took up his abode in the city hall, delivered out a few rusty guns, made speeches, and was in great trouble. Of all which particulars our executive neither brought nor sent us any account whatever.

About midnight our numbers increased, and towards morning I proposed to many persons to march to Toronto, join such of the reformers there as were ready, and endeavor to make ourselves master of the garrison and muskets.

To this it was objected, that I was uninformed of the strength of the fortress, that the other townships had not yet joined the men from the upper country, that we were ignorant of the state of the city, and that gentlemen who had advised and urged on the movements, and even the executive who had ordered this premature Monday rising, stood aloof, and had neither joined us nor communicated with us.

Next day (Tuesday) we increased in number to 800, of whom very many had no arms, others had rifles, old fowling pieces, Indian guns, pikes, &c. Vast numbers came and went off again, when they found we had neither muskets nor bayonets. Had they possessed my feelings in favor of freedom they would have stood by us even if armed but with pitch forks and broom handles.

About noon we obtained correct intelligence that with all his exertions, and including the college boys, Sir Francis could hardly raise 150 supporters in town and country; and by one P.M. a flag of truce reached our camp near the city, the messengers being the Honorables Messrs. Rolph and Baldwin, deputed by Sir Francis to ask what would satisfy us. I replied, "Independence;" but sent a verbal message that as we had no confidence in Sir F's word, he would have to send his messages in writing, and within one hour. I then turned round to Colonel Lount, and advised him to march the men under his command at once into the city, and take a position near the Lawyers Hall [Osgoode Hall], and rode westward to Col. Baldwin's[60] where the bulk of the rebels were, and advised an instant march to Toronto. We had advanced as far as the college avenue, when another flag of truce arrived, by the same messengers, with a message from Sir F. declining to comply with our previous request. We were proceeding to town, when orders from the executive arrived that we should not then go to Toronto but wait till 6 o'clock in the evening and then take the city.

[60]Augustus Baldwin (1776–1866) left his native County Cork, Ireland, to join the merchant navy in 1792. In 1794 he entered the Royal Navy and procured a commission. Retiring on half-pay in 1817 as a captain, he moved to York, where he followed a rather quiet life although involved in various business enterprises and sitting on the Legislative Council, 1831–41, and the Executive Council, 1836–41. He took no strong role in the latter two bodies. In 1862 he was appointed admiral, having formally retired from the navy in 1846.

True to the principle on which the compact was made for our rising, the order was obeyed, and at a quarter to six the whole of our forces were near the toll bar, on Yonge street, on our way to the city. I told them that I was certain there could be no difficulty in taking Toronto; that both in town and country the people had stood aloof from Sir Francis; that not 150 men and boys could be got to defend him; that he was alarmed and had sent his family on board a steamer; that 600 reformers were ready waiting to join us in the city, and that all we had to do was to be firm, and with the city would at once go down every vestige of foreign government in U.C. . . .

B 32   INFORMATION OF GEORGE REED
13 December 1837
[PAO, Rebellion Papers, 1837–8, no. 9]

For other extracts from this document see B 29, B 49.

. . . I was taken with the party down to Montgomery's Tavern very early on Tuesday morning: Silas Fletcher[61] was at Sheppards farm with the rebels, & was the Commander of a part of them: on the way down he presented pistols to my head & breast repeatedly, because my horse walked faster than his. The next morning (Tuesday) I saw Mackenzie, Gibson, Lount, Lloyd, Fletcher & John Montgomery; in deep consultation together for some time, & then they reviewed their men. On this day (Tuesday) We (the prisoners) were marched down with the body of rebels to the gallows hill – Mackenzie, Lloyd – Lound [sic] Gibson & Fletcher were with the party – When they got to the gallows hill, the rebels saw something coming up the road from the City which the leaders took to be a piece of Cannon: they became alarmed – retreated – & ordered the prisoners who were in the rear, to be placed in front, between them & the Supposed Cannon – which turned out to be a Yoke of Oxen coming up the road. – When they found their mistake they marched us over to the house of Captain Baldwin – where they got refreshment and marched us back to Montgomerys – on our way we found that Dr. Hornes[62] house had been set on fire. . . .

[61]Silas Fletcher (1780–1847) was born in Chesterfield, New Hampshire, and came to Whitchurch Township with his brother in 1805. Over the succeeding years he became a land speculator on a large scale, as well as a horse dealer. In 1824 he was a founder and director of the Farmers' Storehouse Company. By the late 1820s he was a radical reformer and a supporter of Mackenzie. In the fall of 1837 he sold or gave to other family members all of his land, and then took part in the rebellion, which he seems to have been actively promoting even before Mackenzie put forward his scheme to remove the government. He and Jesse Lloyd appear to have been Mackenzie's chief allies in planning the uprising. After the defeat, he fled to the United States, where he bought a farm in New York State and began a large dairy operation. He also purchased a woollen mill with Nelson Gorham, giving his share to his son Daniel. For the rest of his life he remained in the United States.
[62]Robert Charles Horne (d. 1845) was born in England. He had served as surgeon

B 33   STATEMENT OF SAMUEL LOUNT
n.d.
*[PAC, Correspondence of the Provincial Secretary's Office, v. 9, file
1209]*

. . . When the flag of truce came up Dr. Rolph addressed himself to
me – there were two other persons with it besides Dr. Rolph and Mr.
Baldwin – he Dr. Rolph said he brought a message from His
Excellency the Lieutt. Governor to prevent the effusion of blood or that
effect – At the same time he gave me a wink to walk to one side – when
he requested me not to *hear* the Message but to go in with our
proceedings [–] what he meant was not to attend to the Message [–]
McKenzie observed to me that it was a Rebel Message and that it had
better be submitted to writing – I took the reply to the Lieutt.
Governors message to be merely a putt off, I understood that the
intentions of the leaders was to take the City of Toronto and change the
present state of Government – I heard all that was said by Dr. Rolph to
McKenzie which is as above related – this was the first time the flag
came up – I was present also when the second flag came up – Dr.
Rolph then observed the truce was at an end – . . .

B 34   PETITION OF SAMUEL LOUNT TO SIR F.B. HEAD
10 March 1838
[PAC, Upper Canada Sundries, v. 192, pp. 107033-8]

For another extract from this document see B 4.

. . . your petitioner on Monday Morning the fourth day of December
last started for Toronto, and on our arrival at Montgomeries Tavern we
began to be suspicious that we had been grievously imposed upon,
seeing we were not immediately marched into the City and received as
friends as we had been led to believe but on the Contrary some one
fired upon and killed Colonal Moody, that this was done in the absence
of your petitioner and without your petitioners knowledge or Consent –
But on the arrival of Doctor John Rolph was again – led to hope that
there would be no other lives lost, and that all would yet be right, as we
were told by Rolph to push on and pay no attention to the Flag of Truce
as he would tell the Governor, we would not hear his proposals unless
committed to writing (which was arranged by Rolph and McKenzie)
but at last we learned the true state of the affair after the Burning of
Doctor Horne's, House which your petitioner and many others
remonstrated against in the most positive terms – – And in desperation,
seeing ourselves Surrounded by a Country determined to resist our

with the Glengarry Light Infantry before coming to York, Upper Canada, in 1815 or
1816. Well connected through marriage to tory business and political circles, he served
as king's printer, 1817–21, after which he became chief teller (manager) of the Bank of
Upper Canada.

approaches to the City, and a Change of Government, after waiting till the last moment we precipitately retreated, previous to which however, W.L. McKenzie had proposed Burning the House of W.B. Jarvis Esquire which becoming known to your petitioner, he with many others interfeared, being determined to stop if possible the destruction of any property whatever in consequence of which W.L. McKenzie with reluctance abandoned the infamous attempt – . . .

B 35   "DR. HORNE'S NARRATIVE OF THE BURNING OF HIS HOUSE"
Toronto, 26 December 1837
[Christian Guardian, *Toronto, 3 Jan. 1838*]

For another extract from this document see B 43.

It has been so often asserted that my house was consumed by accident, that I am induced to set down some of the leading circumstances, if you think them worth publishing.

A severe affection of the lungs had kept me closely confined during the whole of November, and when I went abroad I heard so much of the movements of the factious, that, coupled with the intelligence from Lower Canada, I felt persuaded, the leaders there would urge, at every risk, a rising in this quarter, if only to distract the attention of the authorities in both Provinces. I cannot think that they anticipated to be eventually successful in their undertaking here, but a bold enterprise by even a small number of men, might have proved of the most serious importance, utterly unprovided as we were against any sudden alarm. I did not imagine that any considerable body to act on foot, could be easily collected without the authorities having ample notice, but as they might come in waggons and destroy the town before any effectual resistance could be offered, I began to collect, privately, information of the number of loyal men in my neighbourhood who would be willing to be sworn in as special constables, to keep a look out, and be ready to act at a moment's notice, there being more than one place near me where a very small number of resolute men could keep a much superior force in check for a long time, or until further help came. These views I communicated to the Government House on Monday morning, and had a very polite letter of thanks in reply, accepting my services, if occasion required. In the middle of the day I had an opportunity of stating my views briefly again, verbally, and asked for arms and ammunition. I had not then time to press the request.

In the evening I had prepared a list of about thirty, and went to bed fatigued and ill, and did not hear of the alarm or disturbance of the night until I went to town on Tuesday morning, when I immediately returned on horse-back – The rebels were then at Gallows Hill, less

than a mile distant. I told my family that as their object would be to get
to town as quickly as possible, it was not probable they would lose
time by stopping to plunder private houses, but that as soon as they
came near the house, my wife and children should leave the place, by
the back way to a neighbour's, and as the servants would not be
injured, they were to keep the doors and windows closed, and be
perfectly quiet. After giving these directions I proceeded slowly again
to the city, endeavouring to rouse all on the road to go in for arms,
expecting every moment to meet a piquet sent out to watch the motions
of the insurgents, or at least to be allowed to bring out a sufficient
force. Except a few from above my place, I found a most unexpected
indifference among the great numbers who by this time were on the
road, some actuated by curiosity, but many I fear by worse motives,
and the most seeming to think it was no affair in which they were much
interested, and not a few of the residents appeared influenced by a fear
of suffering from the vengeance of the self-styled *Liberals* should they
take up arms against them.

When I applied at the depot for men to go out on Yonge Street, I was
informed that the quarters requiring protection were so numerous and
important, that the forces then in arms would be insufficient for their
full defence, and in consequence I could not have fifty, nor even
twenty, at that time. It therefore became incumbent on me to
endeavour to get my family by a private road through the woods; but
when half way out, hearing a great deal of firing near the town, I
supposed the action had commenced, and immediately returned to take
a share in the duty of defence – and found it was only caused by trying
the new muskets. Finding that a party of the rebels, who had come
through the woods from the Don, occupied the Toll-gate on Yonge
Street, I determined once more to make my way through the woods,
although at very considerable risk of capture: – and when I arrived at
the opening beyond, I saw my house in flames, and near to me the
females and children of my family, on their sad and lonely way to a
place of shelter, with only the clothes they had on at the time; – From
them I learnt that Mackenzie led the party, (not more than 200, and not
one half of them armed with muskets,) that he assisted in person in
putting fire to the house, and that to increase the rapidity of the flames,
he himself broke up the chairs and tables to throw upon the fire.

Whatever may have been the motives for this atrocious act, the
consequences have been the very reverse of what they anticipated. Far
from being intimidated, those who were before inclined to remain
neutral, instantly came forward with alacrity, and those already
preparing to take up arms, hurried on with increased energy. And a
very considerable number of the malcontents, having at length their
eyes opened to the real character of the movement, at once refused all
further participation in it. . . .

B 36   Evidence of William Ketchum
[PRO, CO 42, v. 447, pp. 181-204, Trial of John Montgomery, microfilm in PAO]

. . . Witness drove back to town – on his way met Mr. Baldwin and Dr. Rolph going out with a flag – they met Lount on the road – – Mr. Baldwin said they were sent out to ask what were their demands and he inquired for their leaders. Rolph then called witness on one side and spoke to him – he told witness that when he returned to the City, he must mind and say to every one that the party out there was very strong. – Witness was convinced from what he heard that they were not very strong – Witness returned to Toronto – . . .

B 37   Col. James FitzGibbon's Account of Events in Toronto, 5 December
[James FitzGibbon, An Appeal to the People of the Late Province of Upper Canada (Montreal, 1847), pp. 18-19, 20]

For other extracts from this document see B 16, B 19.

. . . On the following morning [5 December], at sun-rise, accompanied by Captain Halkett,[63] of the Guards, His Excellency's Aide-de-camp, and four others, mounted, I rode out and reconnoitred the Rebels, who it was said, were felling trees and fortifying their position at Montgomery's. I found they had done nothing; that the road was perfectly open and well macadamized, and that in less than two hours they could be attacked by a force from town. I had already formed in platoons, in the Market square, upwards of five hundred men; and one six pounder field-piece, was manned and loaded in front of the City Hall. I therefore galloped into town to pray of His Excellency to let me take three hundred of those men and the six-pounder, and make an instant attack upon the Rebels. I will not attempt to describe the feelings of exultation which filled my mind while galloping into town. I eagerly begged of His Excellency to let me take that number of the men then formed in the square and the six-pounder, and I assured him that there need be no doubt but that in two hours we would disperse the Rebels. But to my surprise he almost angrily exclaimed, "O no, sir! I will not fight them on their ground, they must fight me on mine!" Filled with such unexpected and deep disappointment I mentally exclaimed, "Good God! what an old woman I have here to deal with!" I cannot, even now, refrain from thus

[63]Frederick Halkett (ca. 1813–1840), a young lieutenant in the Coldstream Guards, accompanied Head, a distant connection, to Upper Canada as his aide-de-camp. After Head left the province in 1838, Halkett stayed on, marrying the daughter of Colonel Robert Moodie. As a favour to Head, Arthur retained Halkett as his military secretary and came to value his services highly. He was consequently shaken by Halkett's premature death from fever and ague. By the time of his death Halkett had assumed the rank of colonel.

declaring these, my thoughts, exactly as they then arose in my mind, unbecoming as, to many, this declaration, perhaps, may appear. And no doubt the expression of my continuance [*sic*] indicated what was then passing within me. In vain did I use every argument I could, to obtain leave to attack the Rebels instantly; for I considered a prompt defeat to be of the utmost importance to our cause in the very outset; but I soon found that my arguments produced upon His Excellency irritation only.

This day, Tuesday, was passed in further preparation. In the evening I was forming a piquet to be placed on Yonge Street during the night; for the one placed there the night before by Judge Jones he withdrew in the morning. His Excellency from a window above saw me, and sent for me and asked what I was doing: I answered, "Forming a piquet to be placed on Yonge Street."He quickly and imperatively said, "Do not send out a man." To which I said, "I cannot endure to leave the City open to the incursions of these ruffians!" He continued: "We have not men enough to defend the City: let us defend our posts: – and it is my positive order that you do not leave this building yourself." To which I said, "I pray of Your Excellency not to lay such imperative orders upon me: I ought to be in many places, and I ought to be allowed to exercise a discretionary power where you are not near to give me orders." But His Excellency only repeated his orders more imperatively. I retired from the presence of those around me, and reflected intensely on all the circumstances by which we were surrounded. I had no doubt of the importance of having a piquet on Yonge Street to stop the approach of the Rebels from Montgomery's, should they attempt to enter the City. From what I had seen of night-fighting, I knew full well that a handful of men opening a fire upon them as they advanced, would at once make them run back. Whereas if they were not resisted they might come in with the more confidence and set fire to the city; and thus give confidence to their friends in town, and also, in the country at large, and thereby paralize [*sic*] the spirit of the Loyalists every where. I therefore formed a piquet in a place where His Excellency could not see me, and placed Mr. Sheriff Jarvis at the head of it, and marched it out myself and posted it; giving the Sheriff such instructions as the place and circumstances seemed to me to require. I then returned to the City Hall; and as I approached it I debated with myself whether I should state to His Excellency that I had so posted the piquet; and I deemed it most candid to do so. I therefore reported to him what I had done, and he rebuked me for it: certainly not angrily, but in milder terms than I expected from him. In the course of an hour, however, a report reached him that the Sheriff and piquet were made prisoners by the Rebels, and then he reproached me in angry terms for what I had done. . . .

Very soon after a second report was brought, that the Sheriff and his piquet were running into town through the fields in twos and threes, which seemed to appease His Excellency a little. In a few minutes more Mr. Cameron, the young student already mentioned, came from the Sheriff to inform His Excelleny [sic] that the rebels had approached his position when his piquet fired upon them, and they fled, leaving some of their men dead upon the road. It was ascertained the following day that they were coming in to set the town on fire. A Captain Mathias, on the half pay of the Royal Artillery, who lived near the Toll Gate on Yonge Street, was coming into town on horseback, when he fell in with the rebels, who made him a prisoner, and he had to ride in their midst towards town, when he learned, from what he overheard of their conversation, that their object was to set the City on fire. . . .

B 38   W.L. MACKENZIE'S ACCOUNT OF THE PIQUET INCIDENT, 5 DECEMBER
[Jeffersonian, *Watertown, reprinted in* Mackenzie's Gazette, *New York City, 12 May 1838*]

For other extracts from this document see B 1, B 14, B 25, B 31, B 48, B 61.

. . . It was dark, and there might be an ambush of some sort [Mackenzie and his men were moving on Toronto on the evening of 5 December], I therefore told six riflemen to go ahead of us a quarter of a mile on the one side of the street, inside the the [sic] fences, and as many more on the other side, and to fire in the direction in which they might see any of our opponents stationed. – When within half a mile of the town, we took prisoners the captain of their artillery, a lawyer, and the sheriff's horse. Our riflemen a head [sic] saw some 20 or 30 of the enemy in the road, and fired at them, the 20 or 30 or some of them, fired at us, and instantly took to their heels and ran towards the town. Our riflemen were in front, after them the pikemen, then those who had old guns of various kinds, and lastly those who carried only clubs and walking sticks. Colonel Lount was at the head of the riflemen. [sic] and he and those in the front rank fired, and instead of stepping to one side to make room for those behind to fire, fell flat on their faces, the next rank fired and did the same thing. I was rather in front when the firing begun, and stood in more danger from the rifles of my friends than the muskets of my enemies. I stept to the side of the road and bade them stop firing and it appeared to me that one of our people who was killed, was shot in this way by our own men. Certainly not by the enemy.

Some persons from town, friendly to us, but not very brave, had joined us during the march, and they, unknown to me, told awful stories about the preparations the tories had made in several streets, to fire out of the windows at us, protected by feather beds, mattrasses [sic], &c. These representations terrified many of the country people and when they saw the riflemen in front falling down, and heard the firing, they imagined that those who fell were the killed and wounded by the enemy's fire; and took to their heels with a speed and steadiness of purpose that would have baffled pursuit on foot. In a short time not twenty persons were to be found below the toll bar!

This was almost too much for human patience. The city would have been ours in an hour, probably without firing a shot; hundreds of our friends waited to join us at its entrance; the officials were terror struck; Gov. Head had few to rely on; the colony would have followed the city; a convention and democratic constitution been adopted, and a bloodless change from a contemptible tyrranny [sic] to freedom accomplished. But 800 ran where no one pursued, and unfortunately ran the wrong way.

I rode hastily back until I got in the rear of the main body, stopt a number of them, and implored them to return. I explained matters to them, told them to fear nothing, offered with half a dozen more to go between them and all danger, and reminded them that the opportunity of that night would be their last – that the moment it was known in the country that the reformers were timid and fearful without cause, Sir Francis would instantly gain numbers. But it was of no use. To successive groups I spoke in vain. Neither threats nor coaxing could induce them to go to the city. I tried to find even fifty or forty to go to town, but the reply was, "we will go in daylight but not in the dark." Of these, many went home that evening, and although about 200 joined us during the night, we were 200 less numerous on the Wednesday morning.

With the steamers in the hands of the government, the city, 4,000 muskets and bayonets, perhaps 60 experienced military officers, the well-paid officials and their sons and dependants, abundance of ammunition, a park of artillery well served, the garrison, and the aid of all who are prejudiced in favor of colonial government, it had become a difficult task for a collection of undisciplined and half armed countrymen, without cannon, scarce of gunpowder, not possessed of a single bayonet, not even of guns or pikes for half their numbers, to contend successfully against the enemy for the city; we therefore stood on the defensive on Wednesday. Gentlemen of influence, who were pledged to join us, and even the executive who had commanded us to make the premature and unfortunate movement, neither corresponded with us nor joined us. To explain their conduct was beyond my power. It discouraged many, and thinned our ranks. . . .

B 39   STATEMENT OF JAMES LATIMER
[*PAO, Rebellion Papers, 1837–8, no. 18*]

For other extracts from this document see B 2, B 51.

. . . When I heard that Dr. Horne's house was burning on Tuesday, I went out to the blue hill where I saw Mr. Mackenzie – and a number of pikemen ranged on the road – I said to Mr. Mackenzie, "Is this all the men you have got? You a'int going into the City with such a small number of men as this, are you?" When he replied "You dont see all of them – there are plenty more" and then asked me how many men there were in town – I said "from five to seven hundred, all well armed, and more were flocking in from every quarter, and every avenue through the streets was well secured" – he swore a harsh Oath – said it was a d————d lie, that he Knew there were not more than two hundred & fifty men in the whole City, and seemed much irritated as if he was afraid that what I said would discourage the men who heard me. He told me to come along up with him to Montgomery's – and I went – He asked me what was the opinion of the reformers in the City, I told him that the City was a good deal agitated, but I did not see any Warlike appearances, as nobody but the Royalists had taken up arms. He made a significant expression of countenance, as *I* thought, of disappointment that the reformers in Town had not taken up arms. In the evening McKenzie marched the men down to take the City – I rode behind, as far as the turnpike gate, when the main body got a little below that, a volley was fired into them when they all began to run, some of them throwing down their pikes: & cursing Mr. MacKenzie for taking them down there in the dark to get Butchered. Mackenzie was exasperated at their conduct in running away: and when he got back to Montgomerys he seemed to me to be under the influence of liquor: some of the men said "Mackenzie has taken his bitters to-night." . . .

B 40 "J.M."[64] TO W.L. MACKENZIE
Chapinville, 16 July 1838
[*PAO, Mackenzie–Lindsey Clippings, no. 6017*]

. . . What a change of scene since we moved your types with the small press out of the city of Toronto last November! I was greatly deceived at the outset at Montgomery's. Some of our greatest pretenders never made their appearance at all, and some who did acted a most cowardly part, which disheartened others. On the Tuesday night when we were surprised, our men acted a poor part, especially the Lloydtown pikemen; they ran and left their pikes when no great danger was near, as the loyalists had all fled as soon as they fired. Mr. William Harrison[65] commanded the company I was in, of which not above ten or twelve stood their ground. When we returned we found the road

---

[64]"J.M." was probably James Mosher (Moshier), who lived on lot 19, concession 1 of York Township. A near neighbour of David Gibson, Mosher had been active in the political union movement prior to the rising of 1837. He wrote to Mackenzie from Chapinville, N.Y.

[65]William Harrison (1784–1838), the son of a United Empire Loyalist, was born in Nova Scotia but moved to Upper Canada in 1796. He fought in the War of 1812 and

strewed with pikes, and one wounded man who died since in the hospital. Mr. Harrison then declared to me he would no longer command or accompany such a band of cowards, and he returned to his home that night, and I heard on Thursday morning that he was very sick, and since, in one of your papers, I saw that the good old patriot had died. . . .

B 41   LADY HEAD TO FRANK HEAD
Toronto, 13 December 1837
[Bodleian Library, University of Oxford, Letters of Sir Francis and Lady Head to Frank Head, microfilm in PAO]

For other extracts of this document see B 17, B 24, B 59.

. . . We saw Dr. Horne's house in flames, but our party were now gaining strength & confidence every hour – however in consequence of a report that Col. Wells s family were prisoners, (they were kept with a guard of rebels round the house, but not insulted or robbed) your father sent the Archdeacon Strachan[66] to me to beg we go on board a Steamer which would take us off [to] the United States, should the rebels succeed – We all went on board, and also Mrs Robinson[67] & Mrs Hagerman[68] (the wives of the Chief Justice & Attorney Genl. and their families) and remained close to the Wharf so that we saw and heard all that was going on & were cheered by seeing fresh steamers arrive with militia troops (all in their working dresses armed with muskets) who were received with loud hurraes by those already assembled – whilst the rebels were stealing off and losing all heart in their wicked cause – . . .

---

was decorated for his actions. He owned several pieces of land in York Township close to Yonge Street by the mid-1830s. He was active in the political union movement preceding the rebellion. His death in New York State was claimed to be the result of his exertions in fleeing Upper Canada after the rising.

[66]John Strachan (1778–1867) spent his early years in his native Aberdeen, Scotland, but, when advancement seemed blocked, he came to Kingston, Upper Canada, in 1799 as a tutor to the Cartwright family. In 1803 he secured a position as a priest in the Church of England, becoming both a parish priest and a teacher at Cornwall, positions he held until 1812. At Cornwall he established the reputation and the connections that were to carry him forward. Appointed rector at York, he moved to the capital and by his conduct during the American invasion in the War of 1812 vaulted himself into a leading role in the affairs of the town. As his ex-pupils came to take leading parts in the government of Upper Canada, he became the pivotal force in the Family Compact. From 1815–35 he sat on the Executive Council and from 1810–41 in the Legislative Council. In 1827 he became archdeacon of York and in 1839 bishop of Upper Canada. Consistently at the centre of controversy, he concentrated his efforts after the union of the Canadas on matters concerning the welfare of the Church of England, spending less time on the other great concern of his public career, the loyalty of the people to British eighteenth-century values.

[67]The wife of Chief Justice John Beverley Robinson was the former Emma Walker, whom Robinson had married in England in 1817.

[68]The wife of Charles Hagerman was the former Emily Mery (d. 1842).

B 42   F.L. BRIDGMAN TO FANNY WEST
Government House, 15 December 1837
[*PAO, Miscellaneous, 1837, typescript*]

For other extracts from this document see B 23, B 66.

. . . We [the women of Head's household] remained at Mrs. Draper's until Tuesday evening, when the Archdeacon came to Lady Head from Sir Francis to say it was his wish that we should go on board the "Transit" steam boat, as he no longer considered Mrs. Draper's house safe. We heard then that the rebels were at the top of the College Avenue, which is close to the town – we saw also the smoke from Dr. Horn's house which they had set on fire. You can have no idea of the state of excitement and terror in which we were. The scene on board the vessel was most distressing. There were several families on board beside Lady Head's, and they were all in the greatest distress and fear for their husbands, brothers, and sons who were all exposed to danger, as every one had taken arms – although I was very much frightened and felt very deeply for them all, I was rejoiced and comforted to know that all who were dear to me were far away and in safety. During the night we were moored out in the lake, and in the morning we came back to the wharf, so that we could see and hear all that was passing in the Town. On this day, Wednesday, volunteers were coming in from all parts, it was a joyous sight to see them arrive and did ones heart good to hear the cheers of those who came down to receive them. We were very much alarmed this night by a schooner coming up close to us and refusing to give any account of herself – Captn Richardson,[69] who is a very determined character, immediately fired into her, this frightened us as we did not know what might be the consequence, and we were still more alarmed by Mrs. Richardson[70] telling us that McKenzie having heard that Lady Head and her family were on board had sent this vessel to take us prisoners. It proved to be a vessel laden with salt from Oswego, and being taken by surprise was too much frightened to answer. . . .

[69]Hugh Richardson (1784–1870) was born in London, England, and went to sea in 1798. He served in the navy until 1810, when he was captured by the French, and was not released until after the war. In 1821 he and his recent bride came to Canada, where he soon became involved in owning and commanding boats on the lakes. The *Transit* was the second vessel he owned and operated on a regular run on Lake Ontario. The *Transit* served the government throughout the rebellion and its aftermath, carrying messages and ferrying troops. In the 1840s Richardson overextended himself by buying two more vessels and in 1846 went bankrupt. After a brief period serving as a captain on ships in the Montreal–Quebec City areas, he was appointed harbourmaster at Toronto in 1850, probably in recognition of much work he had voluntarily undertaken in the 1830s and 1840s on the harbour. He was able to live comfortably on his salary until his death.

[70]Hugh Richardson's wife was Frances; she and he raised a large family.

B 43   DR. HORNE TO THE *Christian Guardian*
Toronto, 26 December 1837
[Christian Guardian, *Toronto, 3 Jan. 1838*]

For another extract from this document see B 35.

. . . It was on my way down Yonge Street a second time, that I found Dr. Rolph and his companion stopping on their return from their pretended mission of mediation, at the rebel corner, where from 100 to 150 of the city lurkers were eagerly swallowing the information Rolph was evidently detailing for their benefit. His object seemed to be to exaggerate the force and condition of the insurgents, and to impress a belief that our authorities were in a terrible fright. I told him that I understood the nature or intent of their mission was, to shew these misguided people the folly and danger to themselves, of their enterprize, and that it was impossible for them to succeed. "Oh, no, no, Sir; such and such were our instructions – and had they been in writing, we might have succeeded better," &c. Unable longer to restrain my indignation, I exclaimed, "What! treat with rebels, with arms in their hands? – Never!" and moved on. . . .

B 44   STATEMENT OF H.H. WRIGHT[71]
[*PAC, Rolph Papers, v. 2, pp. 91-2*]

. . . I came up home again [5 December] and met Dr. Rolph, Carmichael[72] Emery,[73] Armstrong[74] and a number of others in Lot Street. All were expressing great surprise that McKenzie did not come in. Dr. Horne's house had been on fire at this time about ½ an hour. I said I would go out to see the cause of the delay. Some one requested

[71] Henry Hoover Wright was one of Rolph's medical students in 1837. Active in the rebellion, he fled to the United States, where he continued his studies under Rolph. Returning to the province after a few years, he became a prominent and successful doctor. His statement is undated, but was made about 1838 or 1839. Dent later reproduced it in his history of the rebellion.

[72] Hugh Carmichael was a Scot, a carpenter by trade, who operated a business selling groceries and spirits at 11 Lot Street in Toronto in the mid-1830s. A man of reform sentiments, he was chosen to carry the flag of truce on Thursday, 5 December 1837. Not suspected of rebel activities at the time, his house was searched in March 1838 and letters complaining of poor conditions in Upper Canada were found. He was then arrested and held seven weeks, after which he moved to the United States, returning to the province some years later.

[73] Robert Emery was a wheelwright at 32 Lot Street, Toronto, in 1837. A reformer, he carried a message from the city to Mackenzie on Tuesday night, 5 December 1837, and helped to pack Rolph's bags when the latter decided to flee Upper Canada. He also armed himself on Tuesday night in preparation for the arrival of Mackenzie's forces in the city.

[74] This was Alexander Armstrong, carpenter, John Armstrong, axemaker, or Thomas Armstrong, a carpenter who lived at 11 Lot Street. He was a Scot and employed several men. The latter two attended the meeting late in the fall of 1837 at which Mackenzie had proposed seizing the arms in the city hall.

me to take out word that a body of men, to the number of 37. were placed in the lodges at the foot of College Avenue, and in the Brick Houses on the East side of Graves [Simcoe] Street; the market and buildings adjacent were occupied by the Government, who were soliciting volunteers. In going up Yonge Street I saw no guards, and met with no obstruction from the tories. Dr. Horne's house had fallen in only a short time previously to my passing it; in which neighbourhood I was told they were stationed[.] It was about 3.p.m. I found the main body placed on "Gallows Hill", about a mile further from the City than Horne's house, which is about a mile from it. There was a guard of one man on foot with a fusil, & one on horsback. They stopped me, but on telling my name they knew me, and let me pass. When I got up to the main body I asked for McKenzie. I was told he was not there, but that Gibson and Lount were. I saw Gibson first and told him my message. I also saw Lount, and told him the same. I asked why they did not come in[.] "We can not go, till Genl. McKenzie is ready" was the reply or words to that amount. I asked again for McKenzie and was told he was a little further up. I galloped on as fast as I could, being anxious to return to the City quickly with information to Dr. Rolph of the cause of the delay and the time they intended to come in, till I arrived at Montgomery's tavern, no one could tell me where he was, and after searching with other persons over the house, I asked Montgomery who said he supposed he was in his room. We again searched the house thro', and were as long as 20 minutes hunting for him. I went to the stable and found him ordering a man off the ground. This man said he was a patriot, that he had just come out from Toronto, and brot' him Some news. McKenzie said "I don't Know you, and there are too many friends[.] I don't want any thing to do with you." And in the end drove him away. I gave McKenzie all the information I was possessed of – Where he would meet most resistance, &c. – and told him the Patriots in town desired me to request him to hasten into the City. He asked what is Dr. Rolph doing. I said I have just got home and have not had time to learn all the particulars, but that when I started out I was given the message I have delivered to you. I remarked to him that he had a much smaller body of men than persons in town supposed, as they rated them at 2,000. We started for the main body, On the way we were met by small bodies of men making towards Montgomery's, to get their supper. McKenzie tried to pursuade them to return[;] told me to ride on to Gibson & Lount. After riding slowly some distance, & finding he was so long coming down, I rode back to find him. By this time it was dusk, and I found him not ¼ of a mile south of Montgomery's tavern where I left him. He was talking to a group of men who had brot up the prisioners. He told me to go on to the City, and say he would be in, in half an hour. When I got down to Gallows Hill all the men were going back, declaring they would go in, in the day time, but that rifles were little use at night. Gibson & Lount said their men would not make the attempt that night, but that they would be in by daylight nxt (Wednesday) morning.

B 45   "A SCARBOROUGH MAN" TO THE *Palladium*
Scarborough, 19 March 1838
[Palladium, *Toronto, 21 March 1838*]

. . . On the forenoon of Tuesday, the 5th day of December last, I happened to call at the House of Mr. Isaac Cornell,[75] where for the first time I heard a report that the Garrison and City of Toronto were taken by two thousand rebels under the command of W.L. Mackenzie, and that His Excellency the Lieutenant Governor was a prisoner to rebels in the city hall. In consequence of those unpleasant news, I proceeded immediately to the house of Colonel Maclean,[76] to learn if my information could possibly be true. On my arrival at his house, I found Colonel Maclean standing on the new line of the Kingston road in company with Captain James Gibson,[77] the Colonel told me he had heard a similar report to that which I had heard, and added that he had been listening to hear the twelve o'clock gun, but he had not heard it, although it was then past one o'clock.

We then returned into Colonel Maclean,s [sic] house, for the purpose of consulting what was to be done in such an unexpected emergency. About three o'clock Mr. Frederick Stow arrived from Toronto City, and personally gave a true narrative of the Rebellion. There was no longer any hesitation respecting the line of conduct to be adopted. Orders signed by Colonel Maclean were immediately dispatched to the different officers of the Scarborough Regiment of Militia, directing them to assemble what men and arms they could muster by six o'clock that eveeing. [sic] and either rendezvous at Mr. Gate's Tavern, or march directly on to Toronto City. In the meantime Colonel Maclean and myself agreed that he should eollect [sic] what men and arms he could on the Kingston road. [sic] and that I should do the same on the Danford [sic] road, and that we should meet and join our forces at the aforesaid Tavern on the Kingston road at six o'clock that evening. Accordingly we met at the appointed time and place, when our united forces were found to amonnt [sic] to twenty three men, and our fire arms to seven in number, partly rifles and partly fowling pieces. With that number of men, EIGHT of whom were

[75]Isaac Cornell lived on lot 15, concession D of Scarborough Township.

[76]Allan Maclean, a half-pay officer, formerly of the 91st Regiment, had served in India. He bought 100 acres of lot 17, concession D of Scarborough Township in 1832. As well as a militia colonel, he was a magistrate and reputedly a popular figure in the township.

[77]James Gibson, who lived on lot 16, concession D of Scarborough Township, was a captain of militia and a member of St. Andrew's Presbyterian Church, Scarborough, 1835–59.

OFFICERS, we proceeded immediately for Toronto City, leaving orders at the Tavern for the rest of the officers and men to follow us on to Toronto City as fast as possible. A few minutes after our departure from the said Tavern, Mr. Peter Matthews[78] arrived with sixty armed rebels from Pickering, who detained a few of our Scarborough men prisoners. [sic] who were on their march for Toronto City.

Before we reached Ballard's Inn, or the painted post as it called, a tavern situated at the junction of the Dantford [sic] and Kingston road, we met Mr. Peter Milne Junior,[79] of Markham, who enquired of one of our men if this was Mr Matthews' company, and being told in the negative, he darted into the bush, and escaped before he was recognised.

Almost at the same time we met a good Irishman, who told us that Mr. Doyle from Stoverville with forty five armed men was in Mr. Ballard,s Tavern. [sic] watching to take us all prisoners. We however unanimously agreed to proceed and take the unequal chance of an attack, rather than flinch from prosecuting our design. But the brave Captain Doyle, who did not appear to be remarkably fond of fighting, retreated before us, and again took post on both sides of the road immediately opposite to the late Mr. Small's tomb, where we passed his company without being attacked, although some of them levelled their pieces at us from both sides of the hill – they even followed us as far as Mr. Charles Small's house, when they retired, and we then proceeded to Toronto City unmolested. But I do not know the hour at which we arrived, but I think it must have been between ten and eleven, and we were received with three cheers. Thus we were undoubtedly the first Mllitia [sic] that came from any Township to the assistance of Toronto City. Mr. Dalton[80] the Editor of the Patriot, in

[78]Peter Matthews (1789 or 1790–1838) was the son of a United Empire Loyalist officer who himself fought the Americans as a sergeant in the War of 1812. An affluent farmer and a Baptist, he took part in the political union movement prior to the rebellion. A man of considerable local influence, he was persuaded to lead his neighbours to Montgomery's Tavern in December 1837. Captured a few days after the battle of 7 December, he was tried and executed with Samuel Lount in April 1838, as an example to the population.

[79]Peter Milne Jr. was the son of a pioneering cloth manufacturer who had come from Scotland by way of the United States in 1817 and begun producing cloth. A prosperous merchant with considerable property by the time of the rebellion, Milne Jr. does not appear to have taken any part in the rising, but he was an active radical reformer and known to have been in the vicinity of Matthews' party at one time during the rebellion. As a result, he was arrested in March 1838 and, after petitioning, was ordered transported for seven years. In October his sentence was commuted and he was pardoned.

[80]Thomas Dalton (1792–1840) came from his native Birmingham, England, to Kingston, Upper Canada, about 1812 and opened a brewing and distilling business. Selling this in 1831, he moved to York, taking with him the *Patriot* newspaper, which he had started in 1828. He also represented Frontenac in the Assembly, 1828–30. Originally reform-minded, Dalton became a devoted tory and his newspaper became a strong, even intemperate, critic of reform.

his Extra published next day, that is Wednesday the 6th of December, mentions one hundred men who came from Scarborough last night, that was Tuesday the 5th, but that circumstance he has since forgotten in the overwhelming praises of the men of Gore, and in their praise I have no objections to join – for however delightful it may be for men to sound the trumpet of their own praise, still there is a certain sense of propriety in most men's characters, which forbids them from being too noisy in their own encomiums, as well as too loud in the censure of others.

There is one circumstance which does honour to Scarbsrough [sic], as well as to the Province. [sic] and which I cannot forbear to mention, and it is this: – During the the [sic] night of Tuesday, the 5th of December, the Revd. James George,[81] of the Scottish Presbyterian Church in Scarborough, arrived at the Market Square of Toronto City along with a number of Militiamen, for the Scarborough militia continued to arrive through the whole of the night, and the greater part of next day. The same Revd. Gentleman, already mentioned, armed and cross-belted himself for the fight, because he said he could not bear to see the British Ensign trampled in the dust. – Such conduct in a clergyman will be censured by those who are rebels in their heart, but praised by all loyal men, and Mr. George's private character is the best commentary on his political virtues. . . .

B 46   TORONTO THREATENED
[Christian Guardian, *Toronto, 6 Dec. 1837*]

Tuesday Morning.

REBELLION IN THE HOME DISTRICT! – TORONTO IN ARMS!!

While writing the foregoing article, little did we think that it would be our painful duty to state that Mazkenzie's [sic] measures were so far ripened into revolution as to lead already to armed opposition to the constituted authorities.

THIS IS THE FACT. An armed force is collected on Yonge-street, and is threatening an attack upon the City. The Governor, like a brave representative of his youthful Queen, is under arms at the head of several hundreds of loyal men. The streets are being barricaded. The garrison and the market buildings are placed in the best possible state of defence that the short notice would admit. Unless Divine Providence interfere, much blood will be shed.

[81]James George (1800–1870), a native of Scotland who was educated at the University of Glasgow, emigrated to the United States in 1829 and then to Upper Canada. In 1833 he joined the United Synod and was appointed to Scarborough but in 1834 he took his congregation into the Church of Scotland. A firm supporter of the established order, he led members of his St. Andrew's congregation into Toronto in December 1837 to fight the rebels. From 1853–62 he taught at Queen's College, Kingston.

Canadians of every class! *Canadian* REFORMERS! are you prepared to shed the blood of your country-men? Can anything Mackenzie can offer you compensate for the guilt you must incur if you enrol under his revolutionary banner, and *deluge your fruitful fields with blood*? For God's sake pause! Frown down the propagators of discord! Lift up your voices in prayer, and exert all your energies, to save your firesides and families from the untold horrors of civil war. The Royal Standard of Britain yet waves triumphantly, and invites the loyal and the good to unite in its defence, and still avail themselves of its PROTECTION against aggression.

B 47   THE LOYALISTS RALLY
[Christian Guardian, *Toronto, 6 Dec. 1837*]

POSTSCRIPT.

Tuesday, 6 P.M. – The rebel force, with MacKenzie at their head, are encamped on Gallows Hill, about a mile and a half from the City. An attack is threatened to night. May heaven avert it. Hundreds of the assailants must perish before the city can be carried.

Among the armed loyalists we recognize the Chief Justice, Judges Jones and McLean, the Vice Chancellor, and a large portion of the most respectable inhabitants of the place.

The strength of the rebels is variously reported from 600 to 1,500. About 1000 men are already well armed in the city, with some artillery.

Wednesday Morning, 8 o'clock.

Through the Divine mercy no disturbance has taken place in the City during the night. The rebels have fallen back from Gallows Hill, (perhaps there were some unpleasant associations connected with the name,) and have taken up their position, we understand, about three miles from the City. A reinforcement of about 70 loyalists arrived last night from Hamilton, under Colonel Allan MacNab, and about the same number from Scarborough. Constant accessions are coming in, and we understand it is intended to march out to day, and give battle to the insurgents. From the enthusiasm displayed by the loyalists, and the advantage they possess by having field-pieces under their command, and the justice of their cause, there is little doubt of success. . . .

Last night, about eight o'clock, a piquet guard of 32 men, under Sheriff Jarvis, was suddenly attacked by a large party of rifle-men, who opened upon them a smart fire, but happily without effect. It was briskly returned by the little band with more fatal precision. One of the assailants was left dead, and it is said that two others were carried off by the insurgents, mortally wounded.

Yesterday morning His Excellency humanely requested Drs. Rolph and Baldwin to visit the headquarters of the rebels, and to urge them in the name of humanity to desist from their wicked designs, and to return peaceably to their families, and thus prevent the effusion of blood. We understand that the appeal of His Excellency was touching and eloquent; but it was in vain. Mackenzie, who has now ventured his all, dictated terms which no Governor could asset to without forfeiting his honour and his head.

B 48   W.L. MACKENZIE'S ACCOUNT OF THE EVENTS OF 6 DECEMBER
[Jeffersonian, *Watertown, reprinted in* Mackenzie's Gazette, *New York City, 12 May 1838*]

For other extracts from this document see B 1, B 14, B 25, B 31, B 38, B 61.

. . . On Wednesday forenoon, I took a party with me to Dundas street intercepted the great western mail stage and took a number of prisoners, with the stage, mails and driver, up to our camp. The editors state that money was taken from the mail, which was not the case. But the letters of Mr. Sullivan, President of the Executive Council, Mr. Buchanan,[82] and others, conveyed useful information. We found they expected soon to have strength enough to attack us in the country, and I wrote to the executive in the city to give us timely notice of any such attack. Some of the leading reformers in the city had left it, *but not to join us* – others seemed to have lost their energies; neither messenger nor letter reached our camp; the executive was not there. One man on horseback told us we might be attacked on Thursday.

My chief hope lay in this, that if we were not attacked till Thursday night, vast reinforcements would join us from the outer townships, and that reformers at a distance would march to our aid, the moment they heard that we had struck for self-government. With this view, I sought to confine the attention of the enemy to the defence of the city and on Thursday morning selected 40 riflemen and 20 others to go down and burn the Don bridge, the eastern approach to Toronto, and the house at its end, to take the Montreal mail stage and mails, and to draw out the forces in that quarter if possible. I also proposed that the rest of our men who had arms, should take the direction of the city, and be ready to move either to the right or left, or to retreat to a strong position as

[82]Isaac Buchanan (1810–1883), a native of Glasgow, apprenticed with a local merchant in 1825 and was sent to Montreal in 1830 to help open a wholesale firm there. The business moved to Toronto in 1831 and in 1834 Buchanan and his brother Peter bought the firm out. Soon Isaac Buchanan and Company was doing extremely well, expanding to Hamilton in 1840 and to other cities, with various partners, in later years. Buchanan was one of the chief supporters of the Free Church in Canada West when it was created, a strong force in the Great Western Railway, and a vigorous and vocal proponent of various causes. He represented Toronto in the Assembly from 1841–4 and later sat for Hamilton. Though not attached to any party, his ideas were closest to those of the moderate conservatives. He even served briefly in the ministry in 1864. The crisis of 1857 and his devotion to too many other causes contributed to the failure of the various firms with which he was associated, and he lost most of his wealth before he died.

prudence might dictate. At this moment Colonel Van Egmond, a native of Holland, owning 13,000 acres of land in the Huron Tract, a tried patriot, and of great military experience under Napoleon, joined us, and one of the Capt's desired a council to be held, which was done. Col. V. approved of my plan, a party went off, set fire to the bridge, burnt the house, took the mails, and went through a part of the city unmolested. But the councilling and discussing of my project occasioned a delay of two hours which proved our ruin, for the enemy having obtained large reinforcements by the steamers [from] Cobourg, Niagara and Hamilton, resolved to attack us in three divisions, one of them to march up Yonge street, and the others by ways about a mile to the right and left of that road. Had our forces started in the morning, the party at the bridge would have interfered with and broken up the enemy's plan of attack, and we would have been in motion near Toronto, ready to retreat to some one of the commanding positions in its rear, or to join the riflemen below and there enter the city. . . .

B 49   INFORMATION OF GEORGE REED
13 December 1837
[PAO, Rebellion Papers, 1837-8, no. 9]

For other extracts from this document see B 29, B 32.

. . . On Wednesday I saw the rebels drilled at Montgomery's – . . . On Wednesday evening Mackenzie came into the prisoners room – boasted of having robbed the Mail, & found plenty of Money in the mail bags: he said that he would come to no terms with the Government whatever, except they would send home "Bond Head" & have no more such d_____d vagabonds sent to this country – that he would take the City & then have plenty of Money to pay all expences. . . .

B 50   INFORMATION OF JOHN LINFOOT
14 December 1837
[PAO, Rebellion Papers, 1837-8, no. 12]

For other extracts from this document see B 30, B 62.

. . . Mackenzie the next morning [Wednesday, 6 December] promised each man amongst them [the rebels at Montgomery's Tavern] three hundred acres of land if they would adhere to him, still telling them that there would be no difficulty in taking the City as there was a great part of the City would join them if they once made an entrance into it. On Wednesday Capn. Mathews arrived with a party of about Sixty. all this time a number of prisoners had continually been brought in as prisoners[.] On Wednesday night Coll. Van Egmond came and addressing himself to Mackenzie. Gibson & others stated that he could raise an army of about a Thousand men from the Huron Tract. he stated that he had just got the news and had started immediately. that he had five sons who were quite ready to start. On Thursday morning a party of the Rebels were ordered to proceed through the woods and fire the Don Bridge. I do not know who gave the orders. about sixty of their best riflemen accordingly left and I heard some person remark it was under the command of Capn Mathews. . . .

B 51　STATEMENT OF JAMES LATIMER
21 December 1837
[PAO, Rebellion Papers, 1837-8, no. 18]

For other extracts from this document see B 2, B 39.

. . . On Wednesday morning [6 December] I went out to Sheppards in a wagon that was going after flour – staid about three hours, & on my return to Montgomery's the word came that Mackenzie had robbed the Mail. The next morning I saw McKenzie throw some letters and papers out of the up-stairs window & the door below – by arms full – there were a number of Christian Guardians – he read two or three letters which he had taken out of the Mail to the people – there was one from Mr. Sullivan – one from young Thomas Moore,[83] & one from somebody in the Bank – Mr. Sullivans Letter was to his father in Law[84] – they all spoke about the Warlike preparations in the City – some of the passages in the letters excited a good deal of merriment among the crowd. On Thursday morning I told some person, who told McKenzie that I should return to town: when he told me that he wanted me to convey three letters – *all to be left at Dr. Rolph's* – some, proposed, that I should secrete the Letters in my shoes, & some proposed that I should put them between my shirt & my flannel shirt. I told McKenzie that I was afraid that as I was known to belong to his office, I should most likely be arrested, and the letters would be discovered – McKenzie said that on second thought it was better that *I* should not carry the letters, & I did not. . . .

[83]Thomas Moore may have been the son of Thomas Moore, a tailor from England who kept the Crown Inn on King Street at the market.
[84]Sullivan's father-in-law from his second marriage, which occurred in 1833, was Lieutenant-Colonel Philip Delatre of Stamford, Upper Canada.

B 52   STATEMENT OF CHARLES CROCKER[85] AND JOSEPH
MATTHEWS[86]
6 April 1838
[*PAC, Upper Canada State Papers, v. 45, pp. 36-7*]

The *Queen vs. Peter Matthews*

Charles Crocker now a prisoner in the Gaol of the Home District, and
Joseph Matthews also a prisoner in the said Gaol severally make oath
and say that they were of the party seduced by Wm. Lyon McKenzie
on the seventh of december last to proceed to the Don bridge for the
purpose of making a diversion at that point and preventing an Attack
by the Queens forces up Yonge street, that the men selected for this
service were placed under the Command of Peter Matthews, that
deponents verily believe that the most of the men so selected were
strangers to and entirely unknown to the said Peter Matthews, that at
the time of starting, William Lyon McKenzie as deponents were
afterwards informed by some of the Company, but not by Peter
Matthews gave orders to fire the house of the late Simon Washburn[87]
[–] That upon their march it appeared evident to deponents that the said
Peter Matthews had no command of the men as the majority of them
went where, and did, as they pleased; That deponents further say that
they were close to the said Peter Matthews when they got to the house
and bridge and are certain the said Peter Matthews never entered the
said house and they are as certain he did not set fire to either the house
or bridge, and deponents further say that the said Peter Matthews gave
no orders whatever to set fire to the bridge or house or to the house of
any other person which deponents must have heard if such orders had
been given [–] And deponents further say that the said house and
bridge or one of them was set on fire, to the best of their belief by one
Landon Wurtz[88] without the approbation or concurrence of the said

[85]Charles Crocker (b. 1804 or 1805) came from England about 1829 with his father
and settled on part of lot 16, concession 6 of Pickering Township. Active in the
political union movement prior to the rebellion, he took up arms with Peter Matthews.
He was arrested in mid-December and held until May 1838, when he was pardoned.
He, his brother Wickham, and Joseph Matthews fled to the United States in the fall of
1838, having already been there, probably in connection with Patriot activities.
[86]Joseph Matthews was the brother of Peter. He owned half of lot 30, concession 6
of Pickering Township. Arrested in mid-December 1837 for his part in the Toronto
rising, he was pardoned in May. He journeyed to the United States once or twice in
1838 and was reported to have returned with plans to overthrow the government.
[87]Simon E. Washburn (1793?–1837), who was born in Canada, studied law with
William Warren Baldwin. He was called to the bar in 1820 and then became Baldwin's
partner, the partnership being dissolved in 1825. He was clerk of the Home District,
1828–37, and an alderman in Toronto in 1837.
[88]Landon Wurtz, the son-in-law of a United Empire Loyalist, had bought one
quarter of lot 27, concession 5 of Pickering Township in 1831 and one quarter of lot 26
in 1835. It is likely that he belonged to the Wixon Baptist Church on concession 7.
Although indicted for his role in burning the Don Bridge, he could not be tried as he
had fled to the United States. His property, however, was confiscated.

Peter Matthews [–] That upon some person whom deponents do not now recollect speaking of setting fire to the bridge, the said Peter Matthews positively forbid the same[,] giving as a reason that the bridge was of as much use to our party as the other – And deponents further say that after the bridge was discovered to be on fire the said Peter Matthews sent deponents back to put the fire out, that deponents upon such orders returned and used their best endeavours to extinguish the fire, till they were obliged to retreat from being fired upon by some persons on the town side, And this deponent Joseph Matthews further saith that at the two several times that the mails were stoped the said Peter Matthews was in the rear at some distance and gave no orders for their being detained, and that to the best of this deponents knowledge nothing was taken from the mails on either occasion. –

B 53   STATEMENT OF GEORGE AUBURN[89]
ca. 15 December 1837
[PAC, Upper Canada Sundries, v. 180, p. 99017]

I was coming up the road on Thursday last near Mr. Wm. Hewards[.] I heard some shots fired, towards the Don Bridge – I ran up the road as fast as I could [–] when I came to my house I saw the smoke beginning to rise at the house which was burned – then I went into my house. I saw the party under Peter Matthews formed in a line near my house[.] I went to him and patted my hand on his shoulder and begged him to spare my house, he was quite Civil, they then went Eastward [–] he was nearly in the Centre of the body – I heard him distinctly say to some of the persons near him "have you fired the Don Bridge [–"] he swore at them and called the men back [–] they went back [–] I did not go with them but I heard afterwards that the bridge had been fired [–] I saw a Man. a Servant of Mr. Burrow's. shot, and fall off his horse. he was coming up the road and the shot was fired from behind a fence by one of Matthews party –

B 54   STATEMENT OF JOHN ROTH
ca. 15 December 1837
[PAC, Upper Canada Sundries, v. 180, p. 99031]

I was in Company with John Irvine, the witness at Burnetts on Thursday[;] the rebels took us thence[.] I heard they were 53 in number[.] They were all armed. They robbed me of a razor which was in my Coat Pocket. They took a knife from Irvine. On our way to the Don Bridge the rebels fired at some persons near Scaddings[90] – On our arrival at the Bridge they fired at some men running towards the City[.]

[89]George Auburn lived on the Kingston Road on the York Township side of the Don near the river.

[90]This was the house built by John Scadding (1754–1824), who accompanied John Graves Simcoe as property manager to Upper Canada. He only partially developed the

I saw Smith the servant of Mr. Burrows shot from his horse by the Rebels – Matthews and his party passed the Bridge towards the City[.] I and Turner stayed near the toll bar[.] Before they went through the Bridge the houses of Burrows and Stafford were set on fire – I heard Matthews say it was down [done] by his orders[.] I do not know by whose hands the buildings were fired but I saw two of Matthew's party coming out of the premises of Mr. Burrows before the house was in flames: but I saw smoke coming out of the windows[.] I heard Matthews order them to set fire to Smith's[91] house: but John Anderson said there had been enough set fire to – I do not recollect having heard Matthews order the bridge to be burnt: but I saw that it had been set on fire –

B 55   FRANCIS LOGAN[92] TO SIR F.B. HEAD
Toronto Township, 7 December 1837
[*PAC, Upper Canada Sundries, v. 180, pp. 99027-9*]

. . .In consequence of certain occurrences in this neighbourhood yesterday, I trouble your Excellency with this letter, and beg to inform you that Col. Wm. Thompson[93] came to the Village of Cooksville, to call out the Militia, to go to Toronto, when the majority of the inhabitants refused, and I observed a large proportion of them with rifles in their hands, although they had positively refused to join the militia, and I have reason to believe that most of these men were attached to the radical party. Under these circumstances I thought it advisable to propose to the principal inhabitants to meet me there in the evening, intending to see how far I could bring them to their duty, and with some difficulty succeeded in persuading them to sign a document, of which the following is a copy:

We the undersigned loyal subjects of her Britannic Majesty Queen Victoria, inhabitants of Springfield Cooksville and their vicinity having understood that serious disturbances have prevailed in some parts of the province do hereby mutually agree not to take up arms, except for the preservation and safety, of the persons property and families of ourselves and our neighbours residing in the above mentioned places and consider this agreement to be binding on us respectively so long as it does not interfere with the present constitution.

---

grant he was given before returning with Simcoe to England. In 1818 or 1819 Scadding visited the property and had a proper house built so that he could bring out his wife and son.

[91]A William Smith owned this house.

[92]Francis Logan bought half of lot 9, concession N1 (north of Dundas Street), old survey, in 1829.

[93]William Thomson (b. 1796), the son of a United Empire Loyalist, fought in the War of 1812. In 1814 he inherited his father's property. He was appointed colonel of militia in 1830, and was a magistrate and a member of the Church of England. From 1824 to 1828 he sat for York and Simcoe counties in the Assembly.

This document though not so satisfactory as I could have wished was as much as I could obtain from them and indeed knowing that I was acting on my own responsibility and without any orders from higher authority I felt some hesitation in acting in the matter[.] I am carefully watching the motions of the radical party as, I have no doubt, they are attentively noticing mine and shall feel honoured by receiving whatever advice and directions that your Excellency may deem necessary.

B 56   J.E. SMALL TO COL. JAMES FITZGIBBON
Toronto, 7 December 1837
[PAC, Correspondence of the Provincial Secretary's Office, v. 9, file 1157]

Whether the views I entertained of my dismissal from the rank I held in the Militia were correct or otherwise, or whether the political course I pursued as a Reformer in opposition to the views of Government was the correct one, it is not now necessary to discuss – It is only necessary for me to know, to deplore, the fact of my native Country being in a state of Civil war – A state which calls upon every lover of good order to stand forward in Vindication of the Laws of the land – And altho' a Reformer, as I never have, and trust I never shall be a Revolutionist, I cannot witness the lawless destruction of private property that has taken place within the last [ten?] days, without tendering to you my services, as I now do most heartily, should they be deemed acceptable and any further disturbances were to require them – And I am requested by a number of my neighbours, Good Reformers, but not Revolutionists, to state that they will be most happy to accompany me in the protection of the laws, whenever you may signify that our services are required. –

P.S. It may be said by my enemies that I offer my services only when there is no necessity – I can only say let them not flatter themselves that all is over, I trust it may be, but I doubt it –

B 57   JOHN G. HOWARD[94] AND THE EVENTS OF 7 DECEMBER
[MTPL, John G. Howard Papers, Mrs. Howard[95] to her sister, Toronto, Feb. 1838]

. . . at 8 we marched out first, our company consisted of 16[,] a very

[94]John George Howard (1803–1890) was born John Corby at Bengeo, Hertfordshire, England. Trained as a carpenter and architect, he moved in 1832 to Upper Canada, where prospects of employment seemed better, changing his name on the way. His drawings won favour with the lieutenant-governor and he was employed at Upper Canada College, becoming first drawing master in 1839. He remained at the college until the mid-1850s but meanwhile designed many public and private buildings. He also passed the provincial surveyor's examination and, after some work in Toronto, became city surveyor, 1843–55. After 1855 he retired to his estate, doing some painting and speculating in land. His account of his activities is reproduced by Mrs. Howard in her letter to her sister.

[95]Jemima Frances (Meikle) Howard (1802–1877) had married John Howard in

indifferent troop[,] my friend and I had practised rifle shooting together therefore could depend upon each other and resolved should either of us be hit to remain with him, we were informed the rebels were about 5 or 6 hundred strong[,] our whole army amounted to about 15 hundred raw militia but well armed with Muskets and Bayonets, our orders were to scour the Bush and on no account to retreat as the main body would support us[,] our little band of 16 marched out first and left the road[,] I soon found what mettle my Men were made of[,] while the Cannon were at their heels they were regular fire eaters but we no sooner left the road then they said it was not right to send them on so dangerous an expedition, I must confess I thought I had brought myself and friend into a mess and we were within ½ a mile of a thick copse from which I expected the enemy, I therefore advised them to keep a sharp look out or they might have a bullet in them before they could say Jack Robinson[,] my friend I advised to make himself as small as possible and if he saw any one to make for the first stump, we had not gone far before I observed three Men evidently watching our motions[,] one with a pike the other two with cloaks on, between us and them was a deeper ravine full of stumps and fallen trees[,] I and my friend drew upon it by degrees and examined every stump as minutely as we could[,] the three Men were about 400 yards from us[,] I drew up our Men in file and called out to the Men to surrender but they paid no attention[.] I threatened to fire upon them[,] still they would not move[,] I then fired my rifle over their heads and two of them immediately ran down the Hill towards us, the other would not stir, I told my friend to fire[,] this caused him to dodge backwards and forwards[,] still he would not surrender[,] the whole platoon of 14 Men then fired which so frightened him that he ran into the Bush and got away, I found by this what sort of shots my Men were[,] some of their Bullets I do not think went within 50 yards of the Man, we took the two Prisoners, our firing caused the main body to rush forward so that I and my friend had the honor of firing the first shots, we battered down Montgomery's Tavern the rendevouz of the Rebels[,] the enemy would not come to an engagement which was fortunate as we must have wounded or killed some of our people whom they had got as Prisoners[,] I believe about 60[,] most of them respectable people living in and about the town[,] those of course they were obliged to leave who gladly returned to their homes[,] walking or rather running about all day we returned home completely tired about 7 with our Prisoners[,] at 9 went to bed. . . .

London, England in 1827, emigrating with him to Upper Canada in 1832. The couple were childless. She was invalided in her last years.

B 58   SIR F.B. HEAD TO LORD GLENELG
Toronto, 19 December 1837
[*F.B. Head*, A Narrative *(London, 1839), pp. 326-41*]

For other extracts from this document see B 15, B 22.

. . . on Thursday morning, I assembled our forces, under the direction
of the Adjutant-General of militia, Colonel Fitzgibbon, clerk of the
House of Assembly.

The principal body was headed by the Speaker, Colonel Allan
M'Nab, the right wing being commanded by Colonel Samuel Jarvis,[96]
the left by Colonel William Chisholm,[97] assisted by the Honourable
Mr. Justice M'Lean, late Speaker of the House of Assembly; the two
guns by Major Carfrae[98] of the militia artillery.

The command of the militia left in the city remained under Mr.
Justice Macaulay,[99] and the protection of the city with Mr. Gurnett,
the mayor.

I might also have most advantageously availed myself in the field of
the military services of Colonel Foster,[100] the Commander of the

[96]Samuel Peters Jarvis (1792–1857) was the son of a loyalist officer who
accompanied John Graves Simcoe to Upper Canada. Born at Niagara, his studies of
law were interrupted by service in the War of 1812. Called to the bar in 1815, he
served in the provincial secretary's office from 1814 to 1839. From 1837 to 1845 he
was chief superintendent of Indian affairs. From 1825 to 1844 and again in 1846 he
was a director of the Bank of Upper Canada. He saw service in 1837–8, reorganizing
the Queen's Rangers in the process.

[97]William Chisholm (1788–1842) was born in Nova Scotia, his father being a
loyalist soldier. In 1791 the family moved to Upper Canada and settled on Burlington
Bay. The father and three sons served in the War of 1812, William being a lieutenant
in a flank company. In 1816 Chisholm became a captain in the 2nd Gore militia, in
1824 lieutenant-colonel, and in 1831 colonel. He was a magistrate and a very
prosperous merchant. His prosperity was helped by land he received for his war effort,
land which was granted slowly because he supported Robert Gourlay's convention. A
moderate tory, he sat in the Assembly, 1820–4, 1830–4, and 1836–41, losing the
intervening elections. Considered a fair man even by his opponents, he was most
interested in educational and religious issues, being a strong Church of England
supporter. In December 1837 he led the militia from Trafalgar to assist the government
and commanded the left wing of the loyalist force on 7 December.

[98]Thomas Carfrae (1796–1841) came from Edinburgh, Scotland, to York with his
father and family about 1805 when his father opened a store on King Street. Thomas
retired from the business in 1833, one year after his father, who provided him with a
competency. He was appointed collector of customs at Toronto in 1835 and
harbourmaster in 1838, two posts he retained until his death. In addition, he served on
the first city council, 1834–5, and was appointed a magistrate in 1837. He helped to
found the York Fire Company, the York Mechanics' Institute, the. St. Andrew's
Society, the St. George's Lodge of Freemasonry, and several other institutions. He
was a major in the 1st East York Artillery, which he also helped to establish.

[99]James Buchanan Macaulay (1793–1859) was born at Newark (Niagara) and served
in the War of 1812. He was called to the bar in 1822. In 1829 he was appointed to the
Court of King's Bench; in 1849 he became chief justice of the Court of Common Pleas
and in 1857 he was made a judge of the Court of Error and Appeal.

[100]Colley Lyons Lucas Foster (d. 1843), an Irishman, joined the British army in

forces in Upper Canada, of Captain Baddeley of the corps of Royal Engineers, and of a detachment of eight artillerymen, who form the only regular force in this province; but, having deliberately determined that the important contest in which I was about to be engaged should be decided solely by the Upper Canada militia, or, in other words, by the free inhabitants of this noble province, I was resolved that no consideration whatever should induce me to avail myself of any other assistance than that upon which, as the representative of our gracious Sovereign, I had firmly and implicitly relied.

At twelve o'clock the militia force marched out of the town, with an enthusiasm which it would be impossible to describe, and in about an hour we came in sight of the rebels, who occupied an elevated position near Gallows Hill, in front of Montgomery's tavern, which had long been the rendezvous of Mr. M'Kenzie's men. They were principally armed with rifles, and for a short time, favoured by buildings, they endeavoured to maintain their ground; however, the brave and loyal militia of Upper Canada, steadily advancing with a determination which was irresistible, drove them from their position, completely routed Mr. M'Kenzie, who, in a state of the greatest agitation ran away, and in a few minutes Montgomery's tavern, which was first entered by Mr. Justice Jones, was burnt to the ground.

Being on the spot merely as a civil Governor, and in no way in command of the troops, I was happy to have an opportunity of demonstrating to the rebels the mildness and beneficence of Her Majesty's Government, and, well knowing that the laws of the country would have ample opportunity of making examples of the guilty, I deemed it advisable to save the prisoners who were taken, and to extend to most of these misguided men the royal mercy, by ordering their immediate release. These measures having been effected, and the rebels having been deprived of their flag (on which was inscribed in large letters

"BIDWELL, and the glorious minority!

"1837, and a good beginning!")
the militia advanced in pursuit of the rebels about four miles, till they reached the house of one of the principal ringleaders, Mr. Gibson, which residence it would have been impossible to have saved, and it was consequently burned to the ground*. . . .

*By my especial orders.

1799 and came to British North America in 1813 as the aide-de-camp and military secretary of Sir Gordon Drummond. In 1814 he became the assistant adjutant general of the Canadian militia and the next year the assistant adjutant general of the forces in all British North America and commander of the regular troops in Upper Canada. In January 1838, after the *Caroline* affair, Colborne had him take command of the Upper Canadian militia, in addition to the regulars in the colony.

B 59   LADY HEAD TO FRANK HEAD
Toronto, 13 December 1837
[Bodleian Library, University of Oxford, Letters of Sir Francis and Lady Head to Frank Head, microfilm in PAO]

For other extracts of this document see B 17, B 24, B 41.

. . . On Thursday before we thought the troops could have reached Montgomery s Tavern where the rebels were quartered the Mayor came galloping up to the side of the wharf and calling for me presented me with a flag your father had sent me with *Bidwell and Reform*, on it & in an extascy of delight shouted out of the intelligence of the defeat of the Rebels

Orris followed your father the whole day – a man took aim – at your father from the top of a pine tree but it waved about with him & by the mercy of God he missed his fatal purpose – a boy seeing something move in the tree fired & shot him dead – the rebels fired too high so that none of their bullets took effect – On Thursday night we all returned home and your father is now quite well & bears up wonderfully against the press of business which has fallen on him. . . .

Dr Duncome is at the head of 200 men in this Province.

B 60   THE REBELS DEFEATED
[Christian Guardian, *Toronto, 13 Dec. 1837*]

TOTAL DEFEAT OF THE REBELS!

Last week we gave a statement of the commencement of the insurrection in this District, and its progress up to Wednesday morning; . . . During Wednesday large numbers of loyal volunteers were constantly coming in, and most vigourous [*sic*] measures were adopted for the defence of the city, and for the dispersion of the rebels. The state of public feeling was roused to the highest pitch of indignation on learning that Mackenzie and a band of desperadoes had stopped the mails, and *robbed* the bags and the passengers of all the money on which they could lay their hands! as also on learning from various prisoners that were brought in that his plan was to fire the City in various quarters, by force or stealth, and thus reduce it to ashes, and its inhabitants to destitution. All the fire companies were held in readiness, strong patroles paraded all the streets, piquet guards were posted at the various avenues leading to the City; the Bank, the market and parliament buildings, and the garrison were placed in a state of defence, and filled with armed men. Happily for the rebels, they did not venture to advance on the City. Had they done so, scarcely a man could by any possibility have escaped.

On Thursday about twelve o'clock a large armed force marched out in three columns to attack the enemy at their head quarters. The centre column advanced up Yonge Street, led on by the Lieutenant Governor in person, accompanied by two field pieces, (6 pounders) and a company of cavalry. The left column marched up the College Avenue, west of Yonge Street, and the right column, who marched some time before the others scoured the woods to the east. On the centre column approaching Montgomery's Inn, the enemy was discovered drawn up on the road, and about 100 of them advanced down the hill to oppose the progress of the loyalists. On the division in advance opening to the right and left, however, to uncover the artillery, the whole body of the enemy *prudently* fled to the woods, their march being quickened by several discharges of canister. From the edge of the woods they opened a shower of rifle balls, which was promptly returned from the artillery, and from several divisions of infantry, who advanced to dislodge them. After exchanging a few volleys, the enemy fled in every direction. On approaching to Montgomery's house, which was supposed to be occupied by the rebels, three round shot were fired through it, on which *Capt.* Gibson, who with about 30 rifle men had a number of prisoners in charge, retreated, but being closely pressed abandoned his charge and took refuge in the woods, leaving his horse and his arms. Mackenzie is said to have been seen endeavouring to rally his men, and on finding his efforts impracticable galloped off up Yonge Street accompanied by five or six others. . . .

After scouring the woods, and ascertaining the total dispersion of the enemy, an advance was ordered to Hogg's Mills where a party of them was said to be collected. On arriving there, however, not a trace of them could be found, and the volunteers returned to the City, where they arrived about 5 o'clock.

While the main body of the rebels was being dispersed, a detachment of about 70 of their riflemen made a detour through the woods, and came suddenly to the Don Bridge at the east end of the City, which, with a number of buildings, they basely set on fire. Two companies of men were immediately marched out, who dispersed them after killing one of them. The bridge was saved; but the buildings, which were the property of the widow of the late S. Washburn, Esq., were entirely destroyed. . . .

The rebel force, before the action was variously estimated by their partizans at from 1000 to 1400; but since the defeat they report it as having been only from 500 to 600. The volunteer force which marched against them was about 1500 strong. The loss on the part of Mackenzie's dupes is supposed to be 11 killed, (7 have been positively ascertained,) and 14 wounded; some of them, as we know, dangerously. On the part of the volunteers, only three wounded, all slightly, and no loss of life.

B 61 W.L. MACKENZIE ON THE EVENTS OF 7 DECEMBER
[Jeffersonian, *Watertown, reprinted in* Mackenzie's Gazette, *New York City, 12 May 1838*]

For other extracts from this document see B 1, B 14, B 25, B 31, B 38, B 48.

. . . We were still at the hotel, discussing what was best to be done, when one of the guards told us that the enemy was marching up with music and artillery, and within a mile of us. Our people immediately prepared for battle, I rode down towards the enemy, doubting the intelligence, until within a short distance I saw them with my own eyes. I rode quickly back, asked our men if they were ready to fight a greatly superior force, well armed, and with artillery well served. They were ready, and I bade them go to the woods and do their best. They did so, and never did men fight more courageously. In the face of a heavy fire of grape and cannister [*sic*], with broadside following broadside of musketry in steady and rapid succession, they stood their ground firmly, and killed and wounded a large number of the enemy, but were at length compelled to retreat. In a more favorable position, I have no doubt but that they would have beaten off their assaillants [*sic*] with immense loss. As it was they had only three killed and three or four wounded. I felt anxious to go to Montgomery's for my portfolio and papers, which were important, but it was out of the question, so they fell into the hands of Sir Francis. – All my papers previous to the events of that week I had destroyed, except a number of business letters, and these it took my family upwards of an hour and a quarter to burn. But with all my caution, some letters fell into their hands to the injury of others.

The manly courage with which two hundred farmers, miserably armed, withstood the formidable attack of an enemy 1200 strong, and who had plenty of ammunition, with new muskets and bayonets, artillery, first rate European officers, and the choice of a position of attack, convinces me that discipline, order, obedience and subordination, under competent leaders, would enable them speedily to attain a confidence sufficient to foil even the regulars from Europe. About 200 of our friends stood at the tavern during the battle, being unarmed.

Mr. Fletcher, Col. Van Egmond, myself and others, held a consultation near Hogg's Hollow, and concluded that it would be useless to re-assemble our scattered forces, for that without arms success would be doubtful. I instantly determined to pass over to the United States, and accomplished my purpose in three days, travelled 125 miles, was seen by 2000 persons at least, and with a reward of 4000 dollars advertised for my head, speedily reached Buffalo. . . .

As to Sir Francis Head's story of 10,000 men instantly making to the capital to support him, it is a sheer fabrication. If that were true, why has a law become necessary since to suspend the trial by jury? Why were his family confined for two days on board a steamboat? Why did he send us a flag of truce on Tuesday, when all the force he could muster was 150 men and boys, out of a population of 20,000 in and near to Toronto? – The truth is, that thousands were on their way to join us on Thursday evening, that being the regular time for which the towns had been summoned; and they, on learning that we were dispersed, made a virtue of necessity, and professed that they had come to aid the tories! Sir Francis, says in his speech, they were "generally speaking, without arms;" and in fact most of them had none to bring. That was the grand difficulty; and would have been remedied had our movement been delayed till Thursday, as agreed on. Very few Militia men in U.C. had been entrusted with arms, and of these few the government had endeavoured, through Capt. Magrath[101] and others, to deprive them previous to the outbreak.

The burning of Mr. Gibson's house, stables, and outhouses, by the order and in the presence of Governor Head, was highly disgraceful to him, and is a stain upon his reputation. Dr. Horne's premises were head quarters to the spies and trators who infested our camp, and used for the purposes of the enemy, but this was not the case with those of Mr. Gibson. Yet government destroyed them and carried off his cattle! horses, grain, and property, and used or sold it and kept the money.

The moveables of hundreds of others were taken in the same way. Sir Francis' advisers may live to see this example followed more extensively than they desire. When the reformers destroyed the house of Dr. Horne, they did not carry off to the value of one farthing of his effects. As to Sheriff Jarvis's premises, they would have been burnt but for two reasons – 1st, we had no proof that the Sheriff's house was used as a rendezvous for our enemies; and 2ndly, there were sick people in it, whom we did not wish to make war upon.

About 3,500 persons joined us during the three days on which we were behind Toronto. . . .

B 62   INFORMATION OF JOHN LINFOOT
14 December 1837
[*PAO, Rebellion Papers, 1837–8, no. 12*]

For other extracts from this document see B 30, B 50.

. . . about half an hour after this party [the rebels who were to fire the Don Bridge] had departed. the guard brought in word that the enemy were coming up the street. Mackenzie Gibson and Fletcher ordered

[101]"Captain Magrath" was probably James Magrath (b. 1804 or 1805), the son of the Rev. James Magrath of Erindale, Toronto Township. The family had come out from Ireland in 1827. The younger Magrath was a merchant, an Orangeman, and an arch-tory. James was deputy grandmaster of the Orange Lodge of British North America in 1838. He was also a major of militia in 1837 but Mackenzie may have been using a more familiar designation in referring to him as "Captain Magrath."

them all to turn out. After several rounds had been fired. Watson the Elder[102] came in and ordered the prisoners to be brought out[.] Gibson then came in. both of whom took charge and marched them up the Street as far as Mr Hewsons and I saw no more of them. After the first ball had passed through the house I left it and went toward Sniders and I met Mackenzie coming from behind the house, who spoke to Van Egmond who was also there and asked him what was best to be done. he[,] Van Egmond[,] asked him what had become of the men. Mackenzie replied he had no command over them. Van Egmond said we must retreat. Mackenzie got on a horse that was running loose in the street and rode off. . . .

B 63   INFORMATION OF ARCHIBALD MACDONELL
Toronto, 20 December 1837
[*PAC, Upper Canada Sundries, v. 180, pp. 99588-91*]

For another extract from this document see B 21.

. . . We were again kept close Prisoners [of the rebels] until Thursday – on that morning we saw the Militia coming out – we saw a general muster of the Rebels at the front of the House. They marched down the Street and took to the Woods – Additional Guards were put over the Prisoners who were kept in the Ball Room at Montgomery's House – After about six rounds of Cannon were fired an Order was given to turn the Prisoners into the Street where we were strongly guarded – Mr Gibson came up and ordered us to march up Yonge Street – we went up about three quarters of a Mile – we were then countermarched as far as the edge of the Woods in the rear of Mr Hewson's house [–] We were halted there – Mr Gibson went to the top of the hill [–] he soon returned and marched us further towards the Woods – we soon afterwards saw some horsemen coming up the Lane when three Cheers were given by the Prisoners and the Guards decamped – Afterwards one of the Guards on – horseback (whom I have since seen in Gaol and identified to be William Alves[103]) pointed the Gun at my breast with the evident intention of shooting me as I supposed – I seized a gun from one of the Rebels when several persons called out why dont you shoot that man –

---

[102]Leonard Watson (b. *ca.* 1783) was an Englishman by birth and was, in 1837, a road contractor employing a large number of men engaged in macadamizing Yonge Street. A freeholder, Watson and two of his sons were involved in the rebellion. He was arrested after the defeat of 7 December and, after petitioning for pardon, was ordered transported. While passing through England, he and the other Canadian prisoners were released by the courts.

[103]William Alves (b. *ca.* 1816) came with his parents from Torres, Scotland, to Upper Canada in 1834. He worked as a carpenter and joiner in the London District and in the United States until May 1837, when he moved to Toronto to support his parents. In December 1837 he was working at Montgomery's Tavern. Captured after the rebellion was crushed, he petitioned and was ordered transported for fourteen years. He was released by the courts while passing through England.

Judge Jones rode up and Alves and all the party retreated into the woods – On the road I had had a conversation with Alves and expressed my regret at the people being concerned in such transactions when he said "it is a glorious cause and I will die in it". . . .

B 64   DIARY OF REV. FEATHERSTONE OSLER[104]
[Records of the Lives of Ellen Free Pickton and Featherstone Lake Osler *(Toronto, 1915), pp. 171-3*]

Monday [4 December] – Whilst at Captain Hill's[105] the alarming and unexpected intelligence was brought to us of an insurrection, and that a party of rebels had marched that morning towards Toronto, with the avowed purpose of attacking the city and plundering the bank early the following morning. At first we could scarcely give credence to the report, but the neighbouring gentlemen speedily assembling at Captain Hill's house to consult on measures to be adopted for the public welfare put it beyond doubt. As there was every reason to believe that the Governor had not the slightest suspicion of such a movement, messengers were dispatched to try to elude the rebels and give information in the city. These were, however, soon taken prisoners. In the evening Mr. Carthew[106] determined to go on as far as possible to obtain information. After riding nearly the whole of the night he returned on Tuesday morning, bringing with him the intelligence that the rebels had shot Col. Moodie, and that one of the rebels' captains, named Anderson, was also killed. The people seemed panic-struck, and but few assembled for the purpose of defence, the people of Newmarket being mostly a miserable, disaffected set. In the afternoon left Newmarket for Tecumseth. Took dispatches to Holland Landing and Bradford, to raise men and search for arms. Met many small parties of men on the road; many, however, unarmed. Cheered them on and gave as much encouragement as possible, but the general cry was, "We have no arms, what can we do?" At a late hour on Tuesday night I was riding, giving intelligence, stirring up the men, and quieting the women; stating what I believed to be the fact, that the only

[104]Featherstone Lake Osler (1805–1895) was born in Falmouth, England, and went to sea at an early age, later joining the navy. Finding chances of advancement slim, he took religious orders and, because of his travelling experience, was persuaded to go to Canada, arriving in the spring of 1837 in Tecumseth Township. During the rebellion he encouraged the men of his area to go to the aid of the government. He later served the church in the Dundas–Hamilton area.

[105]"Captain Hill" was a captain on half-pay who had come out to Upper Canada with his family in 1833 and settled on lot 93, concession 1 of Whitchurch Township. He was a member of the Church of England.

[106]Arthur Carthew (d. 1878) was of Cornish origin. He came to Upper Canada in 1830 on half-pay from the 64th Regiment. Originally settled near Kempenfeldt Bay, he moved to Yonge Street near Newmarket in 1837, where he bought and developed a farm. He was a member of the Church of England. In 1837 he was lieutenant-colonel of the militia north of the oak ridges.

means of safety was for the men to turn out and meet them boldly. Things, however, wore a very miserable aspect, and the few valuables or rather the little specie I had I buried, that in case of the rebels taking everything else – as there was little doubt but they would should they gain the upper hand – we might not, if our lives were spared, be quite destitute.

Tuesday night. – I lay down, but scarcely to close my eyes for sleep, at Mr. Robinson's,[107] when in the middle of the night Mr. Jeff[108] came to tell me what he had done, and to ask advice.

Wednesday morning. – Gave my gun to Mr. Robinson to arm one man. Met Chapman, who, in the midst of all the excitement, wished me to marry him on that day, which, as he had procured a licence, I could not refuse to do. Just as I was leaving my hut, met Mrs. Phillips, who told me that her husband was apparently sinking fast. Went to see him; found him in a kind of stupor; read and prayed with him. Mr. Hurst[109] also came to ask what he should say to a number of men who had come to ask his advice about going to the war, as the women were half frantic. Told him it was the duty of every man who could possibly go not to hold back in the present emergency. Mr. Hurst also gave me a most gratifying account of the Sunday School which he superintends. Supplied him with some books and tracts.

In the afternoon started for Newmarket; overtook a party of Loyalists on horseback on the way to Bradford. At Bradford found about 200 men collected, the principal of whom begged me to stop and consult with them on the best measures to be adopted. They called a council to elect me a member, and after some discussion it was determined to march with a body of about 500 early on Friday morning, and in the meanwhile to collect all the arms and ammunition possible. Took on dispatches to Holland Landing and Newmarket. Reached Captain Hill's house late in the evening, having met Capt. H. and his eldest son on the road. Between 11 and 12 I was about to retire to bed, when Mr. Carthew called me to say that there was good reason to believe that a party of rebels intended to attack the house that night, and therefore it was necessary to be on the watch. The ladies, Mrs. Hill and Mrs. Carthew, and my E.,[110] with the children, who had all

---

[107]This was the house of W.B. Robinson.

[108]Edward Jeff came with his father and family from County Armagh, Ireland, in 1820 to Penetanguishene. In 1829 he moved to lot 3, concession 6 of West Gwillimbury Township, where he built a house and barn. He was a member of Featherstone Osler's Church of England congregation.

[109]This was probably Thomas Hurst, who lived on lot 16, concession 8 of Tecumseth Township.

[110]This was Ellen Free (Pickton) Osler (1806–1907) who had been born near London, England, into a merchant family. Adopted by her aunt and uncle, she was sent to boarding school at an early age. In 1837 she married Featherstone Lake Osler, whom she had known for some years, and emigrated with him to Upper Canada.

assembled together for mutual support, had retired. Mr. C. and myself, with Captain Hill's two boys, kept guard with four loaded guns. Between twelve and one dispatches came from the Governor stating that he intended attacking the rebels on the following afternoon, and for all the force that could be raised to come down and check the rebels in the rear. Mr C. immediately left to raise men, leaving the two boys and myself to guard the house. At every sound we heard and every bark of the dogs we ran out with our guns, but the Lord protected us and saved us from an attack.

Thursday. – Was a day of anxiety and suspense. No certain intelligence was to be had, though there were rumours innumerable. At night it was reported that the rebels intended probably to burn the property of all who were opposed to them. The inhabitants of Newmarket formed a body of men to watch, which we knew nothing of, and were not a little startled, after retiring to bed, at hearing a great knocking at the doors and the windows. The whole house was in commotion, but we were not a little relieved when we found that the knocking was by the men who had been appointed to watch opposite Capt. H.'s house. After this we slept more composedly.

Friday morning. – Rode into Newmarket for intelligence, and was told that Toronto was burnt by the rebels. This I could scarcely believe, and rode a little distance down Yonge Street to try and pick up some certain information. I then learned that not Toronto but Montgomery's tavern, a very large building near the city, which the rebels used as a barracks, was burnt and the rebels routed.

Friday night. – There was again a dread of fire, and a man came to the house on purpose to tell us that the rebels were determined on burning the property out of revenge. This kept us again on the watch, but no attempt was made, though in the early part of the night we were startled at hearing a shot fired. One of the men on guard was certain, as he said, that he saw something lurking near the farm. He hailed, but as no answer was returned he fired. It was afterwards discovered that he had fired at his own shadow, which, of course, moved as he moved.

B 65   JOURNAL OF MARY O'BRIEN[111]
[PAO, Mary Sophia O'Brien Journals, Journal 118]

. . . last night [5 December] news was brought that they [the rebels] had been assembling on the previous night to the amount of 1000 men

---

[111]Mary Sophia O'Brien (1798–1876) was born Mary Gapper in Charlton Adam, Somerset, England. Her father died in 1809 and, after the Napoleonic Wars, the three sons of the family decided to emigrate, arriving in the area of Thornhill, Upper Canada, in 1825. In 1828 Mary and her mother paid a visit, and after a period of courtship, Mary wed Edward O'Brien; they lived for a period at Shanty Bay on Lake Simcoe before returning to live in the Toronto area around 1845.

& drawing towards Toronto with the intention of entering the town in the morning & seising on the Militia arms stored there – Edd.[112] went to Barry [Barrie] this morning to obtain more certain information[,] deciding what was best to be done – he found that the communication along Yonge St. was so interrupted that no certain intellegence of what was passing below had been obtained but the alarm at New Market was very great & had been spread from thence back into our quiet & loyal townships [–] for the Indians & Militia here it is formed & the true hearted elsewhere to be prepared [sic] – It is Known however that a well equipped Militia regiment of 700 men was within a moments call at Toronto & a loyal country to the west accessible so that there can be little fear as to the result & it is said that the rioters were driven back four miles from the town – The proprietry of seeing the men of his company who have never yet been called together detains Edward for a day or two or he could not resist his anxiety to go and try what might be done below to Relieve the alarms & inconvenis [inconveniences] that our beloved friends there may be suffering – my anxiety on their account is every hour increasing & is but little allayed to say the truth by the prospect of Edd. traveling a road where he is so well known as the strenuous opponent of the disturbing principle – my hope is that a couple of days will send them all sneaking to their homes & hiding places again – but the situation of our Yonge Street party in the meantime is any thing but easy; what part circumstances have given Richard[113] it is impossible to conjecture but we here [hear] that a messenger sent by the Majistrates a little above Thornhill to aprize the town of the intentions of the rioters was interrupted & detained – fighting there has been for firing in the direction of Toronto has been distinctly heard from several places – with very little fear for the political result & with a fair probability perhaps of its being favourable to the general quiet of the province [–] it is impossible to contemplate the bloodshed & the series of necessary punishment falling often perhaps on men whom we have known & regarded as otherwise worthy members of society with the train of moral evil attendant on such an out breaking without a terribly melancholy feeling which added to aprehension for the immediate suffering of those so dear to us almost

[112]Edward O'Brien (1799–1875) joined the navy at the age of 11, returning to Ireland, where his father was stationed, at the end of the Napoleonic Wars. He soon joined the 58th Regiment, and was sent to the West Indies. Returning on half-pay as a lieutenant in 1824, he went to sea again and then emigrated to Thornhill, Upper Canada. After marrying, O'Brien moved in 1832 to Shanty Bay on Lake Simcoe, where he was emigrant agent and in charge of a "negro" settlement. A conservative, he supported tory candidates in the elections and helped to organize assistance for Toronto during the rebellion of 1837. In 1838 he was made lieutenant-colonel. Around 1845 the family moved to Toronto, where Edward owned the *Patriot* newspaper for a few years; he also engaged in railway speculation and was employed by an insurance company. He retired about 1858.
[113]Richard (Dick) Colston Gapper was the brother of Mary. He came out to Upper Canada in 1825 and took his family back to England about 1852.

overwhelms me and seeing Edd. almost equally depressed by the same views encreases the sickening melancholy – (Thursday) The officers of the Militia are all gone in seach of their Major & just after their departure arrived another dispatch urging them to haste [–] the alarm below was encreasing [–] Nothing had been heard from Toronto but one of the Richmond Hill gentl [gentleman] had been killed in attempting to pass thro' to Toronto. Bridgeford (whom A[Anthony][114] will well remember) was in his company[,] escaped & rode on [–] falling in with another post he was stopped again & made prisoner but having a pistol in his breast he shot his captor & road on – if he lives to see the end of the fray full often will this tale be told & glad I am that he was preserved – two gentns. houses near Toronto had been burnt – There has been no attack on the Town & whether on the garrison or not I cannot make out [–] if not, they can have but little spirit tho' McKensie & Lount are hoarse with haranguing – they returned late from the meeting having made arrangements for proceeding with all possible dispatch – Edd. goes on tomorrow without waiting for his company with the first 20 men he can collect – at 10 oclock another dispatch arrived from Barrie giving intelligence that an express had arrived at Newmarket from the Govr. pronouncing that having received the reinforcement from Glengary for which he had been waiting he purposed atta[cking] the rebels (I have learnt to dignify them since alas their number is now stated[)] and calling on the men above to come down uppon them with all their strength [–] All night I was busied in making preparations for Edd. or at least not being disposed to sleep I made it last out the night & in the morning with thirteen men immediately about he departed for Barrie intending to move on as soon as he could make up a sufficient party – in the course of that & the next morning all the remaining gentn. followed leaving me & and [sic] our man in charge of our little settlement – any thing like danger to Edd. was certainly a very remote probability but still there were loaded riffles & unquiet spirits about & I felt more & more anxious about Dick [–] seldom have I passed more painfully anxious hours – on Saturday I relieved myself by a visit to my fellow sufferers in the village & on Sunday I was somewhat farther set at ease by a hasty note from Edd. telling me that Thornhill was in possession of one of the Magistrate officers from Newmarket and that all was well there. This was some comfort tho I saw from the manner of his writing that his information had not been very precise [–] men in numbers were still going down from Penetanguishine with the arms & ammunition stored there & [our?] settlers and indians from the back townships & others were yet to be had if required – . . .

[114]Anthony Gapper (1799–1883) was the brother of Mary. He came to Thornhill, Upper Canada, about 1826 but stayed only long enough to do a zoological study of the area.

B 66   F.L. Bridgman to Fanny West
Government House, 15 December 1837
[*PAO, Miscellaneous, 1837, typescript*]

For other extracts from this document see B 23, B 42.

. . . McKenzie made his escape and has not yet been taken. 1000 pounds are offered for him. You may suppose that the party on board the steamer were most anxious all this time – I never passed so long a day in my life. At length the Mayor came to us and brought the rebels flag, which he presented to Lady Head, he told us that the victory was complete, that the rebels were flying in all directions, and that Sir Francis had pardoned many who were brought up prisoners. This act of mercy must I am sure have gained him the hearts of these poor deluded creatures, many of whom were so affected, that they burst into tears. He is indeed a noble character, uniting great firmness and decision with so much humanity and goodness. He is as kind and amiable in private life as he is just and honorable in his public character. He sent the carriage down to the wharf for us on his return, and on Thursday evening we had the happiness of being once more in safety under the same roof we had left in such alarm and which none of us expected to see again. Everything is now going on well. Government House is a scene of great bustle and business – full of gentlemen from morning till night. Volunteers continue to come in every day – on Saturday 500 came from Yonge Street and on Sunday 1100 more[;] there is now however, thank God, no occasion for their services, the business is done. Sir Francis has issued a Proclamation to say that there is no further occasion for the resort of Militia to Toronto. We are to have a body of 1000 men, who are to be stationed at the Garrison for the protection of Toronto and the neighbourhood. There is a guard round Gt. House night and day. It is really delightful to see so many brave men ready to defend us to the utmost. The town that was so peaceful and quiet is now like a garrison, every one is armed, horsemen are galloping in all directions and bodies of armed men are to be seen marching about. . . . The number of the rebels was, I believe 700 although it was said there were 3000. . . . I really tremble when I think of it, for had Mr. Powell [not] given the alarm they would have been in the Town before we knew of their approach. It was McKenzie's plan to come to Gt. House, and he was heard to say nothing [would] satisfy him but Sir Francis's head. It is very well known now that it was their intention had they been victorious to hang the Governor and his principal officers, to burn the town and put everyone to death. We have heard of one escape Sir Francis had – on Thursday when in pursuit of the rebels one of our party saw a man take a deliberate aim at him from a tree, the ball passed close between him and his servant who was close behind him. The man who saw this went under the tree and shot the villain dead on the spot. The rebels have lost a great many men, but the number is not known. There are 200 prisoners, among whom is Montgomery. . . .

B 67   REWARDS OFFERED
[Upper Canada Gazette, *Toronto, 7 Dec. 1837*]

PROCLAMATION.

By HIS EXCELLENCY SIR FRANCIS B. HEAD, Baronet, Lieutenant Governor of Upper Canada , &c. &c.

To The Queen's Faithful Subjects in Upper Canada.

IN a time of profound peace, while every one was quietly following his occupations [*sic*], feeling secure under the protection of our Laws, a band of Rebels, instigated by a few malignant and disloyal men, has had the wickedness and audacity to assemble with Arms, and to attack and Murder the Queen's Subjects on the Highway – to Burn and Destroy their Property – to Rob the Public Mails – and to threaten to Plunder the Banks – and to Fire the City of Toronto.

Brave and Loyal People of Upper Canada, we have been long suffering from the acts and endeavours of concealed Traitors, but this is the first time that Rebellion has dared to shew itself openly in the land, in the absence of invasion by any Foreign Enemy.

Let every man do his duty now, and it will be the last time that we or our children shall see our lives or properties endangered, or the Authority of our Gracious Queen insulted by such treacherous and ungrateful men. **MILITIA – MEN OF UPPER CANADA,** no County has every shewn a finer example of Loyalty and Spirit than **YOU** have given upon this sudden call of Duty. Young and old of all ranks, are flocking to the Standard of their Country. What has taken place will enable our Queen to know Her Friends from Her Enemies – a Public Enemy is never so dangerous as a concealed Traitor – and now my friends let us complete well what is begun – let us not return to our rest till Treason and Traitors are revealed to the light of day, and rendered harmless throughout the land.

By vigilant, patient and active, – leave punishment to the Laws, – our first object is, to arrest and secure all those who have been guilty of Rebellion, Murder and Robbery. – And to aid us in this, a Reward is hereby offered of

One Thousand Pounds,

to any one who will apprehend, and deliver up to Justice, **WILLIAM LYON MACKENZIE** – and **FIVE HUNDRED POUNDS** to any one who will apprehend, and deliver up to justice, **DAVID GIBSON** – or **SAMUEL LOUNT** – or **JESSE LLOYD** – or **SILAS FLETCHER** – and the same reward, and a free pardon, will be given to any of their accomplices who will render this public service, except he or they shall have committed, in his own person, the crime of Murder or Arson.

WILLIAM LYON MACKENZIE by
Alf. Sandham, *ca*. 1862. *PAC,
C–3918*.

DR. CHARLES DUNCOMBE [date
and artist unknown]. *PAC, C–4500*.

PARLIAMENT BUILDINGS,
Toronto, 1834, by Thomas Young.
*Metropolitan Toronto Public Library,
T–30086*.

DR. JOHN ROLPH in late life. *MTPL, T–15092*.

PETER MATTHEWS [date and artist unknown]. *MTPL, T–16313*.

ROBERT BALDWIN by Francis Hoppner Meyer, 1845. *MTPL, T–10252*.

FRANCIS HINCKS *ca*. 1841 [artist unknown]. *Archives of Ontario, S–14854*.

PETER PERRY [date and artist unknown]. *OA, S–4424*.

GIDEON TIFFANY [date unknown]. *OA, S–13892*.

SIR FRANCIS BOND HEAD by
Nelson Cook, 1837. *PAC, C–18789*.

SIR GEORGE ARTHUR [date and
artist unknown]. *PAC, C–15231*.

JOHN BEVERLEY ROBINSON by
Francis Hoppner Meyer, 1842. *OA,
S–2976*.

ALLAN MACNAB, lithograph by F.
D'Avignon from painting by T. Hamel,
184?. *MTPL, T–13738*.

COLONEL JAMES FITZGIBBON
[artist unknown]. *MTPL, T–30753*.

JONAS JONES [date and artist
unknown]. *MTPL, T–16853*.

JOHN POWELL [date and artist
unknown]. *MTPL, T–15029*.

COLONEL C.L.L. FOSTER [date and
artist unknown]. *MTPL, T–30837*.

SIR RICHARD BONNYCASTLE [date
and artist unknown]. *MTPL, T–30828*.

ANTHONY MANAHAN [date and
artist unknown]. *MTPL, T–30836*.

ABRAHAM A. RAPELJE [date
unknown]. *MTPL, T–81838*.

MAHLON BURWELL [date and artist
unknown]. *OA, S–5551*.

KINGSTON FROM FORT HENRY by James Gray, 1828. *OA, S–971*.

VIEW OF TORONTO, 1834 [artist unknown]. *PAC, C–9351*.

GOVERNMENT HOUSE, TORONTO, 1834, by Jane Harris. *MTPL, T–11868.*

TORONTO JAIL, 1835, by J.G. Howard. *MTPL, T–11963.*

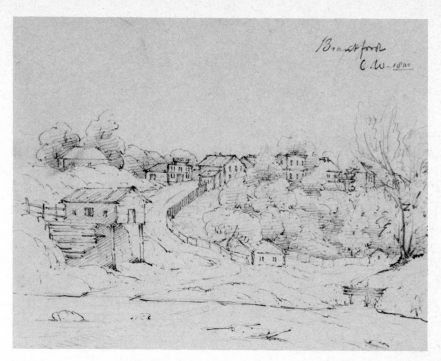

BRANTFORD, 1840, by J.J. Warre. *PAC, C–17694.*

HOUSE OF COLONEL A.W. LIGHT, near Woodstock, *ca.* 1838 [artist unknown].
OA, S–17334.

LONDON, *ca.* 1839, by Dr. Dartnell. *PAC, C–13306*.

THE LONDON COURT HOUSE. *OA, S–14999*.

DEATH OF COL. MOODIE by Adrian Sharp [date unknown]. *PAC, C–4783.*

ESCAPE OF JOHN POWELL [date and artist unknown]. *PAC, C–4784.*

BATTLE AT MONTGOMERY'S [date and artist unknown]. *PAC, C–4782*.

BATTLE AT MONTGOMERY'S [date and artist unknown]. *PAC, C-11322*.

DESTRUCTION OF THE *CAROLINE* by G. Tattersall [date unknown].
PAC, C–4788.

LOYALISTS RETAKE NAVY ISLAND by "Hogarth, Esq." *ca.* 1838–9. *MTPL, T–14653.*

SITE OF THE BATTLE OF THE WINDMILL, Prescott, by H.F. Ainslie, 1839. *PAC, C–508.*

PATRIOTS REPELLED AT DICKINSON'S LANDING, near Cornwall, by C. Smyth, *ca.* 1840. *PAC, C–1032.*

And all, but the Leaders above-named, who have been seduced to join in this unnatural Rebellion, are hereby called to return to their duty to their Sovereign – to obey the Laws – and to live henceforward as good and faithful Subjects – and they will find the Government of their Queen as indulgent as it is just.

GOD SAVE THE QUEEN.

Thursday, 3 o'clock, P.M.

7th December.

The Party of Rebels, under their Chief Leaders, is wholly dispersed, and flying before the Loyal Militia. The only thing that remains to be done, is to find them, and arrest them.

B 68   T.G. ANDERSON[115] TO S.P. JARVIS
Newmarket, 10 December 1837
[*PAC, Indian Affairs, v. 67, pp. 64191-2*]

I have the honor to report to you, that in compliance with information received from Captain Dugan[116] of the Volunteer Cavalry I shall send home the 8 indians who accompanied me to this place.

I arrived at this place today; on my way down I dispersed Couriers to the various hunting Grounds for the Potawatamis &c. &c. to meet me without delay on my route to the Scene of Action, and am hourly expecting parties in from the Bush – I consider it prudent to remain here, for the purpose of receiving those Indians to prevent their

---

[115]Thomas Gummersall Anderson (1779–1875) was born at Sorel, Quebec, but moved to Cornwall in 1783. After apprenticing with a Kingston merchant, he traded with the Indians in the American north-west from 1800 until the War of 1812. He served in the same area during the war, and at its end was attached to the Indian Department as clerk and interpreter, with the military rank of captain, at Drummond Island and then at Penetanguishene. In 1830 he was made superintendent of the Indians at The Narrows (later Orillia), and then on Manitoulin Island. At neither place did the scheme to settle the Indians work, through no fault of his, and in 1845 he was transferred to Toronto as chief Indian superintendent for Upper Canada. He moved the office to Cobourg in 1847 and remained there until he retired in 1858.

[116]"Captain Dugan" was probably George Duggan Jr. (1812–1876), who had come to Hamilton as an infant from Mallow, County Cork, Ireland. In 1828 he had begun the study of law and in 1837 was called to the bar. A strong Orangeman, as were all his relatives, he was district master for Toronto in 1840, deputy county master for East York, 1848–9, and junior deputy grand master, 1849–50. He sat as a Toronto alderman, 1838–40 and 1843–50, losing several other elections and unsuccessfully seeking the mayoralty. From 1841 to 1847 he sat in the Assembly for the second riding of York, after which he was ignored in favour of other candidates. After he made several approaches to the Baldwin-LaFontaine government, he was appointed recorder of Toronto in 1851, in 1868 being promoted to the York County Court as senior judge.

commiting depredations – I avail myself of Mr. Lallys[117] going to Toronto to forward this – And shall await your instructions –

B 69   THE REBELS ROUNDED UP
[Commercial Herald, *Toronto, 20 Dec. 1837*]

. . . On Friday volunteers continued to arrive [in Toronto], and scouting parties were sent out in various directions in seach of the rebels.

On Saturday a datachment [*sic*] of men headed by Colonel Chisholm, left Toronto for Cooksville, for the purpose of suppressing any insurrectionary movements which might be attempted in that quarter.

Fifty-two prisoners were brought into the City who had been engaged in the late battle. These unfortunate and misguided men were taken by a scouting party which had been sent out in search of them.

Towards evening the steamer Traveller arrived from Kingston, bringing a number of well-armed men, 1000 stand of arms, a vast quantity of ammunition, and two pieces of artillery.

On Sunday [should be Saturday] several hundred volunteers arrived from Tecumseh, having in charge a number of prisoners whom they had arrested. Towards evening [Sunday] upwards of 1000 men arrived from Cobourg and Port Hope, under Col. Boulton, bringing along with them 16 prisoners, and among them Dr. Hunter.[118] Col. Macnab, agreeably to a commission received from His Excellency, having embarked about 800 men, on board the Traveller and Burlington left Toronto for the London District, to meet Dr. Charles Duncombe, who, it is said, has 500 armed rebels under his command; and we have no doubt that the same success will accompany Her Majesty's arms there, which has so gloriously crowned them here. . . .

[117]Edmund Lally (1806 or 1807–1889) came to Upper Canada in 1835 and settled with his brother at Shanty Bay before taking up lot 28, concession 5 of Oro Township. He bought a mill from E.G. O'Brien. He was a magistrate and a member of the Church of England.

[118]James Hunter (b. 1790?) came from his native Yorkshire to the Niagara District in 1823, bringing his family. In 1826 he passed the medical board and in 1829 or 1830 moved to Whitby, where he developed an interest in politics. Soon he was the acknowledged leader of the reformers there and a supporter of Mackenzie. In 1837, however, Hunter retired from politics because he felt Mackenzie was going too far. Arrested at home after the rebellion, which he had spoken against, he was released a few days later. He then moved his family to New York State until 1840, when he returned to Upper Canada, eventually settling on Yonge Street near Newmarket.

C. THE DUNCOMBE RISING

C 1   EXAMINATION OF DUNCAN CAMERON[1]
n.d.
[PAC, Upper Canada Sundries, v. 195, pp. 108709-12]

. . . Saith he was at Scotland on or about the Seventh day of December last and Saw Jacob Bemer[2] in his Bemers Bar Room who Said with a degree of authority that George Case[3] had come there and Stated that Toronto was taken by McKenzie & his forces and that the Sheriffs were after Duncombe & Malcolm[4] but said there would be forces enough in Scotland to set all the Sheriffs at defiance – a few hours afterward John Kelley[5] came to Scotland with about forty men [–]

[1]Duncan Cameron was a Burford Township farmer.
[2]Jacob Beamer (Bemer) (b. ca. 1808) was a native-born Upper Canadian farmer and carpenter who kept an inn in the village of Scotland. He owned 300 patented acres. He attended a reform meeting at Oakland in November 1837 and turned out with Duncombe in December. Indicted as a rebel, he fled to New York, joining the Patriots who launched the Short Hills raid in June 1838. Captured, he was tried and convicted and transported to Van Diemen's Land from which he never returned. He left a bitter legacy in the form of accusations from several of his Short Hills comrades that he had betrayed them time and again.
[3]George Washington Case (b. ca. 1820) was the son of a Hamilton doctor and hence was described by authorities as a "gentleman." He was active at Oakland in December 1837, and fled the province after the revolt, joining Mackenzie on Navy Island. Thereafter he continued to be active with the Patriots, and was tried for breaching American neutrality laws after joining in an abortive raid along the Niagara frontier in June 1838. He was fined $20 and sentenced to a year in jail.
[4]Eliakim Malcolm (1801–1874) was a well-known member of the numerous Malcolm family which had fled the America of the Revolution to New Brunswick and then settled in Oakland Township in 1795. The Malcolms had large interests in and about Oakland, Eliakim and his wife Samantha owning in 1837 almost 1,000 acres of property. This helps explain why he schemed unsuccessfully in the mid-1830s to make the Oakland village of Scotland the capital of the proposed Brock District. He was not without influence. Aside from family connections, he himself was a deputy provincial land surveyor, a magistrate, and a commissioner of the Court of Requests. Brother of Finlay, reform MLA for Oxford, 1828–30, Eliakim first flew his radical colours in the election of 1836. He was forward in the reform meetings in the fall of 1837 and second only to Duncombe in organizing the revolt in the west. After the rising's failure, he fled to the United States and was attainted a traitor. Rumour had it that he was active with the Patriots. In 1841 he was pardoned and returned home. He retained his local popularity, being elected to the Brock District Council in 1844 and to the wardenship of Brant County in 1853.
[5]John Kelly (Kelley) was born in the Niagara District and served in the War of 1812, becoming a captain in the militia thereafter. He settled in Burford, acquiring the patent to lot 13, concession 14, which he and his family farmed. He became a commissioner of the Court of Requests and in 1833 was slated to be a magistrate, though, for

Some with Arms and being at the head of the party marched them up & down the Street with Music consisting of 1 dinner horn, a Small Bugle and a Clarionet [–] tune played was "Wha Wallace Bled" – deponent was requested by one Raymond[6] to accompany the party to Hamilton [–] deponent refused when Eliakim Malcolm said to deponent when they returned from Hamilton where they intended to go to for the purpose of liberating John G. Parker from Goal & those who refused to accompany them would fare the worse [–] Jacob Bemer also said they were going to Hamilton for the same purpose and Bemer made many series threatenings – Said he would Blow out the Brains of any sheriff who would come to take any of the above persons – Peter Laden[7] said to deponent on the same morning that he deponent was the only damned Tory in the House and further abused deponent & John Moore Esqr,[8] John Kelly continued drilling his party during the day and Marched them at their Head & E, Malcolm in the rear [–] Peter Laden was in the Ranks with Kelly [–] does not Recollect if Laden had fire Arms – deponent Saw John Willson[9] a discharged Soldier from the late Hundredth Regiment who told deponent that he Willson had consented to conduct their forces to Hamilton and when asking Malcolm how he intended to support his men answered that they would plunder for a living[–]

C 2   DEPOSITION OF DUNCAN MCDIARMID[10]
14 December 1837
[*PAC, Upper Canada Sundries, v. 187, pp. 104471-2*]

. . . on Saturday last the 9th day of the present Month – he went to a place called Scotland in the Township of Oakland in the London District – and there saw a number of men, under training to Arms – in number from one hundred to one hundred and twenty – – They appeared to be under the orders of one McGuire[11] a School Master – Deponent saith that after being at Scotland about five Minutes – he was

whatever reason, he did not receive the appointment. He participated in the 2 November 1837 reform meeting at Oakland and turned out with two of his sons in December to join the rebels. He was jailed at London on 17 December, but was freed in the summer of 1838 after petitioning under 1 Victoria, c. 10.

[6]Cyrenus Raymond (b. *ca.* 1814), a native Upper Canadian, was a bachelor and a resident of Windham Township.

[7]Peter Ladon (Laden, Landon) was an Irish-born, unpropertied Oakland labourer. After turning out with the rebels, he was jailed on 16 December at Hamilton, and, not being indicted, was freed on 15 March.

[8]T. John Moore (1799?–1842?) of Burford was made a justice of the peace in 1835 and a captain in the 4th Oxford Regiment of militia in 1838.

[9]John Wilson (Willson) of Oakland was jailed at Hamilton after the revolt and freed on a date unknown.

[10]Duncan McDiarmid was a resident of Brantford Township.

[11]William McGuire, an Oakland schoolteacher, was forward both in the agitation in the fall of 1837 and in the rising in the west. He seems to have fled the country after the

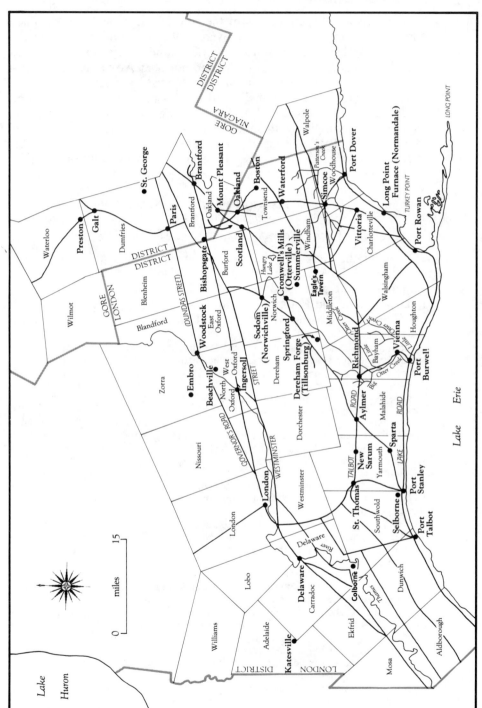

4: Area Affected by the Duncombe Rising

made a prisoner by the orders of the said McGuire and was detained under arrest from the hour of eleven in the forenoon to three in the afternoon – deponent was then liberated under a promise extracted from him, that he should go home and not bear Arms against them – Deponent further saith that he saw Mathews[12] the Auctioneer from Brantford and William Lyons[13] who resides near Merwins Tavern on the Road from Brantford to Burford –: taking an active part among the men under training – on the above day – and at the same time he saw Merwin[14] the Tavern-Keeper put under arrest and immediately after released, in consequence of the interferance of Lyons, who said that he Knew Merwin to be a reformer for some length of time. –

C 3   DEPOSITION OF JOSEPH N. SMITH[15]
7 March 1838
[*PAC, Upper Canada Sundries, v. 187, pp. 104607-8*]

. . . about the time of the rebels assembling at Scotland deponent attended at John Malcolms[16] house in Oakland were [*sic*] a party were gathered for the purpose of preventing John Malcolm being arrested – John Malcolm and Finlay Malcolm[17] were present – Finlay Malcolm took part of the guard away to protect himself at his own house – John

---

revolt and joined the Patriots. Embittered, he suggested to W.L. Mackenzie in 1840 that they draw up a black list of those who had harmed Upper Canada's reformers. He had himself, he said, a small score to settle.

[12]William Matthews (Mathews) (d. 1872?), a young Irishman, was a Brantford auctioneer who actively promoted the rebellion. He escaped official notice, however, after it and lived to become mayor of Brantford decades later.

[13]William Lyons, born in Upper Canada, farmed and owned property in both Brantford town and township. Involved in the reform agitation of the fall of 1837, he joined the Duncombe revolt. Jailed at Hamilton on 21 December, he was tried for treason in March 1838 and acquitted.

[14]Henry Merwin, a native Upper Canadian, was a Brantford Township innkeeper and farmer who owned almost 150 acres. Though the rebels doubted his loyalties on the occasion reported here, he did join their forces, and was examined for doing so and granted bail in March 1838.

[15]Joseph N. Smith (b. *ca.* 1805?) was an American-born Brantford farmer. He attended the Oakland reform meeting of 2 November 1837 and joined the rebels in December. He was jailed at Hamilton on 15 December, and, not being indicted, was freed on 21 March 1838.

[16]John Malcolm (1776–1846) was born in the United States, coming to Upper Canada with his loyalist family in 1795. He fought in the War of 1812, serving as a militia captain. After that conflict, like several in his family, he engaged in a long controversy with the government over war losses claims, a controversy that ended in 1833 with his getting, in common with other claimants, just 25 per cent of his claim satisfied. Like some others in his family, John was a mill owner who built up large properties, owning 820 patented acres by 1837. A rebel, he was jailed at Hamilton on 23 December and was indicted, but the bill against him was ignored. He was freed on 10 March 1838, whereupon he returned to his wife and family.

[17]Finlay Malcolm (1779–1862) was born in Maine, emigrating with his loyalist parents to Upper Canada in 1795. He served in the War of 1812 as a lieutenant in the militia. After, he kept a tavern in Oakland where he also farmed and raised his family.

Hammell[18] of Brantford and George A Clark[19] of the same place were at John Malcolms House – John Hammell had a great deal to say and detailed a plan by which the rebels could take Brantford – Clark and Hammell were there until about one o'Clock of the morning – Hammell said his excuse for leaving Brantford was that he came up to see his daughter who was Keeping a School at Mount Pleasant – but that he must get back soon or he might be suspected [–] Hammell advised the rebels to advance on Brantford in two parties – one to go by Brantford Bridge and the other by the way of Paris – and make the atack at the same time. – Clark and Hammell were present when a party were organized to go off and take the Long-point Mail as it was thought not right to let the Mail go from place to place carrying news – Something was said that Gunpowder and Lead was concealed under Mr Clarks Store House floor at Brantford but cannot say if the information came from Clark himself [–] The names of the party selected to go and take the mail were – McGuire – Robert Elliot[20] – Lyman Chapin[21] – and five others – names not recollected – making the number eight – Eliakim Malcolm was very active at the meeting. – James Malcolm[22] was also there. – The guard that went to take the Mail was all armed[.]

By 1837 he had over 300 patented acres in the township. In 1828 he was elected to the Assembly for Oxford but was defeated in 1834 when he stood as a radical candidate. Chosen a captain by the rebels in December 1837, he was jailed at Hamilton on 23 December and tried for treason in the spring of 1838. He was acquitted.

[18]John Hammell (Hammill) (b. ca. 1791) was a native Upper Canadian. He fought in the War of 1812. In 1837 John, now a carpenter by trade, operated a toll bridge across the Grand River. His involvement in the rebellion puzzled some, for his family seemed most respectable, his brother Thomas being a Gore District magistrate and his brother Patrick a captain in the militia. Jailed on 9 March 1838, John was tried at Hamilton for treason and found guilty before being freed on bail on 17 August 1838.

[19]George Alexander Clark, the son of loyalist parents, was a Brantford merchant. A lieutenant in the militia, he had been a justice of the peace in the Midland District before moving to Brantford and had been slated for appointment to the Gore magistracy until a cleric made representations against him. According to R.B. Sullivan, this drove him into the rebel camp. Indicted for treason in 1838, he fled to the United States with his family, where he enlisted with the Patriots.

[20]Robert Elliott (Elliot), an Englishman, was a tanner and a resident of the village of Scotland. He attended the Oakland reform meeting of 2 November 1837 and joined the rebels in December. His brother John, a lawyer, was secretary of the Toronto political union. Robert was jailed at Hamilton in December 1837, and, reportedly, his property was plundered and his family turned out of their home. He petitioned under 1 Victoria, c. 10 and was freed on bail in June 1838.

[21]Lyman Chapin (b. ca. 1813) was an Upper Canadian-born Oakland farmer who in 1837 had 100 patented acres. He had been active in the reform agitation of the fall of 1837. Jailed at Hamilton on 16 December, he petitioned under 1 Victoria, c. 10, and was freed on bail on 6 June 1838.

[22]James Malcolm (1800–1854), brother to John, Finlay, and Eliakim, was born in Oakland Township. A farmer, by 1837 he owned 176 patented acres which helped support him, his wife, and their seven children. Prominent locally, he had been an assessor and town clerk of Oakland in 1832, and was town clerk once again in 1837.

C 4   EXAMINATION OF MARIA HUNTER[23]
14 April 1838
[PAC, Upper Canada Sundries, v. 202, pp. 112046-6B]

Maria Hunter . . . saith that Doctor Charles Duncomb formerly of Burford came into the said Township of Norwich on or about the sixth of december last past and continued there about the span of six days endeavouring to raise force – against the Government, at the expiration of which period being about the twelfth of that month he left to go to a place in the Township of Oakland called Scotland. . . . a day or two after the said Duncomb came into Norwich as before mentioned, she this deponent had heard that warrants had been issued for the apprehension of the said Snider[24] and others inhabitants of Norwich aforesaid to the number of six or eight who it was reported were to be tried by martial law and forthwith executed. That such report of the expected apprehension & execution of the said Snider and others deponent understood was circulated by said Duncomb who alleged as deponent also understood that he the said Duncomb was to be dealt with in the same manner. That such report to deponents personal knowledge had been extensively circulated and was at that time accredited and received as true very generally throughout the said Township. . . .

C 5   EXAMINATION OF JOHN A. TIDEY[25]
9 February 1838
[PAC, Records of the London District Magistrates, v. I, pp. 126-7]

John A. Tydy was brought up for examination who states that on or

---

He joined the political union formed in Oakland in November 1837. A rebel in December, he fled to Michigan. Family tradition has it that the tories then put his property to the flames. Nevertheless, he returned to Oakland, some time before 1843.

[23]Maria Hunter and her husband Oliver, a "yeoman," lived in Norwich Township.

[24]Elias Snider (b. ca. 1797) emigrated to Upper Canada from the United States about 1811. He taught school for a time, then devoted himself to farming, acquiring 450 patented acres by 1837, on which he and his wife supported six children and Elias' aged parents. Naturalized in 1834, he became an important member of his local community, being elected to various township offices, including that of township commissioner in 1837. He was also in 1837 clerk of the Court of Requests, becoming that September recording secretary of the Norwich political union. A lieutenant-colonel with the rebels, he was jailed at Hamilton on 23 December and tried and found guilty of treason in the spring. He was released on bail in September 1838.

[25]John Arthur Tidey (Tydy) was born in Berkshire, England, and was resident in Sodom, Norwich, by 1828. There he acted as a merchant, farmer, and deputy provincial surveyor. A local scribe, he held various minor township offices and was elected president of the Norwich political union in September 1837. Jailed as a rebel at London on 7 February, he petitioned under 1 Victoria, c. 10 and was granted bail in October, returning to Norwich and his family.

about the 6th Decr. last he was at Mr. Wallace's[26] store in Norwich where a boy brought in an open letter which he thinks was directed to Solomon Lossing[27] & signed by Charles Duncombe – which stated that there had been an outbreak at Toronto and called upon the people to assemble at a public Meeting – About 3 hours afterwards Duncombe and several others came into the village and examinant was sent for by Duncombe to attend at a house belonging to Garry. B De Long[28] where Duncombe was – when he attended, Duncombe called him aside and stated to him that the Government had issued Warrants for the apprehension of one individual in each township as they were determined to shake terror among the Reformers and that his (Tydy's) life was in danger as he knew there was a warrant out for him – It was entirely owing to this conversation that examinant went with Dr. Duncombe to Oakland for his own safety – . . . He occasionally acted as a Clerk for Duncombe – . . . wrote several lines of a letter which Duncombe dictated and which Duncombe afterwards finished – This letter was a sort of Harangue resembling the speech Duncombe made to induce them to take up arms – . . .

C 6   PETITION OF JOHN A. TIDEY TO SIR F.B. HEAD
London Gaol, 9 March 1838
[*PAC, Upper Canada Sundries, v. 203, pp. 112554-6*]

Humbly Sheweth:
   That your Petitioner in the beginning of December last while your Petitioner was assisting Mr. Wallace in Norwich – a Lad presented himself at the Store door with an open letter dictated to one of the

[26]Thomas Wallace, an Englishman, was a farmer and merchant of Sodom, Norwich, who owned property in both Norwich and Brantford townships. Not surprisingly, he was a supporter of the projected London and Gore Railroad. He provided ample demonstration of his loyalty during the rebellion and was rewarded accordingly, being elevated in 1838 from a lieutenant to a captain in the militia and being selected the new postmaster at Sodom.

[27]Solomon Lossing (1781–1844) was born in Dutchess County, New York. When his father Peter purchased an extensive tract in Norwich about 1810 in association with Peter DeLong, he moved his family, Solomon included, to the township. DeLong and Peter Lossing did much to promote Quaker emigration to Norwich. Solomon evidently developed diversified economic interests, owning in 1837 a flour mill and a carding machine. Despite his Quaker heritage, he took an active part in local government, serving as a commissioner of the Court of Requests and a magistrate from 1829 onwards. Jailed at Hamilton on 23 December 1837 on suspicion of having aided the rebels, he was tried in the spring and acquitted, returning to his family. In 1843 he was elected warden of the Brock District.

[28]Garry DeLong (b. *ca.* 1811), the son of Peter DeLong, was known as the first white child born in Norwich. In 1837 Garry had a small family of his own, a tavern at Sodom, and 49 patented acres. In 1836 he held a minor township office. In December 1837 he incited others to rebellion and was jailed at Hamilton on 23 December. Freed on bail on 28 February, he fled the country and was indicted, but soon returned, evidently suffering no legal penalties.

Magistrates, the letter was handed into the Store and read by Wallace before those present, Stating that McKenzie with resistless numbers hemmed in Toronto – and other matters – The Boy after thus shewing the Letter took it to its destination. – About the middle of the afternoon of the same day Charles Duncomb himself came forward – a considerable party had now got together at his rendevous – he called me and several others aside and in his usual specious and insinuating manner – pretending love and confidence (when he possessed no honor himself) told us that Warrants were out for himself and for three or four of the leading Reformers in each and every Township through the Country – That the Governor was intending to inflict such vengeance upon the Land as was never heard of. – This communication alarmed and tearified all those who heard him, and a general meeting was called for the next day [8 or 9 December] to take the matter into consideration – Accordingly next day at a very large Meeting a Body of men for the defence of Norwich was organized – no other particular tendency that Body at first appeared to have. – A few days after, a deputation from the Malcolms came in – after which the Report was that the men should shortly be marched down to Scotland, which was the place of Rendevous. –

In looking back upon those proceedings – it is impossible for me or any person to tell what I did in the business – Like the restless frightened persons about me I did and said many things which cannot now be recalled and for which I must at present content myself by expressing my unfeigned sorrow – . . .

C 7   DEPOSITION OF THOMAS WALLACE
18 December 1837
[PAC, Upper Canada Sundries, v. 180, pp. 99470-1]

. . . about Tuesday last the 12th Inst. deponent read a Letter from Charles duncombe to Squire Lossing, stating that there was going to be a general rising, through the Country – that McKensie was about Toronto with about 1500 men, and that he Duncombe hoped Squire Lossing would join them, or be at the meeting to give them his assistance – verily believes that Lossing received the said Letter, . . . Does not Know for certain that Lossing did attend the meeting. . . . deponent is not aware of his own knowledge that Lossing was one of duncombe's secret committee, but has been told by several people, . . . that he Lossing was on the Secret Committee – . . . deponent further said that George Case, late of Hamilton, in the district of Gore, was one of the men under arms with Charles Duncombe, and that he the said Case did violently and with force of arms did endeavour to take a horse, the property of deponent. for the service of the rebel army. heard said Case say. the Rebels were on their march to attack Brantford – . . . deponent further saith, that he was told to tell the

Magistrates of Brantford, that if they fired a single gun at them they would burn the town – was told so by Paul Bedford[29] and James Dennis,[30] who were both Captains or Lieutenants in the Rebels' Army – . . .

C 8   EXAMINATION OF WILLIAM DARROW[31]
27 December 1837
[PAC, Upper Canada Sundries, v. 181, pp. 99991-2]

. . . He the said William Darrow acknowledgeth that on or about the eighth instant a report came to the Dereham Forge that George G. Parker of Hamilton was in Gaol at Hamilton that he was to have a mock trial and then tobe hung; that he Darrow borrowed a rifle and with six other men volunteered to go to Hamilton and rescue said Parker, that they went to Norwich, joined a rebel party of men. . . .

C 9   INFORMATION OF JOHN BEARD[32]
10 December 1837
[PAO, J.M. Snyder Papers]

. . . John Beard . . . saith – That on Thursday last the 7th day of this instant December this Deponent was in the Township of Norwich in the District aforesaid where he met several men to the amount of fifteen or twenty who told this Deponent that they were going to the Meeting at a Tavern in Sodom that in conversation this Deponent heard several of them, who were strangers to him, say that they were determined to overthrow the British Government: and that they had no doubt that they were able to do it asserting as their reason that the taxes had been raised and that the Government wanted to put tythes upon them as they did in the Old Country – This was at the house of Henry Chase Yeoman who this deponent believes is not disposed to join either party – they said that they wanted to pull every one down to their

[29]Paul Bedford (b. *ca.* 1805) was born in the Newcastle District. He settled in Norwich, where he and his wife farmed. In 1836 he served as an overseer of highways for the township. A rebel, he was jailed at London in December 1837. After petitioning under 1 Victoria, c. 10, he was ordered transported to Van Diemen's Land for fourteen years, but was freed in England. His brother Daniel was not that lucky. A Duncombe rebel and a participant in the Windsor raid of December 1838, he was hanged in 1839 for his Patriot activities.

[30]James Dennis (b. *ca.* 1805) came to Upper Canada from the United States with his parents about 1820. In 1837, still single, he lived with them in the "Dennis settlement" in the north of Norwich. Here James, who owned 100 patented acres of lot 21, concession 2, farmed. He turned out with the rebels in December, subsequently fleeing the province. Attainted a traitor, he was eventually pardoned and returned to Norwich.

[31]William Darrow (b. *ca.* 1807) was an American-born blacksmith. Examined for his part in the rebellion, he was freed on bail on 27 December.

[32]John Beard was an Oxford County resident who described himself as a "gentleman."

own level and make their own laws – Chase afterwards said to this Deponent that he wished the leaders of the disaffected were every one of them hung. On Saturday morning the 9th Instant, this Deponent saw groups of men amounting to a large number going towards Sodom – going to a training – all armed with rifles – On Friday night One man in particular said he knew every thing would turn out (to H Chase's wife) and directed her to desire her Husband not to fail to be at Sodom by Day light the next morning. Yesterday morning (Saturday) Deponent was in Chases House when five or six men went in there, one of whom pulled from his pocket about as many as thirty rifle balls – this man had a rifle and the others told him that they were going to bring their arms – This Deponent also heard from these people that their numbers amounted to five hundred Men under arms – On friday night there was a meeting at a school house about three miles South of Chase's – And as this Deponent, in company with George Hay[33] of Woodstock Carpenter, was returning home they heard several shots fired in the direction of Sodom – The man aforesaid who pulled out the balls said he had *stacks* of them and that he wished they were every one lodged in the hearts of the Tories (meaning the Conservatives) or words to that effect – This Deponent has reason to believe and does believe that Charles Duncombe was in the vicinity and was told that he went from house to house and that there was always a strong guard put over him as Warrants were out to arrest him and Eliaquim Malcolm.

C 10   INFORMATION OF JAMES KINNEY[34]
21 December 1837
[*PAC, Records of the London District Magistrates, v. II*]

. . . The said informant, upon his Oath saith that he was chopping wood near his own premises on Friday the Eight instant when Horatio Fowler[35] of the Township of Burford came to deponent on his way home from Norwich and said to deponent that the fuss had begun, That Toronto city was taken & that it behoved evry one to do all they could to save their leaders head – that they had organized two companies in Norwich & should march the next day or on Sunday to Oakland to join the companies their in Oakland that they had sent to the west for Troops to unite with them & that the Oxford companies would march to Oakland in a few days – deponent Saw Said Horatio Fowler have

[33]George Hay had established a cabinet and chair factory in Woodstock by the 1850s. He may have been the George Hay who was appointed a magistrate for Zorra in December 1836, but this seems unlikely.

[34]James Kinney was a Burford Township "yeoman."

[35]Horatio Fowler (b. *ca.* 1794) was a native of New York State who came as a child to Upper Canada about 1798. He fought in the War of 1812. In 1836 he and his wife were "in good circumstances"; they farmed and owned 195 patented acres. Jailed at London for his part in the rebellion on 19 December 1837, he petitioned under 1 Victoria, c. 10 and was freed in October 1838.

one pistol, and he said Fowler enquired for Garret Van Camp[36] & others to send them to Oakland and said "we had sent a despatch to Toronto City[–]"

C 11   DEPOSITION OF ABRAHAM SACKRIDER[37]
27 January 1838
[PAC, Records of the London District Magistrates, v. II]

. . . he had business at Sodom – and went down there [–] found Duncombes men collected at the Meeting house near Sodom – he was told that a Methodist Preacher of the name of Bird[38] was going to Preach to Duncombes men [–] this was on a Monday as Deponent believes and between the tenth and twentieth of December [–] Deponent went to the Methodist Meeting house and heard Bird Preach – cannot recollect what Bird said Exactly – but the chief object of his sermon appeared to be to Encourage the people to take up arms and fight for their freedom [–] Deponent never saw this Preacher before [–] has heard that he had Preached at Sodom once or twice before – After meeting Dr Duncombe came to Deponent and endeavoured to persuade him to go along. . . .

C 12   A LETTER OF JOHN TUFFORD[39]
recipient unknown, n.p., n.d.
[PAC, Upper Canada Sundries, v. 205, pp. 113447-52]

The following is a correct statement directly & indirectly of all that I have done[.] About the sixth day of december I received a letter from Dr. Duncombe saying that he had just been informed that Toronto was in possession of the reformers and that he (Dr. D.) was to be arrested. however I continued my work, assisting my brother frame a barn for

[36]Garrett Van Camp (*ca.* 1810–*ca.* 1842) was born in New York State. In 1837 he worked as a labourer in Burford. Though he joined Duncombe's force, he was not taken up or indicted for his part in the revolt. Having fled the province, he returned in June 1838 as a Short Hills raider. Captured, he was tried, found guilty of treason, and transported to Van Diemen's Land for life, where he died.

[37]Abraham Sackrider (b. *ca.* 1798) was a native of New York State. He emigrated to Upper Canada about 1811 and fought for his new country in the War of 1812. Though a Quaker, he married a Baptist, James Dennis' sister. In 1837 he, his wife and their seven small children farmed 100 patented acres of lot 18, concession 1 in Norwich. After turning out with Duncombe, he was jailed at London on 21 December and, after petitioning under 1 Victoria, c. 10, was freed in the summer of 1838.

[38]This was probably Francis Bird, who rode the Long Point Circuit for the Methodist Episcopal Church, though it may have been William Bird from the Nelson Circuit.

[39]John Tufford (b. *ca.* 1809) was an American-born farmer. In 1837 he, his wife Eliza Jane (Duncombe's daughter), and their two children lived on 200 patented acres in concession 1 of Brantford Township. Jailed at Hamilton on 15 December, he was tried and convicted as a rebel in the spring of 1838 before being freed on bail in September.

Thos. Coleman Jr.[40] the remainder of the week[.] On monday [11 December] I went to Paris for salt where I met Mr. G. Curtiss[41] who asked me where Dr. D. was. I told him I had heard the Dr. was in Norwich but that I had not seen him for about a fortnight[.] I also told him that I had rec'd a note from the Dr. & what the note contained[.] He (Mr. (G.C.) [sic] told me that he had enquired of every magistrate in the G.D. [Gore District] who said there was no warrant out for the Dr. and begged of me if I had any influence over the Dr. to go to him & say that if he had not taken up arms against the Government to go home and remain quiet and that he would not be molested. . . . I went immediately to Norwich and told the Dr. what Mr. Curtiss told me[;] his answer was I dare not risk it. . . .

C 13   JOHN HAYCOCK TO JOHN JOSEPH
Ingersoll, 11 December 1837
[PAC, Correspondence of the Provincial Secretary's Office, v. 9, file 1172]

For another extract from this document see C 19.

. . . I have just seen a young man from Norwich who says that regular training is going on there, he (simple fellow) thinks it all right, he was summoned to enrol his name for the purpose of going in the direction of Brantford to meet a body from oakland & about 100 from this neighbourhood – in all about 300 to 350 were expected – The avowed object appears to be to liberate the prisoners at Hamilton – Dr. Duncombe (he states) is in Norwich & known there as *Gen:l Duncombe* & has a guard of 12 men about his precious person. An Englishman passed through the village last night from Norwich who stated that he had been regularly warned to attend training in Capt ____'s Company – the notice was signed by some one as Serj:t of the said company – he supposed at the time that it was meant for the regular militia – I believe the militia in this division has not been summoned. . . .

C 14   DEPOSITION OF THOMAS WALLACE
18 December 1837
[PAC, Upper Canada Sundries, v. 180, pp. 99460-1]

. . . Thomas Wallace . . . saith that one Peter de long[42] told deponent

---

[40]Thomas Coleman appears to have been a member of the Coleman family which, along with Hiram Capron and the Curtises, had an interest in the plaster of Paris beds near Paris.

[41]William Granville Curtis (Curtiss) (1804–1843) was born in New York State into a Quaker family of recent English origin. In 1814 his family emigrated to Upper Canada, settling first in Norwich, then in Dumfries. William married in 1831. In the 1830s he, and possibly other members of his family, acquired an interest in Paris' plaster beds. A loyalist in 1837, he was appointed a magistrate for Paris in 1838.

[42]Peter DeLong (de long) (*ca.* 1778–1839) of Dutchess County, New York, emigrated to Upper Canada about 1810, buying, in association with Peter Lossing, an

that he de long was one of Charles Duncombe's Secret Committee – that de long generally took a very active part amongst the rebels and did do every thing in his power to aid and assist them – deponent Supped with de long on Wednesday night last [13 December], and de long told deponent that he deponent must be watched very strictly, as he deponent was an enemy to the righteous cause – that said de long told deponent, if he sent any information of the movements of the Rebels to Brantford, they would take him deponent prisoner and keep him as a hostage – de long told deponent he had no doubt duncombe would succeed – and that if they, meaning the loyal people of Brantford, fired a single shot, they would burn Brantford. or would not leave a house Standing – deponent further saith, that he was arrested and made prisoner by Paul Bedford and six others, and kept in custody about a couple of hours.

C 15   REBEL REQUISITIONS
[Ipswich and East Suffolk Record Office, A.N. MacNab Papers, microfilm in PAO]

We the Norwich Committee Request you to Peaceably to give all your fire arms and amunition up to the Bearers and this shall be your Receipt for the same for the use of the provincial army

Head Quarters   December 13th 1837.
M. Mott[43] Secretary   Abraham Sutton[44] [word illegible]

C 16   JOHN TREFFRY[45] TO GEORGE TREFFRY[46]
Summerville, Norwich, 24 June 1838
[UWO, Society of Friends Archives, Personal Records, Box 24]

. . . Since the rebellion broke out . . . I have been left very quiet

---

extensive tract in Norwich, where he raised his family. In 1837 Peter, who was a farmer and described as "an old and infirm man and very decriped [sic]," owned 1,619 patented acres. In September 1837 he was chosen a delegate of the Norwich political union. After inciting rebellion in Norwich, he fled the province and was attainted a traitor. He died in the United States.

[43]Moses Mott (b. *ca.* 1809) came with his Quaker family to Norwich from Dutchess County, New York, in 1810. In 1837 he leased 100 acres of lot 9, concession 4, which he farmed. He also served as a town fence-viewer. After the rebellion he fled to the United States, returning in 1838. The authorities took no action against him.

[44]Abraham Sutton was an American-born resident of Sodom who had been naturalized in 1835. A member of the Norwich political union, he joined the rebels, fleeing after the revolt. He was subsequently attainted a traitor.

[45]John Treffry (1813–1850) was a native of Plymouth, England. His father John, a merchant, brought out his wife and nine of his children to Upper Canada from England in 1834, and settled on lot 2, concession 10 in Norwich. Young John helped his father farm and worked as a carpenter. He married a Quaker in 1835. Though his family appear to have been Quakers or to have believed in Quaker-like principles, John had not yet joined the Society of Friends in 1838, though he was a devout pacifist.

[46]George Treffry, John Jr.'s brother, lived in Exeter, England.

considering the situation of the country, I was once ordered to appear at rebel headquarters (by a rebel serjeant,) equiped for marching, I asked him for his authority, he replied he had orders from his captain to order out all he saw, I told him I was no fighter and should not go, and if he forced me I should be of no service to *them* [–] with that he went off and I heard no more from him – previous to this the rebels understood I had a good rifle and demanded it of me [–] I told them I could not let a gun of mine fight, I had rather break it in pieces than let him have it, to kill others, he then offered me a 3 year old ox for it but I told him I had rather give it away than sell it to him – he said I was ugly and used threats, against my life, and searched my house but he did not find it, he then went and represented me to their captain and when he returned he told me I was a marked man – – – and again demanded the gun and I refused it – he said he would have it if it was to be found, and would have searched the house but I told him it was not in the house, he turned to many ann[47] and said he wont lie I know, and I wont look – after that 6 others came and looked up stairs and down for it but in vain, . . .

A Doctor Duncombe was the leader of the rebels in this Township [–] I saw him by chance at a neighbours, this was the first I had any Idea of such a disturbance, he (– Dr. D) was just arrived in town, and onc. by. said well John war is declared, I asked, how war? nonsense – "Dr D replied it is a fact, yesterday McKenzie took Toronto and to day they expect a[n] attack from the government party, McNab is gone to Toronto with only 50 men and he might as well stay home [–] the governer is on the lake with His family and specie, and Dr Rolph is looking out with two steam boats to take them all – Papineau has taken Quebec, and there is a large raft of timber sunk in a narrow part of the St Lawrence to stop Brittish vessels from coming up in the spring, now is our time and the story is told, there are also several warrants out against different people who if they are taken will be hung, and it is now our intention to call a meeting in the town immediately and come to some resolution what to do, to protect them," with this and similar stories he excited the minds of the people in general (who were not very well affected before) to take up arms, and they marched about 200 able bodied men out of the township towards toronto gathering as they went, . . . not a single word of the above happened to be true except the warrants, and that was stretched – – thus one man led astray 200 men, many of whom have since left the country farms wives & families and perhaps will never return. . . . Another of Duncombes schemes to deceive those who were more reformers than rebels, kept a flag hoisted at their meetings and head quarters with the words, British constitution and the rights of the people on it but when they were all embodied and about to march he addressed them all and told them that

[47]Mary Ann Southwick (1816–1908), a Norwich Quaker, married John Treffry in 1835. In November 1837 she began working as a governess for Solomon Lossing.

in case they should not succeed they must call on the U.S. for assist-ance and they could not do that with the flag they hoisted, and forthwith orderd a liberty flag to be put up, the foolish deluded people believed it all and went on crying the British Constitution and the rights of the people, but all the rebels knew the cheat – . . .

I should like to know what thou thinkest about fighting, I believe a fighter *cannot* be *a christian* because a christian is an heir of christs Kindom, . . .

C 17   DEPOSITION OF MYRE WETHY[48]
15 March 1838
[PAC, Records of the London District Magistrates, v. II]

. . . on or about the 11th day of December last past he met with Robert Alway[49] M.P.P. at the house of Thomas Pool[50] in Dereham – Charles Christie[51] and Peter Hagle[52] was there and deponent thinks the two young Hagles[53] & several other persons were present – Deponent heard Robert Alway say that McKenzie and the Reformers had risen and Attacked Toronto – and that Duncomb had a body of men at Oakland – he advised those that were there to turn out and join them – said that the reformers were so much the strongest party that if they would turn out they would easily gain their independence and that He did not think they would have to fight – for if they only showed their

[48]Myre (Mire) Wethy (b. *ca.* 1809), a native of New York State, was an Oxford County farmer. Jailed as a rebel at London on 15 December 1837, he was freed on 1 June 1838 after petitioning under 1 Victoria, c. 10.

[49]Robert Alway (1790–1840) was born in England, evidently arriving in Upper Canada about 1816, following his brother Joseph who had come in 1810. In 1824 he was appointed a captain in the 1st Oxford Regiment. He ran unsuccessfully for the Assembly in Oxford in 1828. In the 1834 and 1836 elections, however, he was successful, coming to be regarded by some as western Upper Canada's leading radical. Arrested after the revolt and jailed at Hamilton on 17 December, he was indicted, but as the evidence concerning his complicity in the rising was, at best, inconclusive, the crown did not proceed with his case. He was freed on bail on 28 March 1838. Though, unlike Duncombe and Rolph, he was not expelled by the Assembly as a traitor, he decided to leave the country, moving first to Buffalo, then to Texas, dying there in 1840, leaving his wife Sarah with seven children.

[50]This was likely the Thomas Poole (Pool) of Dereham (*ca.* 1789–*ca.* 1854) who was an English-born farmer. His son Thomas Poole Jr. (b. *ca.* 1818), a labourer, turned out with the rebels. He was jailed at London on 17 December 1837 and granted bail on 12 January 1838.

[51]Charles Christie, an American, owned no property himself and lived in Dereham with the Hagles, probably as a farm labourer. A rebel, he was jailed at London on 17 December 1837 and freed on bail on 18 January 1838.

[52]Peter Hagle (b. *ca.* 1792) was an American who settled in Dereham, where he raised his family and farmed. He attended the West Oxford reform meeting of 16 November 1837. After urging others to rebel in December, he fled the province in 1838, evidently returning thereafter.

[53]Luke Hagle and Mark Hagle were Peter Hagle's sons. Both were labourers, likely on their father's farm. Both became rebels and were jailed at London on 17 December, being granted bail a few weeks later.

strength the other party would give it up – From his general conversation deponent thinks that his object was to notify the people and induce them to go and join Doctor Duncomb – He said that those who turned out would no doubt be successful and get a Grant of Land as a reward for their Services – Deponent was afterwards induced to join the party at the request of Pelham Teeple[54] and Peter Hagle who made deponent believe that they were going to be attacked by a body of Indians and that it was necessary the people should take up Arms in their own defence –

C 18   INFORMATION OF ELISHA HALL
18 December 1837
[*PAC, Upper Canada Sundries, v. 180, pp. 99432-5*]

. . . the first he heard of the present insurrection was [a] letter from Dr. Duncombe to Mr. Haskins[55] he saw which stated that the reformers had taken Toronto that the militia were to be called out and that tomorrow he Dr. Duncombe was to be erested or something to that perport and which was the first information or knowledge he had of an intention to take up Arms Against the Govt. of this Country – Informant saith that he wrote to Dr Duncombe and Stated that he had seen his letter to Mr. Haskins stating that Toronto was taken and he Dr Duncombe expected to be immediately to be errested – And gave it as his opinion that it was a premature thing on the part of McKenzie and that he this informant would not lift his finger in the matter and that he hoped that he Dr Duncombe would not, and further states that if we ware likely to have troublesome times here he would let his farm and take his family and leave the country – & that he was also fearful the Govt. would incurage the Indians and that life nor property would be safe – . . .

[54]Pelham C. Teeple (1809–1878) was born in Upper Canada into a loyalist family. In 1837 Pelham, a "tall stout" bachelor, worked on his father Peter's farm. A temperance advocate and a reformer, Pelham had toured the northern United States and been much impressed with American freedom and prosperity. He attended the reform meeting at West Oxford on 16 November 1837 and turned out with the rebels in December, much to the chagrin of his father, a magistrate. Captured that December, Pelham escaped, fleeing to the United States. Attainted a traitor, he was finally pardoned in 1843, but, having married in 1841, he remained in Illinois, where he lived out his days.

[55]"Haskins" was Luther Hoskins (b. *ca.* 1776). A native of Connecticut, he settled in West Oxford Township in 1794, where he had acquired 400 patented acres by 1837. Over the years he held various township offices. He was an active reformer, and joined the West Oxford political union in November 1837. In December he turned out with the rebels. Jailed at London on 21 December, he was freed on bail on 26 February 1838 but then recommitted. He was finally freed in October 1838, having petitioned under 1 Victoria, c. 10.

C 19   JOHN HAYCOCK TO JOHN JOSEPH
Ingersoll, 11 December 1837

[*PAC, Correspondence of the Provincial Secretary's Office, v. 9, file 1172*]

For another extract from this document see C 13.

. . . Elisha Hall at whose house there was a meeting on Saturday evening was to head the body from this quarter, but this morning his career was suddenly checked by a fall from his horse when (it is since known) he was on his way to join Duncombe – He received a violent kick on his head & the medical man who has seen him tells me that he thinks his back is injured – . . .

There are many pensioners about here who would willingly turn out – & the Scotch settlers in Zorra – It really appears to me that a demonstration should be made on the part of the loyal in this neighbourhood – at present the activity appears on the side of the disaffected

This observation does not apply to Woodstock where great energy prevails but to this immediate neighbourhood where a feeling of fear appears rather encouraged than otherwise – When the accounts reached us on Saturday of the glorious results near Toronto, my boys ran up the British Ensign, but to-day I have been advised that it will be prudent not to keep it up which I was disposed to have done –

A Yankee rascal of the name of H.P. Hoage in Ingersoll has I understand threatened that if any rising took place that the whole of Mr Ingersoll's buildings & property should be burned; – this fellow is a waggon maker – has no stake in the country, but is a perfect fire-brand –

Several circumstances of a trivial nature have occurred which shew the bias of many towards destruction –

I am informed that Elisha Hall's accident has struck dismay among those who looked to him as a leader – – There is a move towards Norwich of many – the Dorchester reformers have decided very wisely to stay at home –

Since writing the above I have been informed that the Scotch are going to turn out under Capt Graham[56] –

[56]Philip Graham (*ca*. 1792–1849) a Royal Navy commander on half-pay, arrived in Upper Canada from Stamford, Lincolnshire, with his large family in 1832 and acquired large properties about Woodstock. A red-hot tory, he was appointed a magistrate for North Oxford Township in 1833. He took up a militia commission and assumed a deep interest in the force, asking unsuccessfully in 1837 to be allowed to form a regiment in Zorra made up entirely of Highlanders. After helping suppress the Duncombe rising, he was made lieutenant-colonel of the 2nd Oxford Regiment on 8 February 1838. In 1839–40 he served as a commissioner of the Court of Requests and 1842–5 as a councillor of the Brock District. He also became county master of the Orange lodge.

Major Holcroft[57] is unfortunately unwell at present & confined to the house [–]

C 20   INFORMATION OF FINLAY MCFEE[58]
20 December 1837
[PAC, Upper Canada Sundries, v. 180, p. 99608]

. . . The said Informant upon his oath saith – That Thomas Putnam[59] asked him, witness, if he would join the people who were to turn out as volunteers to go to join 4000 at Brantford to keep back the tories; and said he expected they would burn Brantford that night – further stated that Toronto was surrounded, and that 700 well armed men were at Queenston ready to come over to assist as soon as the flag would be highstad, and said he had recd. a letter from Dr. Duncombe the evening before – He also said that all who had property ought to go for a change of government [–] would enhance their property to three times its present value – Did not say he intended to go himself but said a party would go from Oxford and Westminster, and that the people of London would have enough to do to keep London – . . .

C 21   TESTIMONY OF DOYLE MCKENNY IN ROBERT COOK'S TRIAL
[PAC, Upper Canada Sundries, v. 193, pp. 107352-3]

Doyle McKennie Esquire – The Witness resides in Malahide and lived there in December last – on the sixth or seventh of December he was at a Tavern in Bayham where he saw about a dozen persons of whom the prisoner [Robert Cook] was one – some of them were armed with guns – . . . one "Fisher"[60] . . . was there and asked the witness if he knew what the assemblage meant – witness said he did not – Fisher then said he would tell him – then he said McKenzie had taken Toronto – he said it is ours – witness asked him what business they had at Toronto – he said the country there had risen en masse from information they had received – he asked witness if he had heard of the insurrection – witness answered he had not – he said the Mails had been secured by McKenzie's party as witness understood him – and that was the reason

[57]William Holcroft (1777–1858) was a British officer who commanded the artillery in three different battles in North America during the War of 1812. At war's end he may have stayed on in Upper Canada. In any case, he eventually settled in West Oxford Township where, in 1837, he served as a major in the militia, being promoted in February 1838 to colonel of the 5th Oxford Regiment. He was also a magistrate, having been first appointed one in 1836.

[58]This was likely the Finlay McFee who was to receive a tavern licence in the London District in 1846.

[59]This was probably Thomas Putnam of Dorchester Township (1804–1880), an Upper Canadian-born farmer and a member of a locally prominent reform family.

[60]This was Henry Fisher, an English-born farmer who owned 100 unpatented acres of lot 5, concession 8 in Bayham. After being active in the Duncombe rising, he fled the province and was attainted a traitor. Later pardoned, he returned to the colony.

the "Tories" here had not received information of the rebellion –
witness asked him if it were possible the people had broken out into
revolt [–] he said "It was" [–] witness then told him that was very
different from what he had always been saying namely "that: they only
wanted redress of grievances"[–] he said they had tried that long
enough, and that they were now going to enforce measures – . . .
witness asked Fisher what they intended to do [–] he answered that
they intended to take every man prisoner whom they found opposing
them in arms – they meant to displace the Magistrates and Militia
officers and as soon as they had a government restored that private
property and persons should be held sacred – the prisoner and the
others remained silent all the while, and apparently listening to what
was said – the party left Bayham about the ninth or tenth of December
for Oakland as witness afterwards understood –

C 22   DOYLE MCKENNY TO JOHN BURWELL
Malahide, 9 December 1837
[*PAC, Adjutant General's Office, Correspondence, v. 22, Middlesex
file*]

I, hasten to inform you that Some thing of the utmost importance has or
is about to take place[,] Several of the Persons called Liberals has been
out about 24 hours gethering all the men they can[,] they Say a Battle
has been fought in Lower Canada and that McKenzie with a Body of
men has attacked Toronto and that Several Persons has been arrested at
Hamilton and Some persons has gone to yarmouth to raise the men
there, Bell[61] and Several others are now at Jesse Paulding[62][,] Say 30
men ready to Start for Hamilton or Toronto tomorrow morning[,]
Expecting to be Joined this night by all the men they Can raise at
yarmouth

this is all I
Know and which I tell you
is real
I write you by James
Johnson and wait your answer
in great haste
yours &c
Doyle McKenny

[61]James Bell was born in Cumberland, England, and emigrated to Upper Canada
about 1817. He acquired a farm of 100 unpatented acres of lot 5, concession 4 in
Bayham. He became a school trustee and was commissioned a sergeant in the 2nd
Middlesex Regiment. He attended the Richmond reform meeting of 23 September
1837 and turned out with the rebels in December. Jailed at London in December 1837,
he petitioned under 1 Victoria, c. 10 and was granted bail in October 1838.
[62]Jesse Paulding, an innkeeper, held 100 patented acres in Bayham. On 23
September 1837 the reformers held a meeting at his Richmond inn. In December he
acted as a commissary for the rebels; consequently, after the rebellion, he fled to
Cleveland and was attainted a traitor.

C 23   JOHN BURWELL TO JOHN JOSEPH
Port Burwell, 10 December 1837
*[PAC, Adjutant General's Office, Correspondence, v. 22, Middlesex
file]*

We have news of the attack upon Toronto by the Rebels & that his
Excellency has taken quarters in the Market House &c. The Rebels are
collecting to march to assist them and encourage their followers by
asserting His Excellency is a Prisoner.

Rebels are going round with Papers requiring Persons to subscribe to
Terms of enrollment in their ranks under Pains and Penalties. Without
force to Carry into effect the Law an arrest, for Treasonable Practices
can not Safely take place. The London District has some desperate
spirits in it, and unless the Militia force be organized no security will
be felt this winter. – The time has now arived for prompt measures and
full execution of criminals else the Rebels will gain strength and
harrass the People. When I had the honor of an interview with His
Excellency I Expressed my belief [mutilated] the revolt in this District,
which is now fully realized – the moment the signal is given in Lower
Canada and at Toronto. Should the Militia be organized, I beg the
honor of tendering my Services among the first volunteers of the
District in any Situation in which His Excellency may command my
Services: On receipt of the enclosed letter [C 22], I dispatched a
Messenger to Col. Talbot and Col. [Mahlon] Burwell with the
intelegent it contains, And I am just now told the 200 Rebels will Start
Tomorrow morning from their place of rendesvous on Talbot Road in
Bayham gathering their friends from Yarmouth & Malahide

The loyal people wait for orders to join the Standard of their
Sovereign and defend the Government with their best Services. . . .

C 24   DEPOSITION OF HOSEA VAN POTTER[63]
23 December 1837
[PAC, Records of the London District Magistrates, v. II]

. . . Hosea Vanpotter . . . saith that on Monday the 11th day of
December instant, in the evening – he this deponent was at a political
meeting held in the Baptist Schoolhouse in said township [Malahide] –
that the said meeting was attended by about sixty persons – That when
this deponent came into the meeting Ebenezer Willcox[64] of Malahide,
yeoman – was making a Speech during which he advised the people to
arm themselves with guns – Said Ebenezer Willcox requested some of
those present to sign a paper which had been prepared for signatures –

---

[63]Hosea Van Potter was a Malahide farmer.

[64]Ebenezer Wilcox (Willcox) was born in New York State. He emigrated to Upper
Canada about 1819, settling in Malahide, where he farmed, owning 359 patented acres
in 1837. He was an active reformer and a temperance advocate, being an officer in
1836–7 of both the Malahide and London District temperance societies. Jailed at
London on 21 December 1837 for his part in the rebellion, he was tried in the spring
and found guilty of treason but was freed on bail in the fall of 1838. He and his wife
then moved to Iowa, where they lived out their days.

Another meeting was appointed to be held on Thursday evening of the
same week – and said Willcox told them that they had all better bring
guns with them who had guns – He requested all who had signed the
paper to attend and bring guns – and also said something about getting
their guns in repair – and said further that they who had two coats had
better sell one and buy a gun – This deponent understood from the
speech that those who signed the paper agreed thereby to defend one
another and their property – They agreed to appoint a captain and other
officers at the next meeting – and afterwards appointed Enoch Moore[65]
of Malahide Captain until the next meeting to be holden on the
thursday evening following –

C 25   DEPOSITION OF ELISHA R. SMITH[66]
23 December 1837
[PAC, Records of the London District Magistrates, v. II]

. . . on Thursday the fourteenth day of December instant – . . . he this
deponent saw Ebenezer Willcox of Malahide. . . . Said deponent told
him the said Willcox of his advising the people at a certain political
meeting an evening or two previous for those who had two coats to sell
one and buy a gun – . . . Said Willcox appeared to be considarably
angry and said that he was well aware that a gang of robbers would
come and take the people's property from them, mentioning guns –
mentioning at the same time that he expected the authority would do so
– and acknowledged that he had advised them to arm themselves for
defence against such authority. . . .

C 26   EXAMINATION OF STEPHEN SECORD[67]
19 December 1837
[PAC, Records of the London District Magistrates, v. II]

. . . on Friday or Saturday the 8th or 9th Int. David Anderson[68] came

[65]Enoch Moore was born in New Jersey before 1776. His loyalist father took his
family, including his sons Enoch, Elias, and John, first to Nova Scotia, then to Upper
Canada in 1811. Enoch fought in the War of 1812 and became for a time deputy sheriff
of the London District. A prosperous farmer, he acquired a large amount of property in
the Malahide area, where he raised his family. Though his family was a Quaker one,
he strayed from the faith. In December 1837 he helped organize a meeting in
Malahide, ostensibly so that the residents could unite to defend themselves from
marauding tories, if need be. He was jailed at London on 21 December 1837, tried that
spring, and found guilty of treason. Draper considered him dangerous, for he was
"intelligent and mischievous . . . crafty and daring." None the less he was freed on
bail on 5 October 1838.
[66]Elisha R. Smith, a Malahide property-owner, was likely a farmer.
[67]Stephen Secord (1801–1884) was born in Upper Canada. In 1837 he lived in
Yarmouth, where he owned 21 patented acres. In the fall of 1837 he attended various
reform meetings and after the rebellion was accused of having helped incite the revolt.
His alleged sins seemed the more noteworthy for his deceased father's having been a
magistrate in the locale. Jailed at London on 21 December, he was evidently not
indicted and was released on 16 April 1838.
[68]David Anderson (d. 1838), an Irishman, kept a tavern in Selborne in Southwold.

to him with a copy of a letter from Mr. Malcolm of Oakville [Oakland], believes it was James Malcolm, the copy or extract of the letter was written by George Lawton[69] and was extracted from a letter written to himself – the purport of which letter that Toronto was taken by Mr. McKenzie, that a body of Men were assembled at Oakland for marching Eastward, to rescue a prisoner at Hamilton – Anderson gave him the letter and requested him to carry it to Montgomery Smith in Southwold – In addition to the extract the letter contained a request that the reformers would meet at Sparta, to deliberate on what measures they should adopt. . . .

C 27   DEPOSITION OF DUNCAN WILSON[70]
23 January 1838
[PAC, Upper Canada Sundries, v. 196, pp. 109199-202]

. . . between the 1st and 10th of December last – Thinks it was on Saturday night – there was a private meeting of certain Reformers at Artimas Hitchkocks[71] chamber [–] Elias Snyder[72] was there – and deponent thinks the meeting was called in consequence of his coming – deponent was not at the meeting but saw Snyder before the meeting –

He had acted as a district constable. Another claim to local fame was that he had been an Orangeman but had recanted. He was active in the reform agitation of the fall of 1837 and was leader of the Yarmouth rebels in December. After the failure of the rising, he fled the province, joining the Patriots at Detroit. Like Robert Davis of Nissouri, he was involved in the *Anne* episode near Fort Malden in January 1838, and, like Davis, was fatally wounded.

[69]George Lawton (*ca.* 1786–1848) emigrated to Upper Canada about 1817, settling in Yarmouth Township, where he taught school for a time. He acquired the 200 acres of lot 14, concession 3 which he patented. He reportedly developed one of the most prosperous farms in the area. A Quaker, he none the less held elective office in 1836, that of township commissioner. He took a deep interest in reform politics and was chosen a delegate in 1837 of the Sparta political union to the projected provincial convention and spoke at the Westminster meeting of 6 October. After inciting revolt in December, he fled to the United States and was attainted a traitor. Pardoned, he returned about 1840 to his family.

[70]Duncan Wilson (b. *ca.* 1801), a native of New York State, came with his Quaker parents to Upper Canada about 1824. They settled in Norwich; he later took up residence in Yarmouth. Though he was evidently a wagon-maker, he practised medicine. In September 1837 he attended the reform meeting in Richmond, Bayham, with some Yarmouth men, and in December he helped fund the Yarmouth rebel party going to Oakland. He was subsequently jailed at London on 30 December. Though released on bail on 26 January 1838, he was recommitted but then freed after escaping indictment. In June 1838 he participated in the Short Hills raid. Eventually captured, he was not tried. He married in Yarmouth in 1839.

[71]Artemas (Artimas) Hitchcock (Hitchkock) was a Sparta tavernkeeper who participated in the reform meeting of 9 September 1837 in his village. No official actions were lodged against him after the revolt, though he had contributed money to the rebel cause.

[72]This was Elias Snider (Snyder) of Norwich who had been sent to Yarmouth by Duncombe to incite rebellion.

Snyder told deponent that Mckenzie was in Arms at Toronto with 2000 men and that Duncomb had 2 Companies of 80 raised – and that he had Come up for the purpose of raising the Reformers in Yarmouth – Snyder showed witness a letter or address Headed – To our Reform friends in Middlesex or Words to That Effect – stating that the time had now arrived for the People to take arms – and calling them to Arms – which was signed by Charles Duncombe [–] Snyder said it was in his (Duncombs) hand writing –

There was a Committee of Vigilance appointed in the letter – Ephriam Cooks[73] name was one mentioned in that committee – does not recollect the others –

On the other side of the Sheet was a Pledge Written which deponent believes to be in Doctor Duncombs writing which appeared to have been copied from an original document – The Pledge was in the following words –

"We the Subscribers pledge ourselves, our lives our propertys our Sacred honors in the Cause of Reform" – to which was signed the names of Charles Duncomb – Thomas Parke – Bela Shaw [–] Peter Delong – Elias Snyder – John Talbot, Robert Alway – & some others that Deponent does not recollect –

Thinks that all the names were written in Duncombs hand – Except Peter Delongs and Elias Snyders which was written in their own hand writing – Snyder said that the letter had been written by Doctor Duncomb at Peter Delongs –

Deponent saw Bela Shaw at St Thomas on Monday the 11th Decr and told Shaw that he understood they were going to train at Sparta [–] that he had better go down or send his son down to stop them – To Which he replied that they had better be stopped but that he durst not go himself nor send his Son – Mr Shaw further Said that McKenzies Striking the Blow as soon as he did was Premature. – he seemed much agitated[.]

C 28   EXAMINATION OF JONATHAN STEELE[74]
20 December 1837
[PAC, Records of the London District Magistrates, v. II]

Saith, that he was one of Andersons company. on Saturday the 9th first heard of the intention of rising. Attended meeting at Sparta in the

[73]Ephraim Cook (b. ca. 1807) was a native of Massachusetts. He emigrated to Upper Canada with his parents about 1829 and in 1831 was licensed as a physician. Living in Norwich with his wife and parents, he had acquired 100 patented acres there by 1837, as well as the position of postmaster. A "surgeon" with Duncombe's forces, he was jailed at Hamilton on 23 December 1837, freed on bail on 28 February 1838, recommitted, tried, found guilty of treason, and in August 1838 banished for life. Officialdom finally relented of this sentence, for Cook was back in Norwich by 1843, and in 1854 was elected South Oxford's representative to the Assembly of the united Canadas.

[74]Jonathan Steele (b. ca. 1806) was born in the Niagara District. By 1837 he owned

evening. George Lawton, John Moore[75] there. A person from Norwich there, thinks his name was Sneider. John Moore Chairman. The party headed by Anderson was organised there & officers chosen. Hitchcock was secretary. Anderson chosen Captain, Joshua Doan[76] Lieutenant, Solomon Hawes[77] Ensign, Isaac Fisher seargiant. Next meeting monday night Elias Moore there, and generally the same persons as before. John Moore chairman again[.] Names of company enrolled. A person of name of Swisher[78] there. who wanted all to go to Toronto and told them the whole country was in their hands. Arranged to assemble in arms to march the next morning[.] Elias Moore did not oppose it, but did not hear him say anything. Assembled again with arms on tuesday morning. Saw John Moore there. George Lawton and Walter Chase.[79] Chase spoke of forces coming from Buffalo under Dr Rolph: would be at Hamilton with Artillery before themselves. Received money from different persons. Hitchcock gave most supposed to be subscribed. abt 70 dollars. . . .

---

100 patented acres of lot 18, concession 5 in Yarmouth, which he farmed. Though a Quaker, he acted as the treasurer of the Yarmouth rebels in December. He was jailed at London on 20 December, bailed on 15 January 1838, and then recommitted. After petitioning under 1 Victoria, c. 10, he was freed on bail late that summer.

[75]John Moore was born in New Jersey before the American Revolution to a Quaker family. His father, a loyalist, took his family, including his sons John, Elias, and Enoch, to Nova Scotia, then in 1811 to Upper Canada. In 1837 John owned 300 unpatented acres in Yarmouth, cultivating a fine farm reportedly worth $8,000. Despite being a Conservative Quaker, he was a political activist, having helped organize an early political union at St. Thomas in 1833 and participating in the reform agitation of the fall of 1837. Jailed at London on 22 December for his part in the rebellion, he was tried the following spring and represented then as being "a passionate but very weak minded man." He was found guilty of treason but was released that summer. Unfortunately, while he was in jail, his son Joseph, who had been a rebel, jailed at London, then freed, had died from an illness contracted during his imprisonment.

[76]Joshua G. Doan (ca. 1811–1839) was born at Sugar Loaf in the Niagara District, the son of a United Empire Loyalist Quaker, Jonathan Doan. Jonathan, an agent for the Baby lands in the south of Yarmouth, moved his family to that township in 1813. Here, Joshua and his brother Joel began operation of a tannery on lot 19, concession 4. Joshua attended the reform meeting in Westminster on 6 October 1837 and turned out with the rebels in December. On the failure of the revolt, he fled the province and was attainted a traitor. In December 1838 he was with the Patriots who launched the raid on Windsor. Captured, he was hanged in 1839 at London, leaving behind a young family.

[77]Solomon Hawes of Yarmouth fled after the rebellion and was attainted a traitor.

[78]This was Martin Switzer (b. ca. 1778), a Streetsville area farmer who cared for a blind son. He was an ardent reformer, an acquaintance of W.L. Mackenzie, Charles Durand, and Elias Moore, among others. In December 1837, having heard of the rising at Toronto, he went to Yarmouth to see Moore and to raise revolt there. On the failure of the Duncombe rising, he fled to the United States, but returned in 1838, only to be imprisoned that July. After petitioning under 1 Victoria, c. 10, he was freed on bail on 28 September 1838. In December he indignantly informed Mackenzie that, while he had been in jail, his own brother, a tory, had asked the government to grant him his farm.

[79]Walter Chase, an Upper Canadian who was of loyalist descent, was in his thirties

C 29   EXAMINATION OF LEVI HEATON[80]
20 December 1837
[PAC, Records of the London District Magistrates, v. II]

For another extract from this document see C 60.

. . . Heaton saith, That on Saturday the 9th Instant Elias Snyder of Norwich came to him when he was at work in Yarmouth and told him that McKenzie had an army at Toronto, and he had no doubt that he would take Toronto, Snyder said that some Companies were formed in Norwich who were to join Doctor Duncomb at Oakland, expected a Company would be formed in Yarmouth also – he wished to have a meeting at Sparta that evening – S [Snyder] Attended the meeting at Sparta in the evening – about twenty five persons enrolled themselves [–] Heaton was one of the number, George Lawton took the lead and spoke most, David Anderson Joshua Doan and Joel Doan[81] were very forward, John Moore was chairman of the meeting, Officers were chosen and the Company organized, David Anderson was elected Captain, Joshua Doan Lieut. Solomon Hawes Ensign, Isaac Fisher Serjeant. On monday the 11th another meeting of the Company was held at Sparta, a person named Swisser from near Toronto, was present, said he came for the purpose of raising men to go to Toronto. said that McKenzie was within four miles of Toronto with five thousand men [–] no doubt if they turned out there would not be a Gun fired as Toronto would be taken before they got there – said they would be well rewarded if they succeeded – he had seen Doctor Duncomb as he came, when the Company got to Oakland it would be under the immediate Command of Docr. Duncombe – on monday more men joined the company – was about fifty strong when marched from Sparta on tuesday morning – . . .

---

in 1837. His activities as a commission merchant and tavernkeeper at Port Stanley supported him, his wife, and their five children. In 1834 he had served as a township road master. He had long demonstrated an interest in politics when he enlisted with the rebels in 1837. After the revolt, he fled to Michigan, and was involved as a Patriot in the *Anne* episode near Fort Malden in January 1838. Captured on that occasion, he was imprisoned, but escaped from Fort Henry that summer.

[80]Levi Heaton, an American, settled in Upper Canada as a child with his family in 1823. In 1837 he lived near Sparta. A Hicksite Quaker, he none the less attended the Westminster reform meeting of 6 October and turned out with the rebels in December. Jailed at London on 16 December, he was bailed on 12 January 1838.

[81]Joel P. Doan was a partner with his brother Joshua in a Yarmouth tannery. Joel had learned his trade in the United States. Although a Hicksite Quaker like his brother, he too turned out with the rebels in 1837. He fled after the collapse of the rising and was attainted a traitor. Evidently pardoned, he had by 1842 returned to Yarmouth and married the widow of his executed brother. He later became a physician and in the 1870s was reported living in western Canada.

C 30   DEPOSITION OF ANDREW MCCLURE[82]
1 January 1838
[PAC, Upper Canada Sundries, v. 184, pp. 103105-6]

Andrew McClure of Yarmouth deposeth and saith that he was one of the party who took up arms and marched under David Anderson to Oakland – that he was induced to do so [from ?] the representations of a man of the name of Switzer who came From Toronto and represented that McKenzie was in arms at Toronto – had surrounded the City and had Double the force that was inside – and that one half of those inside the City were only waiting for an opportunity of joining McKenzie – that switzer stated to the young men whom he urged to go that they need not be afraid as it was not expected that there would be a gun fired as the Governor had made offers of treating with them and would grant the requests that had been required of the Government –

C 31   EXAMINATION OF BENJAMIN PAGE[83]
6 January 1838
[PAC, Records of the London District Magistrates, v. I, pp. 60-1]

. . . they started from Sparta about 12 OClock in the day [–] there were about 56 & went to Paulding's that night – Chase was there the day the party started – He had a handbill from Buffalo stating how many volunteers they could raise in Buffalo & that the Patriots in Lower Canada were driving the Tories in every quarter – Chase was greatly in favour of the party going – . . . Switzer went at the head of the party until they got into the 11 mile woods below Eacle's Tavern[84] and then left them – Witness states that he never got to Oakland – He had taken a horse from a man of the name of Anderson[85] who lives at Lodor's Place[86] [–] was told by two chaps at Hazern[']s that Anderson had horses – he got at old Mr Ostrander[']s place a saddle and Bridle – after he started from there he went on to the next house – after he had stopped there and came out some one came out behind him and fired at

[82]Andrew McClure (McLure) (b. *ca.* 1812) was an Irish cordwainer who settled in Southwold from New York State in the fall of 1837. He immediately acquired a quarter-acre patented lot on the north branch of the Talbot Road. Despite his recent arrival, he joined the rebels in December. Jailed in London in December 1837, he was granted bail on 1 January 1838 but recommitted. After petitioning under 1 Victoria, c. 10, he was released on bail on 6 June 1838.

[83]Benjamin Page (b. *ca.* 1813) was born in the Niagara District. In 1837 he and his wife lived in Yarmouth where he worked as a tanner and currier. He proved to be an oddity, an Anglican rebel. He was jailed at London on 16 December 1837, granted bail on 16 January 1838, but then recommitted, being freed on bail a final time on 9 June 1838 after petitioning under 1 Victoria, c. 10.

[84]Eagle's Tavern was on lot 188, the south side of the Talbot Road in Middleton, near the Middleton-Windham town line. It was owned by Nelson Eagle.

[85]This was Jeremiah Anderson who lived on Little Otter Creek at Lodor's inn.

[86]"Lodor's place" was Lodor's inn on Little Otter Creek.

him and shot him through the arm – stopped at Edmonds[87] that night and started for Oakland – . . .

C 32 EXAMINATION OF AUGUSTUS CHAPEL[88]
15 December 1837
[PAC, Upper Canada Sundries, v. 181, pp. 99925-6]

. . . States – that George Lawton [,] Elias Moore and Bela Shaw; & a man from Toronto advised him to go and fight – they said that all volunteers were to have twelve Dollars a month during the War, and a reward of 200 acres of Land each – that under these promises he was induced to go – . . . was 16 years old yesterday – . . .

C 33 EXAMINATION OF AUGUSTUS CHAPEL
29 December 1837
[PAC, Records of the London District Magistrates, v. II]

For another extract from this document see C 61.

. . . I went in Captain Andersons Company [–] fifty two Started [–] John Moore came to Pauldings the night we stoped at Paulding [–] Said that a Company of Horse was agoing to follow us from St Thomas [–] if they overtook us we[,] he said[,] Should ambush them and Said that he had been informed a Company ment to ambush us at Spring Creek [–] he John Moore Came to fetch the news to us [–] Hervey Brient[89] was with him [–] he went with us on the way [–] we got to oakland after dark [–] it was allowed there was 400: men there. we got our Supper at Scotland. . . .

C 34 JOHN JACKSON[90] TO THE OXFORD MAGISTRATES
Blenheim, 13 December 1837
[PAO, J.M. Snyder Papers]

I am just recd. information that yesterday morning early there was a

---

[87]Edmonds' tavern was in Windham and was probably run by one of the relatives of Oliver Edmonds, a township commissioner who was jailed on 16 December at Hamilton as a rebel and not released until 15 March 1838.

[88]Augustus Chapel (Chaple) (b. ca. 1821) of Yarmouth attended the Westminster reform meeting of 6 October 1837. A youthful rebel, he was jailed in December 1837 and freed on bail on 9 January 1838.

[89]"Hervey Brient" was Harvey Bryant (b. ca. 1797), a native of Massachusetts. He was resident in Yarmouth by 1825, where he married into the Doan family in 1828. He acquired the 200 unpatented acres of lot 25, concession 3, which he farmed. A reformer, he had joined the St. Thomas political union organized in 1833. Jailed at London on 22 December 1837, he was tried in the spring and found guilty of treason, but was released on bail on 28 September 1838.

[90]This may have been the John Jackson who was appointed an Oxford County magistrate in 1836 and/or the John Jackson who was commissioned a captain in the 2nd Oxford Regiment in January 1838.

meeting of the rebels in the School house in this place, – when my children whent to School the [they] had not yet disperced, – a number of them was armed, they stoped a man on the highway. searched his wagon supposing he had arms or munitions of war – some individuals amongst them resolved to shoot me or take me prisoner last night when I should return from woodstock – I am here yet free & determined to die so – Wm. Grintons[91] life is also marked also Mr. Cowen[']s [–] they say he has turned. – I have taken the names of all those who were forward in this rebelious meeting. – . . . Wm. Winegarden[92] is the leader [–] Fifty volunteers left Blenheim yesterday to join the royal army – some Thirty or 40 to join the rebels – I am now going to Paris to get some gun locks mended [–] I am just told Mr Caperon[93] is on the rebel side. . . .

C 35   DEPOSITION OF JOHN DUMON[94]
16 December 1837
[PAC, Upper Canada Sundries, v. 180, pp. 99355-7]

. . . in consequence of notice sent by Wheeler Malcolm & his Brother, Deponent called a Meeting of Neighbours, having been called to join Dr. Duncombe's party, or they would be sent for. and forced to go – . . . at that Meeting Dudley Marble[95] called himself Captain, & took the direction . . . there might have been about twenty present at the Meeting – . . . Deponent and *Horatio H* Hills[96] went down to Little Scotland on the Tuesday, with arms – . . . these arms, carried by H Hills, were taken from houses in the neighbourhood by Horatio Hills & Dudley Marble – but Deponent cannot say whether violence was used – . . .

---

[91]William Grinton was a storekeeper. On 19 January 1838 he was commissioned an ensign in the 2nd Oxford Regiment and a captain in 1844. In 1842 he became a Brock District councillor.

[92]William Winegarden (b. *ca.* 1781) was described as a "Dutch Yankee." He emigrated from the United States about 1799 and fought in the War of 1812. He acquired 300 patented acres in Blenheim on which he farmed. In December 1837 three of his sons helped him try to secure Blenheim and area for the rebels. Jailed at Hamilton on 21 December 1837, he petitioned under 1 Victoria, c. 10 and was released on bail on 6 June 1838.

[93]This was Hiram Capron (1796–1872). Born in Vermont, Capron moved to western New York in 1818, then to Upper Canada in 1822 to run the Normandale iron foundry at Long Point. Leaving the foundry in 1828, he moved to Dumfries Township, where he laid out the village of Paris in 1831 and became a prominent figure in the area. He seems to have been largely uninvolved in the fiery politics of the later 1830s, and there was no truth to the rumour reported here.

[94]John Dumon of Dumfries was released after his examination of 16 December 1837.

[95]Dudley Marble (Marvel) was a Dumfries farmer.

[96]Horatio H. Hills (*ca.* 1813–1838) was an American who settled with his parents in Dumfries about 1835. The authorities considered his family a "rather disreputable"

C 36   DEPOSITION OF JAMES GRIGG[97]
16 December 1837
[PAC, Upper Canada Sundries, v. 200, pp. 110848-9]

James Grigg . . . Depones that he knows Horatio Hills – That on Thursday Morning last, Deponent started about 9 o'Clock from home for Galt, there he was hired to Mr. Harris,[98] the Brewer – that he met a party of armed men who insisted upon him joining them – That he refused to do so, saying that he knew very well who they were, & what they were about, & that he would have nothing to do with them – That a good deal of altercation passed; & then Horatio Hills, who said he had a Commission from Head Quarters, ordered two men to seize the Deponent & compel him to go – That Deponent still resisted; when Horatio Hills drew a dagger, & repeatedly wounded the Deponent to the effusion of his Blood; & compelled him by force to turn – That the party then proceeded to the Schoolhouse on 3d Concession Dumfries, where a halt was made and a fire kindled – That Deponent was soon after allowed to depart, & was told by Hills that he had taken him for a Spy, & had orders to prevent any person from going to Galt. Depones that he cannot write[.]

C 37   EXAMINATION OF JOHN WALKER[99]
23 December 1837
[PAC, Upper Canada Sundries, v. 181, pp. 99809-10]

. . . he attended a Public Meeting at Waterford on Tuesday the twelfth Inst. at which time he subscribed a paper presented to him by Eliakim Malcolm, explained . . . as being for the purpose of distinguishing Reformers from those in favor of the Government – . . . states that an Armed party attended the said Eliakim Malcolm, and that the said Malcolm said to those attending the Meeting that the Lower Province was in the hands of the Canadians – and that Toronto was surrounded by McKenzie and would be taken by him –

---

one. In 1837 Horatio was a bachelor and a labourer. Jailed at Hamilton on 17 December as a rebel, he was tried in the spring for treason, found guilty, and, ultimately, sentenced to fourteen years' transportation to Van Diemen's Land. He died in Toronto's gaol of "rapid consumption" on 11 November 1838. His family then left Dumfries and, possibly, the province.

[97]James Grigg was a Galt labourer.

[98]This was James Harris who in 1842 became town clerk of Dumfries Township.

[99]John Walker (b. *ca.* 1811) was Upper Canadian-born and a farmer's son. A Townsend resident, he was examined for involvement in the rising on 23 December and granted bail.

C 38   DEPOSITION OF EBENEZER THOMAS GILBERT[100]
22 December 1837
[*PAC, Upper Canada Sundries, v. 181, pp. 99928-31*]

. . . on the twelfth instant, he this deponent attended the Waterford meeting called by the rebel party and saw there John Massacre[101] who told deponent that it was their intention to upset the Government and to establish an independent one and that they intended to join McKensie and could take Toronto and there would not be ten guns fired against it, he also said that he had not taken up arms before to day though he had not taken up arms yet: after the meeting was organized deponent saw said Massacre there, who took pen in his hand and went forward as deponent supposed to sign the paper: deponent also saw Oliver Smith,[102] the elder, there who [was] acting as Secretary to the rebel meeting; deponent saith that Oliver Smith the younger, was at the meeting, he enquired of deponent about the Simcoe force and: when told by deponent he replyed it was a damned lie saying he had accounts from Simcoe as correct as deponent could bring: deponent said McKenzie was dispersed: Smith replyed it was a damned falshood for McKenzie was back of Toronto with two thousand men deponent further saith that Smith had a gun, fell in the rebel ranks and drilled with them: deponent further saith that he saw Samuel Lemons[103] at the meeting at Waterford he had a sword and acknowledged to belong to the rebel party, deponent inquired what he was doing there Lemons answerd we are going to have our Liberty: deponent further saith that he saw at the said Waterford meeting Hirman Lemons[104] and Joseph Lemons[105] that each had a gun and fell in the ranks with the rebel[s] and drilled: deponent further saith that _____ Paulding, Innkeeper of Bayham was at the Waterford meeting and said he would bear the yoke no longer he belonged to the rebel party: deponent further saith that

[100]Ebenezer Thomas Gilbert (1798–1871) came with his family to Upper Canada from New Brunswick in 1800 to the Long Point area. In 1837 Ebenezer was a farmer and postmaster.

[101]John Massacre, an Upper Canadian-born Townsend farmer, had a large, young family. He was questioned by the magistrates for his support of the rebel cause at the Waterford meeting of 12 December 1837. Freed on bail on 26 December, he was subsequently indicted, whereupon he fled to the United States and was attainted a traitor.

[102]Though there were several Oliver Smiths who lived in Townsend Township, where the meeting discussed here was held, the Oliver Smith cited may have been the one of Bayham who helped organize the revolt in his area and joined the rebels in Oakland. This Smith was an unlicensed physician and American-born. Jailed at Hamilton on 23 December 1837, he was tried in the spring and acquitted. He then moved to the United States, returning later to the province and settling in Dorchester.

[103]Samuel Lemons, who owned lot 8, concession 14 of Burford Township, was a farmer.

[104]Hiram Lemons was a Burford labourer.

[105]This Joseph Lemons may have lived in Burford or may have been one of the several Joseph Lemons of Woodhouse Township.

John Anderson of Dover blacksmith, attended the Waterford meeting, he joined in with the rebel party, gave them encouragement in what they were doing by saying to his party that without the shedding of blood there is no remission of Sins. . . .

C 39   MILITIA ORDER
Toronto, 7 December 1837
[PAC, Militia General Orders, v. 5]

Col: McNab of the 4th Regt. of Gore will proceed immediately on a special service to the London district taking along with him about 500 volunteers who are appointed to receive pay and allowances for 30 days. . . .

C 40   GEORGE W. WHITEHEAD[106] TO ALLAN MACNAB
Burford, 13 December 1837
[PAC, Upper Canada Sundries, v. 180, pp. 99169-70]

The Express has with difficulty found me out being obliged to travel from House to House after night on my [Ned?] as detached parties of the Rebels are in Search of me – I have just recd correct information from Norwich that Duncomb left yesterday at the head of 220 mostly armed & little or no ammunition – he took with him 11 Empty *Baggage* Waggons promising his men to fill them at Brantford & my *st.* [store] [–] messenger from Oakland says they are 200 to 250 – Duncomb in a letter to a *female* friend of his in this place says he has 200 Rifles about 100 muskets [*mutilated*] intended attacking Brantford tomorro[w] – however having recd intelligence of your arrival & force[,] may be induced to change their plans – their force is divided part at Malcolms Mills the remainder two miles at a [*mutilated*] they call Scotland/

God Give you Victory[.]

[106]George Washington Whitehead (*ca.* 1792–*ca.* 1868) was born in Nova Scotia, moving to Upper Canada with his family to the Burford area about 1812 and serving in the war against the United States. He opened a store and became a prominent figure locally, involved in road projects and schemes for canalization of the Grand River. Politically he wavered between tory and reform camps. In the 1820s he was an agent for Mackenzie's *Colonial Advocate* and ran unsuccessfully in Oxford in the Assembly elections of 1828. Though known as a ministeralist then, he was identified as a reformer when elected a Burford Township commissioner in 1836. His father Thomas was a Methodist minister, and George, following Egerton Ryerson's lead, supported the tories in 1836. Appointed a magistrate in 1835, he proved an active loyalist in 1837–8 and found himself promoted in the militia to the rank of lieutenant-colonel on 29 February 1838. In 1845–6 he was elected a councillor of the Brock District. He became the first manager of the conservative *British American* established in Woodstock in 1848. In 1850 he moved to that town from Burford.

C 41   DEPOSITION OF PETER COON[107]
17 December 1837
[R.C. Muir, The Early Political and Military History of Burford
(Quebec, 1913), pp. 139-40]

Peter Coon of the Township of Burford, in the London District, Blacksmith, being duly sworn, deposeth and saith, that for about a fortnight past frequent meetings have taken place in the neighbourhood of his residence. Isaac Malcolm[108] and Eliakim Malcolm, of the Township of Oakland, were particularly active and industrious in calling these meetings, and inducing people to attend them, that at some of these meetings, violent speeches were made by Eliakim Malcolm and Doctor Chas. Duncombe, and one McGuire a School Master, who advised the people to arm themselves and fight against the Government, and said they would lead and assist them.

Has seen Doctor Charles Duncombe armed with a sword, and the said McGuire armed with a gun. He also has frequently seen these three, so armed, drilling and training men, some armed and some without arms. He has also seen George Case, of the Town of Hamilton, armed, and he appeared to be acting in concert with the leaders before mentioned, has heard the Malcolms say, that Geo. Case was of their party, and that they considered him a very efficient person, who would do them good service. Has also understood, that a person of the name of Matthews, an auctioneer from Brantford, was in company with Case, aiding and assisting the rebels.

Deponent further swears, that on Sunday last, McGuire, the school master, and James Malcolm came to him and required him to manufacture a lot of Pikes, for the purpose of arming some of the rebels who had no other arms. He objected to doing so, and they returned on Monday last and insisted on his making pikes for them, and threatened if he did not do so, they would put their martial law in force against him. They required fifty, and he was compelled to proceed to work and made upwards of 20. On Tuesday evening following Doctor Duncombe came to his neighbourhood with about 180 men, Duncombe and the principal part of his men being armed, Duncombe sent a message to him, that he must make pikes or do any other work they required him to do, and charge the same to the party. George Case was in company with Duncombe and his party at that time

[107]Peter Coon was born in Upper Canada. He ran a blacksmith shop in the village of Scotland in Oakland Township. (Probably his deposition identifies him as a resident of Burford because Oakland had been called the Gore of Burford.) Coon was jailed at Hamilton on 15 December 1837 for his part in the rebellion, but, not indicted, was freed on 21 March 1838.

[108]Isaac Brock Malcolm (1812–1867) was the son of Finlay Malcolm Jr. of Oakland. In 1837 he was a farmer and, like many of his relatives, a Congregationalist. Jailed at Hamilton as a rebel on 23 December 1837, he petitioned under 1 Victoria, c. 10 and was released on bail on 6 June 1838.

he was told. James Malcolm gave orders, that everyone should throw his house open and give lodging to the men under arms. Some of them lodged in Deponent's house. Eliakim Malcolm and McGuire told desponent [sic], that they would plunder everyone who would not turn out with them, in order to procure provisions, arms and other necessities, he knows, that they did take a quantity of arms from a person or persons at Waterford. He has heard Eliakim Malcolm and others of the party, say, that they had pills for the Lieut., Gov., Sir F.B. Head, and that they would shoot him if they could get a chance. Has heard Eliakim and James Malcolm and McGuire state, that if they could succeed they would establish an independant Government, without any connection with the Queen or the Mother Country, Great Britain. After it was known that a battle had taken place near Toronto, he had heard Eliakim Malcolm and McGuire say, that MacKenzie was doing well, and that they had acted and would act in concert with them, or words to that effect.

The Rebels heard on Tuesday that Col. McNabb was coming up with a body of armed men to oppose them. On Tuesday morning George Case and Matthews came in from Norwich, and when they heard that an army was coming against them, they went back to Norwich and returned again the same evening with Duncombe and his men. On Wednesday evening the Rebels forces in his neighbourhood amounted in all to about 200 men. On Wednesday evening the Rebels, amounting in all to about 400, left deponent's neighborhood in a body and in tolerably good order. On Thursday morning Col. McNabb's men came to his neighborhood. He was called out to take care of Capt. Servos'[109] horse, which had been shot. Shortly after that deponent was taken prisoner, as he was told for making the pikes already referred to.

C 42   DEPOSITION OF HENRY FOSTER[110]
15 December 1837
[PAC, Upper Canada Sundries, v. 180, pp. 99288-91]

. . . Depones. – That two neighbours William Webb[111] and Franklyn Kenny came to Deponent upon Wednesday morning last, & told him

---

[109]Daniel Kerr Servos (b. 1792) was born in Upper Canada into a United Empire Loyalist family. He served in the War of 1812 and was appointed a captain of the 3rd Gore Regiment of militia in 1823. He commanded a troop of cavalry in MacNab's descent on Scotland.

[110]Henry Foster was a farmer who owned 50 patented acres of lot 37, concession 7 of Dumfries. After being examined for his part in the rebellion on 15 December 1837, he was released on bail.

[111]William Webb (b. ca. 1787) was a native of New York State who emigrated to Upper Canada about 1825. He settled in Dumfries Township, where he became an overseer of highways in 1826. In 1837, a farmer, he had a wife and three young children and a reputation as a great marksman. Jailed as a rebel at Hamilton on 17 December, he was tried and found guilty of treason the following spring. He was granted bail on 13 August 1838.

that he must now turn out & join the party assembling in arms, or he would be forced to do so by a party from Galt. & forced to serve with the Government boys: That this assemblage was to be at Little Scotland in Oakland. That he did not go to the place of meeting upon the Wednesday. That the above two persons told him that he would find fifteen or sixteen hundred men in arms, & that seven hundred more had landed at Kettle Creek from the States to join them, & had brought over seventeen Kegs of Powder. They also said that McKenzie had taken Toronto, & had an army of between two & three thousand men under arms.

That witness reached Little Scotland on the evening of Wednesday, & found a party of about three or four hundred only, so far as he could judge. That some had arms, & some had none; but they had an appearance of training, or of being embodied like soldiers. That Dr Duncombe was mentioned as the "Commander.["]. . .

C 43   DEPOSITION OF SAMUEL MARLATT[112]
16 December 1837
[PAC, Upper Canada Sundries, v. 180, pp. 99370-2]

Samuel Marlatt Depones that he is acquainted with William Webb – That William Webb, Henry Foster, two Brothers of the name of [Colburn ?] two Stuarts,[113] & others, accompanied the Deponent to see Dr. Duncombe's Army – That Webb had told the Deponent that he must go, & could no longer remain neutral; as a press gang was coming from Galt, who would probably make them turn out in the Queen's Service; & Deponent went, wishing to see how matters really were – That the place they went to is called Little Scotland – That he had been led to expect Dr. Duncombe's army was Sixteen hundred strong, & would be Two thousand before morning. – That in fact, however, the whole number, which Deponent saw, did not exceed, in his opinion, Four hundred men. That Deponent felt himself to have been misled, and determined to make the best of his way home, & be done with them – That he saw Dr Duncombe personally in command, giving the word to the men – "forward – March" That the companies formed a complete Battalion – That from twelve to fifteen went down with him, & more than one half returned along with him. – That Deponent went down to Little Scotland on horseback, without arms.

[112]Samuel Marlatt was an American, naturalized in 1833. He and his wife acquired 50 acres of lot 37, concession 7, Dumfries, which they patented and farmed. In 1833 he served as an overseer of highways for his township. He was jailed as a rebel at Hamilton on 2 January 1838, tried that spring for treason, and acquitted.

[113]These were Daniel and John Stuart (Stewart) of Dumfries. The government took no action against them for their parts in the revolt.

C 44   INFORMATION OF LEWIS BURWELL[114]
22 January 1838
[PAC, Upper Canada Sundries, v. 187, pp. 104399-402]

Lewis Burwell . . . saith, that he knows George Alexander Clark of the said Town of Brantford merchant – That on the Seventh day of December last past, when the men of the 1t Regt. Gore Militia were assembling in the said Town of Brantford for the purpose of preparing for the defence of the country against the late Insurrection, he this deponent was in conversation with the said George Alexander Clark, in Colborne street, near Bogues Inn, and in the presence and hearing of many of the Militia men then assembled and in the act of falling into their Ranks, he the said George Alexander Clark said to this deponent in an Audible voice, that the calling of the militia together was illegal – that it was disturbing the peace of the Town, and an injury to the business of the place – That the officers nor the magistrates, had no orders nor authority to call the militia together – *That the people were fools to obey the orders of Col. Racey*[115] or *the magistrates*, and that if he was in their places he would go home about his business. – That there was no Rebelion of the people in the Country – *that the troubles were occasioned by the Government persecuting and attempting to imprison Mackenzie, meaning William Lyon Mackenzie.* – That *Mackenzie was justifiable, (or right)* – That the people had not rebeled against the Government, but that *a corrupt Government had rebeled against* the people, together with many other words of like import. – That after this deponent turned from the said George Alexander Clark, he saw him, and heard him talking to the people and telling them that the officers had no authority to call them out. That afterwards on the ninth day of the same month, he this deponent, on entering the house of Mr. Pearson[116] the Inn Keeper in the said Town of Brantford, heard the said George Alexander Clark in conversation with Mr. Hart of the Township of Brantford, when the said George Alexander Clark said to the said Hart, that he the said George Alexander Clark *was in possession of the secrets of the Rebels assembled in Oakland* (in the

[114]Lewis Burwell (1794–1865) was born in Upper Canada's Bertie Township. Like his brother Mahlon, he became a deputy provincial land surveyor, helping arrange for the Six Nations' cession of the Brantford townsite. He established a land office in Brantford and raised his family there. Unlike his brothers Mahlon and John, who were ardent Anglicans, he was a Methodist, and seems to have been less involved in politics than they.

[115]James Racey (d. 1851) and his family emigrated from Bath, England, to Upper Canada about 1805 and settled in the Niagara District. In 1816 James moved to Mount Pleasant and was appointed a magistrate in 1818. He took an interest in politics, unsuccessfully contesting the Oxford election of 1824. In 1823 he was appointed the lieutenant-colonel of the 1st Regiment of Gore militia and held that commission in 1837. He later became an associate judge of the Court of Queen's Bench.

[116]Pearson had just recently built his inn at the corner of Colborne and Market streets. It became known at some point as the *British American*.

London District) – and repeated, *that he was in possession of their secrets*, that he knew what they were about, and what they wanted – and wished to get some person or persons to go with him to Oakland to them. – And that a day or two afterwards, after the said George Alexander Clark had been to Oakland to the *Rebels, he told this deponent that he had been there*, and named several persons whom he saw there – and said that they the Rebels, would lay down their arms if Parker was let out of prison, and they have a free pardon granted them. . . .

C 45   AN EXPEDITION TO THE REBEL CAMP
[*UWO, William Wood Diary, typescript*]

MONDAY DECEMBER 11

. . . A request arrived from Simcoe by Dr. Coverton[117] requesting all the gentlemen of the Lake Shore to march for that place as rebellion had already commenced there. We all set out by 7 p.m. myself Mr. Pugsley on his mare. Of course I was left behind. I had a fall in the lake from my horse on leaping a large tree. I reached Dover half after 12 the morning of Tuesday where I found Heathcote[118] who had tumbled into Dover Creek[119] from his horse and unable to proceed to head-quarters. The rest of our party reached Simcoe.

TUESDAY DECEMBER 12

Heathcote and myself got into Simcoe this morning the first news was that a body of rebels to the number of about 80 armed lay between Waterford and Scotland and numbers of others unarmed[;] volunteers were called for and Hall[120] Heathcote Forbes[121] T. Moore Jr.[122] myself from the Lake Shore enrolled our names on the list[.] Lawrence

---

[117]This was Charles William Covernton (b. 1813), a native of Walworth, England. In 1835 he graduated from the University of Edinburgh and then secured a diploma from the London College of Surgeons. He toured Upper Canada in 1836 and, influenced by the decision of his brothers to settle in Norfolk County, did so too, in or near Vittoria. He became a surgeon with the local militia. He married in 1840, and had a long and distinguished career, being appointed to the provincial Board of Health in 1882.

[118]Heathcote lived along the Erie shore near Port Dover. He was evidently a "gentleman," interested as he was in forming a cricket club. In December he went with the Walpole militia to the Niagara District to oppose Mackenzie at Navy Island.

[119]This was likely Patterson's Creek, whose two main branches today are known as Black Creek and the River Lynn.

[120]Hall lived near Port Dover. He, like Heathcote, was interested in forming a cricket club, and he also joined the Walpole militia in the Niagara District against Mackenzie at Navy Island.

[121]Forbes lived near Port Dover in "Waverley Cottage." He went with the Walpole militia in their effort to oppose Mackenzie at Navy Island.

[122]T. Moore Jr., who lived near Port Dover, was evidently the Moore who later left with Wood and others as part of the Walpole militia to oppose Mackenzie at Navy Island.

Mercer[123] bolted home – this evening the party just mentioned nine of us in all with Mr. Evans[124] and some gentleman of Simcoe. We were ordered on a secret march thro the enemies encampment to Brantford after sunset to give intelleigence and form a communication with the Queen's forces there. We marched over a very rough country 15 miles when I was disabled with blistered feet and obliged to lay this night within half a mile of the enemies camp in a rebels house having previously given up my arms to our party. Lucky for me it was for a prisoner I must have been had I kept them – after being examined by several black looking fellows I was permitted to escape, having tried in vain to hire a horse. I quietly went to bed our party reached Brantford in safety having encountered only two men with arms who permitted them to pass for want of strength. I forgot to mention that our party were obliged to procure a guide near Oakland Mr. Evans having lost the road through the woods.

WEDNESDAY DECEMBER 13
I tried among the rebels to hire a horse in vain for a long time as I was very lame and unable to walk however the man with whom I stayed at last consented for his son-in-law to carry me to Simcoe on horse. We got thro the rebels lines in safety from his being well acquainted with them and one of their party and finally arrived in Simcoe safely. I stayed in Simcoe some time and set off home as none of our party were likely to be there some time and there was nothing to be done in Simcoe without arms of any kind. I could not procure a gun. I was unable to get over the creek so I rode back to Simcoe and tried to get a gun again but in vain so I again set off for Dover after dark and stayed on guard there all night with a walking stick – a number of forks were taken in Anderson's shop and several prisoners sent up to Simcoe.

C 46   DUNCAN CAMPBELL[125] TO RICHARDSON
Simcoe, 13 December 1837
[*PAC, Upper Canada Sundries, v. 180, pp. 99167-8*]

Your favour by my man Came to hand ½ past 8 oClock this morning. Containing pleasing intelligence

[123]Lawrence Mercer, who lived near Port Dover, evidently joined the Walpole militia later in December 1837 on their march to the Niagara District to oppose Mackenzie at Navy Island.

[124]Francis Evans (1801–1858) was born in County Westmeath, Ireland. A graduate of Trinity College, Dublin, he became a Church of Ireland cleric, coming to Lower Canada to a parish in Three Rivers in 1824. In 1827 he was ordained a priest, and moved his young family to Woodhouse Township in Upper Canada the succeeding year. Excoriated once by W.L. Mackenzie as the typical idle, bloated Anglican cleric, he received one of the rectories endowed by Sir John Colborne. None the less, he was an active priest, helping found the Anglican diocese of Huron. He died in Ireland while on a trip there to regain his health.

[125]Duncan Campbell (1805–1902) was a Scot whose family emigrated to Lower

I forgot to mention in my letter to you last night that the Revd. F. Evans with other gentlemen had left this place for Brantford at 4 oClock P.M. yesterday. with assurance from our Commanding officers that we were to proceed with all our Forces this day as far as the round plains[;][126] this agreement is Kept inviolate[;] this moment 150 men are under. arms ready to March and intend proceeding as far as the round plains and if we meet no despatches from you we intend returning back to Simcoe this [Evning ?] and wait until we hear your intentions which You will let us Know by the bearer[;] the Forces at Oakland is not so numerous as represented therefore the sooner such scoundrels are dispersed the better –

C 47   REV. FRANCIS EVANS TO SIR GEORGE ARTHUR
Woodhouse, 14 April 1838
[PAC, Upper Canada Sundries, v. 204, pp. 112709-12]

. . . [I] entirely failed in the object of my visit to Scotland on the 13 of December which was to urge the misguided insurgents to avail themselves of the Proclamation issued by Sir F.B. Head and to disperse. . . .

C 48   RANALD MCKINNON[127] TO MARCUS BLAIR[128]
14 December 1837
[HPL, Land Papers, pp. 142-4]

I crossed the [Grand] River at eight oclock this Morning on way to Townsend agreeable to yesterdays arrangment & reach the first House

---

Canada in 1815. Duncan came to Birdtown in 1818, changing the name of that village to Simcoe in 1829. There he ran a general store and acted as an agent of the Bank of Upper Canada, as well as a land agent for the provincial government. He became an extensive landowner in the area. A magistrate, he was also active in the militia, being a captain in 1837 and later a colonel.

[126]The Round Plains were in Townsend, just northwest of Waterford, some ten miles distant from the rebel camp at Scotland. The hamlet of Round Plains later appeared there.

[127]Ranald McKinnon (1801–1879) was born in Ulva, Scotland. His family emigrated to New York State in 1805. Ranald later moved to Upper Canada, becoming a contractor working on the Rideau Canal before settling in Haldimand County at Bryant's Corners (Caledonia) in 1835. He married that year and the next built a sawmill, a store, and a residence in Caledonia. He also became involved in constructing navigation works on the Grand River and, in later life, manufacturing woollens. In the post-rebellion era he was elected warden of Haldimand County and was a successful conservative candidate in the elections of 1851 and 1854 to the Assembly of the united Canadas and of 1867 to the House of Commons.

[128]Marcus Blair (b. *ca.* 1805) of Cayuga, a Scot, was a captain in the 1st Regiment of Haldimand militia. He had spent five years in the 61st Regiment of the British army before settling in Haldimand, where he married in 1835. An Indian agent, he held twenty shares in the ill-fated Grand River Navigation Company. An active loyalist in 1837–8, he was gazetted an adjutant in the 1st Battalion of Incorporated Militia in 1838. He was likely dead by 1842, for in that year his wife remarried.

in the Boston Settlement about 12 Oclock noon which I found to be the house of a man of the name of Olmstead who was not at home[;] his wife informed me that he had two cousins in the Rebel Army under Malcom who had about 300 men and that Dr Dunkum had a large force and it was expected that Malcom's force would cross this River at or near Bryants[129]

About three Miles further on I saw two men[;] they had not heard of the defeat of the Rebels at Toronto nor would they believe me when I told them[;] they said they were not Rebels but were straddle of the fence & Corraberated the former statements about the Rebel force, I was next hailid by a woman who said she was the wife [of] one Slyke[130] who was a Recruiting officer under Malcom & that he was gone to Waterford to ascertain which way the army was to march[;] said Malcom had about 300 men Dunkum 800 & daily increasing from the west & had not heard of the defeat at Toronto & weeped aloud when told[;] wanted to know if they should loose their farm if the Tories gained the day[;] said the Rebels were determnd. [determined] not to burn any Property

I next met one of the name of Egleston who Knewed me[;] he told me he had just Come from Waterford & that Malcom had 300 men Dunkum 800 & that they did talk of Crossing the Grand River at this place[.] He looked to me as if he had not slept for several days. I was next met by a Mr Beildy who is said to be a good subject[;] he told me that Malcom had 380 & Dunkum & Case 800 men & that they sent to Walpoal to Raise a Rifle Company & had secured & had the promise of a general Turnout from that Township and that all would join & make an attack on Brantford an[d] that Malcom's force would come this way[;] he also told me they had not heard of the defeat at Toronto and there were about 200 Loyalists at Simcoe and that they had salli[e]d out in the direction of Brantford yesterday & Returned again unmolested but the country around were generally Rebels, They were in hopes of making Prisoners of all strangers who would not join them[;] he advised me to Return as I was in danger of being taken as a spie by their scouting party and that they Robed a Capt. Slyke of nine stand of arms & while he was talking I saw a party coming about ¼ of mile off[;] four men I saw very plain[;] how many more there was I could not say but think there was more[.] I then turned twoards home & Rode 3 Miles very fast & then stoped about 3 oc After noon to feed my Horse & before he had eaten 6 Qts oats the same party came in sight again[;] they were supposed to [be] looking for Guns[.] I again made off at full speed & soon met Egleston again who told me, he had heard some firing in the direction of Oakland[.] Reached the River at eight oclock PM. P.S I Reach within four Miles of the Rebel camp[.]

---

[129]Bryant's Tavern was on the Grand River at present-day Caledonia.
[130]"Slyke" was probably meant to be Slaght, a common name in Townsend.

C 49   REPORT OF MR. CAMPBELL
n.p., n.d.
[HPL, Land Papers, p. 156]

yesterday about *1 PM*. a man . . . passed Cayuga Bridge from the Westward. – says – there are 200 loyalists mounting guard at Simcoe – about 400 radicals at Waterford – a small armed body of the latter had come to Simcoe, and met a patrol of 30 men, had told them they were not going to use their arms offensively, and were permitted to return to Waterford. – Loyalists estimated at 1000 about Simcoe – Col. [Mahlon] Burwell expected to reinforce them – Passed through Walpole, understood there were many disaffected – but not rising in arms. Radicals had been seizing arms and ammunition in Middleton. Heard it reported that the radicals assembled at Waterford intended to come by the Talbot road up the river to Brantford – General impression was that the Royalists were the strongest party. all along the road he had come from Middleton.

C 50   ADAM FERGUSSON[131] TO JAMES FERGUSSON[132]
Woodhill, 25 December 1837
[PRO, CO 42, v. 454, pp. 108-9, microfilm in PAO]

For another extract from this document see C 75.

. . . a well equipped force, under our *Speaker* of *the House*, McNab a noble gallant fellow & Capt. Macdonald[133] late of the 79th both with Brevet Rank as Lt. Colonels, was ordered to the London District, where the Rebels were said to be in considerable force under a Dr. Duncombe *M.P.*[;] about 500 marched from Hamilton, well provided & armed & McNab told me that he had a carte blanche from the Governor to provide everything the men might require – The Roads were without snow, the weather clear hard frost and fine moon light, the men in the highest glee, & burning for a dash at the rascals. Upon reaching Brantford, information was given of the Rebels having taken a position upon the London road at a village called *Little Scotland* 10 miles west from Brantford – . . .

[131]Adam Fergusson (1783–1862) was born at Woodhill, Perthshire, Scotland. A lawyer and landed gentleman, he was sent by an agricultural society to Upper Canada in 1831 to report on agriculture in and the prospects of emigration to the colony. His mission led to his publishing two books of advice and observations and to his settling himself and his family on his estate "Woodhill" near Waterdown in 1833. He became a large landowner in Nichol Township and a founder of the village of Fergus. In December 1837, acting under MacNab's orders, he brought the Fergus volunteers to Dumfries Township. He was gazetted colonel of the 13th Gore Regiment of militia on 20 March 1838 and appointed to the Executive Council in 1839. In the 1840s and 1850s he allied himself with the moderate reformers.

[132]James Fergusson was Adam's brother. The two were sons of the sheriff of Fife, Scotland.

[133]This may have been the A. M'Donnell who was commissioned lieutenant-colonel of the 4th Gore Regiment, drawn from Dumfries Township, on 7 December 1837.

C 51   A DESPATCH FROM ALLAN MACNAB
Scotland, 14 December 1837
[Patriot, *Toronto, 22 Dec. 1837*]

For another extract from this document see C 62.

I have the honor to report that the detachment under my command halted at Brantford on Wednesday evening, in perfect order, and the men in high spirits; at nine o'clock the same evening I was informed by persons sent by me to this place, (it then being the head-quarters of the Rebels), that Dr. Duncombe, with about four hundred men, were here and preparing to retreat to Norwich. I immediately despatched persons to Simcoe, Woodstock, and London, requesting that all the volunteers that could be mustered should march down and intercept the Rebels, and meet me at this place. . . .

C 52   REGIMENTAL ORDER – 2ND MIDDLESEX
London, 7 January 1839[134]
[*PAC, Upper Canada Sundries, v. 214, pp. 117209-10*]

. . . the conduct of the Regiment at Mackenzie's out-break . . . reminds the Colonel of the propriety of noticing publicly before all their fellows of the Regiment, the two privates Ephriam Cole Mitchell,[135] and John Anderson,[136] who exerted themselves (the moment they heard that the 52 *armed* rebels under Anderson were collected and on the move from the South part of Yarmouth for joining Duncombe in Oakland) to take up the Bridge at Big Otter Creek and prevent their crossing: and also, of those who collected at a moment's notice in the night time, when they got word through Philip Hodgkinson, Esq. of their own Reg't, that the banditti from Yarmouth were on their way down, and marched up to Talbot Road the same night to attack them at the Ravine of the Bayham Spring rill, with all the Fire arms they could muster, which was only *fifteen*; – then finding that they had passed an hour before their arrival, and not having heard that Captains Shore[137] and Nevills[138] were collecting volunteers to

[134]In 1839 Mahlon Burwell reviewed here the conduct and performance of the men of the 2nd Middlesex Regiment during 1837–8.

[135]Ephraim Cole Mitchell (b. *ca.* 1787) was a native of the United States. He emigrated with his family to Upper Canada about 1793. He served as a London District constable in 1810 and as a militiaman in the War of 1812. By 1837 Ephraim, a farmer, and his wife had acquired 234 patented acres in Bayham. They lived on lot 118, on the north side of the Talbot Road.

[136]John Anderson was a Bayham resident.

[137]William Shore was an Anglican resident of Southwold, where he owned property.

[138]James Nevills, who was likely American-born, served as an adjutant in the militia in the War of 1812. In the 1830s, a farmer near Port Stanley, he held several Yarmouth Township offices, including that of town clerk in 1831 and 1833. In the latter year he was also appointed a magistrate. A captain during the rebellion, he was made a major after it.

pursue the rebels, returned, and marched by way of Port Burwell and the Lake Road, to join Colonel Salmon,[139] who had sent an express to Captain [John] Burwell the day before, to say that rebels were collecting in Oakland. It also reminds him of the conduct of Captains Medcalf, and Summers and Ensign Doyle McKenny, who with the men they could collect on the short notice they had, joined Captains Shore and Nevills, on their march down, and went with them to attack the banditti at Oakland, where they met The Honorable Colonel McNab, who with the volunteers under his Command had dispersed that banditti. . . .

M. BURWELL,
Col. Com'g 2d Reg't Middlesex Militia.

C 53   JOHN B. ASKIN TO JONAS JONES
London, 22 December 1837
[C.R. Sanderson, ed., The Arthur Papers . . . I (Toronto, 1957),
pp. 35-6]

For other extracts from this document see C 70, C 78, D 79.

. . . On Tuesday the 12th. I proceeded to St. Thomas to arrest John Talbot and found that he had left that place on the Afternoon of Sunday the 10th. at about 3 o Clock P.M. and subsequently heard that he had crossed the Detroit River on Tuesday afternoon the 12th. Inst.

On the Morning of Wednesday the 13th. after seizing the papers appertaining to the Establishment of the "Liberal" I heard that an Express had been received by Col Bostwick from Col Salmon stating that apprehentions were entertained that an Attack would be made by a Large Body of Rebels under Doctr. Duncombe and Eliakum Malcolm Assembled at Scotland, against Simcoe with a view of destroying the Court House there; and also that a large body of well armed Riflemen fully provided with ammunition and provissions, had been met on Talbot Street on their march to join Duncomb's army and beating up for Volunteers: upon learning this I, immediately tendered my services to Col Bostwick, and requested permission to raise a Body of Volunteers, to pursue the Rebels and defeat them, that being granted me I instantly beat up for Volunteers and in less than three hours was on the march for Scotland (in the township of Oakland) which place I

[139]George Catcheyd Salmon (1777–1843) was born in Gloucestershire, England, the son of a prominent family. He emigrated to Upper Canada in 1809 with his wife, settling in Woodhouse near Port Ryerse. A veteran of the English militia, he began a long association with the Upper Canadian one, serving in the War of 1812. He was a prominent figure locally, being appointed a magistrate in 1813, acquiring large properties, and taking an active interest in the Church of England. Chastised in 1838 by the authorities for needlessly summoning out the Indians in response to an imagined Patriot threat, he resigned his militia commission.

reached at about 12 o Clock noon on Thursday (about half an hour after Col McNab and a very short time after Col Salmons from Long Point) with 260 Volunteers fully ready for action, having travelled a distance upwards of 60 miles within 23 hours. . . .

I want words sufficiently strong to express the Zeal, ardour and patriotism evinced on this occasion by the Loyal Inhabitants of St. Thomas and its neighbourhood Who under every privation and difficulty incident to a turn out without timely notice, to prepare themselves for the Extreme severity of the Weather at this season of the Year, and I beg here to mention that Col Bostwick the Commanding Officer then at St. Thomas, and Assembling the Militia was most active and zealous in forwarding the Volunteers and provissions, in fact he ordered all that could, at the time be got to march instantly. . . .

C 54   EDWARD ERMATINGER[140] TO JOHN JOSEPH
St. Thomas, 16 December 1837
[PAC, Correspondence of the Provincial Secretary's Office, v. 9, file 1211]

. . . Yesterday morning a body of at least 150 volunteers and Militia-men[,] horses and foot[,] well-armed started from this village increasing their numbers till they reached Otter Creek (Bayham) to 300 men in pursuit of the Rebels marching downwards; this loyal band being preceded by others from Malahide and Bayham – probably to the amount of 150 men – 300 men we are informed marched from Simcoe about the same time with the same object in view, as an express had been forwarded the preceding night from this place to apprize the loyalists there of the march of the Rebels, and these different parties we trust will force those Traitors upon Col: McNab's notice –

Col: Hamilton[141] has arrived this Eveng with a respectable body from London and will no doubt tomorrow commence the highly necessary work of weeding this fruitful garden and hotbed of sedition. . . .

[140]Edward Ermatinger (1797–1876) was born on Elba, the son of a British army officer. He was educated in England, then in 1818, along with his brother Francis, he joined the Hudson's Bay Company, in whose employ he remained until 1828. In 1830 he settled in St. Thomas, opening a general store there and a private bank. A tory, he was appointed a magistrate in 1833. In 1859 he produced his valuable Life of Colonel Talbot.

[141]James Hamilton (1792–1858) was born in Upper Canada and served in the War of 1812. In the 1820s and 1830s he was a partner in the Port Stanley firm of Hamilton and Warren and the St. Thomas agent of the Commercial Bank. In 1828 he ran unsuccessfully for election to the Assembly in Middlesex, and, judging by the Liberal's comment in 1833 that he was an honest man and, hence, it could not object to his appointment as a magistrate, seems to have been a moderate tory. A brother to John Hamilton, a legislative councillor, he was appointed sheriff of the London District in 1837. He settled in Westminster Township, remaining the sheriff until his death.

C 55   ADAM HOPE TO ROBERT HOPE
St. Thomas, 24 December 1837
[*HPL, Adam Hope Papers, typescripts*]

For other extracts from this document see C 63, C 71, C 79.

. . . the St. Thomas Volunteers were called out into active service. Dr Chas Duncombe M.P.P. for Oxford was understood to be posted in the Township of Oakland with 500 men, about 10 miles from Brantford, in a westerly direction, and supposed to be meditating an attack upon that village. After the defeat of MacKenzie & his Brother Rebels at Toronto Col. MacNab of Hamilton was dispatched with 400 men to dislodge the Rebels under Duncombe & scour the London District at the same time despatches were sent to the Clerk of the Peace of this District, an active & determined man, – to raise the Militia & effect a junction with MacNab. About 50 or 60 political fanatics, chiefly young men, from the township had gone off in a body to join Duncombe, armed with rifles & toma hawks; this had a corresponding influence upon the loyal disposed inhabitants of St. Thomas who simultaneously resolved to arm themselves & follow the Rebels. It was given out that the only object of our expedition was to overtake the rebels who had gone from Yarmouth & bring them to account for their insolence. The whole company I believe with the exception of one individual was in the dark about the ultimate object of our mission. Waggons were pressed into our service in all directions. Several Barrels of Pork, Beef & Bread followed the army & on the forenoon of the 13th the Volunteers amtg to 50 & the Militia to about as many left St. Thomas. The whole village was in a state of great excitement. I left a few directions with Mr. Hodge[142] who stopped at home to look after matters in the event of accident, about my papers &c, & soon found myself in the *ranks* of the Volunteers with a good Yankee rifle on my shoulder & several rounds of ball cartridge in my pocket. One of the waggons carried also a supply of Powder & Ball. It was cheering to see the enthusiasm of the People who turned out to join our ranks as we passed along the road. Our great difficulty was to procure a sufficient supply of firearms & in order to accomplish this the Magistrate authorized our men to seize what arms they could find in the houses on the road in the "*Queen's name*". Our force amounted to about 150 men bearing arms before we have travelled 20 miles. At this distance we expected to overtake the 60 rebels from the township as rumours in the morning spoke about their halting at this place. In this we were disappointed. We halted here to feed the horses & take some refreshment. Two taverns were filled. We ate our supper, leaning on the butt ends of our rifles & muskets. The scene was odd enough. Strong guards were planted all around with

[142]Thomas Hodge was Adam Hope's business partner. They were successful merchants, agents of the Gore Bank, and brothers-in-law, both sympathetic to the reform cause.

regular pass words in military order. About a quarter of a mile from the Tavern & at the foot of a hill when a bridge crosses the Otter a strong guard was posted & relieved at intervals during our halt. A gun was fired in the direction of the bridge, the alarm was given & out rushed every man from the Tavern, the ranks were formed & "March" "double quick" was no sooner given than off we went every man with his hand on the lock of his firearm. It was a false alarm! At 12 oclock of the evg of the 13th & in the midst of a Canadian winter I found myself walking sentry on the said bridge with a *rifle* on my shoulder. A curious train of reflections arose in my mind. I had not fired a musket of any description with one single solitary exception since I came this side the Atlantic. It is true I tried my rifle before starting to be sure I would make no mistake when the critical moment arrived. Inwardly & internally with curses deep but not loud did I denounce, Radicalism, Liberalism, & a whole host of isms & schisms at being found in such a situation so alien & foreign to my real disposition. The business of the guard was to prevent spies of disaffected people who were in our neighbourhood from breaking down the bridge & also to give timely notice in the event of any body of men approaching. 5 men kept guard at a time. We travelled all night. Our next stage was 20 miles which we reached about 5 oClk A.M. on the 14th[.] Having about 14 or 15 waggons each drawn by two horses & the roads pretty good we were enabled to travel quick as we rode & walked & alternately. Before reaching our second halting place we have to pass through a deep & dangerous ravine. All the men were ordered out of the waggons & formed in two & two abreast. Our *locks* were examined & cautiously & silently we wended our way down one hill & up another. We were apprehensive of an ambuscade. Had an enemy not half of our force been posted in the woods in the ravine, the half of us might have been destroyed. We learn'd at the Tavern that the Rebel force were encamped about 16 miles further on, in Oakland at a village called Scotland. We were told about the Rebels having sworn to *conquer or die. A counsel of war was held.* Various reports were in circulation about the strength of the enemy & doubt & hesitation hung on our minds; scouts were sent out on horseback in all directions in quest of information. At last an *express* arrived from *Brantford* via *Simco* from MacNab with instructions to march as expeditiously as possible & get as near the Rebels as possible. . . .

C 56   INFORMATION OF GEORGE GREGG WARREN[143]
9 January 1838
[*PAC, Upper Canada Sundries, v. 184, pp. 102995-6*]

. . . on Wednesday evening the 13th day of December now last past — he this deponent was on the public highway leading from the Village of

---

[143]George Gregg Warren was an Oakland "husbandman."

Scotland towards Burford Street when he met Thomas [Suples ?][144] of the Township of Burford Labourer on Horseback riding in great haste – Deponent asked him where he was going – when he the said Thomas [Suples ?] replied – that he was going to Doctor Duncombs army to inform them that Colonel McNabbs forces were advancing and would be at Scotland that night or next Morning – and that if Duncombs army did not get out of the way they would be all taken – Deponent further saith that the said [Suples ?] further informed him that he had been told of the advance of Colonel McNabbs forces by one John Van Arnum[145] – Tavern-Keeper – – who said that he Van Arnum had obtained his information from one James Rounds[146] of Burford – and that the said Van Arnum had despatched him the said [Suples ?] as a Messenger to Doctor Duncomb. . . .

C 57   EXAMINATION OF WILLIAM STOREY[147]
27 December 1837
[*PAC, Records of the London District Magistrates, v. II*]

. . . [at Oakland] all the Captains and Colonels for *there was but few Privots* wanted to go and take Simcoe. . . . [at night] word was given to turn out to meet the men from Simcoe[;] we Marched to Swamp and the Rifle Company Staid near the Swamp till they the men from Simcoe Come and have a Battle[;] we all returned to Scotland and laid up our Guns[;] in about half an hour the Colonels Come in the Room and Said be Still[;] the men were Silent[;] they Said all men who has Baggage waggons to git ready and make a final move toward Simcoe[;] the Pugls [Bugles] Sounded and we went toward Edmons and turned towards Norwich[;] we came to a Crook in the Road and made a halt at a white house there.

we went on a gain till we came near Sodom[.] Doctor Duncomb and three of Highest in Commands they Said we was on a Retreat and Must go to Sodom[;] when we got to Sodom they said all the men must Ly down with their guns by their Side. . . .

[144]This was likely Thomas Sirpell of Burford, an Englishman. He was jailed at Hamilton on 3 January and freed on 9 February 1838.

[145]John Van Arnam (Van Arnum) was born in New York State. The Van Arnams came to Upper Canada about 1822. John's father, a British subject, was still alive and living in Brantford in 1837. John, who acquired almost 300 acres in Brantford Township, and his wife raised seven children in the province. Jailed as a rebel on 23 December 1837 at Hamilton, he was released on bail on 20 February 1838 but was later indicted. He fled the province and was attainted a traitor. His request for a pardon, made in 1840, was refused.

[146]A James Rounds had settled in Burford before 1800, coming from the United States. He had a son James; so the one mentioned here might be either the father or the son.

[147]William Storey (b. *ca.* 1805), an Englishman, emigrated to Upper Canada about 1816 with his family. In 1837 he was a farmer who owned fifty patented acres in Bayham of lot 117 of the north side of the Talbot Road. Jailed at London on 20 December, he was granted bail on 2 January 1838.

C 58   EXAMINATION OF FRANCIS DAVIS[148]
14 December 1837
[PAC, Records of the London District Magistrates, v. II]

. . . about or near twelve OClock at night he was awakened by a knocking at his door, Calling out who was there & was answered it is I – on opening the Door . . . Adam Stover[149] and Calvin Austin[150] came in . . . they said that they were retreating into Norwich with all their forces & had some twelve Waggons loaded with ammunition & stores & six hundred men also said that Duncombe was a Coward and that they had recd information by way of the States which caused them to retreat. . . . 5 men came to deponents house armed [–] these stripped themselves of their arms & ammunition leaving them at deponents House saying they would not carry them further as they considered themselves Beat –

C 59   DEPOSITION OF JOSEPH J. LANCASTER[151]
18 December 1837
[PAC, Records of the London District Magistrates, v. II]

. . . On Tuesday Evening They [the Norwich rebels] Marched to Oakland about 100 Strong – Generally armed – and joined the other men – . . . they remained there till Wednesday Evening about 8. OClock. Doctor Duncomb then received intellegence that MacKenzies Army were dispersed and that there was no hopes of success. – and that MacNab was Expected to Attack them next day – as well as the Long Point militia –

[148]Francis Davis, an Irish immigrant, was a Norwich farmer who lived on lot 1, concession 5.

[149]Adam Stover (b. *ca.* 1798) was a native of Dutchess County, New York. His family emigrated to Norwich about 1811. Though the Stovers were Quakers, Adam became a Methodist. In 1837, unmarried, he farmed 175 acres of lot 8, concession 5 granted him by his father. Despite turning out with the rebels, he was not taken up by the authorities.

[150]Calvin Austin (b. *ca.* 1799), an American, was resident in Upper Canada by 1820. He lived in the town of Brantford, where he worked as a watchmaker and gunsmith. Even before 1837 he had a brush with authorities, for in 1835, charged with making counterfeit money, he had fled to the United States. He later returned to the colony. In 1837 he joined the rebels and was freed on bail on 17 December. He was jailed in July for suspected treasonable activities in Norwich and released in September 1838.

[151]Joseph J. Lancaster (1813–1884) was a native of Norwich. He taught school before marrying, but in 1837 he and his wife farmed 80 patented acres on lots 10 and 11, concession 2 in Norwich. A Quaker, he had lost his membership in the local Hicksite society in 1834. He was chosen corresponding secretary of the Norwich political union in 1837 and was an ensign in Duncombe's army in December. Jailed at London that month, he was released on bail within a few weeks. In 1838 he helped the local tories harass reformers. He later became a homeopath. In 1848 he moved to Lambeth. He died in London, Ontario.

Doctor Duncomb had always before concealed the news he received that was unfavorable to the party and communicated only such as was encouraging – The Army was then marched in Confusion to Norwich [–] Anderson who commanded the force from Yarmouth Objected to retreat – and wished to attack Brantford or Simcoe – Anderson said that they need not Expect more force from the west – Doctor Duncomb had been chosen Commander in Chief – and James Wood[152] of Oxford East was chosen his adviser – Doctor Cook Postmaster was Surgeon of the Army – When they arrived at John Kellys [in Burford] Malcom ordered his men back to Oakland and came on himself to Norwich. They then began to disperse as they went on to Norwich and got out of order – Saw Duncomb leave on horseback who said he was going to Michigan[–] he was much frightened, said that if he was taken he should be executed – . . .

Duncomb did not publicly announce to his Army that McKenzies party had been dispersed – but it was whispered privately amongst the men – . . .

C 60   EXAMINATION OF LEVI HEATON
20 December 1837
[PAC, Records of the London District Magistrates, v. II]

For another extract from this document see C 29.

. . . marched into Norwich to a place called Sodom – arrived in the latter part of the night – before day light was informed that the men were dispersing – went into the road[–] met Doctor Duncomb leading a horse – Asked him if he was the Doctor, who said yes and God bless you – asked the Doctor what was to be done – who said that McKenzie was defeated – and the Governor had issued a proclamation stating that all persons who had been in Arms except the leaders and those who had shed blood on returning to their homes would be pardoned – the Doctor advised them all to lay down their Arms, go home and submit to the laws of the Country – . . .

C 61   EXAMINATION OF AUGUSTUS CHAPEL
29 December 1837
[PAC, Records of the London District Magistrates, v. II]

For another extract from this document see C 33.

. . . we was ordered to march to Simcoe to take the Place[;] we went

---

[152]James Wood (b. *ca.* 1789) was a native of New Brunswick. He came to Upper Canada about 1799 and served in the War of 1812. Settled in East Oxford, he married there and worked a farm. In 1837 he owned 200 patented acres of lot 8, concession 8 and he squatted on a further 200 acres. He became an adjutant with the rebel forces in December 1837. Jailed at London on 15 December 1837, he was released on bail on 4 January 1838, but was jailed again in July for suspected treason in Norwich. He was granted bail that September.

Several miles and took the Road to Norwich[;] we herd that Enemy was coming with Cannon and if we got to Norwich we could git rid of them as Cannon Could not git there[;] on gitting to Norwich I went to bed[;] in the morning all the officers were gone and left word for all of us to make our Escape as fast as possible or we would be taken Prisoners. . . .

C 62   A DESPATCH FROM ALLAN MACNAB
Scotland, 14 December 1837
[Patriot, *Toronto, 16 Dec. 1837*]

For another extract from this document see C 51.

. . . At one o'clock on Thursday morning, (to day,) having obtained a plan of the position of the Rebels and the roads approaching thereto, I moved off from Brantford with my own detachment, consisting of about 300 rank and file, and 150 volunteers from Brantford, and 100 Indian warriors under the command of Captain Kerr,[153] with directions that they (the Indians) should take possession of the woods marked on the enclosed plan, *pine woods*. Major Thompson,[154] with 100 men, was to march down the *Back Settlement Road*; while the main body, with myself, were to march down the *Main Road,* and make the attack simultaneously.

I regret to say that the Rebels became alarmed and moved off during the night.

This afternoon I have been joined by not less than one thousand volunteers, with Colonel Salmon, Colonel Askin, and Colonels Rapelje[155] and McCall[156] at their head; volunteers are pouring in at all times and at all places. It is my intention to march at 6 o'clock to-morrow morning, with 1600 men, through the Township of Norwich, the most disaffected part of this District. I have at least six

[153]William Johnson Kerr (1787–1845) was born in Upper Canada, his father a British army surgeon, his mother of Indian ancestry and related to the Brants. William later married a daughter of Joseph Brant. In the War of 1812 he commanded the Six Nations warriors. After that conflict, he was active politically, siding with Robert Gourlay, for a time at least, and serving as a Lincoln MLA, 1820–4. In the 1830s he was a notorious tory, having arranged a physical assault on William Lyon Mackenzie in 1832 which cost him a $200 fine. In the 1830s he was manager of the Burlington Canal. In the summer of 1838 he and the Six Nations warriors helped round up the Short Hills raiders.

[154]Possibly this was George Thompson of the 5th Gore Regiment of militia.

[155]Abraham A. Rapelje (1766–1841) was born in Long Island, New York, emigrating to Upper Canada about 1799 and settling in Charlotteville. During the War of 1812 he raised his own company of men and evidently received a pension thereafter. From 1818 to 1837 he served as sheriff of the London District.

[156]Daniel McCall (1772–1848) was born in New Jersey, moving with his family to the Long Point area in 1796. He married and settled in Charlotteville, and served in the War of 1812 as a militia captain. He later became a lieutenant-colonel. His father Duncan, who died in 1833, had sat in the Assembly as an MLA for Norfolk.

times as many men as I require; but the fact of such an army marching through this country cannot but have a very beneficial effect; and, besides[,] the volunteers joining me in this District would not be pleased to be dismissed, and all left to the men of Gore.

I have taken all Doctor Duncombe's papers, also Mr. Eliakim Malcolm's: the latter (which are of considerable consequence) were discovered buried in a field, together with several of the leading Rebels. The latter I have sent under guard to Hamilton. . . .

It is a matter of no small mortification to me to have failed in capturing the traitor Duncombe and his Rebel Band. And I very much fear he will not give me an opportunity of attacking him, but like the other leaders of the Rebel bands will fly the Country.

C 63   ADAM HOPE TO ROBERT HOPE
St. Thomas, 24 December 1837
[HPL, Adam Hope Papers, typescripts]

For other extracts from this document see C 55, C 71, C 79.

. . . upon hearing him [MacNab] from the opposite direction commence firing we [the Yarmouth volunteers] were to rush forward & attack the enemy from our side; the Simco Militia, who were marching from a different direction, amtg to 284 men, had similar instructions. We had travelled 40 miles overnight without sleep. We had 16 miles further to go through the woods and an engagement to boot before we had the prospect of any sleep. We got pieces of red tape & red flannel tied round our arms to prevent mistakes in case we got to close quarters. It was wonderful to see how the presence of anything like danger chases sleep from the eyelids. When we entered the woods every man had his eyes & ears about him eagerly looking for any sudden surprise. I could not wish to see a more determined resolute body of men. Not a soul but what was animated with a stern determination to do his duty. We mustered nearly 200 men all under arms. Several false alarms were given & it was delightful to see with what alacrity the men were at their posts. The military tactics were extremely simple. It was resolved to bring the rifles first into action & next the guns &c. for closer work, & after two rounds should the enemy keep their ground we were to rush on him & lay about us with our Muskets, bayonets, dirks, etc. &c. There were numbers of Orangemen with us in high spirits at the prospect of a little fun. About 6 miles from the expected field of battle we captured a rebel who assured us Duncombe had dispersed the previous day. A man was stationed over our informant with instructions to put a ball through his head if we were surprised by any body of rebels. We reached the village of Scotland but lo! the Rebels had fled. MacNab & his men had possession of the ground when we arrived. We were received with military honours. I met a number of my Hamilton acquaintances.

Whatever disappointment some, & in fact a great many, expressed at not finding an enemy, I confess I was *quite satisfied* with the result. A Bloodless victory rather than a bloody one any day for me. We found quarters wherever we could. The house where a party of us were sleeping was suddenly entered by several of the guards posted around the place, in quest of an individual, who it was reported was concealed in the house. A man was found concealed between two feather beds in an upper Chamber. It was the Capt. of the Rebel rifle Corps – an American lately from the States.[157] He was a sweetheart of one of the girls in the house who had strip'd the piece of red flannel from the arm of the *Magistrate* that was in our party in order to favor the escape of her lover. It would not do. He is now in Hamilton Jail. It seems Duncombe kept telling his poor deluded followers that Toronto was in the hands of Mackenzie & that after the Western Count[r]y had risen he would lead them on to certain & yet bloodless victory. Duncombe hearing of the movements of MacNab drew off the most of his men under a false pretence, put spurs to his horse & told his victims every one to look to his own safety. His poor men were almost mad with rage when they found themselves duped in such a manner. Had D. not been very expeditious in his movements he would have fallen by the hands of his own followers. He left a detachment to stand sentry where his main body had been stationed; upon the approach of McN's men they fired a few shots without effect & then took to their heels. The *Indians* were let slip in pursuit & three of the unfortunate men were shot down & scalped. Those who stood were taken prisoners & marched to Hamilton. . . .

C 64   A CORRESPONDENT TO THE ROCHESTER *Democrat*
Brantford, 17 December 1837
[PAO, Mackenzie–Lindsey Clippings, No. 6017]

. . . To the eternal disgrace of British chivalry be it spoken, the Indians were sent out at Scotland, against the unresisting radicals, like blood-hounds, to hunt them from the forests – murdering and scalping unarmed men. On my return to that place, two men were found in the same wood through which I passed, with withes about their necks, hanging to small saplings, whicn [sic] had evidently been bent down for the purpose and sprung with them into the air. This circumstance I related to a retired navy effioer [officer] who was amongst them, and who spoke exultingly of the event, and boasted that he had offered one

[157]This was almost certainly Charles P. Walrath (b. *ca.* 1811). A native of New York State, he moved to Windham from Ohio early in 1837 to work on his brother's farm and to sell a race horse. He drilled the rebels at Scotland. Jailed at Hamilton on 15 December, he was tried at Hamilton in the spring, found guilty of treason, and ultimately ordered transported to Van Diemen's Land for fourteen years. He escaped, however, from the Toronto gaol on 7 November 1838.

of the chiefs a dollar a piece for the scalp of every damned rebel scalp
he would bring in. . . .

C 65 MARCUS BLAIR TO THE BRIGADE MAJOR, HAMILTON
Bryant's Tavern, 15 December 1837
[HPL, Land Papers, pp. 153-4]

. . . Word was brought in yesterday that a large party of about 500
were advancing on the South Talbot Road to Cayuga Bridge – my own
opinion however is, that there are not so many, if any – As the ice
about Cayuga Bridge is now passable at all points – . . .

I can not make satisfactory arrangements with the tavern keepers
concerning the supply of provisions – – they will not keep men at
ration allowance – and we have no means here as in towns of subsisting
on rations – I must request explicit directions on this head – the tavern
keepers say they will hold me responsible – and though willing, I am
not able to maintain a party of the Queens troops at my own expence –
. . . you can not depend upon the militia. they have no arms – I tell you
plainly that there is danger here, and it would be pitiful to compromise
the Crown, on a matter of pounds shillings and pence – I assure you
that this is any thing but pleasant to me – my own house is now
deserted – my cattle starving in their stalls – but I will stick to it if I am
supported –

If I had arms I would make a strong party to penetrate the rebels
country – and act in concert with M'Nab – they ought to be driven into
their houses or out of them – as it is, they hang about their own homes
– whilst we are about to leave ours, so they will weary us out, and
ultimately succeed – . . .

C 66 P.B. DE BLAQUIERE[158] TO ALLAN MACNAB
Norwich, 15 December 1837
[PAC, Upper Canada Sundries, v. 180, pp. 99284-7]

. . . The Magistrates having placed me in command of Her Majesty's
Volunteer Force at Woodstock, we moved from thence yesterday at 5
PM with our own force of about 60 and a column of 50 from Ingersoll's
under the command of Captain Rothwell[159] upon Martin's Tavern[160] –

---

[158]Peter Boyle de Blaquiere (1784–1860) was born into the Irish nobility, though he
was not the eldest son of his family. He served in the British navy before arriving in
Upper Canada and settling in Woodstock in 1837 with his family. In December 1837
he commanded the Woodstock volunteers and was appointed lieutenant-colonel of the
3rd Regiment of Oxford militia, 20 January 1838. In 1839 he was made a legislative
councillor.

[159]William Rothwell (b. ca. 1797) was an Irishman. He served as a lieutenant in the
62nd Regiment of the British army. Likely, he was related to the Anglican cleric John
Rothwell who arrived in the village of Oxford (Ingersoll) in 1834.

[160]Martin's Tavern was in West Oxford.

I moved with the Woodstock column this morning to Harris Street[161] near Ingersoll – Finding it by report impracticable for our provision waggon to move by the direct route on the Burford side, a combined movement was arranged with Captain Rothwell who had no waggon, to move upon that line and form a junction with us here – The reports that poured in upon us in the absence of all communication from you, except as above stated, agreed that you had defeated the Rebels under Duncomb, and dispersed them in this direction. Our column searched most of the suspected houses on the line we have scoured, and we have brought forward two prisoners. some arms & a small quantity of ammunition; in the house of Elisha Hall a notorious Radical near Ingersoll we found him confined to his bed by a fall from his horse, and discovered amongst his papers several of which are forwarded to you. herewith your attention is particularly requested to two of them which are separated from the rest; the letter addressed to Mr. Hoskins decided us on taking Hall into custody on a charge of High Treason. I left him in charge of his own house (for I understood he could not be moved in safety) of Mr. Ingersoll's force, with directions to guard him strictly – Previous to our starting from Martin's Tavern at 3 AM., suspicious circumstances had arisen which induced me to direct the arrest of Mr. Hoskins by Captn. Rothwell whom we left behind, but I am sorry to add he was not able to effect his capture. I had detained at that place Captn. Curtis also all night, but at that time I had not sufficiently strong grounds to justify his being detained when we marched, and he was then set at liberty – From Ingersoll's I sent an express to Woodstock to arrest him again immediately, and seize his papers; I have not yet learnt whether this has been done – I beg to direct your particular attention also to another letter from Mr. Diamond of Ohio which clearly proves him to have been long engaged in treasonable correspondence – You will also observe from the general correspondence, the intended tendency of Duncomb's and Always long and bitter hostility to the British Government

Alway is evidently concealed somewhere in this neighbourhood, for he was at Hall's house the evening before we arrived there – of Duncomb we can make out no intelligence. Captain Rothwell has brought up with his force 8 Prisoners and some arms, and it is quite evident since the Rebels were so lately between us and you (Captain Rothwell having seen as he states about 40 of them this day assembled to gether), that much arms must be concealed in this neighbourhood – our force is very much fatigued by the harrassing nature of the latter part of our march upon this place [–] I purpose halting here untill I receive orders from you, and I have therefore dispatched my son [Henry ?] with this Express and directions not to return untill he has seen you – We have a very small quantity of Provisions, and our supplies are very indifferent indeed – We have a little Tea, Biscuit &

[161]Harris Street evidently ran south out of Ingersoll.

some few pounds of Beef, but no spirits whatever; we have very little ammunition made up and our Volunteers have only four rounds – We shall proceed if possible early in the morning, to search the houses around us for arms &c. – I enclose a list given to me from Mr Ingersolls of names known to be lately out in arms against Her Majesty's Government – Captain Rothwell is posted near us –

C 67   ALLAN MacNAB TO F. HALKETT
Scotland, 15 December 1837
[Patriot, *Toronto, 19 Dec. 1837*]

I have the honor to report, that the Rebels have dispersed in all parts of this District, and that I have taken every precaution to intercept them and cut off their retreat.

I have received several Deputations from these misguided men, praying for leave to come in and surrender their arms, take the oath of allegiance if necessary, and join the Troops under my command. In endeavouring to find out those of the leaders who may yet remain behind, so far I have refused their request, unless the leaders are delivered into my hands. On this subject I am to meet several Deputations this day, and will forward a more explicit Despatch respecting it in the morning. . . .

I cannot describe in terms sufficiently strong, the enthusiasm and ardour with which the loyal inhabitants of this county are crowding to my aid.

C 68   "REWARD"
16 December 1837
[Patriot, *Toronto, 12 Jan. 1838*]

By command of His Excellency the Lieutenant Governor.

A **REWARD** is hereby offered, of FIVE HUNDRED POUNDS to any one, who will apprehend and deliver up to justice **CHARLES DUNCOMBE**; and a reward of *Two Hundred and Fifty Pounds* to any one who will apprehend and deliver up to justice **ELIAKIM MALCOLM**, or **FINLAY MALCOLM**,[162] or **ROBERT ALWAY**; and a Reward of *One Hundred Pounds* to any one who will apprehend and deliver up to justice _____ **ANDERSON**, (said to be a Captain in the Rebel Forces,) or **JOSHUA DOAN**.

[162]This likely referred to Finlay Malcolm of Oakland, the former MLA, but it may have referred to his nephew Finlay (b. 1799) of Bayham who had been particularly active in raising rebellion in his area. Born in the Niagara District, Finlay had settled, along with his father Daniel, in Bayham. In 1837 he, his wife, and seven children lived on 200 unpatented acres there. Finlay, a farmer, claimed in 1838 that he was poor. Jailed at London on 21 December 1837, he petitioned under 1 Victoria, c. 10 and was ordered transported to Van Diemen's Land for fourteen years. He was, however, released in England in 1839. He returned to Bayham and his family.

All the above persons are known to have been traitorously in arms against their Sovereign; and to entitle the party apprehending either of them to the Reward, he must be delivered to the Civil Power, at Hamilton, Niagara, London, or Toronto.

GOD SAVE THE QUEEN.

C 69 ALLAN MacNAB TO JONAS JONES
Sodom, 18 December 1837
[Patriot, *Toronto, 22 Dec. 1837*]

. . . yesterday . . . upwards of 200 of the Rebels and disaffected persons marched in and surrendered themselves and their arms. They were received in the centre of a square formed by the Volunteers, under my command, – and I availed myself of the opportunity thus afforded me of explaining to these deluded men the situation in which they had placed themselves – that by their wicked and unnatural conduct they had forfeited their lives and properties, – and I permitted them to return to their homes, on the express condition that they should at any time surrender themselves, should His Excellency not think proper to extend to them the royal clemency. – Their arms are in my possession.

The ringleaders and some of the most wicked and active men amongst them, including many of their officers, are detained prisoners, and I shall send them under a strong escort to London, to await their trials.

In justice to my own feelings, I cannot forbear expressing my entire conviction that from all I have seen and heard, many of these unfortunate men have been grossly deceived by the traitor Duncombe, & his colleagues, & I firmly believe that many of them will return to their allegiance, and yet be numbered among Her Majesty's faithful and loyal subjects.

I have been detained here longer than I expected, but the delay has been owing to the necessity for my maintaining a central position, so that easy intercourse might be kept up with the numerous detachments moving in all parts of the District, to ensure the total capture of the Rebels, which I am proud to say has been done, very few having escaped, – and the gallant Militia volunteers under my command will, I am sure, give a good account even of those few ere we quit the field. . . .

I shall march from this place for Oxford [Ingersoll] tomorrow morning.

P.S. – Robert Alway M.P.P. is a prisoner. He was taken near Simcoe, on his way to the west. I am unable to furnish a complete Return of the prisoners and arms taken, . . . but the number of prisoners amount to nearly five hundred, and from one hundred to one hundred and twenty rifles.

C 70 JOHN B. ASKIN TO JONAS JONES
London, 22 December 1837
*[C.R. Sanderson, ed., The Arthur Papers . . . I (Toronto, 1957),
pp. 35-6]*

For other extracts from this document see C 53, C 78, D 79.

. . . On Friday the 15th. having received a General Order from Col Mc. Nabb I proceeded to Norwich and taking a position about a mile to the right of his Division, remained there on the Saturday, sending out parties to arrest the fugitives, who had fled from Scotland, on this day we captured 18 prisoners. – On Sunday the 17th. having been informed that a large Number of men who had been in Doctr. Duncomb's army were about to surrender, and throw themselves on the Mercy of the Government I remained there, till the afternoon, and moved to Cromwell's Mills[163] on the Otter Creek in Norwich; . . .

C 71 ADAM HOPE TO ROBERT HOPE
St. Thomas, 24 December 1837
[HPL, Adam Hope Papers, typescripts]

For other extracts from this document see C 55, C 63, C 79.

. . . We [the Yarmouth volunteers] were informed on the Friday morning [15 December] that the Rebels were determined to give us battle in the Township of Norwich where they awaited our approach. We were soon on the route in that direction. The village of Sodom in that township was the head quarters of the Rebels previous to the breaking out of the disturbances. It was there Duncombe held his treasonable meetings. It was the strong hold of disaffection & Rebellion. Upon the arrival of the Queen's troups there was no opposition to be found. Every thing was quiet. We came into the place on the Friday forenoon & remained till the Sunday forenoon. We were billeted on the farmers around the village. I got quarters along with a pleasant party in the house of a most respectable Quaker whose house, family & Larder bespoke peace & plenty. We were most kindly and hospitably entertained with vennison, beef, tea, cider apples &c &c. The honest Quaker refused to make out a Bill against us but as the expense could not fall short of £10 cy the Magistrate has taken proper steps to have the money sent to him. The usual way was for the principal person in any party to give a receipt for the amount of the Bill & upon this being transmitted the clerk of the Peace for the District at London funds would be transmitted for the liquidation of the claim. Some of the people whose sentiments were opposed to "the

---

[163]Cromwell's Mills (present-day Otterville) took its name from the Cromwells, a Quaker family who moved into Norwich in 1811. In 1837 the Cromwells had a store and a mill there.

Tories" grumbled about finding accomodation for the troops, but a dozen of rifles & the "Queen's name", with a threat that remuneration was optional, was an argument too powerful to be withstood. The township of Norwich is perhaps one of the best settlements in Upper Canada; the country is thickly settled; well cleared; and you meet with better farms & better houses, gardens & barns in a shorter distance than you will do almost any where else that I know of – The settlers are chiefly from the United States & native Canadians; – *there is an almost total absence* of *European population. It is this*, which has proved the curse of this part of the country. The people read the "Liberal" & the "Constitution". They were wholly ignorant of the state of public opinion in other parts of the Province. The matchless power, greatness, & resources of the British Empire they were utter strangers to. Hence they became the dupes of such a worthless traitor as Dr. Chas. Duncombe, whose false hoods, as related to me by many of the prisoners which we took, appeared to be so glaring & absurd that I felt almost angry to think any sane man could have given a moments credence to them. The good people of Norwich wont forget our visit in a hurry. Quartering the best part of 1000 men on them for 2 days with a promise to repeat the visit should their conduct justify such a step will have a proper influence upon the behaviour of our Norwich friends. Before we left you could not find a man that would avow himself a "Radical Reformer" no! not one. One poor fellow offered to take any oaths *I* pleased to support the Govnt. He was suspected of having been in arms & upon solemnly promising to support the "British Crown" as long as he remained in Canada we dismissed him. Postmaster, Magistrate, all & sundry were implicated & concerned in this business with Duncombe, with the exception of a very few. . . .

C 72   ALLAN MACNAB TO JONAS JONES
Ingersoll, 19 December 1837
[*Patriot, Toronto, 22 Dec. 1837*]

. . . I halted here this afternoon at 4 o'clock, after a very severe march, through ice and snow, of eighteen miles. – The men bear the fatigue well. I hope to reach London tomorrow night. . . .

it is my intention to organize a Volunteer Corps at London, of from 100 to 150 men, which I shall submit for the approval of His Excellency. I shall do the same at Woodstock, Brantford and Simcoe. . . .

It is my intention to allow the Militia, except the Volunteers with me and the Volunteer Companies above mentioned, to return to their homes; as I am satisfied that it is not prudent at this inclement season of the year to harrass them more than there is necessity for, I am assured by all those whose opinion is worth having, that on the slightest intimation they will again fly to their posts. This is also my opinion.

The remaining prisoners, except the notorious offenders, will be immediately set at liberty, after being bound over to appear at the next General Gaol Delivery, as you have directed.

Finlay Malcolm was taken last night by a party of my men, others are still in pursuit of Duncombe. Malcolm has been sent to Hamilton with several other prisoners, . . .

C 73   EDWARD GRIFFIN TO ALEXANDER HAMILTON[164]
Hamilton, 22 December 1837
[PAC, Alexander Hamilton Papers, v. 65, pp. 170-1]

. . . Coln. McNab. . . . is in high Spirits – A paper was found, upon which a resolution was written, "that when they took Macnab prisoner, he was to be placed before the patriots (rebels) & shot at by the whole (*gang of Madmen*)["] – the man who drew up this same resolution is now in Our Gaol here – . . . The "Ancaster" Company arrived here this afternoon – as also 15 prisoners from the West – lots more expected by morng.

C 74   PRISONERS AT SIMCOE
[*Eva Brook Donly Museum, Simcoe, Norfolk Historical Society Collections, McNeilledge*[165] *Diaries, microfilm in PAC*]

Sunday 17th Decr. 1837–
Sleet and snow. throughout the Day – the Country. all in an uproar. the Radicles fled. Several prisoners taken. – Very. fourtantly [fortunately] the Simcoe Court. House finished enough. likewise the Jail. for the prisoners[.] People all under arms – from 16. to 60 years age –

Monday. 18th rather Cold. . . . Went up to Simcoe to see how they get on . . Still takeing prisoners – one Company . . of. Horse left in serch. of. the Malcolms – got Mr. Rt. Allaway begghing – $1000 – reward for him – McKenzie. Rolph. and Bidwell made their escape. & is at Buffalo –

---

[164]Alexander Hamilton (*ca.* 1794–1839) had an unsuccessful career as a Niagara District businessman involved in milling and lumbering enterprises. About 1820 he was appointed a postmaster and in 1833 sheriff of the Niagara District, a position he held until his death. He was a brother of James Hamilton, the sheriff of the London District.

[165]Alexander McNeilledge (1791–1874) was born in Greenock, Scotland. He went to sea with his father in 1800 and sailed the world for a number of years on merchantmen. He secured his first captaincy in 1822. In 1830 he settled with his family on lot 8, concession 2 in Woodhouse, near his brother Colin's milling establishment in Port Dover. Colin served as an MLA for Norfolk in 1833–4. Alexander on 1 January 1838 sailed the schooner *Resolution* to the Niagara frontier to MacNab's forces opposing Mackenzie on Navy Island and stayed on that frontier for two weeks. He often captained vessels on Lake Erie but also worked, in somewhat indifferent fashion, as a farmer. He took his own life in a fit of depression.

tuesday 19th rather Cold. but good wr. for the season . . picking up –
the enemy off. & on . . Now in Simcoe Court House & Jail – 66 –
prisoners –

C 75   ADAM FERGUSSON TO JAMES FERGUSSON
Woodhill, 25 December 1837
[PRO, CO 42, v. 454, pp. 108-9, microfilm in PAO]

For another extract from this document see C 50.

. . . The Troops continued their march in divisions, numerous recruits
pouring in, till they reached the Township of *Norwich*, the great west
of rebellion, and there they remained about a week, scouring the
country, and taking numerous Leaders with Duncombes papers, but
like the other *brave* Commanders he as yet concealed himself – The
poor people had been infamously deceived and misled by the most
barefaced falsehoods, and of course upon laying down their arms &
returning to their allegiance they will be leniently dealt with – . . . I
was at Fergus when the tornado broke out, . . . I went by a
Commission & orders from McNab to Galt and sent an express for the
Fergus lads to meet me there, which they did on Tuesday night, &
welcome guests we were, for it is an important Bridge and if the rebels
had been in any tolerable heart, they would have made a dash at it, and
cut McNab off from communicating with Hamilton, the villagers were
Loyal but had no arms, and the neighborhood contained ma[n]y rebels
– I rode from Dundas to Galt on Tuesday alone with my old Cavalry
sabre at my side and a borrowed pistol, receiving the most terrific
stories as I went along. Mr Shade[166] M.P. lives in Galt & made me take
up my residence in his hospitable mansion – We made one excursion &
took 10 prisoners, fine fun to[o]. Kenny, G. Hamilton Ferrie,[167]
Drysdale[168] &c. – Mr Shade & I sifted them singly & soon discovered
that we had *two* [of] Duncombes Captains – We made out a strong case

[166]Absalom Shade (*ca.* 1793–1862) was born in Wyoming City, Pennsylvania. He
trained as a carpenter, pursuing that trade in New York until 1816 when William
Dickson, who owned most of present-day Dumfries Township, asked him to
superintend his settlement. Shade took his family that year to the site of Shade's Mills
(Galt), becoming a wealthy businessman there, running Dickson's mills, and his own
store and distillery, as well as acquiring much land in the area. The Grand River
Navigation Company, chartered in 1832, was one of the less successful ventures in
which he was engaged. Appointed postmaster of Galt, he kept the post for twenty-five
years. In 1831 he was elected to the Assembly in a Halton by-election, but was
defeated in the 1834 provincial election and then returned in 1836. Politically, he was a
strong tory. He held many posts over the years in local government.
[167]"G. Hamilton Ferrie" was presumably one of the merchant Ferries from
Hamilton, likely Colin Ferrie.
[168]Alexander Drysdale, a farmer, settled near Fergus in 1835 on a clergy reserve lot.
He went with the Fergus volunteers to Galt in December 1837. In September 1838 he
was promoted a lieutenant in the 13th Gore Regiment and in 1842 was appointed a
magistrate for the Wellington District.

against [them ?] and discharged the others upon recognizances, and on Sunday I conveyed my prisoners to Head Quarters at Brantford, and on Monday I came down, leaving orders with Wilson[169] to remain at Galt until relieved. . . .

C 76 REGIMENTAL ORDERS FOR THE 2ND REGIMENT OF MIDDLESEX
MILITIA
Port Talbot, 18 December 1837
[Patriot, *Toronto, 30 Jan. 1838*]

The Colonel commanding is fully aware that the officers and men generally feel with himself deeply the disgrace which has come upon the Regiment, by their Major, *John Rolph*, and their Surgeon, *Charles Duncombe*, two persons who have wormed themselves into the House of Assembly, the former for the County of Norfolk, and the latter for the County of Oxford; joining the rebels against Her Majesty's Government, and being the contemptible tools of the *mendicant arch traitor*, William Lyon Mackenzie; and that some other officers are not free from suspicion of a desire to follow their base and unprincipled example, and of seducing a few of the men to join in the rebellion. This disgrace must be wiped off, and it must be shown to the whole public, that the characters of the many cannot be tarnished, nor their principles contaminated by the villainous actions of the few. There is great excuse for such as have been misled in their opinions under the specious guise of *"reform,"* which has for several years been the watch-word of the rebel leaders, though without attaching to that word any specific meaning but that of general slander and falsehood, unsupported by a single fact, or a word of truth. But every man of sane mind must have known that, in quitting his peaceful home and joining the rebel vagrants with arms in his hands, and putting his loyal and peaceful neighbours in fear of being murdered, and their properties plundered, he was guilty of Treason. Such officers and men as have behaved in the treasonable manner above mentioned, and those who have aided and abetted them, must be arrested and brought to justice; and the officers and men of the Regiment are hereby commanded to arrest any traitors they may know, and take them before Justices of the Peace for examination.

(Signed,)   M. BURWELL,
                                       Colonel Commanding,
                                       2d Regiment Middlesex Militia.

[169]George Wilson (1793–1867) was born in Aberdeenshire, Scotland. He was a lawyer and practised in Glasgow until 1834, when he emigrated to Upper Canada's Nichol Township. He joined the Fergus volunteers in December 1837. In 1838 he emigrated with his wife to Australia to join his brothers there, but returned to the province in 1858.

C 77 MAHLON BURWELL TO COL. JAMES FITZGIBBON
Port Talbot, 18 December 1837
[*PAC, Adjutant General's Office, Correspondence, v. 22*]

. . . There has been no open rising of rebels in this County excepting 52 in the Southern part of the Township of Yarmouth, and some few in parts of the Township of Bayham, all of whom sneaked off and were moving before the loyal men were on the alert – the scamps must have had secret information of the time Mackenzie intended firing the city, and ventured to make their way to Oakland and join a collection of vagrants at that place, who after being united sneaked off in various directions, and the inhabitants were constantly hunting them up, and taking them before the magistrates at St. Thomas for examination and commitment. I fear that all the principal ringleaders will make their escape. . . .

C 78 JOHN B. ASKIN TO JONAS JONES
London, 22 December 1837
[*C.R. Sanderson, ed.*, The Arthur Papers . . . *I (Toronto, 1957),
pp. 35-6*]

For other extracts from this document see C 53, C 70, D 79.

. . . on Monday the 18th. [the Yarmouth volunteers] marched through Dereham, Scouring the Country and reached Richmond, on the Big Otter Creek on Talbot Street, taking several prisoners: – on Tuesday the 19th. marched up Talbot Street, through Bingham [Bayham], Mallahide scouring the Country to New *Sarum*: – thence, turning to the Front of Yarmouth to Sparta a small village noted as a rendesvous or assemblage of Rebels – on Wednesday the 20th. marched to St. Thomas and dismissed the Volunteers, to enable them to return to their homes to provide for their families, leaving a strong guard over the prisoners; – this day the Prisoners taken by the Volunteers 38 in number were brought to this place and committed to Gaol.

In the performance of this service I beg to remark, that the Whole Country through which I had occasion to move (with the Exception of Norwich and the Village of Sparta,) appeared to me to be most Loyal and ready to serve wherever required by the Government – great numbers requesting to be furnished with Arms and Employed.

I beg to request that His Excellency the Lieutenant Governor will be pleased to give his sanction to this Act of Patriotism on the part of the Middlesex Volunteers and that he will in addition be pleased to grant some authority for the payment of the Expences incurred in the performance of this Service.

C 79   ADAM HOPE TO ROBERT HOPE
St. Thomas, 24 December 1837
[*HPL, Adam Hope Letters, typescripts*]

For other extracts from this document see C 55, C 63, C 71.

. . . On the Monday [18 Dec.] we [the Yarmouth volunteers] got to the Otter again with between 20 to 30 prisoners of no note. Our official men were anxious to shew the fruits of their mission by dragging these poor deluded people from their homes to immure them in a jail for no purpose whatever. The whole prisoners taken by McNab's people with few exceptions were discharged with a suitable reprimand. I spoke to the authorities in behalf of the men our party had taken but without effect. To tell the truth *catching* these mistaken & misguided men did not suit my ideas at all. The most of the prisoners surrendered voluntarily & after their deposition was taken it could have been transmitted to the Governor and he could have granted them pardon or not as he might have deemed proper. I got disgusted with the parade which was made of the prisoners before they reached London. We reached the Otter on the Monday night; abt 20 miles from St. Thomas. It was deemed advisable to scour the south of this township. . . . I volunteered on the Guard with the prisoners, And on the Tuesday after . . . [a] pretty severe march *on foot* reached home early in the evening after . . . weeks absence. *Business* had been very good during my absence. . . . [the] London volunteers & great numbers of militia were stationed here all the week. I have thought since this business that after all our St. Thomas Volunteers were not a *legal body*. We *elected* our own Capt and he was governed in a great degree by the gentlemen of the corps. I am not sure that even the *Governor* can sanction volunteer corps without the *consent of Parliament*. I am not apprehensive that the *Law* of the case will be very strictly enquired into. . . .

In the south of this Township a young ruffian defied the Law Officers at the point of his rifle for weeks together previous to this "Break out". I would rather live under a despotism than in a state of anarchy where the Law did not *reign supreme*. I abhor mob law. The leaders of the Rebels, their Captains &c!! from my own personal knowledge of the men were perhaps a sett of as consumate ruffians as ever disgraced humanity. I am perfectly amazed at the number of people of *property* & respectability who are implicated in this matter. The following are part of those who have lent themselves to this Rebellion . . . Dr. Chas. Duncombe M.P.P. a libertine, & proved to have told gross false hoods in a petition to the House of Commons. Robt. Alway M.P.P. a *swindler* & colleague of Duncombe's as M.P.P. for Oxford, £500 reward for each of these two Elias Moore M.P.P. for this County is in Jail, on a charge of treason. I feel for Moore. In many respects he is a good man altho' God & nature never intended him for a Legislator. I hope nothing will be proved against him. His Father lost a beautiful Estate in New Jersey for his adherence to British Interests during the Revolutionary War. Mr. Moore when quite a boy, remembers well of seeing his late Majesty in New York when in the hands of the British. Arrests & Examinations have been going on here in great numbers for this week past. In Hamilton it is the same, in Toronto the same also. . . . "Mack" . . . is said to be encamped on Navy Island with 200 men. It is a small island immediately above Grand Island in the Niagara River. Preparations are making to dislodge and, if possible, capture the Rebels. In the West Duncombe & a good many of his Brother scoundrels are in Detroit trying to organise a band of plunderers from the refuse of society to invade our Western frontier. A thousand stand of arms is to be sent to us from Toronto, which we need much. I had to borrow a *rifle* from a *cousin of Ogle R. Gowans*!! We would be unworthy of the high & honorable priveleges of British Freemen if we were not prepared to take up arms when the Laws are insulted & even *British supremacy* itself threatened to be subverted. The enlightened inhabitants on our frontier now see clearly & admit that the people of this Province do not desire Revolution. Because an attempt at something of the sort has been put down by the "people" themselves, without a European bayonet being employed in the matter. . . .

Numbers of families are said to be on the point of leaving this Province. Property to the extent of $100000 is likely from all accts to be confiscated to the Govnt. In this *township* it will perhaps reach $20,000; *at least* $10,000 will go into the hands of Govnt. It is truly melancholy to see the earnings of a life of honest industry swept away in a minute, in a moment of political insanity. I hope the Govnt will deal mercifully with the deluded & leave no cause for its friends to be ashamed of its proceedings. . . .

Never was a party more completely prostrated than that known under the name of "the Reform Party" in this Province. A general election tomorrow would terminate in the return of not one solitary opponent of the Government. On general grounds I deplore the present state of things. The Tories have unfortunately neither sense nor moderation to profit by their victory. Greedy & intolerant they will disgust numbers of people & compel them to leave the Province. There is one consolation however. I hope we are done with a base anti British faction who have carried this noble Province by their snarling agitation for these some years & we have now the prospect of a party of "juste milieu" reformers arising in the Province, . . . The two Luminaries which enlightened my mental darkness on the affairs of Upper Canada have both perished in the Storm of their own raising. John Talbot is in Detroit. The Press belongs to a friend of mine at present under arrest, but not expecting to be so long. He offered the use of the Press types office &c to a *half Whig* Magistrate of this place & *myself*!! free of rent for *one year* if we would start a *Paper on our own views*! . . .

D. REBELLION DAYS AROUND THE PROVINCE

D 1   GEORGE PHILLPOTTS[1] TO SIR JOHN COLBORNE
Cornwall, 20 November 1837
[J.E. Colborne, Plymouth, England, PAC, Colborne Papers, photostats, v. 11, pp. 002969-71]

. . . I believe I expressed doubts in my last respecting the Highlanders in this neighbourhood, and that Mr Marions the Priest at St Regis is not the only RCatholic Priest who is disaffected to the Br Govt – from what I have since heard I believe that none of the RCatholics are to be trusted. The Protestants in Glengarry are I believe all loyal but I have heard that the R.Catholics are determined not to act agt. [against] the RCatholics in Lower Canada – . . . I am inclined to fear that a spirit of disaffection exists among the R.Catholics generally which has not been hitherto suspected. A person in this neighbourhood has said that a grand effort is to be made this winter when the Troops cannot easily move about, and that 50,000 RCatholic Irishmen are ready to come in and assist when required. . . . In this Province all is quiet at present; but if the Rebels in LCanada shd. by any accident gain any advantages, I believe they wd. find many friends here. Every person who is guilty of uttering seditious language ought immedly. [immediately] to be imprisoned – . . .

D 2   GEORGE PHILLPOTTS TO SIR JOHN COLBORNE
Cornwall, 25 November 1837
[J.E. Colborne, Plymouth, England, PAC, Colborne Papers, photostats, v. 11, pp. 002993-5]

I have delayed . . . in order to be able to give you more decided information respecting the Highlanders, and I am happy to say that I have this day heard from the Sheriff[2] that they are all to be fully

---

[1]George Phillpotts (d. 1853) received a commission in the Royal Engineers in 1811 and served in British North America during the War of 1812. He outraged provincial reformers in 1827 by twice ordering the removal of a private fence built on military land overlooking Niagara Falls. A brother of the Anglican bishop of Exeter, he became Colborne's aide-de-camp in 1833 and, a major, was in 1837 the Assistant Quarter Master General in the Canadas. He served in China, before dying in Bermuda, where he was acting lieutenant-governor.

[2]The sheriff of the Eastern District was Donald Greenfield Macdonell (1778–1861) of Cornwall, who had been born in Greenfield, Scotland. In 1792 his father led a group of Highland settlers to Charlottenburgh Township. Donald attended John Strachan's

depended upon & that they will turn out if called upon – Col. Chisholm[3] has also come forward as well as all the Colonels of Militia here, and they feel confident that their men are to be relied upon –

I have this day heard from very good authority that a few days since 100 men on horseback & armed, passed the Cedars to attend a meeting in that neighbourhood, telling the inhabitants that they wd visit them on their return, & that they wd. have no neutrals – In the neighbourhood of Vaudreuil we hear they are in a state of open rebellion, & fears are entertained that the Mail from hence to Montreal will be stopped ere long – . . .

Many I find still doubt the R. Catholic Highlanders. . . .

D 3   GEORGE PHILLPOTTS TO SIR JOHN COLBORNE
Cornwall, 5 December 1837
[J.E. Colborne, Plymouth, England, PAC, Colborne Papers, photostats, v. 11, pp. 003088-91]

. . . A letter arrived here this eveng. from George Hamilton[4] Esqr. to Mr Jarvis[5] dated Hawkesbury 1st Decr from which I give you an Extract

"We are all here rather in a state of commotion, being on the frontier, our communication with Lower Canada cut off, the mail stopped, & totally unprovided with the means necessary either for

school in Cornwall. He served in the War of 1812 and was commissioned colonel of his militia regiment in 1814. In 1819 he was appointed sheriff, retaining that post until 1838. A tory, he sat in the Assembly representing Glengarry from 1834 to 1841. In 1846 he was appointed assistant adjutant general of Canada West and held that post until his death.

[3]Alexander Chisholm (d. 1854) was born in Scotland. He served with the Royal African Corps until 1817 when he, a lieutenant, retired on half-pay. That year he settled in Glengarry and married there in 1823. In 1825 he was appointed a militia colonel and in 1835 a magistrate. From 1834 to 1841 he served as an MLA for Glengarry and demonstrated his moderate principles.

[4]George Hamilton (*ca.* 1781–1839) was born in Sheephill, County Meath, Ireland. He had arrived in British North America from Liverpool by 1804 when he was resident in Quebec. About 1808 his brother William bought sawmills at Hawkesbury. George came to operate the mills and, in conjunction with brothers William in Quebec and Robert in Liverpool, ran a successful business. The year 1822 was disastrous for George. Both his brothers died, his wife and three of his children drowned, and his home burnt to the ground. None the less, he survived and amassed a considerable fortune. From 1816 to 1825 he served as a judge of the Ottawa District Court and also acted as a magistrate. In 1822 he became a lieutenant-colonel in the militia. He served at Prescott in November 1838, contracting an illness there that claimed his life.

[5]This was likely George Stephen Benjamin Jarvis (1797–1878), who had been born in New Brunswick and who had come with his brother, William Botsford, and the rest of his family to York, Upper Canada, in 1809. He served in the War of 1812. He became a lawyer after the war and from 1825 until his death in 1878 served as a district court judge in the eastern part of the province. In 1835–6 he was mayor of Cornwall and from 1836 to 1840 Cornwall's representative in the Assembly, where he sided with the tories. In 1838 he served as captain of a body of cavalry.

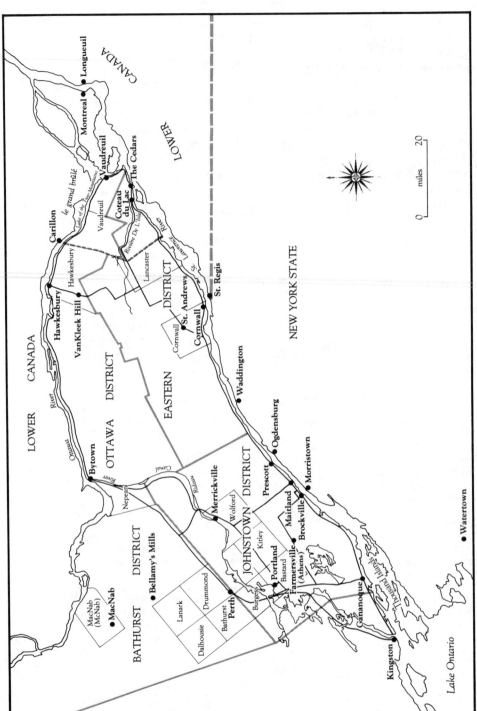

5: Eastern Upper Canada, 1837

defending ourselves or assisting our neighbours – At Carillon it is true there are 120 men of the 32d Regt. but the Rebels are reported upwards of 3000 strong at Grand Brulé, & threaten to attack & burn St. Andrews. All the women are coming up this way –"

"The people have insisted on my calling them together, which I have done for monday at 12 oClock to meet at Van-cleek's Hill. We shall pass some Resolutions which I shall make a little caustic." . . .

All the Militia here are anxious to be armed in order that they may be able to act when reqd – Those twixt [1] 5-50 yrs of age who will remain behind wish also to have arms in order to defend their property here, as they are near the Province Line; which has been crossed in one place by an armed party between Lancaster & the Cotenir [Coteau?], from the River de L'Isle.

Mr. Roebuck[6] fm. [from] Waddington, another brother of the Member for Bath,[7] arrived here yesterday fm. Waddington where he resides – He had provided himself with a Rifle & was on his way down to assist in defending Cotenir [Coteau?] du Lac – he informed me that he saw no one in the State of New York between Waddington & Ogdensburg who was not in favor of the Rebels, but Col. Ogden[8] – That they are now looking on quietly to see what chance the Canadians have of success, & if they appear likely to carry their point; a great number of americans will go to their assistance – At Ogdensburg are a no. of Canadians, and a short time since a number of them hearing that the Steamer Sir Jas. Kempt was going up with a quantity of arms to Kingston, formed a plan for taking them, by going on board at Prescott as passengers, & when the boat was in the middle of the stream to rise[,] take possessn[,] throw the arms overboard & steer her into a port on the American side & make their escape – That a number of the disaffected inhabitants of Prescott, frequently go over to Ogdensburg to concert with & encourage the rebels there – . . .

You will see by Col. McMillan's[9] letter to me, which I have

[6]This was one of John Arthur Roebuck's brothers.

[7]This was John Arthur Roebuck (1802–1879). Born in Madras, India, he came with his mother, stepfather John Simpson, and siblings to Augusta Township, Upper Canada, in 1815. His mother, whose brother had served as Simcoe's secretary, had a grant of 500 acres in the colony. John returned to England in 1824, leaving his family in the province. In England he became a lawyer and a member of Parliament, 1832–7. An independent reformer, he served as the Lower Canadian Assembly's representative in Parliament in 1835. He also sat in the British House of Commons, 1841–7, 1849–68, and 1874–9.

[8]This was likely Gouverneur Ogden (1778–1851), who had been born in New Jersey, the son of one of the founders of Ogdensburg, New York. Gouverneur Ogden studied law and travelled in Europe before settling in Waddington, New York, where he operated flour mills and furnaces and raised a large family.

[9]This was Alexander McMillan (fl. 1817–1849). McMillan, a retired captain, was one of a number of ex-soldiers who settled in a military colony at Perth, Lanark County. In 1825 he became registrar of Carleton County and, at some point, registrar of Lanark also. A tory, he ran for the Assembly but was unsuccessful, though he did

enclosed to Capt. Goldie,[10] that the Lanark Militia will not probably be here for some days – The roads between Brockville & Perth are represented as being in many places knee deep in mud & water, &.

Wednesday Morng – You will be gratified to hear that I have *the best authority fm all quarters* to inform you that the Militia in all directions here will turn out to a man & march agt. [against] the Rebels – The Highlanders say they cannot go without arms, but give them a musquet or a *bayonet*, with a few rounds of ammunition and they will go wherever they are ordered – *They fear no [marauders?] if thus prepared, and I now feel assured* that you may depend upon *all of them*. – Radicalism is quite forgotten, all are ready to turn out under you & fight for the Queen & the Constitution. – All the Glengarry Regts. the 1st Stormont near St Andrews &c. unite in this expression of their feelings – and I am satisfied you may depend upon them – . . .

D 4   DONALD AENEAS MACDONELL[11] TO JOHN JOSEPH
Cornwall, 12 December 1837
[*PAC, Correspondence of the Provincial Secretary's Office, v. 9, file 1244*]

I have the honor to inform you, for the information of His Excellency, the Lieutenant Governor, that since the commencement of hostilities by the Rebels in Lower Canada, the several Regiments of Glengarry Militia have been organising in the expectation, that His Excellency would order them to Lower Canada, at the disposal of Lieutenant General Sir John Colborne, – They are still I regret to say without arms, . . . We intend however going to Montreal in a few days, to bring arms up for the Glengarry Regiments, and as from our distance from those parts of Upper Canada, which appear to be in a state of Revolt, We may not be called above: And as we conceive we are equally contributing in serving our Country, by acting in either Province, We feel anxious to have His Excellency's orders to march to Lower Canada, to assist in putting down the Rebels there. We beg however to inform his Excellency that should our services be required

serve as the president of the Prescott Board of Police in 1834 and 1838. In addition, he was collector of customs at Prescott, 1817–1823(?), and was active on the district Board of Education in the 1820s. Too, he was appointed the first warden of the Bathurst District in 1841.

[10]Thomas Leigh Goldie was in 1837 the acting military secretary of Lower Canada. In 1838–9 he served as the province's civil secretary.

[11]Donald Aeneas Macdonell (1794–1879) was born in Charlottenburgh Township and attended John Strachan's school in Cornwall. He served as a British regular during the War of 1812 and saw duty in England and Nova Scotia after that conflict. In 1817 he retired on half-pay, returning to Upper Canada, where he was active with the militia, becoming a colonel of the 2nd Glengarry Regiment. In 1834 he was appointed a magistrate for Cornwall and in 1834 and 1836 was elected as a reformer to the Assembly from Stormont. In November 1838 he served with the militia in Lower Canada. From 1848 to 1869 he was warden of the Kingston penitentiary.

at Kingston, Toronto, or elsewhere, we can march 1,200 effective men from 18 to 50 years of age, from the County of Glengarry to assist His Excellency in crushing Rebellion in this Province, and supporting Her Majesty's Government therein – . . .

D 5   DONALD AENEAS MACDONELL TO JOHN JOSEPH
St. Andrews, 13 December 1837
[PAC, Correspondence of the Provincial Secretary's Office, v. 9, file 1184]

. . . It gives me great pleasure to be enabled to state that the whole Population of this District are in Tranquillity, . . .

I beg that you will convey to His Excellency the Lieutenant Governor, the assurance that as an individual firmly attached to a monarchial form of Government, that I shall at all times feel it an imperative duty to aid as a magistrate or in any other capacity to put down any attempted Revolution, And that although I have always advocated Reform Principles that I have not in any substance deviated from the duty of a subject –

D 6   DONALD E. MACDONALD TO COL. JAMES FITZGIBBON
St. Andrews, 13 December 1837
[PAC, Adjutant General's Office, Correspondence, v. 22, Stormont file]

It is with extreme regret that I have been informed of what has taken place in the neighbourhood of Toronto, if any person had told me that a portion of the population of Upper Canada could have been instigated to such rash and unlawful proceedings I could not have been prevailed upon to believe it – This section of the Country is in the most profound peace – The disturbances in Lower Canada have been wholly confined to some portions of the District of Montreal and I may say are compleatly quell'd – – . . .

D 7   PHILIP VANKOUGHNET[12] TO JOHN JOSEPH
Cornwall, 14 December 1837
[PAC, Correspondence of the Provincial Secretary's Office, v. 9, file 1190]

I am happy to be able to state for the information of His Excellency the

---

[12]Philip Vankoughnet (1790–1873) was born into a United Empire Loyalist family in Cornwall and was educated at John Strachan's school there. A veteran of the War of 1812, he served thereafter in the militia as an officer. A merchant, he sat in the Assembly for much of the period 1816–34 and identified himself there as a government supporter. In 1836 he was made a legislative councillor. In 1838 as a lieutenant-colonel in the militia he saw action at Prescott in the battle of the windmill. In 1841 he ran once more for the Assembly but, upon losing the election to J.S. Macdonald, withdrew from politics.

Lt Govr. that the Eastern District is *right*. Col. Chisholm has come publickly forward and declared himself in favour of our cause and has offered himself & Regt. to march to any part of the two Provinces to assist in putting down the Rebels – and it has had the effect of deciding the Catholics in our favour – Those under the influence of Donald A. McDonell and belonging to the 1st Regt of Stormont with perhaps the exception of half a dozen have come *nobly* forward – so that we will have nothing to fear in their quarter –

I have been requested by Sir John Colborne to adopt measures to keep open the communication between the two Provinces, and he has authorised me to garrison the Fort at the Coteau du lac with as many men as I may think necessary for the purpose of maintaining possession of that Fort, as well as to keep up the Communication – I have consequently taken upon myself to order 250 of my Regt. to march next week to the Fort – but as there may be some demure on the part of some – I beg His Excellency will upon receipt of this command me to march my Regt. to Lower Canada whenever the Commander of the Forces may require me to do so –

As an appointment has not yet been made to the 1st Regt of Stormont, I would suggest to His Exy. the propriety of placing it under my Command until further orders – both officers & men are applying to me daily for orders –

D 8   THE LAIRD OF MACNAB[13] OFFERS SUPPORT
[Chronicle & Gazette, *Kingston, 27 December 1837*]

The Macnab. – We have of late been wondering what had become of the gallant chief of the Macnabs in these stirring times. The following, which we copy from the Bytown Gazette, shews that he and his kilted followers are on the alert, anxious for the sound of their favorite pipe at Cruinecha na, chlan, – (gathering of the clans)

COPY OFFER OF SERVICE.
McNab, 20th Nov. 1837.

General:

A number of my countrymen have called upon me, for they hope it will not be considered an intrusion in me, to assure you their War Pipe

---

[13]Archibald MacNab (1781?–1860), the hereditary chief of the clan MacNab, fled his creditors and Scotland in 1814. Upon making friends in the administration of Upper Canada, he was granted MacNab Township on the Ottawa River. He brought out twenty-one families from his clan and settled them in his grant, but did not give them title to their property. Although MacNab sold off the settlers' timber, he gave them no aid, treating them as his serfs. After an investigation begun by Lord Durham, he was ousted in 1843 and returned penniless to Scotland. At his death he was living as a pensioner of his estranged wife in the south of France.

can still sound "The Pronach a' cach" – (the charge to battle) The
Ottawa men are desirous to march, if necessary – and as for numbers –
'Their swords are a Thousand,
'Their [hearts?] are but one."
And as we Lads o' the Kilt have ever been more famed for deeds than
lang speeches, I have only to say – DONALD'S READY.

I beg leave to add that many respectable individuals, both Scotch
and Irish, are equally ready to march from this quarter, to support the
honor of their country if need be.

Awaiting your Excellency's commands,
I have the honor to be,
With much respect, General,
Your most obdt. very humble servt,
(Signed)   ARCH. McNAB.

D 9   GEORGE BAKER[14] TO JOHN JOSEPH
Bytown, 30 November 1837
[PAC, Adjutant General's Office, Correspondence, v. 22, Carleton
file]

. . . Since my letter of 21st instant covering a Copy of one to Captain
Bolton – Captain Randolph and Lieutenant Hadden R.E. have been
ordered hence to Montreal; and late events, have tended to create much
excitement in this Section of the Province; the People are very desirous
to obtain some degree of organization in case their Services should be
required. . . .

D 10   VARIOUS MAGISTRATES OF BYTOWN TO SIR F.B. HEAD
Bytown, 2 December 1837
[PAC, Adjutant General's Office, Correspondence, v. 22, Carleton
file, enclosed in G.T. Burke[15] to _____, 5 Dec. 1837]

. . . At this time when every post conveys additional intelligence of the

[14]George William Baker (1790–1862) was born in Cork, Ireland. After serving as a
captain in the Royal Artillery, he came to Upper Canada in 1832 and settled in
Bytown, where he became a member of the local Family Compact. He was a
magistrate, lieutenant-colonel of militia, and postmaster of Bytown, the latter position
being his from 1834 until 1857 when he resigned. Baker served on the Dalhousie
District Council from 1842 until 1850 when he was defeated.
[15]George Thew Burke (1776?–1854), a native of Tipperary, Ireland, is reputed to have
entered the army in 1798. He served with the 99th Regiment in the Canadas
during the War of 1812 and, along with other veterans of the 99th and 100th regiments,
was demobilized at Quebec in 1818 and offered land in Upper Canada. Always
impecunious, he eagerly accepted the post of secretary (manager) of a military
settlement to be established at Richmond in the Johnstown District. A captain or
brevet-major when he retired, he was made commander of the 3rd Carleton Regiment
(it became the 1st in 1825) in 1821. In 1838 he formed the 1st Carleton Light Infantry.
He served as an MLA for Carleton, 1824–8, and was appointed registrar of Lanark

increasing audacity of the malcontents in Lower Canada – Their open resistance to Her Majesty's Forces and the many gross acts of violence committed on the isolated Constitutionalists presiding amongst them –

We the undersigned Magistrates deem it our duty respectfully to submit for your Excellency's consideration, whether it might not be advisable for the reasons hereinafter stated to divide the 1st Battalion of the Militia of the County of Carleton and form a 2nd, by setting off the Township of Nepean or a part of it for that purpose – . . .

D 11   COL. ALEXANDER McMILLAN TO COL. NATHANIEL COFFIN
Perth, 10 November 1837
[*PAC, Adjutant General's Office, Correspondence, v. 22, Lanark file*]

In consequence of the disturbed State of the Lower Province. and His Excellency the Lieutenant Governor having given his consent to the withdrawal of Her Majesty's Troops from this Province – I beg leave to Report for His Excellency's information that I consider the 1st Regiment of Lanark Militia to be one of the most Effective Corps in the Province – it having a number of well drilled old soldiers in its Ranks – And should His Excellency deem it necessary to call out a part of the Militia Force for the Public tranquillity &c. – I hope he will at an early period employ this Regiment on Such Service as he may be pleased to order – . . .

D 12   G.H. READE[16] TO COL. RICHARD BULLOCK[17]
Perth, 28 December 1837
[*PAC, Adjutant General's Office, Correspondence, v. 22, Leeds file*]

. . . The recent events in both Provinces called into play our Military feelings and habits, as for myself devotedly attached to the Army, I exerted myself to the utmost and had a bad account reached us from Toronto, I had every thing in readiness to march off the Parade for the Seat of Government. I had Six Company's of fine Active fellows fit for

---

County in 1824 and then of Carleton County. Although the efficiency of his management of the Richmond colony was at times questioned by higher authorities, the settlers evidently did not complain and he remained in his post until he moved to Bytown and became county registrar, dying there in 1854.

[16]George Hume Reade (*fl.* 1820–1839), an ex-army surgeon, settled in the military colony at Perth, Lanark County. He was made clerk of the peace for the Bathurst District when it was created in 1822, a position he still held at the time of the union of the Canadas. In addition, he was active on the district Board of Education in the 1820s.

[17]Richard Bullock (d. 1857) was probably born in Ireland, for he left that country in 1799 with his parents for Upper Canada. In the colony he pursued a career in the army. From 1834 to 1837 he was sheriff of the Prince Edward District and was appointed sheriff of the Midland District in 1837. The same year he became a colonel of the militia, then on 19 December 1837 was appointed adjutant general of Upper Canada. Arthur judged him gallant but incompetent; none the less, he held his post until 1846. He was an active Orangeman.

any duty, and two other's of Rifles 50 each, the two latter companies had nearly all Rifles, and I got Ball Cartridge and evry thing that I considered necessary, so that if I met any *old Antagonist Red Wig* [Whig], I could have honoured him with a Warm reception – I got these two Companies together at Vast expense but in a righteous cause what sacrifice would not a man make. . . .

Graham[18] had a fine Company of Artillery and well equipped the men were greatly mistified at not being employed. . . .

I formed the Rifle Company's as I could but get them: the remainder of my Regiment I formed into a Reserve Corps. I addressed my Men at great length, and I never witnessed a more Loyal burst of feelings even amongst some of my Men whom I had cause to suspect were not over and above, *ready to fight*, they appeared animated with the like feeling of Loyalty. . . .

D 13   ANTHONY LESLIE[19] TO JOHN JOSEPH
Perth, 22 December 1837
[PAC, Correspondence of the Provincial Secretary's Office, v. 9, file 1257]

I have the honor for His Excellency Sir Francis Head The Lieutenant Governors information to forward herewith a copy of a declaration made and signed by the Catholics of the Town of Perth and the vicinity.

I would have sent the original now in my possession were it not for the following reasons, To get them signed with the greatest expedition I made out five copies which were sent out one for Perth one for Burgesss, one for Bathurst, one for Drummond, and one for Lanark and Dalhousie Townships[;] to have forwarded all of them would have caused a bulky package and their having been signed by persons in the middle of their agricultural pursuits they are a good deal soiled altho I am convinced from all I hear of our deservedly and greatly esteemed Governor that he would not have valued the declaration less on that account, but I thought that a certified copy would do as well to forward

It will be both proper and requisite for me to let the Governor know the occasion why it was considered necessary that the Catholics here should express their Loyalty in the manner they have now done

When the most active Magistrates of this Place found that Lower

[18]This was probably Henry Graham (1794–1846), an Irishman, a wealthy merchant, and a member of the local Family Compact. He was commissioned as a legislative councillor in 1839 but was not sworn into the council and never sat on it. He did, though, later sit in the Assembly of the united Canadas.

[19]Anthony Leslie, a Scot, served as a captain in the British army before settling in Upper Canada. In 1821 he was appointed a magistrate in Perth and he retained that office for a number of years. In the 1830s he was made an agent for the Commercial Bank in Perth and served as such until 1857. In 1840 he married the daughter of Anthony Manahan.

Canada was in open rebellion and that the seditious faction in the Home District were preparing to make an attack upon Toronto it was considered to be highly proper to look into the state of the disposition of our own population as to their attachment to the Government. From all we could discover we were convinced that the Protestant part of the Population were sound and Loyal but there was some doubts felt and expressed as to the Catholics[;] never having my self heard the least whisper that there were any disloyalty amongst them I heard of the report with surprise and grief and I thought that such might be the case and the same carefully kept from my knowledge altho a catholic. So I immediately made up my mind that I would not rest until I should discover how matters stood in that respect

I went first to Mr McDonald[20] the Priest when he in the most confident manner assured me that such could not be without his knowing of it and that it was his firm belief that it was quite the reverse and that they were Loyal to a man[;] after leaving him I went to the most influential men amongst them and they confirmed what Mr McDonald had stated to me[.] I finding things looking so well I wrote out the above mentioned declaration which was exactly the sentiments expressed by those that I had spoken too[.] I informed The Honorable William Morris[21] how I had found matters and showed to him the declaration and I had his approval of what I had done and about to do in it

I immediately dispached five proper persons to have it presented for signature and it is with pride and pleasure I have to assure you for His Excellency's information that the trial was a most triumphant one

The persons that went round assure me that every house that they called at and found the proprietor at home that it was hailed as a blessing to have such an opportunity to express their Loyalty and that they were quite indignant that they should have been so cruelly slandered and expressed the greatest gratitude to me for having fallen on a plan to enable His Excellency and their fellow subjects to be made acquainted how sound and Loyal their priciples [sic] are. . . .

---

[20]John Macdonald (McDonald) (ca. 1790–ca. 1890) ministered to the Catholics of Perth as early as 1829. He surrendered his charge there in 1838.

[21]William Morris (1786–1858) emigrated to Montreal from his native Scotland in 1801. Before the War of 1812, in which he served, he moved to Brockville, and in 1816 established himself in Perth as a merchant. He sat as as member of the Assembly from 1830 to 1836 and was appointed to the Legislative Council in 1836. He was known as a champion of the Kirk, and took that body's claims to a share of the clergy reserve revenues to the British government in 1837. He was also active in the militia, serving in the rebellion period as colonel of a Lanark regiment. From 1844 to 1846 he sat in the Executive Council and was the receiver general of the united Canadas. From 1846 to 1848 he was president of the Executive Council.

D 14   THE CATHOLICS' DECLARATION OF LOYALTY
[*PAC, Correspondence of the Provincial Secretary's Office, v. 9, file 1257, enclosed in Anthony Leslie to John Joseph, Perth, 22 Dec. 1837*]

Copy

We the undersigned Catholics in the Town of Perth and in the Townships of Burgess, Drummond, Bathurst, Lanark, and Dalhousie, have heard with deep regret, that we are suspected of being disloyal

We here solemnly declare, that the said suspicion, is most unjust and false, and that we take thus means, to let our fellow subjects know, that we love and venerate our Young Queen and Her Government; and that we are ready to join with her other Loyal Subjects to put down any Rebellious attempts that may be made to sever the connexion of this Colony from Great Britain and Ireland

The original of the above copy is signed by The Reverend John McDonald and Two Hundred and Seventy seven of the congregation

Perth, 22d December 1837

I certify that I have compared the above with the original declaration and find it to be an exact Copy – . . .

Wm. Morris J.P.

D 15   WORD OF "DISTURBANCES IN UPPER CANADA"
[Recorder, *Brockville, 14 Dec. 1837*]

For another extract from this document see E 40.

On Friday evening last [8 December] we were put in possession of Toronto papers, one day in anticipation of the regular Mails. They contained the important intelligence of an out-break in the Home District, the particulars of which, as contained in the papers received, we gave in slips on Saturday morning. The articles are now embodied with other matter on our first page. . . .

D 16   COL. H. MUNRO[22] TO COL. NATHANIEL COFFIN
Prescott, 11 December 1837
[*PAC, Adjutant General's Office, Correspondence, v. 22, Grenville file*]

In accordance with the general Militia order of the 4th Inst. I called out the division of my Regt residing in the Town of Prescott – and this day about 300 men appeared on parade who are determined to support *the Queen & Constitution* – . . .

[22]Hugh Munro (*fl.* 1797–1837), a captain, was granted over 2,000 acres of land in Edwardsburgh, Oxford, and Johnstown townships in the 1790s and early 1800s. He became a justice of the peace for Edwardsburgh and South Gower.

D 17   ARRESTS IN THE BROCKVILLE AREA
[Chronicle & Gazette, *Kingston, 27 Dec. 1837*]

Sayings and doings at Brockville. – The Statesman of the 16th instant, says:

"Some arms and ammunition have been taken from suspected parties in this Town, and several arrests have been made by the Magistrates, amongst others, who have been arrested, are Wm. Buell Richards,[23] _____ Stephen, Junr., Sylvester Skinner,[24] _____ Shepherd,[25] Rev. W. Wilson[26] (Episcopal Methodist Preacher) Philip Wing[27] (of Farmersville,) 2 Bellamys[28] and young Pike; near Bellamy's Mills. – Warrants have been issued and strict search made for W.B. Wells, M.P.P.[29] Stephen Richards,[30] S.C. Frey.[31] and others, who, it is said, have absconded."

[23]William Buell Richards (1815–1889), a native of Brockville, was called to the bar in 1837 and practised in his home town. He was very active in community organizations and was a reformer in politics. He worked hard to reorganize local reformers in the 1840s after the disruption caused by the rebellion and was elected to the Assembly in 1848 for Leeds. A close friend of Robert Baldwin, he became attorney general under Francis Hincks in 1851. In 1853 he was made a puisne judge of the Court of Common Pleas and spent the rest of his working life on the bench, becoming successively chief justice of the court (1863), chief justice of the Ontario Court of Queen's Bench (1868) and chief justice of the Supreme Court of Canada (1875–9), which he helped to create.

[24]Sylvester Skinner (1800–1874), a native of Hartford, Connecticut, came to Brockville in 1816. He formed a carriage-building company with Gideon Sheppard and was very successful. An outspoken critic of the Family Compact, he was briefly arrested after the rebellion. Subsequent to this he spent several years building locks on the Black River Canal in New York before returning to Brockville. In 1857 he moved to Gananoque, where he manufactured scythes, hames, etc.

[25]Quite possibly this was Gideon Sheppard, Sylvester Skinner's partner.

[26]This was likely Thomas Wilson, a Methodist preacher, who was arrested on 13 December 1837 and released on 15 December.

[27]Philip Wing (1804–1863) was a member of a loyalist family of Quakers who settled at the site of Farmersville (Athens). Primarily a farmer, he owned a store from 1835 to 1846 and opened one of Ontario's first cheese factories in 1859 or 1860. In 1849 Wing was a director of a joint stock company created to build a plank road from Farmersville to Unionville (Forthton).

[28]Samuel J. Bellamy, and his brothers, Edward, Chauncey, and Hiram, came from Vermont to Augusta Township about 1819. Over the next few years they built and operated mills in several locations in Leeds and Grenville counties. Edward, Hiram, and Samuel continued to operate the original mills and a distillery, pot and pearl ash works, and store attached to the mills. Undoubtedly, the Bellamys referred to are one or two of these three and/or their children.

[29]William Benjamin Wells (1809–1881) was born in Augusta Township into a United Empire Loyalist family. William, who became a lawyer in 1833, published the *Vanguard* at Prescott in 1834. A reformer, he was elected an MLA for Grenville in 1834 and 1836. In 1837 he published *Canadiana*, a reform tract which warned the British government that if Upper Canada's grievances were not remedied the province might well break out in rebellion. When rebellion did occur, fearing reprisals, he fled the province and was expelled from the Assembly. He returned to the colony in 1843, becoming a judge in the County Court of Kent and Lambton in 1850.

[30]Stephen Richards (1820–1894) was born in Brockville. He was the younger

D 18 _____ TO ALPHEUS,[32] HENRY,[33] AND SIDNEY JONES[34]
Brockville, 19 December, 1837
[*PAC, Upper Canada Sundries, v. 180, pp. 99503-5*]

I think on friday last[35] a number of persons were arrested by special constables and brought before several Magistrates of this Place suspected of *treasonable practices*, Among the number was one Wilson one Episcopal Methodist Preacher, the prooff against whom (as near as I can recollect) is this; he was warned to train by a serjeant of some company belonging to Colonel Frasers[36] [Batilion?] for training on the 12th instant to do actual service at Maitland in this District, to whom he replied he would not have under the *tory faction and had enough to back him from training, he did not train*[,] nor was he present[,] this was while the rebelion was raging in upper & Lower Canada[,] it was further proven against him that in a sermon he Preached he drew some comparison with the present times and those in former days mentioned in scripture where a rebelion existed; and stated, to his congregation that he had been informed by a *soldier* in Montreal, from whence he had lately come, that the soldiers were *deserting* by twos and threes, for protection to the United States – upon this evidence he was only fined *10s–*. for his not training and held to bail for his good conduct,!

brother of William Buell Richards and a relative by marriage to the Buell family. Educated at Brockville and at Potsdam Academy, New York, he was called to the bar in 1844. From 1867 to 1875 he was MLA for Niagara and he served as commissioner of crown lands and provincial secretary under John Sandfield Macdonald.

[31]Samuel Chollett Frey (b. 1799) was active for some time in support of the Patriots after fleeing Brockville in December 1837. Reportedly, he was involved in the burning of the *Sir Robert Peel* in May 1838, leading the authorities of New York State to offer a $250 reward for his capture. He soon settled in Canton, Ohio, where in 1852 he was involved in promoting a local railroad scheme.

[32]Alpheus Jones (1794–1863), brother of Jonas Jones, was a prominent Prescott merchant. In 1823 he was made Prescott's collector of customs, a position he held until his death. He also became the Prescott agent for the Bank of Upper Canada and postmaster of the town.

[33]Henry Jones (1790–1860) was a cousin of Alpheus Jones. He fought in the War of 1812 and settled in Brockville, where he became postmaster, magistrate, and a well-known merchant and businessman, operating, among other things, a potash works. He was Brockville's first MLA, elected in 1830.

[34]Sidney Jones (1802–1856) and his brother Henry operated a successful shipping business in Brockville.

[35]"Friday last" was 15 December but the arrests actually occurred on 13 December.

[36]This may have referred to Colonel Alexander Fraser (1786–1853) of the 1st Glengarry Regiment, since Wilson had evidently passed through Glengarry on his way back from Montreal. Alexander Fraser was born at Glendonmore, Scotland. He came to Upper Canada about 1800, settling in Charlottenburgh Township and acquiring large properties. From 1812 to 1818 he was the quarter-master of the Canadian Fencible Regiment. In 1822 he was appointed colonel of the 1st Glengarry Regiment and led an expedition into Lower Canada in 1838. From 1828 to 1834, a tory, he represented Glengarry in the Assembly; from 1837 to 1853 he served as the county's registrar, and from 1839 to 1853 as a legislative councillor.

D 19   J. SABINE[37] TO JOHN JOSEPH
Highbury, 27 December 1837
[PAC, Correspondence of the Provincial Secretary's Office, v. 9, file 1271]

In these bustling & troublesome times perhaps we *little people* at Brockville can scarcely expect to be much noticed at the *seat* of *Government*, . . . we know that we have some unquiet spirits who, though they have cross'd the Water to be out of the way, would still, if they could find opportunity, stir up disaffection & promote confusion – – there is one *Mr Wells – M:P:P:* amongst whose papers, when seized – was found (as I understand) a plan for burning this our Town of Brockville – releasing the Prisoners from the Court House & seizing the Arms – a Guard has hitherto been maintained here. . . .

D 20   S.C. FREY TO W.L. MACKENZIE
Morristown, 4 January 183[8]
[PAO, Mackenzie–Lindsey Papers, Mackenzie Correspondence, pp. 1382-5]

Since Mr Fletcher left here the Tories have continued their oppression at Prescott and Brockville[,] Arrests are going on and, the lowest Soundrils among them seem to have most authority, such for instance as J.K. Hartwell,[38] many Americans have been abused and insulted merely for the sin of being americans – . . .

Animosities between the Tories at Prescott and the citizens of Ogdensburgh run high[,] threats are exchanged. they have threatened at Brockville to take me here and smuggle me over, I have no fears on that head – I frequently see friends from the other side, there is no change in the minds of the people, many are still and sullen[,] they wait [and?] pant for vengeance, the poor fellows dare not say any thing. . . . Peter Robertson[39] of Belleville was arrested here at Brockville on the 20 Decr. & gave bail in £1000 to appear before the Magistrates at Bellville on the 5th Inst.[,] he is a fine young fellow and if they do not imprison him he will join you soon. Kingston jail is full of patriots principally from Bellville.

[37]This may have been James Sabine, appointed a magistrate for Elizabethtown in 1840.
[38]J.K. Hartwell, a Gowanite Orangeman, counted some of Brockville's most prominent residents among his friends. He sat on the Brockville Board of Police in 1835 and 1837. In 1836 he was the returning officer for Leeds in an election that saw reform accusations of irregularities when two government supporters were returned. In 1837 he contested the by-election occasioned by Jonas Jones' appointment as registrar of Glengarry County but lost to a moderate. A militia colonel, he offered to march his regiment to Lower Canada in 1837.
[39]Peter Robertson appears to have been a Trenton, rather than a Belleville, merchant. He returned to the Midland District and was arrested on 27 February 1838 for alleged involvement in an abortive Patriot raid. He was freed on 16 May 1838.

It was astonishing to see what the effect was in the county of Leeds among the Orangemen when news first came down that you had taken Toronto – the scoundrils ran about among their nighbors who were reformers and wanted to be good friends. as soon as it was known that you were defeated, they acted like hungry wolves & nothing would satisfy them but to hang & shoot all the damnd radicals. Oh. they want doctoring. May God prosper the glorious cause, . . . Buell[40] is obliged to talk more than half tory or have his press torn down. Many of his subscribers have quit him, . . .

D 21   EXAMINATION OF JOHN GRAFF
[PAC, Upper Canada Sundries, v. 181, pp. 99882-6]

District of Johnstown } Examination of John Graff of the Township of Wolford in Said District, Tailor, for Seditious and Treasonable Conduct against his Lawful Sovereign, and the Constitution of Great Britain, Before Henry Burritt,[41] Stephen Burritt,[42] Truman Hurd,[43] John L Read[44] and Terence Smyth[45] Esquire, five of her Majestyes

[40]William Buell (1792–1862) was born in Elizabethtown, Upper Canada. He served in the War of 1812. A moderate reformer, he edited the Brockville *Recorder*, 1828–49, and represented Leeds in the Assembly, 1828–34. In 1856 and 1857 he was elected the mayor of Brockville. In 1837, a militia officer, he turned out with the loyalists and in 1838 he served at Prescott against the Patriots.

[41]Henry Burritt (b. 1791), a native of Augusta Township, was a son of the founder of Burritt's Rapids, Stephen Burritt, a United Empire Loyalist and one of the first settlers along the Rideau River. Though he came with his family to the Rideau in 1793, Henry may have been the Henry Burritt appointed a magistrate for Augusta in 1821 and who in 1815, a War of 1812 veteran, was appointed a major in the 2nd Grenville Regiment, then in 1830, a resident of Edwardsburgh, appointed a lieutenant-colonel in the same regiment. This Henry Burritt, a tory, in 1839 took William Wells' seat in the Assembly.

[42]This may have been Stephen Burritt Sr., who had been a member of Rogers' Rangers and who, as a loyalist, had been granted land in Augusta Township. Stephen settled at Burritt's Rapids in 1793 and was appointed a magistrate in 1800. From 1808 to 1812 he represented Grenville in the Assembly, and became in 1813 a lieutenant-colonel in the 2nd Regiment of Grenville militia. He lived to be 84 and was still active in his public duties in 1837.

The reference may have been, however, to Stephen Sr.'s son, Stephen (b. 1805), also a magistrate in 1837. Stephen Jr., a native of Burritt's Rapids, assumed his father's role as postmaster there. He later became a district councillor in 1842 and became, as well, a clergy reserves inspector. In 1855 he moved to Thornbury, Canada West.

[43]Truman Hurd (d. *ca*. 1879), the son of a loyalist, was the first settler at Kemptville. In 1821 he was appointed a magistrate for Oxford Township.

[44]John Landon Read (1789–1857) was born in Augusta Township. He served in the War of 1812, then moved from Montreal, where he had been a merchant, to Merrickville, where he opened a general store and became a lumber dealer. In 1833 he was appointed a magistrate for Wolford Township. Though known as a tory, he resisted the threatenings of a tory mob in 1836 when, as returning officer for Grenville, he returned two reformers to the Assembly.

[45]Terrance (Terence) Smyth, presumably a relative of Major Thomas Smyth after

Justices of the peace, in and for Said District, at Merrickville Decr. 20th 1837. –

The Queen	}	
vs	}	Dept. [Deponent] being Arrained
John Graff	}	Pleads Not Guilty

Mathew Hunter being duly sworn *Saith* that he was present at a training, on or about the 15th Novr. last, and heard Dept. say, he was a full Blooded *Papanau man*, thinks he was a Member of the Secrete Meeting held in this Village by Certain Characters, Dept. was inebriated at the time – thinks he would not have Spoken so if he had been sober

John Eastman[46] Sworn Saith that he (Witness) and Dept. have always been friends, that at the last training in this Village, he heard Dept. say, he was a *Papanau man* and would Support his principals, – was in the Road at the time; and appeared to be in a passion, and beat his fist against the Stable – did not appear to be in Liquor – was able to walk about. – Mr. Mathew Hunter was present, but no other person. . . .

Stephen H. Merrick[47] *Sworn* Saith that he and Dept. has always lived on Good terms – Never heard him say anything agt. [against] – the Government – Considered him a reformer he (Witness) was a member of the secrete Meeting spoken of – Mr. Joel Putnam[48] was President – The writings was in the hands of Walter McCrea,[49] Secty. to the Society, and when it was disolved, it was Mutually Agreed, to burn them – they thought it was best to disolve the Meeting on account of the disturbed State of the province – Mr. Fr[e]y sent out a paper from Brockville, Called the Constitution, from which the Constitution

---

whom Smith's Falls was named, built the first mill at Burritt's Rapids. Appointed postmaster of Merrickville, he opened a business there in 1829. He appears to have been a Methodist, for in 1831 and 1832 two children of Terrance and Eleanor Smyth were baptized by a minister riding the Rideau circuit.

[46]This may have been the John Eastman of United Empire Loyalist origin who settled in North Gower Township in 1828.

[47]Stephen Hedger Merrick (b. *ca.* 1807) was born in Merrickville, the son of William Merrick, the founder of that town. In 1842 he appeared on the list of Johnstown magistrates and was later described as a Merrickville hotel owner. He also built and operated a woollen mill, the ruins of which have been preserved by Parks Canada.

[48]This was likely Joel Putnam (1779–1869), who had been born in Vermont. An Episcopal Methodist and one of Wolford's first settlers, he and his wife Elizabeth farmed lot 17, concession 2. Childless, the couple raised several orphans.

[49]Walter McNiffy McCrea (1810–1902) was born in Oxford Township, adjacent to Wolford. He studied law at Merrickville and became a Johnstown District magistrate, evidently in 1842. He later moved to Chatham, where he was elected mayor. He was appointed a legislative councillor of the united Canadas in 1862 and a senator of the new Canada in 1867. He resigned the latter position in 1871 to become judge of the District Court of Algoma. He died at Sault Ste. Marie.

of the Society was taken all but the three latter Clauses, which was omitted – The Constitution was brought from Brockville by Horatio N Church,[50] who said he received it from Mr. Frey – the Clauses Omitted was something eminating from McKenzie – The object of the Meeting was, to take Steps which would enable them to Carry their points at the Next Township Meeting – At the time when the Society was organized, the members Mutually Agreed to support the Magistrates in the execution of their duty, and was friendly to the Government – thinks Alexr. McCrea[51] Objected to have the papers distroyed – there was about 26 Subscribers to the Constitution at the time when the disolution took place – there was no connection between this society, and one of a Similar Kind, in Brockville – each member of the Society was to pay a small sum for the use of the room and Stationary. Alexr. McCrea pd. 10/– Dept. was one of the Members of the society – . . .

Dept. John Graff bound to take his trial at the Next Assizes

John Graff	£50–0.0
Alexr. McCrea	25–0.0
John Welsh	25–0.0[52]

D 22   EXAMINATION OF WALTER McCREA
[*PAC, Upper Canada Sundries, v. 181, pp. 99890-1*]

Johnstown District } Examination of Walter McCrea of the Township of Wolford in Said District Yeoman, . . . who was brought forward on a Charge, for Treasonable and Seditious Conduct, Towards our Sovereign Lady the Queen, and the British Government – Merrickville Decr. 20th 1837 –

The Queen	}	Dept. [Deponent] arrained for Treason
vs	}	Pleads not Guilty
Walter McCrea	}	

. . . John L Read Esquire, Sworn Saith that near Two Years ago, he (Witness) and Alexander McCrea was in conversation upon the subject of Public affairs – McCrea appeared to be dissatisfied with the Govt. he (Witness) asked him what he wanted, Whether it was a republican Government, or a revolution – Dept. replied, that is what we want and will have it – does not think Dept. meant to Carry his point by physical force

[50]Horatio N. Church was presumably a member of the Church family which had arrived in Wolford Township in 1805.

[51]This was Alexander McCrea Sr. (1784–1856), a native of Stillwater, New York, who came to Upper Canada about 1798. He located at Burritt's Rapids before settling in Wolford Township, where he farmed lot 21, concession 3. He married in 1809 and his son Walter was born the next year. Another son, Alexander Jr., was born in 1816.

[52]Graff was bound over for £50 and McCrea and Welsh were his two sureties.

E.H. Whitmarsh[53] Esquire maketh oath and saith, that he was present when Dept. made the Statement mentioned by John L Read Esquire, and that the above Testimony is correct to the best of his Knowledge –

Samuel Furguson *Sworn* saith That he and Dept. has always lived as friends and neighbours – that las[t] month, he met with Dept. at Mr. Millins *Inn* – Dept. said he would support reform, and McKenzie and that he would die in his Country,s Cause, Meaning the system that McKenzie espoused – Thinks Dept. would be glad to have a republican Government, and that he would Join the Rebels, if they had have been successful. . . .

Dept. bound to take his trial at the Next Assizes for Sedition

Walter McCrea	£50–0.0
Alexr. McCrea	25–0.0
John Welsh	25–0.0[54]

D 23   TERENCE SMYTH TO CHRISTOPHER HAGERMAN
Merrickville, 26 December 1837
[PAC, Upper Canada Sundries, v. 181, pp. 99880-1]

In consequence of the Calamitous situation of the country, and the many disaffected Characters which we have much reason to believe are residing among us – The Magistrates of this neighbourhood, have felt it a duty to take up, and examine a number of disaffected Characters, three of whom we have bound to take their trials at the next Assizes – I have been particular in taking the Examinations, a duplicate of which, I have taken the liberty of enclosing for your information and as it is a business, the nature of which Seldom comes under the notice of a Magistrate, you will Confer a particular favour by giving us your advice and instructions in regard to the above cases –

Walter McCrea and John Graff, are no doubt enemies to the Country, and have long manifested a spirit altogether at variance with the Government – and as far as I can Judge from their General Conduct, there can be but little doubt of their hostile feelings towards the constitution of Great Britian – The former is son to Mr Alexr. McCrea, a very wealthy farmer in this Township, and one of *McKenzie,s* warmest friends – but who has managed his Business with so much policy, that although we have been very particular in

---

[53]E.H. Whitmarsh (1809–*ca*. 1877) was born at Edwardsburgh into a United Empire Loyalist family. He worked as a store clerk before opening his own businesses in Unionville and Brockville. In 1835 he settled in Merrickville, where he became involved in the lumber trade. In 1836 and 1837 he was elected a township commissioner and in 1842 a district councillor. In 1838 he participated with the loyalists in the battle of the windmill at Prescott.

[54]Walter McCrea was bound over for £50 and Alexander McCrea and Welsh were his two sureties.

investigating his conduct at the late examinations, yet the only thing we could elicit from the witnesses against him was, that he was an active member of the secrete Meeting Mentioned in the Examination –

Robert Nicholson,[55] is a person in Good Circumstances, his General Character is that of a peaceable man, and although he professes to be a reformer, yet I never heard of his having taken a very active p[art] in political affairs, or of speaking disrespectful of his Excellency before – He sent his wife and money to the States about the time of McKenzies, diabolical rebellion in the Home District, and was to have followed her in a few days – John Graff, is in low circumstances, and not very respectable –

The Hbl. Judge Jones can give you some information about the McCreas –

D 24   COMPLAINT AGAINST B.R. CHURCH[56]
[PAC, Upper Canada Sundries, v. 181, pp. 99961-3]

To

His Excellency Sir Francis Bond Head, . . .

We the Undersigned Magistrates, Militia Officers, and Others, residing in the District of Johnstown on the Rideau Canal, feel it a duty, Respectfully to State for Your Excellencys information, that we have been this day Called upon to act in our Official Capacity to investigate the Conduct, of Alexr. McCrea, Walter McCrea, John Graff, William Bourk, and Archibald Mooney, for Sedition and Treason, Against her Majesty and the Government, and also of holding secrete Meetings in Connection with W.L. McKenzie, And we exceedingly regret to state; that B.R. Church Esquire has long been in the habbit of Associating, and consulting with, the prisoners (Alexr. and Walter McCrea,) and other disaffected Characters in the County; and that during the Examination above Mentioned, the said B.R. Church, went out and Secretely Conversed with the prisoners – That he is in the habbit of promulgating Deisticle principals throughout the country, – and in various ways is Guilty of pursuing a Course, altogether at varience with the true Character of a Justice of the peace – That very recently he declared (to one of the Members of the Secrete Society) that the British Officers could not bring their men into the field to fight the Rebels, in consequence of their disaffection towards her Majestyes Govt – And that it is his Genl. Character, to be

---

[55]This may have been the Robert Nicholson of Montague Township who was a member of the Church of Scotland's Smith Falls congregation.

[56]Basil R. Church was a Merrickville doctor who had been granted his licence in 1828. In 1833 he was appointed a magistrate for Wolford. Married to a Universalist, he evidently became one himself, spreading that sect's peculiar doctrines of universal salvation, thus making himself particularly obnoxious to his fellow magistrates. In 1852 he was elected to the Assembly of the united Canadas.

secretely doing all in his power, with dis disloyal [sic] men, to the injury of the public at large – and also that he does not believe in future punishment, and is at all times doing all in his power to injure the Cause of Religion throughout the Country. . . .

in giving this information, we have not been mooved by feelings of a private nature, but Solely by a Sense of duty –

We have the Honor to be
Your Excellency's
Obdt. and very
Hbl. Servts.

E.H. Whitmarsh

Stephen Burritt J P
T. Hurd J..P..
Terence Smyth J.P.
Edmund Burritt Capt[57]
Stephen Burritt Snr

D 25   LOYALTY OF THE MIDLAND DISTRICT
[Chronicle & Gazette, Kingston, 2 Dec. 1837]

The Magistrates of Kingston have been praiseworthily engaged within the last few days, in bringing to light some treasonable designs, and in arresting a correspondence with some persons in this District hitherto suspected of disaffection to the Government. . . .

Although we are assured that in this District there exists but little of the radical combination which the arch-fiend, Mackenzie, and his rebel crew, boast of in other places, we cannot avoid recommending to the friends of good order and of good government throughout the District to be watchful, as the movements of the disturbers are, in their own language, "quiet but effectual." . . .

D 26   MILITARY OFFICERS TO SIR F.B. HEAD
Kingston, 6 December 1837
[PAC, Correspondence of the Provincial Secretary's Office, v. 9, file 1156]

Your Excellency's Despatch of the 5th inst. (Monday morning 3 o'clock) reached us at 1/2 past 5 o'clock P.M. This day[;] we beg to inform Your Excellency that your Commands will be complied with as soon as possible, Every thing requisite will leave this under charge of a proper officer by the conveyance pointed out by Your Excellency.

---

[57]Edmund Burritt (fl. 1793–1879), the son of Stephen, was reputedly the first white child born on the Rideau. A militia captain, he served in November 1838 at Prescott in the battle of the windmill. For many years he held the rank of lieutenant-colonel in the militia.

D 27   REV. JOSEPH STINSON[58] TO REV. ROBERT ALDER[59]
Kingston, 8 December 1837
[*The School of Oriental and African Studies, University of London,*
Wesleyan Methodist Missionary Correspondence, Canada West,
microfilm in United Church Archives]

Under the influence of great excitement I take up my pen to send you a few lines. The spirit of rebellion has broken out in this Province as well as in Lower Canada and where it will end no human being can at present tell. . . . It was expected that there would be A battle yesterday between the loyalists & rebels about three miles from Toronto – & we are all anxiously looking for the result. We are all mustering here to defend our loyal Town – should the Rebels get possession of Toronto this will be the next place at which they will aim – they will meet with a hot reception here & many of them will bite the earth before the rascally rebel Cry shall displace the glorious banner of old England – our men are in fine spirits & are determined to Conquer or die. I must refer you to the Lower Canada papers for information as to the state of affairs there – but can just say that the rebels appear to be giving way before our brave fellows. This is the most rascally unprincipled rebellion that ever disgraced a country & will bring destruction upon the heads of its abettors – not however, I fear before many valueable lives are sacrificed. . . . Late as the season is a steamer came here last night from Toronto for muskets – cannon &c. &c.

I shall not expose myself unless it be *absolutely necessary* – but if we are assailed by a strong force – as all our regular soldiers are in Lower Canada – any man who can fire a shot will most likely be called upon to do so [–] if so – you know I shall not shrink from the pose of duty [–] I cannot see my family & friends sacrificed to these blood thirsty rebels without doing all I can to prevent it. Pray for us we are in trying circumstances. Our cause is just & we trust in the Lord. . . .

[58]Joseph Stinson (1802–1862) was born at Castle Donington, Leicestershire, England. He came to British North America in 1823, and as a minister of the Wesleyan Methodist Church served several charges in Upper and Lower Canada. In 1839–40 and 1858–61 he was president of the Wesleyan Methodist conference.

[59]Robert Alder (1796–1873) was an Englishman who was both an Anglican priest and a Methodist minister. He served in Nova Scotia and Lower Canada from about 1816 to 1827, then returned to England, where from 1833 to 1851 he laboured as one of the secretaries of the Wesleyan Methodist Missionary Society. He helped achieve the Methodist union of 1833, but his subsequent conflicts with Egerton Ryerson and others helped provoke its dissolution in 1840, despite a trip by Alder in 1839 to Upper Canada to try to heal Methodist divisions.

D 28   R.H. BONNYCASTLE[60] TO JOHN JOSEPH
Kingston, 7 and 8 December 1837
[PAC, Upper Canada Sundries, v. 180, pp. 99055-9]

I beg you will represent to His Excellency the safe reciept of His Excellency's Despatches of the 5 & 6th instants.

all the Boats being dismantled here for the Season, the Respective officers on the receipt of the Despatch of the 5th instant chartered the St. George, had her put in order and she was to sail at 9 o'clock on the morning of the 8th

They were aided in this by the zealous and indefatigable exertions of her owner David John Smith[61] Esquire

The Guns ammunition &c. were about to be shipped and were to proceed this morning under charge of Major Cameron[62] of the Royal Artillery who was detached by Lt Colonel Cubitt[63] Commanding the Royal Artillery. but as the Traveller came in about 1/2 past four on the 7th and is a quicker boat and better adapted to encounter the Lake at this late Season they are sent by her and every thing that can be Spared is in her consisting of the best description of Guns and Stores.

The arms demanded from Montreal have not yet all arrived and the absolute necessity of arming the Militia here and those going from the Eastern Districts to keep open the communication with Lower Canada would not permit the Respective officers to send as many Arms as they wished. . . .

The Respective officers deemed it prudent to call out the Flank Companies of the Frontenac Regiment to day and we are happy to say the best spirit prevails and that 100 men were thrown into the Fortress and 100 men into the Tête de Pont at once. The Fort has also been well provisioned[,] Guns mounted as well as Mortars and all the specie in the Military Chest conveyed there to day as well as that of the Bank of the Midland District.

---

[60]Richard Henry Bonnycastle (1791–1847) received his commission in the Royal Engineers in 1809. He served in British North America during the War of 1812. In December 1837 he described himself as a captain and a major commanding the Royal Engineers. He kept command of the Engineers until 1839. After the rebellion, he was knighted for his services in the Canadas. He later served as the officer commanding the Royal Engineers in Newfoundland. He published several works, including *Canada, as it Was, Is, and May Be*.

[61]David John Smith (*ca.* 1796–1848) was born in Kingston, the son of a local merchant, and became a lawyer in that town. He helped found the Midland District Agricultural Society, becoming its first treasurer in 1830. In 1840 he was appointed treasurer of the Midland District.

[62]Angus Cameron (1797–1880) was a Scot. He rose to the rank of lieutenant-colonel before his death, which occurred in Kingston.

[63]Thomas Cubitt (1783–1840) entered the British army as a cadet in the Royal Artillery in 1799. In May 1836 he was commissioned lieutenant-colonel commanding the Royal Artillery at Kingston, and from 1836 until his death he commanded the Kingston garrison.

There are here many Old Soldiers, perhaps 50, who would willingly serve under our officers orders if called upon and would much relieve the severe Garrison Duty to which the Militia will otherwise be subjected and if approved might be clothed armed and provisioned at perhaps less expence

There has been no visible action on the part of the disaffected in and near this place, but there are, it is well ascertained several very loose and restless characters who would take any advantage against the numerous magazines and stores. The 24th Regt. left some clothing in Store in which the Pensioners and old Soldiers might be made to assume a very good aspect.

The Cavalry turned out last night, (6th inst) and patrolled the roads around the Town and the Magistrates and Public officers all do their duty well and zealously

I have dated this Letter 6th and 7[64] because I wished to give the latest intellegince previous to the sailing of the Boat.

Every *precaution* will be taken by the Respective officers to avoid needless expenditure, but it is right to meet the emergency, by every mode likely to prevent accident to the highly valuable and extensive Buildings and Stores

1/2 past 8. A.M

His Excellencys orders to "deliver Arms and Ammunition to all loyal men" has just reached me. Mr Murney[65] the bearer was stopped & searched near Toronto but escaped. We shall send Arms by a Steam Boat to Belleville to day

Every thing quiet here.

10 o'clock 8th Decbr 37

We are supplying the 1st 2nd Regts of Hastings militia with Arms also the 3rd Northumberland. . . .

D 29 ARMS FOR TORONTO
[Chronicle & Gazette, *Kingston, 9 Dec. 1837*]

The Traveller, Captain Sutherland,[66] left this port for Toronto,

[64]Actually, he dated the letter 7 and 8 December.

[65]This appears to have been Edmund Murney (1812–1861), who was born in Kingston. Educated at Upper Canada College, he studied law with Marshall Spring Bidwell before being called to the bar in 1834. He opened a practice in Belleville, where he married in 1835. In 1836, a tory, he was elected an MLA for Hastings. In 1839 he was appointed clerk of the Victoria District and from 1844 to 1847 sat in the Assembly of the united Canadas. From 1852 to 1856 he was clerk of the peace for Hastings County.

[66]James Sutherland (d. 1857) left his birthplace in Hoy, the Orkney Islands, at an early age to enter the service of the Hudson's Bay Company. After service in the south Atlantic, in the Baltic, and on the Great Lakes, he took command of the *Traveller*, which he partly owned. Very active transporting supplies, troops, and messages during the rebellion, he continued to operate the *Traveller* for some years afterwards, and then captained other ships on the lakes.

yesterday afternoon, having on board a quantity of arms and ammunition, including some pieces of ordnance, for the relief of the Seat of Government, in charge of Major Cameron, of the Royal Artillery, accompanied by fifteen armed Volunteers from this place, as an escort.

D 30   ANTHONY MANAHAN[67] TO THE *Chronicle & Gazette*
Culbertson's Wharf, 9 December 1837
[Chronicle & Gazette, *Kingston, 13 Dec. 1837*]

Interrupted by ice, we could proceed no further on our way to Belleville, in the steamer Kingston, and were forced to land here at four this morning; the arms, ammunition, &c., were all landed and stored at that hour – . . .

Our Kingston Volunteers, who have absolutely suffered severely, from the severity of the weather, and their diligent care of the important trust committed to their charge, have by their excellent conduct and untiring exertions in the fulfilment of their duties, merited my most warm praise – and although they might be relieved by the band of Indians who have offered their services for prosecuting the journey to Belleville, yet they chose rather to march the 20 miles as an escort, than return by wagons which could be provided for them – . . .

In this part of the country there have as yet been no meetings – two it is said are intended for Tuesday next – one constitutional, and another to *declare a neutrality* – singular enough. . . .

D 31   ANTHONY MANAHAN TO COL. JAMES FITZGIBBON
Belleville, 11 December 1837
[*PAC, Correspondence of the Provincial Secretary's Office, v. 9, file 1176*]

I have the honor and great satisfaction of reporting to you for the information of His Excellency the Lieutenant Governor the safe delivery to the custody of the Magistrates of the County of Hastings of one thousand stand of arms one hundred and fifty pistols fifty Rifles and Two hundred Marine sabres with 10+++ rounds of ball cartridge for musquets and 1+++ for pistols which armament is safely lodged under charge of a Captains Guard of the Volunteers of this Town. these arms having been given on my request for distribution to the Three Regiments of this County Militia and the 3d Northumberland, were

---

[67]Anthony Manahan (1794–1849), an Irish Catholic, a merchant and surveyor in Kingston, and later in Belleville, had for a time in the 1820s a share in the Marmora iron works. From 1827 to about 1830 he was the general manager of those works. A magistrate and a militia colonel, he was elected as a tory to the Assembly for Hastings in 1836 and served there until 1841, representing Kingston briefly in that latter year. From 1841 to 1844 he was the collector of customs at Toronto. He stood for election to the Assembly in 1844 in Kingston as a moderate conservative, but lost to John A. Macdonald.

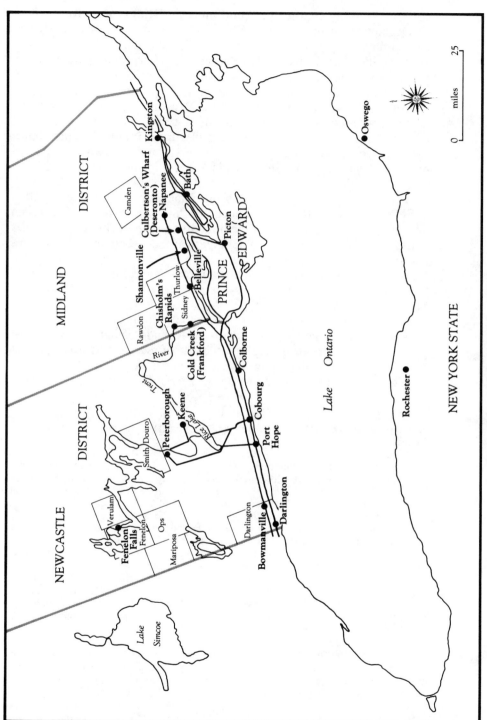

6: Newcastle and Midland Districts, 1837

committed to my charge[.] I accordingly left Kingston on friday night [8 December] in the Steamer Kingston with four of my officers and fifteen men who volunteered their services to secure the safe delivery at Belleville, but we had to land at half past four o'clock on saturday morning at the Indian woods (being prevented by the Ice from proceeding further) when the whole arms &c. were stored by the exertions of two of my officers Lts. Benson[68] and Burton and the laudable willingness of the well disposed inhabitants of that portion of the Country, fourteen waggons were in almost immediate attendance and the whole were put into the waggons and by two o'clock we proceeded on our march to this place accompanied by an additional guard of Thirty of the Indians of the Mohawk Tribe who were [sensibly?] anxious to give us every assistance we required. We halted at Shannonville for the night induced to this by intelligence I received on my way that an attack was meditated in a pine thicket that outskirts that Village by the Rebels of whom there are several in the second third and fourth concessions of Thurlow along the front of which Township we had to pass having used due precaution in guarding the waggons for the night in which I was ably assisted by the Magistrates of the place Messrs. Appleby,[69] Blocker[,][70] Murchison[71] and Lazier.[72] I proceeded on at day light having so disposed the Indians to each of whom I gave a musquet and Bayonet with 10 Rounds of ball cartridge that they cleared the woods throughout the line of march, and we arrived at Ten O'Clock. At Shannonville we were joined by a Company of Volunteers under command of Captn McNabb[73] all armed and bravely

[68]This may have been Charles O. Benson, who in 1838 was captain of the 2nd Hastings Regiment's troop of cavalry and who in 1840 became president of the Belleville Police Board.

[69]Thomas D. Appleby (1778–1865), a native of New York State, emigrated to Upper Canada in 1789, settling first in Kingston, then in Tyendinaga Township, where he farmed. He was elected township clerk in 1832, 1837, and 1838, appointed postmaster at Shannonville in 1833, and made a magistrate in 1834. In that latter year he was a private in the 1st Regiment of Hastings militia.

[70]"Blocker" may have been George Blecker (Bleeker), who in 1837 was a Belleville magistrate and a captain in the 1st Hastings Regiment, or may have been J.H. Blacker, appointed a magistrate for Tyendinaga Township in 1837.

[71]This may have been Donald Murchison, appointed a magistrate for the Midland District in 1842.

[72]This was likely Richard Lazier (b. 1805), a native of Prince Edward County. A son-in-law of T.D. Appleby, he moved to Shannonville in 1828 and opened a grist-mill and a sawmill nearby, settling on lot 5, concession 1 of Tyendinaga Township. He became a collector of customs and both a commissioner and a clerk of the Court of Requests, though evidently not a magistrate. In 1837–8 he captained a body of militia volunteers.

[73]James McNabb (d. 1837) was the son of Scottish miller James McNabb who sat for Hastings in the Assembly from 1816 until the year of his death in 1820. James Jr. lived in Belleville and was appointed a magistrate in 1836 or 1837. He was killed accidently while on duty with the 1st Hastings Rifles in December 1837 (see D 35, D 36).

determined to defend the armament with their lives and on our approach we were joined by a multitude of the Inhabitants of this populous Town within the limits of which there is as far as I can learn but a small proportion disaffected. I must not however conceal the fact that there are in the Rear of Sidney and Thurlow very many of the Inhabitants who have attended seditious meetings and signed Articles of association in direct opposition to the laws of the Country and the Queen's authority and I have seen original one, this day. to which the name of Mr Lockwood[74] formerly a Member of Parliament was attached, the others had been torn away.

I have under the circumstances of the Times and the evidence of discord and arrangement of attack which I have received, thought it an imparative duty to keep a band of Indians here with the Chief John Culbertson[75] at my command as the most efficient guard I could controul to aid immediately in any emergency. and they have expressed a wish to join my Regiment as a Volunteer Rifle Company under Culbertson as their Captain, and two others of their Tribe, provided the plan would meet with the approbation of His Excellency. upon which subject I would further add that if I am to make the depot of arms for my Regiment at Rawdon they would form the most efficient and least expensive guard for that place. That such a guard should be placed there is in my opinion necessary as the Contractors for the works on the Trent at Chisholm's rapids are fearful that the powder required for the purpose of blasting, will be taken from there by the Rebels – hundreds of disaffected persons residing in the neighborhood – In fact I have contravened the sending of powder there and they will forbear until I am made acquainted through you with His Excellency's pleasure respecting this company, for whom I have already the Rifles –

You will be pleased to instruct me how the expenses thus incurred are to be paid. and in how far in the defence of this very disaffected part of the District I am to proceed, and how procuor the means of disbursing the expenses. .

D 32   ANTHONY MANAHAN TO COL. JAMES FITZGIBBON
Belleville, 11 December 1837
[PAC, Correspondence of the Provincial Secretary's Office, v. 9, file 1176, enclosure]

I congratulate you, on your appointment, Adjt Genl – we are not a bit

[74]Joseph N. Lockwood, presumably related to the Joseph Lockwood who received a land grant in Sidney Township in 1800, sat as a representative from Hastings in the Assembly of 1828–30. He was arrested on 17 December 1837 and freed on bail on 2 January 1838. He may have been the Joseph Lockwood who was later postmaster of Brighton.

[75]John Culbertson was a cousin of Joseph Brant.

too loyal in Hastings – for there are a great many of the inhabitants of Mackenzie's Kidney – Bowen the Magistrate Sent off a Prisoner from Cold Creek for Sedition and his brother that is the prisoners brother went before him to Secure a rescue – I [am] despatching a Sleigh with Bowens brother[76] and five Indians to follow – and before he is rescued – he will lose his head at the hands of the Indians – I send you a long official – and I beg of you to think favourably of the Indian rifle company – Such a *company* will do more than a Regiment of Regular Infantry to reduce the turbulent, by the fears they entertain of Scalping – &c.

Rifles guns & Powder have been purchased here under fictitious pretences – and 7 Guns & rifles have been found in a vacant house in Town –

There is a Muster of the 1st Regt. to day and I here had a Meeting of officers &c. and you will see by the printed order that they will assemble on Thursday at Rawdon – His Excellency in Council ought to authorize the Magistrates to administer the oath of allegiance – Parker[77] is the only Comr. in this country –

Monday night – 11 Nov. [*sic*] 1837

My advice to the Magistrates is: make Prisoners of the Ring leaders – commit without bail – Search their papers & take Arms from all that are disaffected –

D 33   EDMUND MURNEY TO JOHN JOSEPH
Belleville, 12 December 1837
[*PAC, Correspondence of the Provincial Secretary's Office, v. 9, file 1178*]

Late last evening I received Your despatch enclosing the various proclamations & immediate steps were taken to distribute them through the Country – Our Magistrates are very active and have made arrangements for two Companies from the first one from the second and one from the third regiments of Hastings to be on duty in Belleville for the protection of the Town and Country – Many of our Farmers and Townsmen have refused to take the oath of allegiance which through my suggestion is tendered to every militia-man & they the farmers have organised societies through every part of the Country the ostensible object of which are not to take up arms on *Either* side –

[76]The references here to "Bowen the Magistrate" and his brother are probably to William Bowen, a Belleville innkeeper and an Indian Department official who became registrar of the Surrogate Court of the District of Victoria in 1840, and to Daniel Bowen, who became a militia officer in 1838 and who later moved to Marmora.

[77]This was Thomas Parker, postmaster in Belleville, 1817–48. He was first appointed a magistrate for Belleville in 1829, and in 1837 was chairman of the Court of Quarter Sessions. In that latter year he was also a major of the 2nd Hastings Regiment. In 1841 he chaired a Belleville meeting which commended Arthur for his administration of Upper Canada.

These societies are very strong, they commenced no doubt through MacKensie, but he has rebelled too soon for them, public opinion was not sufficiently ripe for him in these parts & they condemn him not for his rebellion but for his rashness – I have seen many of their resolutions, but they are so vaguely expressed that without having their watchwords it is impossible to make treason of them.

D 34   COL. THOMAS COLEMAN[78] TO COL. JAMES FITZGIBBON
Belleville Park, 14 December 1837
[PAC, Adjutant General's Office, Correspondence, v. 22, Hastings file]

I have the honor to communicate for the information of His Excellency the Lieutenant Governor Sir Francis Bond Head – Baronet K.C. H. &c. &c. that the First Regt. of Hastings Militia assembled here on Monday last 11 Inst. to the number of at least 1000 men – several of the Magistrates and other respectable individuals having joined the Ranks, with a voluntary offer of their Services, in case of emergency – making a most formidable and impressive appearance – . . .

D 35   ANTHONY MANAHAN TO JOHN JOSEPH
Belleville, 16 December 1837
[PAC, Upper Canada Sundries, v. 180, pp. 99380-2]

I have satisfaction in reporting to you as Colonel of The Second Regiment of Hastings Militia, and as a magistrate commonly[,] when off other duty[,] attending the Special Sessions of the Justices of this County. That several Prisoners, suspected on strong – some on unequivocal grounds of treasonable acts and designs and seditious practices – have just been sent under an escort of forty men under Arms to the District Gaol at Kingston

There are eight – namely "Clifton A McCallum",[79] a man whose general conduct has had a tendency to republicanize his neighbours for several years – arrested upon a letter of his found in the papers of the Archrebel McKenzie – and who would be second to him only in attrocity of conduct had he but the opportunity of showing his character

[78]Thomas Coleman (*fl.* 1812–1838) captained a troop of volunteer cavalry during the War of 1812, but he dropped from government favour after attending one of Robert Gourlay's conventions and was, in fact, charged with sedition by James McNabb, his neighbour in the Belleville area and a government supporter. In 1825 Coleman begged forgiveness from the government and was subsequently appointed major commanding the Hastings Cavalry Troop. In 1837 he commanded the 1st Regiment of Hastings militia. He is known to have owned grist and sawmills at Thurlow, near Belleville, in 1816 and to have acquired extensive lands. From 1824 to 1828 he was the MLA for Hastings.

[79]Clifton McCallum, a Belleville merchant, was arrested on 17 December and released three days later. He took refuge in the United States after his arrest and returned when he felt the danger of persecution had passed.

– This man has Petitioned His Excellency to be allowed to leave the Province, a prayer which I hope will not be granted – & I am joined by most of the Magistrates of this portion of the Country in this hope –. Joseph N Lockwood formerly a member of the Provincial assembly, whose signature is found to one of their republican constitutions and whose general character has been always under Suspicions – Peter Davidson[80] Gideon Turner[81] Joseph P Caverley,[82] Joseph Caniff[83] Reuben White[84] formerly M.P.P. whose countenance and Signatures to the Seditious meetings, (and Aaron H. Hearns[85] who has acknowledged his Signature) can be proven – as well as that Several of them were identified with the purchase of Arms and the accumulation of ammunition – and with whom arms and amunition in unwonted quantities were found – The hope is expressed here that Several others will be taken and sent after them, and that the ring leaders thus treated, and brought to the just punishment their Seditious conduct merits. The example will prove effectual in checking any tendency to revolt within the County –

There is a manifest disposition upon the part of the loyal inhabitants of this county to hope that these characters will be dealt with as they deserve and not permitted to leave the Province – for the general belief is that they will in that event be found active in procuring resources & men on the other side to annoy us hereafter –

I hope to have the satisfaction of Seeing you on Thursday – in the meantime it is with painful feelings of regret I have to inform of a Second sad accident which is likely to deprive us of one of the most deserving and useful members of this Society James McNabb Esq – who last night on the turning out of the Guard upon the alarm of fire –

[80] Peter Davidson, a farmer, was arrested on 17 December 1837 and freed on bail on 2 January 1838.

[81] Gideon Turner, the Sidney Township clerk, was arrested on 15 or 17 December 1837 and freed on bail on 1 or 2 January 1838. Evidently he was later arrested on 23 February and freed on 17 May 1838.

[82] Joseph Caverley, a farmer, was arrested on 17 December 1837 and freed on bail on 2 January 1838.

[83] Joseph Caniff (1798–1872) was born in Adolphustown into a United Empire Loyalist family. He settled in Thurlow Township, where he operated a saw and grist-mill and where in 1837 he served as a township commissioner as well as a tax assessor and collector. Arrested on 17 December 1837, he was bailed on 2 January 1838. In February 1838 he was arrested for suspected Patriot activities and not released until 12 May 1838. In 1844 he ran unsuccessfully for election to the Assembly.

[84] Reuben White (d. 1857) settled in Sidney Township from New York State. He and his wife established large properties in Sidney, operating a general store as well as a lumber mill there. From 1820 to 1828 and from 1830 to 1834 he sat as an MLA for Hastings. He was arrested on 17 December 1837 and released on 2 January 1838. In 1841 he purchased the land for the Episcopal Methodist Church at Bayside.

[85] Aaron H. Hearns, a farmer, was arrested on 17 December 1837 and freed on bail on 2 January 1838.

unhappily ran counter to one of the Guard, and hit against a bayonet which perforated the abdomen – and his death is hourly expected –

D 36   COL. THOMAS COLEMAN TO COL. JAMES FITZGIBBON
Belleville, 16 December 1837
[PAC, Adjutant General's Office, Correspondence, v. 22, Hastings file]

I have the honor to make known to you for the information of His Excellency The Lieutenant Governor. . . . That the following arrangements have been this Day made (viz)

Detachments from the 1st 2 and 3rd Regiment of Hastings Militia. . . . Total 240 men which are now stationd in Belleville under my Command until further Orders to aid and assist the magistrates in the execution of their Duties, to preserve the Peace and tranquillity of The Town and County, to arrest all suspicious Characters, and seize on their Persons and Papers – until disposed of by the Laws of their Country. – The following Persons have been this Day sent down to Kingston under an escort of militia . . .

Rhuben White –
Joseph Lockwood
Peter Davidson
Joseph Canniff
Clifton McCollan

I regret to inform you that last Evening about 10 oClock a Fire Broke out in Belleville and nearly consumed a House belonging to Martin Ryen, on going to which, Capt McNabb came in contact with the Bayonet of One of the militia men who was trailing a musket near the Fire, in a very careless manner – tho' purely accidental, and no suspicion attachd to the Person, who was unfortunately the cause – No hopes are entertaind of Capt McNabbs recovery – another similar accident occurd to Capt Wm. Church of the 3rd Regt Hgs. Mil who had carelessly placed a large Horse Pistol within side his Surtout Coat, which on unbuttoning, fell to the ground and lodged the contents in his Body – whereof he died in a very short time afterwards – . . .

D 37   COL. THOMAS COLEMAN TO COL. RICHARD BULLOCK
Belleville Park, 22 December 1837
[PAC, Adjutant General's Office, Correspondence, v. 22, Hastings file]

. . . We are well prepared for a brush with the Rebels – several notorious Characters have been sent down from this Neighbourhood to Kingston and [we] are keeping a sharp look out for several others – . . .

D 38   GEORGE BENJAMIN[86] TO THE ADJUTANT GENERAL
Belleville, 26 December 1837

[*PAC, Adjutant General's Office, Correspondence, v. 22, Hastings file, enclosed in George Benjamin to John Joseph, Belleville, 26 Dec. 1837*]

I know the circumstances under which the enclosed petition was gotten up – The person petitioned against [Nelson Reynolds][87] is now under arrest for Treason – is & has been a leader of a party whose object has been subversion of the Govt. & giving him Every allowance for good conduct. he has suppressed information from the Govt. which every loyal man should have given – having been aware of p[ersons] holding seditious meetings – He never should have recd. the appointment of Lieutenant & the men never will act under him as Captn. – . . .

D 39   PETITION OF VARIOUS BELLEVILLE RESIDENTS

[*PAC, Adjutant General's Office, Correspondence, v. 22, Hastings file, enclosed in George Benjamin to the Adjutant General, Belleville, 26 Dec. 1837*]

. . . The undersigned inhabitants of the Town of Belleville, . . . beg leave to represent, that an individual named Nelson G. Reynolds, at present a Lieutenant, one of the late leaders & agitators in the Country, a man who has ever opposed the Government, and was a leader in Urging many individuals of this County, to petition for stopping the supplies, and as they are fully convinced, has done the utmost in his power to create discontent in the Country, and supported the late leaders of the rebel faction in this & the Lower Province, that it is in Contemplation . . . to recommend him . . . for the Commission of a Captain.

[86]George Benjamin (1799–1864) was born in Sussex, England. When a young man he emigrated to the United States before arriving in Upper Canada about 1830. Settling in Belleville he became a printer and in 1834 published the *Intelligencer*. A conservative and an Orangeman, his connections secured him various local positions. From 1836 to 1847 he was clerk of the Board of Police. A captain in the Belleville militia, he served as a volunteer against the Patriots. In the later 1840s he was registrar of Hastings County and its warden from 1846 to 1861. From 1856 to 1863 he was MLA for North Hastings. Although in earlier years Benjamin had supported George Brown, in this latter stage of his career he supported John A. Macdonald and the conservatives. In 1848 he unseated Ogle R. Gowan as grand master of the Orange Lodge and, when Gowan defeated him in 1852, Benjamin formed a schismatic lodge which continued until 1856 when both men resigned to make way for a compromise candidate.

[87]Nelson G. Reynolds (1814–1881), who was born in Kingston, is supposed to have served as a lieutenant of the British army in the west, for the Hudson's Bay Company. A resident of Belleville during the rebellion, he was tried and acquitted of treason. A very active businessman, he was interested in banking and transportation particularly. At one point he served as president of a steamship company and at another as president of the Marmora foundry. In the 1850s he moved to Whitby and became sheriff of Ontario County.

Wherefore we most respectfully beg leave to disclose, that as British Subjects, as men attached to the Constitution, and having a regard for our own safety, we do not consider, that, we should be safe in obeying orders under an individual like the said Reynolds, . . .

D 40   "R.V.C." TO THE *Upper Canada Herald*
Belleville, 18 December 1837
[Upper Canada Herald, *Toronto, quoted* Chronicle & Gazette, *Kingston, 27 Dec. 1837*]

In such times of alarm it is gratifying to witness the spirit of loyal devotion, shown throughout the whole Country by the FAITHFUL MILITIA.

On Sunday week it was a stirring sight to behold a long train of wagons with a strong guard coming into Town with arms and munitions of war for the different Regiments. – Nor was it the least cheering, to find our brethren of the Mohawk Tribe of Indians, with their Flags waving, accompanied by their Chief, leading on the whole as the advance escort.

On Monday there was a muster of the 1st Regiment, and any rebel if there, must have felt their insignificance!

Capt. Perry[88] inspected his Troop on Thursday – they appear to be very respectable men, mostly farmers. He read to them a letter which he had written on the breaking out of the rebellion in Lower Canada, tendering their services to the Lieutenant Governor, and His Excellency's reply. . . . He addressed them at considerable length, upon the unfortunate excitement in our own Province, and . . . the whole body marched forward and pledged themselves to be ready if required, to go with him to any part of the Upper Province. I should judge he has more than sixty men. . . .

If you think by publishing the above, it will serve the Constitutional Cause, you are at liberty, as well as the Chronicle and Gazette, to do so.

D 41   REV. SALTERN GIVINS[89] TO SAMUEL PETERS JARVIS
Napanee, 13 December 1837
[*PAC, Indian Affairs, v. 67, pp. 64202-6*]

I feel it but justice to the Mohawk Indians of the Bay of Quinte to

---

[88]D. Perry was the commander of the 1st Hastings Yeoman Cavalry, formed in 1835, which contained about fifty men.

[89]Saltern Givins (1809–1880) was the son of Col. James Givins. Born at York, Upper Canada, he was educated by John Strachan. In 1831 Givins became deacon and in 1833 priest of the Church of England. He served as missionary to the Mohawks at the Bay of Quinte and priest at Napanee until 1850. From 1851 until 1856 he served in several parishes west of Toronto. From 1856 until his death he was rector of St. Paul's, Toronto. He remained a close associate of his old teacher, Strachan.

inform you for the satisfaction of of [*sic*] His Excellency The Lt. Governor in these exciting time, how very readily they volunteered their Services for the support of the Government of the Country. –

The number of adult males of the Mohawks is about 75 & although a great portion of these, when the startling news that rebellion had broken out, reached us, were absent in their hunting grounds many miles distant, two days had scarcely elapsed before sixty warriors, were only detained from proceeding to Belleville to place themselves at the disposal of the Magistracy, by the delay in obtaining arms.

Under the peculiar circumstances of the case, I took the liberty of forwarding immediately a requisition for the necessary Equipment of arms for the Indians, upon the Commissariat at Kingston, having first obtained to it the signature & recommendation of A. McPherson[90] Esqr. the leading magistrate here. The arms were forwarded after a short delay, & the indians attended to receive them, from the Magistrate, but that functionary having received His Excellency's Proclamation, stating it to be unnecessary for Volunteers to proceed to Toronto; & The Hon. John Macaulay having informed him that he understood His Excellency was disinclined (for. reasons which we immediately Surmised) to accept, in the present juncture of affairs, of the services of the Indians: – the Magistrate therefore deemed it most agreeable with His Excellency's wishes to retain the arms till such time as they might be required, – or in event of their not being needed, to return them to Kingston. And after thanking the Indians in the Queen's name, for their loyal & zealous tender of services, dismissed them. –
. . .

D 42   LT.-COL. JOHN S. CARTWRIGHT TO COL. RICHARD BULLOCK
Toronto, 4 January 1838
[*PAC, Adjutant General's Office, Correspondence, v. 28, Lennox file*]

I have the honor to enclose the return of the State of the 2nd Regt of Lenox Militia as it appeared on parade on the 19th day of December last – I would remark that the Officers and men were in good spirit and that all the Officers and upwards of One Hundred and fifty men volunteered for immediate service in any part of Upper or Lower Canada –

[90]Allan McPherson (d. 1875) was the son of a Scottish officer, Major Donald Macpherson, who had come to Kingston in 1809 and had decided to stay in Upper Canada. Allan leased mills on the Napanee from Richard Cartwright in 1812 and over the next few years added a store, distillery, and other businesses. He acquired much land in the Napanee area, became its first postmaster and a magistrate, and built a fine house, where he entertained members of the province's social elite. In 1848 or 1849 he became crown lands agent at Kingston and moved to that centre, but he retained his interest in the Napanee area.

D 43   JOHN McGUAIG[91] TO COL. JAMES FITZGIBBON
Picton, 16 December 1837
[PAC, Adjutant General's Office, Correspondence, v. 22, Prince Edward file]

I have the honour to state to you for the information of His Excellency, that the 2 Regt. under my Command met on the 14th at the Consecon[92] pursuant to orders, . . .

I now proceed to detail our proceedings on the parade ground which are as follows, vizt. – On the Regiment being formed into line, and Equalized into Companies a hollow square was formed Eight deep with a view to reduce the Erea as much as possible, all the Magistrate[s] present within the Square Mr. Wilkins[93] and myself mounted[,] I proceeded to read the General order next the Proclamation with several other documents Eminating from His Excellency. regarding the disturbed state of the province the whole body of the people, there being no less in the Judgement of good Judges that one Thousand present, manifested great indignation at the proceedings of the rebels, and at the Close of Each paper three loud and long cheers were given for the Queen and Constitution and our gallant Sir Francis Bond Head. with tremendous cries["] where are the detested rebels, where are they, we shall put them down we shall hunt them like blood hounds." then Mr. Wilkins addressed them as a Magistrate in a short but impressive speech, told them to be true and faithful to themselves and the Government. that His Excellency had shewn them an Example worthy of their imitation that he had led the Civil Authorities from the City of Toronto. Met the rebel faction and disperced them, with considerable loss. on the rebel side! – Tremendous cheering

The Regiment was then thrown back into line, and Each Captain was ordered to call for Volunteers. When I am happy to say that the whole Regiment turned out, . . .

---

[91]John McGuaig (b. ca. 1792) was in 1837 the senior captain commanding the 2nd Regiment of Prince Edward militia. In 1840 he became the Surrogate Court registrar for Prince Edward County. His family was prominent in shipping in Picton.

[92]Presumably McGuaig meant Consecon Creek, which rises to the north of Picton and flows into Consecon Lake in the northwestern part of Prince Edward County.

[93]Robert Charles Wilkins (1782–1866) was the son of a British soldier demobbed in New York State during the American Revolution because of his wounds. After the revolution Robert's father, also named Robert, took his family to Nova Scotia, then in 1789 to England before bringing them to Upper Canada in 1792. Robert Jr. served in the War of 1812, reaching the rank of captain, also being appointed the Midland District's commissary officer. Very successful in the timber, importing, and distilling businesses, he was appointed to the Legislative Council in 1839 but was not reappointed after the union. In 1837 he was commissioned colonel in the militia. He died at Belleville.

D 44   COL. HENRY RUTTAN[94] TO COL. JAMES FITZGIBBON
Colborne, 10 December 1837
[PAC, Upper Canada Sundries, v. 180, pp. 99280-3]

In obedience to the Militia General orders issued by you a Copy of which I accidentally fell in with I immediately assembled the 3d Regt. Northumberland Militia under my Command and have now on permanent duty 2 Compys. of 60 men each, one at the River Trent and one at this place where I intend Keeping them until I receive further orders – I moreover have ordered the Batallion Companys to assemble at the respective places of their Company training every Wednesday for drill until further orders. I have upward of 100 stand of Govt. Arms and accoutrements[,] all of which I have at this place[,] leaving the Compy at the Trent to receive arms from Kingston by the Bay Steam Boats.

The whole Regiment have displayed the most gratifying enthusiasm in the Cause, not a Rebel is to be heard of that I Know of in the whole District unless the Refusal of the Smith's[95] of Port Hope to turn out or to call their men out be sufficient to characterise them as Traitors.

I am Keeping a Guard and Sentries at every road and pass by which it would be likely that the Traitors might fly in attempting to leave the Country.

You may rely upon this District for 3000 effective men in any Case of Emergency[.]

D 45   COL. HENRY RUTTAN TO COL. JAMES FITZGIBBON
Colborne, 12 December 1837
[PAC, Upper Canada Sundries, v. 180, pp. 99277-9]

I yesterday sent you a statement of my proceedings informing you that out of my Regt. (which I had assembled on Saturday last) I placed two volunteer Companies of 60 men each on permanent duty, one here and one at the River Trent, since which I have learned that various detachments of militia on their march to Toronto have been ordered back, in consequence of the dispersion of the Rebels.

[94]Henry Ruttan (1792–1871) was born in Adolphustown into a United Empire Loyalist family. He settled in Cobourg, where he became a merchant. A veteran of the War of 1812, he played an active role in the militia and was, in 1837, colonel of the 3rd Northumberland Regiment of militia. From 1820 to 1824 he served as an MLA for Northumberland County, and was elected as a government supporter to the House chosen in 1836. From 28 December 1837 to 24 January 1838 he served as Speaker of the House in MacNab's absence. Appointed sheriff of the Newcastle District in 1827, he retained the post until 1849. Towards the end of his career he became an inventor of ventilation systems.

[95]This may be a reference to John David Smith (1796–1849) and his family. Smith was born in New York State and came with his parents to Port Hope in 1797. He rose to a position of local prominence, serving as an MLA for Durham County, evidently as a government supporter, from 1828 to 1830. In 1843 he became the president of the Port Hope Board of Police. He raised a large family, including nine sons.

I also informed you that it was my intention to Keep the two Companies on duty until further orders should be received from you. Will you therefore be good enough to drop me a line upon receipt of this

My Opinion is that they ought *not* to be reduced Just now. The whole of the Newcastle District it is true is quiet and if there are any Rebels in it they have not made the least attempt at shewing themselves, but how far this state may be the effect of the prompt answer of the Loyalists to their countrys call is uncertain. But admitting that there are none who would dare commit any overt act of Treason yet there are disaffected persons who would, unless musseled by an organised Force be very busy with their Tongues

Another reason for Keeping up this Force is that the County of Hastings lying Contiguous to my Regiment, I am informed has a few refractory spirits who require Keeping in order and it is by this means the most effectually done[.] I await a reply.

D 46   COL. HENRY RUTTAN TO COL. JAMES FITZGIBBON
Colborne, 14 December 1837
[*PAC, Upper Canada Sundries, v. 180, pp. 99274-6*]

. . . All right here in this District and the Midland & Prince Edward, All *profess* Loyalty & in truth there *is* very little else here. A few no doubt who if they saw their way clear & in the majority who would take up arms but they are few and far between. I have just returned from *Hastings* about which I wrote you, all quiet there but I still Keep up my two volunteer Companies 60 men each well armed & ammunitioned – one here and the other at the Trent bordering upon *Hastings*, and I shall continue so to Keep them until I receive counter orders from you.

On leaving the Trent this morning I heard that Mr. McAulay and Mr. Cartwright had arrived at Bellville. I have Just seen a Mr. Ham and Mr. Davey, son-in-law to Peter Perry who say that Lenox & Addington are firm as a Rock to a man for the Queen & Constitution.

Major Gorlie, my Major, has this moment returned from Cobourg & says that Mr. Ebenr. Perry[96] expressed himself warmly in favour of the Govt and said that the word "Reform" could never again be mentioned without disgrace[.] As I have not time at this moment to write to Mr Joseph will you communicate the substance of this to him. –

[96]Ebenezer Perry (1788–1876) was an elder brother of reformer Peter Perry. A veteran of the War of 1812, Ebenezer settled in Cobourg in 1815, where he worked as a merchant, pork packer, and miller. He was active in the militia, holding a captaincy in the 1st Northumberland Regiment. In 1837–8 he served as Cobourg's first president of the Board of Police. He also became a deputy sheriff of the counties of Durham and Northumberland and in 1855 was appointed to the Legislative Council of the united Canadas.

D 47   REGIMENTAL ORDER FOR THE 3RD NORTHUMBERLAND
Colborne, 16 December 1837
[Star, *Cobourg, 27 Dec. 1837*]

. . . I feel myself called upon to express, in the most unqualified manner, my thanks to the officers and men composing it [the 3rd Regiment], for their prompt answer to the call of their country, to rally round its constitution, and protect it from the unhallowed and polluted touch of a band of Traitors, secretly organised under the name of *Reform*. You have nobly performed your duty; nothing can be a clearer proof of this than the fact that, notwithstanding it was generally understood that the Regiment was forthwith to march to Toronto, the scene of action, there never before were so many "present on parade." . . . Notwithstanding all this, it cannot be denied that a few who ought to have made their appearance, from whatever cause, were not to be found at their post.

It cannot be denied – and the time has now come when it would be criminal in us to conceal the fact – that there are those residing amongst us, some of whom may even belong to the Regiment, who are suspected of disaffection to the government. *They are known and marked*. . . .

You all know that there are those residing within the bounds of our Regiment, who are, perhaps vulgarly, but expressively, termed *Skulkers*, and we have no other means of singling them out, in order that the finger of scorn may be pointed at them wherever they go, – that they may receive this punishment in addition to that which the Law awards. And I am happy to say that they are few, and a majority of that few are persons excused by Law from training – as aliens – as being over age, and otherwise. This is no time for half measures; whoever is not for us is against us:. . .

H. Ruttan
Col. Commanding.

D 48   THOMAS LANGTON[97] TO WILLIAM LANGTON[98]
Fenelon Township, 23 December 1837
[*Anne Langton*, Langton Records: Journals and Letters from Canada, 1837–1846 . . . *(Edinburgh, 1904), p. 46*]

For another extract from this document see E 23.

In this province the insurrection was suppressed and tranquillity restored before we had heard of its interruption. . . .

[97]Thomas Langton (1770–1838) was born at Kirkham, Lancashire, England. He was the father of Anne and John Langton whose comments on settlement in Upper Canada were later to be published. Thomas lost his business interests in the 1820s because of poor management and in 1837 came out to visit his two children in Fenelon Township in the backwoods of Upper Canada. He died within a year of arriving.

[98]William Langton, a successful banker, was the only child of Thomas to stay in England.

D 49   COL. ALEXANDER MCDONNELL[99] TO JOHN JOSEPH
Peterboro, 6 December 1837
[*PAC, Correspondence of the Provincial Secretary's Office, v. 9, file 1155*]

I have the honor to acknowledge the receipt of his Excellency the Lieutenant Governors dispatch of yesterdays date calling upon me to proceed to Toronto with as efficient a force as I could readily obtain, forthwith. –

I beg therefore to acquaint you for the information of his Excellency that I have communicated the necessary orders to the officers of the Regiment under my command, and hope to be under March for head quarters on tomorrow or the following day, which will be soon as circumstances will possibly admit with what force I can muster –

D 50   C.P. TRAILL'S DECEMBER DIARY
[*C.P. Traill, The Backwoods of Canada . . . (Toronto, 1929),
pp. 325-9, 331-3, 335*]

Thursday, December 7th. – This morning my brother Sam[100] came over to communicate the startling intelligence that an armed force was on the march for Toronto. Despatches had just reached Peterborough to that effect, with orders for every able man to hasten to the Capital to assist in driving back the rebels. They are headed by Mackenzie and Lount. God preserve us from the fearful consequence of a civil warfare. It seems we have been slumbering in fancied security on a fearful volcano, which has burst and may overwhelm us. Let us devoutly and earnestly ask the assistance of Him, whose arm is powerful to save. Assured of His help we need not fear, for greater is

---

[99]Alexander McDonnell (1796–1861) was a Scot who came to Upper Canada in 1804 with his uncle Alexander, who was later the Roman Catholic bishop of Regiopolis. During the War of 1812, Alexander served as an ensign or cadet and then moved to the Peterborough area, becoming one of the first residents there. He served as guide and then clerk, 1825–9, to Peter Robinson during the latter's successful attempt to found an immigrant settlement. When Robinson became commissioner of crown lands in 1827, McDonnell became agent for the department in the Newcastle District. He remained agent for Northumberland and Durham until 1843, although his importance diminished as the area became populated. In 1834 he was elected MLA for Northumberland, being re-elected in 1836. In 1841 he was defeated in his attempt at a third term. He also served as a commissioner for navigation work in the Newcastle District through the 1830s. In 1837 he commanded the 2nd Northumberland Regiment of militia. In the 1840s and 1850s he had extensive business interests, most notably in timber.

[100]Samuel Strickland (1804–1867) was born in Suffolk, England. He sailed for Upper Canada in 1825 and settled in Douro, where his two sisters, Susanna Moodie and Catharine Parr Traill, and their families joined him. From 1828 until 1832 he worked as manager of the Canada Company at Guelph but then returned to Douro. For twenty years he served the Lakefield area as magistrate, president of the Court of Requests, and captain in the 4th Northumberland militia. He set up an agricultural school in the area to train young men in the skills needed for pioneer farming.

He that is for us, than those that are against us. "The hand of the Lord is not shortened that it cannot save." Surely ours is a holy warfare; the rebels fight in an unholy and unblessed cause. My dear brother has already left home for Peterborough, and my beloved husband[101] goes at daybreak. It is now past midnight; the dear children are now sleeping in happy unconsciousness of the danger to which their father and relatives are about to expose themselves; they heard not the fervent prayer of their father as he kneeled beside their bed, and laid his hands in a parting blessing upon their head. O, my God, the Father of all mercies, hear that father's prayer, and grant he may return in safety to those dear babes and their anxious mother.

Friday night, Dec. 8th. – My heart is lonely and sad; this morning was only beginning to dawn, when Mr. Traill departed; he went off in good spirits, and I rallied mine till the snow drifts that were whirling before a keen sweeping wind hid him from my sight. I sent word to my sister Susan,[102] telling her and Mr. Moodie[103] what had happened. They both came down to dine with me. Moodie is resolved – in spite of his lameness, from a recent fracture of the small bone of his leg – to go down to Peterborough. I hope he will be detained on home duty, for he is quite unfit for moving. This has been a day of suspense, no word from my husband; I know not whether he marches forward to Port Hope, which seems to be proposed as a rallying point of rendezvous. It is said a steamer is to meet the volunteers there to convey them to Toronto.

Saturday 9th. – Moodie came in to adjust his knapsack, and bid me good-bye. God bless him and restore him to my dear sister and her little ones. Snow has been falling at intervals all day, much suffering must have been endured by those who were encamped, or on the march. Siboons came in about three o'clock and brought me a kind note from Mrs. Stewart;[104] she had seen my husband and brother, previous to their leaving the town, which they did under the command

---

[101]Thomas Traill (d. 1847), a retired army officer from the Orkneys and friend of J.W.D. Moodie, came with his wife to Douro Township in 1832. He was a farmer while in Upper Canada.

[102]Susanna (Strickland) Moodie (1803–1885) was born in Suffolk, England. She married John W.D. Moodie and they emigrated to Cobourg, Upper Canada, in 1832. In 1834 they moved near her sister and brother in Douro Township. In 1839 the couple moved to Belleville. Susanna wrote extensively for the *Literary Garland* in later years and published several books, including the classic *Roughing It in the Bush; or Life in Canada*.

[103]John W.D. Moodie (1797–1869) was a native of the Orkneys. He retired from the army on half-pay and married Susanna Strickland in 1831, taking her to Upper Canada the following year. Always impoverished, he secured an appointment as sheriff of Hastings County in 1839, an office which he later lost as a result of several lawsuits. He was a moderate reformer and in later years a friend of Robert Baldwin.

[104]Frances Stewart (1794–1872) and Thomas Alexander Stewart (1786–1847) were married in Ireland in 1816, she having been born in Dublin and he in Wilmot, County

of Captain Cowells. A report has reached us that 400 Indians had come down on Toronto and slaughtered a number of the inhabitants – this seems to be unfounded. Five hundred Mohawks and Hurons have joined our party, and Colonel Anderson[105] from Rice Lake has led up 170 Rice Lake Indians. Parties are arriving constantly from the back townships. Colonel Brown's[106] troop, 4th Northumberland, are to go off to-night.

Saturday night. – The day has been piercingly cold, dark and gloomy; just at dusk I went to see my sister-in-law Mary,[107] to hear if she had had any news. The cold was so intense, and myself so agitated and unwell, that when I reached by [sic] brothers [sic] warm parlor I fainted. No news; no news of Sam and my dear husband, or *anyone*. All in painful suspense and anxious fears. *Later* – have just received a hasty note from Mary. One of her brothers had ridden up from Peterborough, no post in, no despatches up to eight o'clock – rumour speaks of a Colonel Moody having been killed and six men at Toronto. This is bad news. The muster of loyal men continues hourly to increase – Cowen sent 400 men, and Cobourg proved loyal beyond expectation – much fear had been entertained of the disloyalty of this town, but to their honour, be it recorded, that they proved faithful on trial.

Sunday evening. – I became so restless and impatient, I felt in a perfect fever. Snow has been falling thickly, the ground is quite covered; this change will prove beneficial to our friends. I resolved on despatching Marten (the hired man) to hear if Moodie went on or was on guard at the Government House, on account of his lameness – it will relieve poor Susan of a load of care, if we hear this is the case. About three o'clock I noticed a person on the road, slowly making their way through the snow, which by this time was several inches deep. I watched the traveller up to my brother's house, and felt certain she was the bearer of news from below. Soon Mary sent the lad Tom over, with the glad tidings that the rebels were all dispersed and twenty of them

---

Antrim, Ireland. When he lost heavily in his business, they emigrated to Douro Township in 1823, along with his brother-in-law Robert Reid and his family. Having government connections, the Stewarts received 1,200 acres of land. When Peter Robinson and his colonists arrived in 1825, Stewart and Robinson became close friends. Stewart was appointed to the Legislative Council in 1833.

[105]Charles Anderson (d. 1844), an interpreter with the Indian Department, was promoted to lieutenant and then captain in 1813 for distinguished service in the War of 1812. He later settled in Otonabee Township and became a trader and teacher with the Indians at Rice Lake.

[106]This might have been John Brown (*ca.* 1790–1842) of Port Hope, a very successful businessman and politician who was on the Board of Police in 1838, who was an MLA for Durham, 1830–6, and president of the Port Hope Harbour Company in 1829. If this is the Brown referred to, he was living a considerable distance from his regiment.

[107]Mary (Reid) Strickland (d. 1852) was the wife of Samuel and the daughter of his ex-neighbours, the Reids.

killed on the other side of Toronto. Miss Reid[108] had walked up by herself from Peterborough, through the snow – a distance of nine miles – with a devotion of purpose that reflects great credit on her heart, being anxious to be the bearer of the first good news to her sister Mary. What a change of feelings has a few words wrought in me; I no longer feel that dead weight on my heart – or that restlessness, that kept me constantly moving. The feverish impatience that made me chide the dear children for their innocent mirth has gone; I could now listen to them and take part in their amusements. I sent off Marten to Susan to let her share in our good news.

Mr. Moodie rode out this morning at the head of two hundred men from Smithtown. He would not remain in Peterborough on guard, but in spite of his lameness went on to join the rest of his brothers in arms. Ten thousand well-appointed militiamen are now in Toronto, and hundreds hourly flocking in. It is a glorious thing to think how few traitors, and how many loyal hearts, the Province contains. I feel now a proud satisfaction that my dear husband was among the first to volunteer – and with him my brother and brother-in-law. Two spies were taken up in Peterborough and sent in charge of Moodie and his two hundred men to be safely lodged in the jail at Amherst.

The Saturday night's mail did not come in till ten; it brought the news of a skirmish having taken place, in which twenty of the rebels paid the forfeit of their lives. Reward of £1,000 is offered for Mackenzie and £500 for either of the other leaders – Lount, Gibson, Lloyd and Fletcher.

God be praised, who has confounded the malice of the enemies of our adopted country. To His name be the honour and the glory, now and forever. I shall lie down this night with a light heart. This morning I sent up Martin [sic] in the ox-sleigh for Susan and the dear children to spend the day with me. In the afternoon I had a letter from my dear husband from Cobourg. Up to Saturday they had been detained in that place, for on account of the tempestuous state of the weather, the steamboat did not arrive, but the whole party were summoned to meet the men at the Court House and march forward to Toronto. My brother and husband are under the command of Captain Cowell [sic]. He enclosed a printed proclamation of the Governor's. At the end of his address to the loyal militiamen of Upper Canada he says. – "The party of rebels under their chief leader is dispersed and flying before the loyal militia – the only thing that remains to be done is to find them out and arrest them." . . .

December 12th. – Enjoyed a quiet day; no news of the rebels this day. I suppose our gallant volunteers are in Toronto by this time – where it seems probable they will be detained till public confidence is restored.

---

[108]"Miss Reid" was a daughter of the Reids, who had been Samuel Strickland's neighbours in the 1820s and who were related by marriage to the Stewarts.

Nine o'clock p.m. – While preparing for my tea, I heard the parlor door open, and looking up was greeted by my dear husband, a sight that was as welcome as it was unexpected. It seems that the party of volunteers – of which my husband was one – had proceeded only as far as Port Hope when their Colonel, Alex. MacDonnel, received a despatch countermanding their further progress. According to report, Silas Fletcher, one of the proscribed leaders, and several others had been taken prisoners. By the confession of some of them, it appears the plan originally proposed was to march to the Capital at night, seize the Governor and any of the men in office whose principles were opposed to theirs, take possession of the arms and amunition [*sic*] and public money. Taken by surprise, naked and unarmed, the inhabitants could have made but little resistance against even a few hundred men, well armed and bent on accomplishing their purpose, but fortunately the leaders of the rebellion were not unanimous in their opinions as to the fittest time for the assault, and Mackenzie was prevailed upon to sit down quietly and encamp beyond the city, thus giving the Governor time to make preparations for defence, and to rally round the standard of loyalty – the militia of the province – and well the summons was answered. From every part of the country came men of all ages and degree, anxious to prove their attachment to their Queen and the established government, by whose laws they were protected, and to protect their homes. It is currently reported that Sir Francis himself went out at the head of 300 militia and had a skirmish with the rebels, but till we hear further particulars we do not know if this is correct. Sixty prisoners were brought in – taken between Lake Simcoe and Toronto – among them the son of the rebel Lount.

December 14th. – It is reported that Mackenzie is somewhere in the township of Mariposa – endeavouring to raise fresh troops, either with the view of renewing hostilities in the Upper Province, or making his way down to aid the insurgents in the Lower. The latter scheme I should think the most probable as by this time he must consider any attempt to raise a revolution in this Province as a forlorn hope. Among other rumors it was said he was skulking in some of these back townships – one man asserts that he passed through Smithtown disguised as a woman – a story that savours more of romance than probability, and by no means agrees with his being in Mariposa. The latter report is confidently believed and a meeting of the Volunteers is to take place early to-morrow, to go on an expedition in search of the traitor. My husband goes down to attend the meeting and, if required, to join Captain Cowell [*sic*] and his volunteers.

Again I am left alone, but this time parted from my dear husband with less feeling of dread, and in reasonable hope of his safe and speedy return. *Nine o'clock.* – Moodie just rode his horse home with the distressing intelligence that Mr. Traill had fallen and sprained his ankle, so severely as to be unable to get further on his way home than our friends the Stewarts, where I am certain he will be paid every kind attention. I am to send Martin [*sic*] with the horse for him in the morning.

16th. – My husband returned today, but so hurt as to require assistance to dismount from his horse. His foot and leg are dreadfully swollen and discoloured. This accident will, I fear, make him an unwilling prisoner for some time to come.

25th, Xmas Day. – . . . The party of volunteers returned from Mariposa and Opps [Ops] – no trace of rebels there. We hear that Mackenzie is trying to stir up the Americans on the other side, and promises them large rewards for their services in endeavouring to tear from us our Government and laws, and force us to become a free and independent people. Surely our freedom would be a blessed gift so obtained!! And with the traitor Mackenzie for our President our independence were most honourable and admirable!! God forbid we should change our dependence on a gracious Sovereign to become the tools and victims of the most despicable of rebels. It is commonly reported that Mackenzie offered a reward of 3,000 pounds for the head of Sir Francis – at all events he considers it worth 2,000 more than his own. Our gallant Lieut.-Governor did go forth at the head of the party that attacked the rebels, and after having put them to flight returned to the city with many prisoners, amid the greetings and tears of a grateful multitude. Shall we not lift up our hearts in thanksgiving to Him who hath given us the victory over our enemies.

D 51   MAJOR STRICKLAND'S REMINISCENCES
[*Major Strickland*, Twenty-Seven Years in Canada West . . . *II* (London, 1853), pp. 259-64]

I HAD been a resident in Douro about five years, when an event of vast importance in the history of Canada occurred, which threatened the dismemberment of the colony from the parent country, and involved the immersion of both Provinces in anarchy and civil war.

For several years preceding the rebellion of 1837–8, the country had been agitated by the inflammatory speeches and writings of William Lyon Mackenzie and his political coadjutors. Little danger, however, was apprehended either from them or their writings, especially by the loyal inhabitants of the counties of Northumberland and Peterborough, who were completely taken by surprise on hearing that a body of rebels, headed by William Lyon Mackenzie, were actually in arms and on their march to invest Toronto. . . .

The next morning [7 December],[109] accompanied by my brother-in-law and several other gentlemen who had joined us during the night, we attended the rendezvous and enrolled ourselves in the band of Peterborough Volunteers. At this very time I held the commission of a

[109]Strickland's account indicates that the date was 5 December, but it was 7 December.

lieutenant in the 2d Regiment of Durham Militia; but as the distance prevented me from joining them at once, I thought it best in the meantime to march with the volunteers.

At eleven o'clock A.M., everything being in readiness, we got the order to march, which was received with the most enthusiastic cheering, both by the volunteers and the inhabitants, who escorted us out of town, bidding us "God speed in the good cause." Thus, within twenty-four hours from the reception of the Governor's proclamation did a fine body of nearly four hundred well-armed and well equipped volunteers, leave Peterborough to assist in putting down rebellion, and upholding the cause of legality and order. . . .

At Port Hope we were joined by the 2d battalion of the Northumberland Militia, under the command of Colonel M'Donnell, and the 4th Northumberland, under Colonel Brown: these two battalions left Peterborough the day after the volunteers. We found several other bands of loyalists already assembled in Port Hope, which swelled our little army to upwards of a thousand men.

Many and contradictory had been the reports which reached us – every hour brought different intelligence. The first news was, that Toronto was burnt and the loyalists in full retreat; that seven thousand "patriots," as they styled themselves, were assembled at the Rush Hill to intercept the Militia marching to the relief of Toronto; and various reports of the same kind, which only served to inflame the ardour of our little band, who were anxious for the coming fray. Judge, then, of our astonishment when our Colonel received a despatch, accompanied by a proclamation from Governor Head, informing us of the action at Montgomery's Tavern – Gallows-hill, as it is generally called – and the dispersion of the rebels; thanking us, at the same time, for our loyalty and devotion, and permitting us to return to our homes and families.

Of course, the news of the dispersion of the rebels was received with great cheering along the whole line; though the well-deserved epithet of "cowardly rascals," was freely bestowed upon Mackenzie's rabble army by men who wished to fight, yet found their services were no longer required.

On our return to Peterborough the volunteers were again in request, and received orders to march to the rear townships of Ops and Mariposa, to intimidate the disaffected in those townships, and intercept some of the rebel leaders who, it was supposed, had escaped in that direction. The country was found perfectly quiet, and the volunteers once more returned to the comforts of their homes. . . .

D 52   REV. EGERTON RYERSON TO JAMES STEPHEN,[110] DRAFT
Kingston, 9 March 1838
[*United Church Archives, Ryerson Papers*]

. . . I was on my way from this town to Toronto when the insurrection

[110]James Stephen (1789–1859) was born in London, England. Educated at Cambridge, he became a lawyer, then permanent counsel to the Colonial Office and

broke out, – I was in Cobourg, Newcastle District, when the volunteers rallied from all parts – & the report was there that Rolph & Bidwell were under arms in defence of the City *against* Mackenzie[111] – you may judge of the effect of this report throughout the province – it doubled the number of volunteers in defence of the government; . . .

D 53   REV. EGERTON RYERSON TO _____ OF KINGSTON
Cobourg, 6 December 1837
[Egerton Ryerson, "The Story of My Life," edited by J.G. Hodgins (Toronto, 1883), pp. 176-7]

You will recollect my mentioning that I pressed upon Sir Francis the propriety and importance of making some prudent provision for the defence of the city, in case any party should be urged on in the madness of rebellion so far as to attack it. He is much blamed here on account of his overweening confidence, and foolish and culpable negligence in this respect. There was great excitement in this town and neighbourhood last night. To-day all is anxiety and hurry. The militia is called out to put down the rebellion of the very man whose seditious paper many of them have supported, and whom they have countenanced.

The precepts of the Bible and the example of the early Christians, leave me no occasion for second thoughts as to my duty, namely, to pray for and support the "powers that be," whether I admire them or not, and to implore the defeat of "fiery conspiracy and rebellion." And I doubt not that the sequel will in this, as in other cases, show that the path of duty is that of wisdom, if not of safety. I am aware that my head would be regarded as something of a prize by the rebels; but I feel not in the least degree agitated. I trust implicitly in that God whom I have endeavoured – though imperfectly and unfaithfully – to serve; being assured nothing will harm us, but that all things, whether life or death, will work together for our good if we be followers of that which is good. Let us trust in the Lord, and do good, and He will never leave nor forsake us!

About 700 armed men have left this district to-day for Toronto, in order to put down the rebels. There is an unanimity and determination among the people to quash rebellion and support the law that I hardly expected. The country is safe, but it is a "gone day with the rebel party."

---

the Board of Trade, 1825–34. In 1834 he was appointed the assistant under-secretary of state for the colonies and in 1836 the under-secretary. So efficient was he in his duties that he became known to those in his department as "King Stephen" or, alternately, "Mr. over-secretary." He resigned his post in 1847 and received a KCB the next year. In 1849 he was made Regius Professor of Modern History at Cambridge.

[111]The rumour was just one of the many which circulated in the province in December 1837, and certainly had no basis in fact.

D 54   MILITIA MOVEMENTS AT COBOURG
[Star, *Cobourg, 13 December 1837*]

. . . On Tuesday night, (the 5th inst.) expresses arrived in Cobourg, bearing orders to the different Colonels to turn out their regiments; the flank companies to advance on Toronto, and the others to hold themselves in readiness to march at an hour's notice.

Early on Thursday morning the several volunteer companies began to assemble. A few days previously, several young gentlemen had formed a rifle company, in case their services might be required, and the alacrity with which those youth, accustomed to all the luxuries of life, advanced in their country's cause, reflects on them the greatest credit. They mustered about forty, under the command of Captain Warren, late of the 66th. This company formed the advance: they were succeeded by Captains Clark and Calcutt's companies, and Capt. Conger,[112] with his men in fine order and in excellent appearance, brought up the rear. After the volunteer companies had left the town, Col. Burnham[113] inspected the remainder of the regiment, and an additional company, under the command of Captain McKyes, was organized. On Friday, Col. Burnham proceeded with the volunteer cavalry, commanded by Captain Rogers, and measures were taken to insure the advance of the others in case of necessity.

On Saturday afternoon the regiment from Peterboro' under the command of Col. McDonell, arrived at Cobourg, on their way up, and a finer body of men cannot be imagined: all private interests were deserted when their country called. . . .

D 55   THE RADICALS MUSTER WITH THE LOYALISTS
[Chronicle & Gazette, *Kingston, 9 Dec. 1837*]

We learn from Cobourg, that Ebenezer Perry and his brother, Peter Perry, Esq. together with Wilson S. Conger, Esq. have already

[112]Wilson Seymour Conger (1804–1864) was born at Hallowell, Upper Canada. He began a long career of public service in Cobourg at the beginning of the 1830s. He was secretary of the building committee of Upper Canada Academy in 1831 and ran as a radical reformer in the 1834 provincial elections, but was defeated. He served on the Cobourg Board of Police, 1837–41. In 1835 he helped form the Cobourg and Peterborough Railway Company. After the rebellion, which he opposed, he moved to Peterborough to become sheriff of the Colborne District in 1841. He served as sheriff of Peterborough County, 1849–56, and as mayor of Peterborough in 1856. He was MLA for Peterborough, 1856–7, and from 1863 until his death.

[113]Zaccheus Burnham (1777–1857) came to Cobourg about 1798 from the United States and became one of the most successful men in Northumberland and Durham counties. In 1820 he received the first land title, to almost 4,000 acres, in Otonabee Township. In 1825 he helped survey Peterborough County and in 1850 he laid out the village lots for Lakefield. In 1834–5 he had a grist and sawmill built for him near the village of Burnham (Warsaw). He was Newcastle District registrar, 1826–44?, and was elected MLA for Northumberland, and Durham when combined, in 1816, 1824, and 1852. From 1831 to 1841 he sat in the Legislative Council. He was active in the militia and was in 1837 colonel of the 1st Northumberland Regiment.

proceeded with a strong volunteer party to Toronto, to join the Royal Standard.

These gentlemen have been long known as reformers of the first water. It is most gratifying to observe, that notwithstanding their reforming motives they are true and loyal men.

D 56   DIARY OF FRANCIS COLEMAN[114]
[MTPL, Diary of Francis Coleman]

December 1837

An account of a march to Toronto for the purpose of putting a stop to rebelion On Wednesday the 6 of December I was warned to join the Darlington Millitia I among several others went to Bowmanville and on Friday morning we started for Toronto weather cold Marched through Whitby in Company with about five hundred men that night we got as far as post tavern in the Towmiship of Pickering had rather poor fare and lodgings Started from there at five in the morning broke open a door and took several prisoners and after Marching all the day we got in Toronto[.]

D 57   LT.-COL. GEORGE HAM[115] TO COL. ZACCHEUS BURNHAM
Darlington, 8 December 1837
[Star, Cobourg, 13 Dec. 1837]

I beg to inform you that the brigade under my command is now in this place. We have taken this day, and made prisoners of war, some of McKenzie's principal men, and we are marching them up to Toronto under guard. We understand that McKenzie's forces are in a very great degree dispersed. These prisoners very much fear they will be hung. – We allow no one to pass us without knowing who he is and what is his business, and if a satisfactory account is not given of himself, we make him a prisoner. . . .

We now form, . . . six hundred effective men, and we are determined to force our way through to Toronto. We are all in good health and most excellent spirits. . . .

D 58   DEPOSITION OF DAVID PARSONS[116]
29 December 1837
[PAC, Upper Canada Sundries, v. 185, p. 103594]

. . . met with Aaron Glover[117] of Nelson, at Oakvill, on Sabbath day

[114]Francis Coleman (1813–1900), a native of Cornwall, England, emigrated to Darlington Township in 1833, where he farmed. He died in Hamilton.

[115]George Ham was a resident of Cobourg. He became that town's mayor in 1838–9. In the document cited here he described himself as lieutenant-colonel of the 1st Brigade. He may have been the George Ham who served on the Niagara frontier in December 1837.

[116]David Parsons was an East Flamboro "yeoman."

[117]Aaron Glover (b. ca. 1805) was a native Upper Canadian. By 1837, a married

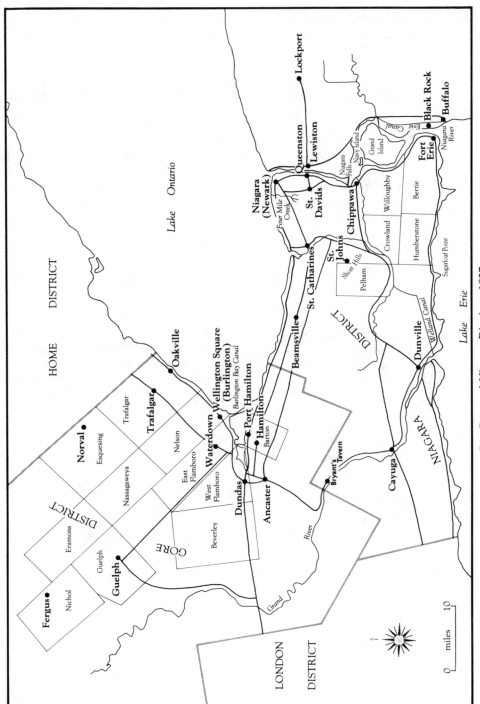

7: Gore and Niagara Districts, 1837

the 10th Decr inst. [,] understood from him that he was a prisoner, asked him where he & the others with him, were taken, ansd, at, or near Posts Inn,[118] in Trafalgar, were armed with rifles, had a number of balls, powder &c. [,] told witness when he left home, & that he had been at Montgomery's on Yonge Street the day after the battle was fought, on being asked who he went to fight for, the Queen or McK. answered, he meant to join the Strongest party, but as the rebels were dispersed, they returned home, meaning himself, N. Kerns[,] ____ Irvine[119] & his brother Samuel Glover[120] –

Sometime last fall Witness met with A. Glover & D. Ghent[121] in the road near Ghents house, had some talk with them on political matters – they, or one of them, cannot say which, after expressing the high esteem in which they held W L MKenzie, went on to say, that if these matters could not be settled peaceably, they were afraid if things continued on, it would result in a war or bloodshed, or something to that effect –

D 59   DEPOSITION OF JOHN ANDERSON[122]
14 December 1837
[PAC, Upper Canada Sundries, v. 180, pp. 99241-2]

. . . he was with others who took arms &c. from some, . . . A [Angus] MK [Mackenzie][123] with 2 others come to Dep [Deponent's] house the eveng [evening] before[,] said the Gov his 6 counsellors & the city of Toronto was taken by the reform party – & asked Dep what he meant to do, sd. did not Know, was told a meeting wd be at his[,] A [Angus] M [Mackenzie's][,] house next day & he best come – they went away – . . . went next morng to the meeting, a great number, took his Musket, as others who had arms did – the conclusion of the meeting was, that nearly all, Dep among the number[,] turned out viz, volunteered to go

man, he had lost property he had once owned and was working as a labourer in Nelson Township. In November he attended a reform meeting in Wellington Square and suggested the establishment of a rifle company there. He was jailed at Hamilton on 25 January 1838 and released on bail on 3 February. He later farmed in Nelson.

[118]Post's Inn was on the seventh line of Trafalgar and was operated by Ephraim Post (1776–1851), a New Englander.

[119]This may have been John Erwin of East Flamboro who, along with others, had urged fellow reformers meeting at Wellington Square in November to form a rifle company.

[120]Samuel Glover was a labourer. He and his brother Aaron worked for the same employer in Nelson Township.

[121]David Ghent (b. ca. 1806), a native of Upper Canada, and his wife farmed in Nelson. Aside from their Nelson property, they owned 200 acres in neighbouring Nassagaweya. In November 1837 Ghent attended the reform meeting in Wellington Square. He was jailed at Hamilton on 3 January 1838 and freed on bail two days later.

[122]John Anderson farmed in the Nassagaweya area. After taking his deposition, the magistrates freed him on bail.

[123]Angus Mackenzie, a Nassagaweya area farmer, was indicted for his part in the events of December. He fled and was attainted a traitor.

to assist WLM & his party who, as the[y] heard & believed, had taken the Gov[,] the city of Toronto &c. – AM appeared to take the lead, Donald Black[,][124] T. [Thomas] G. [Galloway] was there, but as they spoke Gaelic which Dep does not understand, was at a loss to Know many things was said, – but no orders shewn no force used, but was told by A M. he wd be in danger of losing his life if he did not go with them, from the Tories who wd shoot him [–] they seperated, Dep went with those who took a gun from A Gallaway[,] 2 at J. yourt[']s, did not say any thing to dissuade them from doing so[,] went with the party. A M. leader, past his own home, to Shepherd[']s in E [East] F. [Flamboro] & afterwds seperated, did not use any compulsion with Dep to force him to go with them – they were to meet next morning at A.Mks to go off to Toronto, to assist the reform party – Dep did not go did not hear any news but considered he had went rather too far – nothing sd. when they parted about returning or paying for the guns &c. taken,. AM & the others took them with them[.]

D 60   DEPOSITION OF WILLIAM CAMPBELL[125]
13 December 1837
[PAC, Upper Canada Sundries, v. 186, pp. 103773-4]

. . . he was present at a Meeting held at the Central School-House in Eramosa aforesaid District aforesaid – upon the Eighth day of December current – at which Meeting James Benham[126] acted as Chairman – & deponent heard the said Chairman declare and state as follows – "now is the time to strike the blow and have a free nation of our own – The French in Lower Canada have taken possession of that Province and we ought to join with them and be free" – with other language equaly Treasonable & Rebellious – which deponent Cannot now recollect sufficiently to particularize – and deponent farther states – that Calvin Lyman[127] of Eramosa . . . proposed to him – (deponent) – that shd. said deponent turn & join with them that they would acknowledge him as Captain & train with him immediately for the purpose of assisting McKenzie's party – and deponent farther states –

[124]Donald Black, a Scot, and his brothers settled in the southwestern part of the province in 1798. Donald moved to Nassagaweya in 1823, where he acquired 100 unpatented acres of lot 17, concession 5. In 1837 he was the township clerk.

[125]William Campbell of Eramosa was a "yeoman" and a militia officer. On 9 November 1838 he was gazetted captain of the 5th Gore Regiment.

[126]James Benham (1794–1879) was born in Surrey, England, and served in the Napoleonic wars. He arrived in Upper Canada in 1827, settling in Eramosa, where in 1837 he and his wife rented clergy reserve lot 10, concession 3. In later life they accumulated a considerable estate. James was jailed at Hamilton on 16 December 1837 and freed on bail on 3 February 1838, but was recommitted and tried for treason at Hamilton in the spring when he was acquitted of the charge.

[127]Calvin Lyman, an Englishman, was granted bail by the magistrates on 14 December 1837, but was tried at Hamilton in the spring for treason and acquitted.

that James Butchard[128] also made use of similar inducements to Deponents to join them – as did also William Armstrong[129] – Blacksmith – in Eramosa . . . and Deponent farther states – that the Resolutions passed at said meeting were in his (depts) [deponent's] opinion highly Treasonable & calculated to disturb the peace of her Majesty's government in this province – deponent farther states that James Peters[130] of Eramosa . . . acted as Secretary of said Meeting – and that among those who signed the Resolutions of said Meeting he recognized James Parkinson[131] of Era [Eramosa] . . . Deponent farther states that Henry Tolton[132] of Guelph . . . Farmer. did also sign said Resolutions – & Robt M Cullaugh[133] did sign said resolutions – farther deponent saith not[.]

D 61   EXAMINATION OF HIRAM DOWLAN[134]

n.d.

[PAC, Upper Canada Sundries, v. 186, p. 103777]

Hiram Dowlan – was present at the latter part of the Meeting. Benham was speaking when he entered – Benham said that now was the time to

---

[128]James Butchard (b. ca. 1788) was one of John Galt's Scottish La Guaryia settlers. He came to Upper Canada in 1827, settling in Eramosa, where in 1837 he and his wife rented one of the lots granted King's College for its support, lot 13, concession 3, which they farmed. He was jailed at Hamilton on 16 December 1837, released on bail on 3 February 1838, then later recommitted. Tried for treason in the spring, he won acquittal.

[129]William Armstrong (b. ca. 1813) emigrated with his parents from Roxborough-shire, Scotland, in 1819 to New York State. In 1822 they settled in Eramosa. In 1837 William was working as a blacksmith. Examined and released on bail by the magistrates on 14 December 1837, he was tried for treason that spring at Hamilton and found not guilty.

[130]James Peters (ca. 1801–1869) was born in Lancashire, England. He came to Upper Canada in 1826, settling in Eramosa, where he became the first township clerk and where in 1837 he and his wife farmed 100 patented acres of lot 23, concession 2. He was jailed at Hamilton on 16 December 1837 and granted bail on 31 December. He was later recommitted and tried at Hamilton in the spring of 1838 for treason but was acquitted.

[131]James Parkinson (1815–1880) emigrated from England with his father Joseph and the rest of his family to Pennsylvania in 1818. In 1824 the family moved to Eramosa from New York. Joseph established large properties in Eramosa, and became a prominent settler there, being appointed a magistrate. In 1837 James worked on his father's farm. Granted bail by the magistrates on 14 December 1837, he was tried for treason at Hamilton in the spring and acquitted.

[132]Henry Tolton, an Englishman, emigrated with his parents to Upper Canada, settling in Guelph in 1830. Henry's son Edwin later became a member of the House of Commons.

[133]Robert McCullagh (M Cullaugh), who was likely Irish-born, was granted bail by the magistrates on 1 January 1838.

[134]Hiram Dowlan (Dowling) (b. ca. 1804) and his wife farmed lot 14, concession 4 in Eramosa, a lot to which they held the patent. Hiram was freed on bail by the magistrates on 14 December 1837, but was tried for treason in the spring at Hamilton and acquitted.

strike a blow – or to rise or words to that effect – . . . Benham announced that Toronto was taken by the reformers. . . . Benham said England was so disturbed that she could not send out Troops – heard Benham say that the Country would be better off if we had nothing to do with England – Benham spoke of Papineu & said that the Lower province were gaining their independence & that now was the time to Strike the Blow –

D 62 EXAMINATION OF WILLIAM ARMSTRONG
n.d.
[PAC, Upper Canada Sundries, v. 186, p. 103777]

William Armstrong – was present at the Meeting on Friday the 8th Decr. – had heard that if they did not turn out & train – would be tried [sic] to a tree & shot – met to tak[e] means of remaining neutral – the object of the Meeting was to join the strongest party – Benham said that the object was to remain neutral until they shd. hear reports confirmed – was of the committee – who sent a messenger – to ascertain whether Toronto was taken – paper was signed by the committee – James Benham mentioned that if they were called out in militia – they shd. not obey the call – Benham said that Lower Canada was in the hands of the french & who ever had lower must have upper Canada. James Peter was Secritary – the emisary . . . was to report to Benham on his return – . . .

D 63 EXAMINATION OF ROBERT ARMSTRONG
11 December 1837
[PAC, Upper Canada Sundries, v. 187, p. 104647]

The Examination of Robert Armstrong of the Township of Guelph in the said District Blacksmith, taken this Eleventh day of December in the Year of Our Lord One thousand Eight hundred and thirty seven, before us William Ellis[135] and William Scollick[136] Esquires two of Her Majesty's Justices of the peace for the District aforesaid, The said Robert Armstrong, being charged before us the said Justices with having on this said Eleventh day of December purchased at the Store of Adam Ferrie Junior & Co.[137] in Preston in the said District the following Articles to Wit, Eight pounds of Canister Gun Powder and four and a half Pounds of Keg Gun Powder, also Twenty five Pounds

---

[135]William Ellis was appointed a magistrate for Waterloo County in 1818.

[136]William Scollick was appointed a magistrate for Waterloo County in 1827. From 1825 to 1828 he represented Halton in the Assembly.

[137]The Ferrie firm was founded by Adam Ferrie (1777–1863), who was born in Irvine, Scotland. A Glasgow merchant, he came to Montreal in 1829, where he established a general importing business. In 1830 he sent two sons, Adam Jr. and Colin, to Hamilton to establish a branch of the business there. The Hamilton concern developed a series of branches in turn.

of Bar Lead and three Boxes of percussion caps, all the above named Articles we the said Justices believe were intended for the use of the Rebels in this Province, the said Robert Armstrong is now asked by us if he wish to say any thing in his own behalf whereupon the said Robert Armstrong saith that he Bought the above mentioned Articles to sell again as there were no powder and Lead to be purchased in Guelph.

D 64   DEPOSITION OF JOHN NICHOLSON
19 December 1837
[PAC, Upper Canada Sundries, v. 189, p. 105487]

John Nicholson, – being sworn deposeth that he brought from Waterdown to Hamilton Goodes in M. Mills waggon some time during this present month[,] a quantity of Powder in a Keg and some shot[,] which powder & shot were buried in the orchard of M.M. Mills & by him[,] said Mills[,] & deponent who assisted to bury the same at the desire of Mills. Willard Sherman[138] was present when the same was buried –
deponent is in the employ of M.M. Mills.

D 65   MILITARY PREPARATIONS IN HAMILTON
[Gazette, Hamilton, 19 Dec. 1837]

. . . Our town, during the whole week [since the news of the Toronto outbreak arrived], has been like a garrison, drillings, reviews, fortifications, &c. The gaol has been strongly fortified. . . . The bank has been protected in a similar manner, and the Hamilton people have scarcely slumbered or slept since the York ruffians plunged the country into the vortex of rebellion. . . .

D 66   REV. JAMES MARR[139] TO REV. ABSALOM PETERS[140]
Beamsville, 8 December 1837
[University of Chicago Divinity School, American Home Missionary Society Congregational, Correspondence, microfilm in United Church Archives]

. . . With regard to the commotions in the Canadas, I will state further,

---

[138]Willard Sherman, an Upper Canadian-born farmer's son from East Flamboro, was jailed at Hamilton on 17 December 1837. Tried for treason the following spring, he was judged not guilty.

[139]James Marr was the Beamsville pastor of the Niagara Presbyterian Church, an American sect. In 1838 he took his ministry to St. Thomas, but soon left when the parent American Home Missionary Society abandoned the Upper Canadian field. Marr littered his letters with hyphens. To make his letters (D 66, E 98) more intelligible, we have removed much of his peculiar punctuation.

[140]Absalom Peters (1821–1894), a native of Vermont, was a graduate of Dartmouth College and Princeton Seminary. He served as pastor for five years in Bennington, Vermont, before moving his family to New York City in 1825, where he became the secretary of the American Home Missionary Society. He was the society's secretary

that brother Furman[141] and his family came to my house last evening quite lait, and to my astonishment, said – that he was leaving Canada on account of the war, and that – a member of his church[,] a prominent individual in the place [John G. Parker], was arrested, and imprisoned upon a charge of high treason, which occasioned a very great excitemen[t] in the place. He said he has no doubt but that the court house, and prison is burnt before this, or will be in a very short time[.] He stated further, that 1500 men were expected that night for the purpose of rescuing the prisoner, and burning the public buildings, and that there wd. no doubt be a struggle between the two parties (Radicals, and Tories)[.] Hamilton is about 20 miles distant from Beamsville. They are now calling out the malitia, and vollunteers in this disct. [district]. A few days since there was an attack made upon Toronto which resulted in the loss of several lives, and the burning of several important building[s]. The radicals are considerably the strongest, and in my opinion will come off victorious. I hope and pray that they may – Thus you see that we are in the midst of scenes of of [sic] war, and confusion. I however have no fear, and do not feel the least disposition to leave it. . . .

D 67 FATE OF THE RADICALS
[Gazette, *Hamilton, 12 Dec. 1837*]

. . . The only arrest of any consequence *at present* made here, was that of Mr. J.G. Parker, on whose case, prudence urges our silence.

Since the above was put into type Mr. McIlroy,[142] the Smith, and one of the *sympathisers* of the Irish, with two or three other *worthies*, have been arrested and placed in the cells. We have often faithfully warned some of these deluded men, but we well recollect the thanks we received. . . .

M.S. Bidwell, Esq. of radical notoriety, "the highly gifted personage," has got liberty to quit the Canadas for ever. We could spare a few others from this town, who are now chuckling in their sleeves, as if they were not known. But "wait till yet." . . .

---

for twelve years and was the first editor of its magazine. After surrendering his post with the society, he became pastor of a Congregational church in Massachusetts.

[141]Charles Edwin Furman (1801–1880) was born in Clinton, New York. From 1826 to 1828 he attended Union College, New York, and in 1828–9 served as the Ohio agent of the American Tract society. Ordained by the Cayuga Presbytery of New York, he was sent to Hamilton in 1835. After fleeing Upper Canada in 1837, he settled in New York State, where he ministered to several charges. In the 1870s he published various theological works.

[142]This was John McIlroy, a Hamilton blacksmith who was freed on bail on 16 December. He had participated in the radical reformers' meeting of 24 November in Hamilton.

D 68   SAMUEL RYCKMAN[143] TO COL. ROBERT LAND,[144] CAPTAINS
DANIEL SERVOS OR JOHN SNIDER[145]
10 December 1837
[*PAC, Upper Canada Sundries, v. 180, pp. 99073-5*]

This morning being informed by two women travellers from Malkum's
Mills, long point settlement, that the Rebels are in that place collecting
themselves to gather to rescue Mr. Parker, it is said that the attack will
be made upon Hamilton to day or tomorrow – probabley not so soon
and as they must know there is Guard kept at Brantford it is my opinion
should they made the attack, their rout will be by the way of Briants,
Grand River[;] in that case you may be taken on surprise[.] Therefore
your prudence will direct you as Commanding Officers of this Post
whether there should be a guard placed at the Grand River or Hamilton
re-enforced.

D 69   LOYALTY AT THE HEAD OF THE LAKE
[*Gazette, Hamilton, 26 Dec. 1837*]

. . . The whole population of Hamilton were under arms – Ancaster,
with a population somewhat less than 500, turned out 170 men! whilst
Dundas, with a population exceeding 1,000, turned out but NINE!!!
. . .

In fine, this pestilent swamp, true index of the character of its
population, is a foul blot on the fair fame of Upper Canada. Many of its
merchants, brewers, wharfingers, canal-men, upholsterers, masons
and *others*, are steeped to their very chins in sedition. . . .

D 70   ALLAN MACDONELL[146] TO JOHN JOSEPH ?
Hamilton, 13 December 1837
[*PAC, Upper Canada Sundries, v. 180, pp. 99128-30*]

Having had information that a meeting had been secretly held at

[143]Samuel Ryckman (1777–1846) was born in Pennsylvania. He emigrated with his
parents to Upper Canada about 1784. He became a land surveyor, and in 1837 appears
to have been the same Samuel Ryckman who maintained a boarding house in Hamilton
and who acted as that town's police bailiff.
[144]Robert Land (1772–1867) was born in Pennsylvania. In 1783 he and his mother
moved to New Brunswick, joining his father Robert, Hamilton's first settler, in Upper
Canada in 1791. Robert Jr. served in the War of 1812, maintaining a connection with
the militia at its end. He was gazetted colonel of the 1st Gore Regiment on 25 May
1830, and in 1837–8 commanded at Hamilton. He surrendered his commission in
1847. A farmer, he was prominent in his locality, holding various minor public
offices.
[145]John Snider of Ancaster was gazetted lieutenant of the 3rd Gore Regiment on 29
April 1830 and captain on 13 December 1838.
[146]Allan Macdonell (1808–1888) was born at York, Upper Canada, into a Loyalist
family. He was admitted to the bar in 1832 and appointed sheriff of the Gore District in
1837, a post he held until about 1842. In 1837–8 he raised and equipped a troop of

Dundas on Monday night last [11 Dec.] by several suspected persons, I yesterday afternoon proceeded to Dundas for the purpose of taking the arms of those persons and also whatever papers there might be in the possession of their secretary, or other person acting with that party; The only papers I could discover of any kind are those herewith enclosed[.] I took some arms for which I gave receipts[.] There is no appearance of disturbance here nor is there any excitement: excepting such as is occasionly made in consequence of reports reaching us of intended attacks for the purpose of liberating Parker[.] I have now before me two letters from the London District informing me that 100 men were to march from Oxford and that 150 had commenced their march under a person of the name of Elisha Hall with the avowed object of liberating Parker and others[,] that Mr Hall had fallen from his horse and was killed, McNab left this yesterday with about 500 men. It was expected that about 200 more would join them on their march.

His Excellency may rest assured that every exertion shall be made to bring to justice every rebel in the District and that every suspected person will be well looked after

I send this by express, Arms have been sent up for the militia here[.] None have been given me for the protection of the Gaol[;] if his Excellency would allow me 50 or 60 stand of muskets and bayonets for the defence of the Gaol I am confident[,] attack it when or as they may[,] Parker shall never leave this thru their means[.]

D 71 BRIGADE ORDER
Hamilton, 12 December 1837
[PAO, H.H. Robertson Papers, Captain Daniel D. Lewis[147] Book]

Several reports have been made of the irregular and disorderly conduct of the Guards and picketts on the outposts[;] the officers commanding such will in the future be held responsible for the conduct of their men and they are hereby ordered to report all persons who may be found to supply them with spirits excepting in their presence and by their authority

The tavern keepers will be warned by each officer or non commissioned officer immediately on their arrival at this post that his license will be taken from him on the very first complaint of a contravention of this order

John [McDermid?]
Brigade Major

---

cavalry. After resigning as sheriff, he explored the country north of Lake Superior for minerals.

[147]Daniel Lewis (b. 1790) was a native of Grimsby, Upper Canada. A resident of Saltfleet and a veteran of the War of 1812, he was commissioned captain of the 3rd Gore Regiment on 16 April 1823 and on 24 December 1838 captain of the 12th Gore.

D 72   COL. ROBERT LAND TO ALLAN MACNAB
Hamilton, 19 December 1837
[HPL, Land Papers, Robert Land Papers, pp. 796-800]

. . . I regret to state that no communication has yet been received by me from any public department in Toronto, and that therefore I am wholly in the dark as to providing ways and means for the Commissariat department in this Garrison – For the supplies required in Town credit can easily be procured but the Commissary has frequent and pressing demands from the outer stations at the Grand River, Burlington Canal &c. and money is absolutely required for the use of the Express department –

I shall therefore esteem it a particular favour if you will give directions for a reasonable sum of money to be furnished for the use of the Commissariat here – . . .

I have the satisfaction to acquaint you that the best spirit continues to animate the officers and men under my command, and that few mistakes have had to be corrected than under all circumstances might have been expected – I have taken upon myself to relieve Col Lamprey[148] and the troops under his command from further duty here but have recommended that officer to cause the Nicol volunteers to be relieved from guard at the Bridge in Galt – . . .

From the moment that I took the command in this Garrison I have exerted myself to establish a confidential communication with the civil authorities and have requested them to give information to the Brigade office of any thing which might transpire. – assuring them that a perfect reciprocity would be established by the departments under my command. – but no communications relative to any suspicious characters have yet been received from that quarter –

Immediately after Receit of your General order of 12 Decr I appointed a strong party to put it in effect, directing however that Cap [Captain] Gourlay[149] who was to take command of the same should request the Sheriff &c. to name any places which he might consider suspicious and that Cap Gourlay was desired to cooperate with the civil power in any way – He was informed that it was not for the present necessary to make any search –

On Saturday last I dispatched a strong party to apprehend some suspicious persons in Flamboro – two of whom Ashel Davis[150] & one

[148]George Lamprey (d. 1838) was born in Dublin, Ireland. He fought in the War of 1812, and in 1837 served as the colonel of the 6th Gore Regiment. He died at Guelph.

[149]William Gourlay (1794–1867) was born in Berwick-on-Tweed, Scotland. From 1815 to 1836 he was a lieutenant in the Royal Welsh Fusiliers, serving in France, Spain, and Malta. In 1836 he settled in Binbrook, Upper Canada, becoming a captain in the militia. Towards the end of December 1837 he led a body of incorporated militia to Chippawa, and in March 1838 became a major in its 1st Battalion. On 10 April 1839 he was gazetted lieutenant-colonel of the 12th Gore Regiment.

[150]Asahel (Ashel) Davis (1774–1850) was born in North Carolina. He came to

of his sons[151] were brought in at night delivered at the Court House and instantly liberated by the civil authorities there –

The differences of opinion between the civil authorities and myself have been matters of deep regret to me – more especially as both are acting from the best motives – but I have now resolved to take depositions myself in Barracks and act independently. . . .

D 73   DEPOSITION OF WILLIAM JOHNSON KERR
19 December 1837
[PAC, Upper Canada Sundries, v. 180, pp. 99507-8]

. . . on Saturday the sixteenth day of this present month of december at Wellington Square Asahel Davis came to this deponent and enter'd into conversation with him relative to certain charges made against him [–] the said Asahel Davis. as having been connected or concerned in treasonable plots or practices – the deponent told him (davis) that he was personally not aware of any charges agt [against] him but gave him to understand certain reports which he had heard, which were first. that he had understood said davis had harbor'd John Rolph and provided him with a horse and guide to further his Escape, and he admitted that it was so and that his son Wm had accompanied him[.] Secondly. deponent told davis that he had understood that he had harbor'd Charles Durand and given him a horse to make his escape with – he said he had received & was glad to see Durand because he was his Lawyer and that his son Gilbert had furnished him with a horse – deponent then said he understood there had been a meeting at his (davis house) in order to form a rifle corps. – he admitted there had been a meeting at his house for said purpose but he thought it would not amount to much unless they got a good fusle [fusil] man who could train them properly. – deponent then said there was another charge he had heard & that was holding a meeting at his house to receive subscriptions or voluntairs contributions towards McKenzie – which Davis admitted –

and further deponent sayeth not.

Upper Canada in 1792 with his father and the rest of his family. The Davises settled first in the Niagara District, then located in Nelson in 1794, where Asahel later raised a family and farmed. Asahel was active in the reform agitation of the fall of 1837, and was jailed at Hamilton on 17 December and freed on 24 December. He later became a Gore District magistrate and was active in the Great Lakes grain trade.

[151] Actually, two of Davis' sons were jailed. Gilbert (b. 1804), a native Upper Canadian, was jailed at Hamilton on 17 December and freed on bail on 24 December, and William (b. 1809), an Upper Canadian, was jailed on 16 December and granted bail on 24 December also.

D 74   CATHARINE R. MERRITT[152] TO DR. JEDIAH PRENDERGAST[153]
St. Catharines, 8 December 1837
[*PAC, Merritt Family Papers, Correspondence of W.H. Merritt,*
v. 13, pp. 002031-4]

No doubt, you have heard before this, of the disturbance in the lower Province. and also in this; Toronto has been Beceaged, and we have heard this morning, by way of Niagara, that the Radicals (Rebels) have been defeated; & driven back 15 miles, they had 40 killed, & 30 taken Prisoner. it took place yesterday – will probably get the official report before I close this, but to give you, some Idea of the state of exitement; must go back a few days,. all last week, the papers were filled with (our cavelry – the young Men of this village, have this instant, returned from Niag [Niagara], galaping round & Hurawing, at every corner. they went down yesterday 2 oc P.M. for to cross over, get there Horses on Board a Steam B. but the wind was too strong a head, to proceed. & the news this Morning, fortunately prevented them going.) accounts of the Proseedings in L. Canada, not to the advantage of Papinos party. the People never dreaming of any disturbance in this Province; the Governor had let all the troops go from Toronto (and there was none any where elce to assist Lr. Canada) when on tuesday afternoon [5 Dec.], we were surprised by the inteligence, that Toronto was taken – that they had possession of the Bank, & the Gov. a Prisoner. this caused a goodeel of exitement, & not a little stur, but it was contradicted that night, & we could not get any imfourmation that could be credited till the Boys got home,[154] last night at 12 oC, as the Mail had been taken – we had heard of the Radicals having meetings & Exercising back on young street – & of meetings being held in the short Hills[.] H. [William Hamilton Merritt] went up, & saw there Chairman, a Mr Brady[155] – Mr B said they were all of one mind – wished a reform. but was very sorry to hear of the Proseedings in other Places, wished it Brought about in a Peaceable way – had no intention of taking up armes – it was determined here, to prepare for defence and go to there assistance at T. [Toronto] if kneeded, [H ?] had prepared to leave this morning, & about one Hundred more – there was four Hd

---

[152]Catharine R. (Prendergast) Merritt (*ca.* 1793–1862) was born in the United States. She married William Hamilton Merritt in Mayville (Chautauqua), New York, in 1815. The couple had four sons and two daughters.

[153]Jediah Prendergast (1766–1848) was born in Dutchess County, New York. His father was neutral during the American Revolution. In 1804–5 Jediah brought his family, including daughter Catharine, to the site of present-day Thorold, but returned to the United States months before the outbreak of the War of 1812, settling in Mayville, New York.

[154]The Merritt boys were students at Upper Canada College.

[155]Moses Brady, a Pelham Township merchant, was chairman of the Short Hills political union. Mackenzie's Navy Island journal shows that he expected Brady to bring him 100 men.

went in St [Steam] Boats from Hamilton – & a number from Niag. several of our vilegars were there on Business – . . .

Saterday afternoon, there is no Mail from Toronto since monday & no intelegence Since yesterday by way of the lake – the troop that is formed in this place, are exercising. Mr McDonald[156] (the Lawyer) seems very anxious to be busy[.] H. says he is a smart fellow. they wish H. to Drill – & have the direction of them – he may ocasionly. but says he has not time – they went out last night, through the Short hills, to look for MK [Mackenzie] & 4 others, that is expected will make there escape – the ferrys is watched – they returned 6 oC this morning brought in 2 suspicious characters, who they met armed, one had a Rifle the other a gun – they acknoweledged they were agoing to meet. to defend themselves as they were afraid of being taken up – the Magistrates reprimanded them, and let them go, they were Strangers – labourers – . . .

D 75   HENRY MITTLEBURGER[157] TO JOHN JOSEPH
St. Catharines, 12 December 1837
[PAC, Correspondence of the Provincial Secretary's Office, v. 9, file 1179]

. . . the St. C. Troop delivered one musket & a rifle (similar to those taken from the rebels on Yonge Street) to the Magistrates – and on Sunday Evening [10 Dec.] a person by the name of McKenny[158] was detained under the impression that he was a spy from the Short Hills – During a momentary absence he was however contrary to my intention allowed to return home, upon his promise to appear here to enter into examination the next day, but instead of doing so he returned to Pelham and reported he had made his escape, which with other reports has tended to create an alarming excitement among the disaffected – I am happy however to state, with the exception of a few persons, the main movers at their Meetings have desisted from appearing – and that a Meeting which was to have been held on Saturday night [9 Dec.] near Rice's[159] to determine *finally* what stand they were to take, only fifteen

[156]Rolland Macdonald (McDonald) (1810–1881) was born near Fort William, North-West Territories. A lawyer, he settled in St. Catharines and married there in 1835. During the revolt, he raised a cavalry troop. After it, he evidently moved to Cornwall, serving as that town's MLA, 1844–6. He later moved back to the Niagara peninsula, however, and became a judge of the Welland County Court.

[157]Henry Mittleburger (1802–1879) was first appointed a magistrate for St. Catharines in 1833. He became the St. Catharines postmaster, the manager of the Bank of Montreal branch, and the founder of the town's fire department. In 1850 he was the town treasurer.

[158]This may have been William McKenny, a Pelham labourer bound over on 28 June 1838 for suspected "treasonable practices."

[159]Rice's tavern was three miles south of the village of St. Johns and was operated by Eber Rice (b. *ca.* 1789), a native of Upper Canada. Rice was arrested on 27 June 1838, suspected of having helped the Short Hills raiders, was tried at Niagara that August and acquitted.

persons of low Character are said to have mustered and that they did not assemble at the School House where it was to have been held, & consequently no resolutions were adopted –

It seems tolerably well ascertained that Mr. Moses Brady & other leaders disavow any intention & discountenance every thing in the shape of taking up arms, & that their wish to effect reform was to be done peaceably & with moderation – Yet there are those among them who seem desirous of taking more active steps to effect their wishes & Among the most active a man by the name of Winchester[160] seems zealous – It cannot however be denied under the circumstances of the times that any Meetings must be looked upon with suspicion; and that it was exceedingly indiscreet even in the moderate men of their party to call, and much less to preside at any Meetings with the view of adopting a form of constitution (such as has appeared in the "Constitution") and to move, discuss & adopt resolutions to sympathize with the rebellious faction in L. Canada, and to reform our present form of Government –

As Chairman of the Committee of Magistrates here I shall therefore be happy to learn what course it may be deemed expedient by His Excellency, we may here pursue with such persons as have urged Militia men not to turn out in this crisis – & what measures may be taken to prevent the formation of Meetings & of Union & other Societies, by the disaffected, under the specious name of reformers –

Mr. Keeler,[161] of St. Johns – informs me that Mr. Thorburn[162] addressed the people in Pelham on Saturday last to return to their duty as loyal subjects but that he was not happy as to the mode he took to do so and that he did little or no good –

Some persons at the Solicitation of Mr. Keeler will go to Pelham, if deemed expedient by the Justices, to disabuse them of the unfounded reports in circulation which I think will tend to restore order –

D 76   JOHN JOSEPH TO HENRY MITTLEBURGER
Government House, 14 December 1837
[PAC, Lieutenant-Governor's Internal Letter Books, v. 3, No. 42]

. . . With regard to the question you ask namely "what Course it may

[160]This was Aaron Winchester, an Englishman and a farmer who had several sons. He was evidently an old man. He was bound over on 6 March 1838 to keep the peace for one year, but that summer provided the Short Hills raiders with supplies. Indicted, he fled the province and was attainted a traitor.

[161]This was likely John Kalar of St. Johns. In June 1838 Kalar was taken and then released unharmed by the Short Hills raiders.

[162]This was David Thorburn. Born in Roxboroughshire, Scotland, Thorburn emigrated to Upper Canada in 1817, settling in the Niagara peninsula, where he became a shopkeeper. A reformer, he represented the third riding of Lincoln in the Assembly from 1835 to 1844. From 1844 to 1862 he was a superintendent of the Six Nations Indians. He also served as a director of the Suspension Bridge Bank and of the Gore Bank and as a warden of the Niagara District.

be deemed expedient by His Excellency we may here pursue with such persons as have urged Militia Men not to turn out in this Crisis – and what measures may be taken to prevent the formation of Meetings and of union and other societies by the disaffected under the spurious name of reformers", I am directed to state to you that His Excellency Conceives no measures of any kind can be taken with respect to such Individuals, and that all that can be done is to watch their proceedings and gain whatever information may be obtained Concerning their Conduct and disposition.

D 77   GEORGE RYKERT[163] TO COL. JAMES FITZGIBBON
St. Catharines, 13 December 1837
[C.R. Sanderson, ed., The Arthur Papers . . . I (Toronto, 1957),
pp. 25-7]

I commenced writing you two or three times during the past week, but owing to the great excitement, and frequent alarms, could not get time to finish a letter, and even now, cannot say much – as I expect every moment to be called upon again to turn out – Matters here since yesterday are a little more tranquil. A Report however reached us last night that McKenzie and his party had reached Buffalo, (of which I have no doubt) that a very large Meeting was assembled at that place on Monday night. . . . I understand there is a strong feeling of "sympathy" as they state in Buffalo in favour of the "Canadian Patriots" – I am also aware that we have a desperate set here in our rear who are only awaiting the sound of the "tocsin" in some other quarter, to pounce upon us like hungry wolves – to pillage and plunder us – Undoubted information has been received that a considerable number of rebels have organized themselves into a body with Arms in the Short-Hills, ready to turn out in the rebel cause – I am not apprehensive that they will make any attack unless there is a rupture elsewhere –

I have been in favour of our turning out with sufficient force to disarm them, and bring the ringleaders to justice. A majority however of the Magistrates deemed it bad policy at this time, thinking it would create an unnecessary excitement – especially now that their party was so happily and gloriously defeated at Toronto – I am of opinion they will disperse, at same time I am not disposed to slumber at my post –

Disaffection I regret to say prevails to a great extent in the Southern Townships of this District – The Township of Palham [Pelham] has not more than 6 to 8 loyal men in it – Bertie, Willoughby, Arnland [Crowland], & Humberstone are very little better – And I am

---

[163]George Rykert was a surveyor who was involved in surveys of the Welland Canal. He was appointed a magistrate in 1833, and in 1834 and 1836 was elected to the Assembly from the second riding of Lincoln. Though commissioned a lieutenant in the militia by Sir John Colborne in the early 1830s, his appointment had not been gazetted by 1837, though he served as captain in 1838.

persuaded that if the rebels had succeeded at Toronto, a large force would have been collected from those Townships against us –

It behoves us therefore in my opinion to be vigilent in this quarter, and follow up our glorious and timely victory –

There is little doubt of the Fugitives having passed through the front of our district on Friday last, – A boat with 5 persons landed along the Lake Shore a little above the 4 Mile Creek – where they were driven by the severe storm on that day – near where they landed there was a person burning Coal, from whom they enquired the way to Queenston stating they were going there after goods – they had no arms – nor anything with them except a bag containing a ps. of bread a few cold boil'd potatoes and 2 fishes which they warmed upon the Coals and ate – I examined the boat, and also took the description of the persons in writing, which answers to those of McK. & Son, Gibson, Lount and Fletcher, their clothes it was stated, seemed altogether inferior to the station of the individuals who wore them – they left the boat [with] the man, and proceeded towards St. Davids, they [were] tracked to within a short distance of St. Davids, where they crossed the road & went into the woods – And I have no hesitation in saying that in my opinion they were protected and forwarded from that neighbourhood[.] The two smaller ones had on grey clothes – and were subsequently seen with cloaks over them –[164] . . .

Although I have great confidence in the Militia in this quarter, a very strong force can be collected here in a short time, I am sorry to find to great a deficiency in Officers, we have not more than 8 or 10 who can be depended upon, the rest are really a disgrace to the battalion. In addressing an Officer of your experience I feel it unnecessary to comment upon the importance of having good officers to render the Regt. efficient and respectable – In the first place we are greatly deficient in the proper no. Secondly there are some 6 or 8 drinking fellows unfit for office, under whom the men do not like to serve – then again we have about as many disaffected ones who decline attending to their proper duty – You may perhaps deem it a little officious in me, but I do beg of you to take early steps to officer our Militia more efficiently, otherwise it will "go to the dogs", but in order to do so you will require to be exceedingly cautious to prevent ill feeling at this time – I understand there are a few young officious chaps who have been trying to "shove" themselves in, but I trust they may not succeed, as it will give very general dissatisfaction to the Regt – and create a great apathy in their duty – . . .

[164]Rykert may have had grounds for his suspicions, at least with respect to Lount. He and Edward Kennedy were captured in a small open boat on Lake Erie. The craft was handled by James Dace (Dease), a Charlotteville labourer.

D 78   DEPOSITION OF EDWARD ALLEN TALBOT
8 January 1838
[*PAC, Records of the London District Magistrates, v. II*]

. . . he was at Flanagans [in London] on Friday Evening [8 Dec.] after the news from Toronto arrived – . . . After the party had assembled at Flanagan's there was a good deal of conversation respecting McKenzie's attack on Toronto – All who did speak respecting it deprecated the measure with the exception of William Hale[165] who approved of it and said as a commencement had to be made and the sooner it was made the better – and he knows this was responded to by Mr. Latimer – William Niles[166] expressed his apprehension that should McKenzie succeed and shed blood at Toronto, that the Tories would revenge it by attacking the Reformers here – William Hale said the same and if an attack was made that the first step the Reformers took, should be to secure the Treasury as he thought that a good deal of money was there – to which Deponent replied that from circumstances within his knowledge he knew there was not a shilling in it – Some person proposed that some effective mode of defence should be adapted [*sic*] and in consequence a Resolution was drawn up which was signed by all present – Mr. Latimer commenced drawing the Resolution but Deponent perceived that he was drawing it in a way that could not meet his approbation and deponent took a pen and drafted the Resolution in the following words "The Undersigned Reformers of the town of London do solemnly pledge ourselves that in the event of any attack being made upon the lives liberty or property of any reformer in this Town we will to the utmost of our power aid each other in any Constitutional way in repelling any such attack" [–] Deponent thinks these are the exact words – That in order to give effect to this in the event of any attack as aforesaid, it was concocted that they should assemble in the neighbourhood of the Scotch Church on a signal being given, which signal was to be the firing of two Guns and the blowing of a Bugle – Three persons were appointed to cause this signal to be

[165]William Hale, an Upper Canadian-born carpenter, lived in London Township in 1837. He owned property both in the town and township of London. In 1835 he had served as a roadmaster and in 1836 as a poundkeeper for the township. In October 1837 he attended the reformers' Westminster meeting. Jailed at London on 15 December 1837, he was tried for treason in the spring and acquitted.

[166]William Niles (1799–1873) was born in Coeymans, New York. He came to Upper Canada while still a child. In 1821 he settled in Dorchester Township, where he farmed, ran a sawmill and store, and raised a family. In 1827 and 1829 he served as an overseer of highways for Dorchester and in 1837 was chosen a delegate to the projected reform convention from neighbouring Westminster. He was questioned about his reform activities and released on bail in London on 17 January 1838. He served on the District of London/Middlesex County Council, 1842–54, and was warden, 1847–54. In 1849 he was made a magistrate and sat in the Assembly of the united Canadas, 1854–7.

given without whose consent it should not be given – John ONeil[167] was one of these persons [–] Deponent was another and Thomas Gibbins[168] or William Niles the third – It was the impression of deponent that Mr Latimer was to have kept the paper for the signature of the other reformers in the town afterwards

At the meeting after the signal was concocted a conversation took place about who had arms [–] believes all who were present said that they had arms except Deponent who said he had no need of arms. – Latimer was asked if he had powder and replied that he had 30 or 40 pounds – it was proposed that he should keep this but he objected on account of his partner and said if they wanted it to come and buy and some said they would take a pound some half a pound and so forth – There was some conversation as to the probability of John Talbot being arrested – who said that he hoped that would not take place [–] if it did it would make the Liberal party the aggressors for nothing could stop the people South from rescuing him – for that it was with great difficulty they were prevented from attacking the Gaol on the day of the Westminster meeting[169]

Deponent further says that. on enquiry of Mr. Latimer whether they [the authorities] had found any papers – Mr. Latimer stated that they had found with him a minute or minutes of the meeting at Westminster meeting or Lobo. does not recall which – and also a List of the names of the Reformers in the town of London [–] Dept. [Deponent] then asked what he had done with the paper drawn up at Flanagans to which he replied that whilst they were searching Yeomans[170] papers he had destroyed it – Deponent then said he was sorry he had done so as the paper was intended to speak for itself – –

D 79   JOHN B. ASKIN TO JONAS JONES
London, 22 December 1837
[C.R. Sanderson, ed., The Arthur Papers . . . I (Toronto, 1957), pp. 35-6]

For other extracts from this document see C 53, C 70, C 78.

I have the honor to report for the information of His Excellency the

[167]John O'Neil was appointed high constable of the London District in 1831. He kept the Mansion House tavern in London.

[168]Thomas Gibbins opened a store in London in the early 1830s and, as a merchant, supported the projected London and Gore Railroad. In 1837 he owned 100 patented acres and two patented town lots. He was examined at London on 17 January 1838 and thereafter bound over.

[169]It is not entirely clear why the reformers wanted to attack the gaol, but they may have believed that the three reformers taken for their parts in the Richmond riot were being held there. In fact, true bills had been found against the three on 2 October and they had been released on bail on 5 October. The Westminster meeting was held on 6 October.

[170]Yeomans was Latimer's partner.

Lieutenant Governor, that on the receipt of a communication from Her Majestys Attorney General on Monday Morning the 11th Inst. at 5 o Clock, to arrest the Editor of the "Liberal" Newspaper and such papers as might be found with him, I immediately consulted with Col Hamilton the High Sheriff, and upon consideration it was agreed between us, that I should wait till the following day, (tuesday the 12th.) having heard that morning that an attack was intended to be made on the town that night, at about 10 O Clock P.M. intelligence (which I had reason to believe could be relied on) reached me to prepare and to be on the alert at the same time giving me the signal intended to be used by the attacking party for assembling, which was the firing two Guns and to be immediately followed by the blowing of a Bugle, and their place of rendezvous the Scotch Church; this notice enabled me to rouse all the inhabitants that could be relied upon who instantly repaired to the Court House with all the Arms and Ammunition within their reach, in all about 200 strong, who soon put that building in a state of defence, capable of resistance for a period. I am fully satisfied now, that the Zeal displayed by the Loyalist[s] on that night frustrated such plans as might have been in progress of maturity by the Rebels.

On Tuesday the 12th. I proceeded to St. Thomas to arrest John Talbot and found that he had left that place on the Afternoon of Sunday the 10th. at about 3 o Clock P.M. and subsequently heard that he had crossed the Detroit River on Tuesday afternoon the 12th. Inst. . . .

D 80   AMELIA HARRIS[171] TO HENRY BECHER[172]
London, 14 December 1837
[UWO, Harris Family Papers]

. . . after you left information was sent here yesterday that the Rebels are assembling in Oakland about 9 miles this side of the Grand River[;] to day the London Militia were called out & they have marched for St Thomas. . . . old Longworth[173] with about 200 men have arrived in

[171]Amelia (Ryerse) Harris (1798–1882) was born at Long Point, Upper Canada, into a United Empire Loyalist family. She married John Harris, a naval master, in 1815. The couple settled near Port Ryerse in 1817 after Harris retired on half-pay, and moved to London in 1834, where they built Eldon House, which became the social centre of that community. The two had twelve children.

[172]Henry Cory Rowly Becher (1817–1885) was born in London, England. He came to London, Upper Canada, in 1835, where he studied law under John Wilson. From 1839 to 1849 he was the registrar of the London District Surrogate Court. He was called to the bar in 1841. From 1850 to 1854 he was a member of the town council.

[173]John Longworth (1790–1883) was born in Westmeath, Ireland. A veteran of the Peninsular war and an engineer, he came to Upper Canada in 1830, deserting his wife and children. He worked on the Rideau Canal for a time and then married a Toronto barmaid. In 1836 a court found him guilty of bigamy, and he became for a time a notorious character, though it is not clear to what extent his career suffered from his notoriety. In 1836 he was appointed superintendent of the Huron Tract by the Canada Company, and he settled in Goderich, designing the harbour there.

Town this evening from Goderich[;] the Lobo Scotch who have nearly all turned tories & the Adelaide people are to be here to morrow[;] all is enthusiasm now and the Rads have no chance but there was a great deal of appathy in our Sherriff & Col Commandant at the commencement[;] he will never be able to recover the confidence of the Towns people[;] there was a meeting of the Radicals that is all the leaders in the middle of the night preceeding our news of their defeat at Toronto[.] Mr Harris[174] urged & entreated to have them arrested but his answer was oh no we must re main quiet, we must not irritate them[;] there was Mr john Talbot Mr Obrien[175] Tommy Park old Proudfoot, Bill Hale[,] Putnam[,][176] Little[177] the Carpenter & would you believe it Morrel[178] was one of them[,] Mr Latimer [also][;] in all they mustered about thirty which had I been a man & clothed with any authourity they should have all been lodged in the cells to keep them out of harms

[174]John Harris (1782 or 1783–1856) was born in Devon, England. He entered the Royal Navy in 1803, rising to the rank of master. In 1815–17 he worked under Admirals Bayfield and Owen in their charting of Canadian waters. In 1815 he married Amelia Ryerse, and in 1823, then on half-pay, became treasurer of the London District, a post he held until 1846. After the district capital was moved from Vittoria to London, he settled his family there, becoming a stellar member of that town's elite, helping found a mechanics' institute, serving as a district school trustee, and so on. In 1836 he was appointed a commissioner of the Court of Requests. In December 1837 he participated in the cutting out of the *Caroline*; indeed, the idea was evidently his. Over the years he profited considerably from his land speculations.

[175]This was Hugh O'Beirne. A prominent local Catholic, he was a St. Thomas grocer and dry goods merchant. In 1836 he acted as the reformers' agent in the Middlesex elections, and in 1837 was chosen vice-president of the St. Thomas political union. In the latter year he was also tax collector of Yarmouth Township. He was examined in London on 30 December for his participation at Flannagan's meeting and for his reform activities generally. In 1838 he left Upper Canada for the United States, where he seems to have become involved with the Patriots.

[176]This was in all likelihood William Putnam (*ca.* 1793–1838). Born in the United States, he settled in Upper Canada with his parents about 1797 in Dorchester Township. He became a farmer, a sawmill owner, and a building contractor. A veteran of the War of 1812, he was made an adjutant in the militia but he resigned his commission in 1836. In 1837, though then a resident of Delaware, he was chosen the Dorchester representative to the projected reform convention. Jailed at London on 15 December 1837 on suspicion of treason, he was tried the following spring and acquitted; however, while he was in jail his house burned down, evidently at the hands of vengeful tories. He went to Michigan and enlisted with the Patriots, shooting and killing a militia officer at Bear Creek in June. He himself was shot and killed during the Windsor raid of December 1838, though two of his sons escaped.

[177]James Little, an Irishman, emigrated to Upper Canada about 1821. In 1837 he owned three lots in the town of London. He was jailed at London after the revolt and released on bail on 17 January.

[178]Simeon Morrill (Morrel) (1793–1871) was born in Vermont. By 1817 he was resident in Kingston, working as a tanner there. In 1829 he moved to London to work his trade. A temperance advocate, he inclined to reform politics, running unsuccessfully for the Assembly in 1844. He was appointed a magistrate in 1841 and in 1848, 1850, and 1851 served as mayor of London. His tannery and shoe manufactory became quite extensive, though he was forced to declare bankruptcy in 1868.

way[;] on Saturday night [9 Dec.] when the news came the Rebels were defeated Col. H — said dont Hurrah do not Hurrah, it will excite them but I am happy to say it was not in his power to suppress the true British feeling. Latimer was weighing out Powder to the Radicals untill yesterday[;] the Sheriff & Magistrates could not be prevailed upon to seize it[;] yesterday Mr. Harris & Mr Wilson where determined to take the responsibility upon them selves[;] I persuaded them to insist upon his[,] Co. H[,] saying yes, or no[;] it was placing him in a awkward situation for he was afraid to do either[;] he at last said if they thought best they might do it, & it was done, last Sunday during the hours of Service the children & myself were employed runing Bullets[;] I was rather abashed when Mrs. Cronyn[179] came in & caught me at it but she displayed a pair of Bullet Moles [moulds] she had just borrowed & was going home to employ her self in the same way[;] we have been several times notified that Mr Harris was to be shot & our house burned[;][180] Mrs. Cronyn was notified that her house would be Burned as it was church property but she need not be alarmed as her & the children would be allowed to walk out – very civil – two of the leaders in this place Hale & Little disappeared last night; whether they have gone to join the Rebels in Oakland or Detroit we cannot tell[.] Goodhue[181] has come out on the right side and behaved most handsomely and Mr. Shaw also at St Thomas, our kitchen is turned into a guard room and it appears to me it is not the same world we where living in when you left us[.] I hope God will protect my husband & restore him safe to us[;] how happy shall I be to see you all to gether again enjoying the blessings of home & peace. . . .

D 81   MAGISTRATES LAURENCE LAURASON AND THOMAS BALL TO
LT. JAMES PARKINSON[182]
London, 14 December 1837
[PAC, Upper Canada Sundries, v. 180, p. 99237]

You are hereby authorized to require for The use of Her Majestys

---

[179]Benjamin Cronyn's wife was the former Margaret Ann Bickerstaff. The couple, who married in 1826, had seven children.

[180]The Harris' home, Eldon House, was renowned as the social centre of London's elite. Today it is a museum.

[181]George J. Goodhue (1799–1870) was born in Vermont. By 1820 he had established a store in Westminster Township and was operating a distillery. He served as a township tax collector and poundkeeper. In 1826 he moved to London and in 1830 was appointed postmaster there, a position he held until 1852. In 1832 he entered a partnership with Laurence Laurason, and, though his partner was an avowed tory, Goodhue took little interest in politics in the turbulent 1830s. In 1840 he became the first president of the village of London and in 1842 a legislative councillor. Over the years, as one of London's leading merchants, he amassed considerable wealth.

[182]James Parkinson was gazetted an ensign of the 4th Middlesex Regiment in 1824 and a lieutenant in 1838.

Government, all the arms, and ammunition which you find within the Township of London in possession of such as have not come forward to serve and Lodge the Same at the Court House in London for Her Majestys Service – granting to Every person from whom you receive the Same a receipt –

By order of Colonel Hamilton

D 82   INFORMATION OF JOHN BURGESS[183]
18 December 1837
[PAC, Upper Canada Sundries, v. 180, p. 99468]

. . . on Friday the 15th Instant Informant met Robert Davis With Seven others in the woods of Nissouri Armed with Guns – Informant Knew Hugh Davis,[184] George Burgess,[185] and Henry Hall [–] the others he did not Know – Davis Said they were armed for the purpose of Resisting the Tories who They Heard were coming out to Seize arms for the Queens service. Also said that He had 130 men armed under his Command ready to resist the Authority [–] Informant Knows several other disaffected persons in Nissouri who are all armed –

D 83   EXCITEMENT IN AND AROUND LONDON
14 December 1837
[Sarnia Public Library and Art Gallery, Henry Jones[186] Diary]

Breakfasted at Nash's dined at Delaware and reached London about 7 p.m. Met numbers of young men with light packs making their way west. They were all radicals but took good care to keep their opinions to themselves. Every bar room was full of politicians the greater part of whom who if not radically inclined, showed no great attachment to the other side – I heard from no single individual any thing like a warm expression of loyalty. Long before our arrival at London we learnt that there was nothing like danger there, arrived, it was as far to the East as ever. Symptoms of the military mania now however began to be apparent, the loyal citizens were keeping guard and drinking grog with much perserverance, heroes might be seen walking around in Buffalo

[183]John Burgess was a Nissouri Township resident.

[184]Hugh Davis, Robert's brother, was born in Ireland. He emigrated with his parents to Upper Canada in 1819; the family settled in Nissouri Township. Hugh was not taken up by the authorities for his part in the events of December 1837.

[185]George Burgess was evidently the brother of the complainant, John Burgess.

[186]Henry John Jones (1809–1885) was born in Exeter, England. In 1827 he came with his father Henry, who was connected to Sir John Colborne by marriage, to the Sarnia area of Upper Canada. Here Henry Jones Sr., who had a large land grant, established a cooperative community, Maxwell. In 1834, after a disastrous fire, the community folded. Young Henry stayed on in British North America, becoming a crown lands agent in Sarnia and Chatham and later a clerk in the Crown Lands Department in Toronto and Quebec City.

robes and armed with sundry weapons[,] raggamuffins were in much demand for volunteers and were proportionably drunk and impertinent. Took up my quarters at O'Neil's which appeared to be the head quarters of the tories and was on the whole tolerably quiet.

Various reports of battles fought or to be fought at or about Oakland (10 m. west of Brantford) between the rebels under Duncombe and the loyalists under Askin, Bostwick & c. – Weath. Cold and Cloudy.

D 84 LONDON ON THE ALERT
[UWO, Proudfoot Family Papers, Proudfoot Diary 28]

Sabbath Decr. 17. 1837. –

Preached in London from Heb. 1. 6-14 to about 49 persons. – The whole town taken up with catching the radicals so that no body had time to attend meeting for the worship of God. Such a scene I never witnessed. . . .

Monday Decr. 18. 1837. –

on my way home called . . . at Henry Shenic's,[187] was examined by a military picket, and got a *passport* for London !! . . .

D 85 INFORMATION OF ALVARO LADD[188]
27 December 1837
[PAC, Records of the London District Magistrates, v. II]

. . . After the news of the Commencement of the insurrection at Toronto, had, reached Delaware, there was a special meeting of the Society [the political union] convened on the 16th December instant for the purpose of Embodying and organising the members of the Society for their own personal protection, as they were apprehensive that the Government would call out the Indians to Act against the Reformers – Examinant was led to his belief from having personally called upon Mr. Clench, Superintendant of the Indians to request him to induce the Muncey Indians to keep quiet if any collision should take

---

[187]Henry Shenick (Shenic) (b. *ca.* 1793) was a native of Holland. His family emigrated to New York State in 1796 and then to Upper Canada's Westminster Township in 1810. Henry's second marriage was to Charles Duncombe's sister, Huldah, and about 1821 the couple had a son, Charles Duncombe Shenick. The family farmed lot 28, concession 1, Westminster. Henry was the first clerk of Westminster, Delaware, and Dorchester townships, and from 1838 to 1843 he served as a tax collector. Family tradition has it that in December 1837 he hid Charles Duncombe on his flight west.

[188]Alvaro Ladd (1801–1842) was born in Vermont. He emigrated to Upper Canada about 1814 and settled in Delaware Township, where he operated the first stage between Delaware and Ancaster and where he ran a store. A Universalist, he was well respected in his community. He was elected town clerk in 1837. An active reformer, he was jailed at London on 15 December 1837 and freed on bail on 1 January 1838. He was, however, recommitted and tried for treason that spring. Found guilty, he was finally released on bail and in ill health on 25 September 1838. He moved his family to Michigan, but later returned to Upper Canada, where he died.

place between the parties [–] and Mr. Clench having stated to him in answer, that being at the head of the Indians he could not interfere, but if ordered by the Government he should of course call them out – the Union met on the 16th instant – McKenzies defeat at Toronto and Dr. Duncombe's army having. dispersed was canvassed and the meeting adjourned until the day for the Town Meeting, as there would be likely to be a larger Attendance – . . .

D 86   J.B. Clench to S.P. Jarvis
Colborne on Thames, 18 December 1837
[*PAC, Indian Affairs, v. 125, pp. 70334-5*]

I have the honor to inform you that I have taken every precaution in my power to rally the Indians under my Superintendence to defend the Queens Government and I rejoice to be able to bear testimony to their devoted Loyalty, the Munsees, Moravians, and Chippewas to a man are ready and willing to take the field notwithstanding that every effort has been used by the People of the surrounding Country to seduce them from their duty. I have requested the Civil authorities to call on me for assistance whenever the Exigency of the Service shall require the Co-operation of the Indians; I regret that not more than a fourth of the Warriors are armed and I beg to suggest that Rifles would be preferred, if to be had. . . .

I feel it my duty to transmit the enclosed letter from the Chiefs of the St. Clair which I am sorry to say breathes sentiments so selfish, unfeeling and disloyal that the parties deserve, in my humble opinion, the severest Censure. – . . .

I beg to add that there is a body of about 700 Indians (called Black Hawks) who are Chippewas from Green Bay, hunting in the rear of the settled Townships in this District, they have about 180 men, and I have had a Conference with three of them who professed loyalty and devotion to the Government and I have also directed them to Capture any suspicious Persons and to bring them to me for examination.

D 87   Joshua Wawanosh,[189] Edward Ogeebegun, and Gordon Megezeez to Kanoodung,[190] Maushkenoozha,[191] Wannedegoosh,[192] and John Kiya Ryley[193]
St. Clair mission, 14 December 1837
[*PAC, Indian Affairs, v. 125, pp. 70337-8*]

Dear Brothers,

we last evening received a letter bringing us bad new respecting the troubles which exist in our country, of which we were sorry to hear.

You enquire whether we think it best to take any part in these affairs. we can inform you that we consider it best to spread our matts to sit-down & smoke our pipes and to let the people who like powder & ball fight their own battles.

We have some time ago counselled with the Indians around us & we are all agreed to remain quiet and we hope that all the Indians will do so, as we can gain nothing by fighting, but may lose every thing.

We should be glad to see you but cannot come at present, we send this by one of our Chiefs who will have a talk with you on the subject.

We have no fear that you who are wise will go astray, but we fear that some of those who are in the west on Lake Huron may be misled by designing white men & should such as are yet foolish be induced to commence war on the whites of any party, we should all be more hated by the whites than we are now.

We would just observe that we cannot be compelled to go & fight for any party, we mention this fact in order that should you be called on you may know that you are free men & under the controul of no one who has authority to make you take up arms.

D 88 CHIPPEWA CHIEFS TO S.P. JARVIS
Colborne on Thames, 21 December 1837
[PAC, Indian Affairs, v. 67, pp. 64211-14]

Be pleased to lay before our Father the Governor this our second Petition of grievances, . . .

Father

. . . It was with sorrowful hearts we learned the mail was stoped, and that our Father was in great trouble, we your children were all ready to fly to your assistance, but the fog was so dense we could not see through it, and we anxiously awaited Mr. Clenches return to drive the mist from our eyes by bringing your Orders for your Red children to

---

[189]Joshua Wawanosh, "White Elk," (*ca.* 1792–1871 or 1879) became a chief of the Chippawas along the St. Clair when still a youth. He fought in the War of 1812, and was the first head chief of his people; he was that when they ceded much of their land to the government in 1827. In 1829 he converted to Christianity and was first a Methodist, then an Anglican. In 1837 he and others evidently planned a mission to England to protest Head's Indian policies. He was deposed as chief of 1844 but was later restored as such. One of his four sons graduated from Victoria College in 1862.

[190]Kanoodung (Canoting, Kanotang), was a veteran of the War of 1812. In 1828 the Rev. Peter Jones came to him, the chief of the Bear Creek Ojibway, in order to convert him and his people. Kanoodung refused to desert his ancestral religion. Though he signed a letter of the Munceytown and area chiefs in 1837 avowing support for the Church of England mission, he remained resolutely non-Christian, as did his people.

[191]Maushkenoozha (Mas-Kan-oou-je) was one of the Munceytown area chiefs who, in 1837, claimed to be identified with the Church of England, rather than the Methodists.

[192]Wannedegoosh (Wen-ta-gashe) was another Munceytown area chief who, in 1837, claimed an Anglican, rather than a Methodist, orientation.

[193]John Kiya Ryley was evidently a Métis. He developed a reputation for being a great hunter. He lived originally along the St. Clair frontier but by 1837 he was a chief on the Muncey-Chippawa reserve on the Thames. In 1837 other chiefs near Munceytown disputed his right to be a chief, in part because he was a Methodist while they inclined to the Church of England. Also, they claimed he planned to go to England with Wawanosh to protest Head's Indian policies. The upshot of this dispute is unclear, but he was probably not deposed, for he was reported a chief in 1851.

raise the Tom-a-hawk-, Mr. Clench returned to us last week when he called a council, he then told us he had not received any orders whatever for us, and advised us to prepair ourselves in case we should be called upon, we informed him we had before his return expressed a desire to assist you but our weapons were few and out of repair, that if our Dear Father would put forth his arms and give us our blankets, for to make our woman, and children, warm and guns, and amunition, we would then be better prepaired to destroy his enemies. –

We have been frequently advised by the Liberals, and Messrs. [Waldern ?],[194] and Carey,[195] to remain quiet, and let the white men fight their own battle. we tell them the War Cry of the Britains, will raise the war club of the Red men, and at a moments warning we will be prepaired to go where duty calls us to make it red with the blood of their enemies –

We sent immediately for Pa-shik-ka-shik-ques-cum[196] of Walpole Island, and Wa-wa-nosh of the St Clair, the former is now with us and is ready with his young People to fight for his Father the Governor. Wa-wa-nosh would not come. but sent us a very bad letter[.] Mr. Clench would neither read it to us; nor let us have it to send to you – We are not pleased with Mr. Clench for so doing, and fearing he would not write our determination to die for you, we have caused it to be written by the Young Man You was pleased to allow us to Keep.

We think Mr. Clench has neglected us very much, and is too great a friend to Missions, to be friendly desposed towards your dutiful, and Loyal subjects, the Chipewas of the Thames –

> Canoting
> Mas-Kan-oou-je[197]
> Mus-Ko-Koo-mon[198]
> Wen-ta-gashe
> Chicken Mas-Kan-oouje[199]
> Yan Cause[200]

[194]Waldern or Waldron appears to have been a Methodist minister in Munceytown. In October 1837 various chiefs there asked Head to remove him, blaming him for the troubles they were encountering amongst themselves.

[195]This appears to have been John Carey, who came to the Muncey reserve in 1825 from the United States to teach school. He seems to have married Peter Jones' widow about 1858.

[196]Pa-shik-ka-shik-ques-cum, "the one who makes footsteps in the sky," (d. *ca.* 1842) was the head chief of the Walpole Island Ojibways. He was a non-Christian, having resisted several attempts to persuade him to convert, and was a man of considerable influence.

[197]See n. 191, supra.

[198]Mus-Ko-Koo-mon fought under Tecumseh in the War of 1812. In 1837 he was one of the Munceytown chiefs who claimed an Anglican, rather than a Methodist, orientation.

[199]Chicken Mas-Kan-oouje was another of the "Anglican" Munceytown chiefs.

[200]"Yan Cause" was likely Yahvance who had fought with Tecumseh in the War of 1812. In 1837 Yahvance was one of the Munceytown chiefs who claimed an Anglican, rather than a Methodist, orientation.

D 89 INFORMATION OF JAMES EDWARDS[201]
22 December 1837
[*PAC, Records of the London District Magistrates, v. II*]

. . . James Edwards . . . maketh oath and saith That on Friday the fifteenth day of December current – this Deponent was at Alexr. Wards[202] Tavern having been called out to march with Col: Craigs[203] Reg.t: – was induced not to go along with it from what Alexr. Roberts[204] and others said to prevent their going – Christopher L[an]g[205] was one of these Persons, who declared that he would not go – There were several others said the same, but Dept. [Deponent] does not recollect their names – After Capt. Ward & the Company had marched – A. Roberts & those who refused to go, held a meeting – there were about 50 or 60 – A. Roberts said it was best to get arms from Detroit – He offered to go for them – along with John Ward[206] & Wm Gardiner[207] – That in case any attempt was made to take any of them Prisoners, – they were to warn their friends out to resist – That a person of the name of White[208] read a printed paper which he called the "Constitution of Upper Canada" – That the meeting approved of this Constitution & said they would endeavour to get it introduced into Upper Canada – That the People cheered this Constitution – That the People then went home – Understands a Political meeting was held by A Roberts & Philips[209] – & others at Christopher Langs Tavern last

[201]James Edwards, a "yeoman," was the son of James Edwards, likely the same James Edwards who settled in Mosa in 1814, becoming one of the township's first settlers.

[202]Alexander Ward was a member of the large and locally prominent Ward family of Mosa. George Ward, the founder of Wardsville, settled in the township in 1810 and is often credited with being its first settler. Alexander's tavern may have been the Ward's Tavern on Longwoods Road, though there were at least two taverns owned by Wards in the township in 1837.

[203]James Craig (*ca.* 1783–1848) of Caradoc, a farmer, was one of the first settlers along the Longwoods Road. He rose to the rank of colonel in the militia and served with his regiment in the winter of 1837–8 on the Detroit frontier. His men complained to the militia authorities that he badly mistreated them there.

[204]Alexander Roberts was a Mosa farmer. In December 1837 he fled the province, leaving behind him large debts, a court fine, and his wife and children. To one local resident, he was "a swindling, scamp, cheating & overreaching every person he could." In Michigan he became involved with the Patriots.

[205]Christopher Lang ran a tavern and owned 100 patented acres in Mosa. In June 1838 he was suspected of treasonable activities, and a warrant, which was evidently never enforced, was issued for his arrest.

[206]There were several John Wards in Mosa in 1837, members of the large Ward family.

[207]This was probably the William Gardiner who was the son of Singleton Gardiner who died in 1834. This William (b. *ca.* 1811) was in 1837 the operator of his dead father's saw and grist mills.

[208]This was John White, a Mosa millwright.

[209]This could have been one of four members of the Philips family active with the radicals in and about Mosa in December 1837 – Peter, Isaac, Ira, or H. Philips. In

Sunday [17 Dec.], but does not know what took place as he did not attend it. That on Monday the 18th inst. A. Roberts & the six following Persons came about dark to the House of Amos Thomas[210] Junr. of Aldbourough where this Dept. was – They remained all night – their names are Joseph Hendershott[211] of Talbot st. – Joseph McClements Joshua Wilcocks[212] Caleb Wilcocks[213] Wm. Wilcocks[214] all of Mosa and Ira Philips of Eckfrid – They came they said to Defend A. Roberts – Daniel Thomas of Mosa was also there – They all went away about three OClock in the morning except Roberts – who afterwards went back into the Bush – They all said when they were in A. Thomas's House, that they meant to leave the Country – Daniel Thomas went away with the above six men – Deponent has never seen any of them since – except A. Roberts on Tuesday, who persuaded this Deponent & George Stafford to leave the Province with him. That they accordingly accompanied Roberts into the Bush [–] That Roberts strongly advised them *not to join the Regt. as they would be sent to Lower Canada to fight & probably lose their lives* – That this Dept. was a good deal *scared* – but before he had made up his mind his mother sent a message across the River to him to come home & accordingly he & G. Stafford returned & left A. Roberts alone in the Bush – whom he has never seen since – believes that A. Roberts has left the Province as well as all the other persons above mentioned, except Hendersott [*sic*] & Stafford – They were all armed with Rifles & Guns. They resolved to go by Bear Creek to Michigan – said if there were any Americans coming over to assist the Canadian Reformers – that they would join them – Does not know of any men assembled on the aldborough side of the River – with arms; and does not believe that there are any such assembled. –

D 90   JOHN PRINCE[215] TO JOHN JOSEPH ?
Sandwich, 15 December 1837
[*PAC, Correspondence of the Provincial Secretary's Office, v. 9, file 1197*]

I this morning received your Summons to attend Parliament on

December 19-year-old Ira fled to Michigan while Isaac and Peter were both jailed at London on suspicion of treason and released on 4 January 1838. H. Philips, though at the Mosa meeting, escaped official notice.

[210]This may have been Amos B. Thomas, jailed at London on 30 June 1838 for suspected treasonable activities and freed shortly thereafter.

[211]Joseph Hendershott of Mosa, a labourer, gave the local magistrates a deposition on 18 December and was evidently not troubled further.

[212]Joshua Wilcocks fled to Michigan in December.

[213]Caleb Wilcocks, who owned one patented acre in Mosa, fled to Michigan in December.

[214]William Wilcocks fled to Michigan in December.

[215]John Prince (1796–1870) was born in Hereford, England, and trained as a lawyer before coming to Upper Canada in 1833. He established Park Farm at Windsor and

Thursday next. Even if I could start instanter it would be quite impossible to reach Toronto by that day. The roads are in such a state (so rough without snow) that a carriage cannot travel beyond 3 or 4 miles an hour. But however desirous, nay most anxious, I am to attend to the Summons with punctuality in these extraordinary times, I am yet more anxious to compleat the work I have undertaken of satisfying our opposite neighbours in Detroit & Michigan that the Lower Canadians are undeserving of their, sympathy, and that nothing can justify their sending volunteers into the Canadas. An agent from L. Canada is actively engaged in Detroit – And I hear (and have some reason to think) that McKenzie or Dr. J. Rolph or both are there. Also Talbot the Editor of the St Thomas *"Liberal"*. I have an appointment with the Governor (Mr. Mason)[216] *for next Monday*, then to confer with him generally upon Canadian affairs. They are altogether uninformed, or rather misinformed, upon that subject; And their sympathies are alive to the supposed grievances complained of. The Citizens of Detroit have been with me, and I have informed them of the absurdity of the complaints: *I do not* think that a single volunteer will cross the line to this Country or L. Canada. But I am anxious to keep my appointment with Governor Mason for Monday. I shall get from him, if possible, a few Kegs of G. [Gun] Powder & balls or Cartridges, in case of anything happening here during my absence. We have no ammunition in these parts of any consequence. Hitherto we have been quiet in this County & District[.] *But there are some disaffected pers[ons]* – & many will, I apprehend, fly, fro[m] the London & other dis-tricts to *Detroit*, and preach sedition here & hereabouts.

I shall set out on Tuesday or Wedny for Toronto, thro' Michigan, via Buffal[o]. I am told that the Rebels denounce me in particular, because I was the author of the Bill to prevent the dissolution of Parliament by the demise of the Crown. I shall travel armed – and "Let them come if they dare" . . . .

---

became a magistrate there. In 1836 he was the chairman of the Court of Quarter Sessions, and was elected to the Assembly as an independent who approved of Head's course. In December 1838 he led the loyalists who repulsed the Windsor raiders and he had four of the latter summarily shot. Erratic in his political orientation, he represented Essex in the Assembly until 1854. From 1856 until 1860 he sat in the Legislative Council. In 1860, appointed a judge, he moved to Sault Ste. Marie and the Algoma District.

[216]Stevens Thomson Mason (1811–1843) was born in Virginia, though his family moved to Kentucky in 1830. Andrew Jackson appointed Stevens' father secretary of the Michigan Territory in 1830, and, when his father moved to Texas in 1830, gave the appointment to 19-year-old Stevens, who helped conduct the campaign for statehood. A Democrat, he became Michigan's first elected governor in 1835, though Michigan, embroiled in a territorial dispute with Ohio, was not admitted to the union until 1837. In November 1837 he was re-elected, retiring from office in 1840 and moving to New York, where he practised law until his death.

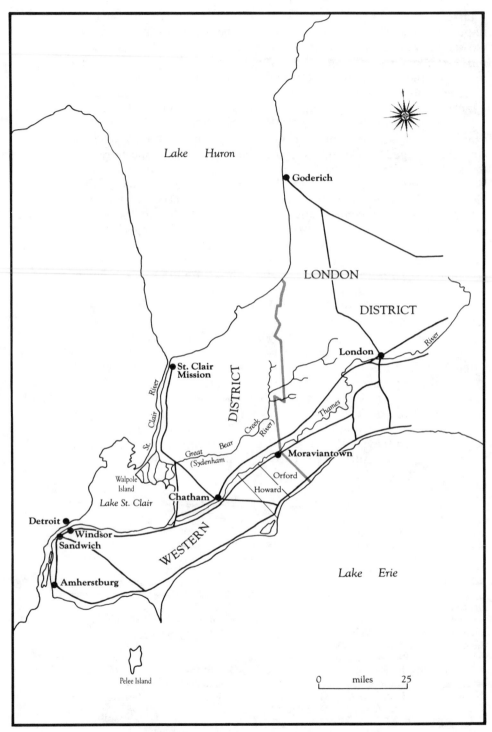

Lake Huron

Goderich

LONDON

DISTRICT

St. Clair
Mission

London

River

DISTRICT

Thames

St. Clair River

Creek

River

Great
(Sydenham

Bear

Moraviantown

Walpole
Island

Orford

Chatham

Howard

Lake St. Clair

Detroit

WESTERN

Windsor
Sandwich

Lake Erie

Amherstburg

Pelee Island

0   miles   25

8:    Western District and Adjacent London District, 1837

D 91   JAMES READ[217] TO JAMES HAMILTON
Chatham, 26 December 1837
[*MTPL, James Hamilton Papers*]

. . . The whole of the Malitiae Have been Called out Here and with very few acceptions Have Shewn a determination to stand for the *Queen & Constitution* with the *Motto* Death or *Victory*. They Resound to the *Cry* of *Ready* yes *Ready* but Armes are Scarse, All that is wanted by the Yeomanry Here is a possitive Call to Defend. the property of Their Neibours as well as themselves. Let the Enemy Come from where they may. If it is thought possitively Nessesary for the protection of the Frontier from Robbers or Rebbells or Invaders All is wanted is a Possitive Order to attend and Protect Property and Liefs [Lives]. If Nessesary Send an Order to the officer in Command or to the Magistrates and there will be no Time Lost in making the Genrall Call to Armes. . . .

D 92   COLIN C. FERRIE[218] TO W.H. DRAPER
Hamilton, 22 December 1837
[*PAC, Records of the London District Magistrates, v. II*]

. . . I have just been told by Mr [Wm.?] Davidson[219] (brother in law to Mr Shade) who is a customer of ours doing business in Wilmot – that about 500 Michigan Indians are near in some of the C. [Canada] Coy. [Company] Townships beyond Wilmot – & some of them just a few miles from his place – Mr. D. says they have been breaking into peoples houses stealing guns & committing other outrages – also that they make a great cry in favour of Papineau McKenzie – I cant conceive what right they have in this country – Possibly they may have been sent into this Province by Political emissaries in the U. States – or they may have come in on other business and may have been tampered with by some evil disposed persons – Mr. D. got his information from

[217]James Read (*ca.* 1811–1841), a wharfinger and merchant who ran a general store in Chatham, was in 1835 president of the Chatham Vigilante Society for the Suppression of Felony. In 1837 he was appointed a magistrate and during the rebellion served as a volunteer commissary. In 1838 he was made quarter-master of the local militia. He thereafter became postmaster of Chatham. On his death he left a wife and two young children.
[218]Colin Campbell Ferrie (1808–1856) was born in Glasgow, Scotland. He was sent by his father on business to Montreal in 1824. In 1830 he and his brother Adam opened a branch of the store their father had established in Montreal the preceding year. In 1833 he was appointed a magistrate and in 1833 and 1834 sat on the Hamilton Board of Police. In 1836 he was elected to the Assembly from Hamilton and pursued an independent course there. In 1847 he was elected Hamilton's first mayor and from 1839 to 1856 was president of the Gore Bank.
[219]Absalom Shade married Isabella Davidson, who had come with her family, including her four brothers, John, James, William, and Alexander, to Winterbourne, near Elora, in 1834. It is not known to which of the brothers the document refers, though it might well be William.

some of our own Indians who were trading with him – he says the people in that part of the country are in great terror – and I think the matter is worth enquiring into – Mr. D. says he was told by our own Indians that these American Indians were going to Toronto to fight for McKenzie – I give you the story exactly as I have got it, and you can give it what weight you may think it entitled to –

D 93   DESPOSITION OF CYRUS SUMNER[220]
[PAC, Records of the London District Magistrates, v. I, pp. 76-7, 12 Jan. 1838]

. . . says that the Militia were being called out, was at Goderich on the 11th Decr. last and saw Joseph Alway[,] that Alway said the Country was revolutionized and Toronto and the Governor were taken and that the Americans were coming into the Country by hundreds and had seen the handbills stating this in the hands of the Tories themselves – and stated it was of no use resisting for that if they did they would lose their property – spoke this to deponent and others [–] deponent states that there had been a meeting at Goderich for the purpose of calling out Volunteers [–] prisoner [Joseph Alway] seemed to use this language to prevent them Volunteering – J.W. Garrison heard him – Mr. Longworth and his hired man was along with Garrison – Always conversation was entirely to excite the Volunteers not to go out and against the Government and he seemed to make it his whole business – deponent had a quarrel with prisoner which arose from political circumstances, the next day Alway overtook him on his road to London [–] Alway commenced the conversation with deponent when Alway said he [Sumner] was foolish for taking the part he did as he would lose his property as the Radicals had got the better and that he would be liable to be popped off at any time [–] deponent understood him to mean that he would be liable to be shot at any time –

D 94   WILLIAM DUNLOP[221] TO THE ATTORNEY GENERAL[222]
Goderich, 23 December 1837
[PAO, Rebellion Papers, 1837–8, no. 20]

. . . Mr Lizars[223] supported by a party of his Co: [Company] is busily

[220]Cyrus Sumner was a young man and a resident of Westminster Township.

[221]William "Tiger" Dunlop (1792–1848) was born at Greenock, Scotland. He became an assisant surgeon with the 89th Regiment of the British army and served in British North America in the War of 1812. He then saw service in India, returning to Britain on half-pay before coming to Upper Canada with John Galt in 1826. He gained employment with the Canada Company and settled in Goderich. A notable literary figure, he sat in the Assembly for Huron County from 1841 to 1846.

[222]The attorney general was Christopher Hagerman.

[223]Daniel Lizars, an Edinburgh engraver and publisher, followed his brother to Upper Canada in 1833, bringing his own family with him. He settled in Goderich and,

employed in investigating how far the treason of Van E.[224] may have spread[;] from all accounts he has made few converts & these of the most unimportant classes – . . .

appointed a magistrate in 1835, became a fast friend of William Dunlop and a leading member of the Colborne Clique. Members of that clique argued that the Canada Company had not lived up to its obligations to its settlers. In 1841 he was appointed clerk of the peace of the Huron District.

[224]Dunlop had seized Anthony Van Egmond's papers.

E.   AFTERMATH

E 1   PRISONERS TO BE DETAINED
Government House, 10 December 1837
[Upper Canada Gazette, *Toronto, 14 Dec. 1837*]

HIS EXCELLENCY the LIEUTENANT GOVERNOR directs, that no Officer, whatever may be his rank, or on whatever service he may be employed, shall take upon himself to release any Prisoner taken in arms against the Government, or any one apprehended on suspicion of Treasonable practices; but all such persons are to await the decision of the Government, upon a careful investigation of the charges against them.

E 2   E.G. O'BRIEN TO JOHN JOSEPH
Lloydtown, 10 December 1837
[*PAC, Correspondence of the Provincial Secretary's Office, v. 9, file 1166*]

I beg leave to state for the Information of His Excellency that early this morning I came to this place; and on my way hither from the West Gwillimbury causeway as well as here found every thing perfectly quiet, but the families of all in a terrible state of alarm and agitation – I assured them all of protection, and as I came along visited several houses where one or more members of the family were absent, hiding from Justice, to assure the women that excepting the ringleaders and those guilty of murder and arson there would be no lives taken, but that tho punishment must necessarily follow such crime, yet all those who voluntarily gave themselves up, together with any arms or ammunition they might have, would be considered as much less guilty – that all who came into me should be allowed, on proper security for their appearance being given, to return quietly to their own homes; messengers were immediately dispatched after Several; and I am most happy to find by His Excellency's Proclamation I have been acting according to his wishes: The comfort it gave to the unfortunate women in the utmost wretchedness and distress was very great. I have already released 4 or five on such conditions, and shall give every facility to persons to take advantage of the proclamation.

Mr. Lally with his party of the 1st Simcoe Militia (45 men) came in here from Younge Street at noon, and will remain here untill instructions are sent to dismiss them: the country is now perfectly quiet, and I have no doubt but that special constables can now do all the necessary duty. Mr. Lally being a magistrate will remain here with me; and we beg to be informed how those who come in, or are arrested, or have gone to their own homes (having been known to have been [in] arms) are to be disposed of, – whether bound over to the "Peace & Good behaviour"; to appear at Qr. [Quarter] Sessions for rioting, or at the Assizes? May I further request to be informed what is to be done with arms seized, found or delivered up? There is also a horse taken from a Prisoner who acknowledged having been in the fight on Thursday, but says that he seized the horse at Montgomery's to escape on, does not know whose it is, but that it belonged to one of the party – Thanking God for the Speedy and complete termination of this wretched business. . . .

E 3   JOHN JOSEPH TO E.G. O'BRIEN
Government House, 11 December 1837
[*PAC, Correspondence of the Provincial Secretary's Office, v. 9, file 1166*]

His Excellency has perused Your Letter addressed to me, from Lloyds Town, 10th Decr. 1837. and highly approves of the zeal and activity which you have shewn in proceeding with a party to Lloyd Town, to protect the public Peace. and afford aid to the civil power.

In reference to the assurances which you appear to have held out respecting the treatment of Prisoners, who have been in open Rebellion against their Sovereign, or have adhered to those concerned in treasonable practices I am directed to enclose to you, a copy of a Proclamation which His Excellency has issued on the subject, and further to explain to you, that the General Proclamation first issued to which you refer. was published, in the hope that it might lead, the band of armed Rebels, and their Adherents to disperse and desist from their traitorous designs and not to use their arms in open resistance to their Government

Since His Excellency Signed that proclamation, an opportunity was afforded to those Rebels who assembled in arms, to abandon their treasonable design and submit themselves to the laws. but they unhappily failed to avail themselves of it by volunteering to surrender their Arms. and many have continued to the present time, without coming Forward and making that submission which their duty to their Government, to their fellow subjects and themselves required –

Under these Circumstances, His Excellency feels it to be due to the loyal Inhabitants of this Province, and to the Security of the Public peace, that the Case of every Individual. who may be apprehended or who shall deliver himself up to Justice shall be deliberately Investigated. by a Committee of Magistrates Appointed for that purpose and shall be disposed of as shall appear proper after a full Knowledge of his Character and Conduct.

You will therefore clearly understand that no Magistrate or public officer. or other person is Authorized to release any Prisoner or give him any assurance. that his Conduct will not be enquired into and himself detained until a proper Investigation shall have been made.

E 4   J.H.S. DRINKWATER[1] TO SIR F.B. HEAD
North Brook, Orillia, 16 December 1837
[*PAC, Correspondence of the Provincial Secretary's Office, v. 9, file 1214*]

. . . I do myself the honor of addressing Your Excellency in consequence of information I have just gained from Your Excellencys Proclamation issued on the 10th Inst. in which you have commanded that no Prisoners should be released by any Officer untill the[y] were properly examined.

I therefore beg leave to state to Your Excellency that I commanded the 5th Batt. Compy. of the 1st Regt. of Simcoe Militia; that I arrived at the Holland Landing on Sunday morning the 10th Inst. and finding that none of the Militia had taken possession of Davids. Town. I immediately marched my men of on and possession [*sic*] of the Place (and here I beg leave to remark I did so without the slightest opposition on the part of the Inhabitants) A short time afterwards I was told by an Officer of the advance Guard of a Troop. from Toronto/commanded by Captn. Duggan that I might liberate the Prisoners I had made. I refused to do so but when Captn. Duggan arrived and informed me he had instructions to liberate any Prisoners, I delivered them up to him in presence of my company, he then released them all and thanked me for my services. He also said I had done perfectly right in not releasing the Prisoners untill his arrival

I therefore hope that Your Excellency will not think that I have intentionaly acted contrary to Your commands and I beg to assure Your Excellency that I shall ever be ready to come forward in support of Our Queen's Government and the wishes of Your Excellency. . . .

E 5   SPECIAL COMMISSION ESTABLISHED AT TORONTO
Government House, 11 December 1837
[*PAC, Upper Canada Sundries, v. 180, pp. 99090-3*]

Upper Canada

Victoria, by the Grace of God, of the United Kingdom of Great Britain and Ireland, Queen, Defender of the Faith &c. &c. &c.

To the Honourable Robert Sympson Jameson, our Vice-Chancellor,

---

[1]J.H.S. Drinkwater came to lot 1, concession 3 of North Orillia Township in 1832, thus being one of the earliest settlers in the area. He was captain of the 5th Battalion Company, 1st Regiment Simcoe militia in December 1837.

the Honourable Robert Baldwin Sullivan, the Honourable William Allan, members of our Executive Council, and to Alexander Wood,[2] and John Godfrey Spragge,[3] Esquires, Greeting.

Whereas, divers evil minded persons, forgetting their allegiance to their Sovereign, have lately appeared in arms against our royal authority, with the treasonable design of subverting the constitution of this Province, as by law established, and Whereas it is necessary to enquire into the origin and design of the conspiracy that has just resulted in open Rebellion, and to examine all such persons as may be arrested upon the charge of being concerned therein, that they may be brought to justice, and peace and security be established throughout our Province. NOW KNOW YE, the said Robert Sympson Jameson, Robert Baldwin Sullivan, William Allan, Alexander Wood, and John Godfrey Spragge, that reposing full confidence in your Loyalty, Skill and Integrity, we have appointed you, or any two of you, our Justices to enquire into, and take evidence upon such charges of Treason, Felony, or Sedition, as may be brought before you, against any person or persons whatever, within our said Province, and to do all such matters and things in the Premises as to you, or any two of you, may seem meet, in as full and ample a manner as might or could be done, by any of our Justices of the Peace, in our said Province, And we do hereby charge and command our Sheriffs, Constables, and other Peace Officers, as well as all our Loving Subjects throughout the several Districts of Our said Province, to be obedient unto you in the lawful exercise of the Powers herein given you and for that purpose to execute all warrants, that shall or may be issued by you, or any two of You, and generally, to be aiding and assisting you, the said Robert Sympson Jameson, Robert Baldwin Sullivan, William Allan, Alexander Wood and John Godfrey Spragge, in the execution of the duties hereby assigned to you, and each, and every of you. In Testimony whereof, we have caused these our letters to be made Patent, and the Great Seal of our said Province to be hereunto affixed, Witness our Trusty and

[2]Alexander Wood (1772?–1844) came to Kingston, Upper Canada from his native Aberdeen, Scotland, about 1793 and became a partner in a brewing concern. In 1797 he moved to York, opening a store in partnership with William Allan. After 1801 Wood was on his own and was very successful. He had retired from business by 1821, occupying himself with his duties as a magistrate and with various philanthropic activities. Three times after 1793 he returned to live in Scotland for extended periods, including the last two years of his life.

[3]John Godfrey Spragge (1806–1884) was born near London, England, coming to Upper Canada in 1820 with his father, who became master of the Upper Canada Central School. The younger Spragge articled with James Buchanan Macaulay and then with Robert Baldwin before being called to the bar in 1828. In 1838 he formed a partnership with John Hillyard Cameron, but much of his time was spent on the bench. He was surrogate judge of the Home District, 1836–41, master of Chancery, 1837–44, registrar of Chancery, 1844–50, vice-chancellor, 1850–69, chancellor, 1869–81, and chief justice of the Court of Appeal and chief justice of Ontario from 1881 until his death.

well beloved, Sir Francis Bond Head, Bart. K.C.H. &c. &c. &c. &c. Lieutenant Governor of our said Province, this eleventh day of December in the year of our Lord one thousand eight hundred and thirty seven and in the first year of our Reign

(Signed)
F.B. H.

E 6   MILITIA GENERAL ORDER
Toronto, 14 December 1837
[Recorder, *Brockville, 28 Dec. 1837*]

GENERAL ORDER

It is His Excellency the Lieutenant Governor's desire, that no further arrests shall be made by Officers of the Militia on duty, except in the case of notorious offenders.

The arms of the disaffected are, however to be secured as heretofore; and all officers will continue to act under the directions of the Civil Magistrates for arresting and securing those for whom warrants shall be issued.

By Command,
(Signed)   JONAS JONES,
                                                     A.D.C.

E 7   ALEXANDER CLUNAS[4] TO W.L. MACKENZIE
Caledon, 26 May 1840
[*PAO, Mackenzie–Lindsey Papers, Mackenzie Correspondence*]

. . . after the defeat on Yonge Street, as you may know Toronto Public Buildings were all crowded to excess with Your Followers and whoever the Loyal Worthies took for such[;] amongst the rest there was a goodly number of my neighbours thrust into the Market Buildings and on the night of Wednesday 13th Or Thursday 14 Decr. 1837 The Worshipful George [Gurnett] addressed himself to ninety two Prisoners (my neighbours included) calling upon any that chose to state what they had to say in their own defence[;] about the number of Thirty spoke, one after another, all protesting they knew of nothing that warranted their being Confined[,] when the Loyal Man that at One

[4]Alexander Clunas bought in 1825 lot 5, concession 2 west of Hurontario Street, 200 acres, in Caledon Township as well as the east half of lot 6. He was active in the political union movement prior to the rebellion. Among those rounded up after the rebellion was put down, Clunas was in custody by 13 December, but was not officially arrested until 5 January 1838. He was discharged by the investigating commission two days later. There is no evidence to link him to the rising.

time was "Casting about in his minds eye for a new state of Political existence" made for answer to one and all them, (upon each of them admiting they were reformers) what reform would you want[;] you need none. If you were tied to a Cows tail and dragged about or if you were sent to Botany Bay and Lashed about like the slaves there you would need some reform but here you need none[;] you are too well already. – . . .

E 8   PETITION OF VARIOUS NORWICH INHABITANTS
[Patriot, *Toronto, 22 Dec. 1837*]

To Allan Napier MacNab, Esq., Colonel Commanding the Queen's Forces in the District of London, &c. &c. &c.

The humble petition of certain inhabitants of the Township of Norwich, lately in arms against the Government of this Province.

SHEWETH – That we your petitioners being truly sensible of the great error and wickedness which we have lately committed in taking up arms against Her Majesty's Government, a Government on whose part we do not pretend to say that we have any real wrongs or grievances to complain of, but we have been led away by Charles Duncombe, Eliakim Malcolm, and other wicked and designing leaders, who have induced us by promise of large grants of land and great pay for our services, to take up arms against Her Majesty's Government, and who have now basely deserted us and left us to answer with our lives and properties for those crimes which they have themselves committed, do therefore most humbly beseech you, Sir, to take our case into your kind consideration, and to intercede with His Excellency the Lieutenant Governor of this Province, to grant us a pardon for our offences.

We acknowledge ourselves to be completely subdued, and we throw ourselves entirely upon your mercy; and we hereby promise, one and all, if such mercy be extended to us, that we will from henceforth live as peaceable and loyal subjects to the Government of Her Majesty Queen Victoria; and that we will not only bring in our arms, but also use our utmost endeavours to apprehend the ringleaders of the late insurrection and bring them to justice.

We are thus induced to address you, Sir, not only from the exalted position which you hold as the first Commoner in the land, and Commander of the Queen's Forces in this part of the Province, but also from our knowledge of your kind and benevolent disposition, of which we have had ample proof in the protection of the lives and properties of the inhabitants, since your arrival amongst us, and which we trust you will exert in our behalf to relieve us from our present unfortunate situation; and we, your petitioners, as in duty bound, will ever pray, &c.

Signed by one hundred and three petitioners.

E 9   JOHN JOSEPH TO ALLAN MACNAB
Government House, 18 December 1837
[Patriot, *Toronto, 22 Dec. 1837*]

. . . His Excellency desires that you will answer the Petitioners by stating, that he sincerely regrets that any number of Her Majesty's subjects in this Province should have been prevailed upon to commit Treason against a Government which had always protected them, and treated them with justice and kindness, – that, trusting to the truth of the declaration by the Petitioners, that they have seen their error, and not doubting but they must be ashamed and astonished at their own misconduct, His Excellency consents to your liberating such of them as are not known to have committed acts of violence against the persons or property of their fellow-subjects, upon their entering into recognizances, with sufficient sureties, to appear at the next Court of Oyer and Terminer and General Gaol Delivery, in the District of London, to answer any complaint that may be brought against them at the instance of any of their fellow-subjects.

E 10   ESTABLISHMENT OF THE LONDON DISTRICT COMMISSION
Toronto, 8 December 1837[5]
[*PAC, Records of the London District Magistrates, v. I*]

(Signed)

F.B. Head.

His Excellency the Lieutenant Governor is pleased to direct that John B. Askin Esquire do institute examinations against any person in the London district suspected of treasonable or seditious practices and to cause any such persons to be arrested and their papers to be seized and examined and to transmit such of their papers as may be thought necessary to his Excellency[.]

In Council

E 11   J.B. ASKIN TO JOHN JOSEPH
London, 22 December 1837
[*PAC, Upper Canada Sundries, v. 180, pp. 99759-61*]

I have the honor to inform you, that immediately on my return to this place (from Scotland in the Township of oakland) yesterday, having received a Copy of the order of the Honorable the Executive Council of

---

[5]After the agitation of the fall of 1837 in the west and the breaking out of the Home District rising, the authorities at Toronto, as soon as 8 December, expected difficulties in the London District. Consequently, they established a commission of inquiry there, which served the local authorities well after the flight of the Duncombe rebels on 13 December. The commissions established at Toronto and London were the only two in the province.

this Province, of the 8th Instant I formed a com[mission] of Examination in pursuance thereof, and have taken Laurence Laurison, Thomas H. Ball, William Robertson and Thomas Radcliff[6] Esquires magistrates to aid and assist; there being a very large number of persons to Examine independent of information &c[.] I have taken the liberty to Employ James Givens[7] and John Stewart[8] Esqrs. Barristers with Mr Muttleberry[9] as Clerk, in order that all the proceedings may be carefully arranged and submitted to the crown officer[.] This you will please submit for the approval of His Excellency the Lieutenant Governor.

E 12   J.B. ASKIN TO JOHN JOSEPH
London, 22 December 1837
[C.R. Sanderson, ed., The Arthur Papers . . . I (Toronto, 1957), p. 34]

I have the honor to enclose you a Return of the Prisoners now in Gaol at London, some of whom are fully committed, and others in progress of Examination under charges of High Treason, Sedition and Treasonable practices; and to inform you that Col Radcliff with a detachment of 200 officers and men are doing duty – Guarding the Gaol, under the orders of Col McNabb. . . .

P.S. I beg to add, amongst those committed a number will be found, to have been induced under most plausable, insiduous, and false representations to take up Arms, and who, since appear most repentant and sorry; and some few of less than 21 years of age, who I think have been completely beguiled into Error, – under such circumstances I would beg that His Excellency would be pleased to permit the Magistrates who act with me, to use such discretion as the particular circumstances of cases of the sort, which I represent may admit, and to allow such as are not most implicated to be allowed admitted to Bail

---

[6]Thomas Radcliff (1794–1841) was born in Castle Coote, County Roscommon, Ireland, the eldest son of a Church of Ireland priest. He enlisted in the British army, served in the Peninsular war, and retired on half-pay in 1816. In 1832 he brought his family to Adelaide Township in Upper Canada. He was appointed a magistrate in 1833 and a colonel in the militia in 1837. In January 1838 he commanded on the Detroit frontier and in November 1838 was commissioned lieutenant-colonel of the 11th Provisional Battalion of militia. In 1839 he was appointed a legislative councillor.

[7]James Givens, a lawyer, lived in St. Thomas before moving to London, where he acted for the Bank of Upper Canada. In 1841 he was elected president of the London Board of Police, and in 1847 was appointed judge of the London District Court.

[8]John Stewart was a law student of John Wilson. In 1841 he divorced his wife, a granddaughter of William Dummer Powell, for adultery, thus securing perhaps the first divorce in the province. He later settled in Goderich.

[9]Rutherford Muttleberry boarded in London in the same house with Charles Latimer, who was suspected of treason in December 1837. Muttleberry, a tory, had attended the Westminster meeting of 6 October 1837 and in December was active with the authorities in ferreting out suspected traitors.

for their Appearance to Answer at the next Court of Oyer and Terminer and General Gaol Delivery, such Charges as may be alledged against them[.]

E 13   THE LONDON COMMISSION QUESTIONS RECALCITRANT
WITNESSES
[*PAC, Records of the London District Magistrates, v. I, pp. 29, 30, 46, 49, 107, 108, 111, 119*]

Decr. 29th 1837. –

The Commissioners met – Present
John B Askin Esquire
Laurence Laurason Esq –
Harry Cook[10] Esq –
Thomas Radcliff Esq –
William Robertson Esq
Thos Ball Esq. . . .

It was put to the Magistrates whether *Moore Stevens*[11] should be discharged on Bail –
It was decided that he should be –
Upon his appearance and the promise read to him that hereafter he should behave himself as a loyal and faithful subject of our sovereign Lady the Queen and the Government of Great Britain – He replied he would as long as he remained in the province that he intended to live in the United States and might probably become a subject in which case he would not deprive himself of the opportunity to take up arms against Gt. Britain if the United States should be at war with her – It was therefore decided that he should not be admitted to Bail.
Prisoner was therefore remanded. . . .

Thursday 4th January 1838

The Commissioners met – Present
Laurence Lawrason Esq
Harry Cook Esq – . . .

Uriah Emmons[12] brought up – admits that he took up arms in order to get men out of Gaol at Hamilton – Would not undertake the pledge

[10]Harry Cook was appointed a magistrate in 1835. In 1837 he farmed on 217 patented acres in Caradoc Township.
[11]Moore Stevens, who had been born in Dublin, Ireland, and his brother ran a store in Delaware. Jailed for treason on 19 December 1837, he was freed on bail on 16 January 1838. He was then recommitted and tried in the spring but acquitted.
[12]Uriah Emmons, who had been born in the London District, lived in Norwich with his mother and worked as a labourer. He was jailed on 21 December 1837 and petitioned under 1 Victoria, c. 10 and ordered banished for life on 13 August 1838.

offered by the Magistrates to be a Loyal and faithful subject to the Queen so was remanded to Gaol – . . .

January 25th 1838 –

the Commissioners met – Present
Laurence Laurason Esq
Harry Cook Esq

Charles Latimer called up states that he does not choose to give any evidence concerning a meeting at Flanagans Tavern in London on 8th December 1837 –
Upon the Information of E.A. Talbot[13] being read to him he declined at present asking the witness any questions – . . .
The Prisoner upon being asked why he did not apply to the Magistrates for protection at the time the Meeting was formed at Flanagan's – He said they were the very people from whom he expected an attack – The Prisoner being asked what he had to say in answer to the charges alledged against him said "That he did not see proper to reply at present that he was sorry he had not done more for the cause of Reform than he had" –
He was fully committed. . . .

January 26th 1838 –

Harry Cook Esq –
Laurence Laurason Esq – . . .

Charles Laurence[14] Is still a Reformer and does not regret going to Oakland says that if the party had been attacked he would have fired and fought – He would have done any thing his Commander had told him – If Dr. Duncombe had told him with others to go to take Simcoe if they had been resisted in any way he would have fired – He was finally committed – . . .

E 14   J.B. ASKIN TO JAMES HAMILTON
London, 30 December 1837
[*MTPL, James Hamilton Papers*]

. . . here we are going on as usual Examining the Vagabonds and discharging all we can on Bail calling the least offensive, & most

[13]For Talbot's information, see D 78.
[14]Charles Lawrence (Laurence) (b. *ca.* 1820), a native of Hampshire, England, lived in Yarmouth, where he worked as a labourer. He was jailed on 19 December, and, after petitioning under 1 Victoria, c. 10, was released on bail on 11 June 1838. He later married and ran a sawmill in Yarmouth. *The Rising in Western Upper Canada* (p. 113), in referring to Laurence and his testimony here, incorrectly identifies him as Charles Scrivener, noting that hereafter "Scrivener" disappeared from the historian's view.

penitent for that purpose, not many new arrest[s] and those made are all admitted to Bail, Col Radcliff & the Light Infy. are as yet on duty, Guarding the Gaol, the town beging [beginning] to assume the appe [appearance] of a garrison town, sentry Boxex [sic] are shuth [sic] up in all directions – . . .

E 15   MEDICAL REPORT ON GORE DISTRICT PRISONERS[15]
31 December 1837
[HPL, Land Papers, Robert Land Papers, pp. 3067-70]

I find the prisoners generally in a tolerably good state of health – but all complaining more or less of the effects of the close and crowded state in which they are at present. 1st I would therefore most urgently recommend that the prisoners be separated as much as possible, and that *one* or Two efficient persons at least, be appointed to assist the gaoler in keeping the apartments clean – &ct.
2nd That the provisions of the prisoners be removed from the tainted air in which they are now kept, to some place of security where the prisoners might be certain that they would not be interfered with. –
3d. I consider also that it would be highly conducive to the maintaining the health of the prisoners that all the cooking required for them, be performed in the kitchen of the Gaol.
4th If considered consistent with security I would recommend that parties of 4 or 5 prisoners at a time be allowed to take exercise in the hall, of course under proper guard –
5th That the prisoners be allowed to have access to the yard for the calls of nature, as nothing vitiates the air so much as having any collection of filth in confined apartments
6th As several of the prisoners are totally without money or provisions, they have hitherto been compelled to subsist on bread and water alone, – now setting aside the claims of humanity I consider such a sudden alteration in diet to be highly injurious to the health, and might lead to the development of serious disease among the prisoners – I would therefore recommend that rations be provided to such as cannot afford to purchase provisions for themselves.
7th That as some of the prisoners are totally without any change of clothing the filth caused by wearing the same linen for weeks must evidently be a fruitful source of disease – I would therefore recommend that if possible some shirts should be supplied to them –
8th That the bed clothes of the prisoners be aired in the yard for several hours every day that the weather will permit

[15]Because so many prisoners were taken up at Toronto, Hamilton, and London after the rebellions, the jails in those centres quickly became overcrowded. This document is the only contemporary one extant detailing prisoner conditions in any of the three centres. The picture it presents suggests that conditions were at their worst in Hamilton.

Should the above recommendations be carried into effect I consider that it would be possible to keep the prisoners in good health for a considerable time notwithstanding the situation in which they are placed.

Duncan Campbell[16] M.D.
Physician to State Prisoners

E 16   WILLIAM CHISHOLM TO CHRISTOPHER HAGERMAN
Oakville, 11 December 1837
[*PAC, Upper Canada Sundries, v. 180, pp. 99097A-C*]

Mr Dear Hagarman

I have this moment learnt that Mr. A. Lewis[17] of Cooksville was taken Prisoner by one of the Mr. McGraws [Magraths],[18] and sent to Toronto. It is my opinion, not only imprudent, but unjust of Mr. McGraw, and only done to Gratify his own mallice. Capt. Chalmers[19] and mySelf had the Advance on our way up on Friday, and called on Mr. Lewis who was ready and willing to Join us, which he did and accompanied us as far as Springfield. I have known Mr Lewis since he first Came in the Province and I know him to be an honest worthy and Good man, and owns a large property. and if it was required Captain Chalmers and my Self would be his Security for Five Thousand Pounds, And I assure you from what I know of Mr. Lewis I would depend much more on him than on those who arrested him at this time. it is not the wise course to annoy and irritate the peaceble People[.] The example is set by our worthy Governor and if Mr McGraws go on as they have with Mr Lewis, they will do more harm than they ever will do good, with all there boast of Bravery. I trust that Mr. Lewis may be sent amediately home to this family. Mr McGraw well knew that Mrs Lewis was very ill expecting every moment to be confined[.] She has not been able to leave her room for many days. The County of Halton is now all alive to catch Mr. McKenzie[,] he is now in or about this

---

[16]Duncan Campbell (1811–1879) was born in Edinburgh, Scotland, and secured his degree from the University of Edinburgh in 1833. The following year he emigrated to Upper Canada. During the rebellion, then a Hamilton resident, he served as surgeon to a militia regiment. Shortly after the rebellion he moved to Niagara, and in 1858 he and his large family settled in Toronto.

[17]A. Lewis was a merchant of American origin.

[18]The Magrath involved was either James or Charles (b. *ca*. 1807), the sons of the Rev. James Magrath of Erindale, Toronto Township, who had come out from Ireland in 1827. Charles, like James, was a merchant and an Orangeman.

[19]"Capt. Chalmers" was either James or Joseph Chambers. James owned lot 14, concession 6 east, new survey, of Toronto Township, patented 1834, and Joseph owned 100 acres of lot 14, concession 5 east, patented 1834. In 1834 Joseph Chambers was master of No. 5 Orange Lodge and county grand treasurer; James was county master. In 1840 Joseph was on the grand committee for British North America and James was grand master of York County.

Township[,] there is not less than 2 to 300 men now on parties both night and day hunting him and searching every Suspicious House. he was so very near being caught that he left his waggon and horses which we now have here, they are said to be Wm J Comforts[20] of the township of Toronto. What shall we do with them[?]

E 17   DIARY OF JOSEPH RICHARD THOMPSON[21]
[C.P. Stacey, ed., "The Crisis of 1837 in a Back Township of Upper Canada . . .," Canadian Historical Review, XI (1930), pp. 228-31]

11. [December] This morning a public Meeting[22] was held at which fresh signatures were affixed to the Enrolment List & the Regulations of the Society agreed to. Two additional Committee men were appointed for the front of Brock and for Mariposa.
12. It is reported that several persons from this neighbourhood have been killed in the tumults of the week – P. Shell[23] – a son of F. Maybe[24] &c
13. While winnowing here this morning K. McCaskill[25] & I. McKay came & informed me that they brought unpleasant news – that a mob of orangemen were going about threatening to burn down the houses of such persons as they chose to visit – carrying away fire arms &c

Mr. McKay stated they have been to his house & ransacked every thing and refused to shew any authority for what they did.

From these representations we concluded that they must be acting illegally and that the Society for protecting property &c ought to be forthwith summoned. Accordingly K. McCaskill undertook to give notice to the members in his neighbourhood & McKay was to send a special messenger to the members on the front concessions.

[20]William J. Comfort was a farmer who owned 100 acres of lot 1, concession 4, new survey, of Toronto Township, purchased in 1828. A reformer who knew nothing of the rebellion, he agreed to assist the fleeing William Lyon Mackenzie to reach the United States, by loaning his waggon and team. Arrested for this, he was held until April 1838 when he was discharged by the investigating commission. While in gaol his wife was terrorized by a "loyalist" gang and died in premature childbirth. In 1842 Comfort sold his farm and settled near London, Canada West, where he became a partner in a mill.
[21]Joseph Richard Thompson (1803–1855) was born in Salisbury, Wiltshire, England, the son of a major. He trained at the bar before emigrating to Brock Township in 1835. He lived on lot 18, concession 10.
[22]This public meeting was held to create an organization to protect the local inhabitants from perceived dangers. In various places about the province such organizations sprang up. Some were anti-rebel, others anti-loyalist, and others, like the one discussed in this document, were strictly neutral.
[23]Peter Shell lived in Markham but obviously had connections with Brock Township, since the Brock party going to Montgomery's Tavern spent one night at his house. He was active in the political union movement prior to the rising. He may have been a member of the Schell family which came to Vaughan Township from New York State around 1805.
[24]The "son of F. Maybe" was probably John Maby, who went to Montgomery's Tavern in December 1837.

Having subsequently heard that the party were at G. Maybe's[26] we proceeded in that direction, and met G. Maybe in person followed by Thos. Jackson[27] armed with an old sword – on enquiry it was stated by the latter that warrants had been issued by the Magistrates here for arresting certain persons accused of having been engaged in the recent disturbances and that these warrants were in the hands of certain headmen who were dispersed for the purpose of executing them. G. Maybe was safely lodged in Cowan's.[28] M. Cowan promised to send us a copy of the warrant which however he neglected to do.

The same morning a woman named Harris called at our house to state that the preceding night a mob had surrounded her house & taken her husband[29] forcibly from his bed.

After dinner the following procession marched past our house – first came Harris with his arms bound behind him, then Ferguson[30] with a gun – next an ox sleigh with a lame man on it – behind it Low[31] of Mariposa – next came several persons armed as a Guard & last of all on horseback the aforesaid T. Jackson on horseback with his sword.

The Jacksons stated to me that the prisoners were to be taken to Toronto.

In the course of the afternoon two of the McKaskills & two other persons came to attend the meeting which had been summoned, to whom I explained that the arrests & search appeared to me from what had been stated to me to have been made under legal authority.

K. McKaskill informed me that he was now of the same opinion, though he had at first thought that they were the mere outrages of an orange mob, which ought to be suppressed. It was wrong of the

---

[25]Kenneth McCaskill may have lived on the same lot, lot 20, concession 11, of Brock Township as William McCaskill, who was presumably his brother.

[26]Godrey Maybe bought lot 19, concession 11 of Brock Township in 1846, a lot which he had lived on for some years. He was active in the political union movement prior to the rebellion.

[27]Thomas Jackson Sr. lived on lot 9, concession 11 of Brock Township.

[28]Matthew Cowan came to Brock Township with his family in the 1820s or 1830s from Tipperary, Ireland, where he had been a lieutenant in the yeomanry. He settled on lot 18, concession 11 but did not own it. A devoted Orangeman, he served as a member of the grand committee of the Order in British North America in 1840. He was a magistrate and a member of the Church of England, retaining his magisterial post for thirty years until his death at the age of 89.

[29]This was probably James Harris, who lived on lot 12, concession 12 of Brock Township.

[30]Edward Ferguson lived on lot 21, concession 11 of Brock Township.

[31]Charles Low was born in Lower Canada of loyalist parents. His father commanded the gun boats on Lake Champlain during the War of 1812, and Charles was an ensign. He came to Upper Canada in 1832 with very good references. Active in the political union movement prior to the rebellion, he was elected captain of the Brock company that went to Montgomery's Tavern. He, however, took little part in the events at Toronto. Arrested in mid-December, he was originally sentenced to fourteen years' transportation but in July 1838 was pardoned.

constables to refuse to shew their warrant. He had requested Ferguson to shew it to him, which the latter had refused to do & at the same time threatened to go down to the mill and seize all arms found there which he said he had a right to do. K. McCaskill told him if he did come for any such purpose without producing his authority he had better bring his coffin along with him.

These members then returned to their homes. . . .

14. This day we resumed our regular occupations hoping that all annoyances were at an end – no such thing – Wm. Cowan[32] – John Brandon[33] & M. Gaunt came over brimful of loyal zeal – their fine sense of honor was hurt at having their names signed on the same paper with McKay whom they stated to be a rebel, and M. Gaunt wished to have his erased. He was accordingly allowed to erase it.

The same day Wm. Brandon[34] & Ward came under some excitement, for the same purpose but were requested to make their statement to the Committee which would meet to-morrow.

15. No members of the Committee attended this day, though several Members of the Society were present & Mr. Bagshaw[35] brought over a Proclamation dated 7th inst. in which authentic information relative to the late rebellion was given. It was discussed whether any measures should be taken to express the opinion of the meeting as to the danger of allowing the prisoners sent to Toronto, to return to the Township. It was ultimately decided that a Meeting of Loyalists shd. be held at the School House on Saturday the 23d inst. to consider of this.

19. While busy chopping, Emily came out to inform us that McKay was arrested & at Cowan's – further that one of the McCaskills and some one else were copying some of the papers relating to the Society. Lavinia & Elizabeth afterwards came to us & requested that we would go in as three persons were waiting for us.

On reaching home we found McKay, one of the McKaskills & Hall[36] – McKay stated he would be liberated on giving Bail and requested me to become one of the Securities, Mr. McKaskill having consented to be the other. I refused of course, and I afterwards heard that Kenneth McKaskill had agreed to join with his brother for that purpose.

21. I walked over to Bagshaw's this morning according to promise,

[32]William Cowan probably lived with Matthew Cowan on lot 18, concession 11 of Brock Township and was almost certainly his son.

[33]John Brandon lived on lot 18, concession 13 of Brock Township.

[34]William Brandon lived on lot 18, concession 13 of Brock Township.

[35]William Bagshaw (1783–1861), though born in Alstonfield, Staffordshire, England, lived in various parts of the country before emigrating to Upper Canada in 1817. His wife and children followed him in 1819. The family settled in Brock Township on lot 5, concession 9 (Walton's 1837 directory says he was on lot 15), acquiring more property in Brock and Reach in later years. In 1833 he was appointed a magistrate and in 1836 was made the first postmaster of the township.

[36]David Hall lived on lot 21, concession 11 of Brock Township.

when he stated to me that on the 15th after the meeting, he had met Cowan, on his return, who told him that he had directions from the Lt. Governor to prevent any meetings.

He further promised to acquaint us & the other persons who had agreed to meet on the 23d therewith, & he (Bagshaw) was much surprised that he had not done so. . . .

During the week numerous parties of armed men have been observed passing our house & several more prisoners have been taken.

From this day to the 1st January nothing of moment has occurred, but having heard that Lieut. Johnson[37] had been arrested & sent to Toronto, I went over to his House on the 2d & found that he was taken into custody on 25th ulto. & had gone to Toronto where after having been questioned by the Special Commission and nothing appearing agst. him he had been discharged on his own Recognizance. He informed me that Captn. Baldwin one of the Commissioners[38] had told him "they have been making some very improper arrests."

E 18   FRANCIS LEYS[39] TO CHARLES BERCZY[40]
Pickering, 23 December 1837
[PAC, Upper Canada Sundries, v. 181, pp. 99840-2]

I have just this moment learned that Abraham Anderson[41] is made a prisoner by Charles Hadley[42] who is Ravaganing this and the adjoining Townships to a far greater extent than the Laws of the Country admits of – this man says he is Acting by orders of the Executive Council, he can show no written authority, he has now in Custody I am told upwards of Thirty persons, not 6 of which has done any further offence than signing some paper which they never Knew the contents – he is

[37]William Johnson (1784–1851), born in Berwick, Scotland, joined the navy as a midshipman in 1801, rising to the rank of lieutenant in 1810. Placed on half-pay in 1813, he emigrated to Georgina Township in 1819 and took up lot 6, concession 7. According to his diary, which is in the PAO, the crime for which he was taken into custody in 1837 seems to have been that he would not "levy war against reformers." He was thus a rare creature, a half-pay officer suspected of disloyalty or treason.

[38]There was no Captain Baldwin who was a commissioner. Possibly Johnson meant Robert Baldwin Sullivan.

[39]Francis Leys emigrated from Aberdeenshire, Scotland, to Upper Canada, where he obtained lot 12, concession 1 of Pickering Township. By the mid-1830s he was the most important man on the Front Road, being a magistrate, a commissioner of the Court of Requests, a major of militia, a deputy postmaster, and having several other appointments. He kept the only store in his part of Pickering. He also set up a school for the area which doubled as a church. In 1837 he was one of those tories who attended political union meetings to try to prevent the passing of disloyal sentiments.

[40]Charles Albert Berczy (1794–1858) was born in Newark, Upper Canada, the son of William von Moll Berczy. He served in the commissariat during the War of 1812 and in 1837 served as a confidential agent of F.B. Head. When James Scott Howard was dismissed as postmaster of Toronto in that year, Berczy was given the position.

[41]Abraham Anderson lived on lot 30, concession 6 of Uxbridge Township.

[42]Charles Hadley lived on lot 33, broken front, of Pickering Township.

doing more injury than even this present Rebellion has done – I see no use of sending men to Toronto to be immediatly discharged. when this will end I Know not if the thing is not put an End to – . . .

E 19 FRANCIS LEYS' WARRANT
Pickering, 15 December 1837
[PAC, Upper Canada Sundries, v. 181, p. 99843]

Home District   To Charles Hadley of the
                                                 Township of Pickering Consta-
                                                 ble – and to all other Peace
Pickering to Wit   officers in the Said District –

For as much as Landon Worts [Wurtz][,] George Barclay Jr[43][,] Joseph Wixon[44][,] Allan B Stevens[45][,] Falkener John Rammerfielt[46] and all others that has taken up arms against Her Majestys Government in the present Rebellion Yeomens and Labourors – hath this day been charged before me Francis Leys Esq. one of Her Majestys Justice of the Peace for the District aforesaid. . . . then are therefore in Her Majestys name to command you forth with to apprehend and bring before me or some other of her Majestys Justices of the Pease in and for the said District the Bodys of Landon Worts[,] George Barclay Jr[,] Joseph Wixon[,] Allan B Stevens[,] Falkener John Rummerfielt and all other that is known to have taken up arms. . . .

[43]George Barclay Jr. (b. 1800 or 1801) came from his native Scotland to Pickering with his family in 1816, where the family settled on part of one of the Matthews' farms. George Jr. bought several pieces of land in York Township, where he lived in 1837. His father, a Baptist minister, was an active radical reformer, and George Jr. followed his lead, participating in the rebellion. Arrested in December 1837, he petitioned for pardon and was sentenced to three years in prison and then banishment. In 1839, while in prison, he was pardoned.

[44]Joseph Wixon came to Pickering Township with his brother Joshua from Steuben County, New York, around 1800 and settled on concession 9. Between 1813 and 1819 Joseph acquired lot 17, concession 9, selling most of it by 1837. He was very active in the political union movement prior to the rebellion and went with Peter Matthews to Montgomery's Tavern. Although not arrested for his participation in the revolt, he was arrested for alleged Patriot activities in February 1838. The one witness against him was of dubious character and the grand jury ignored the indictment.

[45]"Allan B. Stevens" was Allen R. Stevens, who lived on lot 12, concession 9 of Pickering Township.

[46]"Falkener John Rammerfielt" was John Rummerfeldt, who was working in Uxbridge in 1837. His family had come to Pickering Township from the United States early in the nineteenth century. Arrested after the suppression of the rebellion, Rummerfeldt petitioned for pardon, having been with Matthews' party throughout the rising, and was sentenced to three years in prison, followed by banishment. In 1839, while in prison, he was pardoned.

E 20 _____ TO FRANCIS LEYS
n.p., n.d.
[PAC, Upper Canada Sundries, v. 181, p. 99844]

I am directed by the Commission of Inquiry to acknowledge the Rect. of your Letter of the 23rd Inst. addressed to Charles Berczy Esq. and to inform you that your communication has been submitted for the Consideration of His Ecy the Lt. Governor –

I am also instructed to Call your attention to the Proclamation of His Ecy in which it is expressly stated that no further arrests are to be made unless the parties have been leaders in the late rebellion, or against whom regular informations have been preferred and to Convey to you the opinion of the Commission that under warrants of so general a nature as the one addressed by you to Mr. Hadley it is scarcely possible to prevent the evils of which you complain. The Commission also desire me to add that General Warrants are illegal –

E 21 "P"[47] TO THE *Palladium*
Toronto, 26 December 1837
[Palladium, *Toronto, 3 Jan. 1838*]

. . . one half of the prisoners who have been taken into custody have been discharged as perfectly guiltless, and are men who alone owe to the petty spite of some of their officious neighbors, the misery of being dragged from their families, and being lodged in a crowded, and hence unwholesome jail for ten days or a fortnight, till they could be examined and discharged. This has been carried to a great extent, and men have actually been arrested, in one instance charged with having attended Mackenzie's meetings *five years ago*, in another with being *a bad man*, and in another with being *a very bad man*. Of course, the moment these parties were brought before the Magistrates here they were discharged, and I impute no blame to the Government for their apprehension, but I submit it would be well if His Excellency would issue a proclamation that should put a stop to this system of persecution, and direct that no parties shall henceforth be apprehended but upon the warrant of a Magistrate, and that if a Magistrate shall again be found from folly or from worse motives to resort to this system, his name shall be erased from the Commission. . . .

E 22 EXTRACT OF A LETTER FROM REV. ROBERT THORNTON[48]
Whitby, 28 April 1838
[United Secession Magazine, *VI (July 1838), pp. 381-2*]

. . . No sooner did the disturbance break out, than every man who had

[47]"P" was likely "Guy Pollock," the *nom de plume* of a regular contributor of letters to Toronto's reform newspapers.

[48]Robert H. Thornton (b. 1806) trained as a minister of the United Secession Church in Scotland, and came to Whitby, Upper Canada, in 1833. There he lived on lot 16, concession 2, serving a large area east, west, and north of Whitby.

either ground for a boast of loyalty, or who had dexterity enough speedily to assume the cloak, seemed to view with his neighbour in getting all who differed, dragged forward to examination or imprisonment. The name of reformer soon became synonymous in the vocabulary of such with that of rebel; and, in innumerable instances, the man of character and he who had none, the loyal and the disaffected, the constitutional reformer and the revolutionary firebrand, were dragged before the same magisterial court: . . . These things were done moreover, not by magistrates only, who had a right and a call to exercise authority, but oftener, by some officious partizan, some obsequious office-hunter, and not seldom some villain, for a piece of bread. . . .

My congregations, in this place [Whitby], were in tumult, and not a little said about many of the members who would doubtless have been greatly troubled, but for the prudent interference of magistrates, and other influential individuals, with unjust proceedings. I am glad to say, that I believe nothing but their general character saved many from party violence. But, alas! it was far otherwise in Pickering. That station I thought, for some weeks, would be scattered and dismembered, after all my labours. One of the elders, and seven members, were taken up at the first, all men of excellent character, and not rebels. This could not for a long time be distinctly traced home to the author, and, till that was done, everthing was at a stand; many believed the parties had been secretly guilty, and not a few tried to affix a blot upon the *whole body*, whose views, they say, are necessarily hostile to the Government. I spent several days every week among them, endeavouring to get at the truth, preventing further mischief, and, I am happy to say, was successful beyond my expectation. The real author of the charge, which caused the apprehension, I, after going to the authorities in Toronto, found to my regret, but as I had begun to suspect, to be *another elder*, who, to gratify a private grudge, and bring himself into notice with "the powers that be," acted a part, which he thought secrecy would prevent being charged to *him*. . . . Suffice it to say, that, without *any very material injury*, this station is again rallied, and nearly as it was. . . .

E 23   THOMAS LANGTON TO WILLIAM LANGTON
Fenelon Township, 23 December 1837
[*Anne Langton*, Langton Records: Journals and Letters from Canada, 1837–1846. . . (*Edinburgh, 1904*), *pp. 46-7*]

For another extract from this document see D 48.

. . . Our invitations had gone forth to twelve gentlemen to dine with us on Christmas day, when on the 19th a message was received from the Government by Wallis recommending the whole force of the townships of Fenelon and Verulam being called out to beset two roads into the Lower province – one about ten miles, the other about forty miles north of Fenelon Falls, by which it was thought Mackenzie might endeavour to escape. . . .

This put an end to our party, as we expected; but this morning intelligence was received that Mackenzie had succeeded in escaping into the States, so that there was an end to our soldiering for the present, and our party again revived with but short time for preparation.

E 24   EXAMINATION OF JOHN DENT[49] AND WILLIAM BARROW
7 March 1838
[PAC, Upper Canada Sundries, v. 187, pp. 104588-90]

. . . the said Dent declares that he heard William Barrow of Darlington, Shipwright say that David Gibson of the Home District a rebel leader was to have gone to the States in the Schooner Prosperity[,] Trull,[50] owner, had she not been detained by getting in the ice[,] the said Barrow being a seaman on board the said schooner – and further states that he understands the said Gibson went on board the schooner Industry, Sutherland, Master – . . .

William Barrow being examined states that the Schooner Prosperity in his last trip took over a number of passengers, among them some who came on board outside the bar – one of the passengers taken on board in the harbour was named Samuel Pegg[51] son of William Pegg[52] in North Gwillim [Gwillimbury] [–]

E 25   STEPHEN J. FULLER[53] TO R.B. SULLIVAN
Toronto, 7 April 1838
[PAC, Upper Canada State Papers, v. 31, pp. 10-19]

. . . After leaving Toronto in January I travelled west, and ascertained

[49]John Dent was a labourer who lived in Darlington Township.

[50]John Casey Trull was the son of one of the original three settlers in Darlington Township. His father settled there in 1794, having emigrated from the Isle of Wight, via New York. John Casey, known as Captain Trull, was the first white child born in Durham County. He was a lieutenant in the 1st Regiment of Durham militia in 1830, a captain in the 3rd battalion in 1846, and lieutenant-colonel of that battalion in 1856. In 1838 he served as a township commissioner.

[51]Samuel Pegg (b. 1785) was a native of Pennsylvania who came to Upper Canada with his father at some time prior to 1825. In 1836 he was naturalized. He lived on a rented lot, lot 6, concession 4 of East Gwillimbury Township, not North Gwillimbury, as indicated here. In 1825 he inherited lot 8, concession 4 of East Gwillimbury, probably from an uncle, and lot 1, concession 4 from his father in 1847.

[52]William Pegg lived on and owned lot 35, concession 4 of Whitchurch Township.

[53]Stephen John Fuller (*ca.* 1799–1856), a native of Kerry, Ireland, for several years captained a ship for the East India Company. He emigrated to Upper Canada in 1832. In 1838, engaged in "general business," he lived near Port Dover with his family. He died at Simcoe.

at Oakland that the uncaptured Malcolm [Eliakim] was still lurking in the vicinity of his own residence; and that he had in fact been seen in his own house the night before. He was not however a person of sufficient importance to induce me to delay there to look after him and I proceeded west. I may as well observe here that I have never seen, or heard any thing of said Malcolm, any where on the American side; and that I believe he is still in the Vicinity of Oakland.

From information received I felt it right to proceed to- Turkey Point and Long Point furnace where *Lount* had been for two days. At Turkey Point I got into the house where Dr. C. Duncombe had been concealed, but after a close search I found that he was gone and that I should lose time which might be better employed than hunting after him if I proceeded further. I therefore retraced my steps, and passing thro Dunville . . . got into the U.S. at Black Rock. . . .

E 26   M.S. BIDWELL TO ROBERT BALDWIN[54]
Toronto, 9 December 1837
[PAC, Correspondence of the Provincial Secretary's Office, v. 9, file 1212]

I am obliged to leave without having an opportunity to see you. I wish you to understand that I have been as ignorant of this lamentable affair as yourself was; but you will not require to be informed of considerations which oblige me without hesitation and even thankfully to comply with Sir Francis Head's request that I should expatriate myself. This is not a time when any body, however innocent, could successfully contend against the expressed wish of the Lieut. Governor. A flag was found at Mongomery's [*sic*] with the words "Bidwell and the glorious Minority 1837." This of course would be conclusive evidence of my guilt, with many. I should be arrested, and plenty would be found to furnish all necessary evidence to support the step thus taken by Government. But I need not go through the detail. The Victim would be offered up beyond a doubt.

I am obliged to leave without a moment's delay. My affairs of course will be in great confusion, and your assistance may be needed. . . .

I leave my Sister and Child here, and depend on a gracious Providence for their preservation and on the kindness of my friends for whatever Counsel Sympathy and assistance they may need.

E 27   PETITION OF JANNET MARSHAL TO SIR GEORGE ARTHUR
Chinguacousy, 3 July 1839
[PAC, Upper Canada State Papers, v. 52, pp. 259-61]

. . . Your Pettioner jannet Marshal, an Aged Widdow of the Township

---

[54]This letter was delivered by hand to Baldwin.

of Chinguacousy, had her house voilently entered into on the night of the 11th of Decr. 1837 by a party of Men some of them armed, and that after they had used a great deal of insulting language and plundered and destroyed a many things her property, they took away a valuable Gun beloning to her Son a youth of 18 years of age residing with her – And her son has repeatedly applied to the said parties to have it returned without effect [–] Your pettioner would therefore humbley pray Your Excellency to require the Magistrates of this Township to enable her to obtain justice, in either having the Gun restored or the value thereoff paid. . . .

E 28 JOHN SCOTT[55] TO S.B. HARRISON[56]
Chinguacousy, 23 July 1839
[PAC, Upper Canada State Papers, v. 52, pp. 262-3]

The widow Jennet Marshall and her sons being strangers to me, and living about ten miles off, I went to their place on monday in compliance with yours of 13th inst., and found, that a party of twenty one men from the neighbourhood of Norval, under one John McNabb as their leader, came to her house on the night of 11th Decr 1837 (as stated in her petition) and it appears behaved in a rude tumultuous manner towards the widow and her sons, taking with them a shot gun of considerable value, besides plundering the house of several articles, as a silver half dollar, some stockings, clasp knives, and other articles, at the same time making free with her provisions. – They gave me the names of eight of the party that were known to them, besides their leader, who, is now in United States prison under a ten years sentence, . . . I am not aware of what authority McNabb had for seizing arms, but have heard him and his party much complained off [*sic*], for their rude and unwarrantable conduct in many cases[,] with regard to the widow's sons, they are said to have been disaffected to the Govt. and supporters of McKenzie to the last altho they were not known to take any active part in the rebellion; this character may have been the cause of the rough treatment they met with, . . .

A great many guns were taken about the same time from persons in

---

[55]John Scott lived on lot 6, concession 1 east of Hurontario Street in Chinguacousy Township.

[56]Samuel Bealey Harrison (1802–1867) was born in Manchester, England. He was called to the bar in 1832, but ill health decided him to cut short his legal career and emigrate to Upper Canada. He settled near Bronte in 1837, operating mills and a farm. His legal and administrative talents, however, were not unnoticed and in 1839 he accepted the offer to become Arthur's civil secretary. That same year he was admitted to the Upper Canadian bar and the next made a magistrate. A moderate reformer, he became involved in politics, serving as virtual government leader in the Assembly of the united Canadas for much of the period 1841–4. In 1845 he left politics, becoming a judge of the Home District's, and later of York County's, Surrogate Court. In 1848 he was appointed a judge of the Home District Court. He remained on the bench until his death.

this township and Caledon known to be disaffected and many of them known to have been in arms. – and served out to Volunteers who took them to Chippewa and which are not now forthcoming, – . . .

E 29   JOHN M. SWEENEY[57] TO THE *Chronicle & Gazette*
Kingston, 22 December 1837
[Chronicle & Gazette, *Kingston, 23 Dec. 1837*]

Having arrived in Kingston on Thursday last, from Hartford, (Connecticut,) after an absence of six months, I find from the statements of my friends, that my unexpected appearance here has caused some sensation. This, doubtless, must have arisen from the agitated state of the public mind at present; aided, perhaps, by the exaggerated views which the fears of some of my acquaintances contributed to impart, to the simple statement I gave respecting the *Rebel* forces on the frontier.

I said that "the number of the so called "patriots" should not be underrated." My object was that the spirit of British loyalty should not be lulled into a fatal security; . . .

But the expression, that "the number of the "Patriots" should not be underrated," coupled with the intelligence I gave, that Messrs. Papineau and O'Callaghan[58] were within sixteen miles of the place wherein I was, on Thursday the 14th instant, gave serious alarm to some even of my warmest friends. . . .

E 30   NOTICE OF THE BANK OF THE PEOPLE
Toronto, 1 January 1838
[Christian Guardian, *Toronto, 3 Jan. 1838*]

Bank of the People.

FALSE REPORTS injurious to the credit of this Institution having been industriously circulated, and the Chartered Banks and the Post Office having thought proper to discontinue receiving their notes, the Directors feel it their duty to give Public Notice that they continue to redeem their Bills in Specie, as heretofore, and have no intention of

---

[57] John M. Sweeney was a deacon in the Catholic church.

[58] Edmund Bailey O'Callaghan (1797–1880) was born at Mallow, Ireland. He emigrated to Quebec City in 1823, where he completed his medical education, begun in Dublin and Paris. In 1827 he was licensed to practise medicine. From his arrival at Quebec, he worked to publicize the Irish question and to reconcile Irish and French Canadian Catholics and reformers. In 1833 he moved to Montreal to edit the radical *Vindicator*, and in 1834 was elected to the Assembly, where he quickly rose to prominence. In November 1837 his offices were sacked by a tory mob and he fled to the Richelieu area, which was soon in open revolt. He subsequently fled to the United States, never returning to Canada. In 1848 he became the archivist of New York State, a position he held for many years.

ceasing so to do.[59] They also think it right solemnly to declare, that the Bank of the People has had no connexion with the late rebellion in this Province, and that not a shilling of its funds has ever been applied to any illegal purpose.

By order of the Board
JAMES LESSLIE
President.
F. HINCKS, *Cashier.*

E 31   MILITIA GENERAL ORDER
Toronto, 23 December 1837
[Upper Canada Gazette, *Toronto, 28 Dec. 1837*]

Militia General Order

HIS EXCELLENCY the LIEUTENANT GOVERNOR has been pleased to authorize the formation of a City Guard, . . .

Two Companies to be embodied, each consisting of one Captain, one Lieutenant, one Ensign, three Sergeants, three Corporals, and fifty Privates, who will be supplied by Government with the pay, rations, and allowances of their respective ranks, with Arms to such of the men as may be unprovided therewith; any extra expenses are to be defrayed by the City, . . .

This Force is intended more immediately to aid the City Police, and will afford assistance at all times to the Mayor, upon his requisition. . . .

In addition to the above, it is to be distinctly understood, that these Companies shall at all times afford their assistance to the Government in any part of the City or its vicinity, that may (in case of necessity) be required. . . .

RICHARD BULLOCK,
Adjutant General.

E 32   MILITIA GENERAL ORDER
Toronto, 15 January 1838
[Upper Canada Gazette, *Toronto, 18 Jan. 1838*]

Militia General Order

The Commandant of the Militia Force in this City, will please to issue

[59]By the date of the document reproduced here, 1 January 1838, one of the chartered banks, the Commercial Bank of the Midland District, had taken advantage of the legislation allowing banks to discontinue payments in specie. The other two chartered banks, the Gore Bank and the Bank of Upper Canada, followed suit in March 1838. The three concerns did not resume specie payments until 1 November 1839 after several extensions of the deadline for resumption established by the suspension legislation of June 1837. The Bank of the People, which was not a chartered bank, could not have suspended payments in specie under the legislation passed in 1837.

proper instructions to all Guards and Military Posts of his superintendence, to prevent any undue annoyance or hindrance (after Tattoo beat,
and before Reveille,) being offered to peacable [sic] citizens, who are
mere passengers in the pursuit of their respective avocations. From
them, no Password, Parole or Countersign is to be on any account
required; and the only concern of the Sentries, as regarding them, is to
prevent, with due civility, their crowding upon their Posts, or
obstructing the passage. . . .

The Patroles [sic] will also be instructed not to interfere with
ordinary passengers, and not to impede any one unless strong
circumstances of suspicion should warrant the detention, in which case
they will civilly conduct the persons to the nearest Officer's Post. . . .

E 33   REPORT OF CAPTAIN W.B. VANEVY[60]
Hamilton, 12 January 1838
[HPL, Land Papers, Robert Land Papers, pp. 1887–8]

Report of Grand Rounds

1st   Visited the Castle Guard 11 1/4 P.M.[.] Guard turned out all in
perfect order. . . .
2nd   Visited Beasley Hollow[61] Guard 12 1/4[.] Guard turned out
disorderly, Sentinal quite drunk on his post. I consider the Guard a
nuisance to the public in the state I found them
3d   Visited Bank Guard 12 1/2[.] all in order. . . .
4th   Visited Mountain Guard 1 1/4 a.m.[.] all in perfect order. . . .
5th   Visited Main Guard 2 o.c. a.m. was not challenged by Sentinal.
passed on to the Goal [sic] door[.] called out officer of Guard. allowed
to pass without demanding countersign. could have taken complete
possission of the Goal with fifteen armed men without difficulty – I am
extremely sorry that an officer in charge of such an important Post as
the Main Guard Should be so very rimiss in the discharge of his duty –
6th   Visited Barrack Guard 2 1/4 a.m. Guard turned out in proper
order. nothing extra[.] dismissed escort 2 1/2 a.m.

E 34   JOHN BEVERLEY ROBINSON TO SIR JOHN COLBORNE
Toronto, 13 January 1838
[J.E. Colborne, Plymouth, England, PAC, Colborne Papers,
photostats, v. 13, pp. 003624-8]

. . . Intercepted letters from the interior of Michigan. to people about
Brantford & London confirmed expressly the accounts we hear otherwise

---

[60]W.B. Vanevy (Vanevry) was from a United Empire Loyalist family. A clerk of
the quarter sessions, he was appointed a magistrate for Hamilton in 1827 and
commissioned captain of the 3rd Gore Regiment of militia on 27 October of that year.

[61]Beasley Hollow was named after Richard Beasley, an early Hamilton settler and
merchant.

that a large force is forming there – to cross the river Sinclair [St. Clair] & come down upon London, to release the prisoners – kill & plunder the Tories, & do other pleasant things – I apprehend more danger from Ohio & Kentucky than any state that has yet taken the field if this state of things be not speedily checked by Congress – . . .

E 35   WILLIAM SALMON[62] TO GEOFFREY B. HALL
Simcoe, 17 January 1838
[Ipswich and East Suffolk Record Office, A.N. MacNab Papers, microfilm in PAO]

– By report we hear that Navy Island has surrendered[,] particulars not known, but 300 of the regulars are going past to the Westward which looks as if an attack was expected in that quarter, neither MacNab or any one else writes or sends one word to us and we are left entirely in the dark as to the movements on the frontier, and we are very fearful if the Rebels have left the Island it may be to land here where they would no doubt be joined by many and we have direct information that meetings are again taking place in Norwich and near Scotland to which place the Troop go to night to endeavur to seize some arms, we are very desirous that you should go with the Trooper who takes this to you to Chippawa and state fully our exposed situation to the Commanding officer, and particularly that Troops landed at Dover in the night might march to Hamilton before a force could be sent either from Chippawa or London (to which latter place the 24th are going) and overtake them, we have only 100 stand of arms in this District. (Talbot)[63] and very little ammunition, If they could be spared 150 Regulars ought to be stationed here – very suspicious meetings of some 5 or 6 of the disaffected are frequently held in this neighburhood, for no good purpose – about 600 of the Rebels took Possession of an Island opposite Sandwich & Bombarded the Town[,] our Troops made an attack upon them[,] killed 1 – wounded 8 – prisoners 12 – took 400 stand of arms & a quanty [quantity] of ammunition & a Schooner – a Steamer full of men was seen to go down the Detroit River into Lake Erie[,] they are as likely to land here as any where else[,] we want for both Rgts – 500 stand of arms & ammunition &c- – send the Trooper

[62]William Salmon (1802–1868) was a native of Alveston, England. He emigrated to Upper Canada and practised law in Simcoe. He ran unsuccessfully in Norfolk in the 1836 elections to the Assembly, but gained a seat on 27 February 1838 after Rolph had been expelled. In 1845 he was appointed a Talbot District Surrogate Court judge and a judge of the Talbot District Court. He died at Simcoe.

[63]Legislation passed in 1837–8 contemplated the creation of several new districts. The Talbot District (Norfolk County) was proclaimed on 30 December 1837 and was the only new district proclaimed that year.

back from Chippawa the moment you can with every information you can Collect –

Yrs in haste
Wm Salmon

P.S.

Wilson[64] goes to Hamilton & if necessary to Toronto for the same purpose[.]

E 36   DAY OF PUBLIC THANKSGIVING ORDERED
22 January 1838
[Upper Canada Gazette, *Toronto, 25 Jan. 1838*]

PROCLAMATION.
UPPER CANADA.

F.B. HEAD.

VICTORIA, *by the Grace of* **GOD,** *of the United Kingdom of Great Britain and Ireland, Queen, Defender of the Faith, &c. &c. &c.*

To all our loving and faithful Subjects, in our Province of Upper Canada –

GREETING:

KNOW YE, that taking into our most serious consideration, the merciful interposition of **DIVINE PROVIDENCE,** and that it hath pleased **ALMIGHTY GOD** to deliver us from the dangers and calamities of the unnatural Insurrection and Rebellion with which we have been lately afflicted: **WE** have resolved, and by the advice of our Executive Council, for our Province of Upper Canada, do hereby command, that a day of **PUBLIC THANKSGIVING** be observed throughout our said Province, on **TUESDAY,** the Sixth day of February next, so that all our people therein may humble themselves before **ALMIGHTY GOD,** and in the most devout and solemn manner send up their Prayers, Praises and Thanksgivings, to the Divine Majesty, for having removed the heavy Judgments which our manifold provocations have most justly deserved; and for beseeching GOD still to continue to us His mercies, favour and protection: **AND WE** do strictly charge and command, that the said day of **PUBLIC**

[64] "Wilson" may have been William Mercer Wilson (1813–1875), who was born in Perthshire, Scotland, and who emigrated to Upper Canada in 1832. He settled in Simcoe in 1834, where he established a distillery two years later. He was appointed a commissioner of the Court of Requests. Active in the rebellion period, he was involved in the cutting out of the *Caroline*. In 1838 he was appointed clerk of the peace and clerk of the court of the Talbot District. In 1868 he was made a judge.

"Wilson" may also have been the William Wilson (*ca.* 1789–1847) born in the Niagara District, who settled in Simcoe in 1817, where he established a grist and a sawmill as well as a carding factory. He became a captain of the 3rd Regiment of Norfolk militia in 1823 and a magistrate in 1829. In 1830 he was elected to the Assembly for Norfolk. He died in Simcoe.

THANKSGIVING be reverently and devoutly observed by all our loving Subjects, in our said Province of Upper Canada, as they tender the favour of **ALMIGHTY GOD,** and would avoid His wrath and indignation, and upon pain of such punishment as we may justly inflict on all such as contemn or neglect the performance of so Religious and necessary a duty. . . .

E 37   REACTION OF REV. WILLIAM PROUDFOOT AND HIS
CONGREGATION TO THE DAY OF THANKSGIVING
[*UWO, Proudfoot Family Papers, Proudfoot Diary 28*]

Monday. Feby 5 1838. – . . .
Held session, of the Congregations – . . .
In consequence of tomorrow being appointed a thanksgiving day by the Governor, it is likely that no business will be done, it was therefore agreed that as it will be an unemployed day, we May profitably spend it in devotional exercises, The sessions therefore agreed so to spend it, at the same time agreeing unanimously, that said meeting shall not be held because the Governor has appointed a thanksgiving for tomorrow, as we do not admit his right to appoint any such service nor do we approve of the unchristian and tyrannical language employed in his proclamations –

E 38   EXTRACT OF A LETTER FROM REV. JOHN ROAF[65]
Toronto, 15 March 1838
[Colonial Missionary Society Report (1838) *(London, 1838), App. B, pp. 30-4*]

"I will inclose to you a small pamphlet, containing two letters, written by myself. After the publication of the former, the municipal authorities quartered six soldiers upon me, and upon no other minister, and no one of my neighbours. Having the alternative of submitting to a small fine, I refused to receive these soldiers, and was immediately plundered of furniture to four times the amount of the fine. I took all without saying a word; and the parties have become ashamed of their conduct, and are about sending my furniture back again. The principle contained in my two letters is said to be *now* admitted almost universally in the city, and I hope a great object has been advanced."
. . .

[65]John Roaf (1801–1862) went from his native Kent to London, England, to learn printing. He was converted, however, by an evangelical preacher and in 1819 began studying for the ministry. From 1823 to 1837 he was a minister in Wolverhampton, coming in the latter year to Upper Canada to manage the finances of the Congregationalist Missionary Society. In early 1838 he became minister of a small Congregationalist body in Toronto. This grew into the mother church for other Upper Canadian congregations. Roaf was very active in organizations opposed to state-church connections and in the temperance movement. He retired in 1856.

To the Editor of the Palladium

Sir,

His Excellency the Lieutenant-Governor of this Province has issued a Proclamation for the observance of the 6th of February, as a day of "Thanksgiving," and, as in this case, I must publicly refuse obedience to authority, I feel bound to submit my reasons for so doing to the Government and the public. Will you allow me the requisite space in the columns of your next number?

It is with me a religious duty to "honour," "pray for," "submit to," and pay due "tribute to" the "powers that be," wherever I reside, – *religious*, because required by God. I also admit that every man in this country is under immense obligations to love and praise God for preventing conflict and slaughter in the late insurrection, and so soon restoring peace. I cannot, however, obey the present "command" to "humble ourselves before Almighty God, and in the most devout and solemn manner send up our prayers, praises, and thanksgivings to the Divine Majesty;" because I cannot recognize any secular authority in religion where "Christ is all and in all," and claims to himself our entire faith and service. The Lieutenant-Governor bears the commission of the Queen – but not that of Christ. Conscience is not his province; and spiritual allegiance to him would be treason to heaven, . . . I cannot for a moment admit the promise of God's favour, and threat of his wrath and indignation, by a human being and a mere political officer. . . .

E 39   EXTRACT OF A LETTER FROM REV. THOMAS GREEN[66]
London, 19 February 1838

[*Rev. W.J.D. Waddilove*, The Stewart Missions . . . *(London, 1838), pp. 248-50*]

. . . I suppose you are aware that the Home and London Districts were the only disaffected parts of the Upper Province. I was not much surprised, as from personal observation in the various parts of the country which I visited as Travelling Missionary, I can ascribe the existing spirit of insubordination simply to *one cause* – the absolute lack of sound scriptural education, and faithful preaching. A large body of the disaffected are Universalists, whose teaching may be truly and briefly described – blessed are they who die in their sins, and whose practice in the various relations of life, amply verifies this to be their doctrine. I believe nearly two-thirds of the prisoners at present confined in the jail here are connected with this most unscriptural body. Not a few also of the Quakers of Norwich township have been

[66]Thomas Green (1809–1878) was a graduate of Trinity College, Dublin. In 1832 or 1835 he was sent to British North America by the Travelling Mission Fund to act as an itinerant priest. In 1838 or 1839 he became the first rector of St. Luke's Anglican Church in Wellington Square (Burlington), where he served for many years.

suspected; and very many *professed* Baptists have been found arrayed in the ranks against their Sovereign Liege Lady the Queen. I am happy to be able to say that as far as I can learn, (and I have pretty good means) the Wesleyan Methodists here, as connected with the *British* Wesleyans, have all rallied on the side of order and good government and I am also happy to say that *I know not of one member of the Church of England,* nor have *I heard of any*, where my personal knowledge does not extend, being detected in aiding or abetting the unnatural and unwarrantable outbreak; . . .

E 40 BROCKVILLE *Recorder* ADVOCATES REFORM, NOT REBELLION
[Recorder, *Brockville, 14 Dec. 1837*]

For another extract from this document see D 15.

. . . It is well known since the dismissal of the Executive Council, which incurred the displeasure of Sir F.B. Head by their firm adherence to what they, and we conceive to be the true spirit of our Constitution, that we have looked upon the administration of his Excellency as unwise and impolitic; as tending to engender and foster feelings of dissatisfaction and distrust. Such being our views in relation to our Colonial administration we have from time to time expressed our opinions freely, in opposition to the course pursued, as well by his Excellency as by the Provincial Parliament, which under the circumstances of their election, we have never looked upon as a body calculated to express the true feelings of the people whom they ostensibly represented. Our aim has, therefore, been to show the impropriety of the acts of the Assembly on many important questions, (but more particularly the conduct of those who have been styled the Representatives of Leeds[67]) as connected with the administration, with a design of producing an ultimate and beneficial change. But we have never entertained the desire or inculcated the sentiment, that a resort to arms should be had for the accomplishment of the several objects of reform. Although we confess that we have for some time past, nearly despaired of any beneficial change in our Colonial affairs; yet we would rather suffer the èvils under which we labour, than plunge the country into others we know not of. . . . We are an advocate of Reform so far as is consistent with the true principles of the British Constitution. We go no further. – In the present state of things there is but one course, that which we have ever endeavored to pursue, namely, to discharge our duty to the Government, at the same time that we use all lawful and proper means for the removal of such abuses as are known to exist. . . .

[67]Here the *Recorder* likely intended referring to the conduct of both Ogle Gowan and Jonas Jones. The latter, however, was no longer a representative for Leeds. He had been appointed registrar of Dundas County on 20 June 1837 and had resigned his seat. James Morris won the electoral contest that ensued, but he did not take his place in the Assembly until 30 December 1837, two days after the opening of the new session.

E 41 REFORM ENDANGERED, I
[Mirror, *Toronto, 3 Feb. 1838*]

The Election for a member to represent the inhabitants of the 1st Riding of the County of York, commenced on Monday last. . . . Mr. Ketchum[68] has not gone to the Hustings, his crime only, having the man[l]iness to declare himself a Reformer. Is the goddess of Reform expelled from Upper Canada. MUST we be compelled to say, "Oh! breathe not her name." – Can no Candidate offer professing himself her devotee? Surely there can be no crime in Reform – if there be, the splendid men of Great Britain and Ireland are deeply ingulphed in treason. . . .

Can the people of Canada ever behold her flourish, in her legal and constitutional beauty? Yes, we shall see her in the same brilliancy, that the seaman beholds Sol, after being 3 days without his shining beams, and as many nights without a sparkling star. But the mode of obtainment must be lagal [*sic*]; and without shedding a drop of blood.

E 42 REFORM ENDANGERED, II
[Reporter, *Niagara, quoted* Journal, *St. Catharines, 27 Feb. 1838*]

Danger. – There is danger in imagining that we are safe – the loyalty we have recently exhibited, may be made the means of enslaving us. Let us convince our rulers, that it was not for the purpose of perpetuating their tenure of office that the people of this province buckled on their armour. There is danger of a re-action on the part of that "family influence" which has so long ridden rough shod over the liberties and interests of this glorious appendage of the British empire. Now is the time to urge the repeal of partial laws, and to demand the enactm:nt of liberal ones. Now is the time to insist on some provision being made for the EDUCATION of the people; the removal of incompetent and tyrannical Magistrates; the abolition of that baneful system of favouritism by which the appointments to office have hitherto been regulated – in short, now is the time for REFORM. The people have shown themselves worthy of all the privileges which the British Constitution is intended to confer; and it will be their own fault if they do not obtain them. . . . If the magnates of the land are permitted to suppose, for a moment, that the Loyalists of Upper Canada rose to secure to them the possession of that power which too many of them abuse, our rights will be trampled upon, and there is danger of another and a worse rebellion. –

[68]Jesse Ketchum (1782–1867) was born at Spencertown, New York, and settled in Upper Canada in 1799. He established a tannery at York and became a wealthy man. Though he fought in the War of 1812, some doubted his loyalty during the capture of York. A temperance advocate, he sat for York in the Assembly, 1828–34. In the rebellion he tried to disassociate himself from the rebels, though his son William fled to the United States. In 1845 he followed, settling in Buffalo.

E 43   HARSH PUNISHMENTS DEMANDED
[Gazette, *Hamilton, 9 Jan. 1838*]

It is a matter of regret and serious alarm to many worthy members of
the community, to witness the conduct of some of those misguided
men who have been the objects of the Governor's clemency; and we
cannot but express our serious and solemn conviction, that unless a
very severe example is made of the ringleaders of this most accursed
rebellion, we shall have the same scenes enacted over again in this
province, and next time, perhaps, with more success. We ask what is
treason? The widow's wail, and the orphan's coy [*sic*] – devastated
hamlets – plundered families – villiages [*sic*] in ashes – confidence
destroyed – trade stagnant – public securities diminished in value –
dismay, terror, anarchy, and confusion – in fine, every vice and villany
[*sic*], in the whole catalogue of human crimes, concentrated in one;
and that is treason! And shall this destruction of life, property, liberty –
the great expenditure of the public treasure – the weeping and anxious
families this outbreak has produced, be treated as naught? Shall it pass
over, without solemn and effectual punishment? The government owe
it to themselves, whose contemplated destruction has been prevented –
and they owe it to us, who have escaped a general massacre; – they
owe it to insulted virtue, outraged innocence; to the families who have
suffered from murder, robbery, and arson, to punish signally and
effectually the guilty perpetrators of these audacious crimes! . . .

E 44   HABEAS CORPUS SUSPENDED
[Upper Canada Gazette, *Toronto, 18 Jan. 1838*]

AN ACT *to authorise the apprehending and detention of Persons*
suspected of High Treason, Misprison [Misprision] of Treason, and
Treasonable practices.
  [Received the Royal Assent, 12th January, 1838.][69]
WHEREAS a traitorous conspiracy hath been formed for the purpose of
overthrowing, by means of insurrection, the Government, Laws and
Constitution, of this Province, and the happy connection thereof with
the Mother Country: *And whereas*, designs and practices of a
treasonable and highly dangerous nature are now carrying on in some
parts of this Province: Therefore for the better preservation of the
peace, laws and liberties, of this Province, *Be it enacted*, . . . That all
or any person or persons that are or shall be in prison in this Province,
at or upon the day on which this Act shall receive the Royal Assent, or
after by warrant by the Lieutenant Governor of this Province, in
Council, for High Treason, suspicion of High Treason, or treasonable
practices, may be detained in safe custody, without bail or mainprize,
during the continuance of this Act; and that no Judge or Justice of the

---

[69]The square brackets occur in the original.

Peace shall, during such continuance, bail or try any such person or persons so committed, without an order from the Lieutenant Governor of this Province, in Council, any law or statute to the contrary notwithstanding: . . .

5. *And be it further enacted by the authority aforesaid*, That for and during the continuance of this Act, in all and every case in which application shall be made for Her Majesty's Writ of Habeas Corpus to any Court or Courts, Judge or Judges, within this Province, by any person or persons who are or shall be in prison . . . by any public authority, with High Treason, misprison of High Treason or treasonable practices, such Writ of Habeas Corpus, if allowed, shall not be made returnable in less than thirty days from the time of its being allowed; and in all and every such case and cases, it shall be the duty of such Court, or Judge or Judges , . . . when and so soon as such application . . . shall to them be respectively made, to give notice and information thereof in writing, together with copies of such application, and of the affidavit or affidavits, or other paper or writings, on which such application shall be founded, to the Governor, Lieutenant Governor, or Person Administering the Government, for the time being.

6. *And be it further enacted by the authority aforesaid*, That this Act shall be and continue in force to the end of the next Session of Parliament, and no longer.

E 45   DUNCAN WILSON TO DR. BURNSIDE[70]
London, 23 February 1838
[*PAC, Upper Canada Sundries, v. 196, pp. 109191-3*]

. . . Benjn. Page . . . was one of Duncombe's rebels, on his way to join Duncombe, stole a horse, [Cald?] at a house near by[,] attempted to steal a saddle, was shot thrugh the fleshy part of the arm, his testemony was as follows[,] heard that Doct Wilson gave $40 Dollars to the rebbels, this sir is exactly the Testemony, and all the testemony that I was commited on. I have been admitted to bail for the limits of the town four weeks, I am anxious to be admitted to permanent bail until the assises, which is not to take place until may, The commissioners say they cannot admit to Bail nor any one Else without an order from the Attorney General. . . . All I ask from the authority is to be admitted to Permenant bail till the assises, you Dear Sir knowing the respectability of my parents as respects Character, prompts me to take this liberty with you, Will you please have the goodness to lay my case before the Attorney General, and such other Authority as may be

---

[70]Alexander Burnside (d. 1854), a New Englander, emigrated to Upper Canada and was licensed by the provincial medical board in 1822. He frequently visited Norwich, his wife having relatives there. A resident of Toronto, he became a wealthy man and a director of the British America Fire and Life Assurance Company. He gained a reputation as a philanthropist.

necessary, Presumeing that the Authority will not hesitate to Issue an order for Permenant Bonds[.] It is very unhealthy in my neighbourhood[,] the Scarlatina [scarlet fever] is very alarming, which makes me much more anxious, to get home[,] the inhabitants are suffering for the want of medical aid, you will see that my case is not a very bad one[,] if it was the commissioners would not admit me to bail for the limits of the Town. If you can attend to this you will confer a lasting favour, on your humble friend[,] should you get an order I wish it might be directed to me[,] if such a course would be propper. Since I have been here my horse a valuable animal has been taken and sold to defray the expences of conveying me to London. Sd horse was taken and sold by the order of John Burwell & Doyle M Kinney Esqrs. . Should like to have the opinion of the Attorney General what course to pesue to regain my horse. was sold for $45. have refused $150 for him frequently[.] Perhaps the Attorney can advise me some legal course to pesue to get him immediately, I suppose where property is taken illegally, in such a manner as my animal was taken, The law I expect will point out some way to regain it immediately. . . .

E 46 PARDON POSSIBLE FOR GUILTY REBELS
[Patriot, *Toronto, 6 Mar. 1838*]

A BILL granting to His Excellency in Council the power to pardon Criminals charged of High Treason.

Whereas, there is reason to believe that among the persons concerned in the late treasonable insurrection in this Province, there were some to whom the lenity of the Government may not improperly be extended on account of the artifices used by desperate and unprincipled persons to seduce them from their allegiance. Be it therefore enacted &c. that upon the Petition of any person charged with High Treason committed in this Province, preferred to the Lieutenant Governor before the arraignment of such person and praying to be pardoned for his offence, it shall and may be lawful for the Lieutenant Governor of this Province, by and with the advice and consent of the Executive Council thereof, to grant, if it shall seem fit, a pardon to such person in Her Majesty's name, upon such terms and conditions as may appear proper, which pardon being granted under the Great Seal of this Province, and reciting in substance the prayer of such petition, shall have the same effect as an attainder of the person therein named for the crime of High Treason, so far as regards the forfeiture of his Estate and property real and personal. Provided always, that in case a pardon shall not be granted upon any such Petition, no evidence shall be given of any admission or statement therein contained upon any trial to be afterwards had.

2. And be it &c. That in case any person shall be pardoned under this Act upon condition of being transported or of banishing himself

from this Province either for life, or for any term of years, such person if he shall afterwards voluntarily return to this Province without lawful excuse contrary to the condition of his pardon shall be deemed guilty of Felony and shall suffer death as in cases of Felony.

3. And be it &c. That the Provisions of this Act shall not extend, or be construed to extend, to such persons as have fled and are still absent from this Province under a charge of High Treason, and for whose apprehension a reward has been offered.

E 47   PETITION OF VARIOUS PRISONERS

[PAC, Upper Canada Sundries, v. 187, pp. 104450-1]

To his Excellency the Lieutenant Governor and the Honorable the executive council of Upper Canada. The petition of us whose names are hereunto annexed prisoners in the London Jail humbly sheweth that your petitioners are confined in said Jail on charges of high Treason against her Majesty's Government. and having received a communication. informing us to petition Your Excellency and council for Pardan. agreeable to an act of assembly passed at its last session touching our cases. we have therefore to state, that having borne arms through the articifices [*sic*] of designing men we have been led into error. and consequently into crime although we have not either or any of us been guilty of Murder, arson, or Robery nor had we any hand in distraining any Government or private property. As our cases are all of the same nature and similar to each other in circumstance. having been to Oakland Under Dr. Duncombe, We therefore hope that Your Excellency in council will mitigate as far as it lies in your power the punishment due to our offence, We therefore humbly request that if we cannot have a free pardon, to be allowed a Voluntary Banishment. for a period of Time at the Discretion of your Excellency and the Honorable Council, and your petioners [*sic*] as in Duty Bound will ever pray –

London Jail	Amos S Bradshaw[74]
March 5th 1838	his
Alexander Neely[71]	Thomas x Archer[75]
	mark
Uriah Emmons	
Edward Carmon[72]	Joseph Bowes Jr[76]
William Watts[73]	George Hill[77]

[71] Alexander Neilly (Neely) (b. *ca.* 1816) came to Upper Canada from Ireland about 1830 and settled in Yarmouth, where he became a carpenter. In December 1837, propertyless, he turned out with the rebels. He was jailed on 19 December, and, having petitioned, was admitted to bail on 11 June 1838.

Stephen Brunger[78]

Lewis Norton[79]

his
James x Coville[80]
mark

his
Ezekiel x mans[81]
mark

Charles Lawrance

his
Mire x Wethy
mark

his
Patrick x Malada[82]
mark

---

[72]Edward Carman (Carmon) (b. *ca.* 1815) came with his Quaker family to Upper Canada from New York State in 1826. He grew up in Yarmouth, where in 1837 he was an apprentice hatter. He attended the Westminster reform meeting of 6 October 1837 and turned out with the rebels in December. He was jailed that month, and, having petitioned, was ordered imprisoned at Kingston for three years and then banished from the province. The full force of his sentence, however, was not carried out, for he married in 1840 and was resident in Port Stanley in 1842.

[73]William Watts (*ca.* 1816–1838) was born in Berkshire, England. He emigrated to Upper Canada in the 1820s with his parents, settling in Yarmouth. In December 1837 he joined the Yarmouth rebels. He was jailed on the thirtieth of that month, and, after petitioning, was ordered pardoned on 21 May 1838. However, he had died on 5 May of "jail fever." Nevertheless, official documents show him as released on bail on 9 June.

[74]Amos S. Bradshaw (b. *ca.* 1815), a Pennsylvanian, emigrated to Upper Canada in 1835, settling in Yarmouth, where he worked as a propertyless labourer. In 1837 he attended the Westminster reform meeting of 6 October and turned out with the rebels in December. He was jailed on 28 December, and, having petitioned, on 13 August was ordered freed and banished for life.

[75]Thomas Arker (Archer) (b. *ca.* 1821), an Oxford County resident, joined Duncombe's men at Scotland. Jailed on 15 December 1837, he was admitted to bail on 19 June 1838 after petitioning.

[76]Joseph Bowes (b. *ca.* 1797) was a native of Philadelphia. His English-born father settled in Upper Canada in 1816, and Joseph joined him on his Bayham farm in 1834. In 1837 Joseph turned out with the western rebels. He was examined and freed on bail on 17 December, but, after declaring his intention to take up arms again, was jailed on 2 February 1838. After petitioning, on 13 August, he was ordered freed and banished for life.

[77]George Hill (b. *ca.* 1799) was born in Massachusetts. In 1837 Hill, a Bayham blacksmith, was appointed a rebel officer. He was taken after the rising but freed on bail on 28 December, then re-arrested at Sandwich while trying to flee to Michigan. Jailed on 3 January 1838, he petitioned and on 13 August was ordered freed and banished for life.

[78]Stephen Brunger (b. *ca.* 1816) was a native of Kent, England. He settled in Upper Canada about 1834. In 1837 the propertyless Southwold clothier married; at that time, too, he joined the western rebels. He was jailed on 26 December, and, after petitioning, was ordered pardoned on 21 May 1838.

[79]Lewis Adelbert Norton (b. 1819), a Vermont native who had numerous relatives in Westminster Township, settled in the area about 1834. In 1837 Norton worked on a fishing boat that sailed from Yarmouth. In December he joined the rebels. Captured, he was jailed first at Simcoe, then at London. After petitioning, he was freed in August 1838 and banished for life. He spent the remainder of his life in the United States, and in 1887 published his colourful reminiscences.

E 48   W.H. DRAPER'S COMMENTS
London, 9 April 1838
[*PAC, Upper Canada Sundries, v. 187, p. 104452*]

The petitioners Stephen Brunger – Alexander Neilly – Amos Bradshaw, Uriah Emmons – Edward Carman – William Watts – Lewis Norton – James Coville – Charles Lawrence and Patrick Malada formed part of a body who under David Anderson went from Yarmouth and joined Dr. Duncombe at Norwich – There are no peculiar circumstances to distinguish their case from that of numbers who joined in the late insurrection

Mire Wethy is an important witness as he implicates Robert Alway Esq. M.P.P. for Oxford and I propose using him for that purpose

Thomas Arker lived in Oxford – His case is of a similar description to those of Stephen Brunger and the others who followed David Anderson

The same observation applies to the cases of Ezekiel Manns – Joseph Bowes Junior and George Hill – and I believe the principal evidence against them is derived from their own confessions.

E 49   DECISION IN COUNCIL
[*PAC, Upper Canada Sundries, v. 187, p. 104453*]

In Council 21st May 1838.
Stephen Brunger, Alexander Neely, William Watts, Thomas Archer, Ezekiel Munns, Charles Lawrence, Patrick Malada, pardoned upon giving and entering into Bail for good behaviour for three years.[83]

Joseph Bowes Junior, George Hill, Uriah Emmons, Amos S. Bradshaw, Lewis Norton & James Coville, to be banished during the Term of their Natural Lives.[84]

Edward Carman, to be transported for 14 years to the Colony of Van Dieman's Land.

---

[80]James Coville (b. *ca.* 1816) was a native of New York State. In 1821 he and his orphaned brothers and sisters were sent to Yarmouth, to be raised there by the Quakers. In 1837 the unmarried Coville worked on Harvey Bryant's farm. He turned out with the Yarmouth rebels in December. He was jailed on the thirtieth of that month, and, after petitioning, on 13 August 1838 was ordered freed and banished for life.

[81]Ezekiel Manns (Mans) (b. *ca.* 1817) was a native of the London District. He joined the Norwich rebels in December 1837. He was jailed on 21 December and granted bail on 12 June 1838 after petitioning.

[82]Patrick Malada (b. *ca.* 1821), an Irish-born Yarmouth labourer, attended the Westminster reform meeting of 6 October 1837 and joined the rebels in December. He was jailed on 1 January 1838, and, having petitioned, was freed on bail on 7 June 1838.

[83]These prisoners were released on bail in June.

[84]The sentences of these prisoners were not implemented until August.

In Council 29th May 1838

Edward Carman, Order revised, to confinement in the Penitentiary for three years and subsequent banishment for Life.

Mire Wethy, discharged, admitted as Witness for the Crown.

E 50 PETITION OF REUBEN A. PARKER[85] TO SIR F.B. HEAD
Toronto, 13 March 1838
[*PAC, Upper Canada State Papers, v. 63, pp. 228-9*]

. . . The Petition of Reuben A Parker a prisoner confined confined [*sic*] in the Gaol of the City of Toronto late of Hamilton. humbly, Showeth, that Your Petitioner was on the night of the Twenty third February last past, at the hour of one o clock in the morning, at his then temporary abode in this City taken out of his bed arrested and taken to the Said Gaol by George Gurnett Esquire Accompanied by an armed body of men

That he was then lodged in the Said Gaol where [he] has has [*sic*] been Since detained without any examination or without Knowing for what Crime he is detained That Mr. Gurnett at the time Your petitioner was arrested Said he arrested him on his own cognizance of his Your petitioners being Suspected of conspiracy with others to release the prisoners out of Gaol. As Your petitioner is wholly innocent of any Such charge and as the Suspicion is altogether Unfounded he humbly prays Your Excellency to cause an enquiry to be made in to his case And to discharge him from Prison. . . .

E 51 DECISION IN COUNCIL
[*PAC, Upper Canada State Papers, v. 63, p. 230*]

In Council 15 March 1838.

On reading the report of the Commission of Enquiry, on the Petition of Reuben Alexander Parker – Recommended that a Warrant [be] issue[d] for the detention of said Reuben Alexander Parker suspected of treasonable practices.

The Council do not doubt the propriety of the arrest of the prisoner and therefore are willing that it should be sanctioned by Your Excellencys warrant[,] they however do not apprehend danger from his release at this time and after he shall be legally in custody by virtue of

---

[85]Reuben Alexander Parker (d. 1858) was one of three brothers who came from New Hampshire to Upper Canada in the 1820s. He was a merchant, first at York, then in partnership with his brother, John Goldsbury, for two or three years in Hamilton. Both brothers were arrested in connection with the rebellion of 1837, and, perhaps because of the publicity surrounding their case, their store in Hamilton went under in 1838. In later years Reuben lived in Toronto, where he derived considerable revenue from the rental of several prime downtown properties and from the sale of the land on which he lived, where the village of Yorkdale was built in the early 1850s.

the warrant. would respectfully recommend his discharge on bail to be taken for his good behaviour. before the Commission of enquiry.

R B SULLIVAN
PC [President of the Council?]

E 52   LOYALISTS PROTECTED
[Upper Canada Gazette, *Toronto, 15 March 1838*]

AN ACT *for indemnifying persons who since the Second of December, one thousand eight hundred and thirty-seven, have acted in apprehending, imprisoning, or detaining in custody, persons sus-pected of High Treason, or Treasonable Practices, and in the suppression of Unlawful Assemblies, and for other purposes therein mentioned.*

[Passed, 6th March, 1838.][86]

WHEREAS a late armed insurrection of certain Subjects of Her Majesty, in this Province, with intent to subvert the Government, and to plunder and destroy the property of the loyal Inhabitants, has been happily subdued, but not until the insurgents had committed acts of murder, robbery and arson, and had occasioned much alarm for the peace and security of the Province: *And whereas*, immediately before and during the said insurrection, and in consequence thereof, it became necessary for Justices of the Peace, Officers of the Militia, and other persons in authority in this Province, and for divers loyal Subjects of Her Majesty, to take all possible measures for apprehending, securing, detaining and bringing, to Justice, persons charged or suspected of joining in the said insurrection, or of aiding or abetting the same, or of other Treasonable Practices dangerous to the peace of this Province, and the security of its Government, and also for the purpose of defeating and putting down the said insurrection, and for maintaining the peace of this Province, and securing the lives and properties of the Inhabitants thereof: *And whereas,* some of such acts may not have been strictly legal and formal, but it is nevertheless just and necessary that the persons doing or advising the same should be kept harmless, and indemnified against actions at Law, or other proceedings, with which they might otherwise be harrassed: *Be it therefore enacted*, . . . That all personal actions, suits, indictments and prosecutions, heretofore brought, . . . or to be hereafter brought, . . . and all judgments thereupon obtained, . . . and all proceedings whatsoever against any person or persons, for or on account of any act, matter or thing, by him or them done or commanded, ordered or directed, or advised to be done, since the second day of December, in the year of our Lord one thousand eight hundred and thirty-seven, for apprehending, commit-ting, imprisoning, detaining in custody, or discharging any person or persons who hath or have been imprisoned or detained in custody for

[86]The square brackets occur in the original.

High Treason, or suspicion of High Treason, or treasonable practices, or for apprehending, committing, imprisoning, or detaining in custody, any person or persons who hath or have been imprisoned or detained in custody, for having been so tumultuously, unlawfully and traitorously, assembled in arms as aforesaid, or for dispersing by force of arms any persons so assembled as aforesaid, or for suppressing the said traitorous insurrection, and discovering and guarding against any other [of] the treasonable proceedings aforesaid, or for the discovering and bringing to justice the persons concerned therein, or for maintaining the public peace and the security of Her Majesty's Subjects in their persons and property, or for supporting the Government and Constitution of this Province against the treasonable practices and proceedings aforesaid, shall be discharged and made void, and that every person by whom any such act, matter or thing, shall have been done, or commanded, ordered, directed, or advised to be done, shall be freed, acquitted, discharged and indemnified, . . .

And be it further enacted by the authority aforesaid, That if any action, suit, indictment, information, prosecution or proceeding, shall be brought, commenced, preferred, exhibited or had in any Court, against any person or persons, for or on account of any such act, matter or thing as aforesaid, it shall be lawful for the Defendant or Defendants in any such action, . . . to apply by motion, petition, or otherwise, in a summary way to the Court . . . and upon proof, . . . that such action, . . . is brought, . . . for or on account of any such act, matter or thing as aforesaid, to make an order for staying execution and all other proceedings in such action, . . . and the Court . . . shall also order unto the Defendant or Defendants, and he or they shall have or be entitled to double costs for all such proceedings as shall be had or carried on in any such action or suit, after the passing of this Act, . . .

And be it further enacted by the authority aforesaid, That all and every person or persons discharged out of custody as aforesaid, although he shall not have been discharged according to Law, shall be deemed and taken to have been legally discharged out of custody.

E 53   MILITARY TRAINING PROHIBITED
[Upper Canada Gazette, *Toronto, 15 March 1838*]

AN ACT *to prevent the unlawful Training of Persons to the use of Arms, and to practice Military Evolutions and Exercises, and to authorise Justices of the Peace to seize and detain Arms collected or kept for purposes dangerous to the public Peace.*

[Passed 6th March, 1838.][87]
WHEREAS in some parts of this Province, men clandestinely and unlawfully assembled have practised military training and exercising in arms, to the great terror and alarm of Her Majesty's loyal Subjects, and the imminent danger of the public peace: *Be it therefore enacted*, . . .

---

[87]The square brackets occur in the original.

That all meetings and assemblies of persons for the purpose of training or drilling themselves, or of being trained and drilled to the use of arms, or for the purpose of practising military exercises, movements or evolutions, without any lawful authority for so doing, shall be and the same are hereby prohibited, . . .

2. *And be it further enacted by the authority aforesaid*, That it shall be lawful for any Justice of the Peace, or for any Constable or Peace Officer, or for any person acting in their aid or assistance, to disperse any such unlawful meeting or assembly as aforesaid, and to arrest and detain any person present at or aiding, assisting or abetting, any such assembly or meeting as aforesaid; . . .

4. *And whereas*, Arms and weapons of various sorts have, in some parts of this Province, been collected, and are kept for purposes dangerous to the public peace, . . . *Be it therefore enacted by the authority aforesaid*, That it shall be lawful for any Justice of the Peace, upon information on oath of one or more credible witness or witnesses, that any pike, pike-head or spear, is in possession of any person or persons, or in any house or place, or that any dirk, dagger, sword, pistol, gun, rifle or other weapon, is, for any purpose dangerous to the public peace, in the possession of any person, or in any house or place, to issue his warrant to any Constable or other Peace Officer, to search for and seize any such [weapon]. . . .

5. *Provided always, and be it further enacted by the authority aforesaid*, That it shall be lawful for any person from whom any such arms or weapons shall be so taken . . . in case the Justice of the Peace . . . refuse to restore the same, to apply to the next General or Quarter Sessions of the Peace, . . . and the Justices assembled . . . shall make such order for the restitution or safe custody of such arms or weapons, or any part thereof, as upon such application shall appear to them to be proper.

6. *And be it further enacted by the authority aforesaid*, That it shall and may be lawful for any Justice of the Peace, or for any Constable, Peace Officer or other person, acting under the warrant of any Justice of the Peace, or for any person acting with or in aid of [the above] . . . to arrest and detain any person found carrying arms, in such manner and at such times as in the judgment of such Justice of the Peace, to afford just grounds of suspicion that the same are for purposes dangerous to the public peace; . . .

E 54   BELLA FLINT[88] TO SIR GEORGE ARTHUR
Belleville, 26 March 1838
[PAC, Adjutant General's Office, Correspondence, v. 28, Hastings file, enclosed in Bella Flint to Col. Richard Bullock, Belleville, 27 March 1838]

To His Excellency Sir George Arthur K.C.H Lieutenant Governor of

[88]Bella Flint (1805–1894) was born in Elizabethtown and came to Belleville in

the province of Upper Canada. Major General commanding her Majesty's forces therein &c &c &c

The memorial of the Justices of the peace in and for the Midland District in Special Sessions assembled at Belleville –

Humbly sheweth –

That upon the twenty second day of February last a conspiracy in which a large number of persons in the county of Hastings were Engaged was discovered by the Magistrates: That it was made known to the Magistrates of the county on the twenty third of the same month. that a very considerable number of the persons engaged in that conspiracy were under arms on the night previous[,] some of whom had been arrested between this town and Bath. That arrests of persons Engaged in that conspiracy have continued up to a very late period and that there are many of the same persons lurking within or adjacent to the county at this time as your memorialists have every reason to believe: That your memorialists have gone through a long and tedious investigation of the circumstances attending that Conspiracy and Examination of the persons arrested and that in the course of their investigations they were not a little surprised at discovering from testimony before them that so long ago as last November. discussions had taken place at secret meetings within the county as to the signal for burning this town: That on the twentieth of February last upon written instructions to Major Parker of the second regiment of Hastings Militia from Major Samson[89] and also verbal instructions accompanying the Same: Three companies of the Hastings militia were called out and ordered to Kingston where two of them arrived on the twenty first and twenty third of that month one of which was sent to Gananoquè and the other two ordered to return to Belleville.[90] . . .

1829, where he became a successful merchant. In 1836 he was appointed a magistrate and served as president of the Belleville Board of Police, as he did in 1838–9. In 1837 he acted as commissary of the 1st Hastings Regiment of militia. From 1847 to 1851 and from 1854 to 1857 he sat in the Assembly of the united Canadas. He later became a legislative councillor and a senator.

[89]"Major Samson" was James Sampson (1789–1861), born at Banbridge, Ireland. He studied medicine and became the assistant surgeon to the 85th Foot in 1811 and was sent to British North America. In the War of 1812 he served with the Royal Newfoundland Fencibles. In 1817 he retired on half-pay and in 1820 settled in Kingston, where in 1821 he was made a magistrate. From 1835 to 1861 he served as the first surgeon of the Kingston Penitentiary. He held various other offices, including a majorate in the 3rd Regiment of Frontenac militia, and in December 1837 he commanded the Kingston town guard. In 1839, 1840, and 1844 he was mayor of Kingston.

[90]The magistrates felt they had discovered a plan of the disaffected about Belleville to attack Belleville, Kingston, and possibly other points, in concert with Patriot raiders. In fact, a small band of Patriots did land at Hiccory Island in the Upper St. Lawrence in February 1838. The scare produced by the entire episode led to over forty arrests, and though some of those arrested languished in jail for months, none were ever found guilty of treason.

E 55   COL. GEORGE C. SALMON TO COL. FOSTER
Simcoe, 17 March 1838
[*PAC, Adjutant General's Office, Correspondence, v. 29, Norfolk file*]

. . . I am called on daily by persons residing on or near the Lake Shore to urge upon upon you the necessity of having troops of some kind stationed on this frontier by the time the Ice is out of the bay, threats are constantly made by the rebels who have fled from here that they will return & plunder us as soon as the navigation is open, and many families are preparing to move into the interior of the Country should troops not be sent to protect them, and they feel the more dissatisfaction because so large a force is kept at London (a place more than 30 miles from the Lake); . . .

E 56   COL. GEORGE C. SALMON TO F. HALKETT
Simcoe, 24 April 1838
[*PAC, Correspondence of the Military Secretary, v. 608, pp. 140-1*]

I think it necessary to acquaint you without delay that information has been brought me by a person on whom I have reason to place reliance, that it is the intention of a large body of armed Americans to make a descent on three points of our coast on the night of the 25th Inst. viz one detachment between Fort Erie & Sugar Loaf – another at Port Dover (only six miles from this place) & the third between this place and Port Stanley with a view of obtaining a footing in this part of the Province & giving the malcontents an opportunity of joining them. – I have ordered out the Norfolk Troop of Cavalry & 200 men of 1st & 2d Regts. of Norfolk Militia & must urgently request that your Excellency will send forward some Regular Troops (if only one company) to give confidence to the Militia –
I think it also necessary to inform your Excellency that the disaffected in this part of the Country (and they are very numerous) far from being humbled, are as violent as ever and they openly declare that the country will yet be occupied by the Americans and only yesterday a man was arrested here, from its being discovered that he had written to a rebel man at Detroit who had absconded from this neighbourhood, informing him of the undefended state of the country & that the troops were in a state of mutiny in consequence of not obtaining their pay[.]

E 57   T.W. MAGRATH[91] TO JOHN MAITLAND[92]
Brantford, 1 May 1838
[*C.R. Sanderson, ed.*, The Arthur Papers . . . I *(Toronto, 1957)*,
pp. 95-6]

According to instructions received (verbally) from His Excellency The

[91]Thomas William Magrath (b. *ca.* 1804) was the eldest son of the Rev. James

Lieut. Governor, I left this with twenty men and proceeded to Port Dover on the 29th. Inst. [*i.e.* ultimo], leaving two officers & thirty five men here ready to march if your orders arrived before my return.

At every tavern we halted we found the people extremely insolent and abusive, and it was with the greatest difficulty I prevented my men resenting it however I am happy to say no row occurred;

Numbers of persons met us at the different cross roads, and made use of the following expressions repeatedly. *we are getting ready for you*: our friends have only left this to *shew others the way here*: if *one* of *you* stay behind we will treat *him* as *you did Lount & Mathews*:

On my arrival in Simcoe I found the Company of your Regt: commanded by Capt: Markham[93] there, several persons to whom I spoke in the village said we are *rebels* and *will* be *again* but what can any of you make of it.

From thence I marched to Pt: Dover 10 Miles. Capt: Markham came with me, on our arrival there we found the steam boat still aground,[94] but 25 miles from the Port, not close to it, as had been represented by some of the Inhabitants at Toronto.

With very few exceptions they are all rebels there and I am confidant only wait for an opportunity to begin a row, in speaking to a fellow of the name of Herries, he said that did *their friends* come to Port Dover the red coats would not be a bit a piece for them as there were 1000 men between Scotland, Oakland, & there ready to turn out

The Magistrates in general seem not to make that exertion that they ought, and I think a Magistrate ought to be sent there that would act. they all have property in the neighbourhood. & are evidently *afraid* of *those fellows,* I think it would be as well, as was done in Ireland repeatedly, to make all the officers in command Magistrates of the District in which they are stationed. . . .

Magrath who emigrated with his family from Ireland to Erindale, Upper Canada, in 1827. Several of Thomas' letters appeared as chapters in *Authentic Letters from Upper Canada*, published in London in 1833. In 1838, a major, he commanded a troop of militia cavalry. He eventually rose to the rank of lieutenant-colonel. In later years Magrath was prominent on the Toronto sports scene.

[92]John Maitland (1788–1839), the third son of the Earl of Lauderdale, enlisted in the British army in 1807 and served in the Peninsular war. He saw action in suppressing the 1837 rebellion in Lower Canada, and in 1838 was given the military command of the forces in western Upper Canada. He then commanded, as he had done for twenty years, the 32nd Regiment. In 1838 he received the Order of the Bath for his services in the two Canadas. He died in London, Upper Canada, where his regiment was stationed.

[93]Captain Frederick Markham was appointed deputy assistant quartermaster general of the forces in the Canadas on 24 August 1838. He rose to the rank of major shortly after.

[94]On 24 April 1838 the *Bunker Hill* grounded on Long Point. It got off on 5 May.

E 58   CHIEF JUSTICE'S CHARGE TO THE GRAND JURY IN THE CASE OF
SAMUEL LOUNT AND PETER MATTHEWS
Toronto, 8 March 1838
[Charge of the Honorable John B. Robinson . . . *(Toronto, 1838),*
pp. 5-7, 20-1]

. . . Until the close of the past year, this Province wore the appearance
of universal peace, and of perfect security; the pressure of commercial
difficulties, which so much distressed the neighbouring country, was
of course felt by us, but in a much less degree; our Legislature had
occupied themselves sedulously in advancing various works of public
improvement, and in endeavouring to ward off from this Province the
difficulties which seemed to beset almost every other country; the laws
were every where submitted to, and justice was administered through
its usual channels, as free from any circumstances to create
excitement, or disturb its ordinary course, as could have been the case
in any country, at any time. It is ascertained that Upper Canada
contains about 400,000 souls; and I believe I may say, with that strict
adherence to accuracy which becomes this place, that it would have
been difficult to point out any portion of the world where an equal
number of persons were at the same time living in a state of more
general tranquillity and contentment – in the more perfect possession
of every right and liberty which is consistent with human happiness,
and apparently enjoying in more entire security the fruits of their
labour, and all other advantages which it is the object of good
government to guard.

I do not mean to say that there were no efforts used to excite
discontent, or that there were no exceptions to that cheerful and
grateful acknowledgment of blessings enjoyed, which will generally be
exhibited by the great majority of a virtuous people. Undoubtedly there
were such exceptions, and so there always have been, and always will
be, while human nature is imperfect, and until envy, jealousy, and a
restless ambition, shall be no longer suffered to mar the happiness of
mankind. But the workings of these bad passions, from which no
community is free, had hitherto led to no acts of violence, nor indeed
to any interruption of the ordinary current of affairs. They had chiefly
shewn themselves in those railing accusations at public meetings, and
in public papers, against the Civil Authorities of this Province, and of
our Parent State, which have of late years become so common
throughout the world, that it has been perhaps imprudently concluded
that they had nearly lost their influence over the minds of men. . . .

There is no setting limits to the irregular desires and unreasonable
expectations of ill constituted minds. If it were otherwise, one would
have supposed that rebellion against the Government of this Province
could scarcely have found a single adherent. I have long been
intimately acquainted with that portion of this District from whence the

principal armed band of people came to threaten this town with devastation, and to insult and defy the laws, under whose protection many of them had lived in security and peace from their childhood. I have always regarded it as the most favored portion of the Province. – Enjoying the advantage of a climate as decidedly healthful and agreeable as can be found in this Province, or perhaps upon this Continent, and a soil remarkably fertile, with the general aspect of the country such as cannot be seen without attracting admiration, I have often thought the industrious possessors of this inviting land were perhaps the most to be envied of any of the people of Upper Canada; and I must confess myself to have been among the last, who could believe it possible, that those who were in the enjoyment of such blessings could prevail upon themselves fatally to renounce them all, either for the gratification of some unaccountable resentment, or in the mad and guilty pursuit of such imaginary advantages as no form of Government ever did, or ever can confer. But I will not urge these reflections farther. . . .

E 59   CHIEF JUSTICE'S ADDRESS TO SAMUEL LOUNT AND PETER
MATTHEWS
[Christian Guardian, *Toronto, 4 April 1838*]

. . . On Thursday, the 29th March instant, **SAMUEL LOUNT** and **PETER MATTHEWS,** who on the preceding Monday had pleaded **GUILTY** to the Indictment preferred against them for **HIGH TREASON,** were again placed at the **BAR,** when the **ATTORNEY GENERAL** moved for Judgment against them. Silence having been proclaimed, **HIS HONOR,** the **CHIEF JUSTICE,** pronounced the awful sentence of the **LAW,** preceded by the following impressive Address:

SAMUEL LOUNT and PETER MATTHEWS!

You have been arraigned upon several indictments charging you with High Treason. In accordance with the humane provisions of our law, many days have necessarily elapsed between the time of your being indicted and arraigned; and in that interval you were furnished with full and exact copies of the charges preferred against you, together with lists of the witnesses by whom those charges were to be proved, and with the names of the jurors who were to pronounce upon the awful question of your guilt or innocence. Having had all these advantages for disproving the charge, if that were possible, you have each of you upon your arraignment pleaded "*guilty;*" that is, you have confessed that upon the day named in the indictments, you were in arms against your SOVEREIGN, and did traitorously levy war in this Province, for the purpose of subverting the constitution and government.

You are, neither of you, I dare say, so ill informed of the laws of your country as not to know that the offence of which you now stand convicted, upon your own confession, is the highest in the scale of crimes – so high, that the law annexes to it the severest punishment, and leaves to this Court no discretion to dispense with, or to mitigate its awful sentence. . . .

It may, therefore, not be necessary (and I hope it is not) that I should insist upon the enormity of your crime, with a view to convince you of the justice of that law under whose severest condemnation you have brought yourselves; . . . But it may be of some public service, and possibly may in a small degree assist in turning others from the path which you have followed to your destruction, if I use this occasion for expressing some reflections to which your conduct and its consequences have very naturally given rise.

A few months ago, you were, both of you, living in the enjoyment of health and liberty, under circumstances as favourable, perhaps, to happiness, as the condition of human nature admits of. The wants of life cannot be supplied without labour; and in all countries the great majority of the inhabitants must, in some shape or other, make their living by their own exertion. No form of government can do away with this necessity; nor is that to be wished for, since there is little satisfaction or pleasure in mere idleness. On the contrary, the honest labourer, whose industry raises him above poverty, is frequently found among the most cheerful and contented members of the community; and here, as in all countries, where he is peaceful and well disposed, he is respectable and respected. But if the lot of the mere industrious labourer should seem a *hard* lot, you were, both of you, raised above that condition. A long residence in this Province had given you the opportunity of acquiring property, and had enabled you to find a suitable field for your exertion.

You were not the tenants of rigorous and exacting landlords; you were not burthened with taxes for the State, further than the payment perhaps of a few shillings in the year, to support the common expenses of the District in which you lived; you held that middle station of life than which none is happier; you were your own masters. Regularity and industry would always have ensured you a competency. Higher rank and greater wealth might have enabled you to live with less actual labour of your hands; but it is not certain that they would have increased your enjoyment. On the contrary, they often bring with them care and anxiety, while they attract jealousy and envy; and whoever will look with candour upon human life, will find that those who possess these supposed advantages, are not by any means the most contented.

When men are raised, as you were, above the danger of want, and above the evils of poverty and dependence, their happiness is for the most part in their own power. It depends upon the disposition of the mind and heart, upon their being grateful and contented, upon their

"doing justly, loving mercy, and walking humbly with their God."
Without these dispositions no condition of life can give happiness.
With them, millions are contented and happy, who have far less to be
thankful for than had fallen to your lot. You lived in a country where
every man who obeys the laws is secure in the protection of life,
liberty, and property; under a form of government, which has been the
admiration of the world for ages. No man could deprive you, by force
or fraud, of the smallest portion of the fruit of your labour, but you
could appeal to a Jury of your country for redress, with the certainty
that you would have the same measure of justice dealt out to you, as if
you were the highest and wealthiest persons in the Province. . . .

It was open to you, if you were discontented with the Government
that protected you, to sell your possessions here, and transfer
yourselves to any other country whose laws and institutions you liked
better than your own. *That* you could have done, without injuring
others, without violating your oaths of allegiance, and without loading
your consciences with crime. You might, perhaps, have found, after
making the experiment, that you had gained nothing by the change; but
you would have *incurred* no guilt by the attempt. . . .

I hope you have endeavoured to retrace in your minds the causes of
your dreadful fall. – There is no doubt the chief cause has been your
wilful forgetfulness of your duty to your Creator, and of the purposes
for which life was bestowed upon you. Instead of being humbly
thankful to a kind Providence, which had cast your lot in this free, and
prosperous country; you have, I fear, too long and unreservedly
indulged in a feeling of envy and hatred towards your rulers – which
was sure to undermine every just and generous sentiment, and to lead
in the end to the ruin of your happiness and peace.

It is one of the miserable consequences of the abuse of liberty, that a
licentious press is permitted to poison the public mind with the most
absurd and wicked misrepresentations, which the ill-disposed, without
inquiry, receive and act upon as truths. It is, to be sure, in the power of
the laws to restrain this evil to a certain extent, or, at least, they may
attempt to do so; but such is the perverseness of a great portion of
mankind, that whenever it is endeavoured to exert this power, the
attempt is felt, and resented, as an infringement upon liberty. The viper
unhappily is cherished in the bosom, till, as in your case, it gives the
deadly sting; and then it is acknowledged, when it is too late, that it
would have been mercy not to have spared so long. . . .

We have no discretion to exercise. The awful sentence of death must
follow your conviction. But although a power to pardon resides only in
the SOVEREIGN whose authority you endeavoured to subvert, if I could
conscientiously encourage in you a hope that pardon would be
extended, I should gladly do so – . . . I know no ground, however, on
which I can venture to hold out such a hope; and I do therefore most
earnestly exhort you to prepare yourselves for the execution of the

sentence which is about to be pronounced. In the short time which may remain to you, I pray that you may be brought to a deep sense of the guilt of the crime of which you are convicted; and that you may be enabled to address yourselves in humble and earnest sincerity to the infinite mercy of the SAVIOUR whose divine commands you have transgressed. . . .

E 60 MINUTE OF SIR GEORGE ARTHUR IN EXECUTIVE COUNCIL
31 March 1838
[*PAC, Upper Canada State Papers, v. 50, pp. 2-18*]

. . . The Lieutt. Governor particularly invites the attention of the Council to that part of the despatch in which Lord Glenelg makes the following observation;

"Great circumspection will I think also be requisite in carrying into effect any capital sentences which may be passed on Persons convicted of Political Offenses. It may indeed be necessary that a sentence of this nature should be carried into effect, and without any considerable delay; but, unless under circumstances of peculiar and pressing urgency, I am strongly of opinion that sound policy as well as humanity dictates an abstinence on that part of the Executive from having recourse to this extreme penalty." –

3. The Council will perceive by the above extract that Her Majesty's Government unless in cases of extreme urgency is desirous of reserving to itself much discretion on the subject of the infliction of severe or extreme penalties, and the Lieut: Governor sees, in addition to the arguments so forcibly set forth in this dispatch an additional inducement to follow the humane course pointed out by His Lordship, in the necessity under which the local authorities, and the loyal Canadian people must feel themselves placed, not only to act in a manner which they know to be right and becoming to the best of their own judgment; but, also in such a way as to secure the good opinion, sympathy, and assistance of the British Government and people to which this Colony must in a great measure look for the preservation and security of the institutions which it has been proved to hold so dear. . . .

5. The cordial approval by the Secretary of State of the distinction made by his Predecessor Sir Francis Head between the few leaders and instigators of the late revolt and their deluded followers, leads the Lieutenant Governor irresistably to the conclusion that it is not the desire of Her Majesty's Government to visit with prosecution and punishment the great mass of offenders engaged in the late insurrection. He is therefore induced to request the assistance of the Council in selecting from the numbers who have brought themselves within the penalty of the Law such as from their influence or importance or from the aggravated nature of the offenses committed by

them may appear the most proper to be made examples of severe punishment. . . .

E 61   EXECUTIVE COUNCIL MINUTE
31 March 1838
[PAC, Upper Canada State Papers, v. 50, pp. 19-29]

. . . [The Honorable The Chief Justice being in attendance was called in, and His Excellency having communicated to him the Documents above enumerated, was pleased to request his Opinion as to the necessity of Capital punishments for High Treason, committed during the late revolt and to what extent the actual State of the Province required that such punishment should be inflicted, and also as to the time when it would be most calculated to be of public benefit to carry the Sentences of the Courts into effect in cases in which it would be considered that the Royal mercy ought not to be extended.

The Chief Justice stated, that in his Opinion it was necessary for the ends of Justice, and due to the Loyal Inhabitants of the Province, that some examples should be made in the way of Capital punishments.

He also said that he conceived the extent to which this was actually required to be done would be very limited.][95]

The Chief Justice having attended the Council at the request of His Excellency The Lieutenant Governor the Despatches of The Right Honorable The Secretary of State for the Colonies and His Excellency's Minute were laid before him, and being desired to state whether having considered these Documents, there was any ground upon which he would recommend that the Sentence of the Court in the two cases reported by him should not be carried into execution, The Chief Justice stated in answer that he saw no ground upon which he felt that he could properly recommend a pardon or respite in those cases.

[The Chief Justice also remarked, that if the Nature of the punishment of Transportation to a penal Colony were generally understood, and if he thought many in the Community could be brought to concur with him in Opinion he would be most willing to recommend a forbearance from the infliction of capital punishment in all the cases of persons now in custody for crimes arising out of the late Rebellion, but this course he thought could not be pursued in the state of the public mind. with a due regard to the necessity of example and the prevention of future crimes of a like nature.

The Chief Justice was of Opinion that all the good to arise from carrying Sentences of death into effect, would be lost by the delay which must take place, if references were had to Her Majesty and that

[95]The various square brackets in this document occur in the original. The sections within those brackets are marked "cancelled," presumably to indicate that the material therein was confidential and not part of the public record. The material inside the brackets is much more revealing of J.B. Robinson's reasoning and arguments than the material outside them.

however his feelings might lead him to give the unfortunate Convicts every chance of Mercy, he felt himself bound by an imperative sense of public duty, not to advise such a reference in all cases.

His Excellency was pleased to ask the Opinion of The Chief Justice as to whether it would be legal or proper for the Government after selecting for prosecution and punishment those whose cases might be considered as most Aggravated and requiring exemplary punishment to direct a Stay of proceedings against others until the pleasure of Her Majesty should be known?

The Chief Justice answered, that an interference with the ordinary course of Justice, on the part of the Government and without Parliamentary Sanction was liable to many objections, but that before giving any decided recommendation he would take pains to inform himself more fully as to the course usually pursued on like occasions, and that he would if it was His Excellency's pleasure, wait upon His Excellency in Council at such time as His Excellency should desire his attendance.

Upon which The Lieutenant Governor informed the Chief Justice that it was his intention to meet his Council on Monday next at Noon and would feel obliged by the Chief Justice's attendance.]

His Excellency was pleased to require the attendance of the Attorney General, and on that Officer appearing, His Excellency proposed to him the same questions as had been before asked of the Chief Justice, and moreover directed his attention to the Cases of the two Convicts reported by the Chief Justice to be under Sentences of death.

The Attorney General said that after giving the matter great consideration he felt himself bound to give it as his Opinion that a necessity existed for the infliction of Capital punishment in some instances, he however thought that the number of Cases of Capital punishment might, if such was the desire of Her Majesty's Government, and of His Excellency be very limited

The Attorney General called the attention of His Excellency to the fact that the Lives of several of Her Majesty's Loyal Subjects had been taken by the Insurgents during the late revolt, and that the peculiar and appropriate punishment for this crime was death, and that he did not consider the crime at all mitigated, but on the contrary aggravated by its being accompanied with Treason, and committed in the attempt to overthrow the Government by violence.

The Attorney General said that he had selected the persons reported to be under Sentence of death from amongst the number in custody, as being to the best of his knowledge more peculiarly accountable than the others actually within the reach of Justice for the Crimes Committed, that they were not of a class liable or likely to be misled, or deluded by others, and most certainly had been most active in assisting and leading into the Rebellion many who had that excuse such as it was to offer.

The Attorney General further said that he regretted exceedingly that some had succeeded in escaping to the United States who well deserved to be substituted for these prisoners as objects for the extreme penalty of the Law, but that he knew of no circumstances in their Cases in extenuation of Guilt which would warrant him in recommending them as proper objects of Royal Clemency.

The Attorney General said that as the Plea of Guilty by these Prisoners prevented the facts of their respective cases from coming before the Chief Justice, and therefore could not enter into his report, he would collect such informations as the proceedings of the Commission of Enquiry placed within his reach and would have the honor of transmitting them for the information of His Excellency

The Attorney General further said, that although he knew it was expected by the Public that a Sacrifice of Life to a greater extent should take place, and that extreme leniency on the part of the Government might produce dissatisfaction, he nevertheless hoped His Excellency might feel himself justified in compliance with the Views of Her Majesty's Government, and with his own feelings of humanity in limiting the number of Capital punishments even to the two Cases reported. . . .

E 62   EXECUTIVE COUNCIL MINUTE
2 April 1838
[*PAC, Upper Canada State Papers, v. 50, pp. 33-9*]

. . . The Council having considered with great deliberation the Despatch dated 30th January 1838, the Copy of a Despatch to Sir John Colborne, bearing date 6th January 1838, transmitted with the former Despatch and referred to therein, and also to the Opinion delivered by the Chief Justice and the Attorney General before the Council, with the Report of the Attorney General.

The Council have also considered attentively the Minute of His Excellency and with every disposition to recommend the extension of Royal Clemency so far as at all compatible with the Public Safety, feel bound respectfully to advise His Excellency not to interfere with the course of Justice in favor of Samuel Lount and Peter Matthews.

The Council respectfully conceive that in advising this course, they are not in any respect departing from the Spirit of the Despatch addressed to Sir John Colborne, the Council are of Opinion that the Cases in question are of great urgency, that Severe Public example is actually required in some instances and that the Crimes of which these Prisoners are shewn to have aided, abetted and Countenanced the committal of. in addition to the Crime of High Treason, point them out as particularly fit to be selected for Capital Punishment.

They are not the deluded followers of the instigators of Treason, but on the contrary the Leaders and instigators of others. Lives have been taken by the men which they led, and Houses have been burned by those amongst whom they held command, they appear to have been present aiding in robbery of the Public Mail and their conduct appears to have but too well justified the apprehensions entertained of the horrible consequences which would have attended a successful revolt.

The Council believing that the execution of the Sentence of the Law with promptitude will do much to its beneficial Operation and they feel they cannot consistently with their duty, recommend the delay which must take place on a reference to Her Majesty. . . .

E 63   PETITION OF SAMUEL LOUNT
7 April 1838
[PAC, Upper Canada State Papers, v. 45, pp. 43-4]

To His Excellency Sir George Arthur . . .

The Petition of Samuel Lount now a Prisoner under Sentence of death in the Gaol of the Home District

Most Humbly sheweth

That Your Petitioner stands convicted of the crime of High Treason in having been concerned in the late Criminal Rebellion in this Province

That Your Petitioner deeply sensible of the heinousness of his Offence and desirous of making the only reparation in his power by a candid avowal pleaded Guilty to the Indictment formed against him and now humbly throws himself upon Your Excellencys Mercy for that Life which stands forfeited to the offended Laws of His Country

That your Petitioner before his arraignment petitioned Your Excellencys Predecessor praying for a Pardon under the Provisions of the Late Act of Parliament[,] That though His Excellency Sir Francis Head did not deem it proper to grant the prayer of that Petition Your Petitioner makes this new appeal in humble hope that though it may have been thought expedient for the purpose of example to put Your Petitioner upon his Trial the sacrifice of his life may not be considered absolutely necessary to the ends of Public Justice

That Your Petitioner in the prosecution of the criminal attempt in which he was concerned exerted his influence as much as possible to prevent the wanton outrage as he trusts will appear by the accompanying affidavits to which Your Petitioner begs leave most respectfully to refer Your Excellency

That Your Petitioner has a wife and six children now plunged in the deepest distress by the awful situation in which your Petitioner is placed. Your Petitioner therefore humbly prays that Your Excellency will be graciously pleased to take his case into Your Excellencys most favourable consideration and Grant to Your Petitioner Her Majestys most Gracious Pardon upon such Terms and Conditions as in Your Excellencys opinion the Public Interest may require or if you should not deem this within your power or consistent with your duty that Your Excellency would be pleased to respite the Execution of the Sentence under which Your petitioner now lies until Your Petitioner should have an opportunity of appealing to the mercy of Her Most Gracious Majesty

And Your Petitioner as is duty bound will ever pray &c.

E 64   EVIDENCE OF PETER SOULES[96]
30 March 1838
[PAC, Upper Canada State Papers, v. 45, pp. 45-7]

The Queen } In the Kings Bench –
vs   Peter Soules of Vaughan in the Home District,
Samuel Lount} Yeoman maketh oath and saith, that he this deponent was before day light on Tuesday morning the 5th day of December last made a prisoner by the party of Rebels who were then in Arms on Young Street[,] that he was at Montgomery's Tavern about two hours after Colonel Moodie was killed[,] that this deponent was then a prisoner and was asked for by Samuel Lount, that the desire of the said Samuel Lount, was to set this deponent at liberty and to send word to the Widow of the deceased that he would cause her to be permitted [to] have the body of the deceased, that the said Samuel Lount, appeared to be very much distressed at the death of Colonel Moodie, and desired that his family might have his body as this deponent verily beleives from motives of pure humanity, that the said Samuel Lount did eventually succeed in getting the body of deceased from McKenzie tho with much difficulty, That the said Samuel Lount regretted very much the, situation in which he had placed himself, and said to this deponent that in the outset he never believed that there would be any Blood shed, in the late insurrection

And this deponent further saith that he this deponent took a very deep interest in all that passed[,] that this deponent was extremely ill used when first taken[,] that when Mr Lount seen this deponent he caused this deponent to be well treated, as also the rest of the Prisoners as this deponent has reason to beleive.

And this deponent further Saith that from all the circumstances that passed under this deponents notice he this deponent is convinced that the said Samuel Lount did Sincerely oppose the destruction of any property whatever[,] that he always expressed his regret at what had happened and appeared to be much distressed in mind in consequence of the death of Colonel Moodie. And this deponent further Saith that he

[96]Peter Soules lived on lot 32, concession 1 of Vaughan Township. The Executive Council considered his petition along with Lount's petition of 7 April 1838.

hath reason to beleive and doth really beleive that it was the said Samuel Lount that Saved the property of Sheriff Jarvis from being burned by McKenzie And this deponent further Saith that the Conduct of the said Samuel Lount towards the Prisoners was very mild and that he was extremely Kind to them, that he did permit Several of them to write letters to their families, and always received from the Prisoners, their thanks for his exertions in their favor, – And this deponent further saith that when the said Samuel Lount delivered to this deponent the letter for Mrs. Moodie he, told this deponent that if this deponent, should meet his son on the road Coming to Join the Rebels that he this deponent should not use any persuasions to induce him to refrain from joining the Rebels but that he this deponent should take him by Force and compel him to go home in order/as this deponent was given to understand/ that his, the said Samuel Lounts son might be prevented from joining the said party as the said Samuel Lount expressed a wish that he should not, –

E 65   EVIDENCE OF LUTHER ELTON[97]
31 March 1838
[PAC, Upper Canada State Papers, v. 45, p. 49]

The Queen } In the Kings Bench
vs   Luther Elton of Newmarket in the Home District
Samuel Lount } Tailor maketh oath and saith that he this deponent is one of the unfortunate persons who was seduced from his allegiance[,] that he this deponent was at Montgomerys, that this deponent heard the above named Samuel Lount condemn the Conduct of McKenzie in burning Doctor Horns house, that the said Samuel Lount was much grieved that the said property should have been destroyed, and this deponent further saith that he Knows that it was through the exertions of the said Samuel Lount that the property of the Sheriff on Young Street was saved[,] that he heard Samuel Lount the above named defendant declare positively that he would prevent the burning of Sheriff Jarvis house or the disturbance of his Family at all hazards —

[97]Luther Elisha Hall Elton (b. 1808 or 1809) came to Canada in 1833 from Vermont and set himself up as a tailor in Newmarket. He was active throughout the rebellion and was arrested a few days later. After petitioning for pardon in May 1838, he was sentenced to three years in prison and then banishment. Elton was pardoned in January 1839, along with several others then in prison. In 1841 he was naturalized and bought a small part of lot 94, concession 1 of Whitchurch Township. The lot was in Newmarket. The Executive Council considered his petition along with Lount's petition of 7 April 1838.

E 66   PETITION OF PETER MATTHEWS
6 April 1838
[*PAC, Upper Canada State Papers, v. 45, pp. 34-5, 39*]

To His Excellency Sir George Arthur . . .

The petition of Peter Matthews late of the Township of Pickering, now a prisoner in the Gaol of the Home District under sentence of death for High Treason –

Humbly Sheweth,

That he has been given to understand that there is a strong suspicssion abroad against your petitioner as having set fire to the house of the late Simon Washburn deceased and the Don Bridge, and as also having given orders to set fire to other houses – That your petitioner[,] duly sensible of the awful situation in which he stands, solemnly declares that he not only did not set fire to either the house or the bridge, but used his utmost exertions to prevent the bridge from being fired – that he was not aware of the house being set fire to until he saw the flames, being at the time about half a quarter of a mile on the west side of the bridge – that the men who were sent with him were the most of them perfect strangers to your petitioner and over whom he had no controul; That altho sworn to, as your petitioner is informed, he solemnly denies as he shall answer to his Maker ever giving orders to set fire to the house of William Smith or that of any other person – Your petitioner further states, that he took no active part in stopping the stage that was going down from Toronto, that as your petitioner was informed it was stoped by some of the advanced party but that nothing whatever was taken from it – That with regard to the mail horses which were detained on their way up to Toronto, it was done without any orders from your petitioner and by a portion of the men over whom petitioner had no controul, that no mail was taken upon this or any other occasion by your petitioner or any of the men under him, the whole of which facts your petitioner is of opinion he can substantiate by affidavit –

Your petitioner would further beg leave to state that during the last war with the United States of America he served as a Sergeant in the Militia under Capt. Duncan Cameron,[98] Capt. Howard and other officers; That your petitioner never attended but one public meeting upon politics in his life, and should never have been seduced from his allegiance but for a number of his neighbours coming to his home on Saturday the second day of december last and insisting upon your petitioner being their Captain – That he has a wife and eight children[,] the youngest only about six months old[,] besides two step children

[98]This was probably the Duncan Cameron who had arrived in York, Upper Canada, from Scotland by 1801. This Duncan Cameron served in the War of 1812 and commanded a company of York militia at Queenston Heights. In 1817 he served as provincial secretary and was appointed to the Legislative Council in 1820. He held the latter appointment until his death.

who depend upon your petitioner for support [–] Under all these circumstances, and the crime with which he now stands charged and convicted tho' heinous being the first of his life, your petitioner humbly prays that your Excellency in the exercise of the prerogative with which you are invested will be pleased to respite the awful sentence under which your petitioner is most justly placed, in order to afford your petitioner an opportunity of pleading at the foot of the Throne of Her Most Gracious Majesty by petition for mercy and such a commutation of his Awful sentence as to Her Majesty may seem meet, and your petitioner as in duty bound will ever pray with a broken hearted and distressed family for your Excellencies happiness here and in eternity. –

E 67   "A Friend" to the *Christian Guardian*
Toronto, 8 June 1838
[Christian Guardian, *Toronto, 27 June 1838*]

THE LATTER DAYS OF LOUNT AND MATTHEWS. – (No. ii.) . . .

REV. AND DEAR SIR, – My second and last visit to them was on the evening of Wednesday, about twelve hours before the solemn event of their execution. They were alone; and scarcely had the door closed upon us, when Lount, in cheerful accents, announced to me that a most happy change had taken place in his state of mind since our previous interview, and that he now had no doubt of his peace with God through our Lord Jesus Christ. In the earlier part of the day, while engaged in meditation and prayer, pacing his room, and lifting up his heart to God, divine comfort arose within him, and he obtained such an assurance of mercy from heaven, as that he was obliged to fall on his knees, and weep and praise and pray. "Since then," he added, "all my fears have been entirely removed." . . .

I ventured to ask his views of the late Rebellion, and of his conduct in relation to it; when he readily admitted its unlawfulness, and deeply regretted the part he had taken in it. Notwithstanding his character for shrewdness and good sense, he himself assured me he had been beguiled to become a party in the conspiracy by the most flagrant misstatements of Mackenzie, who visited him, in the country, for that object. Some particulars of these Lount mentioned to me, and which I knew to be outrageously false. He remarked that he discovered the delusion on reaching Montgomery's; but then he appeared to have been too far committed to the proceeding to retrace his steps from it. . . . Both the prisoners had declared that the punishment of death was nothing more than what they had expected from the first moment of their apprehension. Both had acknowledged the justice of their sentence. Lount said, "Life is sweet; and I should be glad to live, and endeavour to train up my children in the fear of God, which great duty I confess I have most criminally neglected." "However," he added, "who can tell? No man ought to put any trust in himself. Perhaps were we to live, we might turn back again to sin as formerly; and it may be best for us to go now."To which Matthews, who spoke but little, immediately replied, "Yes; and we ought to be thankful we were not suddenly cut down during the fighting, and that we have had time and space to turn to God!" . . .

E 68 W.L. MACKENZIE'S AND CHARLES DURAND'S COMMENTS ON THE EXECUTIONS
[The Caroline Almanack . . . for 1840 *(Rochester, 1839), pp. 40-1]*

APRIL 12. 1838, Messrs. LOUNT and MATTHEWS, two of the bravest of the Canada patriots, were executed this day, by order of Sir George Arthur, and at the urgent request of Chief Justice Robinson; Hagerman the Attorney General; and Sullivan, Baldwin, Elmsley,[99] Allan and Draper, the Executive Council. Petitions to Arthur, signed by upwards of 30,000 persons were presented, asking him to spare their lives, but in vain. He knew that Victoria and the English Ministry and Peerage thirsted for Canadian blood – he had been told to follow Head's example, by Lord Glenelg, and he obeyed orders. Capt. Matthews left a widow and fifteen fine children, and Colonel Lount a widow and seven children. He was upwards of six feet in height, very good looking, and in his 47th year. Arthur was earnest to know of Lount who the leaders were, but, except that he told him that Dr. Rolph was the Executive, he answered him not a word. They behaved with great resolution at the gallows; they would not have spoken to the people, had they desired it. The spectacle of LOUNT after the execution was the most shocking sight that can be imagined. He was covered over with his blood; the head being nearly severed from his body, owing to the depth of the fall. More horrible to relate, when he was cut down, two ruffians seized the end of the rope and dragged the mangled corpse along the ground into the jail yard, some one exclaiming "this is the way every d___d rebel deserves to be used." Their families are impoverished. . . . Mr. Lount's wife was, for two months prevented from even seeing her husband, by the monster Head. When she was allowed to enter his dungeon (his son writes, that) "his eyes were

[99]John Elmsley (1801–1863) was the son of John Elmsley Sr., former chief justice of Upper and then Lower Canada. Born in Toronto, young Elmsley joined the Royal Navy in 1818, serving until 1824, when he retired as a lieutenant on half-pay. In 1825 he returned from England. He was welcomed onto the Executive Council in 1830 and the Legislative Council in 1831. He served for several years as a director of the Bank of Upper Canada and founded the Farmers' Bank in 1835.

In 1833 he converted to Catholicism and resigned from the Executive Council over the lieutenant-governor's criticism of his land speculations (he was reappointed in 1836). In 1837, as a militia officer, he helped Drew cut out the *Caroline* and later served on the Great Lakes. A disagreement over his commission led to his dismissal from the Legislative Council in 1839. He spent his later years operating ships on the Great Lakes, looking after his properties, and serving the Catholic Church.

settled in their sockets, his face pale as paper, he was worn down to the form of a living skeleton, and bound in heavy chains. . . ." . . .

Mr. Charles Durand, then under sentence of death, gives the following account of the last days of these glorious martyrs: – "Matthews always bore up in spirits well. He was, until death, firm in his opinion of the justice of the cause he had espoused. He never recanted. He was ironed and kept in the darkest cell in the prison like a murderer. He slept sometimes in blankets that were wet and frozen. He had nothing to cheer him but the approbation of his companions and his conscience. Lount was ironed, tho' kept in a better room. He was in good spirits. He used to tell us often, in writing, not to be downcast, that he believed 'Canada would yet be free,' that we were 'contending in a good cause.' He said he was not sorry for what he had done, and that 'he would do so again.' This was his mind until death. Lount was a social and excellent companion, and a well informed man. He sometimes spoke to us under the sill of our door. He did so on the morning of his execution! he bid us 'farewell! that he was on his way to another world.' He was calm. He and Matthews came out to the gallows, that was just before our window grates. We could see all plainly. – They ascended the platform with unfaltering steps like men. Lount turned his head at his friends who were looking through the iron-girt windows, as if to say a 'long farewell!' He and Matthews knelt and prayed, and were launched into eternity without almost a single struggle. Oh! the horror of our feelings, who can describe them!" . . .

E 69   EXTRACT OF A LETTER FROM REV. JOHN RYERSON
[*Egerton Ryerson, "The Story of My Life," edited by J.G. Hodgins (Toronto, 1883), pp. 183-4*]

At eight o'clock to-day, Thursday, 12th April, Lount and Mathews were executed. The general feeling is in total opposition to the execution of those men. Sheriff Jarvis burst into tears when he entered the room to prepare them for execution. They said to him very calmly, "Mr. Jarvis, do your duty; we are prepared to meet death and our Judge." They then, both of them, put their arms around his neck and kissed him. They were then prepared for execution. They walked to the gallows with entire composure and firmness of step. Rev. J. Richardson[100] walked alongside of Lount, and Dr. Beatty[101] alongside of Mathews. They ascended the scaffold and knelt down on the drop.

[100]James Richardson (1791–1875) was born at Kingston and educated there. Joining the provincial marine in 1809, he gained a lieutenant's commission in 1812 and served with distinction in the War of 1812, losing an arm. He was appointed magistrate and collector of customs at Presqu'ile at the end of the war but gave these posts up in 1825 to pursue a life as an itinerant Methodist preacher. Before long Richardson emerged as a major figure in Canadian Methodism, serving as editor of the *Christian Guardian*, 1832–3, and holding other important posts. When the Wesleyan Methodist Church joined the British Wesleyan Church in Canada, he gradually became disillusioned with

The ropes were adjusted while they were on their knees. Mr. Richardson engaged in prayer; and when he came to that part of the Lord's Prayer, "Forgive us our trespasses, as we forgive those that trespass against us," the drop fell!

E 70   SIR GEORGE ARTHUR TO THE EXECUTIVE COUNCIL
[*PAC, Upper Canada State Papers, v. 50, pp. 48-51*]

Executive Council Chamber
10th April 1838

. . . It is respectfully recommended that an order in Council do issue in the following Terms. . . .

1st That the Attorney General do forbear to institute proceedings by indictment against all or any persons liberated upon bail by the Commission of Inquiry unless it shall appear upon Information.

That the person to be indicted.

Was active as a leader amongst the rebels during the late revolt.

Was personally concerned in any murder robbery or arson done or committed during the said Revolt.

Was active in instigating and seducing others to join in the said Revolt

Continued traitorously to conspire against Her Majesty after the suppression of the said revolt.

or who absconded from the Province. and fled from Justice –

And in case any person or persons not coming within the above exceptions shall be hereafter arrested committed or presented by the Grand Jury, the Attorney General is directed to report the case, and to forbear proceedings until the Pleasure of His Excellency be Known.

And it is further ordered that all such cases in which such forbearance or stay of proceedings shall take place be laid before Her Majesty, and shall await the signification of Her Majestys pleasure thereupon.

And it is further ordered that this order shall be held to apply to persons admitted to bail by the magistrates in the other Districts of The Province and to persons not arrested or committed in these Districts. . . .

Geo Arthur. . . .

---

the growing connection between his church and the state. In 1836 he left the Wesleyans and, after a short time, joined the Methodist Episcopal Church, rising to be bishop in 1858, an office he retained until his death.

[101]John Beatty (1782–1864) was born in County Tyrone, Ireland, in 1782. Converted from the Church of England to Methodism at the age of 21, he emigrated to New York, where he practised as a class leader. In 1819 he came to the Credit River area of Upper Canada, being both a farmer and a class leader. In 1828 he was accepted into the ministry. He was an itinerant in various parts of Upper Canada, 1827–35. He also spent eight years in various positions with the Upper Canada Academy. In 1842 he retired at Cobourg.

E 71   W.H. DRAPER TO JOHN JOSEPH
London, 24 April 1838
[*PAC, Upper Canada Sundries, v. 192, pp. 106856-65*]

. . . an example of some severity is in my opinion necessary in this district as well for the subduing the spirit which even yet exists in some quarters, particularly in Norwich and the South part of Yarmouth, as for the protection of Her Majesty's loyal subjects. – I have only lately heard of some of the Crown Witnesses who were bound to appear, having left the country – and though I have not information sufficient to warrant any proceedings, I have enough to lead me to conclude that they have been got out of the way by the friends of those who are indicted. I will only add, that all who are not forthcoming are witnesses against Elias Moore Esq: M.P.P. and some of his near relations. . . .

E 72   PETITION OF STEPHEN SMITH[102] TO SIR GEORGE ARTHUR
Hamilton Gaol, n.d.
[*PAC, Upper Canada Sundries, v. 194, pp. 108090-1*]

. . . I beseech you to spair my life for my soul sake (1) spair my life until I can be better prepaired for eternity[,] dont put me out of the world in my sins if I can be spaired to once more enjoy my family to bring them up in the fear of the lord and that I may serve my God and Country better (1) spair my life[,] spair it[.] Confine me in any dungeon or send me – to any part of the erth but spair my life until I can be better prepaired to meat my God –

(1) [s]pair my lif and I wil prais you and serve my God and Country while I liv[.]

E 73   MERCY MUST BE DISPENSED SPARINGLY
[Gazette, *London, 19 May 1838*]

As the Special Commission for the Trial of persons suspected of Treason and Treasonable Practices has closed in this, it becomes necessary to indulge in some general remarks on the result of its investigations. All the principal traitors petitioned for executive mercy, which according to the act must be granted inasmuch as the life of the prisoner is concerned; but those who had any hopes of getting clear threw themselves upon the country for trial, six of whom have consequently been convicted and three condemned.[103] The question

[102]Stephen Smith (b. *ca.* 1813), an American, settled in Norwich from the United States in 1835. In 1837, a husband and father, Smith, a tradesman who described himself as being poor, collected weapons for the rebels. He was jailed at Hamilton on 23 December 1837 and tried that spring for treason and found guilty. He was freed on bail in September 1838.

[103]The six were Alvaro Ladd, Ebenezer Wilcox, Robert Cook, Enoch Moore, John Moore, and Harvey Bryant. The first three had their cases reserved for further consideration. The last three were condemned to death but their sentences were later respited.

now discussed is whether or not the sentence will be executed. As the trials took place merely for ascertaining their guilt or innocence – not from any desire to single them out as the most prominently guilty – it seems unreasonable to suppose that they will be denied those benefits which are secured to their equally guilty confederates. . . . Justice to the loyal and peaceable portion of the community certainly requires, that so enormous a crime as treason should receive the heaviest penalty; but the government, founded as it is in the affections of the people, is powerful enough to say, "let us be unjust that we may be generous." Mercy on the other hand pleads for lenity to the unfortunate beings, many of whom have no other fault than a fanatic desire to kill those who are contented to live in peace. . . .

Before the insurrection commenced we saw it approaching and raised our warning voice; we also foresaw its results, and told the disloyal that, although they might be allowed for awile [sic] to tamper with the British lion, yet when once aroused from his apparent slumber, he would arise in his might and crush them to the dust. They heeded us not: but where are they now? They are on their knees – pitiful, prostrate, and repentant – begging for that mercy which the enormity of their wickedness forbids us ever to have expected from them. . . . Notwithstanding their speedy defeat, they still attribute it to want of precaution and unforeseen accidents on their part, rather than to the numbers, the loyalty, and the bravery of their opposers – they are the same incorrigible dunces they always were; but were it possible to convince them of our power, we might then say to the guilty wretch, "Your crimes are forgiven you: go sin no more;" but lest the native malignancy of a traitorous spirit should again tempt them to rebel in defiance of the feelings of gratitude, which a traitor never did and never can possess, they must be removed from the possibility of ever again attempting to drench the land with the blood of unoffending citizens. He who would clench the murderous steel to enslave his fellow-man, deserves not to be free – pepetual [sic] slavery is his natural doom; but in consideration of their total inability to do much mischief, we pity them for pity's sake, and not because we think the severest punishment too great for them.

But while we wish a degree of mercy to be shown, we by no means advocate the doctrine of a general goal [sic] delivery. This would be fraught with the worst of consequences. To turn loose upon society, after a deal of expense, those who have disturbed its repose, would be giving a premium for treason, and inciting them on to farther deeds of wickedness. At the same time it would deter the loyal from again entering so freely into the service of the Crown upon the next attempt being made – an event which will as certainly follow as an effect follows a cause. When the insurrection began, it was proclaimed by the government to "leave punishment to the laws." The people of Upper Canada obeyed this injunction to the letter, trusting that the government would not allow crime to be committed with impunity. . . . Now it remains to be seen whether the laws are to be enforced – so far at least as is consistent with mercy to a weak & fallen enemy, who wanted neither the will nor the wickedness to execute their horrid purposes but strength and adequate means.

E 74   SOLICITOR GENERAL'S[104] OBSERVATIONS ON THE WESTERN
RISING AND THE WESTERN PRISONERS
Toronto, 28 May 1838
[PRO, CO 42, v. 447, pp. 133-150, microfilm in PAO]

Although the rising of the insurgents in the London and the Western extremity of the Gore Districts was so nearly simultaneous with that at Toronto, and though the object of all was identical, little has appeared in the course of the whole investigation to establish any previous concert or general agreement to co-operate. There is no room to doubt that the principal leaders were in correspondence with each other, and had perhaps resolved upon their desperate course some time before they carried their designs into effect; but the circumstances tend strongly to shew that no period was actually fixed for the outbreak, and that the great mass of their followers, though their minds had been excited and prepared for a movement of some description, had been Kept in total ignorance of the designs of the leading conspirators. . . .

The whole number of prisoners committed to the Gaol at Hamilton in the Gore District or bound to appear there, was Sixty five; of these sixteen were discharged for want of evidence or used as witnesses on behalf of the Crown; five were discharged upon sureties to Keep the peace and be of good behavior; bills of indictment against three were ignored, and forty one were indicted. – Of these fourteen petitioned under the statute confessing their guilt; ten were convicted, and the remainder were acquitted. –

In the London District there were seventy prisoners committed to gaol, and about one hundred and thirty admitted to bail, against whom pursuant to the Order in Council of the 10th April, no indictments were preferred. – of these seven were discharged for want of evidence, some of them on finding sureties to Keep the peace and be of good behaviour; three were made Crown witnesses; Bills of indictment against four were ignored and fifty four were indicted; of these thirty nine petitioned under the Statute; Six were tried and convicted, and the residue were acquitted; – Two cases remained untried; one in consequence of the severe illness of the prisoner, who in consideration of danger to his life from further confinement was admitted to bail; and one indicted for misprision of Treason, also admitted to bail, whose trial was deferred partly on the ground of the Crown witnesses having absconded, and partly on account of some technical difficulty. –

[104]W.H. Draper was the solicitor general.

Of the persons indicted as above mentioned, Twenty two were natives of the United States who have from time to time settled in this province. – It is also worthy of remark, that of those who were indicted and petitioned, a large portion are young men, between the ages of seventeen and twenty five and possessed of little or no property. – Thirty one indictments were preferred and returned true bills against persons who had taken a leading part in the treasonable proceedings in the Gore and London Districts, and had fled, with a view to their attainder under the provincial Statute of last Session. –

It is necessary however to state that although the number of the actual insurgents in these two Districts was thus limited, had any success attended their movements, there is but too much reason to believe their numbers would have received great additions, particularly in the London District. – . . .

A meeting was held at London as soon as the news of the insurrection at Toronto reached that place of a very suspicious character; none but well Known reformers were present and consequently no evidence of their proceedings could be obtained but from some of the parties, and one of them refused to give evidence of what took place at that meeting, because he could not do so as he said without criminating himself. – Three of the leading parties at this meeting however [were] indicted, and the principal [Charles Latimer] after a long trial having been acquitted, no evidence was offered against the other two [William Hale, William Putnam]; enough however appeared to satisfy the mind of any unprejudiced person that all was not right, though the evidence given by reluctant witnesses did not bring conviction to the minds of the Jury. –

At Delaware too, a meeting was held on the Second of December to form a political Union; when news of McKenzies outbreak arrived, another meeting was called: – it was held on the Sixteenth of December. – The propriety of arming for *"self defence"* was discussed. – It was agreed that the indians should be spoken to, to remain quiet; and they were spoken to, and inducements held out to them of advantage if the insurgents were successful, and the Indians did not interfere. –

The principal actor in holding these meetings and speaking to the indians [Alvaro Ladd] was tried and convicted. –

There were some other demonstrations of an unfavourable character in one or two other places, but the rapid discomfiture of the rebels prevented any thing further; –

Still the flight of many important witnesses for the Crown in the interval between the service of the list containing their names and the trials; the violent though anonymous threats used against other witnesses of great importance; the absconding of many who had been bailed and against whom no prosecutions were instituted and even of some in whose favor verdicts of acquittal had been rendered, compel the admission that disaffection has spread in the London District more widely than from the actual numbers of the insurgents might have been imagined, and that it is mainly owing to the prompt and determined spirit of the loyal part of the population, and to the total absence of previous organization and preparation for revolt that the rebellion was so effectually and rapidly put down. – . . .

E 75   EXTRACT OF A DESPATCH FROM LORD GLENELG TO SIR GEORGE ARTHUR
London, 30 May 1838
[PRO, CO 42, v. 446, p. 59, microfilm in PAO]

I HAVE received your despatch of the 14th April last (No. 4), reporting the execution, on the 12th of that month, of Lount and Matthews, who had been convicted, on their own confession, of "high treason,"and explaining, at considerable length, the views adopted by yourself and the Executive Council with regard to these prisoners, and the considerations which appeared to you imperatively to demand that the law in this case should be allowed to take its course.

Her Majesty's Government regret extremely that a paramount necessity should have arisen for these examples of severity. They are, however, fully convinced that you did not consent to the execution of these individuals without having given the most ample consideration to all the circumstances of the case, and they have no reason to doubt the necessity of the course which, with the entire concurrence of the Executive Council, you felt it your duty to adopt.

With respect to the disposal of the other prisoners, Her Majesty's Government cannot give you any specific instructions, until they shall have received the report which you lead me to expect. But I cannot defer expressing our earnest hope that, with respect to these persons, your opinion that no further capital punishments will be necessary, may have been acted on. Nothing would cause, Her Majesty's Government, more sincere regret than an unnecessary recourse to the punishment of death, and I am persuaded that the same feeling will influence not only yourself, but the Executive Council. The examples which have been made in the case of the most guilty will be sufficient to warn others of the consequences to which they render themselves liable by such crimes, and this object having been accomplished, no further advantage could be gained by inflicting the extreme penalty of the law on any of their associates.

E 76   PETITION OF VARIOUS PRISONERS
London Gaol, 5 June 1838
[PAC, Upper Canada Sundries, v. 195, pp. 108425-6]

To His Excellency Sir George Arthur Lieutenant Governor of the Province of Upper Canada &c &c &c

The Petition of certain persons – Prisoners *now* confined to the Cells of London Prison. –

Most humbly sheweth –

That your Petitioners are among the number who in March last addressed Petitions to the Lieutenant Governor, in consequence of a communication made to us by the honorable Allen N McNab, pointing us to an Act of Parliament, which empowered the Governour to dispose of the cases of such Petitioners – and to extend lenity according to His will and pleasure. –

With joy we cherished the strongest hopes, and with speed we hastened to lay our cases before the power to pardon; believing confidently that but a short time would elapse, before our missteps would be viewed with lenity; the mantle of charity cast over our motives and delusions; a pardon magnanimously extended and the Petitioners restored to their suffering wives and families. –

Long delays occurred, which excited wonder: But when the Petitioners heard of the release of about fifty persons, who had petitioned similar to ourselves, in the City of Toronto, hope revived, and the Petitioners confidently expected from day to day a similar act of noble generosity and clemency to be extended to them. But alas! It is now the fifth day of June and no friendly or consoling eye or hand that can help us, appears to be turned towards the Petitioners. They wonder the more at this, as they truly consider their cases to be much more mitigated than the Toronto characters: – in their rising valuable property was burned; murders committed – and other violent depredations openly threatened and daringly executed. – While your Petitioners declare that no such motives actuated them; and they appeal to all that has happened from the breaking out of the disturbance to the time of their imprisonment for proof of the assertion. – No person was injured – No Property was unrespected: – no violation or indecency whatsoever was committed. And we earnestly appeal to your Excellency who alone can dry the tear, and ease the heart, whether we can compare our two different cases together and reconcile them to that sense of Equity, which exists in every individual. –

That our means are exhausting: – our Property wasting: – our wives and families suffering both mentally and corporally. –

And above all, that the Petitioners, who were through the Winter, in a comparatively comfortable Room, were suddenly, on the second instant selected from their fellow Prisoners, and removed therefrom into the Cells of this Jail – where were six other Prisoners making altogether fifteen persons. –

The Petitioners are assigned to three Cells, not more than Eight feet square each, into which these fifteen persons are nightly crowded. In the day permission is given to a narrow passage, in which, two persons can hardly walk abreast leading into a small room, very little larger than one of the Cells, in which the Prisoners take their meals – a door with wide openings between the boards, opens from this, into a very badly calculated place of necessity – which from its very bad construction, continually pours into the adjoining Room the most intollerable smell. Within four feet of this bad place is a Stove in which the Petitioners are obliged to keep a fire on account of the chilliness and dampness of the place – Three narrow apertures in the wall opposite the cells and across the narrow passage is all by which light and air are admitted – no circulation of air therefore can be enjoyed – The air is damp and heavy and hard of respiration. – one of our number is taken already violently ill: – and without doubt the most of the Prisoners will shortly be deprived, in consequence of their numbers and confined situation of that little health which they now enjoy, and probably of that life which as human beings they cannot but prize. –

Your Petitioners therefore most humbly pray, that your Excellency will at your earliest convenience, take the cases & afflictions of the Petitioners into your Excellencys kind consideration, and extend to us that lenity and compassion, which from the representations of high and leading individuals, in the confidence of Government, we have been led to expect – and particularly that your Excellency would give directions for our removal into a more tolerable and healthy part of this Jail – as we assure Your Excellency could be done, without any inconvenience to any person whosoever

And your Petitioners as in duty bound will ever pray. –

June 5th 1838.

Joseph Hart[105]
Paul Bedford
Nathaniel Deo[106]
Finlay Malcolm
Edward Carman
John A Tidey
Jas. *Bell*
John Kelly
Horatio Fowler[107]

[105] Joseph Hart (b. *ca.* 1797) was born in New York State, moving with his wife and family to Norwich about 1833. Hart, who was evidently poor, served as a lieutenant with the rebels in December 1837. He was jailed on 18 December, and, after petitioning, was freed in October 1838.

[106] Nathaniel Deo (b. *ca.* 1797), a native of New York State, settled in Upper Canada about 1809 with his family. In December 1837 Deo, who lived in Dorchester Township, helped organize meetings of local residents to discuss what actions, if any, to take in response to the rebellion. He went into hiding after the failure of the risings, but was captured and jailed in March 1838. After petitioning, he was freed on bail in September.

[107] Fowler and five others were freed some months after submitting their petition, while Bedford and Malcolm were transported and Carman sent to penitentiary.

E 77   PETITION OF JESSE CLEAVER[108]
[*PAC, Upper Canada Sundries, v. 200, p. 110662-3*]

To His Excellency Sir George Arthur . . .
The Petition of Jesse Cleaver a prisoner Confined in the Jail of the City of Toronto for the Crime of high treason,
Humbly Sheweth
That your Petitioner has been now Confined in Jail nearly five months.
That his health is daily suffering from his Confinement. He is a poor man and has a large family of young Children who are dependent on his daily labor for a livelihood
Your Petitioner was never examined by the Commissioners and is unaware of what is laid to his Charge –
He took but little part in the late Rebellion and the part he did take he was foolishly persuaded to do by others. . . .

E 78   HENRY SMITH[109] TO JOHN MACAULAY
Kingston Penitentiary, 30 July 1838
[*PAC, Upper Canada Sundries, v. 200, p. 110884A*]

As it appears from the statements of the seventeen prisoners who were received into this Establishment in obedience to His Excellency's the Lieutenant Governor's Warrant dated the 11th Instant that they have never been informed of the particulars of their several sentences I beg leave to request that instructions may be given to me as to whether I am to make known to the said prisoners their respective sentences, as by the terms of the Warrant I am only directed to receive them into my charge and to discharge them at the expiration of their imprisonment.

E 79   "J.E."[110] TO THE *Examiner*
[*PAO, Mackenzie–Lindsey Clippings, No. 4687*]
n.p., n.d.
The Canadian State Prisoners in London

. . . The ill-fated prisoners it will be recollected, petitioned the

[108]Jesse H. Cleaver (b. 1802 or 1803) came to Upper Canada from Pennsylvania in 1833. He was either born in that state or had come to Pennsylvania from England, but he was an American citizen when he entered Upper Canada. He worked as a cooper in King Township, likely in Lloydtown. Arrested in March 1838, he petitioned for pardon but was banished. In September 1838 he advertised in Rochester, New York, for work as a carpenter and joiner, or as a model maker.

[109]Henry Smith (d. 1866) emigrated from his native England to Montreal before 1818. In the early 1820s he and his family moved to Kingston, where in 1835 he became the first warden of the new penitentiary. In 1849 a commission appointed by the Baldwin–LaFontaine government, with George Brown as its secretary, condemned Smith's administration, particularly for its harsh treatment of prisoners, and he was dismissed.

[110]"J.E." may have been reformer John Elliott of Toronto.

government for pardon under the provisions of the Provincial statute, acknowledging their guilt. After suffering long and tedious imprisonment, they were at length informed (as if by way of mockery) that their PARDON was granted under the condition of being transported to a penal colony *for life*. At a moment's warning they were conveyed from Fort Henry to Quebec heavily ironed, exposed [on] the open deck of a vessel during a severe frosty night, and even obliged to lie down among horses; – and subsequently shipped to Liverpool, in a vessel the accommodation in which is described to be equal to any slave ship. Doubtless it must have been some compensation to them on their arrival in England, after the cruelties inflicted on them, to find that the authorities there treated them with great humanity and respect, and all classes of the people with kindness and consideration. Trusting that they may be eventually restored to their afflicted families.

E 80   DIARY OF JOHN G. PARKER
28 November 1838
[PAO, Mackenzie–Lindsey Papers, Mackenzie Correspondence, Narrative of John G. Parker, filed in John G. Howard, Statement Regarding the Rebellion of 1837]

We were taken on board this vessel on thursday the 22nd instant [Nov. 1838] in the forenoon and have proceeded thus far on our Voyage without accident having a favourable wind – I procured in Quebec a sufficient supply of sea stores, but we are so crowded that they will probably do us but little good – through the mercy of God I am favoured with good health although numbers are sick around me – this is not surprising as 17 of us are confined in a space 5 feet by 10 and a less space for 17 others on the other side of the hatchway, making 34 prisoners – the only light we have is through a piece of glass in the deck called a deadlight – it is dark between 3 & 4 when we go to bed and lay (not sleep) untill 8 or 9 oClock next morning – Mr Wait[111] and myself are still chained together and have a berth to ourselves [–] others are more crowded having to stow 3 or 4 in ea: berth. . . .

[111]Benjamin Wait (1813–1895) was a native of Markham Township. In the 1830s he ran a sawmill near York on the Grand River but later worked as a clerk in Port Colborne. He appears to have left Upper Canada in the summer of 1837 after being jailed at Niagara for debt. He joined Mackenzie on Navy Island in December 1837 and the Short Hills raiders in June 1838. Captured after the raid, he was tried. At his trial he described himself as a law student. He had been very prominent with the raiders and it was no surprise he was found guilty of treason and condemned to death. His sentence was later commuted to transportation to Van Diemen's Land for life. His wife Maria tried desperately to persuade the authorities to free him, but he eventually freed himself, escaping from Van Diemen's Land in 1842. The next year in Buffalo he published *Letters from Van Dieman's Land*, which presented his and Maria's accounts of their combined ordeal. He later lived in Duluth, Minnesota, and Grand Rapids, Michigan.

E 81   PETITION OF MARY ANN KENDRICK[112] TO SIR F.B. HEAD
York Township, 12 December 1837
[*PAC, Upper Canada Sundries, v. 180, pp. 99110-11*]

. . . Humbly Showeth,

That your Petitioner is the Wife of William Kendrick[113] of said place [York Township] Inn Keeper who is at present a prisoner in the Gaol of this city. Petitioner begs to state that your Excellency immediately released her husband on his first being taken prisoner in his own house and brought before you and on Petitioner having addressed your Excellency on Saturday last for the release of her husband, (he having been arrested a second time) you were graciously pleased to order his release in writing on the back of the said Petition, which Petition was kept from her after she presented it and the order for his release has not been complied with. Petitioner was therefore obliged to return to her house without her husband who is still detained a Prisoner. She humbly begs to state, that since her husband has been made prisoner her house has been robbed of almost every thing of value it contained[,] her person ill treated and abused, every particle of provision taken from her, which she had for the maintenance of her husband, herself and eight children which were all living with her.

Petitioner begs to state that amongst the number of pretended friends to the Government that resides in her neighborhood, there is no person more deserving of reprehension than Mr. Hogg the Miller, nor is there she sincerely believes one whose disposition is more inimical to the Government than him. McKenzie and his family has been his constant visiters during the last Summer, and no two persons could be on a more intimate footing, he having at one particular period paid four Dollars in treating McKenzie and his men, altho now pretending to extraordinary loyalty. The said Mr. Hogg has entered your Petitioner's house last night and violently threatened to ill use herself and family, and to such a pitch was his violent conduct carried, that Petitioner had to go above half a mile in her bare feet to seek protection. Petitioner therefore humbly begs, that your Excellency will be graciously pleased to order the Gaoler where her husband now is to release him, and your humble Petitioner as in duty bound,

Will ever pray –

[112]Mary Ann Kendrick lived with her husband William on lot 6, concession 1, west side, of York Township.
[113]William Kendrick was probably a son of one of the four Kendrick brothers who took up lots 6, 7, 8, and 9 on concession 1, west side, of York Township. They acquired the lots after the American Revolution, in which they had been pilots. They took up milling at York Mills and served in the provincial marine during the War of 1812. In 1837 William bought a quarter of an acre of lot 9 on concession 1, where he ran his tavern. He was arrested on 7 December and freed on 21 December after being examined.

E 82 SAMUEL MCMURRAY[114] TO JOHN JOSEPH
House of Assembly's Office, 7 June 1838
[*PAC, Upper Canada Sundries, v. 199, pp. 110376-8*]

May it please Your Excellency
Sir,

Permit me, through the Kindness you have always shewn to listen to any enquiry which has been made to you in reason, to reply, and as I have a particular favor to ask, I hope I do not do so without a cause sufficient to bear me out.

I will briefly mention the circumstances for His Excellency's consideration – A woman of the name of Watson[115] whose husband[116] has undergone the penalty of the law and is now at Kingston Gaol, called upon me and informs me that two individuals have two Horses belonging to her, and have Kept them since the day of Battle and worked them, and now refuse to give them up to her or her poor *starving* family – I pity the poor woman and family, but I cannot pity *Watson* – She will have no object[ion] and has no objection (not the least) for the Government to use them, but she thinks that private individuals, after having them all Winter and working them should either give them up to the Government or return them to her, to support her poor helpless family – I have undertaken this as a heavy task, but I think Justice commands me and I am sure you will not think hard of me for thus addressing you – Being enrolled and always was a British subject I can have no other reason, than saving a poor widow (and I may call her) and Children from Starvation –

I could not thus have written to you on the subject before me, but Knowing too well the generosity of the English government, I am willing to venture the case before me [–] I have done it with pure principles and honesty – Because as the poor woman says, that if the Government takes them, they are welcome to them, and she would think no more about them –

I shall add nothing more except if His Excellency would wish to hear, or to Know, any thing more particular, Mrs. Watson will attend His Excellency's pleasure – . . .

---

[114]Samuel McMurray was a clerk for the Assembly. His letter was considered by the Executive Council when it deliberated the petition of Joseph Watson of 19 July 1838.

[115]Mrs. Watson was the wife of Joseph Watson of Lloydtown. The couple had eight children in 1837.

[116]Joseph Watson came from Scotland to Lloydtown, where in 1833 he bought half an acre on lot 31, concession 9. A carpenter by trade, he was also postmaster of Lloydtown and painted flags for use during elections. He was active in the political union movement prior to the rebellion. During the rising he painted a flag for the rebels and was active at Montgomery's Tavern. He surrendered in mid-December 1837, petitioned, and was sentenced to three years in penitentiary, followed by banishment. In 1839 he was pardoned.

E 83   Petition of Phoebe D. Willson[117]
Hope, 14 July 1838
[PAC, Upper Canada Sundries, v. 199, pp. 110263-4]

To the high Commissionor of the british provinces Earl of Durham,[118] &c. &c.

Sir hear with patence the voice of the afflicted – many are Crying unto you and my words Shall be few – I am the disconsolate wife of Hugh D Willson[119] who has departed from Toronto Jail after seven months Close Confinement – I attended the prison with Crumbes through the winter leaving my Children and home to Cry after me hoping his long Imprisonment and his testimonal desire to stay in the Country with fidelity to the Queen would be accepted for his offence – but it hath pleased the Government to send him away to me unknown and to where unseen – you are the last I can look to under heaven for a remady – many tears are shed for him because he was much beloved but all in vain [–] his Crime hath apeard to be unpardonable – but my hope is in you to Consider me and my little ones – his affectionate father[120] and mother[121] weeping in there old age over the son of there bosom – and abate dear parant the tears of the afflicted – he is a dutiful son a loving Husband and tender farther – have mercy and heaven reward you the like again –

[117]Phoebe D. Willson was the wife of Hugh D. Willson, a member of the Children of Peace or Davidites. Since members of that sect usually married other members of the sect, Phoebe was probably a Davidite also. The couple lived in the village of Hope (later Sharon).

[118]John George Lambton (1792–1840) was elected a British MP in 1814, and gained a reputation for being a radical. Elevated to the peerage in 1828, he became a member of Lord Grey's ministry in 1830. In 1836 he was appointed British ambassador to Russia, and in 1838 selected to investigate the causes of the rebellions in the Canadas and make recommendations on the political state and future of the two colonies. His massive report, finished in England after he had returned there having resigned his post because the Colonial Office had overturned an executive order of his, aroused a storm of controversy but did lead to the union of the two Canadas. He died of consumption, as had many in his family.

[119]Hugh D. Willson was the younger son of David Willson, founder of the Davidites. Hugh was a merchant who for some years prior to 1832 was in partnership with Charles Doan; thereafter he was on his own. He engaged in some land speculation, keeping for himself lot 9, concession 2 of East Gwillimbury. He became postmaster of Hope and in 1851 served as the township clerk of East Gwillimbury.

[120]David Willson (1778–1866) was born in the colony of New York, and went to work at an early age after being orphaned. Before 1800 he married a fellow Quaker and they emigrated to Upper Canada with their two sons in 1801, settling near Hope. David joined the local Quaker meeting in 1805 but was ill at ease with it, as were most of its members with him. In 1812 he was expelled and, with a few who followed him from the meeting, he established the Children of Peace, a group that had certain doctrinal differences from the Quakers and a strong belief in the use of music to inspire worship. Willson's teachings were at best obscure, serving to encourage many of the young men in the community to join the uprising in 1837, even though he himself opposed the rebellion.

[121]Phoebe (Titus) Willson, a Quaker, married David Willson near Poughkeepsie,

E 84 PETITION OF ANNA CODY
September 1838 ?
[PAC, Upper Canada Sundries, v. 206, pp. 113978-81]

To His Excellency Sir George Arthur . . .

The petition of Anna Cody of the township of Whitchurch wife of Jay Cody[122]

Humbly Sheweth,

That your petitioners husband Jay Cody was unfortunately induced by evil minded persons to leave his home on Monday morning the fourth of December last with a number of his neighbours, to join in the late attempt at revolution, that having on Wednesday the sixth of the same month wandered south-wards from the party to which he was attached and lost his way, he was taken prisoner and confined in the Gaol of the Home District, where he remained till sent from thence to the Fort at point Henry with the exception of six or seven weeks that he was confined in the Hospital with fever & small pox; that during his illness your petitioner attended her said husband for two weeks in the Hospital when she herself was taken ill with Typhus fever under which she laboured for four weeks – That your petitioner has two young Children who with their Mother have suffered severely from the folly and criminality of their father, who born and brought up in this Country, has ever conducted himself as a loyal subject and peaceable Citizen until the occasion of the late unfortunate and criminal outbreak – That his aged mother now upon her death bed, broken hearted, prays as her last earthly consolation to see him once more before she closes her eyes in death; In this prayer your Excellencies petitioner most fervently joins, and that he may be once more restored to an affectionate but wretched family – In the respectful but confident hope of influencing your Excellencies kindly feelings in her behalf your petitioner would mention that her father John Richard and his family are well known for their loyalty and attachment to the Government and constitution of the Country, he having served in defence of the Country during the last war with the United States of America [–] Wherefore your petitioner humbly prays that your Excellency will be pleased to extend the Royal mercy to her unfortunate husband who has suffered now nearly nine months of imprisonment, six weeks of this time in irons, and permit him to return to his family and friends upon such security for his good behaviour as to your Excellency shall seem meet and proper –

New York, prior to 1800 and accompanied him and their two sons to Upper Canada in 1801.

[122]Jay Cody, a Canadian-born farmer, lived on part of lot 83, concession 1 of King Township, which was owned by his mother in 1837. He, however, owned two and one half acres of lot 68 from 1835 until 1838. After being captured on 6 December, he was held until October of 1838, when he was pardoned.

E 85   PETITION OF JAMES AND WILLIAM LESSLIE[123]
Toronto, 9 January 1838
[*PAC, Upper Canada State Papers, v. 45, pp. 82-93*]

To the Queens Most Excellent Majesty –

The Petition of James Lesslie of the City of Toronto in the Province of Upper Canada Banker and William Lesslie of the same place Merchant –

Humbly sheweth. . . .

That on the eighth of December last a few days after the first insurrectionary movements in this Province their dwelling and premises were violently entered, taken possession of and kept by a Body of armed men under the direction of a person named Alexr. Dixon[124] one of the Aldermen of the City [–] That the persons of your Petitioners without any examination, warrant or commitment were consigned as criminals to the Common Jail of the District [–] That upon demanding of the said Alexr. Dixon by what authority he had instituted those proceedings he replied that he acted under the special direction and authority of Christopher Alexander Hagerman Esquire Your Majesty's Attorney General of this Province – that application was therefore immediately made by Your Petitioners to the said Attorney General for a copy of their Commitment and earnestly soliciting an examination into their case and also offerring if liberated to give bail to any required amount for their appearance when demanded [–] That the said Attorney General declared that "there was no Commitment drawn out, neither was any necessary: that no examination would be had until certain Commissioners were appointed and that no bail would be taken"

Your Petitioners applied further both to the Sheriff and Jailer for a Copy of their Commitment but were informed also by them that there was none and in consequence thereof up on Your Petitioners making application to the Judges of Kings Bench, to be released under the act of Habeas Corpus failed to obtain the protection of that "second great charter of the rights of Britons"[;] thus violently and unlawfully deprived of their liberty Your Petitioners were imprisoned for thirteen days in the Common jail ignorant of the cause of that imprisonment[,]

---

[123]William Lesslie (d. 1843) was a son of merchant Edward Lesslie of Dundee, Scotland. In 1820 Edward began sending out some of his sons to establish a business in Upper Canada. William came with his parents and other members of his family in 1825. The family established stores in York, Dundas, and Kingston, all called Lesslie and Sons, after a brief partnership in York and Dundas with William Lyon Mackenzie. William operated the Dundas store briefly and then took over in Kingston. Gradually the business concentrated on stationery, books, and pharmaceuticals. At the end of the 1830s William's business was merged with that of James in Toronto as Lesslie Brothers.

[124]Alexander Dixon (1792–1855) arrived in York from the north of Ireland in 1830, setting himself up as a saddler. He was a city councillor in 1835 and an alderman, 1837–44. A member of the Church of England, he was also a very active Orangeman.

their dwelling and Premises occupied for nine days by armed men who were also quartered upon them[,] their business almost suspended[,] the peace and Comfort of their household invaded, and their credit and reputation exposed to serious and irreparable injury. – That finally when your Petitioners were brought before the Commissioners alluded to they found that there existed no charge against them whatever nor did there appear to be the shadow of any ground for arrest far less for imprisonment, an imprisonment accompanied by the foregoing circumstances of high aggravation and increased by the peremptory refusal to admit any of their friends to visit them during the latter days of their confinement [–] to consummate this violation of the most sacred rights of the subject, committed in the Name of British Justice Your Petitioners were required prior to their liberation, to give each their recognizance in the penalty of £500 – to keep the peace for one year which they had in no respect violated nor intended to violate, and to appear at any of the Courts of Justice in the Province to answer to any charge which might afterward appear against them – with the hope that there exists in the Imperial Government a desire to maintain inviolate the freedom of the subject although resident in a Colony and to visit with just displeasure the unconstitutional and despotic proceedings of persons holding office therein your Petitioners hereby humbly submit their case to the gracious consideration of Your Majesty. . . .

E 86   EXECUTIVE COUNCIL ON THE CASE OF JAMES AND WILLIAM
LESSLIE
Government House, 27 July 1838
[PAC, Upper Canada State Papers, v. 45, pp. 76-9]

. . . His Excellency the Lieutenant Governor was pleased to direct the attention of the Council to a despatch from Her Majestys Secretary of state for the Colonies enclosing a petition from James Lesslie & William Lesslie – complaining of their having been illegally arrested, and of their house having been occupied by a Militia guard. and of their papers having been searched. & detained for some time from them. Also to a report from Her Majestys attorney General upon the same subject. with certain papers annexed thereto.

These documents having been read and considered. The Executive Council. beg to express their opinion That the Messrs. Lesslie have no reason to complain of their being strongly suspected of adherence to the rebels then in arms or that being suspected, they were subject to the inconveniences, of which they complain. and which they have so much exaggerated in their Statement.

The Council are aware that it was with great pain and reluctance, the Government felt forced to believe that grounds of suspicion existed against the Messrs Lesslie. The manner in which they were treated bears no appearance of a desire to oppress insult or injure them. Their arrest was a measure which the public safety seemed imperatively to require, at a time when it was apparently very much jeopardized. There was no time or opportunity for the taking of regular informations, and the investigation of their cases and their release took place as soon as the pressure of business of a like nature would permit.

The members of the Council can vouch personally for the correctness of the statements of the attorney General & the Vice Chancellor and they desire to state that they are now by no means convinced that the petitioners were free from all Knowledge of or participation in the insurrection –

They believe that it must be apparent to all reflecting minds that in cases of sudden danger from armed insurrections strict regard to private legal rights must in many cases give way to the more pressing and paramount consideration of public safety. and had the Messrs – Lesslie been sufferers from false or malicious misrepresentations, or from unfounded, or unreasonable prejudices entertained against them, It would under all the circumstances be more a matter of regret than surprise. But the Petitioners even if perfectly innocent of treasonable intentions, or of guilty concealment of them when entertained by others, cannot deny that they were active in promoting the seditious and dangerous sentiments which ended in rebellion loss of life and property and other calamities with which the Province has been visited. or that they had allowed their names to be mixed up with transactions which have since been found to lead to treason and rebellion. To their own improper conduct. or in the most favorable sense their own great imprudence they ought to attribute the proceedings against them. in the course of which it is believed they cannot allege a single act of contumely, insult. or oppression, or the visitation of any inconvenience upon them which could be avoided consistently with their safe custody, and a proper investigation of their papers. which the public safety seemed [to] require.

E 87   SIR GEORGE ARTHUR AND THE EXECUTIVE COUNCIL ON THE
CASE OF JAMES S. HOWARD
Government House, 27 June 1838
[*PAC, Upper Canada State Papers, v. 36, pp. 28-32*]

. . . His Excellency The Lieutenant Governor was pleased to lay before the Council, a Despatch from His Lordship The Secretary of State for the Colonies, on the Subject of the Suspension, OR removal, of James S. Howard Esquire, from the Office of Deputy Post Master, at Toronto, with the Accompanying Documents – upon which His Excellency desires the advice of the Council.

It appears that Mr. Howard desires an investigation of the Charges against him which occasioned his removal.

The Council beg leave on this Subject to inform Your Excellency, that previous to the rising in Arms of the Rebels near Toronto, there was much reason to suspect that an extensive Correspondence had been carried on between the disaffected through Her Majesty's Post Office, as well at Toronto, as at other places –

That there appeared no means of preventing this Correspondence, or of discovering the designs of the disaffected but by the establishing a Strict Surveillance over the Post Office and by causing suspected Letters to be opened and intercepted.

That for the adoption of this course it was necessary that the Government should have the utmost confidence in all persons in charge of the Post Office Department.

That Mr. Howard in private Life, was said to associate with persons whose Violent Course in party politics gave good ground of Suspicion of their being connected with the Rebels, or friendly, or at least not adverse to them.

That Mr. Howard's not coming forward with alacrity to offer to take up Arms, added to the Suspicions which naturally arose, from the above circumstances.

That although Mr. Howard might have been neutral as regards politics, a man in his situation at least could not be neutral, or desire to be so without blame, when the Enemy was in Arms and the Lives and property of Her Majestys Loyal Subjects supposed to be in extreme danger.

That Mr. Howard's excuse of not taking up Arms, because he was not required to do so, can hardly be received in his exculpation, in asmuch as no one at the time could have been formally required to Arm himself, the Enemy being said to be on the advance and the Alarm Bell of the Town and the Assembling of the Citizens being the only Summons which any one received.

That although the above circumstances may not be sufficient to implicate Mr. Howard in any connection with the Rebels, which implication would amount to High Treason, Yet it must be apparent that a person who allowed any grounds of Suspicion to exist against him could not be permitted to remain in a Situation on the faithful and zealous discharge of the duties of which so much depended.

The Executive Council do not desire to charge Mr. Howard with any treasonable intentions, or Actions, nor do they intend to intimate that his assiduity in his office and his long Services should not be favorably considered but Mr. Howard can have no reason to complain because in a Country, in an Actual State of Civil War, it was not thought fit to intrust him with a Department in which the Safety of the Province was liable to be compromised to an extent which was out of all proportion either as regarded Mr. Howard's character, his hopes, or his Claims.

The Executive Council do not see that a failure of proof in any actual charge against him will prove that he is fit to be a Post Master, however fit he may be to hold another Situation.

Mr. Howard not being actually charged with any Crime, the

Executive Council do not recommend An investigation. For all purposes not connected with the Post Office, Mr. Howard has a right to be presumed Innocent, until he is proved to be Guilty, As regards the Post Office Suspicion for which there was any ground, would seem to be Sufficient for his removal. Mr. Howard Cannot be expected to prove a Negative, and to establish what can only be Known to himself And therefore there is no way for him to shew his fitness for the Situation of Post Master in a time of political excitement, and of danger from an Enemy, the trust which would be required to be placed in him must be in the mind and belief of his Superiors in the Department, and in the opinion of the head of the Government, who could not be expected to undergo the charge and responsibility of their respective offices without being morally certain of the most positive Loyalty and discretion of persons holding subordinate offices of high trust and political importance.

> R B Sullivan
> PC [President of the Council?]

I think the advice of the Council, under the present circumstances of the Country, is judicious; and Sir Francis Head's suspicions, from all I have heard, were, I have no doubt, well founded.

> Geo Arthur
> 28 June 1838

E 88   W.L. MACKENZIE ON THE CASE OF JAMES S. HOWARD
[Mackenzie's Gazette, *Rochester, 9 Nov. 1839*]

A BRITISH POSTMASTER! – James Scott Howard, an Irish protestant, has come over to Rochester from Canada to reside. He was 18 years assistant to Hon. W. Allan in his various offices, and afterwards obtained the P.O. of Toronto, worth $3000 a year, from which Head removed him on suspicion of his being *a reformer*. In March, 1838, Mr. Howard wrote the postmaster general,[125] London – "My Lord, I am ready by OATH to prove that I do not hold, that I never held, any republican principles." He next petitioned Sir Francis Head, stating that he "was suspected of being a radical," and felt deeply "under the false insinuation." A supple German genius of the name of Berczy, however, outwitted him; and Howard, who, as he declares, hates democracy, eschews radicalism, and is one of the most loyal of Canada's officials, had to plunge indignant into that hot bed of sympathizers, radical Rochester.

[125]The postmaster general was the Earl of Lichfield, who had been born Thomas William Anson (1795–1854). He succeeded as Viscount Anson in 1818 and was elevated to the earldom in 1831. He served as postmaster general from 1835 to 1841, and witnessed the introduction of penny postage in 1840, an innovation he had opposed on the peculiar grounds that the flood of letters it would bring into the post offices would lead to their physical collapse.

E 89   PETITION OF JOSEPH HARR[126]
Goderich, 26 July 1838
[*PAC, Upper Canada Sundries, v. 200, pp. 110683-5*]

To His Excellency Sir George Arthur, . . .

The humble petition of Joseph Harr of the Town of Goderich. Watch & Clock Maker

Sheweth

That your petitioner was forced away on Her Majesty's service on the 6th day of January last, and altho pleading his exemption as a foreigner (being a native of Germany and only three years in this province;) Captn Prior[127] of the Huron Militia, told him unless he joined the Company in one hour – he would send him to London jail, consequently, petitioner took a number of Watches and left them in charge with one of his next neighbours, together with the key of his workshop giving strict orders not to suffer any person into his house till he returned, but instead of so doing – she suffered another man together with her son to sleep in petitioners room. which contained a quantity of Jewelry, Clocks, and one Watch and various other articles – On Petitioners return in March, he found a number of those articles were taken away, and on asking this woman about them – she denied knowing any thing of them – Petitioner then brought her before the Magistrates, considering her to be responsible for the property missing: as she had the Key. but the Magistrates gave petitioner no redress or satisfaction, but took bail of her in ten pounds till further proof and would not hear petitioners witness after, but caused him to pay all costs and suffered this woman to go to the United States – Petitioner has been sued by a person (whose watch was taken away) to the Court of Requests and judgment given against him for the value of the Watch – petitioner feels greatly aggrieved having no friends in this country being a single man, should he be sued for the articles taken away the property of several persons, it would ruin him as it would exceed Fifty Pounds. independant of what was his own

petitioner hopes your Excellency will see his grievance redressed. . . .

[126]Joseph Harr was a watch and clockmaker in Goderich from 1835 to 1838. Presumably the situation he described in his petition forced him out of business in the latter year.

[127]Charles Prior was the personal assistant and secretary to John Galt when the latter took up his post as head of the Canada Company's operations in Upper Canada in 1825. Under Galt's successor, Thomas Mercer Jones, Prior became general agent, responsible for the Huron Tract, with his headquarters at Goderich. An engaging and witty man with his peers, he dealt with the settlers in an overbearing and heavy-handed manner. He became increasingly dissolute, accepting Jones' cast-off mistresses and cheating both settlers and the company. In 1836 he was dismissed for dishonest conduct, rather than the careless business practices that had always characterized his management. He then operated a large farm at Goderich, serving the area as a

E 90   PETITION OF JAMES LOCKHART[128]
[*PAC, Upper Canada State Papers, v. 46, pp. 275-7*]

To His Excellency Sir George Arthur . . .

The Petition of James Lockhart of the Town of Niagara in the District of Niagara, Merchant Humbly Sheweth

That in the month of December 1837 he was possessed of a case of Fowling Pieces of the value of upwards of £100 and had deposited the same with Mr Cathcart,[129] a Merchant in Toronto, for sale.

That the said Fowling Pieces were seized and taken possession of by Alexander Dixon Esquire, one of the Aldermen of the City of Toronto at the time of the Rebellion in the said month of December, and as he alleged either to arm the Inhabitants of the neighbourhood, or to prevent their falling into improper hands, and that he has frequently applied to the said Alexander Dixon, either to return the same to him or to pay for them.

That the said Alexander Dixon alleges that they were taken for the public service and that he knows not what has become of them.

That not being able to get any satisfactory account of his property from the said Alexander Dixon, he some time since, caused an Action of Trover to be brought against him to recover the value thereof, which action was tried at the Assizes for the Home District in October last and a verdict rendered in your Petitioner's favor for £106, subject to the opinion of the Court of Queen's Bench whether the said Alexander Dixon was protected by the Provisions of the Act 1st Victoria Cap 12.

That the Court of Queens Bench upon argument, determined that the said Defendant was protected by the Provisions of the said Act and that your Petitioner consequently had no redress for the loss of his property save in the Justice of the Government, who, the Court expressed a strong opinion, could not avoid indemnifying your Petitioner.

That your Petitioner has incurred an expense of £17/10 in prosecuting his said suit and has been called upon by Her Majesty's Attorney General, who defended the said Alexander Dixon, to pay the further sum of £13/0/2 for the costs of the Defense.

That had his property been taken away never so illegally while done bona fide for the public service he would have disdained seeking any

---

magistrate. During the rebellion of 1837 local officials created the Huron militia where none had existed. Prior became its captain and proved no better a militia officer than a Canada Company agent.

[128]James Lockhart was a major figure in Niagara, active as a merchant, banker, and shipowner. In 1831 he was secretary of a harbour and dock company which was given land in the town to develop. In December 1837 it was Lockhart's ship, the *Britannica*, that carried the Niagara and St. Catharines volunteers to Toronto.

[129]Robert Cathcart opened a general dry goods store on King Street in York in the late 1820s, taking on one of his employees, William McMaster, as partner in 1834. In the 1830s Cathcart's store was also the depository for the Upper Canada Religious Book and Tract Society, and the Bible Society. In the mid-1840s Cathcart retired from the business and moved to Bathurst Street, where he died about a decade later.

recompense had it been returned to him again after the emergency had terminated, which has been made the ground of its original seizure, but your Petitioner cannot conceive that the total abstraction of Property, without any shadow of Right and the keeping thereof altogether and without a Order of any payment whatever could have been contemplated by the Legislature as one of those necessary acts for not quelling the Rebellion which by whomsoever committed was to be justified by this ex post facto Law.

The Court however have decided that the Statute operates to the indemnifying of such acts as that of which he complains and therefore that he must appeal to the Justice of the Government for redress.

Your Petitioner therefore humbly prays that Your Excellency will take his cause into consideration and order him to be paid the sum of £136/10/2, being the amount of the said verdict and the costs he has been put to, with Interest.

E 91   EXECUTIVE COUNCIL'S COMMENTS ON JAMES LOCKHART'S
CASE
[PAC, *Upper Canada State Papers, v. 46, p. 272*]

In Council 13th August 1840
The Council having inquired into and recalled their individual recollections of the circumstances under which the arms were seized, are of opinion that the act of seizure was fully justified by the public Danger at the time existing. and that in the hurry & confusion of the time It was Impossible to take care of the property so that it might be returned in safety.

The Provincial Parliament having passed an act of Indemnity to the Magistrates, and having provided no means from which losses incurred should be paid the Council Know of no fund from which they can recommend the petr. [petitioner] to be indemnified[.]

R B Sullivan
PC [President of the Council?]

E 92   JOHN VAN ARNAM TO SIR GEORGE ARTHUR
Lockport, 22 March 1838
[PAC, *Upper Canada Sundries, v. 189, pp. 105267-70*]

Knowing of no other source from which to obtain justice for the wrongs which I have suffered, I take the liberty of addressing you personally, and beg that your Excellency will condescend to acknowledge the receipt of this as soon as convenient

I have been a resident of the Province of Upper Canada for the last 15 years, early became attached to the constitution and laws, and have ever been a loyal and peaceable citizen

Immedeately after the commencement of these unhappy difficulties,

I was arrested and immured in prison, without even knowing of what I was accused. having taken no part in the affair except to advise the disaffected to desist from adopting violent or unconstitutional measures to bring about that reform in the Administration which myself with many others deemed necessary for the happiness of the subject and the prosperity of the province, and which we believe the British government wish us to enjoy

After near 3 months imprisonment I procured bail, through the clemency of the Government, and the indefatigable exertions of my wife[130] who made several journeys from Burford (my place of residence)[131] to Toronto, alone in the most inclement season of the year, – when I returned to my family and my farm

But the spirit of persecution was abroad in the land and ere I had enjoyed the society of my family 6 days, I was informed that a warrant was out for my arrest. – Preferring banishment to illegal imprisonment I sought a temporary shelter from my persecutors in this land of strangers

Warm with the love of my adopted country and conscious of my innocence I would gladly return to Upper Canada and assert my innosence. But I have too much reason to fear that British freedom and British justice have been frightened from the once happy province. and oppression and injustice have usurped their place

In behalf of my suffering fellow countrymen I would inform your Excellency that thousands of the most respectable and most loyal of her Majestys subjects, are now in exile; (driven from their farms, their shops, their professions, their families, and their homes by the lawless violence of an excited and unprincipaled soldiery) who claim the sympathies of your Excellency, and who are impatiently and confidently looking to you for that protection, justice and liberty, which has so long been the boast of every British subject.

E 93   MATTHEW WAITE AND ISAAC WAITE JR.[132] TO THEIR UNCLE
Toronto Township, 30 April 1838
[PAO, Diaries of Isaac Wilson,[133] typescripts]

. . . But owing to the unsettled state of the Province at this present

[130]Chloe Van Arnam described herself as a British-born subject. In 1838 she and her husband John had seven children, the eldest only thirteen.

[131]Actually, good reason exists for thinking that Van Arnam lived in Brantford Township, rather than Burford, for he customarily described himself as a resident of the former.

[132]Matthew Waite and Isaac Waite Jr. were residents of Toronto Township.

[133]Isaac Wilson (d. 1838) was Matthew Waite's and Isaac Waite Jr.'s uncle. Wilson came to York Township from Cumberland County, England, in 1811 with his father and became a farmer. He served in the militia in the War of 1812 and fought at the first battle of York. However, Isaac Wilson was not the uncle to whom the Waites wrote, since he had died before this letter was written. The letter is not part of Wilson's diary but has been filed with it. It too is a typescript.

time, it is a matter of doubt whether we shall be able to collect much of this money[134] this year as the excitement caused by the late rebellion is still very great. A great many are daily leaving the Province for the United States, some through dread of punishment, others disgusted with the administration of government. There are also many others going with a sect called Mormons to the Missouri, all of which tends to reduce the value of property and the difficulty of getting money. . . .

E 94   DEPRESSION AND EMIGRATION
[Mirror, *Toronto, quoted* Spectator, *Kingston, 18 May 1838*]

The people are, in truth, now flying from this Province as if it were "a land of pestilence and famine." The Transit, which left here on Wednesday last from [for ?] Lewiston, contained upwards of two hundred persons. Many of them were our most wealthy and enterprising farmers. We learn further, that the applications at the "Mississippi Emigration Society" in this city, are so numerous as to be almost beyond belief. We trust Sir George Arthur will disentangle himself from the baneful oligarchy that surrounds him. Almost all our merchants are suffering, owing to the impolitic conduct of the late Executive regarding the Banks; our substantial farmers are leaving for what they call more liberal institutions, where they will have a voice in the selection of the men that will govern them; In short, if something be not done soon by Sir George, we are likely to become nothing but Province a [*sic*] of paupers.

E 95   ELIJA DUNCOMBE[135] TO BENJAMIN FULLER
St. Thomas, 28 May 1838
[*London Public Library, Edwin Seaborn Collection, Diaries,
pp. 1132-4, typescript*]

I Recd your Second letter yesterday, dated May 13, 1838. When I Recd the other I answered it Immediately – but I cannot now tell you what I wrote, and a few weeks after that I wrote to you again. I know that letters have been Intercepted and my letters were all broken open, before I Recd them. . . . Nearly 1/3 of the Inhabitants have left and are leaving – for the United States and all the Leading Reformers are gone and a great many Moderate Tories – . . . the Country is in a confused

---

[134]This was a legacy, evidently in the form of debts, left by Isaac Wilson to his family.

[135]Elija Duncombe (1795–1870) was born in the United States, and moved with his brother David to St. Thomas in 1822, so that the two could study medicine with their older brother Charles. The two both concluded their studies at Fairfield Academy in Herkimer, New York, and were then licensed to practise in Upper Canada. Elija settled in St. Thomas and helped organize a political union there in November 1837. Though suspected by some of involvement in the revolt, he stayed clear of it. He remained in St. Thomas, a prominent local physician.

state. The Tories Say there will be another Skirmish in a few weeks –
. . . Money is ten times as scarce as it was when you left . . . but if the
Patriots do come over I cannot tell what will be done – there was about
120 Rebels as they call them in London Jail. 50 from Yarmouth – 6 of
them were found guilty of high treason[136] and 3 Harvey Bryant old
John Moor and Enoch Moor Brothers to Elias Moor – were condemned
to be hung on the 25 of this month but they were Respited till the
Queen's Pleasure is known and 46 have petitioned to Leave the
Province and their Property – Under an act that was passed this winter
– the Liberal Papers in the Province are all Put down – not one goes,
and we have no News but Tory News – and every letter is opened that
there is any prospect of conveying any Intelligence – hard Times
indeed. There is not now only 3 companies of Volunteers here but
Report says that 3 companies of Regulars are to be Stationed here –
while the Regulars were situated here they Conducted themselves very
well – But You Cannot say that about the Volunteers. I Suppose You
know that my brother Charles is proscribed & Report says that he left
the Province in women's Clothing – and a man is now in jail accused of
helping him away[137] – And his Property is all Siezed – his Son in Law
John Tufford that married his Eldest daughter Eliza Jane[138] Under
Sentence of Death at Hamilton –. Dr. Charles is now at Lockport at the
head of from 800-1200 men the Tory Papers say. What the intention is
cannot be known. But the Tories carry every thing they Please here
now – . . . There is two thousand Dollars Reward offered for My
brother Charles. Excuse my bad writing etc. Love to Mrs. Fuller.

E.E. Duncombe

Enclosure
A bout Sale of Your Place – Now is no time to Sell – People all offer
their Property for less than half what they could have taken 3 years ago
– . . . We are all in Tolerable good health now and your acquaintances

[136]The six were Alvaro Ladd, John Moore, Harvey Bryant, Robert Cook, Enoch
Moore, and Ebenezer Wilcox.
[137]This was Charles Tilden (*ca.* 1807–1896), born in Compton, Lower Canada.
Tilden had settled in London Township, where he worked as a carpenter. He acquired
200 acres from his in-laws in Dereham Township in 1837. After the dispersal of the
Duncombe rebels, he helped Duncombe reach the Detroit frontier. He was jailed at
London on 15 February 1838, not for his aid to Duncombe but for his having incited
rebellion in December. He was freed on bail because of ill health and was never tried.
Family tradition has it that Duncombe gave Tilden's infant son 200 acres in Caradoc
Township for Tilden's having helped him escape, though the documents involved
show the date of the transaction as 2 August 1836. In 1844 Tilden acquired sizeable
acreages from Duncombe, however.
[138]Eliza Jane Tufford was Duncombe's first child, born in the United States before
1816. In 1834 she married John Tufford and bore him eleven children. In 1836 she and
John bought 200 acres of land from her father in Brantford Township, but in 1842 the
Executive Council refused to grant the Tuffords a patent because the property involved
had belonged to an attainted traitor. Eliza later wrote a sketch of the life and times of
her father, available in the Duncombe Family Papers in the PAC.

generally are well but there has been more death in this Part of the Country than there was 5 years Past but Principally old People and Children –. The Scarlet fever and Canker Rash has been the Principal cause – some severe colds from Military Exposure – but every thing is Possible now here –. Crops are not very Good – nor very bad – but a very backward Spring – & now very wet & cold. Hay is cut Pleanty – Yet you Must not feel Discouraged with the times for you are a Tory and they do well. . . .

E 96   HAMILTON *Express* ON EMIGRATION
[Mackenzie's Gazette, *New York City, 30 June 1838*]

To English, Irish and Scotch Emigrants. – The Hamilton Express, an Upper Canada modern tory paper, conducted by an Irish protestant,[139] has the following remarks on the condition of Upper Canada. . . .

Emigration from this Province to the United States still continues, notwithstanding the immense numbers who have already left; but it has changed its character, and now, instead of being composed of men of strong political feelings, embraces the more cautious and industrious classes – old countrymen as well as natives. Military clangor keeps one portion of the people from brooding over the general depression, while a morbid melancholy seems to have seized others, who are apathetic as to the consequences of passing events, and look upon emigration as a panacea for all their ills.

To such an extent has emigration been carried on, that in some parts of the London District, we have credibly been informed, there are not males enough left to gather in a tithe of the crops. Some farmers have sacrificed their homesteads for a trifle, whilst others have actually abandoned them "flying from the province as from a land of famine and pestilence." But this is not all. The spirit of change is extending like an epidemic, and several parties from different parts of the province are now traversing the western states, looking for locations to provide for an extensive emigration.

E 97   COMMENTS ON EMIGRATION
[Spectator, *Kingston, 13 July 1838*]

From the [Brockville] Statesman June 30.

BROCKVILLE – MOVING OFF. – We have had occasion frequently to allude to the constant emigration which is taking place from this

---

[139]This was Solomon Brega, an Orangeman of Irish background who had worked in London, England, on the *Morning Chronicle*. He moved to Baltimore, then to Hamilton, where he published the *Express*, a reform, rather than a "modern tory" paper. In 1855, appointed sheriff in another locale, he left Hamilton.

District to the Far West. It seems, however, that the moving spirit, which has taken possession of so many of our inhabitants, is no longer to be confined to individual or isolated cases, but has seized them *en masse*.

A public meeting has been held within the last few days, at Portland, in the township of Bastard, at which, we have been informed, not less than the heads of sixty families subscribed their names as intended emigrants. The sum of 400 dollars was subscribed to defray the expense of sending the two agents to the "land of promise," in order to lay out the site for the intended location of the emigrants. . . .

From the Mt. Morris Spectator.

EMIGRATION FROM CANADA. – Sixteen covered wagons, mostly drawn by oxen, passed through the city of Buffalo on the 6th inst. carrying the persons and effects of about 20 families or Canadian emigrants, on their way to the "far west." They were all from one town in the Brockville District.

E 98   REV. JAMES MARR TO REV. ABSALOM PETERS
St. Thomas, 5 July 1838
[*University of Chicago Divinity School, American Home Missionary Society Congregational, Correspondence, microfilm in United Church Archives*]

. . . I Know of no American ministers now in Canada, with the exception, of brother Close,[140] and myself, and I am not certain but that he has left –. He talked of it some time since, if the disturbance should continue. The country is in a very tumultuous condition, indeed, and things are still bearing a more threatening aspect. There is a perpetual commotion throughout the country; but more particularly along the lines. We are hoping, and praying that it may soon come to an end –. I sometimes feel affraid to stay here, . . . but again when I consider the moral condition of the country, it seems to call upon me a loud, to stay and blow the gospel trumpet, and to look for my reward in another world; Which undoubtedly must-be the case without a great change in public sentiment. There is very little preaching now in the country with the exception of the Established churches of England and Scotland. Public opinion, or rather the Government party being against them. Many are affraid to preach, and indeed some would not be allowed the privilege. I have however never felt myself under an restraint. but am looked upon with suspicion, and frequently called a rebel. I have never been attacked nor insulted by any of them,. I pursue a straight-forward course. . . .

---

[140]The Rev. Mr. Close was a Niagara Presbyterian minister in the Hamilton area. He abandoned the province, as indeed Marr did, in 1838.

E 99   REPORT OF REV. JOHN ROAF TO THE COLONIAL MISSIONARY
SOCIETY

[Colonial Missionary Society Report (1838) *(London, 1838), p. 13*]

. . . Some, too, of our warmest and most efficient friends are irrecoverably gone from the Province, – many are leaving, – others have lost their situations; all are suffering from the Overthrow of commercial business; while the spirit of the ascendant party and their laws is such as must depress and diminish the classes, within which we might have looked for attention and success. . . .

E 100   REV. WILLIAM PROUDFOOT TO AN UNIDENTIFIED
COMMISSIONER OF THE UNITED ASSOCIATED SYNOD
London, 14 August 1838

[*Knox College, William Proudfoot Papers, Series I, Reel 3, microfilm
in PAO*]

. . . The past year has been one of many privations and difficulties, not in the way of direct loss but in the stagnation of all business. Of the nature of these difficulties I need not dwell, suffice it to say that our Churches being all known to be voluntary, have been the object of particular dislike to the Tory party, and as that vile faction has gained for the present the ascendancy, they have in this district particularly done everything in their power to hurt our cause – some members have left the Church on political grounds – and almost all occasional hearers have left. The discomfort in which the liberals have lived has produced a desire to leave the Country and go to the States. Indeed I scarcely know any one who would not remove if he could get his farm sold. – The multitude of farms for sale and the fewness of purchasers has reduced the value of property one half at least, – there is therefore no money – debt [*sic*] are to be paid with cash which it is impossible to get – such is the state of matters here at least, that some of my best members, who used to contribute $8 per annum have not for the last 3 quarters of an year contributed one cent. Some who have a little money are keeping it to take them out of the country. – . . .

E 101   ARTHUR CARTHEW TO JOHN JOSEPH
Toronto, 2 May 1838

[*PAC, Upper Canada Sundries, v. 193, pp. 107240-4*]

I have the honor to communicate to you for the information of His Excellency the Lieut. Governor the following suspicious circumstances which have recently come to my knowledge – they serve to corroborate the statement made by one of my Officers of what occur'd during his journey from "Medonte" – a rough note of which I have already handed to His Excellency –

I have lately been in the Neighbourhood of Newmarket where I was informed that a number of men from the surrounding Townships, known to be adverse to the British Government had left their families and gone to the States with the intention of joining an armed Force assembling on the Frontier – I thought proper to gain every possible information on the Subject of this wild scheme, which I could only do by indirect means –

The people in the neighbourhood of my residence are chiefly Quakers, and are, with the exception of one or two altogether disloyal – Many of them have connections implicated in the Late Rebellion – One of them, a quiet simple man, has a wife who formerly lived as servant in my family – she associates with them, and has of course had frequent opportunities of hearing their opinions and intentions – I have been able to gather from her the fact that the rebel party speak and feel very confident of regaining possession of their forfeited farms with the assistance of a strong force now gathering on the American side for the purpose of invading Canada – that a great number of men from different parts of the Province had gone over to join them, altho' many of them had not been previously suspected – that scarcely a young man was left in the Township of "Pickering"

She mentioned the circumstance of a woman (a school mistress) having lately arrived from near "Lockport" who told her "that great preparations were making for war on the other side" –

A man called Wm. Lundy,[141] a suspected character, absconded a short time since – he has returned from Buffalo and brings the same report – he tells his friends that none of them have cause for alarm, for if their Land should be taken from them, the people from the other side would soon regain them possession –

A woman named "Mosier"[142] sent a message, by a person going to Buffalo, to "Silas Fletcher" (for whose capture a reward has been offered) desiring him to remit her some money which he owed her Husband, and reproaching him for having led her family into trouble – Fletcher returned an answer saying that in a very short time he would return and settle every thing –

Many people have been lately offering their farms for half their value – they now decline selling – a man who owns a farm adjoining my own, wanted some time since £ 400 for it – very recently he wished to sell it and requested one of my servants to inform me that I should have it for £ 250. the man thought he would take less – now he will not sell – or to use his own words "not until I see how the business

[141]William Lundy Jr. lived on 50 acres of lot 35, concession 4 of Whitchurch Township, a property owned by his father until 1849 when he inherited it. The younger Lundy was active in the political union movement prior to the rebellion, but there is no evidence that he participated in the uprising. The family probably came from Pennsylvania just after the turn of the century.

[142]There were a number of Mosier families in the area of Newmarket. The woman referred to here was probably the wife of James Mosier.

on the other side turns out" – this person has a brother in goal for treason.

I enclose a Report given me by an Officer of my Regt. who was lately on Detachment at Windsor Bay, And I beg to notice that when their guns were demanded from the prisoners and their houses searched, about David Wilsons village & elsewhere after the first disturbance, they invariably said they had lost them or thrown them away –

The few facts I have stated, altho' unimportant in themselves, may when united with information received from other Quarters, perhaps, assist His Excellency in forming an opinion as to the state of things –

I have resided in the Country seven years, which together with having been in the Command of the Militia north of the Ridges when they first turned out, has enabled me, with the assistance of information I can rely on, to form a tolerably correct Idea of the reliance which may be placed on the Inhabitants of each Township in case of emergency, . . .

E 102   JAMES REID[143] TO W.L. MACKENZIE
Rochester, 8 June 1838
[PAO, Mackenzie–Lindsey Clippings, No. 3860]

. . . Mother[144] tells me that there is a Magazine of guns, breastplates, stocks &c less than twenty rods from her house, to be used when the movement arrives, which commences the second campaign in Canada! that there are 500 stand of arms missing in the City Hall! of which nothing can be heard, but which are nevertheless buried in coffins not very far from Toronto! – And that she never saw so much disaffection, among those who were once the most loyal, since the troubles commenced. Every one now must take up arms pay forty dollars, or go to jail. . . .

E 103   ROBERT RIDDELL[145] TO JOHN MACAULAY
Woodstock, 28 June 1838
[PAC, Upper Canada Sundries, v. 197, pp. 109590-3]

I have the honor to inform you for the information of His Excellency the Lieutenant Governor that a Statement has this day been sworn to

---

[143]James Reid worked as a clerk in one of the banks in Toronto in 1837. Implicated in the rebellion, he fled to Rochester, where he became a miller.

[144]Mrs. Reid had been a classmate of Mackenzie in Scotland.

[145]Robert Riddell (d. 1863) was born in Dumfries, Scotland, and settled in Zorra Township in 1833, where he amassed considerable property and farmed. He married in 1836. In 1835 he was appointed a magistrate and was, in 1838, chairman of the quarter sessions. On 20 January 1838 he became a major of the 3rd Oxford Regiment of militia, rising to the rank of lieutenant-colonel in 1846. In 1844, a tory, he was elected to the Assembly and served until 1847. He thereafter returned to Scotland.

before the Magistrates of this neighbourhood, of an attack having been made upon two Constables in charge of a prisoner accused of treasonable practices,[146] and his release affected by a body of 30 men well armed – the Horse of one constable[147] was shot, and by evidence since obtained the person of the other constable[148] secured –

Under such circumstances the Commanding officer of the Second Oxford Militia[149] has ordered a company for immediate pursuit and capture of the same. –

Having Mentioned this simple fact, I have to lay before His Excellency the opinion of the Magistrates assembled to take into consideration the state of the County – They would submit that of the Townships Composing it, Norwich Oakland and Dereham, a great part of Blenheim, Oxford and Nissouri & Burford are either wholly disaffected, or so indifferent to the cause of the Government, as to remain inert in its support; the three first may be said to be entirely disaffected, while the four latter consist of Equal parts of Loyal and the reverse – Zorra and Blandford may be said to be loyal. . . .

I have further to say that the breach of the law was committed on the high western road, only six miles from this place, and at 10. o'clock in the forenoon . . . men openly and unhesitatingly proclaim the immediate occurrence of some state of things, that is to prostrate the Goverment. . . .

E 104   A.W. LIGHT TO COL. RICHARD BULLOCK
Woodstock, 6 July 1838
[PAC, Upper Canada Sundries, v. 197, pp. 109678-82]

Since my letter to you from Woodstock of the 28 June, wherein I informed you, from the information I had received, of a body of armed rebels being in Norwich and Dereham, that I was about sending a

[146]This was Dr. Duncan Wilson, who was recaptured in Malahide a few days later.

[147]The constable was "Crazy" Cyrus Sumner of London, who escaped.

[148]The constable was Philo Bennett (b. ca. 1813) of London, who was soon released by his captors. Bennett, a mason, had been a Methodist exhorter, but had reportedly been disavowed. During the rebellion he had been vocally loyal, putting himself at considerable risk in the village of Sparta. In 1848 and 1849 he served as a London town councillor.

[149]This was Alexander Whalley Light (1779–1856). Light, a son of the stipendiary of the Presidency of Madras and postmaster general of India, had served in the Royal Engineers and become a lieutenant-colonel of the 25th Regiment of Foot. He served in the Napoleonic wars and when settled in Upper Canada in 1831, he was described as the former surveyor-general of "Australia." An acquaintance of Sir John Colborne, he certainly had credentials as a draftsman and topographer. Though he was evidently in straitened financial circumstances when he arrived, he built a fine residence for his family in West Oxford Township. An active loyalist, he helped cut out the Caroline in December 1837, and on 19 January 1838 was gazetted colonel of the 2nd Oxford Regiment of militia, a commission he resigned on 29 August 1839. A strong tory, he had published works on the employment of the British poor before emigrating to Upper Canada.

detachment there to disperse them, under the command of Major Beale[150] and Captn. Gibson[151] of 2d Oxford, who marched that night to Dennis's Settlement, where a prisoner was taken up – From thence Captn Gibson was induced to proceed to Sodom in Norwich, as being the hot bed of the rebels. He then met with Lt Col Whitehead Col Brailey[152] Captn. Dailey[153] Capt Doby and Capt Wilsons (Indians) detachments the whole amounting to 307 men; soon after which Captn Jackson & Capt Burns[154] detachments of 2d Oxford also arrived, so that the force amounted to about 400 men.

on saturday the 30 June Col Whitehead and Brailey had information from a man named Hill, that he believed the rebels in Norwich and Dereham had received a reenforcement of Americans, rifles, and amunition, by a Schooner which had landed at or near Long Point. He, Hill, believed the rebel force to be altogether little short of 800 men. When I received this information from Capt Gibson at 12 o clock on Sunday the 1st July, from my military experience, I thought I should be of some service – if I joined the 2d Oxford. I proceeded therefore to Sodom – determined to attack the rebels wherever to be found. This day Col Whitehead had made a reconnoissance of many miles thro' the woods round, without discovering any clue to the rendezvous of the rebels. On Monday the 2d I went with Lt Kirby[155] and 16 Indians to Hungry lake near Scotland, with the same want of success. On tuesday the 3d I went again with the Indians and detachments of each of the corps, extending ourselves as much as possible, to more fully examine the Woods; but still without the desired effect. On Wednesday night the 3d July I received Col Maitlands dispatch of 2d July desiring me to collect my division of 50 armed men at Woodstock to cooperate with his forces when desired. there being 1 1/2d a day allowed for rations with 1 1/4d a day for pay to each man. On thursday Morning when I was about to return home, Col Whitehead requested me to Keep my detachment at Sodom, till a witness was examined from whom he expected to recieve important information, but it turned out a Yankee

[150]This was C. Beale who had served with the 32nd Fusiliers and had seen service in Holland in 1815.

[151]This was likely James L. Gibson (*ca.* 1795–1839) who settled in Oxford County in 1833 with his family. He received his commission as captain of the 2nd Oxford Regiment of militia on 19 January 1838. He may also have been the James Gibson appointed a magistrate for Zorra and Woodstock in 1835.

[152]This was William Brearley, an English barrister who had recently settled in Norwich. On 8 February 1838 he was promoted lieutenant-colonel of the 2nd Oxford Regiment from the rank of major. He resigned his commission in 1840.

[153]J. Dailey became captain of the 5th Oxford Regiment in March 1838.

[154]In January 1838 D. Burns was made a captain of the 2nd Regiment of Oxford militia.

[155]The only Kirby known to be an officer in an Oxford regiment at this time was William Kirby of Brantford, a distiller, who was appointed an ensign in the 4th Oxford Regiment on 23 April 1838.

story to release a prisoner of the name of Doxy.[156] That evening therefore the 2d Oxford departed for Woodstock (sleeping at Dennis's settlement) where we arrived on the morning of the 5th July. The Blenheim detachments of 2d Oxford also returned home, Capt Johnson[157] of 2d Oxford being stationed at Burford. where there are many rebels. On the 5th July at 2 o clock I received another express from Captain Gibson, who with Col Whitehead had remained behind at Sodom to examine some prisoners, to say, that since all the detachments had departed, two of the prisoners had turned Queens evidence, and had divulged the rebel secrets; That from only from having 25 men to guard the prisoners, he and Col Whitehead expected an attack that night, calling earnestly for our assistance. On this information, I thought it advisable to obtain as many mounted volunteers as possible, and send them to Sodom – they amounted to 14 horsemen and six foot who went in a baggage waggon, under the Command of Capt Edmund Deeds,[158] and would arrive there at about 12 oclock the same night of the 5th[.] I have to remark that in our various reconnoissance, that in all the houses we examined, the male inhabitants were generally absent, not working on their estates, or we should have seen them; and I learn that they are all embodied in the Woods, with arms, and purposely keep out of the way, to avoid being made prisoners. There is therefore no possibility of taking these ruffians. Their names are well known, and a proscription or outlawry can be the only means of reaching them, that unless they deliver themselves up by a certain day, to be examined touching their delinquency. their estates shall be confiscated, or sold to the highest bidder – to their exclusion. They are all Yankees or decendants of Yankees, who have bought estates from settlers. and the country can never be at peace till all these be extirpated root and branch. Capt Jackson also informs me that between 60 and 70 men in Burford and Blenheim have gone to the United states, leaving their estates to join the rebels – and those still left behind mob the loyal men who turn out, to endeavour to intimidate them from doing their duty. I humbly conceive such a state of things ought not to exist – or we shall have rebellion every 4th July and every winter –

I have to state that the men of the 2d Oxford have all turned out with the greatest zeal, and altho receiving many of them 1 1/2 dollars a day for work, cheerfully obeyed my summons to the amt [amount] of my arms, and have behaved with the utmost propriety. . . .

[156]Enoch D. Doxy (b. *ca.* 1807) was a native of Upper Canada. On 20 December 1837, a shoemaker who lived in Norwich with his young family, he was arrested as a rebel and jailed at London before being freed on bail a week or so later. He was jailed once again during the Norwich scare, on 29 June 1838, and not released until that October.

[157]M. Johnston (Johnson) was commissioned a captain of the 2nd Oxford Regiment on 25 April 1838.

[158]Edmund Deeds was appointed a magistrate for Blenheim Township in 1836 and a

E 105   ANONYMOUS TO SIR GEORGE ARTHUR
Norwich, 15 July 1838
[PAC, Upper Canada Sundries, v. 200, pp. 110690-3]

An Individual residin[g] for 27 years in the Township of Norwich begs leave humbly to represent that through misrepresentations and other causes easy explained (if opportunity offered) the peaceable and Loyal Inhabitants of this Town are deprived of the protecti[on] of the Laws due to british subjects[;] a few designing men who it is honestly believed have by Intrigue crept into offices which it is visible to the weakest understanding they are not capable of filling taking advantage of the fact that Charles Duncomb did in december last collect a body of men in Norwich for Insurrectionary purposes of whom a large number were from Burford Oxford and other adjoining Towns are continually representing that Norwich is one mass of corruption and disaffection which I can assure your Excellency is entirely fals as Norwich Contains a large majority of as Loyal Inhabitants as can be found in the province[.] I do not wish to tire your Excellencys patience but as a specimen of the Administration of the Law in this portion of her majestys colony I will give the following brief sketch[.] A young man named Willson a resident of Yarmouth being on his Way to Norwich where his father resides calld at the house of one Doyal of Burford[159] (a man who has been riding his neighbors horses without authority all the last winter) he and said Doyal had some altercation and a few days thereafter on a complaint made by the said Doyal one Bennet and Sumner from London were employed to apprehend him in which they succeeded[160] and after passing through Norwich Burford and part of Oxford he was taken from them by a company of men not more according to the testimony of the witness than 8 or 9. Bennets horse was killed and Sumner's Wounded[.] Sumner pursued his way to London and Bennet Returned to Burford[,] gave Information of the circumstances and declared that he recognized three of the men and that they lived in Norwich[.] And the day following A body of of [sic] Militia from Woodstock accompanied by their respective officers to gether with Col Whitehead and Major Wier[161] with the Burford Militia With about 60 Brantford Indians in all amounting to about 3 hundred

captain of the 2nd Oxford Regiment on 19 January 1838. On 19 February 1840 he was made a major. From 1836 to 1840 he was secretary and treasurer of the Oxford Agricultural Society and its president from 1844 to 1847. In 1850 he sat on the Board of Public Instruction and in 1851 on the West Oxford Township council.

[159]This was possibly Benjamin Doyal of Burford.

[160]Actually, Duncan Wilson was a Short Hills raider and was captured fleeing from the scene of the raid. There may have been, however, a germ of truth in the story told here.

[161]"Major Wier" was John Weir, a Burford innkeeper, who in 1827 had been active in trying to secure canalization of the Grand River and improvement of the Oxford-Burford Road. In 1832 he ran unsuccessfully in an Oxford County by-election for the Assembly, losing to a radical candidate. In 1835 he was appointed a magistrate

stationed themselves in Norwich[;] they Committed one man named
Doxie to Gaol on Bennets oath Notwithstanding the driver of the one
horse waggon containing the prisoner at the time he was rescued
testified that Doxie was not the man who took Bennets pistols from
him which Bennet declared was the case also another man present
declared under oath that Doxie was not the man[.] Doxie also proved
abundantly that he was at his own work all that day – they then
proceeded to arrest a number of others on suspicion – But what I would
wish chiefly to re mark is the abuse receved by the Inhabitants during
their stay in Norwich which was about a fortnight – after they had
remained in Norwich several days Imposing most shamefully on the
peaceable farmers especialy the Quakers[,] a despatch was sent from
our officers to Charlotteville Blenheim and other places that there was
a body of armed rebels in the Norwich and Dereham Woods and that
they had burned Col Brearlys house and committed various outrages
which Information called about 2 hundred additional Militia men into
the neighbourhood who entered farm houses to the number of
40-50-and 60 in a place and caused the inmates of the house to provide
food for them until their family stores were all exhausted[;] they
compelled females to leave their beds in the dead of night and give
place to militia officers[.] They went to the Quaker Meeting house
during the hours of worship[,] watched their coming out and turned
feeble women and young children out of their waggons 3 and 4 miles
from their homes and took their teams for the purpose of conveying the
Indians without any baggage the distance of 6 miles but the Indians
being more humane chose to walk and the teams were suffered to
follow their owners home. . . .

One instance more I would venture to mention of an Unoffending
Individual named Babbet[162] who was taken from his house by Joshua
Corbin[163] who is [in ?] the service and so beaten with the musket that
he is still confined to his bed[;] also many horses were taken from the
farmers employ by armed men without any legal authority and ridden
during the extreme heat to their serious Injury And there is even now a
guard of 30 men Kept in this Town on the Queens expense without the
least necessity and 50 men would have been more than any of the late
seccurrencies required[.] The above Instances are only a small portion
of what can be duly attested if called for. . . .

the reason of my writing this anonymously is because that any man
who will at present venture to expose any of the unjust proceedings

---

for Burford and on 8 February 1838 was commissioned a major of the 4th Oxford
Regiment.
[162]This was Russell Babbit (Babbet).
[163]This was likely Joshua H. Corbin (b. *ca.* 1798), a farmer whose family had
settled in Norwich in the second decade of the century from New York State. Though
his family was a Quaker one, he later became an Anglican. In 1832 he served as the
town clerk of Norwich.

openly would be branded as a rebel and confined in Gaol untill the assizes as various Instances have occurred of men being confined in London Gaol 3 months without Knowing for what and then set at Liberty for the same reason[.]

E 106   THE ARGUMENT FOR CONTINUED IMPRISONMENT
[Western Herald, *Sandwich, 17 July 1838*]

From the London Gazette

During the early part of Saturday last, expresses from the West were arriving in rapid succession, representing that the patriots, from one to two thousand strong, were marching toward London, and that they had got nearly to Moravian town. In consequence of this the Militia were ordered out, the bridges barricaded, and the regulars ordered to hold themselves in readiness for battle. Such was the excitement that early on Sunday morning the streets were filled with loyal hearts, demanding arms and anxious for the affray. – About two o'clock they were discharged as no enemy arrived: the Militia of the west always on the alert, determined to ascertain their strength, and if possible to teach them the art of a backward march. Patrols went to view their camp; and found that at the farthest they did not exceed 130, who on hearing of the reception they were likely to get made their way off with all possible speed – some taking to the bush and others recrossing the river. Great preparations were made by the local rebels to join their expected friends – secret and even open meetings were held for the purpose of raising recruits, and many were seen under arms on their way to meet them. The principal part of these fellows, we are informed, have been sworn, to fight for one another – never to lay down their arms until they have accomplished their purposes – and to massacre all who will not assist them, sparing neither age nor sex. This fact came to the knowledge of the Magistrates of Chatham in a manner mysterious, at all events to the patriots: in consequence of which 26 of them were arrested & on their road to London Gaol, before they knew what strange vision had come across them. Two of them we understand were taken on suspicion; but the remainder are those who have sworn to lay down their lives in the attainment of liberty; they are now however in a fair way of proving to the world, that, whatever may be their guilt, they cannot fairly be accused of *perjury*. They were on Sunday evening last locked up safely in our Gaol, where we hope they will remain until they are fairly tried and the guilty punished; and we shall still cling to that hope until we again hear Sir Geo. Arthur talk about "tempering justice with mercy;" for we, as formerly consider that expression as a passport to guilt and as the surest guarantee that crimes may be committed with impunity. We shall patiently await the result, in a spirit of forgiveness for the past and a hope for amendment in the future – firmly adhering to our old political axiom founded on the immutable laws of human nature, that a *"traitor* can never possess a feeling of *gratitude*," any more than, by the mere powerof [*sic*] the will, "an African can change his skin, or a leopard his spots."

E 107   THE ARGUMENT FOR AMNESTY
[Mirror, *Toronto, 18 Aug. 1838*]

. . . The conduct of the government in respect to the state prisoners here, compared to the leniency in the Lower Province, is enigmatical and cruel. The most violent partizan admits the injustice, and makes it a pretext for abuse of Lord Durham. Thirty-five prisoners, charged with state offences, are now confined in Hamilton gaol; some of them from last December! Does the government intend they shall rot there? *Hamilton Express.*

E 108   SIR GEORGE ARTHUR TO LORD DURHAM
Government House, 18 June 1838
[*PAC, Lieutenant-Governor's Internal Letter Books, v. 5, no. 3, pp. 11-14*]

. . . With regard to the criminals who have been convicted of Treason, or have confessed Treason & taken the benefit of the Provincial Act, [1 Victoria, c. 10] so far as it extends – I have throughout been under the impression that they should be treated with as much lenity as the circumstances of the case would possibly admit.

The worst and most mischievous of the Traitors, followed the example of Papeneau, and fled from Justice – certainly, some remain whose conduct was very guilty; but I do not think that it can be necessary, as a deterring example, to transport at the utmost more than 20 or 25 – indeed, if it were not for the respect I have for the feelings of the loyal part of the Population, I would pardon all except perhaps a dozen of the worst

In my last Despatch to the Secretary of State your Lordship will observe that I have asked for great latitude of action in the final disposal of the cases, and I am not without hope that the public sentiment will undergo some change before the instructions arrive. . . .

E 109   SIR GEORGE ARTHUR TO SIR JOHN COLBORNE
Montreal, 11 October 1838
[*C.R. Sanderson, ed.*, The Arthur Papers . . . *I (Toronto, 1957), p. 300*]

I have the honor to inform your Excellency that I have been in communication with the Earl of Durham upon the subject of granting an amnesty to the Parties, in the Upper Province who are implicated in the charge of Treason.

As a means of carrying this measure into effect, I have proposed to the Governor General –

First. That the proclamation which is required by law should be forthwith published preparatory to the outlawing of those persons who have been indicted for treason, and who have fled from the Province. – None of these persons are to be permitted to return to Upper Canada except upon Petition, and giving security for their future good behaviour.

Second. That the most guilty and dangerous of the Traitors concerned in the Rebellion in December last, and whom the Council will not recommend for any further remission – about ten in number – should be forthwith removed to England for the purpose of being transported to New South Wales or Van Diemen's Land.

Third. That in like manner the convicts who were tried and convicted for being concerned in the incursion and insurrection in the Niagara and Western Districts, in the month of June last, whom the Council will not recommend for any further remission of their sentences – about 13 in number – shall also be removed to England forthwith, for transportation.

Your Excellency is fully aware of the strong feeling amongst all the Loyal Population of Upper Canada – Canadians as well as British – against further lenity – and that they almost unanimously call out for the punishment of the traitors, – but, I think if the measure of severity be carried into effect which I have described, that – that [*sic*] a General Amnesty may be extended to all other persons, and that it may have a good effect –

The Earl of Durham has expressed his entire concurrence in this proceeding, and having at his Lordship's request, conferred with Mr. Secretary Buller[164] upon it – I was happy to find that he also considered it a proceeding well adapted to the exigency of our present position. –

Still – as the effect of this measure may, in one way or another, produce an immediate and striking effect upon the Public Mind, I shall feel much obliged – without wishing to be relieved from the slightest responsibility – if Your Excellency will favor me with your opinion upon the measure – it can of course be delayed, if you think at the present crisis, delay important –

---

[164]Charles Buller (1806–1848) was a British MP from 1830 to 1848. He was secretary to Lord Durham and wrote much of his report. On 28 June 1838 he was appointed to the special council of Lower Canada.

E 110 AMNESTY
[Upper Canada Gazette, *Toronto, 25 Oct. 1838*]

PROCLAMATION.
UPPER CANADA.

GEO. ARTHUR. . . .

WHEREAS in cases arising out of the late unhappy revolt, and in the course of the administration of justice against persons implicated therein, it has been our anxious desire to extend our Royal mercy and forgiveness to our deluded and misguided Subjects, to the utmost limits compatible with the public peace, and the security of our loyal and faithful people: And whereas, in furtherance of our desire to extend our Royal clemency as above declared, we have heretofore granted our pardon to numerous offenders who have been convicted, and have also forborne to prosecute others who had rendered themselves, by their misconduct, liable to punishment; and we being resolved still further to extend our Royal clemency, and to make a final declaration of our will and pleasure with respect to all such of our Subjects as are, or have been in any way implicated in the said revolt, we have this day issued our several Royal Proclamations, in pursuance of an Act of our Provincial Parliament . . . passed in the first year of our reign, entitled, "An Act for the more speedy attainder of persons indicted for High Treason, who have fled from this Province, or who remain concealed herein to escape from justice" – calling upon and requiring such of our Subjects . . . to surrender themselves to justice, that their several cases may undergo legal investigation and final adjudication.

And we do now make known and declare to all our Subjects who have not been indicted for any Treason, Misprision of Treason, or Treasonable offence, or who are not now in custody, charged, or liable to be charged with Treason, invasion, or hostile incursion into this Province, or who being charged with either of the said offences, have made their escape from any of our Gaols, or other place of confinement, that they may return to their homes, and that no prosecution for or on account of any offence by them done or committed, and in any way relating to, or connected with the said revolt, shall be instituted or continued, . . . hereby freely offering to all those of our Subjects who may have been implicated in the said revolt, (excepting as aforesaid) our gracious amnesty, pardon and forbearance, . . .

E 111 EXECUTIVE COUNCIL RECOMMENDS CONFISCATIONS
16 July 1839
[*PAC, Upper Canada State Papers, v. 24, pp. 86-7*]

The Council feel it their duty, respectfully to represent to your Excellency, that the very heavy burden of different descriptions, which have been thrown upon the loyal and well disposed inhabitants of the Province by the late rebellion, might be greatly relieved if prompt and decisive measures were taken to confiscate the property of convicted or absconding traitors. It appears strange, that the revenue should be exhausted by expenses attending the trial and transportation of many of these offenders, while their property remains untouched, and the Council have great reason to believe that judgments have been obtained in many instances against these parties colourable only to cover the disposal of their property, and enable themselves to enjoy the proceeds and possibly to use them for the invasion or destruction of the Province.

E 112   JOHN GEORGE BRIDGES TO SIR GEORGE ARTHUR
Norwichville, 30 October 1838
[PAC, Upper Canada Sundries, v. 208, pp. 115015-18]

I address'd Your Excellency some two months since, through Your Excellency's secretary – I then narrated circumstances that came within my own immediate observation, which led me to believe that the disaffected in this part of the country were again plotting trouble, I am now Your Excellency, fully assured that my apprehensions were well founded – For this past month, secret meetings have been held in this Township, and the adjoining one of Deerham, persons have been seen daily going in the south direction of Norwich with fire arms, generally singly, never exceeding two together, and return without them, as yet, I cannot ascertain for a certainty the exact spot where they assemble – Strangers are frequently seen at the houses of those most disaffected, and it has of late been remarked that several residents have left their homes for days together. Your Excellency, I am not an alarmist, but from vigilant watching, and the opportunities afforded me by my profession (that of Physic) of access to all classes, and at all times, I glean information which enables me to form generally a correct prognosis, and I have no hesitation in declaring to Your Excellency, my conviction that the rebels in this part hold regular correspondence with their coadjutors in the United States, and *are prepared*, whenever they may show themselves in Canada to join them – One of them, more indiscreet, and more bold than the rest, declared that they in a days notice could muster six hundred armed men, in the Townships of Norwich, Deerham and Burford – I doubt the number, but I believe Your Excellency, they can raise a formidable force, especially when compared with the loyalists for I think, Sir, it would be difficult in the two first Townships to select, one hundred heads of families, truly loyal, there may be other [sic], whose fears having been acted on, have espoused the Cause of loyalty, but who are likely to throw their weight to the strongest, of whatever party. – . . .

E 113   EXTRACT OF A REPORT OF GEORGE GURNETT[165]
Toronto, 24 November 1838
[PAC, Upper Canada State Papers, v. 33, pp. 36-46]

. . . With respect to the persons concerned in the late rebellion & pardoned by the Executive, and generally of all that class of persons I beg to observe.

That it is my firm conviction that no change for the better has, or ever will take place in their political sentiments. That to a man they entertain & cherish the same sentiments, while their personal feelings are more hostile to the Government, & to the loyal party by whom they have been defeated, than they were previous to the late rebellion. It is but fair to presume that at least the greater proportion of the persons engaged in that rebellion had succeeded in persuading themselves – however false and fallacious their reasonings – that they were engaged in a just cause. Their subsequent defeat & punishment were not likely to convince them of their error. Instead of feeling grateful to the Executive for the pardon which has been extended to them, they look upon the punishment which they have received as persecution which they have sustained in a good cause – a cause which they yet evidently confidently believe will ultimately succeed. "Our day is coming" or sentiments to that effect are constantly expressed by them when irritated or excited. The feelings of these people have been greatly aggravated too by the manner in which most of them have been received on returning to their former neighborhoods. By the taunts, sneers & open insults, to which they are continually subjected from their political opponents – "Rebel" "Jail bird" & other similar offensive expressions being frequently hurled at them. This is calculated greatly to exasperate their feelings, & not the less so because they do not at present feel themselves in a condition to resent the insult. Upon the whole therefore, altho these people are too much awed & subdued by recent events to risk any overt act of rebellion under existing circumstances, yet they must ever be looked upon as determined & irreconcileable enemies of the Government of the Country – who will be ever ready – in the event of any *successful* demonstration of the enemy – to flock to the standard of that enemy. . . .

E 114   W.L. MACKENZIE ON ORANGE TORY REPRESSION
[Mackenzie's Gazette, *New York City, 15 Dec. 1838*]

. . . Thomas Conat or Conant[166] of Darlington has been cruelly

[165]Arthur instructed Gurnett to investigate conditions north of Toronto and to report to him on his findings.

[166]Thomas Conant (1792–1838) came with his family from Bridgewater, Massachusetts, in the year he was born. The family settled at Whitby, where Thomas'

murdered. An express rider belonging to the government orange volunteers, in riding past Conat, knocked off his hat with his sword. Conat had taken an extra glass, and he made some angry reply to this gross insult. The Express rider started on, but undertook to ride over Conat for his amusement. Conat, when he saw the trooper turning on him for that purpose, seized the bridle to save himself, on which the minion of European royalty hewed the poor countryman dead on the spot. . . .

E 115   MILITIA BRUTALITY
[Mackenzie's Gazette, *Rochester, 20 April 1839*]

HORRIBLE SITUATION OF UPPER CANADA.
[From the Toronto Examiner, April 17.][167]
The country, is, it is said, in a horrible state. This is true of those parts where regiments of militia are quartered to oppress and maltreat the people, but not elsewhere. . . . The curses showered on Sir George Arthur in all parts of this district are beyond what any one can imagine. The people are exasperated almost beyond bearing by a set of armed ruffians who maltreat them in the most brutal manner, and who are protected if not countenanced by the government. . . .

On Saturday last, as James E. Small, of this city, was walking on the public highway, in the town of Whitby, in company with two freeholders of the riding, he was assaulted by a body of about 15 of Capt. Low's company of Militia, who were mustered at the roll of the drum with a Sargeant at their head, and most cruelly beaten, the ruffians having kicked him in a most brutal manner after they had knocked him down.

E 116   ANONYMOUS TO W.L. MACKENZIE
Toronto, 8 February 1839
[Mackenzie's Gazette, *Rochester, 30 March 1839*]

Some time last December (I think it was the 20th) George W. Meyers[168] son of Colonel Meyers[169] of Belleville was standing on McDonell's [MacDonell's] wharf in this city, going over to your side.

---

son became a shipowner. The man who likely killed Conant was tried but not convicted because the key witness saw the killing through a window whose glass was of poor quality. The witness consequently could not swear positively to the identity of the killer.

[167]The brackets occur in the original.

[168]George W. Meyers was one of James W. Meyers' four sons.

[169]John W. Meyers (1745–1821), a native of Albany, New York, had served among the loyalist troops during the Revolutionary War. After that conflict he moved to the Bay of Quinte area, 1784–5, and then to the future site of Belleville in 1790, and was one of the founders of that place. He built extensive mills and a store, becoming one of the pre-eminent men in the area.

A spy of the government stept up and accosted him asking what he was going over about. "I am going to look after Mackenzie," said Meyers. Off posted the spy to the Solicitor General (Draper) and made oath to the young gentleman's words, and his arrest followed as a matter of course, but what for he did not know. His father was an old loyalist, and after lying in Jail for a fortnight he sent for his brother, who called on Mr. Draper to ascertain in what he had offended. After much reluctance the affidavit was shewn him, on which he turned round on the public functionary and said – "I believe that my brother never saw William Lyon Mackenzie; I am sure that he never had any business to do with him – but you have taken his (George's) pocket book, and you will find in it a heavy note payable to him by Sheldon Mackenzie, whom he was going to look after, as he truly told your officer." The pocket book was produced and proved this, and Meyers was let out of jail, with an apology, that information had reached them that you was about to throw yourself into the back country again to rouse the inhabitants into action, and hence the mistake.

E 117   JOHN B. ASKIN TO JOHN MACAULAY
London, 26 May 1839
[*PAC, Upper Canada State Papers, v. 22, pp. 60-3*]

. . . those who have been permitted to return, . . . are only the more Cautious of Exposing their Conduct, and less *daring*[.] Yet not one jot less determined when the favorable moment shall Arrive to do all in their power to Effect the overthrow of this Government & to Establish a Republic – I have no faith in their regret, true it is, they regret; – not the Participation they had with the Rebels; but, that they failed in their attempt, which is only permitted to slumber for a time only to revive with more Energy[.]

BIBLIOGRAPHY

PRIMARY SOURCES
GOVERNMENT RECORDS

Archives of Ontario, Toronto (PAO)
   Colonial Office 42 Series, vols. 437-76, microfilm of originals in
   Public Record Office, London

Public Archives of Canada, Ottawa (PAC)
   Adjutant General's Office Correspondence (RG9, I B1), vols. 22, 26,
   28, 29, 33-47, 68-9
   Correspondence of the Military Secretary of the Commander of the
   Forces, 1767–1870 (RG8, I C Series A1), vols. 95, 173, 608-15,
   707.
   Correspondence of the Provincial Secretary's Office (RG5 C1), vols.
   7-14
   Governor General's Office, Lieutenant Governor's Internal Letter
   Books, 1805–6, 1818–41 (RG7, G16A), vols. 2-15
   Indian Affairs (RG10, A7), vols. 5, 10, 66-9, 124-8, 717
   Militia General Orders (RG9, I B3), vols. 5, 10
   Military Letter Books (RG8, I C Series A2), vols. 1271-3, 1292-3
   Petitions and Addresses (RG5, B3), vols. 9-10
   Records of the London District Magistrates Relating to the Treason
   Hearings, 1837–8 (RG5, B36), vols. I-II
   Upper Canada State Papers (RG1, E3), vols. 3-10, 18-19, 22, 24, 29,
   31, 33, 34, 36, 41, 43-6, 50-4, 57, 63-4, 75, 84-91, 97
   Upper Canada Sundries (RG5, A1), vols. 99-221

MANUSCRIPTS

Archives of Ontario, Toronto (PAO)
   Bishop Alexander Macdonnell Papers
   C.H. Graham Papers
   David Gibson Papers
   Diaries of Isaac Wilson, typescripts
   Diary of John Thomson
   H.H. Robertson Papers
   James R. and Ogle Gowan Papers
   J.M. Snyder Papers
   John Arthur Tidey Memoranda and Diary
   John Beverley Robinson Casebook

John Beverley Robinson Papers
John Strachan Papers
J.W. Hunt, "The Stirring Times of Fifty Years Ago"
Letter, F.L. Bridgman to Fanny West, Miscellaneous 1837, typescript
Letters of Sir Francis and Lady Head to Frank Head, microfilm of originals in University of Oxford, Bodleian Library
Macaulay Papers
Mackenzie–Lindsey Papers, Mackenzie Correspondence and Clippings
Mary Sophia O'Brien Journals
Osler Family Papers
Proudfoot Papers, microfilm of originals held by the Presbyterian Church in Canada Archives, Knox College
Rebellion Papers, 1837–8
Rev. J. Doel, "Some Recollections of the "Rebellion" so called in 1837 & 1838"
Rev. William Bettridge Papers, Bettridge Manuscript, typescript
Rev. William W. Smith, unpublished reminiscences
Samuel Rose Papers
Samuel Street Papers
Scrapbook donated by Mrs. Lucy Dent
Scrapbook, "The Canada Company and Anthony Van Egmond – The Story of 1837 in Huron County"
Sir A.N. MacNab Papers, originals and microfilm of originals in the Ipswich and East Suffolk Record Office
Wallbridge Family Papers

Dundas Historical Society Museum, Dundas
Lesslie Diaries

Hamilton Public Library, Hamilton
Adam Hope Letters, typescripts
Land Family Papers

Hiram Walker Museum, Windsor
Military Papers

London Public Library, London
Dr. Edwin Seaborn Collection
Local History Scrapbooks

Metropolitan Toronto Public Library, Baldwin Room, Toronto
Diary of Francis Coleman
James Hamilton Papers
James Lesslie, "Resumé of events and people in Toronto 1822–38"

John G. Howard Papers
Reminiscences of Dr. James H. Richardson, 1905, no. 3, typescript
Robert Baldwin Papers
William Dummer Powell Papers
W.W. Baldwin Papers

Norwich District Museum and Archives, Norwich
Diary of William F. Barns
Throckmorton Diary

Presbyterian Church in Canada Archives, Knox College, University of Toronto, Toronto
William Proudfoot Papers

Public Archives of Canada, Ottawa
Allan Macdonnell Papers (MG24, I83)
Alpheus Jones Papers (MG24, B98)
Colborne Papers (MG24, A40), photostats of originals held by J.E. Colborne, Plymouth, England
Diary of Colonel A.W. Light (MG24, I74)
Diary of George Leith (MG24 H17)
Diary of Pellum C. Teeple (MG24, H45)
Dr. Charles Duncombe Family Papers (MG24, B38)
Dr. John Rolph Papers (MG24, B24)
Durham Papers (MG24, A27), Series 2, vol. 49
Gilkison Family Papers (MG24, I25)
Merritt Family Papers (MG24, E1)
Norfolk Historical Society Collections (MG9 D8 24), microfilm of originals of Norfolk Historical Society, Simcoe
Rebellion Exiles (MG24, B43)
Sheriff Alexander Hamilton Papers (MG24, I26)
William Lyon Mackenzie Papers (MG24, B18)

Queen's University Archives, Kingston
Grubb[e] Family Letterbook, typescript

Robin Harris, Toronto
Harris Papers

Sarnia Public Library and Art Gallery, Sarnia
Henry Jones Diary

Trent University Archives, Peterborough
Stafford Kirkpatrick Letters, photostats of originals in Public Archives of Manitoba

United Church Archives, Victoria University, University of Toronto, Toronto
American Home Missionary Society Congregational, microfilm of originals in the University of Chicago Divinity School
Ryerson Papers
Wesleyan Methodist Missionary Correspondence, Canada West, 1830–50, microfilm of originals in the School of Oriental and African Studies, University of London

University of Toronto, Fisher Library, Toronto
De Grassi Papers

University of Western Ontario Library, Regional History Collection, London
Dennis O'Brien Papers
Elijah C. Woodman Diary and Letters
Fred Landon Papers
Harris Family Papers
Proudfoot Family Papers
Society of Friends Archives, Personal Records, Box 24, John Treffry Letters
Thomas Talbot Papers
William Wood Diary, typescript

PRINTED PRIMARY SOURCES

CHURCH AND GOVERNMENT PUBLICATIONS

Appendix to the Journal of the House of Assembly of Upper Canada, Session of 1835 to Session of 1839–40
Baptist Magazine, xxiv (April 1832) – xxx (Nov. 1838)
Canada Baptist Magazine, and Missionary Register, i, 1 (June 1837) – ii, 5 (Oct. 1838)
Canadian Christian Examiner and Presbyterian Review, i, 1 (March 1837) – ii, 4 (April 1838)
Colonial Missionary Society Report, 1838
Evangelical Magazine and Gospel Advocate, i, 1 (2 Jan. 1830) – x, 26 (28 June 1839)
United Secession Magazine, iii (1835) – vii (1839)

CONTEMPORARY NEWSPAPERS

British Colonist (Toronto), 1 Feb. 1838 – 27 Dec. 1838
Christian Guardian (Toronto), 7 June 1837 – 26 Dec. 1838
Chronicle & Gazette (Kingston), 2 Dec. – 27 Dec. 1837
Church (Cobourg), 6 May 1837 – 29 Dec. 1838
Commercial Herald (Toronto), 11 Dec. 1837 – 17 May 1838

Correspondent and Advocate (Toronto), 29 June 1836 – 2 Aug. 1837
Constitution (Toronto), 4 July 1836 – 6 Dec. 1837
Gazette (Hamilton), 4 Jan. 1837 – 16 Jan. 1838
Gazette (London), 28 Oct. 1837, 18 Nov. 1837, 19 May 1838, 26 May 1838
Journal (St. Catharines), 1 June 1837 – 1 Nov. 1838
Liberal (St. Thomas), 20 Sept. 1832 – 10 Oct. 1833; various issues 1834, 1835, 1836, 1837
Mackenzie's Gazette (New York City and Rochester), 17 April 1838 – 23 Dec. 1840
Mackenzie's Weekly Message (Toronto), 31 March 1854, 7 April 1854
Mirror (Toronto), 28 Oct. 1837 – 21 Dec. 1838
Oxford Star and Woodstock Advertiser (Woodstock), 15 Dec. 1848
Palladium (Toronto), various issues from 20 Dec. 1837 – 27 June 1838
Patriot (Toronto), 15 July 1836 – 20 Nov. 1838
Recorder (Brockville), 14 Dec. – 28 Dec. 1837
Star (Cobourg), 13 Dec. – 27 Dec. 1837
Upper Canada Gazette (Toronto), 6 July 1837 – 28 Dec. 1838
Upper Canada Herald (Toronto), 12 Dec. 1837
Western Herald (Sandwich), 3 Jan. 1838 – 6 Nov. 1838

AUTOBIOGRAPHIES, REMINISCENCES, AND PERSONAL ACCOUNTS

BROWN, THOMAS STORROW. *1837 – My Connection with It*. Quebec, 1898.
FITZGIBBON, JAMES. *An Appeal to the People of the Late Province of Upper Canada*. Montreal, 1847.
HEAD, F.B. *The Emigrant*. London, 1846.
_____. *A Narrative*. London, 1839.
LEONARD, ELIJAH. *The Honourable Elijah Leonard – A Memoir*. London, 1894.
MORPHY, E.M. *A York Pioneer Looking Back, 1834–1884, at Youthful Customs of Fifty Years Ago, also at the Cranks Met with in the Emerald Isle and Canada; with Amusing Incidents and Anecdotes of the Early Settlers in the Latter Place*. Toronto, 1890.
NORTON, L.A. *Life and Adventures of Col. L.A. Norton, Written by Himself*. Oakland, California, 1887.
"Resident Here in 1810 – Settler Tells Life Story." *Era & Express* (Newmarket), 20 Dec. 1946.
RYERSON, EGERTON. *"The Story of My Life."* Edited by J.G. Hodgins. Toronto, 1883.
THOMPSON, SAMUEL. *Reminiscences of a Canadian Pioneer for the Last Fifty Years [1833–1883]: An Autobiography by Samuel Thompson*. Toronto, 1968, reprint.
YOUNG, JAMES. *Reminiscences of the Early History of Galt and the Settlement of Dumfries*. Toronto, 1880.

PAMPHLETS, TRAVELLERS' AND SETTLERS' ACCOUNTS

Charge of the Honorable John B. Robinson Chief Justice of Upper Canada to the Grand Jury, At Toronto Thursday 8 March, 1838 on Opening the Court Appointed by Special Commission to Try Prisoners in Custody on Charges of Treason. Toronto, 1838.

CHISHOLM, DAVID. *Annals of Canada for 1837–38.* n.p., n.d.

DAVIS, ROBERT. *The Canadian Farmer's Travels in the United States of America, in Which Remarks Are Made on the Arbitrary Colonial Policy Practised in Canada, and the Free and Equal Rights, and Happy Effects of the Liberal Institutions and Astonishing Enterprise of the United States.* Buffalo, 1837.

HANSHAW, JOHN P.K., ed. *The Late Bishop of Quebec's Upper Canadian Travelling Mission Fund – Reminiscences of the Late Hon. & Rt. Rev. C.H. James Stewart, Lord Bishop of Quebec by the Rev. John P.K. Hanshaw, D.D..* Piccadilly, 1840?

[Mackenzie, W.L.] *The Caroline Almanack and American Freeman's Chronicle.* Rochester, 1839.

PRESTON, T.R. *Three Years' Residence in Canada, from 1837 to 1839. With Notes of a Winter Voyage to New-York, and Journey Thence to the British Possessions to Which is Added, a Review of the Condition of the Canadian People.* 2 vols. London, 1840.

Return to an Address of the Honourable the House of Commons, dated 8 May 1838; for Return of the Names and Quality or Station of the Several Persons Arrested in Upper Canada and Placed in Confinement in the Prisons in Toronto, and Other Places in the Province, on a Charge of Insurrection or Treason; the Dates of Their Arrest and Discharge; and, if Tried, Whether by Court Martial or Civil Court, with the Result of the Trials Severally; also, the Number in Prison at the Time of the Last Despatch; Prepared from Returns Furnished by the Respective Sheriffs; – to Which is Added, a Schedule of Persons Who Have Absconded. Toronto, 1839.

[Ryerson, Egerton.] *The Affairs of the Canadas. In a Series of Letters. By a Canadian.* London, 1837.

The Speech of the Hon. John Rolph, MPP. Delivered on the Occasion of the Late Inquiry into Charges of High Misdemeanours at the Late Elections, Preferred against His Excellency Sir Francis Bond Head, before The Commons' House of Assembly of Upper Canada. Toronto, 1837.

STRICKLAND, MAJOR [Samuel]. *Twenty-Seven Years in Canada West; or, the Experience of an Early Settler.* Edited by Agnes Strickland. 2 vols. London, 1853.

THELLER, E.A. *Canada in 1837–38: Showing by Historical Facts, the Causes of the Late Attempted Revolution, and of Its Failure, the Present Condition of the People, and Their Future Prospects, together with the Personal Adventures of the Author, and Others Who Were Connected with the Revolution.* 2 vols. Philadelphia, 1841.

Trial of Dr. Morrison, M.P.P. for High Treason at Toronto, on Wednesday, April 24, 1838. Toronto, 1838.

WADDILOVE, W.J.D. *The Stewart Missions: A Series of Letters and Journals Calculated to Exhibit to British Christians the Spiritual Destitution of the Emigrants Settled in the Remote Parts of Upper Canada.* London, 1838.

WILKIE, K. DAVID. *Sketches of a Summer Trip to New York and The Canadas.* Edinburgh, 1837.

CONTEMPORARY MATERIAL OF LATER PRINTING

BECK, J. MURRAY. *Joseph Howe: Voice of Nova Scotia.* Toronto, 1964.

CARELESS, J.M.S., ed. "Letters from Thomas Talbot to John Beverley Robinson." *Ontario History,* LXIX (1957), 25-41.

COVENTRY, GEORGE. "A Concise History of the Late Rebellion in Upper Canada to the Evacuation of Navy Island 1838." Notes by W.R. Riddell. *Ontario Historical Society Papers and Records,* XVII (1919), 113-74.

COYNE, JAMES H., ed. "The Talbot Papers." *Proceedings and Transactions of the Royal Society of Canada,* I (1907), sec. II, 15-210.

GRAY, LESLIE R., ed. "The Letters of John Talbot." *Ontario History,* XLIV (1952), 139-64.

HEAD, SIR FRANCIS BOND. *A Narrative, with Notes by William Lyon Mackenzie.* Edited by S.F. Wise. Toronto, 1969.

LANGTON, ANNE. *Langton Records: Journals and Letters from Canada, 1837–1846, with Portrait and Sketches.* Edinburgh, 1904.

LUCAS, SIR C.P., ed. *Lord Durham's Report on the Affairs of British North America.* 3 vols. Oxford, 1912.

MILLER, H. ORLO, ed. "The Letters of Rebels and Loyalists." *Canadian Science Digest,* 1 (1938), 70-8.

MILLER, LINUS W. *Notes of an Exile to Van Diemen's Land, Comprising Incidents of the Canadian Rebellion in 1838, Trial of the Author in Canada, and Subsequent Appearance before Her Majesty's Court of Queen's Bench, in London, Imprisonment in England, and Transportation to Van Diemen's Land. Also an Account of the Horrible Sufferings Endured by Ninety Political Prisoners during a Residence of Six Years in that Land of British Slavery together with Sketches of the Island, Its History, Productions, Inhabitants, etc. etc.* East Ardsley, England, 1968.

Records of the Lives of Ellen Free Pickton and Featherstone Lake Osler. Toronto, 1915.

REED, T.A. "Extracts from the Diary of a Loyalist of 1837." *York Pioneer and Historical Association Report* (1948), 15-16.

SANDERSON, CHARLES R., ed. *The Arthur Papers: Being the Canadian Papers, Mainly Confidential, Private, and Demi-Official of Sir George Arthur, K.C.H. Last Lieutenant-Governor of Upper Canada in the Manuscript Collection of the Toronto Public Libraries.* vols. 1, 2. Toronto, 1957.

STACEY, C.P., ed. "The Crisis of 1837 in a Back Township of Upper Canada, Being the Diary of Joseph Richard Thompson." *Canadian Historical Review*, XI (1930), 223-31.

TRAILL, C.P. *The Backwoods of Canada, Being Letters from the Wife of an Emigrant Officer, Illustrative of the Domestic Economy of British America.* Toronto, 1929.

WAIT, BENJAMIN. *The Wait Letters.* Introduced by Mary Brown. Erin, Ontario, 1976.

SECONDARY SOURCES

BOOKS, THESES

AITKEN, HUGH G.J. *The Welland Canal Company: A Study in Canadian Enterprise.* Cambridge, Massachusetts, 1954.

BOYCE, BETSY. *The Rebellion in Hastings, a New Look at the 1837–38 Rebellion in Hastings County, Based on the Rebellion Losses Claims of 1845.* Belleville, 1982.

BULL, W.P. *From Brock to Currie: the Military Development and Exploits of Canadians in General and of the Men of Peel in Particular, 1791 to 1930.* Toronto, 1935.

CLARK, SAMUEL DELBERT. *Church and Sect in Canada.* Toronto, 1948.

――――. *Movements of Political Protest in Canada, 1640–1840.* Toronto, 1959.

CONANT, THOMAS. *Upper Canada Sketches.* Toronto, 1898.

CRAIG, GERALD M. *Upper Canada: The Formative Years, 1784–1841.* Toronto, 1963.

CREIGHTON, DONALD G. *The Empire of the St. Lawrence.* Toronto, 1956.

DAWE, BRIAN. *"Old Oxford is Wide Awake!": Pioneer Settlers and Politicians in Oxford County, 1793–1853.* Toronto, 1980.

DENT, J.C. *The Story of the Upper Canadian Rebellion; Largely Derived from Original Sources and Documents.* 2 vols. Toronto, 1885.

DUNHAM, AILEEN. *Political Unrest in Upper Canada, 1815–36.* London, 1927.

ERMATINGER, C.O. *The Talbot Régime – or the First Half Century of the Talbot Settlement.* St. Thomas, 1904.

GATES, LILLIAN F. *Land Policies of Upper Canada*. Canadian Studies in History and Government, vol. IX. Toronto, 1968.

GUILLET, E.C. *The Lives and Times of the Patriots: An Account of the Rebellion in Upper Canada, 1837–1838 and of the Patriot Agitation in the United States, 1837–1842*. Toronto, 1938.

The History of the County of Brant, Ontario. Toronto, 1883.

History of the County of Middlesex, Canada. Toronto, 1889.

History of the County of Peterborough, Ontario. Toronto, 1884.

KEILTY, GREG. *1837: Revolution in the Canadas*. Toronto, 1974.

KINCHEN, OSCAR A. *The Rise and Fall of the Patriot Hunters*. New York, 1956.

LANDON, FRED. *Western Ontario and the American Frontier*. Toronto, 1941.

LIZARS, ROBINA AND KATHLEEN. *In the Days of the Canada Company: the Story of the Settlement of the Huron Tract and a View of the Social Life of the Period. 1825–50. By Robina and Kathleen MacFarlane Lizars*. Toronto, 1896.

McCALLA, DOUGLAS. *The Upper Canada Trade, 1834–1872: A Study of the Buchanans' Business*. Toronto, 1979.

MARTYN, JOHN PARKS. "Upper Canada and Border Incidents, 1837–38, A Study of the Troubles on the American Frontier Following the Rebellion of 1837." Master's thesis, University of Toronto, 1962.

MUIR, R. CUTHBERTSON. *The Early Political and Military History of Burford*. Quebec, 1913.

PRINGLE, J.F. *Lunenburgh, or, the Old Eastern District, Its Settlement and Early Progress: with Personal Recollections of the Town of Cornwall, from 1824: to Which Are Added a History of the King's Royal Regiment of New York and Other Corps, the Names of All Those Who Drew Lands in the Counties of Stormont, Dundas and Glengarry, up to November, 1786 and Several Other Lists of Interest to the Descendants of the Old Settlers*. Cornwall, 1890.

READ, COLIN. *The Rising in Western Upper Canada, 1837–8: The Duncombe Revolt and After*. Toronto, 1982.

REDISH, ANGELA. "The Optimal Supply of Bank Money: Upper Canada's Experience on and off the Specie Standard." Ph.d. Thesis, University of Western Ontario, 1982.

REVILLE, F.D. *History of the County of Brant*. 2 vols. Brantford, 1920.

RYERSON, STANLEY. *1837: The Birth of Canadian Democracy*. Toronto, 1937.

_____. *Unequal Union: Confederation and the Roots of Conflict in the Canadas, 1815–1873*. Toronto, 1968.

STAGG, RONALD J. "The Yonge Street Rebellion of 1837: An Examination of the Social Background and a Reassessment of the Events."Ph.d. Thesis, University of Toronto, 1976.

WILSON, ALAN. *The Clergy Reserves of Upper Canada: A Canadian Mortmain*. Canadian Studies in History and Government, vol. VIII. Toronto, 1968.

WOOD, W.R. *Past Years in Pickering: Sketches of the History of the Community*. Toronto, 1911.

BIOGRAPHIES, GENEALOGIES

BAILEY, THOMAS MELVILLE, ed.-in-chief. *Dictionary of Hamilton Biography*, I. Hamilton, 1981.

CHADWICK, EDWARD MARION. *Ontarian Families: Genealogies of United Empire Loyalist and Other Pioneer Families of Upper Canada*. New Jersey, 1970.

CRUIKSHANK, E.A. *A Memoir of Colonel the Honourable James Kerby, Welland County Historical Society Papers and Records*, IV. Welland, 1931.

FITZGIBBON, M.A. *A Veteran of 1812*. Toronto, 1898.

GRAHAM, W.H. *The Tiger of Canada West*. Toronto, 1962.

HALPENNY, FRANCESS G., gen. ed. *Dictionary of Canadian Biography*, IX: *1861–1870*. Toronto, 1976.

———. *Dictionary of Canadian Biography*, X: *1871–1880*. Toronto, 1972.

———. *Dictionary of Canadian Biography*, XI: *1881–1890*. Toronto, 1982.

HAMIL, FRED COYNE. *Lake Erie Baron; The Story of Colonel Thomas Talbot*. Toronto, 1955.

HIGGINS, W.H. *The Life and Times of Joseph Gould*. Belleville, 1972, reprint.

KILBOURN, WILLIAM. *The Firebrand: William Lyon Mackenzie and the Rebellion in Upper Canada*. Toronto, 1956.

LINDSEY, CHARLES. *The Life and Times of William Lyon Mackenzie, With an Account of the Canadian Rebellion of 1837, and the Subsequent Frontier Disturbances, Chiefly from Unpublished Documents*. 2 vols. Toronto, 1862.

LONGLEY, R.S. *Sir Francis Hincks, A Study of Canadian Politics, Railways and Finance in the Nineteenth Century*. Toronto, 1943.

MACDONELL, JOHN ALEXANDER. *A Sketch of the Life of the Honourable and Right Reverend Alexander Macdonell, Chaplain of the Glengarry Fencibles or British Highland Regiment, First Catholic Bishop of Upper Canada, and a Member of the Legislative Council of the Province*. Alexandria, Ont., 1890.

MACPHERSON, IAN. *Matters of Loyalty: The Buells of Brockville, 1830–1850*. Belleville, 1981.

MALCOLM, JOHN KARL. *The History and Genealogy of the Malcolm Family of the United States and Canada*. Ann Arbor, Michigan, 1950.

MERRITT, J.P. *Biography of the Hon. W.H. Merritt, M.P. of Lincoln, District of Niagara, Including an Account of the Origin, Progress and Completion of Some of the Most Important Public Works in Canada: Compiled Principally from His Original Diary and Correspondence.* St. Catharines, 1875.

SISSONS, C.B. *Egerton Ryerson, His Life and Letters,* I. Toronto, 1937.

WILKINSON, KATHRYN MORRIS. *Duncombes in America, with some Collateral Lineages.* Milwaukee, 1965.

ARTICLES

BARNETT, J. "Silas Fletcher, Instigator of the Upper Canadian Rebellion." *Ontario History,* XLI (1949), 7-35.

LANDON, FRED. "The Common Man in the Era of the Rebellion in Upper Canada." *Canadian Historical Association Report* (1937), 76-91.

_____. "The Duncombe Uprising of 1837 and Some of Its Consequences." *Proceedings and Transactions of the Royal Society of Canada,* XXV (1931), sec. II, 83-98.

_____. "London and Its Vicinity, 1837–38." *Ontario Historical Society Papers and Records,* XXIV (1927), 410-38.

LONGLEY, R.S. "Emigration and the Crisis of 1837 in Upper Canada."*Canadian Historical Review,* XVII (1936), 29-40.

READ, COLIN. "The Duncombe Rising, Its Aftermath, Anti-Americanism, and Sectarianism." *Histoire sociale – Social History,* IX (1976), 47-69.

_____. "The Short Hills Raid of June, 1838, and Its Aftermath."*Ontario History,* LXVIII (1976), 93-115.

RIDDELL, W.R. "A Trial for High Treason in 1838." *Ontario Historical Society Papers and Records,* XVIII (1920), 50-8.

SENIOR, ELINOR KYTE. "The Glengarry Highlanders and the Suppression of the Rebellions in Lower Canada, 1837–38." *Journal of the Society for Army Historical Research,* LVI (1978), 143–59.

WATT, R.C. "The Political Prisoners in Upper Canada." *English Historical Review,* LXI (1926), 526-55.

WISE, S.F. "Upper Canada and the Conservative Tradition." In *Profiles of a Province: Studies in the History of Ontario: A Collection of Essays Commissioned by the Ontario Historical Society to Commemorate the Centennial of Ontario.* Edited by Edith G. Firth (Toronto, 1967), 20-33.

INDEX

Italics indicate main biographical entry in footnotes.

THE CHAMPLAIN SOCIETY

Officers and Council

PUBLICATIONS OF THE CHAMPLAIN SOCIETY

Ontario Series

1. *The Valley of the Trent*. Edited with an introduction by Edwin C. Guillet
2. *Royal Fort Frontenac*. Translations by Richard A. Preston, edited with an introduction by Léopole Lamontagne
3. *Kingston before the War of 1812*. Edited with an introduction by Richard A. Preston
4. *The Windsor Border Region*. Edited with an introduction by Ernest J. Lajeunesse, C.S.B.
5. *The Town of York 1793–1815: A Collection of Documents of Early Toronto*. Edited with an introduction by Edith G. Firth
6. *Muskoka and Haliburton 1615–1875: A Collection of Documents*. Edited with an introduction by Florence B. Murray
7. *The Valley of the Six Nations: A Collection of Documents on the Indians Lands of the Grand River*. Edited with an introduction by Charles M. Johnston
8. *The Town of York 1815–1834: A Further Collection of Documents of Early Toronto*. Edited with an introduction by Edith G. Firth
9. *Thunder Bay District 1821–1892: A Collection of Documents*. Edited with an introduction by Elizabeth Arthur
10. *Ontario and the First World War: A Collection of Documents*. Edited with an introduction by Barbara M. Wilson
11. *John Prince, 1796–1870: A Collection of Documents*. Edited with an introduction by R. Alan Douglas
12. *The Rebellion of 1837 in Upper Canada*. Edited with an introduction by Colin Read and Ronald J. Stagg